EurographicSeminars

Tutorials and Perspectives in Computer Graphics

Edited by G. Enderle and D. A. Duce

EurographicSeminars

Tutorials and Perspectives in Computer Graphics

Eurographics Tutorials '83. Edited by P. J. ten Hagen.
XI, 425 pages, 164 figs., 1984

User Interface Management Systems. Edited by G. E. Pfaff.
XII, 224 pages, 65 figs., 1985

Methodology of Window Management.
Edited by F. R. A. Hopgood, D. A. Duce, E. V. C. Fielding,
K. Robinson, A. S. Williams.
XV, 250 pages, 41 figs., 1985

Data Structures for Raster Graphics.
Edited by L. R. A. Kessener, F. J. Peters, M. L. P. van Lierop.
VII, 201 pages, 80 figs., 1986

Advances in Computer Graphics I.
Edited by G. Enderle, M. Grave, F. Lillehagen.
XII, 512 pages, 168 figs., 1986

Advances in Computer Graphics II.
Edited by F. R. A. Hopgood, R. J. Hubbold, D. A. Duce.
X, 186 pages, 97 figs., 1986

Advances in Computer Graphics I

Edited by
G. Enderle, M. Grave, and F. Lillehagen

With 168 Figures

Springer-Verlag
Berlin Heidelberg New York
London Paris Tokyo

EurographicSeminars
Edited by G. Enderle and D. A. Duce
for EUROGRAPHICS –
The European Association for Computer Graphics
P.O. Box 16
CH-1288 Aire-la-Ville

Editors
Günter Enderle
Standard Elektrik Lorenz AG (SEL)
Lorenzstraße 10
D-7000 Stuttgart 40

Michel Grave
CRAY Research France
7, rue de Tilsitt
F-75017 Paris

Frank Lillehagen
President METIS A/S
P.O. Box 149
N-3191 Horten

ISBN-13: 978-3-540-13804-4   e-ISBN-13: 978-3-642-46514-7
DOI: 10.1007/978-3-642-46514-7

Library of Congress Cataloging-in-Publication Data.
Advances in computer graphics I. (EurographicSeminars: tutorials and perspectives in
computer graphics) 1. Computer graphics. I. Enderle, G. (Günter), 1944-. II. Grave,
M. (Michel), 1952-. III. Lillehagen, Frank M., 1943-. IV. Series: Eurographic-
Seminars.   T385.A36   1986   006.6   86-13057

2145/3140-543210

Editors' Introduction

This book is the sixth issue in the EurographicSeminars Series. This series has been set up by Eurographics, the European Association for Computer Graphics, in order to disseminate surveys and research results out of the field of Computer Graphics. Computer Graphics constitute a powerful and versatile tool for various application areas. The rapidly increasing use of Computer Graphics techniques and systems in many areas is caused by the availability of more powerful hardware at lower prices, by the concise specification of Computer Graphics Interfaces in commonly agreed standards, and by the invention of new and often astonishing methods and algorithms for composition and presentation of pictures and for graphical interaction.

While some issues of this series contain latest research results, e.g. the issues in window management systems or user interface management systems, this book has the character of a state-of-the-art survey on important areas of Computer Graphics. Starting from current practice and agreed consens, it will lead to the latest achievements in this field. The contributions in this issue are largely based on tutorials and seminars held at the Eurographics conferences 1984 in Copenhagen and 1985 in Nice.

The first book in the EurographicSeminars Series, in which the Eurographics 83 tutorials were published, contained a thorough introduction into this field, which is still valid today. This new book also contains an introduction into Computer Graphics, however, this introduction is in French. Eurographics will, of course, continue to use English as the technical and organizational language, the "Introduction à l'Informatique Graphique" highlights the fact that Eurographics is a European organization with living relations throughout the world. Note that the authors of our French introduction are not from France, but from Canada. The second contribution, as all the others in this book, is in English. It covers the mathematical fundament of Computer Graphics. All the sophisticated algorithms rely on these basic mathematics.

A second group of contributions (Part II) is dedicated to hardware, i.e. Computer Graphics devices and device-related algorithms. Main hardware trends are intelligent workstations and high-resolution raster devices incorporating specialized VLSI circuits.

Part III is dedicated to Computer Graphics Standards. In 1985, the Graphical Kernel System GKS was published as the first Computer Graphic Standard. GKS was covered by several previous issues in this series. This book reports on important extensions of GKS for three-dimensions and dynamic picture structures, on graphical meta-files and on the device interface, which are under development as standards. The relation between these interfaces is explained in the framework of a Computer Graphics reference model.

Whereas in the first three parts of this book, fundamentals of Computer Graphics are presented, Part IV covers the application of Computer Graphics for several important application areas. Business Graphics is a very widespread application. Devices and trends for this area are presented.

There is no doubt that CAD (Computer Aided Design) and CAM (Computer Aided Manufacturing) are major application areas for Computer Graphics. It could even be said that without Computer Graphics, CAD/CAM would be impossible in the way it is used today. The contributions in this issue cover the spectrum of CAD/CAM from geometric modelling to interactive production planning.

The Computer Graphics application area with the widest and most spectacular visibility for the public is perhaps the area of computer animation. Films, such as "Star Treck" or "Tron" are impressive examples on what can be done by Computer Graphics today. Three contributions of this book cover image synthesis and computer animation. The composition of realistic or fantastic images from computer models and the addition of dynamical movement to the pictures are among the most exciting developments within Computer Graphics.

This book starts with an introduction in French, it is published for the European Association for Computer Graphics and it contains contributions from all over the world. The Computer Graphics Society is an international one and Computer Graphics is a universal language. We hope this book will help to spread and disseminate the knowledge of this universal language to a world-wide audience.

G. Enderle
M. Grave
F. Lillehagen

List of Authors

Gregory D. Abram
Department of Computer Science
University of North Carolina at Chapel Hill
Chapel Hill, NC 27514, USA

John D. Austin
Department of Computer Science
University of North Carolina at Chapel Hill
Chapel Hill, NC 27514, USA

Norman I. Badler
Computer and Information Science, Moore School D2
University of Pennsylvania
Philadelphia, PA 19104, USA

Patrick Baudelaire
TANGRAM
18, rue Hoche, F-92130 Issy-les-Moulineaux, France

Peter R. Bono
Graphic Software Systems
P.O. Box 648
Gales Ferry, CT 06335, USA

H. G. Bown
IDON Corporation
P.O. Box 3728, Station C
Ottawa, Canada K1Y 4J8

I. C. Braid
SHAPE DATA
Parker's House, 46 Regent Street
Cambridge CB2 1DP, England

Frederick P. Brooks, Jr.
Department of Computer Science
University of North Carolina at Chapel Hill
Chapel Hill, NC 27514, USA

Ingrid Carlbom
Schlumberger-Doll Research
P.O. Box 307
Ridgefield, CT 06877, USA

Franklin C. Crow
Ohio State University Columbus
OH 43210, USA

J. Encarnação
Institut für Informationsverwaltung und Interaktive Systeme
Technische Universität Darmstadt, Fachbereich 20 (Informatik)
Alexanderstraße 24, 6100 Darmstadt, FRGermany

John G. Eyles
Department of Computer Science
University of North Carolina at Chapel Hill
Chapel Hill, NC 27541, USA

Henry Fuchs
Department of Computer Science
University of North Carolina at Chapel Hill
Chapel Hill, NC 27541, USA

Michel Gangnet
TANGRAM
18, rue Hoche, F-92130 Issy-les-Moulineaux, France

Jack Goldfeather
Department of Mathematics
Carleton College
Northfield, MN 55057, USA

W. T. Hewitt
Computer Graphics Unit
University of Manchester, Computer Building
Oxford Road, Manchester M13 9PL, United Kingdom

Jeff P. Hultquist
Department of Computer Science
University of North Carolina at Chapel Hill
Chapel Hill, NC 27514, USA

Jacob Hygen
Production Engineering Laboratory
NTH-SINTEF
N-7034 Trondheim, Norway

Gary P. Laroff
ISSCO
10505 Sorrento Valley Road
San Diego, CA 92121, USA

Gray Lorig
Gray Research Inc.
1440 Northland Drive
Mendota Heights, MN 55120, USA

Carl Machover
President Machover Associates
White Plains, NY 10601, USA

Nadia Magnenat-Thalmann
Département d'Informatique et de Recherche Operationnelle
Université de Montréal
C.P. 6128 Succ. "A"
Montréal, Canada

Bjørn Moseng
Production Engineering Laboratory
NTH-SINTEF
N-7034 Trondheim, Norway

S. P. Mudur
National Centre for Software Technology
Tata Institute of Fundamental Research
Colaba, Homi Bhabha Road, Bombay 400 005, India

C. D. O'Brien
IDON Corporation
P.O. Box 3728, Station C
Ottawa K1Y 4J8, Canada

Alan Paller
AUI Data Graphics/ISSCO
1655 North Fort Myer Drive, Suite 940
Arlington, VA 22209, USA

John Poulton
Department of Computer Science
University of North Carolina at Chapel Hill
Chapel Hill, NC 27514, USA

M. J. Pratt
Department of Applied Computing and Mathematics
Cranfield Institute of Technology
Cranfield, Bedford MK43 OAL, England

J. Schönhut
Fraunhofer-Gesellschaft
Arbeitsgruppe für Graphische Datenverarbeitung (FhG-AGD)
Bleichstraße 10–12, 6100 Darmstadt, FRGermany

Susan Spach
Hewlett Packard Labs
Palo Alto, CA 94303, USA

Daniel Thalmann
Département d'Informatique et de Recherche Operationnelle
Université de Montréal
C.P. 6128 Succ. "A"
Montréal, Canada

Table of Contents

Part I

Overview and Concepts
of Computer Graphics

Introduction à l'Informatique Graphique

N. Magnenat-Thalmann and D. Thalmann

Plan du cours

1. Le rôle de l'informatique graphique et ses applications

2. L'architecture matérielle et logicielle des systèmes graphiques

3. La modélisation des objets

4. Les transformations ponctuelles

5. Les transformations visuelles

6. La couleur

7. La synthèse d'images réalistes

8. L'animation par ordinateur

Références

1. LE ROLE DE L'INFORMATIQUE GRAPHIQUE ET SES APPLICATIONS

1.1 Introduction

Il y a déjà 30 ans que les premiers dessins par ordinateur ont été produits notamment pour le système de défense et de contrôle aérien SAGE et au M.I.T. avec l'ordinateur TX1. Pendant plus de 20 ans, certains scientifiques ont utilisés la capacité des ordinateurs pour produire des diagrammes et des graphes dans leurs rapports, thèses et articles. Pendant toute cette période, le public, même le public averti tel que la communauté universitaire, ignorait littéralement les possibilités graphiques de l'ordinateur. Il faut tout de même convenir que le matériel était encore cher, pas toujours très maniable et les résultats pas toujours très spectaculaires.

Aujourd'hui, la situation a radicalement changé, tous les micro-ordinateurs personnels ont des capacités graphiques. Les millions de télespectateurs des pays occidentaux sont envahis par les génériques et logos produits par ordinateur. On est d'ailleurs parfois ébahi par le réalisme et la perfection de certaines images générées par ordinateur. Que ce soit dans le domaine technique, médical ou simplement artistique, ces images forcent notre admiration et nous questionnent. Dans le domaine de la synthèse d'images réalistes, en moins de dix ans, on a assisté à des progrès spectaculaires, autant du point de vue matériel que du point de vue logiciel. Il faut d'ailleurs remarquer que leur évolution est intimement liée. Il serait difficilement concevable de produire des images réalistes sans disposer d'un terminal graphique de haute résolution avec au moins quelques centaines de couleurs affichables simultanément.

1.2 Les applications de l'informatique graphique

L'informatique graphique trouve ses applications dans presque tous les domaines de la création, de la conception, de la fabrication, de l'information.

En **architecture**, on peut représenter des bâtiments avec tous leurs détails; on peut visionner ces bâtiments avec n'importe quel point de vue.

En **cartographie**, l'ordinateur peut produire très rapidement des cartes avec différents types d'éléments géographiques. Dans une carte météorologique, par exemple, on peut utiliser des symboles comme des nuages ou le soleil pour indiquer quel temps il va faire dans chaque région. Notons que ce type d'application est utilisée par la télévision et dans le cadre des système vidéotex.

Dans le domaine des **transports**, des cartes de réseaux de bus, de chemins de fer ou d'avions peuvent être produites par ordinateur, aussi bien pour les réseaux existants que pour la planification de nouveaux réseaux.

L'ordinateur joue un rôle de plus en plus important dans la **conception** et la **fabrication industrielle**. La conception **assistée par ordinateur (CAO)** est particulièrement développée dans le domaine de l'automobile, de l'aéronautique, de la mécanique et de l'électronique. L'ordinateur joue un rôle fondamental puisqu'il permet de calculer des formes graphiques à trois dimensions en un temps très court. Ainsi le concepteur peut faire varier interactivement des paramètres et voir immédiatement le résultat visuel de son action. Etant donné la diversité et la complexité des formes graphiques et des structures pouvant intervenir dans les dessins de CAO, des bases de données graphiques sont nécessaires pour stocker cette masse d'informations. L'intégration de la CAO et de la **fabrication assistée par ordinateur (FAO)** prend de plus en plus d'essor. Par exemple, dans le domaine du textile, on peut, par CAO, concevoir les motifs d'un tissu et ceux-ci sont transmis directement aux machines produisant les textiles.

Dans les domaines de pointe tels que la **bureautique** et la **télématique**, l'édition graphique joue un rôle de plus en plus important. L'usager conçoit des dessins, les transforme et les conserve pour un usage ultérieur. Ces dessins peuvent servir aussi bien à illustrer des livres ou des textes (*celui que vous avez en mains en est un exemple typique!!*) qu'à être transmis à des milliers de personnes via des circuits de télécommunications.

Il ne faut évidemment pas oublier tous les **dessins illustrant des données numériques**, tels que les courbes, histogrammes et autres diagrammes qui servent aussi bien au **scientifique** pour comprendre les conséquences de ses expériences qu'au **gestionnaire** pour prendre des décisions.

En **médecine**, de nombreuses applications existent. Grâce au traitement d'images, on peut facilement détecter certaines maladies. Par exemple, en cardiologie, on peut déceler l'infarctus du myocarde par reconstruction d'images. Et on commence déjà à avoir des modèles humains entièrement synthétisés pour simuler des expériences.

Un aspect qui connaît un essor considérable est **l'animation par ordinateur**. Dans ce domaine, deux approches sont à considérer: **l'animation assistée par ordinateur** et **l'animation modélisée**. Dans la première approche, l'ordinateur est utilisé pour améliorer le rendement dans la production de dessins animés traditionnels. En particulier, la tâche ingrate de production de dessins intermédiaires est automatisée. Dans l'animation modélisée, les objets synthétisés évoluent dans l'espace tridimensionnel et ce nouveau type d'animation spectaculaire est visible aussi bien dans certaines scènes de films comme TRON ou Star Trek II que dans la publicité et les logos des chaînes de télévision.

Finalement, dans le domaine des **arts** autres que l'animation, l'ordinateur a encore de la peine à acquérir ses lettres de noblesse. Poutant, des peintures et des sculptures sont produites chaque année et des expositions font de plus en plus leur apparition.

CAO	
-circuits VLSI	électroniciens
-architecture	architectes
-génie civil	ingénieurs-électroniciens
-construction navale	ingénieurs-mécaniciens
-industrie aérospatiale	constructeurs de bateaux
Applications biomédicales	
-aide au diagnostic	médecins
-radiothérapie	
-chirurgie plastique	
-médecine nucléaire	
-simulation de modèles	biologistes
-simulation de modèles moléculaires	chimistes
Graphiques en gestion	
-bureautique	employés de bureau
-prédiction de marché	administrateurs
-statistiques	
-système d'information	presse
-analyse financière	financiers
-éditeurs de graphiques	imprimeurs, éditeurs
Apprentissage et éducation	
-applications pédagogiques	enseignants
-didacticiels	étudiants
Cartographie	
-planification urbaine	urbanistes
-cartes géographiques	cartographes, géographes
-cartes géologiques	géologues
-systèmes d'information géographiques	géographes
-météorologie	météorologues
Traitement d'images et reconnaissance de formes	
-reconnaissance d'images médicales	médecins
-vision des robots	ingénieurs
-contrôle de qualité par la vision	industriels
-reconnaissance de signatures	gestionnaires
-intelligence artificielle	
Technologie du vidéo	
-vidéotex	informateurs
-téléconférence	conférenciers
-résultat d'élections	réalisateurs TV
-sondages	commentateurs
-jeux	grand public

Arts visuels	
-conception graphique -conception de produits industriels -architecture d'intérieur -peinture et décoration	designers, graphistes industriels architectes d'intérieur peintres, décorateurs
Synthèse d'images et animation	
-production d'images réalistes -animation -publicité TV et journaux -simulation de vols aériens -architecture, paysages	publicitaires, designers animateurs, cinéastes publicitaires pilotes, contrôleurs architectes, paysagistes

Fig.1.1 Les domaines d'applications de l'informatique graphique et
l'impact sur les professions

La Figure 1.1 nous montre un tableau des domaines d'application de
l'informatique graphique et quelles sont les professions touchées par cette
nouvelle technologie.

2. L'ARCHITECTURE MATERIEL ET LOGICIEL DES SYSTEMES GRAPHIQUES

2.1 Les composantes des systèmes graphiques

On appelle **système graphique**, un ensemble de composantes matérielles et logicielles qui permettent de produire des dessins et des images par ordinateur. Un tel système doit permettre l'entrée, le traitement et la sortie d'informations de nature graphique. Il peut être représenté par un modèle comme celui de la Figure 2.1 où les parties matérielles et logicielles ne sont pas indiquées.

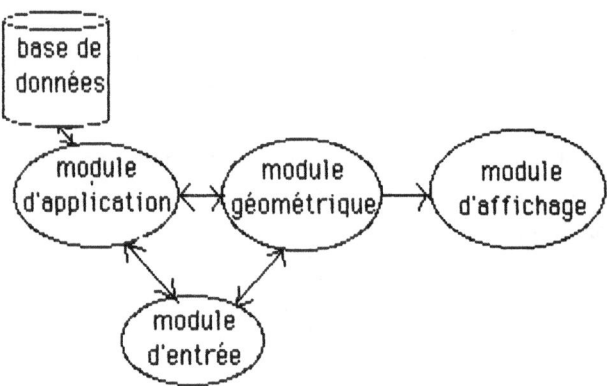

Fig. 2.1 Un modèle de système graphique

Dans ce modèle, on distingue quatre modules principaux:

1. **le module d'entrée**: il est responsable de l'entrée des dessins et comprend normalement des dispositifs d'entrée tels qu'une tablette graphique, par exemple, et le logiciel de contrôle de ces dispositifs.
2. **le module géométrique**: il est formé essentiellement de logiciel et son rôle est de créer et de manipuler des objets graphiques; il faut noter que les terminaux graphiques les plus récents offrent de plus en plus de facilités matérielles pour créer et manipuler des objets graphiques: rotations matérielles, générateur de cercles
3. **le module d'affichage**: il est responsable de la sortie des dessins et comprend le matériel de sortie, tel que les terminaux ou les traceurs ainsi que le logiciel d'affichage qui peut aller du simple ensemble de sous-programmes de traçage de lignes jusqu'au logiciel super sophistiqué de synthèse d'images avec multiples sources de lumière, ombre portée, transparence.
4. **le module d'application**: ce module est celui orienté vers l'usager; il diffère évidemment suivant le type d'application et se présente généralement comme un programme interactif.

Ce modèle est évidemment théorique et pratiquement, on peut plutôt considéré qu'on a un ensemble de dispositifs matériels d'entrée et de sortie, un logiciel graphique de base et un logiciel d'application. Le logiciel graphique de base comprend généralement des opérations d'entrée, de sortie et de création et manipulation d'objets graphiques.

2.2 Les dispositifs d'entrée graphique

Ces dispositifs ont deux fonctions principales:

1. l'**entrée** des objets graphiques
2. la **désignation** des objets graphiques

On distingue normalement 5 sortes de dispositifs d'entrée graphique:

1. **les locateurs** qui permettent d'entrer une position ou une suite de positions.
   Les principaux dispositifs de ce type sont:

   - la **tablette graphique**, surface rectangulaire accompagnée d'un crayon qui permet de donner à l'ordinateur la position de ce crayon sur la tablette.
   - la **souris**, dispositif se déplaçant sur roulettes ou glissant sur une surface plane; un ou plusieurs boutons permettent d'entrer une position correspondant à l'emplacement de cette souris
   - la **boule roulante** (trackball), formée d'une balle que l'on peut faire tourner dans toutes les directions avec la paume de la main pour indiquer les déplacements que l'on souhaite
   - le **manche à balai** (joystick), sorte de tige que l'on peut aussi mouvoir dans toutes les directions pour indiquer un déplacement

2. **les instruments de désignation** (pick) qui permettent de pointer un objet; le plus connu est le **photostyle** (light pen) qui est une sorte de crayon qui détecte la lumière. Ainsi en le déplaçant sur la surface d'un écran, on peut pointer des objets dessinés à l'écran et un signal est envoyé à l'ordinateur, ce qui permet de recueillir les coordonnées de l'objet pointé.
3. **les valuateurs** qui permettent d'entrer une valeur numérique comme un angle, une taille ou un rayon; ce sont typiquement les **potentiomètres** qui se présentent généralement sous la forme de boutons que l'on peut tourner pour faire varier la valeur choisie.
4. **les claviers** qui permettent d'entrer des objets en tapant des commandes
5. **les boutons** qui permettent de choisir une action parmi un choix donné; la réalisation la plus courante est très certainement sous la forme des **clés de fonction** dans la plupart des terminaux.

Signalons encore les possibilités d'entrer des images à partir d'une caméra vidéo. Néanmoins, dans ce cas on se trouve confronté à des problèmes d'analyse d'images relevant du domaine du traitement d'images et de la reconnaissance de formes.

2.3 Les dispositifs graphiques de sortie

Les principaux dispositifs de sortie sont les écrans de visualisation. Même s'il en existe d'autres variétés comme les écrans à plasma, les deux principaux types sont les **écrans calligraphiques** et les **écrans à balayage récurrent** (raster scan).

Dans les écrans calligraphiques, les images sont produites par une suite de segments de droite, ce qui a l'avantage de produire des lignes de très bonne qualité, mais rend difficile le remplissage de polygones. La technologie repose sur les écrans à tube cathodique dont le principe illustré à la Figure 2.2 est le suivant:

Un canon à électrons (émission thermo-électronique) émet un faisceau d'électrons à haute vitesse. Un dispositif de concentration permet d'assurer la convergence du faisceau. Un dispositif de déviation permet de commander la position d'impact sur l'écran. Ce dernier est fait de matériaux luminescents et fonctionne selon le principe photoélectrique. Les électrons incidents provoquent une excitation des électrons de la matière de l'écran qui en revenant au repos provoque l'émission d'un photon (émission lumineuse).

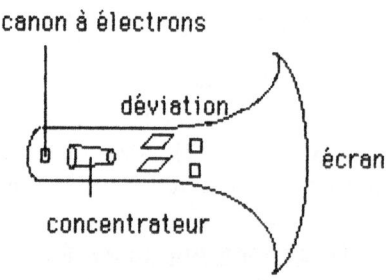

Fig. 2.2 Principe du tube cathodique

Les écrans à balayage récurrent, que nous nommerons plus simplement **écrans raster**, sont proches d'un poste de télévision mais ils sont munis d'une mémoire d'image (**frame buffer**) qui permet de stocker l'image. Cette mémoire se présente comme une matrice d'informations. La taille de la matrice correspond à la résolution du terminal et chaque information est une élément d'image ou **pixel**. Pour chaque pixel, on a un nombre de bits, ce qui fixe les possibilités de couleurs pour ce pixel. Par exemple, si on a 8 bits par pixel, on pourra colorier le pixel selon 256 couleurs différentes. En fait, beaucoup de terminaux ont un grand nombre de couleurs à choix, et la valeur d'un pixel est une adresse dans une table de couleurs choisies parmi toutes les couleurs disponibles. Prenons quelques exemples:

MacIntosh:
>résolution: 512x342
>couleurs: 1 bit, noir/blanc

Tektronix 4027:
>résolution: 640x480
>couleurs: 8 parmi 64

AED 767:
>résolution: 768x580
>couleurs: 8 bits, 256 parmi 16.7 millions

Raster Technologies One/80:
>résolution: 1280x1024
>couleurs: 24 bits, 16.7 millions

Le principal défaut des terminaux raster est la mauvaise qualité du tracé de lignes droites. En effet, comme on peut le voir à la Figure 2.3, les droites sont formées d'une suite de pixels, ce qui cause des effets d'escalier ou **aliasing**. On peut y remédier par des techniques d'**antialiasing**, mais elles sont souvent coûteuses en temps de traitement.

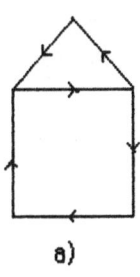

a)

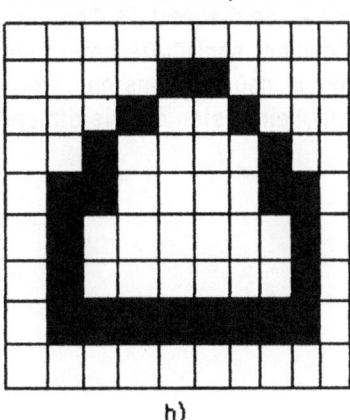

b)

Fig. 2.3 maison   a) sur un terminal calligraphique
b) sur un terminal raster

2.4 Les logiciels graphiques

Ces logiciels peuvent se présenter sous différentes formes:
1. **Ensemble de sous-programmes** pouvant être "appelés" depuis un langage de programmation (typiquement FORTRAN); le principal défaut est

l'absence de syntaxe dans la construction des objets. Parmi les principaux logiciels de ce type, citons Plot-10, GINO, GPGS, DISSPLA, MOVIE.BYU, GSPC Core packages, GKS packages

2. **Langages graphiques**; aucun n'a eu de réel succès, car cela nécessite d'apprendre un nouveau langage

3. **Extensions de langages généraux**: on a l'avantage de profiter de structures existantes et seules les extensions doivent être apprises. Dans cette catégorie, on trouve des extensions de FORTRAN, PASCAL (MIRA), SIMULA, ALGOL 68, ADA.

4. **Systèmes interactifs**: ils regroupent tous les programmes d'application, les systèmes de modélisation et les éditeurs graphiques.

Nous n'entrerons pas en détail dans les opérations de ces différents logiciels, puisqu'en fait, on retrouvera dans les prochains chapitres l'essentiel des ces opérations. Mais il faut signaler l'énorme effort de standardisation des logiciels graphiques, qui a conduit à deux principales propositions de standards:

ACM GSPC Core system: ce standard propose un ensemble de primitives comprenant des transformations visuelles (caméra synthétique), des transformations d'images, des primitives de manipulation de texte et des extensions pour la couleur, le traitement raster, la visibilité des surfaces.

GKS: ce standard créé en Europe semble avoir pris le leadership et devrait devenir le premier standard international. Son principal avantage est le concept de station de travail, ensemble virtuel d'une zone d'affichage et de dispositifs d'entrée. La manière de définir des attributs à l'aide d'index est particulièrement souple. Le défaut principal de GKS est sa restriction à deux dimensions, mais des groupes de travail sont déjà penchés sur l'extension à trois dimensions.

3. LA MODELISATION DES OBJETS

3.1 2D versus 3D

L'être humain vit dans un monde à trois dimensions, mais lorsqu'il dessine, il utilise généralement des feuilles de papier qui n'ont que deux dimensions. Il se trouve donc confronté à un problème de représentation en deux dimensions d'un monde à trois. Deux solutions s'offrent alors:

1. représenter seulement une face plane des objets, par exemple la façade avant d'une maison ou le dessus d'une table

2. tenter de dessiner la scène choisie en tenant compte de lois de projection telle que la perspective.

En informatique graphique, comme les supports matériels (écrans) sont à deux dimensions, ces deux approches se retrouvent et donnent lieu à deux types de modélisation, de systèmes graphiques et d'applications.

On dira qu'un système graphique est **à deux dimensions** (2D) si la représentation interne de l'information graphique dans l'ordinateur est à deux dimensions. Un système graphique sera **à trois dimensions** (3D) lorsque l'ordinateur a connaissance de l'information tridimensionnelle. Cette distinction est fondamentale. En effet, lorsqu'on voit une image produite par ordinateur d'une maison en perspective, il est impossible de savoir si l'image a été produite avec un système à 2 ou à 3 dimensions. En effet, la maison a pu être dessinée en perspective et fournie ainsi à un système graphique à 2 dimensions qui s'est contenté de la restituer ou la vue en perspective a été synthétisée par un système tridimensionnel à partir de données tridimensionnelles. Ceci nous amène à préciser que lorsque nous parlerons d'images tridimensionnelles, il s'agira toujours d'images produites à partir d'un modèle tridimensionnel connu de l'ordinateur et non d'images réellement en trois dimensions, telles que celles produites par des techniques comme l'**holographie** ou la **stéréoscopie**.

Il faut aussi remarquer que l'espace à deux dimensions peut être considéré comme un cas particulier d'espace à trois dimensions dont la troisième dimension Z est toujours nulle. Pour cette raison, nous conviendrons de présenter la plupart des notions dans l'espace tridimensionnel. Nous choisirons également des systèmes de coordonnées tels que la troisième dimension puisse simplement s'ajouter comme le montre la Figure 3.1.

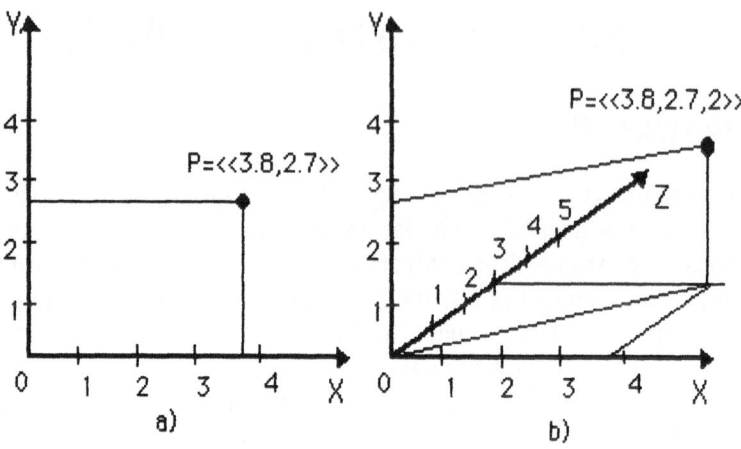

Fig. 3.1 Systèmes de coordonnées   a) 2D   b) 3D

3.2 Points et vecteurs

L'objet graphique le plus simple est évidemment le **point** caractérisé par ses coordonnées et noté $P = <<P_x, P_y, P_z>>$. Des exemples sont montrés à la Figure 3.1. Nous utiliserons une notation semblable pour représenter les vecteurs qui jouent un rôle fondamental en informatique graphique. Un **vecteur** sera considéré comme la direction donnée par la flèche reliant l'origine du système d'axes au point donné par les composantes du vecteur (Fig. 3.2).

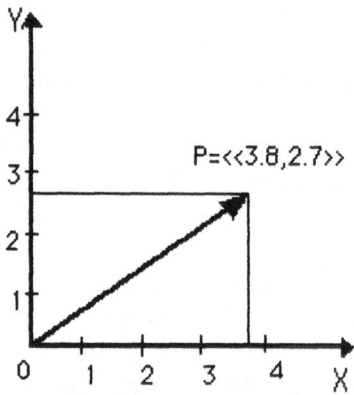

Fig.3.2 Représentation d'un vecteur

Nous noterons un certain nombre d'opérations importantes sur les vecteurs:

norme : $norme(V) = sqrt(V_x^2 + V_y^2 + V_z^2)$

addition : $V1 + V2 = <<V1_x + V2_x, V1_y + V2_y, V1_z + V2_z>>$

produit scalaire: $V1*V2 = norme(V1)*norme(V2)*cos A$ où A est l'angle entre les 2 vecteurs il faut noter que le résultat est un nombre

réel et que dans un système orthonormé, on a :
$$V1*V2 = V1_x*V2_x+V1_y*V2_y+V1_z*V2_z;$$
ce qui permet de déduire l'angle entre les vecteurs.

produit vectoriel: V1 **cross** V2=<< $V1_y*V2_z$ - $V1_z*V2_y$, $V1_z*V2_x$ -
$$V1_x*V2_z, V1_x*V2_y - V1_y*V2_x >>$$

L'intérêt principal du produit vectoriel est qu'il fournit un vecteur perpendiculaire au plan des deux vecteurs intervenant dans le produit. On peut encore noter que
$$norme(V1 \text{ cross } V2) = norme(V1)*norme(V2)*sin A$$
où A est l'angle entre les 2 vecteurs V1 et V2.

3.3 Droites, segments de droite et modélisation en lignes

La droite est une figure très courante bien que l'on utilise plutôt le segment de droite. La différence est simple, une **droite** passe par deux points, tandis qu'un **segment de droite** est limité par 2 points.
Pour tracer un segment de droite AB, nous utiliserons deux instructions, une pour se positionner au point A et une pour tracer le segment de A à B:
   moveabs A;
   lineabs B

Pour tracer la maison de la Figure 3.3, on écrira donc:

```
moveabs <<1,6>>;
lineabs <<9,6>>,<<5,7>>,<<1,6>>,<<1,1>>,<<9,1>>,<<9,6>>;
moveabs <<4,1>>;
lineabs <<4,3>>,<<6,3>>,<<6,11>>;
```

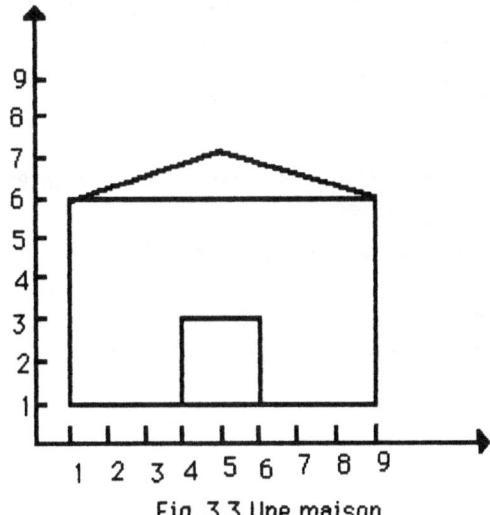

Fig. 3.3 Une maison

Le défaut d'une telle approche est l'utilisation de **coordonnées absolues**, on préfère donc souvent les **coordonnées relatives**. On fixe une origine du dessin (le premier point) et tous les déplacements sont relatifs à cette origine. Notre exemple devient alors.

```
moveabs <<1,6>>;
linerel <<8,0>>,<<-4,1>>,<<-4,1>>,<<0,-5>>,<<8,0>>,<<0,5>>;
moverel <<-5,5>>;
linerel <<0,2>>,<<2,0>>,<<0,-2>>
```

Ce style de programmation peut suffire à réaliser la plupart des dessins en ligne simples et à deux dimensions. En fait, les opérations **lineabs**, **moveabs**, **moverel** et **linerel** sont très primitives, mais présentes dans la plupart des langages, notamment sur micro-ordinateur (BASIC). On peut d'ailleurs construire des abstractions basées sur ces simples instructions. Par exemple, notre maison peut être paramétrisée et construite comme un type graphique de haut niveau dans le langage **MIRA-2D** (Magnenat-Thalmann and Thalmann, 1981). En se basant sur le dessin de la Figure 3.4, on obtient la programmation suivante:

```
type
  MAISON=figure(REF:VECTOR;HAUTE,LARGE,HTOIT,HPORTE,LPORTE:REAL);
         var DEMI:REAL;
         begin
           DEMI:=LARGE/2;
           moveabs REF;
           linerel <<LARGE,0>>,<<-DEMI,HTOIT>>,<<-DEMI,-HTOIT>>,
                   <<0,-HAUTE>>,<<LARGE,0>>,<<0,HAUTE>>;
           moverel <<-DEMI-LPORTE/2,-HAUTE>>;
           linerel <<0,HPORTE>>,<<LPORTE,0>>,<<0,-HPORTE>>
         end;
```

On peut alors aisément définir deux maisons différentes
```
         var M1, M2 : MAISON
```
et les créer avec des dimensions différentes :

```
create M1 (<<1,6>>,5,8,1,2,2);
create M2 (<<10,4>>,2.5,6,2,1.25,1.75)
```

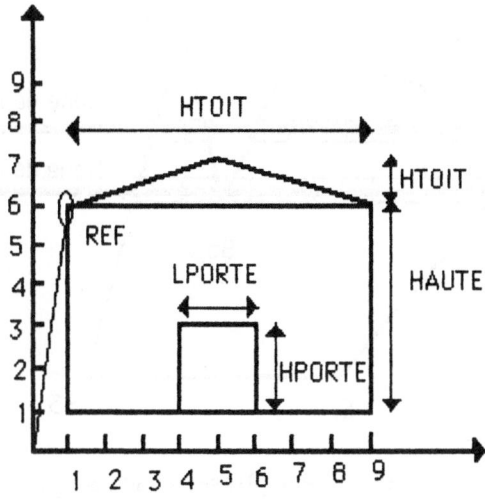

Fig. 3.4 Maison paramétrisée

3.4 Modélisation en polygones

Qu'on travaille en deux dimensions ou en trois, le **polygone** joue un rôle extrèmement important. Sa définition n'est pas toujours rigoureuse et varie selon les auteurs. Nous entendons par polygone une figure plane definie par une liste de points (**les sommets**) reliés par des segments de droite (**les arêtes**). Les sommets sont supposés tous différents, les arêtes ne doivent pas se croiser et une arête relie le dernier sommet au premier. Un polygone est **concave** s'il existe au moins un angle interne supérieur à 180^0; il est **convexe**, s'il n'est pas concave.

A deux dimensions, les polygones sont utilisés sur les terminaux graphiques, car en les remplissant de couleurs, on peut rapidement construire des images attrayantes. En fait, le remplissage en deux dimensions des polygones est devenu une opération de base de la plupart des terminaux raster disponibles sur le marché.

Algorithme de remplissage

L'algorithme de base le plus populaire pour remplir un polygone est un **algorithme de balayage**. On balaye le polygone par des lignes horizontales (lignes de balayage). A chaque ligne, on répète les trois étapes suivantes:

1. trouver les intersections de la ligne de balayage avec toutes les arêtes du polygone
2. trier ces intersections dans l'ordre croissant des coordonnées x
3. mettre à la valeur donnée tous les pixels situés entre les paires d'intersection.

La Figure 3.5 montre un exemple; il faut noter qu'à la ligne de balayage 6, on doit prendre garde au sommet double S5.

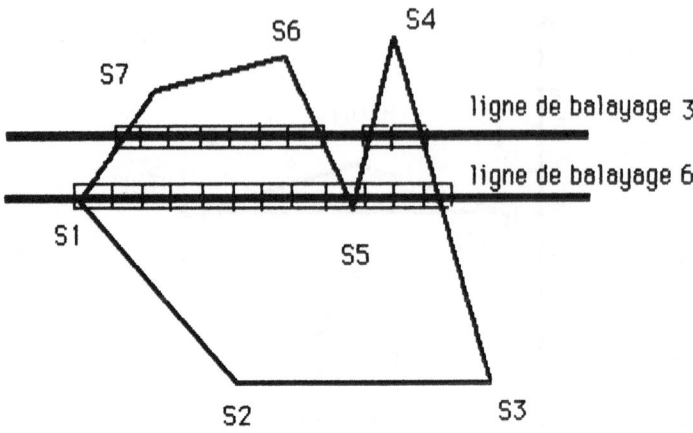

Fig. 3.5 Remplissage par balayage

Bien qu'il soit souvent coûteux en temps d'exécution, **le modèle de représentation d'objets tridimensionnels par polygones** est le plus courant. Dans ce modèle tous les objets sont découpés en faces polygonales. Pour des objets tels que des cubes ou des polyèdres réguliers, ce découpage est évidemment approprié, pour des objets tels que des sphères ou des surfaces de révolution, on est obligé de procéder à des approximations.

Pour construire un objet modélisé par polygones, le principe est toujours le même, il faut une liste de sommets et une liste de faces avec pour chacune les références aux sommets de la face dans la liste globale. Pour illustrer le modèle, nous allons prendre l'exemple d'une boite (parallélépipède) définie par 4 sommets A,B,C et D. L'exemple est implanté en **MIRA-SHADING** (Magnenat-Thalmann et al., 1985) et correspond à la boite de la Figure 3.6.

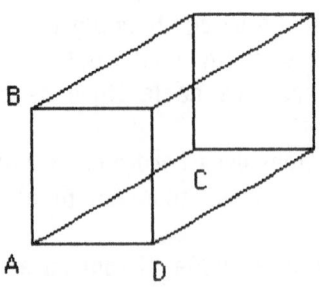

Fig. 3.6 Une boite

```
type BOITE=figure(A,B,C,D:VECTOR);
var CORI, BORI, DORI: VECTOR;
spec
  name 'BOITE', shading CONSTANT,
  figure of 8 vertices, 6 faces;
begin
  CORI:=C-A;
  BORI:=B-A;
  DORI:=D-A;
  vertices:=A,C,B+CORI,B,D,C+DORI,D+BORI+CORI,D+BORI;
  createface 1 to 6 with 4 edges;
  face 1:=1,2,3,4;  face 2:=2,6,7,3;  face 3:=3,7,8,4;
  face 4:=5,1,4,8;  face 5:=1,5,6,2;  face 6:=6,5,8,7
end;
```

3.5 Surfaces courbes

La plupart des objets que l'on désire construire ont des propriétés de courbure; comme nous l'avons dit précédemment, il est possible de les approximer par des polygones. On peut aussi les représenter sous forme de polynomes de degré 3 ou plus. Quelque soit la forme interne de telles surfaces, celles-ci jouent un rôle important. Nous pouvons distinguer trois types de surfaces de ce genre:

1. **Les surfaces réglées** telles que les cônes, les cylindres, les cônes paraboliques, les surfaces de révolutions, les conoïdes
2. **Les surfaces paramétriques** données par leurs équations
   $X=X(U,V)$ $Y=Y(U,V)$ $Z=Z(U,V)$
3. **Les surfaces libres,** ce sont ces dernières qui permettent le plus facilement de modeler des objets compliqués; on distingue 4 principaux types de surfaces libres: les surfaces de Coons, les surfaces de Bézier, les surfaces B-splines et les surfaces béta-splines

Surfaces de Coons

Cette méthode (Coons, 1964) construit une surface $S(U,V)$ à partir de 4 courbes $P(U,0)$, $P(U,1)$, $P(0,V)$ et $P(1,V)$ (voir Fig. 3.7) selon la formule suivante:

$$S(U,V) = P(U,0)*F_0(V) + P(U,1)*F_1(V) + P(0,V)*F_0(U) + P(1,V)*F_1(U)$$
$$- P(0,0)*F_0(U)*F_0(V) - P(0,1)*F_0(U)*F_1(V) - P(1,0)*F_1(U)*F_0(V)$$
$$- P(1,1)*F_1(U)*F_1(V)$$

Les fonction F_i sont des fonctions qui doivent être choisies adéquatement. Les plus simples sont:
$$F_0(U) = U \quad \text{et} \quad F_1(U) = 1-U$$

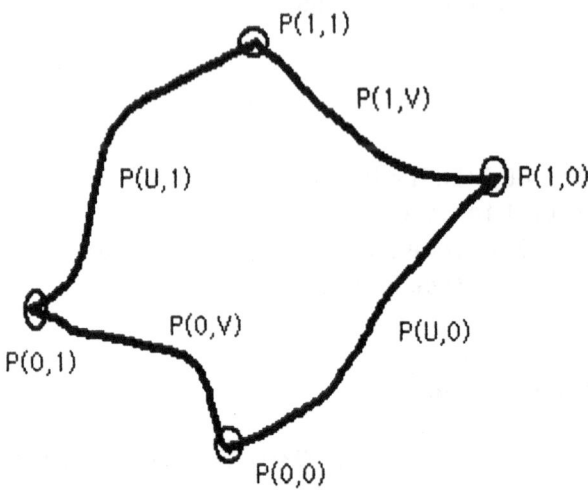

Fig. 3.7 Surface de Coons

Surfaces de Bézier

Dans cette méthode (Bézier, 1972), la surface est calculée à partir d'une grille de M*N points de contrôle selon les formules suivantes:

$$S(U,V) = \sum_{i=0}^{N} \sum_{j=0}^{M} P_{ij} * B_{iN}(U) * B_{jM}(V)$$

où U et V sont compris entre 0 et 1 et les B_{ij} sont les polynomes de Bernstein:
$$B_{iN}(U) = N!/(i!*(N-i)!)*U^i*(1-U)^{N-i}$$
$$B_{jM}(V) = M!/(j!*(M-j)!)*V^j*(1-V)^{M-j}$$

La surface est donc contrôlée par les P_{ij}, malheureusement une modification d'un point de contrôle change toute la surface et le degré des polynomes est intimement lié au nombre de points de contrôle, ce qui entraîne une très grande complexité de calcul quand le nombre de points de contrôle devient grand.

Surfaces B-splines

Ces surfaces remédient en grande partie aux défauts des surfaces de Bézier; leur formulation est d'ailleurs assez proche de la formulation des surfaces de Bézier:

$$S_{k,1}(U,V) = \sum_{i=0}^{N} \sum_{j=0}^{M} P_{ij}*N_{i,k}(U)*N_{j,1}(V)$$

Les $N_{i,j}$ sont les fonctions B-splines de base que l'on définit récursivement. Sans entrer dans les détails, on peut indiquer qu'un contrôle local est possible; ainsi la modification d'un point de contrôle ne change pas toute la courbe. D'autre part, k et 1 contrôlent l'ordre des B-splines, ceci signifie que pour la même grille de points de contrôle, on peut obtenir une surface qui adhère plus ou moins à cette grille en faisant varier k et 1; cependant, lorsqu'on augmente k ou 1, on augmente aussi considérablement la complexité des calculs. De plus k et 1 étant des ordres, ils sont entiers ce qui empêche toute variation continue.

Surfaces béta-splines

Ces surfaces (Barsky, 1981) également produites à partir d'une grille de points de contrôle ont l'avantage d'être basées sur des considérations géométriques. Ainsi, on a :

$$S_{i,j}(U,V) = \sum_{r=-2}^{1} \sum_{s=-2}^{1} V_{i+r,j+s}*b_r(\ 1,\ 2,U)*b_s(\ 1,\ 2,V)$$

où b_k (k=-2 à 1) est un polynome cubique appelé la k-ième fonction de base béta-spline. Dans cette fonction, 1 et 2 sont deux paramètres appelés respectivement le biais et la tension. Le premier permet de contrôler la symétrie de la surface engendrée par rapport à la grille et le second contrôle le degré d'adhérence de la surface à la grille. La Figure 3.8 nous montre l'effet de ces paramètres dans le cas d'une courbe.

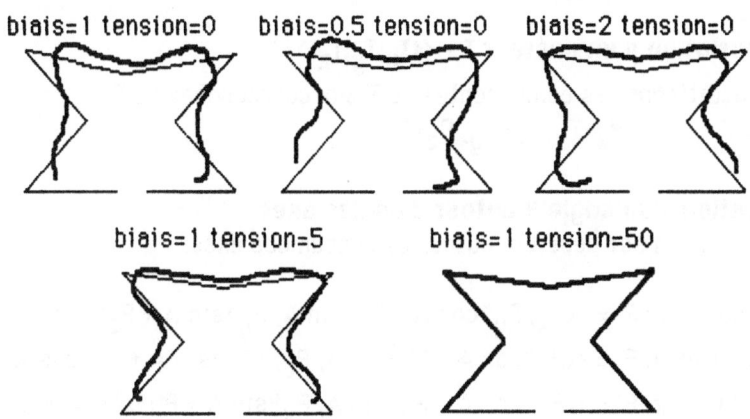

biais=1 tension=0   biais=0.5 tension=0   biais=2 tension=0

biais=1 tension=5   biais=1 tension=50

Fig. 3.8 Effet du biais et de la tension dans une courbe béta-spline

4. LES TRANSFORMATIONS PONCTUELLES

4.1 Les transformations de base

Une fois que l'on a construit des objets graphiques, on désire généralement les manipuler, c'est-à-dire changer leurs **attributs**. Considérons donc les attributs d'un objet graphique, on peut relever:

- **la position**
- **l'orientation**
- **la taille**
- **la forme**
- **la couleur**
- **la transparence**
- **la texture**

La forme est un attribut particulier et sa modification peut s'avérer très compliquée. La couleur sera traitée au chapitre 6 et la transparence et la texture sont des attributs seulement présents dans les images réalistes traitées au chapitre 7. Les trois premiers attributs ont en commun qu'ils peuvent être modifiés par des **transformations** dites **ponctuelles**. Ainsi:

- on modifie la position par des **translations**
- on modifie l'orientation par des **rotations**
- on modifie la taille par des **transformations d'échelle**

Ces transformations sont ponctuelles car elles s'appliquent sur tout point P de l'objet pour donner un nouveau point P'. On peut donc définir chaque transformation par la relation permettant de passer de $P = \langle\langle P_x, P_y, P_z \rangle\rangle$ à $P' = \langle\langle P'_x, P'_y, P'_z \rangle\rangle$. Ainsi, on a:

translation d'un vecteur $T = \langle\langle T_x, T_y, T_z \rangle\rangle$
On additionne les composantes de T aux coordonnées de P:
$P' = P + T = \langle\langle P_x + T_x, P_y + T_y, P_z + T_z \rangle\rangle$

rotation d'un angle A autour d'un des axes
La rotation est possible autour de chacun des axes:

autour de **x**: $P' = \langle\langle P_x, P_y * \cos A - P_z * \sin A, P_y * \sin A + P_z * \cos A \rangle\rangle$

autour de **y**: $P' = \langle\langle P_x * \cos A + P_z * \sin A, P_y, -P_x * \sin A + P_z * \cos A \rangle\rangle$

autour de **z**: $P' = \langle\langle P_x * \cos A - P_y * \sin A, P_x * \sin A + P_y * \cos A, P_z \rangle\rangle$

transformation d'échelle d'un facteur E = $\langle\langle E_x, E_y, E_z \rangle\rangle$

Cette transformation revient à effectuer le produit scalaire de P par le vecteur E:

$$P' = P*E = \langle\langle P_x*E_x,\ P_y*E_y,\ P_z*E_z \rangle\rangle$$

Plutôt que d'employer ces équations, on préfère utiliser une notation matricielle. Mais s'il est aisé de définir des matrices de rotation et de transformation d'échelle, pour intégrer la translation, il faut introduire le concept de coordonnées homogènes.

4.2 Coordonnées homogènes (4D)

Avec ces coordonnées, on travaille dans un espace **à 4 dimensions** où chaque point P est défini comme $P = \langle\langle P_x,\ P_y,\ P_z,\ 1 \rangle\rangle$. Inversément, tout point de coordonnées $\langle\langle x,y,z,w \rangle\rangle$ dans l'espace 4D représente le point $\langle\langle x/w,\ y/w,\ z/w \rangle\rangle$ dans l'espace 3D. Dans cette représentation 4D, les transfomations ponctuelles s'expriment par des matrices 4x4.

translation d'un vecteur T:

$$T = \begin{bmatrix} 1 & 0 & 0 & 0 \\ 0 & 1 & 0 & 0 \\ 0 & 0 & 1 & 0 \\ T_x & T_y & T_z & 1 \end{bmatrix}$$

rotation d'un angle A autour de l'axe X:

$$R_x = \begin{bmatrix} 1 & 0 & 0 & 0 \\ 0 & \cos A & \sin A & 0 \\ 0 & -\sin A & \cos A & 0 \\ 0 & 0 & 0 & 1 \end{bmatrix}$$

rotation d'un angle B autour de l'axe Y:

$$Ry = \begin{bmatrix} \cos B & 0 & -\sin B & 0 \\ 0 & 1 & 0 & 0 \\ \sin B & 0 & \cos B & 0 \\ 0 & 0 & 0 & 1 \end{bmatrix}$$

rotation d'un angle C autour de l'axe Z:

$$R_z = \begin{bmatrix} \cos C & \sin C & 0 & 0 \\ -\sin C & \cos C & 0 & 0 \\ 0 & 0 & 1 & 0 \\ 0 & 0 & 0 & 1 \end{bmatrix}$$

transformation d'échelle d'un facteur E:

$$E = \begin{bmatrix} E_x & 0 & 0 & 0 \\ 0 & E_y & 0 & 0 \\ 0 & 0 & E_z & 0 \\ 0 & 0 & 0 & 1 \end{bmatrix}$$

4.3 Concaténation de transformations

Pour effectuer plusieurs transformations ponctuelles de suite, il suffit de multiplier les matrices de transformations et d'appliquer la matrice résultante comme matrice de transformation globale. En effet, on a:

$$P' = P*T1*T2 = P*(T1*T2)$$

Prenons par exemple, la rotation d'un angle C autour d'une droite arbitraire d, donnée par un point P et un vecteur directeur unitaire N.

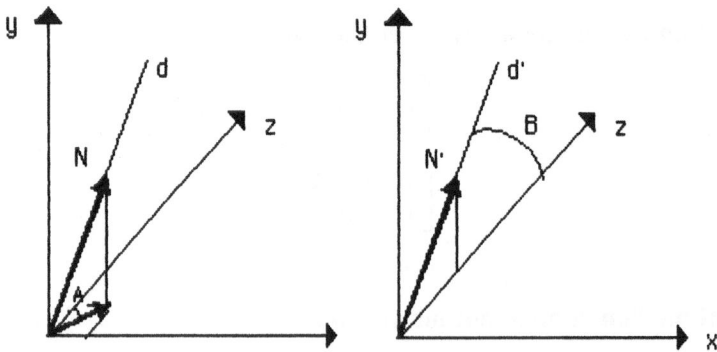

Fig. 4.1 Rotation pour faire coïncider une droite d avec l'axe z

Les étapes de réalisation sont les suivantes:

1. Translation de -P pour amener d à passer par l'origine
2. Rotation de A autour de l'axe x, puis de B autour de l'axe y pour amener la droite d à coïncider avec l'axe z. En observant la Figure 4.1, on peut en déduire les matrices suivantes:

$$R_{xA} = \begin{bmatrix} 1 & 0 & 0 & 0 \\ 0 & N_z/N_{yz} & N_y/N_{yz} & 0 \\ 0 & -N_y/N_{yz} & N_z/N_{yz} & 0 \\ 0 & 0 & 0 & 1 \end{bmatrix}$$

$$R_{yB} = \begin{bmatrix} N_{yz} & 0 & N_x & 0 \\ 0 & 1 & 0 & 0 \\ -N_x & 0 & N_{yz} & 0 \\ 0 & 0 & 0 & 1 \end{bmatrix}.$$

où N_{yz} est la projection de N sur le plan yz.

3. Rotation autour de l'axe z de l'angle donné C
4. Rotation inverse de R_{yB} et rotation inverse de R_{xA}
5. Translation de -T

En remarquant que les transformations inverses s'expriment aisément:

$$T_P^{-1} = T_{-P}$$
$$R_A^{-1} = R_{-A}$$
$$E_S^{-1} = E_{\langle\langle 1/Sx, 1/Sy, 1/Sz \rangle\rangle}$$

on obtient pour la matrice de rotation générale:

$$R_C = T_P * R_{xA} * R_{yB} * R_{zC} * R_{y(-B)} * R_{x(-A)} * T_{-P}$$

4.4 Autres transformations

Parmi les autres transformations ponctuelles, on peut noter les symétries et l'homothétie.

Les **symétries** par rapport aux trois plans principaux sont fréquemment utilisées. On peut les exprimer en coordonnées homogènes par les matrices suivantes:

$$S_{xy} = \begin{bmatrix} 1 & 0 & 0 & 0 \\ 0 & 1 & 0 & 0 \\ 0 & 0 & -1 & 0 \\ 0 & 0 & 0 & 1 \end{bmatrix}$$

$$S_{yz} = \begin{bmatrix} -1 & 0 & 0 & 0 \\ 0 & 1 & 0 & 0 \\ 0 & 0 & 1 & 0 \\ 0 & 0 & 0 & 1 \end{bmatrix}$$

$$S_{xz} = \begin{bmatrix} 1 & 0 & 0 & 0 \\ 0 & -1 & 0 & 0 \\ 0 & 0 & 1 & 0 \\ 0 & 0 & 0 & 1 \end{bmatrix}$$

L'**homothétie** est une opération bien connue en optique géométrique qui multiplie toutes les distances par un facteur R (rapport d'homothétie) à partir d'un point (centre d'homothétie). La Figure 4.2 nous montre un exemple. La matrice d'homothétie peut être obtenue en effectuant une translation de −C, puis une transformation d'échelle de <<R,R,R>> puis une translation de C. Donc:

$$H_{RC} = T_{-C} * E_{<<R,R,R>>} * T_C$$

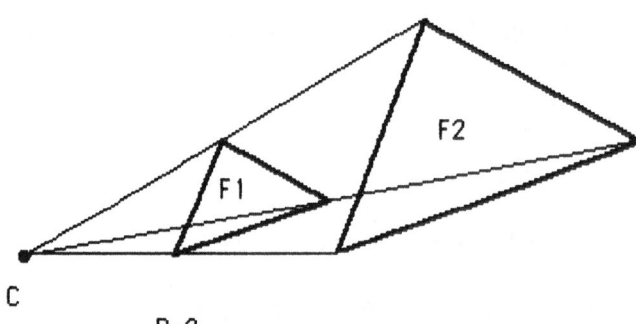

C

R=2

Fig. 4.2 Exemple d'homothétie

5. LES TRANSFORMATIONS VISUELLES

5.1 Fenêtre et clôture

Même si on est capable de modéliser un objet dans l'ordinateur et de le transformer, il n'en reste pas moins que pour le voir sur un écran graphique, il faut passer de l'espace de l'usager (généralement tridimensionnel) à l'espace de l'écran. Non seulement ce dernier est à deux dimensions, mais les constructeurs de matériel graphique se sont ingéniés à définir des espaces d'adresses compliqués et très différents d'un modèle à l'autre. Le but des **transformations visuelles** est donc de passer de l'espace de l'usager à celui du dispositif graphique.

Nous commencerons par le cas simple d'un monde de l'usager à deux dimensions. Ceci nous amène à définir deux concepts fondamentaux: la **fenêtre** et la **clôture.**

Pour ne pas s'occuper de l'espace d'adresses d'un terminal particulier nous allons considérer que l'écran se représente par un rectangle dont le sommet inférieur gauche est à <<0,0>> et le sommet supérieur droit est à <<1,1>>. Ainsi toute portion de l'écran que nous utiliserons sera nécessairement limitée par des vecteurs de composantes comprises entre 0 et 1. Cette portion du dispositif graphique est appelée la **clôture.**

Notre monde réel, supposé à deux dimensions, est évidemment illimité et nous devons spécifier quelle portion du monde réel nous voulons représenter. Cette portion est un rectangle, nommé **fenêtre**, et nous le donnerons par son sommet inférieur gauche et son sommet supérieur droit. C'est ainsi que le contenu de la fenêtre sera toujours représenté dans la clôture. En considérant la Figure 5.1, on peut montrer comment on passe d'un point P dans la fenêtre à un point P' dans la clôture:

$$P'_x = (CH_x - CB_x)*(P_x - FB_x)/(FH_x - FB_x) + CB_x$$
$$P'_y = (CH_y - CB_y)*(P_y - FB_y)/(FH_y - FB_y) + CB_y$$

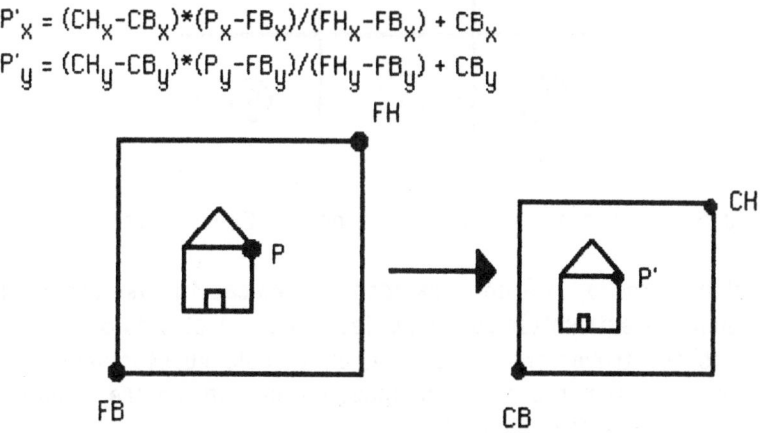

Fig. 5.1 Passage de la fenêtre à la clôture

5.2 Coupage selon la fenêtre

Nous avons encore un problème à résoudre: comment couper les objets qui sortent de la fenêtre ? Il s'agit, dans le cas de dessins en lignes, de couper chaque segment selon les bords de la fenêtre comme le montre la Figure 5.2.

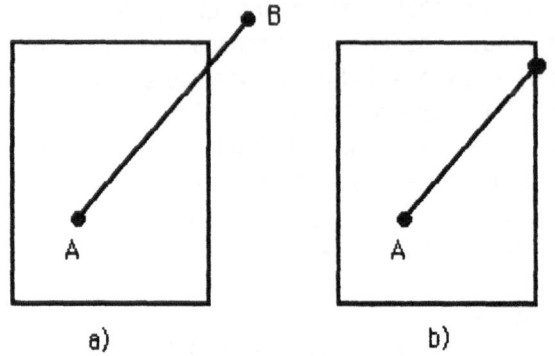

Fig. 5.2 coupage d'un segment   a) avant   b) après

La méthode la plus connue pour effectuer cette opération est **la méthode de Cohen-Sutherland**. Cet algorithme est basé sur une division du plan en 9 régions dont la région centrale est la fenêtre. La Figure 5.3 nous montre cette division.

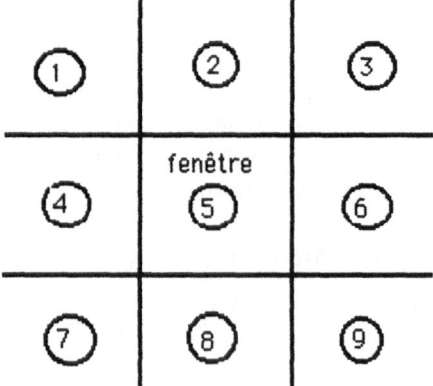

Fig. 5.3 Les 9 régions dans l'algorithme de Cohen-Sutherland

Avec cette approche, on élimine rapidement des cas simples comme des segments dont les extrémités sont dans les régions 1 et 3 ou 6 et 9. Pour les segments qui traversent la fenêtre, on calcule successivement les intersections des segments avec les lignes bordant la fenêtre, comme on le voit dans l'exemple de la Figure 5.4.

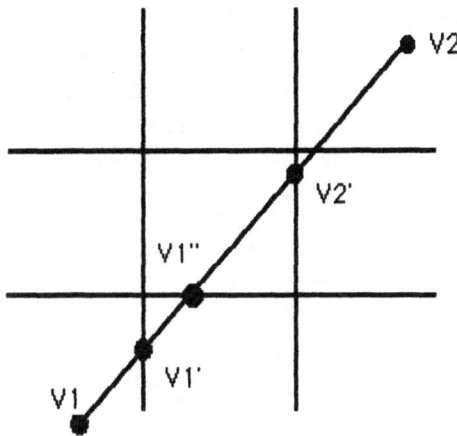

Fig. 5.4 Principe de l'algorithme de Cohen-Sutherland

5.3 Projections parallèles et perspectives

Revenons maintenant au cas général de l'espace à trois dimensions. Le problème principal est de passer de trois à deux dimensions, ce qui suppose la projection des objets de l'espace sur un plan, que l'on appelle **le plan de vue.** On distingue deux grands types de projections: la **projection parallèle** (Fig. 5.5a) et la **perspective** (Fig. 5.5b). dans les deux cas, la projection de l'objet s'obtient en faisant passer des droites (**les projecteurs**) par chaque point de l'objet et en cherchant l'intersection avec le plan de vue. Dans le cas d'une perspective, toutes les lignes émanent d'un seul point : le **centre de projection.** Pour une projection parallèle, toutes les droites sont parallèles à une **direction de projection.** Si la direction de projection est perpendiculaire au plan de vue, on a une **projection orthographique** sinon elle est **oblique.**

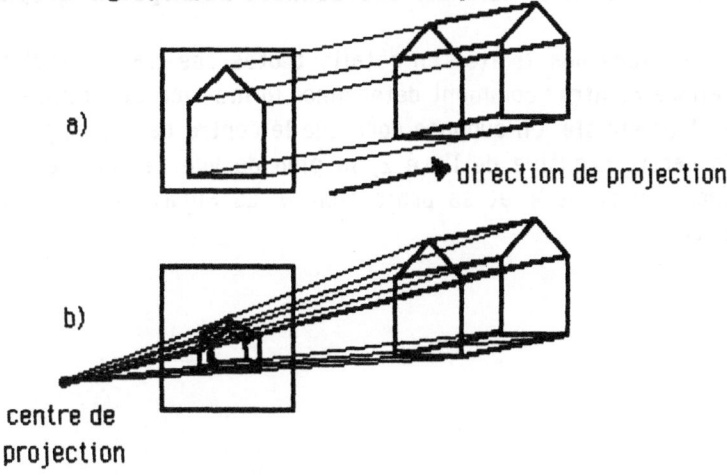

Fig. 5.5 a) principe de la projection parallèle
b) principe de la perspective

On va définir la **fenêtre** comme le rectangle délimitant ce qui doit être vu dans le plan de vue. La fenêtre est spécifiée selon un système d'axes UVW où V est la projection sur le plan de vue d'un vecteur particulier appelé le **vecteur viewup** et W le vecteur normal au plan de vue. L'axe U est alors à 90^0 comme on le voit dans la Figure 5.6.

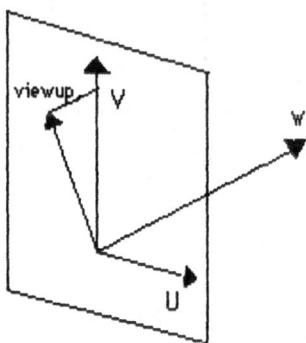

Fig. 5.6 Système d'axes de la fenêtre

On définira aussi un **volume de vue** qui contiendra tous les objets susceptibles d'être projetés. Dans le cas d'une perspective, le volume de vue est une pyramide semi-infinie dont le sommet est le centre de projection et la fenêtre une section. Dans le cadre d'une projection parallèle, le volume de vue est un parallélépipède.

Nous pouvons maintenant décrire les étapes de traitement d'une scène tridimensionnelle:

1. Coupage selon le volume de vue
2. Projection sur la fenêtre dans le plan de vue
3. Passage de la fenêtre à la clôture
4. Passage de la clôture aux coordonnées du dispositif graphique

Nous n'allons pas traiter en détails toutes ces transformations, mais nous allons montrer comment déterminer la **matrice de perspective** dans un cas très simple. On suppose donc que le centre de projection est placé sur la partie négative de l'axe Z, le plan de vue est sur le plan XY. On considère un point V et sa projection W. La Figure 5.7 nous montre la situation.

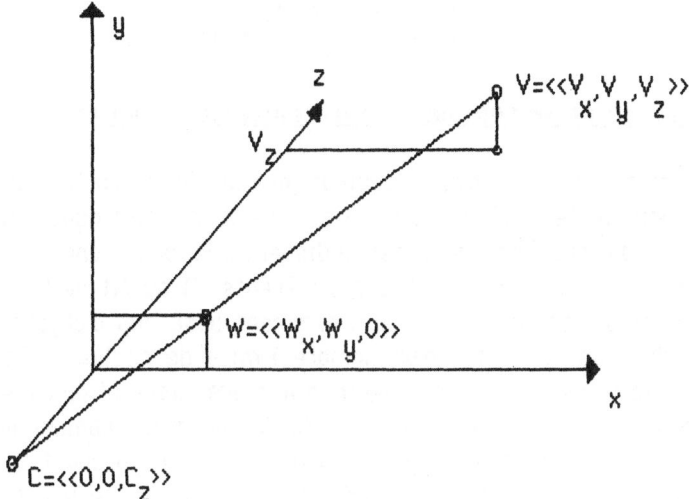

Fig. 5.7 Perspective d'un point V

On voit aisément qu'on a les relations suivantes:

$$W_x = V_x/(1-V_z/C_z) \quad \text{et} \quad W_y = V_y/(1-V_z/C_z)$$

Or si on applique la matrice suivante :

$$M_{per} = \begin{bmatrix} 1 & 0 & 0 & 0 \\ 0 & 1 & 0 & 0 \\ 0 & 0 & 0 & -1/Cz \\ 0 & 0 & 0 & 1 \end{bmatrix}$$

sur le vecteur 4D $V = \langle\langle V_x, V_y, V_z, 1\rangle\rangle$, on obtient $V' = \langle\langle V_x, V_y, 0, 1-V_z/C_z\rangle\rangle$ en ramenant à trois dimensions, comme on l'a vu dans le chapitre 4, on obtient $\langle\langle V_x/(1-V_z/C_z), V_y/(1-V_z/C_z), 0\rangle\rangle$ ce qui est W. Donc M_{per} est la matrice de perspective et plus généralement, on peut affirmer que toute matrice de coordonnées homogènes (4x4) qui a des termes non nuls dans les trois premiers éléments de la quatrième colonne est une matrice de perspective.

Pour terminer, il faut signaler que pour l'usager d'un système tridimensionnel, on lui donne généralement une spécification très simple sous forme d'ine caméra virtuelle comprenant:
- un **oeil**, c'est-à-dire le point d'où l'on regarde
- un **point d'intérêt**, c'est-à-dire le point que l'on regarde
- un **angle de vue** (45o pour un être humain moyen)
Le système va alors calculer la matrice de perspective correspondante.

6. LA COULEUR

6.1 Le rôle de la couleur en informatique graphique

En informatique graphique, la couleur joue un rôle fondamental pour deux raisons principales. D'une part, elle permet de distinguer des objets différents, d'autre part, elle est indispensable pour rendre les images réalistes. Pour distinguer N objets différents, il suffit de N couleurs et souvent moins; comme on manipule rarement beaucoup d'objets à la fois, on peut donc se contenter d'un nombre limité de couleurs. Dans le cas d'images réalistes, on fait intervenir la lumière; mais, si on considère, par exemple, un objet complexe rouge, il faudra un grand nombre de nuances rouges pour le représenter. Plus généralement, la production d'images réalistes avec transparence, texture, ombrage nécessite une très grande quantité de couleurs.

On constate donc que selon le type d'applications envisagées, le besoin en couleurs est variable. Il faut pourtant des moyens standards de spécifier ces couleurs. Avec un nombre limité à 8 par exemple, on peut évidemment se servir des noms des couleurs; mais pour des milliers voire des millions de couleurs, des systèmes numériques sont indispensables.

Il existe plusieurs systèmes dont les principaux sont : **RGB, CMY, YIQ, HSV** et **HLS**. Nous ne décrirons que les systèmes RGB et HLS.

6.2 Le système RGB

Ce système est dérivé du système instauré en 1931 par **la Commission Internationale de l'Eclairage** (CIE). Le système de la CIE définissait un espace basé sur trois couleurs primaires: Rouge (**R**ed), Vert (**G**reen) et Bleu (**B**lue). Toute couleur visible devenait une combinaison linéaire des trois couleurs primaires. Le système RGB correspond au principe des moniteurs TV, puisque dans ces moniteurs, les couleurs sont créees par des phosphores rouges, verts et bleus.

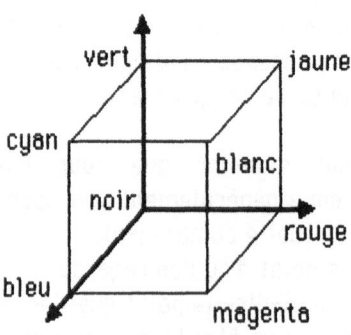

Fig. 6.1 Le cube RGB

Le modèle RGB utilise généralement un cube dont les arêtes sont de longueur 1 et qui est représenté à la Figure 6.1.

Le noir est à l'origine et le blanc au point ‹1,1,1›. Les trois couleurs primaires se trouvent évidemment le long des trois axes. Enfin, les couleurs cyan, magenta et jaune sont situées aux trois autres sommets du cube. Toutes les couleurs peuvent ainsi être exprimées par des vecteurs de composantes comprises entre 0 et 1. On aura donc:

Rouge = ‹1,0,0›	Vert = ‹0,1,0›	Bleu=‹0,0,1›
Jaune = ‹1,1,0›	Magenta = ‹1,0,1›	Cyan = ‹0,1,1›

Il faut encore remarquer que le long de la diagonale du cube, on trouve une échelle des gris allant du noir (‹0,0,0›) au blanc (‹1,1,1›).

6.3 Le système HLS

Ce système spécifie aussi toute couleur à l'aide de trois nombres, mais ces trois nombres ont une toute autre signification. Ce sont la nuance ou teinte (Hue), la clarté (Lightness) et la saturation (Saturation).

La **nuance** ou **teinte H** peut se représenter à l'aide d'un cercle; on considère alors l'angle au centre du cercle. En degrés, la teinte va donc de 0^0 à 360^0 comme le montre la Figure 6.2. Les trois couleurs primaires et les trois couleurs complémentaires forment un héxagone régulier.

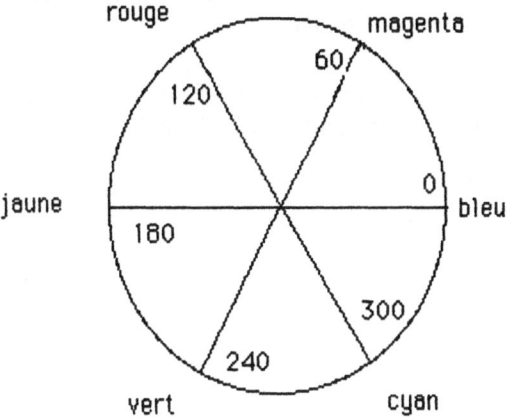

Fig. 6.2 Le cercle des teintes dans le système HLS

La **clarté L** est définie selon une échelle allant de 0 (noir) à 1 (blanc) en passant par tous les gris.

La **saturation S** mesure la pureté des couleurs, c'est-à-dire le pourcentage de couleur pure par rapport au blanc. Une valeur de 1 représente donc une couleur pure ou saturée tandis qu'une valeur de 0 correspond à un gris de même clarté.

Le système HLS peut être illustré à l'aide d'un double cône (Fig. 6.3). A la surface du cône, toutes les couleurs ont une saturation de 1. La saturation est représentée le long du rayon d'une section circulaire du cone. La teinte est décrite par l'angle au centre d'un cercle tandis que la clarté est sur l'axe vertical.

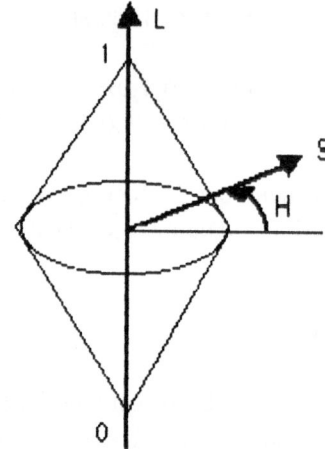

Fig. 6.3 Le double cône HLS

Remarquons que la teinte est souvent exprimée en fraction de tour de cercle, ce qui permet de noter les couleurs par des vecteurs à trois composantes comprises entre 0 et 1 : <H,L,S>. Ainsi, les couleurs primaires et complémentaires peuvent s'écrire:

Rouge = <0.33,0.5,1>   Vert = <0.67,0.5,1>   Bleu=<0,0.5,1>
Jaune = <0.5,0.5,1>   Magenta = <0.167,0.5,1>   Cyan = <0.833,0.5,1>

7. LA SYNTHESE DES IMAGES REALISTES

7.1 Les lignes et les surfaces cachées

Si nous considérons le dessin de la Figure 7.1a, nous sommes tout-à-fait incapables de décider si ce dessin représente deux cubes, comme ceux de la Figure 7.1b ou deux cubes comme ceux de la Figure 7.1c. En effet, le premier dessin est ambigü, tout simplement parce que les lignes qui devraient être cachées ne le sont pas.

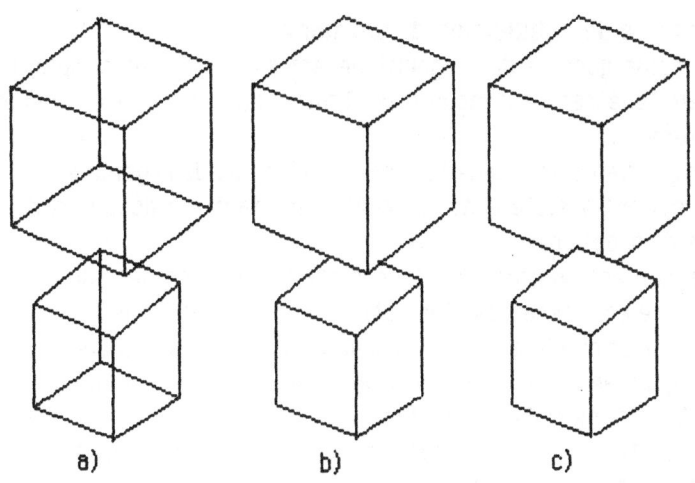

a)   b)   c)

7.1 Le rôle des lignes cachées

Le problème des lignes cachées dans les objets a été étudié très tôt (1967) et on trouvera une description des principales techniques dans l'article de Sutherland et al. (1974). Mais on peut distinguer trois catégories d'algorithmes:

1. **les algorithmes se déroulant dans l'espace de l'usager** (3D). Dans ces algorithmes, tous les calculs et les comparaisons sont effectués entre les éléments géométriques définis par l'usager dans son espace. Ces algorithmes sont appelés **algorithmes de lignes cachées** , car ils produisent une liste de lignes visibles comme résultat. Le principal défaut de ces algorithmes est leur lenteur d'exécution; ils ont par contre l'avantage d'être exacts et de s'adapter particulièrement à la sortie sur traceur digital. Parmi de tels algorithmes, signalons celui de Appel (1967) et celui de Galimberti et Montanari (1969).

2. **les algorithmes se déroulant dans l'espace du dispositif graphique**. Ces algorithmes sont basés sur la technologie des terminaux. En particulier, ils conviennent aux terminaux de type "raster". En effet, ils sont généralement basés sur le principe que les objets sont composés de faces polygonales et on doit décider quelle face est

visible à chaque pixel de l'écran. Les plus connus de ces algorithmes sont les algorithmes de Warnock (1969), de Watkins (1970) et de la mémoire de profondeur (Catmull,1975). Ces algorithmes sont encore actuellement les plus utilisés et nous les décrirons brièvement.

3. **les algorithmes mixtes.** Ces algorithmes forment un compromis entre les deux autres types d'algorithmes. Ils comportent deux phases principales: 1^0 construction dans l'espace 3D d'une liste des priorités des objets selon leur profondeur, 2^0 détermination de la visibilité des objets dans l'espace du dispositif graphique. Le principal algorithme de ce type est la méthode des priorités de Encarnacao (1970).

Algorithme de subdivision de Warnock

Le principe général de l'algorithme est extrèmement simple: l'écran est divisé en fenêtres rectangulaires. Trois cas sont alors considérés pour chaque fenêtre:

1. Il n'y a rien à voir dans la fenêtre, donc pas de problème.
2. Ce qui est visible dans la fenêtre est facile à dessiner, donc il n'y a pas de problème.
3. Ce qui est visible est trop difficile à dessiner, donc divisons la fenêtre en 4 fenêtres plus petites et recommençons récursivement.

Il faut noter que le processus récursif s'arrête dans trois cas:

a) Il n'y a rien à voir, donc la fenêtre est coloriée avec la couleur de fond
b) la fenêtre se reduit à un pixel
c) la fenêtre est facile à colorier, car un seul polygone la recouvre ou a une intersection avec

algorithme de balayage de Watkins

Cet algorithme est basé sur le même principe que l'algorithme de remplissage de polygones vu au chapitre 3. Mais cette fois, on conserve deux tableaux à une dimension de longueur égale à la résolution en x du terminal. Le premier tableau contiendra les couleurs des pixels de la ligne courante et le second tableau contiendra la profondeur courante en chaque pixel de la ligne. Le principe de l'algorithme est alors le suivant et s'applique à chaque ligne de balayage: on commence par initialiser le tableau des profondeurs à une valeur maximale et le tableau des couleurs à la couleur de fond; ensuite pour chaque projection de polygone de la scène, on cherche les pixels de la ligne de balayage qui sont dans le polygone. Ensuite pour chaque pixel, on calcule la profondeur Z, si elle est inférieure à la profondeur courante (stockée dans le tableau), on remplace la valeur dans le tableau par Z et on modifie la valeur de couleur correspondante. A la fin du traitement de la ligne de balayage, le tableau des couleurs contient exactement la ligne à afficher. L'algorithme peut être considérablement amélioré en tenant compte de la cohérence des arêtes et en effectuant des tris judicieux selon x et y.

algorithme de la mémoire de profondeur (z-buffer)

Si on suppose qu'on est capable de mémoriser les profondeurs à chaque pixel pour toute l'image, on peut appliquer un algorithme semblable à celui de Watkins, mais beaucoup plus efficace, car on n'a plus besoin d'ordonner les polygones. En effet, dans un algorithme de balayage, à chaque ligne, il faut trouver tous les polygones concernés; dans l'algorithme de la mémoire de profondeur, on peut traiter les polygones dans un ordre quelconque. Si l'algorithme est simple, il nécessite néanmoins une mémoire considérable et rapide. Un z-buffer typique, comme celui que l'on trouve dans les terminaux Raster Technologies One/25 S et One/80 S, a une instruction qui écrit un pixel seulement si la valeur z est plus petite que la valeur courante.

7.2 La lumière synthétique

Dans les algorithmes que nous venons de voir, on devait colorier un pixel d'une couleur; mais laquelle ? La réponse n'est pas simple, en effet, si on veut dessiner une boule verte et qu'on colorie tous les pixels de la boule avec une même couleur verte, on aura un cercle vert qui n'aura absolument pas l'allure d'une sphère. Ce qui donne l'impression de volume est la répartition des intensités de couleurs sur la surface. Chaque point peut avoir une intensité différente et cette intensité est fonction de la lumière présente. Donc pour synthétiser une scène tridimensionnelle par ordinateur avec de la couleur, il faut aussi **synthétiser de la lumière**. On distingue généralement plusieurs types de sources de lumière:

1. **la lumière ambiante**, c'est une lumière qui éclaire toute la scène uniformément
2. **les sources directionnelles**, ce sont des sources de lumière, supposées à l'infini et qui éclairent la scène avec des rayons parallèles à une direction donnée
3. **les sources ponctuelles**, ce sont des sources de lumière, supposées placées en un point précis et qui rayonnent la lumière radialement

Il faut remarquer que dans les trois sortes de sources de lumière, on doit spécifier leur couleur dans un des systèmes HLS ou RGB.

Phong (1975) a introduit un modèle très utilisé pour le calcul de la lumière en un point donné. Dans ce modèle, l'intensité en un point P est donnée par:

$$I = I_a + I_d + I_s$$

ou I_a est l'intensité due à la lumière ambiante, I_d est l'intensité de la lumière due à la diffusion sur la surface et I_s est l'intensité de la lumière réfléchie vers l'observateur formant un reflet (highlight) sur l'objet. Notons qu'un objet très mat a une forte composante de diffusion, tandis qu'un miroir a une forte composante I_s.

La diffusion se calcule facilement, car elle ne fait pas intervenir l'observateur, on peut donc utiliser la loi de Lambert qui calcule I_d comme la somme sur toutes les sources de lumière du produit scalaire **L*N**, où **L** est un vecteur dirigé vers la source de lumière et **N** le vecteur normal à la surface au point considéré.

La composante I_s est beaucoup plus difficile à calculer et c'est là que Phong a introduit une expression qui est proportionnelle à la somme pour chaque source du produit scalaire des vecteurs **N** et **L'** à la puissance **n**, où **L'** est un vecteur dirigé vers le point milieu entre l'observateur et la source de lumière, **N** est le vecteur normal à la surface au point considéré et **n** est un exposant qui contrôle le reflet.

Une fois qu'on sait calculer la lumière en un point, il faut trouver le moyen de calculer la lumière pour tous les points d'une surface. Trois modèles principaux existent:

le modèle de Lambert
une seule intensité est calculée pour chaque polygone; ce modèle n'est normalement valable que pour une source de lumière directionnelle et un observateur très loin. De plus, le modèle n'est réaliste que pour des objets dont on souhaite voir les faces: cubes, polyèdres.

le modèle de Gouraud (1971)
l'intensité est calculée en chaque sommet de polygone, en déterminant un vecteur normal moyen à partir des normales des faces auxquelles appartient le sommet; ensuite, on calcule en chaque point du polygone, une intensité par interpolation linéaire des intensités des sommets.

le modèle de Phong (1975)
ce modèle, très populaire, repose sur une interpolation des normales plutôt que des intensités, ce qui réduit les discontinuités, mais rend les calculs plus complexes.

7.3 La transparence

Généralement, lorsqu'un objet se trouve devant un autre, il le masque. En informatique graphique, on simule cette propriété en utilisant un algorithme d'élimination des surfaces cachées. Pourtant, la lumière peut traverser certains matériaux et dans ce cas, ces matériaux sont dits **transparents** et on ne doit plus cacher les objets situés derrière. Il faut alors représenter différemment ces objets vus à travers un corps transparent. La technique la plus simple peut s'expliquer par un exemple: supposons qu'on regarde une boite rouge à travers une vitre verte. La couleur de la boite sera un mélange de rouge et de vert. La proportion de rouge et de vert est dépendante du coefficient de transmission (transparence) de la vitre. Si la vitre était complètement opaque, on n'aurait que du vert; si la vitre était complètement transparente, la boite serait vraiment rouge; entre ces deux extrêmes, tous les mélanges sont possibles. On peut donc appliquer la formule suivante:

$$I = t*I1 + (1-t)*I2$$

ou I1 est l'intensité du point P1 situé derrière le point P2 dont l'intensité est I2 ; t est le facteur de transparence du polygone auquel appartient P2, sa valeur varie entre 0 (opaque) et 1 (complètement transparent).

Cette technique donne des résultats acceptables avec des objets non courbes. Pour un objet comme une sphère, il faut tenir compte de la courbure, en effet, la transparence est plus grande en direction du centre qu'aux bords.

Si on veut réellement tenir compte de tous les phénomènes physiques tels que la réfraction, il faut utiliser une méthode comme le **traçage de rayons** (ray tracing) que nous allons brièvement expliquer.

7.4 Le traçage de rayons

Un **algorithme de traçage de rayons (ray tracing)** revient à tirer des rayons à partir de l'observateur pour chaque pixel, calculer les intersections de ces rayons avec les objets de la scène et obtenir les informations photométriques nécessaires pour colorier le pixel courant. La figure 7.2 nous montre le principe.

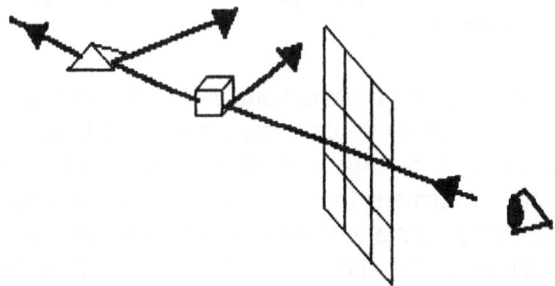

Fig.7.2 Principe du traçage de rayon

A chaque surface touchée par un rayon, un rayon réfracté et/ou un rayon réfléchi peuvent être engendrés. Pour ces nouveaux rayons, il faut évidemment appliquer récursivement le même processus pour déterminer les intersections de ces rayons avec d'autres surfaces.

L'algorithme est extrèmement puissant et permet de traiter pratiquement tous les aspects du réalisme. Malheureusement, les calculs d'intersections sont très coûteux en temps de calculs et seules des machines puissantes peuvent permettre de tels calculs dans un temps raisonnable.

Dans les problèmes de transparence, le traçage de rayons permet de tenir compte de la réfraction. Ainsi, Kay et Greenberg (1979) ont proposé une méthode qui calcule de combien de pixels est déplacée une image réfractée.

Signalons également que l'algorithme de traçage de rayons permet aussi de produire élégamment des **ombres portées**, alors que dans d'autres méthodes, il faut carrément utiliser un algorithme du genre ligne cachées en considérant la source de lumière à la place de l'observateur.

7.5 La texture

Les objets synthétisés par ordinateur ont très souvent une apparence artificielle; il est en effet difficile d'empêcher cet aspect lisse et "plastic" des objets. Un exemple typique est la représentation de la peau humaine qui paraît toujours trop parfaite et donne aux humains synthétisés une allure de mannequin de cire ou de marionnette de bois. Pour réduire cet aspect lisse, on peut utiliser des méthodes de texture. Une texture est définie comme une microstructure de la surface à représenter et différentes techniques sont possibles qui sont toutes disponibles par exemple, dans le système **MIRANIM** (Magnenat-Thalmann et al., 1985):

1. **Application d'une image bidimensionnelle sur la surface de l'objet tridimensionnel**.
La technique revient à découper l'image plane selon une grille puis à faire correspondre à chaque case son équivalent sur la surface. On peut alors transformer la partie d'image contenue dans la case plane selon la forme du polygone équivalent.

2. **Perturbation de la lumière.** Nous avons vu que la lumière en chaque point d'un objet est dépendante de l'angle que forme l'objet en ce point avec la direction de la lumière; plus précisément le calcul de la lumière en un point dépend de la normale (perpendiculaire) en ce point. En modifiant judicieusement cette normale selon une technique due à Blinn (1978), on peut créer des zones de lumière et d'ombre qui simulent une texture. Pour modifier la normale, on utilise des fonctions mathématiques. La Figure 7.3 nous montre le principe.

3. **Simulation de relief par des fractales**
4. **Simulation de corps flous par un ensemble de particules** .
Ces deux dernières techniques vont être traitées plus en détail dans les paragraphes suivants.

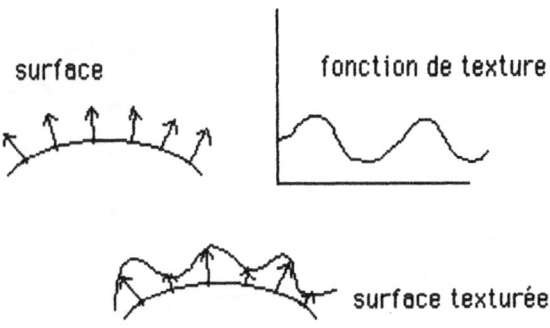

surface

fonction de texture

surface texturée

Fig. 7.3 Principe de la texture par perturbation de la normale

7.6 Les fractales

Pour synthétiser des montagnes réalistes, la représentation classique par des modèles géométriques est peu esthétique. La technique des systèmes de particules (voir 7.7) ne s'adapte évidemment pas, puisque les montagnes "n'évoluent pas". Par contre, la **théorie des fractales** de Mandelbrot (1975) est parfaite. Pourtant, dans la production de nombreuses images, comme c'est le cas en animation, l'application directe de cette théorie est très coûteuse. C'est pour cette raison que Fournier, Carpenter, et Fussell (1982) ont introduit une simplification de la méthode de Mandelbrot. Pour expliquer le principe prenons un exemple simple basé sur des objets construits à l'aide de faces triangulaires. Nous divisons chaque triangle en 4 triangles en reliant "les points milieux" des arêtes des triangles. Mais là où la théorie des fractales intervient, c'est que "le point milieu" d'une arête est décalé du vrai milieu en utilisant des processus stochastiques. On obtient donc, comme on le voit à la Figure 7.4, 4 triangles qui ne sont plus dans le plan du triangle original, mais dans 4 plans différents. On recommence alors le processus récursivement pour chaque triangle.

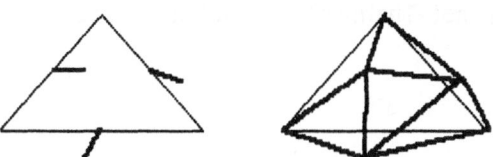

Fig. 7.4 Principes des fractales avec triangles

Un des problèmes importants à résoudre est celui de la **consistance externe**: comment élever le milieu d'une arête partagée par plusieurs triangles toujours de la même façon ? La Figure 7.5 nous montre que dans le cas d'un objet formé de faces quadrilatères, on peut aussi appliquer une méthode semblable où chaque face donne naissance à quatre faces dans des plans différents.

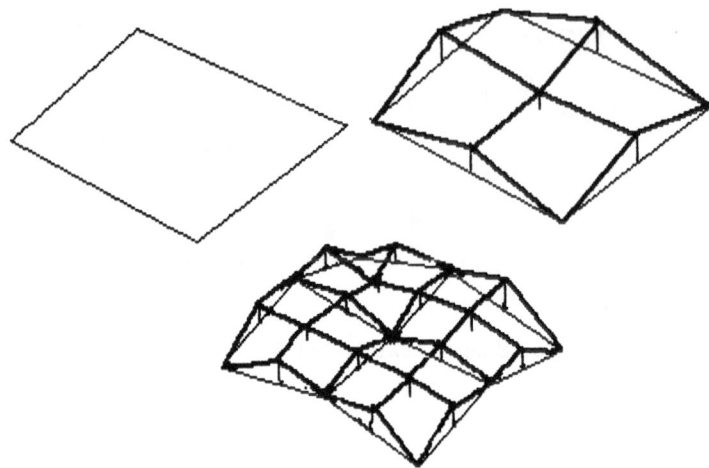

Fig. 7.5 Trois stades de génération de fractales quadrilatères

7.7 Les systèmes de particules

La technique de base a été mise au point par Reeves (1983). Il s'agit de faire évoluer des particules dans un système donné. Les particules naissent, meurent, se déplacent, changent de couleur, de taille. Les particules sont générées selon des processus stochastiques. L'apparence réaliste des particules pourrait être difficile à rendre à cause des problèmes de transparence et d'ombre portée. Cependant dans le cas d'explosions ou de feu, l'algorithme est simple car chaque particule peut être considérée comme une source de lumière ponctuelle. Chaque pixel va alors "gagner" de l'intensité lorsqu'elle couverte par une particule. Ce que nous avons introduit de nouveau dans **MIRANIM**, c'est la possibilité pour l'animateur de définir lui-même les lois d'évolution des couleurs, des tailles et la possibilité d'appliquer n'importe quel mouvement aux particules (Magnenat-Thalmann and Thalmann,1985).

8. L'ANIMATION PAR ORDINATEUR

8.1 Le rôle de l'ordinateur dans l'animation

Traditionnellement, on appelle **animation** le principe consistant à projeter à une cadence rapide (12, 18 ou 24 images par secondes) une suite d'images presqu'identiques pour simuler un mouvement ou une transformation.

L'ordinateur peut jouer différents rôles dans l'animation:

1. dans la création des dessins
2. dans la création des mouvements
3. dans le coloriage et le gouachage
4. dans le tournage
5. dans la postproduction

Si on considère les systèmes d'animation par ordinateur, on peut définir 5 niveaux de systèmes:

niveau 1
systèmes utilisés pour créer, colorier et modifier des dessins; ils ne prennent pas le temps en considération

niveau 2
systèmes permettant de calculer des dessins intermédiaires (inbetweens) et de déplacer des objets le long d'une trajectoire

niveau 3
systèmes prévoyant des opérations applicables sur des objets et des mouvements de caméras virtuelles

niveau 4
systèmes permettant de définir des **acteurs** (objets doués d'animation propre)

niveau 5
systèmes extensibles, basés sur la connaissance et doués d'apprentissage, basés sur l'intelligence artificielle

On sépare aussi très souvent l'animation par ordinateur en **animation assistée** par ordinateur et en **animation modélisée**.

L'animation assistée par ordinateur correspond à une animation de type traditionnelle où certaines tâches sont simplifiées et rationnalisées grâce à l'ordinateur.

L'animation modélisée correspond généralement à l'animation

tridimensionnelle où tous les mouvements et transformations sont générés par ordinateur et où il existe un modèle de haut niveau de ces mouvements et de ces transformations.

Dans la Figure 8.1, on peut voir le rôle de l'ordinateur dans chacun des types d'animation.

	assistée par ordinateur	**modélisée**
création d'objets	-digitalisation -édition graphique	-reconstruction 3D -modélisation
mouvement	-interpolation -P-courbes	-transformations -acteurs
couleur	-systèmes à peindre	-réalisme
caméra	-contrôle de caméra	-caméras virtuelles
post-production	synchronisation assistée	-édition automatique

Fig. 8.1 Le rôle de l'ordinateur dans l'animation

On trouvera au paragraphe suivant, les fondements de l'animation assistée par ordinateur et dans le paragraphe 8.3, un exemple de système d'animation modélisée.

Signalons encore la différence entre l'animation en **temps réel** et l'animation **image par image**. Dans le premier cas, on est capable de produire des dessins et de les modifier, dans une temps suffisament court (environ 1/15 de seconde), ce qui fait que l'animation peut se dérouler directement sur le terminal. L'animation image par image est analogue à l'animation traditionnelle et l'ordinateur peut prendre le temps nécessaire pour chaque image, ce qui peut être des heures dans le cas d'images réalistes très complexes.

8.2 L'animation assistée par ordinateur

On peut distinguer différentes fonctions dans ce type d'animation: l'interpolation, le déplacement selon une trajectoire et les systèmes à peindre.

L'interpolation

Le but consiste à produire des dessins intermédiaires entre deux dessins donnés (appelés dessins-clés). La technique utilisée est l'interpolation; mais il faut pour cela tout d'abord préparer les deux dessins-clés en leur ajoutant des points et en les séparant en sections que l'on fera correspondre. L'interpolation linéaire donne des résultats souvent insatisfaisants et on peut utiliser des interpolations courbes, notamment en se servant de courbes telles que les béta-splines.

La technique des squelettes

Pour éviter de faire des transformations complexes sur des dessins eux-mêmes complexes, Burtnyk et Wein (1976) ont introduit une technique consistant à définir un dessin plus simple appelé le **squelette** et à transformer ce squelette plutôt que le dessin complexe.

Les P-courbes

Cette technique due à Baecker (1969) définit des courbes qui non seulement décrivent la trajectoire d'un objet, mais aussi la variation de vitesse. En effet, dans ces P-courbes, les points ne sont pas équidistants en espace, mais en temps; donc lorsque deux points sont rapprochés, la vitesse est plus petite que quand les points sont éloignés. On contrôle ainsi le mouvement de manière graphique.

8.3 Décors, acteurs, caméras et lumières avec MIRANIM

MIRANIM (Magnenat-Thalmann et al, 1985) est un système permettant de créer des séquences d'animation tridimensionnelle par ordinateur. Les séquences peuvent être arbitrairement complexes et longues. Grâce à sa structure modulaire, **MIRANIM** peut être aussi bien utilisé par des artistes non-informaticiens que par des programmeurs expérimentés. Une séquence d'animation est caractérisée par son **script** qui décrit toute la mise en scène. La séquence peut comporter plusieurs **scènes**. Chaque scène comprend des objets inanimés que l'on regroupe sous le terme de **décor**. Les objets animés, appelés **acteurs** changent au cours du temps, grâce à des **transformations** et des mouvements que l'animateur définit. Ces transformations sont régies par des **lois** et contrôlées par des **variables** obéissant à ces lois. Les transformations peuvent être aussi simples que des rotations ou aussi complexes que des torsions, des flexions ou des déformations. Les objets qui servent aussi bien pour les décors que pour les acteurs sont construits à l'aide de commandes regroupées dans un système évolué nommé **BODY-BUILDING**. Les décors et les acteurs sont colorés et éclairés par des **sources de lumière**. Finalement, le décor et les acteurs sont vus par des **caméras** dites virtuelles. Ces caméras peuvent évoluer dans le temps comme si elles étaient manipulées par des cameramen; on peut donc faire tous les effets tels que zoom-in, zoom-out, tracking, panoramique ou travelling. Toute cette construction d'une scène se fait sans aucune programmation grâce à un certain nombre de commandes très simples. Cependant, il est toujours possible de programmer des objets ou des transformations lorsqu'on veut faire des effets très compliqués non possibles dans le système de base. Dans ce cas, on introduit des **modèles procéduraux.** Cette approche est très intéressante, car elle permet enfin de briser l'incommunicabilité fréquente entre informaticiens et artistes. L'animateur non-informaticien peut littéralement commander au programmeur un modèle procédural en spécifiant la commande qu'il souhaite avoir pour le faire fonctionner; par exemple, on peut introduire une commande EXPLOSION qui nécessite de

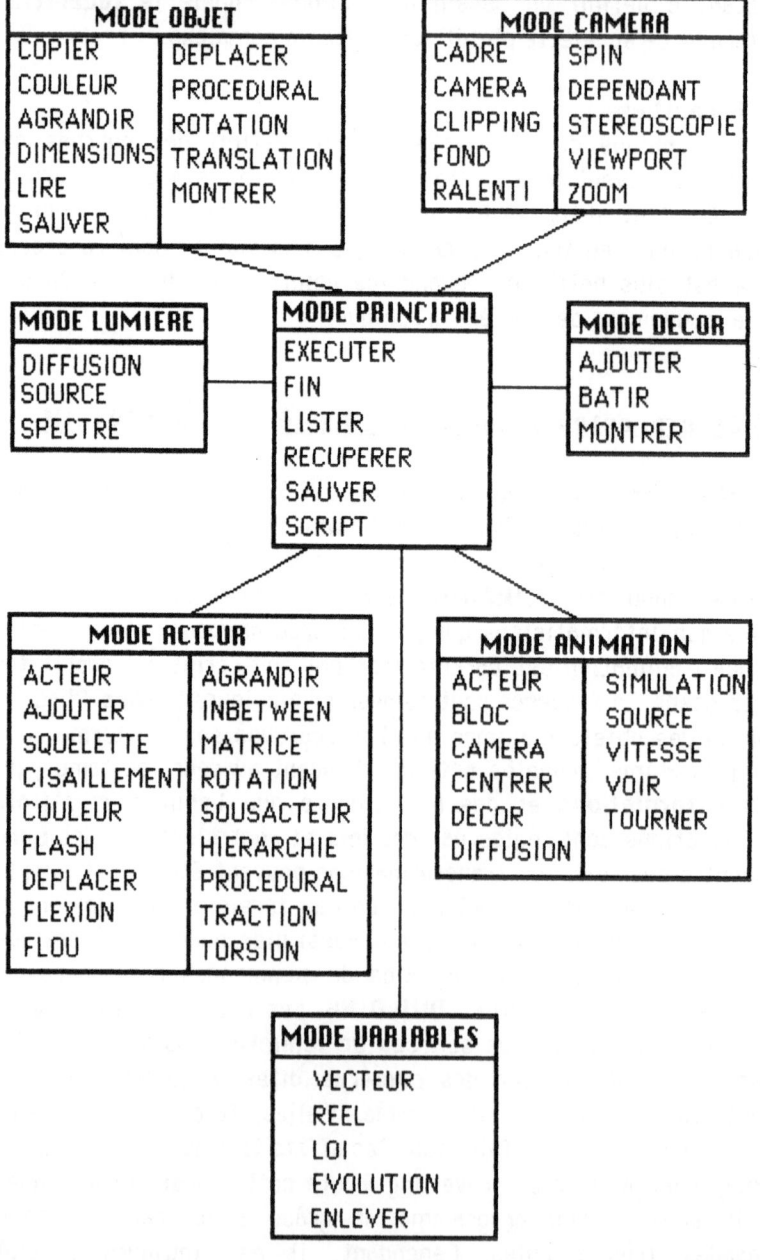

Fig. 8.2 Les commandes interactives d'animation du système **MIRANIM**

donner le centre de l'explosion et son intensité. L'animateur n'a évidemment pas besoin de connaître le contenu du modèle procédural. L'approche procédurale a notamment été utilisée pour réaliser des systèmes de particules, pour modéliser des explosions et pour permettre l'utilisation de lois d'animation seulement exprimables sous forme d'équations différentielles.

La Figure 8.2 nous montre le tableau des commandes interactives d'animation.

REFERENCES

Livres

Foley, J. and Van Dam A., **Fundamentals of Interactive Computer Graphics,** Addisson-Wesley, 1981

Newman, W.M. and Sproull, R.F., **Principles of Interactive Computer Graphics,** McGraw-Hill, 1973

Giloi, W., **Interactive Computer Graphics, Data Structures, Algorithms, Languages**, Prentice-Hall, 1978

Rogers, D. and Adams, J.A. ,**Mathematical Elements for Computer Graphics**, McGraw-Hill, 1976

Rogers, D. **Procedural Elements for Computer Graphics**, McGraw-Hill, 1985

Harrington, S. , **Computer Graphics: a Programming Approach**, McGraw-Hill, 1983

Magnenat-Thalmann N. and Thalmann, D. **Computer Animation: Theory and Practice**, Springer-Verlag, Tokyo, 1985

en français:

Magnenat-Thalmann, N. and Thalmann, D., **Informatique Graphique: Concepts et Techniques avec le langage MIRA**, Gaetan Morin, Chicoutimi, 1983

Périodiques

IEEE Computer Graphics and Applications
ACM Transactions on Graphics
The Visual Computer, Springer Verlag
Computer Graphics Forum, North Holland
Computers and Graphics, Pergamon Press
CAD journal, Butterworth Co
Computer Vision, Graphics and Image Processing, Academic Press
Computer Graphics World, PennWell Publ. Co.
Informatique et Image, Science et Technologie, Québec

Conférences annuelles organisées par des associations

SIGGRAPH (USA)
National Computer Graphics Association (USA)
Graphics Interface (Canada)
Eurographics (Europe)
Computer Graphics Tokyo (Japon)
CAD (Grande-Bretagne)
Computer Graphics, Online (Grande-Bretagne)
CAMP (Allemagne)

Bibliographies

Pooch, U.W. **Computer Graphics Interactive Techniques, and Image Processing 1970-1975: A Bibliography**, Computer, Août 1976

Schrack,G.F. **Computer Graphics: a Keyword-Indexed Bibliography for the Years 1976, 1977 and 1978,** Computer graphics and Image Processing, Academic Press, Vol.14, 1981

Barsky B.A. **Computer-Aided Geometric Design: a Bibliography with Keywords and Classified Index**, IEEE Computer Graphics and Applications, Juillet 1981

Magnenat-Thalmann, N. and Thalmann, D., **An Indexed Bibliography on Computer Animation,** IEEE Computer Graphics and Applications, Juillet 1985

Articles et publications choisies

Nous pouvons citer les principaux articles référencés dans ce cours ainsi que ceux qui ont servi à son élaboration.

Standards et langages

Bono, P.R.; Encarnacao, J.L.; Hopgood, F.R.A. and ten Hagen, P.J.W., **GKS - The First Standard,** IEEE Computer Graphics and Applications, July 1982, pp.9-23

Status Report of the Graphics Standards Planning Committee, Computer Graphics, Vol. 11, 1977

Magnenat-Thalmann, N. and Thalmann D., **A Graphical Extension of PASCAL Based on Graphical Types**, Software-Practice and Experience, Vol 11, 1981, pp. 55-62

Magnenat-Thalmann, N.; Thalmann, D. and Fortin, M. **MIRA-SHADING: A Language for the Synthesis and the Animation of Realistic Images**, <u>Frontiers in Computer Graphics</u>, Springer-Verlag, Tokyo, 1985

<u>Modélisation géométrique</u>

Bezier, P. **Numerical Control-Mathematics and Applications**, Wiley, London,1972

Coons, S.A. **Surfaces for Computer Aided Design**, Techn. Report, Design Division, MIT,1964

Barsky, B.A. **The Beta-Spline: A Local Representation Based on Shape Parameters and Fundamental Geometric Measures**, PhD Thesis, Univ. Utah, 1981

<u>Réalisme</u>

Sutherland, I.E., Sproull, R.F. and Schumacker, R.A., **A Characterization of Ten Hidden-Surface Algorithms**, <u>Computing Surveys</u>, Vol.6, No1, 1974, pp.1-55

Appel, A. **The notion of quantitative Invisibility and the Machine Rendering of Solids**, <u>SJCC</u>, AFIPS, Vol. 32, 1967, pp. 37-45

Galimberti, R. and Montanari, U. **An Algorithm for Hidden-line Elimination**, <u>Comm. ACM</u>, Vol.12, No 4, 1969, pp. 206

Catmull, E. **Computer Display of Curved Surfaces**, <u>Proc. IEEE Conf. on Computer Graphics, Pattern Recognition and Data Structures</u>, 1975

Encarnacao, J. **Survey of and new solutions for the hidden-line problem**, <u>Proc. GC Symp. Delft</u>, 1970

Warnock,J. **A Hidden-Surface Algorithm for Computer Generated Half-Tone Pictures**, Univ Utah Comp. Sc. Dept. ,TR 4-15, NTIS AD-753 671

Watkins, G.S. **A Real-Time Visible Surface Algorithm**, Univ. Utah Comp. Sc. Dept., UTEC-CSc-70-101,1970,NTIS AD-762 004

Phong, Bui-Tuong **Illumination for Computer-Generated Pictures**, <u>Comm. ACM</u>, Vol.18, No6, 1975, pp. 311-317

Fournier, A.; Fussell, D. and Carpenter, L. **Computer Rendering of Stochastic Models**, <u>Comm. ACM</u>, vol.25, NO 6, 1982, pp. 371-384

Gouraud, H. **An Improved Illumination Model for Shaded Display,** <u>Comm. ACM</u>, Vol 23, NO 6, 1980, pp. 343-349

Kay D.S. and Greenberg, D. **Transparency for Computer Synthetized Images**, <u>Proc. SIGGRAPH '79</u>, pp. 158-164

Mandelbrot, B. **Stochastic models for the earth's relief, the shape and fractal dimension of coastlines, and the number area rule for islands**, <u>Proc. National Acad.-Sc USA</u>, Vol 72, No 10, pp. 2825-2828

Reeves, W.T. **Particle Systems - a Technique for Modeling a Class of Fuzzy Objects**, <u>Proc SIGGRAPH '83</u>, pp. 359-3

Animation

Baecker, R.M. **Picture-Driven Animation**, <u>SJCC</u>, 1969, AFIPS Press, Montvale, N.J., pp.273-288

Burtnyk N. and Wein, M. **Interactive Skeleton Techniques for Enhancing Motion Dynamics in Key Frame Animation**, <u>Comm. ACM</u>, Vol 19, No 10, 1976, pp. 564-569

Magnenat-Thalmann, N. and Thalmann, D. **The Use of High Level Graphical Types in the MIRA Animation System**, <u>IEEE Computer Graphics and Applications</u>, Vol. 3, No 9, 1983, pp. 9-16

Magnenat-Thalmann, N.; Thalmann, D. and Fortin, M. **MIRANIM: An Extensible Director-Oriented System for the Animation of Realistic Images**, <u>IEEE Computer Graphics and Applications</u>, Vol. 5, No 3, 1985, pp. 61-73

Mathematical Elements for Computer Graphics

S. P. Mudur

PRELIMINARY REMARKS

In the early days of Computer Graphics primary attention had to be given to the mathematics of simple geometric elements like points,lines and planes. Homogeneous coordinates and space transformation using matrices also received considerable attention. This is much less true today, since most of this mathematics has now become standard, is available in most computer graphics texts, is usually incorporated as part of many of the available graphics software packages and is even being incorporated into some of the more sophisticated graphics workstation processors. In this tutorial therefore the emphasis has been shifted to the mathematics of more complex geometric entities such as polygonal regions, curves and surfaces. Emphasis has also been placed on algorithms for processing these shapes and in particular generating various kinds of images of these geometric shapes.

In addition to supplementing the lectures these notes have been written so as to serve as a reference to some of the basic mathematical formulations/algorithms in common use in computer graphics.

Chapter 1 covers basic geometric concepts. This includes
. Homogeneous coordiantes and matrix transformations
. Analytical and computational techniques for lines and planes, for representation, display and simple geometric computations.
. Efficient algorithms for detecting intersection between sets of line segments.

Chapter 2 discusses regions in a plane, particularly representation issues and alogrithms for some typical operations with special emphasis on polygonal regions. This chapter includes a lot of the recent research in computational geometry, material that is not presently available in any book on computer graphics. It discusses
. Regions as point sets in R^2 and the basis for using boundary representations
. Fill area algorithms for displaying boundary defined regions
. Point location problems
. Clipping, intersection and other Boolean operations
. Decomposition and Convex Hull problems

Chapter 3 presents curve and surface representation both in the implicit and in the parametric forms. The matrix notation is used uniformly to present all the forms. The various curve forms discussed are:
. Plane curves, including conics and super-conics in their implicit and rational forms.
. Twisted Curves, both interpolating and approximating forms, including Hermite, Cardinal, Bezier, B-Spline, Tensioned splines and Beta-Splines.

The surface forms presented are:
. Quadrics and super-quadrics in their implicit and rational forms.
. Parametric bi-cubics such as Coons, Bezier, B-Spline Beta-spline forms.
. Product surfaces in parametric form, which are shown to include the quadrics and superquadrics as spherical product surfaces as well as some swept and spun surfaces such as a torus.

Chapter 4 discusses the processing of curves and surfaces in their implicit and/or parametric forms. Much of the material in this chapter is not covered in full in any text. A variety of tasks are considered including rendering and display, some mass properties and intersection detection. The chapter reviews algorithms/techniques for the following tasks:
. Transformation, display, arc length of curves and surface area of patches.
. Intersection of curves
. Intersection of surface patches and curves and surface patches.
. Silhouette detection
. Hidden line, rendering and visible surface algorithms.

It has been possible to produce these notes only because of the excellent environment provided by the National Centre and the help and encouragement received from my colleagues in the centre and the Tata Institute of Fundamental Research.

1. BASIC GEOMETRIC CONCEPTS

1.1 COORDINATE SYSTEMS AND TRANSFORMATIONS

We begin by discussing some of the concepts fundamental to geometry. In school geometry the so called elementary Euclidean geometry of the ancient Greeks - the main objects of study are various metrical properties of simple geometric figures or objects. The main aim of analytic (or coordinate) geometry is to describe geometric objects by means of algebraic formulae referred to a Cartesian system of coordinates of the plane or 3-dimensional space. In differential geometry subtler techniques of differential calculus and linear algebra are brought into play for describing geometric figures. Being applicable to general "smooth" geometric objects, these techniques provide access to a wider class of such objects.

Our most basic conception of geometry is set out in the following two points:
. We do our geometry in a certain space consisting of points P,Q, ...
. Associated with each point in space is an ordered n-tuple $[x_1, x_2, ..., x_n]$ of real numbers, the coordinates of the point, in such a way that the following two conditions hold:
(i) Distinct points are assigned distinct n-tuples. Points $P = [p_1, p_2, ..., p_n]$ and $Q = [q_1, q_2, ..., q_n]$ are one and the same point if and only if $p_i = q_i$ for all i between 1 and n.
(ii) Every possible n-tuple is assigned to some point in space.

A space furnished with a system of cartesian coordinates satisfying conditions (i) and (ii) above is called an n-dimensional space and is denoted by R^n.

1.2 TWO DIMENSIONAL TRANSFORMATIONS

[Maxwell,Newman/Sproull,Foley/van Dam,Coons-1,Carlbom/Paciorek]
A point in two dimensional space 'a' defined by coordinates is represented as a vector $[x,y]_a$. We shall use the subscript only when it is necessary to distinguish between vectors in different spaces,say, a,b,c etc. Otherwise we shall be using the unsubscripted vector without any ambiguity.

A unit square would thus be described by four vectors, [0,0], [1,0], [1,1], [0,1].

Suppose we wished to define an operation which could change an arbitrary vector $[x,y]_a$ to a new vector $[x,y]_b$. This operation is known as a two dimensional transform and may be thought of as a two dimensional function. One way of writing this transformation is

$$x = ax + cy$$
$$y = bx + dy$$

where a,b,c,d are constants that depend on the nature of the transformation (scale change, rotation etc). Using matrix notation this can be written as:

$$[x,y]_b = [x,y]_a \begin{bmatrix} a & b \\ c & d \end{bmatrix}$$

We can investigate some special cases of this 2 x 2 matrix and see what the geometric interpretation is. Take:

$$[x,y]_b = [x,y]_a \begin{bmatrix} a & 0 \\ 0 & 1 \end{bmatrix} = [ax,y]$$

This is scaling along x by the factor a. Similarly take

$$[x,y]_b = [x,y]_a \begin{bmatrix} a & 0 \\ 0 & d \end{bmatrix} = [ax,dy]$$

This is scaling along x by 'a' and along y by 'd'. Now consider

$$[x,y]_b = [x,y]_a \begin{bmatrix} 1 & b \\ 0 & 1 \end{bmatrix} = [x,bx+y]$$

Here $x_b = x_a$ but y_b is given by the linear equation $bx_a + y_a$. In particular let us apply this transformation to our unit square.

$$\begin{bmatrix} x1,y1 \\ x2,y2 \\ x3,y3 \\ x4,y4 \end{bmatrix} = \begin{bmatrix} 0 & 0 \\ 1 & 0 \\ 0 & 1 \\ 1 & 1 \end{bmatrix} \begin{bmatrix} 1 & b \\ 0 & 1 \end{bmatrix} = \begin{bmatrix} 0 & 0 \\ 1 & b \\ 0 & 1 \\ 1 & 1+b \end{bmatrix}$$

The square has been transformed into a parallelogram. This is customarily referred to as the 'shear' transformation in the y direction.

$$\begin{bmatrix} 1 & 0 \\ c & 1 \end{bmatrix} \text{ yields a shear in the x direction.}$$

Let us now combine the y-shear and the x-shear in that order.

$$[x,y]_b = [x,y]_a \begin{bmatrix} 1 & b \\ 0 & 1 \end{bmatrix}$$

$$[x,y]_c = [x,y]_b \begin{bmatrix} 1 & 0 \\ c & 1 \end{bmatrix} = [x,y]_a \begin{bmatrix} 1 & b \\ 0 & 1 \end{bmatrix} \begin{bmatrix} 1 & 0 \\ c & 1 \end{bmatrix} = [x,y]_a \begin{bmatrix} 1+bc & b \\ c & 1 \end{bmatrix}$$

The unit square when subjected to this transformation results as follows:

$$\begin{bmatrix} x1,y1 \\ x2,y2 \\ x3,y3 \\ x4,y4 \end{bmatrix} \begin{bmatrix} 0,0 \\ 1,0 \\ 0,1 \\ 1,1 \end{bmatrix} \begin{bmatrix} 1+bc & b \\ c & 1 \end{bmatrix} = \begin{bmatrix} 0 & 0 \\ 1+bc & b \\ c & 1 \\ 1+bc+c & 1+b \end{bmatrix}$$

It can be easily shown that this is a parallelogram. If we combine the two shearing transformations with the two scale changes we obtain

$$\begin{bmatrix} 1 & b \\ 0 & 1 \end{bmatrix} \begin{bmatrix} 1 & 0 \\ c & 1 \end{bmatrix} \begin{bmatrix} a & 0 \\ 0 & 1 \end{bmatrix} \begin{bmatrix} 1 & 0 \\ 0 & a \end{bmatrix} = \begin{bmatrix} a+abc & bd \\ ac & d \end{bmatrix}$$

It can be shown that this represents the most general possible 2 x 2 transformation matrix.

Consider the figure alongside: Now obviously

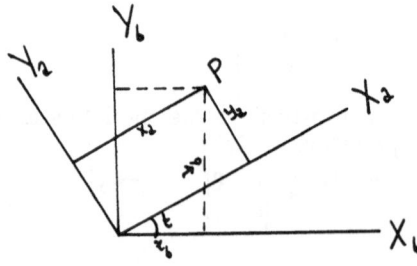

$$x_b = x_a \cos t - y_a \sin t$$
$$y_b = x_a \sin t + y_a \cos t$$

$$[x,y]_b = [x,y]_a \begin{bmatrix} \cos t & \sin t \\ -\sin t & \cos t \end{bmatrix}$$

This is the well known two dimensional rotation function.

Note that the inverse of the rotation transformation matrix is its transpose. This is because its determinant evaluates to 1. All the transformations investigated so far change points in the plane but leave one point unchanged. This point is the origin of coordinates. Thus it is impossible to do pure translation, where every vector is moved a definite dx and dy.

Consider the following matrix product:

$$[x,y,1]_b = [x,y,1]_a \begin{bmatrix} 1 & 0 & 0 \\ 0 & 1 & 0 \\ e & f & 1 \end{bmatrix} = [x+e,y+f,1]$$

The combined effect of first performing a general origin preserving 2-x 2 transformation and then subsequently a translation is given by the matrix product below:

$$\begin{bmatrix} a & b & 0 \\ c & d & 0 \\ 0 & 0 & 1 \end{bmatrix} \begin{bmatrix} 1 & 0 & 0 \\ 0 & 1 & 0 \\ e & f & 1 \end{bmatrix} = \begin{bmatrix} a & b & 0 \\ c & d & 0 \\ e & f & 1 \end{bmatrix}$$

Incidentally, if we perform the translation first and then the origin preserving transformation we get a different result.

The right hand side matrix above which represents a general two dimensional transformation with translation is a special case of the three dimensional transformation, say T

$$T = \begin{bmatrix} a & b & c \\ d & e & f \\ g & h & i \end{bmatrix} \qquad \text{In general } [x,y,z]_b = [x,y,z]_a.[T]$$

As before the elements of T will depend on the nature of the transformation. Further it can be shown again that this is the most general form of the 3D transformation incorporating scale changes, shear and rotation.

However, the origin (in 3D) is preserved by this transformation too!

Consider the unit cube given by the series of vectors and transformed by this 3 x 3 matrix.

$$
\begin{aligned}
[x1,y1,z1] & \\
\cdot & \\
\cdot & = \\
\cdot & \\
\cdot & \\
\cdot & \\
\cdot & \\
\cdot & \\
[x8,y8,z8] &
\end{aligned}
\begin{bmatrix} 0,0,0 \\ 0,0,1 \\ 0,1,0 \\ 0,1,1 \\ 1,0,0 \\ 1,0,1 \\ 1,1,0 \\ 1,1,1 \end{bmatrix}
\begin{bmatrix} a & b & c \\ d & e & f \\ g & h & i \end{bmatrix} =
\begin{bmatrix}
0 & 0 & 0 \\
g & h & i \\
d & e & g \\
d+g & e+h & f+i \\
a & b & c \\
a+g & b+h & c+i \\
a+d & b+e & c+f \\
a+d+g & b+e+h & c+f+i
\end{bmatrix}
$$

It can be easily shown that the faces of the transformed unit cube are all parallelograms, and hence that the original cube transforms into a parallelepiped.

1.3 PROJECTIVE TRANSFORMATION

[Newman/Sproull,Foley/van Dam,Coons,Carlbom/Paciorek]
Consider the matrix transformation

$$[x,y,z]_b = [x,y,1]_a \begin{bmatrix} a & b & c \\ d & e & f \\ g & h & i \end{bmatrix} \qquad \text{so that } z_b = (cx_a + fy_a + i)$$

Now consider the figure obtained by dividing the vector $[x,y,z]_b$ by z_b. The result is $[x,y,1]_c$ say, P_c. The point $[x\ y\ z]_b$ has, by this division, been "projected" into point P_c in the plane $z_b = 1$ with coordinates $[x,y,1]_c$ and the resulting figure, of which this is a typical point, is two dimensional. We often refer to coordinates $[x,y,z]_b$ as the homogeneous coordinates of a point in two dimensions. They are also the ordinary coordinates of a point in three dimensions.

In order to distinguish normal coordinates form homogeneous coordinates we shall use the notation $[wx,wy,w]$ for homogeneous coordinates. Note that wx,wy are 2 letter symbols and not the multiplication of two symbols. The normal coordinates are obtained always at the end by performing the division operations wx/w and wy/w. If after some transformations $w = 0$ this division must not be performed and we know the point is at infinity.

Now consider the transformation

$$[wx,wy,w]_b = [wx,wy,w]_a \begin{bmatrix} a & b & c \\ d & e & f \\ g & h & i \end{bmatrix} = [wx,wy,w]_a [T]$$

In two dimensions this homogeneous transformation carries one plane figure into another. As we shall see later straight lines in a plane are also transformed into straight lines.

1.4 THREE DIMENSIONAL TRANSFORMATIONS

[Newman/Sproull,Foley/van Dam,Coons,Carlbom/Paciorek]
We shall now extend these ideas to three dimensions. One must use a 4 x 4 transformation matrix.

$$[wx,wy,wz,w]_b = [wx,wy,wz,w]_a \begin{bmatrix} a & b & c & d \\ e & f & g & h \\ i & j & k & l \\ m & n & o & p \end{bmatrix}$$

Let us look at some particular matrices and what they do geometrically.

Identity Transformation

$$[wx,wy,wz,w]_b = [wx,wy,wz,w]_a \begin{bmatrix} 1 & 0 & 0 & 0 \\ 0 & 1 & 0 & 0 \\ 0 & 0 & 1 & 0 \\ 0 & 0 & 0 & 1 \end{bmatrix} = [wx,wy,wz,w]_a$$

Scale changes

$$[wx,wy,wz,w]_b = [wx,wy,wz,w]_a \begin{bmatrix} a & 0 & 0 & 0 \\ 0 & b & 0 & 0 \\ 0 & 0 & c & 0 \\ 0 & 0 & 0 & 1 \end{bmatrix} = [awx,bwy,cwz,w]_a$$

This amounts to independent scale changes along each axis. Uniform scaling can be achieved by setting a=b=c or as below:

$$[wx,wy,wz,w]_b = [wx,wy,wz,w]_a \begin{bmatrix} 1 & 0 & 0 & 0 \\ 0 & 1 & 0 & 0 \\ 0 & 0 & 1 & 0 \\ 0 & 0 & 0 & d \end{bmatrix}$$

So that $x_b = (wx/w)_b = (wx/wd)_a = (x/d)_a$ Similarly $y_b = y_a/d$ and $z_b = z_a/d$

Single axis rotations

It is obvious that the wz_a coordinates remain unaffected by any rotation about z axis. It has effect only on wx_a and wy_a. Thus using the earlier derived two dimensional transformation matrix we have

$$Rz = \begin{bmatrix} cost & sint & 0 & 0 \\ -sint & cost & 0 & 0 \\ 0 & 0 & 1 & 0 \\ 0 & 0 & 0 & 1 \end{bmatrix}$$

Similarly we can derive

$$Ry = \begin{bmatrix} cost & 0 & -sint & 0 \\ 0 & 1 & 0 & 0 \\ sint & 0 & cost & 0 \\ 0 & 0 & 0 & 1 \end{bmatrix} \qquad Rx = \begin{bmatrix} 1 & 0 & 0 & 0 \\ 0 & cost & sint & 0 \\ 0 & -sint & cost & 0 \\ 0 & 0 & 0 & 1 \end{bmatrix}$$

Translations

$$[wx,wy,wz,w]_b = [wx,wy,wz,w]_a \begin{bmatrix} 1 & 0 & 0 & 0 \\ 0 & 1 & 0 & 0 \\ 0 & 0 & 1 & 0 \\ k & l & m & 1 \end{bmatrix}$$

Skew or shear

As in two dimensions the yz-shear transformation is as given below:

$$Syz = \begin{bmatrix} 1 & 0 & 0 & 0 \\ e & 1 & 0 & 0 \\ i & 0 & 1 & 0 \\ 0 & 0 & 0 & 1 \end{bmatrix}$$

Similarly

$$Szx = \begin{bmatrix} 1 & b & 0 & 0 \\ 0 & 1 & 0 & 0 \\ 0 & j & 1 & 0 \\ 0 & 0 & 0 & 1 \end{bmatrix} \qquad Sxy = \begin{bmatrix} 1 & 0 & c & 0 \\ 0 & 1 & s & 0 \\ 0 & 0 & 1 & 0 \\ 0 & 0 & 0 & 1 \end{bmatrix}$$

1.5 PERSPECTIVE TRANSFORMATION

[Newman/Sproull,Foley/van Dam,Coons,Carlbom/Paciorek]
Any combination of the transformations discussed so far will result in the general

transformation of the form

$$\begin{bmatrix} a & b & c & 0 \\ e & f & g & 0 \\ i & j & k & 0 \\ m & n & o & p \end{bmatrix}$$

In this the upper left partition of the matrix contains nine numbers that describe shear, scale change and rotation transformation; the bottom 3 elements row represents a translation and the single bottom right number describe a uniform scaling factor. We can now proceed to investigate the fourth column of this matrix. We take the matrix below:

$$[wx, wy, wz, w]_b \; = \; [x, y, z, 1]_a \begin{bmatrix} 1 & 0 & 0 & 0 \\ 0 & 1 & 0 & 0 \\ 0 & 0 & 1 & n \\ 0 & 0 & 0 & 1 \end{bmatrix}$$

So that

$$[x \; y \; z]_b = [x/(nz+1), y/(nz+1), z/(nz+1)]_a$$

This mapping is accomplished by a transformation in 4 dimensions followed by a projection and a section to yield a 3 dimensional space. By similar triangles

$$x_a/a = x_b/(z_a+a) \text{ so that } x_b = x_a/(\tfrac{z_a}{a}+1)$$

Similarly $y_b = y_a/(\tfrac{z_a}{a}+1)$ and $z_b = a$.

This is equivalent to applying above matrix and performing the mapping.

In order to make some qualitative remarks of this mapping we consider the following four homogeneous points $[1,0,0,0]$, $[0,1,0,0]$, $[0,0,1,0]$, $[0,0,0,1]$. These first three are respectively the points at infinity along the x,y and z axis. The fourth is the origin of the space. Applying the above transformation will show that three of the points are mapped into themselves; but the point on the z axis maps into the point $[0,0,1]$. It is no longer at infinity.

To give a more geometrical interpretation to this consider the projection of a point P_a into a point P_b in the $z = 0$ plane taking the centre of projection at $[0 \; 0 \; -a]$.

This is nothing but the perspective projection on the $z = 0$ plane. Often called the one point perspective because all lines parallel to the z axis will appear to converge after the mapping to the point $[0,0]_b$. This point is called as the "principle vanishing point". It should however be noted that any set of parallel lines not parallel to the projection plane will converge to a vanishing point. Thus even in the so called "one point perspective" there are an infinity of vanishing points. However, there are at most three principal vanishing points corresponding to the number of principal axes cut by the projection plane. For example, if the projection plane is normal to the z-axis then only lines parallel to the z-axis have a principal vanishing point, since lines parallel to the x- or y-axes are also parallel to the projection plane and have no vanishing point.

Perspective projections are categorised by the number of principal vanishing points they have and therefore by the number of axes the projection plane cuts. The figure below illustrates these. The two point perspective is the one most commonly used in architectural, industrial design and advertising drawings with the projection plane cutting both x and z-axes and vertical lines remaining parallel.

The transformation matrix for the two or three point perspective is obtained very easily as a combination of successive simpler transformation. For example, specifically the 30-60 two-point perspective could be obtained as below:
(1) rotate about y axis by 30
(2) translate so that projection plane is at $z_b = d$ and the centre of projection is at $(0,0,0)_b$
(3) perspective with n = 1/d

In a general specification of the perspective view the centre of projection also need not be along any of the principal axis. Both the core system and GKS 3D have adopted a general viewing transformation for the specification; which include in addition the specification of a view volume and a view up vector and view reference point. For details of this and a derivation of the transformation matrix for this the reader is referred to [Foley/van Dam,Carlbom/Paciorek].

1.6 AXONOMETRIC TRANSFORMATION

[Newman/Sproull,Foley/van Dam,Coons-1,Carlbom/Paciorek]
A special case of the projective transformation puts the projection point at infinity. So that in that transformation, n = 0. These are known as axonometric projections in descriptive geometry and are also referred to as parallel projections. Parallel projections are categorised into two types based on the relation between the direction of projection and the projection plane. In an orthographic projection the direction is normal to the projection plane while in an oblique projection it is not.

The plane, elevation and end view are the most common tyes of orthographic projection used in engineering drawings. In each of these the direction of projection is one of the principal axes. These are used mainly because distances and angles are preserved and measurements can be made on the drawings. However the 3D nature of the object is difficult to deduce. So projection planes not normal to a principal axis are used so that several faces of an object are simultaneously visible. Parallelism of lines is preserved but angles are not. Distances can be measured along each principal axis but possibly with different scale factors. Three specific cases need attention:
Isometric : the projection plane normal makes equal angles with all three principal axes.
Dimetric : the projection plane normal makes equal angles with two of the principal axes and a different angle with the third axis.
Trimetric : the projection plane normal makes unequal angles with the three principal axes.

The transformation matrices for the orthographic projections are very simple to derive. Basically we are given the projection plane normal,say, [a,b,c] in the space. We apply transformations so that this vector aligns with the transformed z-axis and then project orthographically along the z-axis. For this we first rotate about the y axis so that the vector [a,b,c] now lies in the YZ plan to obtain the matrix below:
Note : $\cos(t_y) = c/sqrt(a^2+c^2) = A$; $\sin(t_y) = a/sqrt(a^2+c^2) = B$;

$$R_y = \begin{bmatrix} A & 0 & -B & 0 \\ 0 & 1 & 0 & 0 \\ B & 0 & C & 0 \\ 0 & 0 & 0 & 1 \end{bmatrix}$$

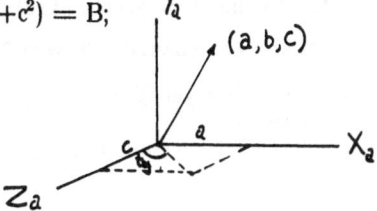

Now rotate about x_b axis by $-t_x$

Note : $\cos(t_x) = \text{sqrt}(a^2+c^2)/\text{sqrt}(a^2+b^2+c^2)$, $\sin(t_x) = -b/\text{sqrt}(a^2+b^2+c^2)$
$= C$ $= D$

So that

$$R_x = \begin{bmatrix} 1 & 0 & 0 & 0 \\ 0 & C & D & 0 \\ 0 & -D & C & 0 \\ 0 & 0 & 0 & 1 \end{bmatrix}$$

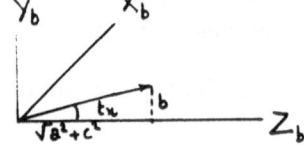

For an isometric projection we can choose the normal as [a,a,a] so that

$$T_{isom} = \begin{bmatrix} 1/\text{sqrt}(2) & 0 & -1/\text{sqrt}(2) & 0 \\ 0 & 1 & 0 & 0 \\ 1/\text{sqrt}(2) & 0 & 1/\text{sqrt}(2) & 0 \\ 0 & 0 & 0 & 1 \end{bmatrix} \begin{bmatrix} 1 & 0 & 0 & 0 \\ 0 & \text{sqrt}(2)/\text{sqrt}(3) & -1/\text{sqrt}(3) & 0 \\ 0 & 1/\text{sqrt}(3) & \text{sqrt}(2)/\text{sqrt}(3) & 0 \\ 0 & 0 & 0 & 1 \end{bmatrix}$$

Similar matrices may be obtained for the dimetric with equal scaling of x and y axis by choosing (a,a,b) as the normal.

In the oblique projections the projection plane may be chosen normal to one of the three principal axes. But the direction of projection makes some non-zero angle with the normal. Two special cases are the cavalier projection (45°) and the cabinet projection (arccot(1/2)). As a result for the cavalier projection a line perpendicular to the projection plane projects into a line of the same length as the line itself. Lines parallel to the other two axis remain orthogonal. For the cabinet projection the length is halved. In order to derive the transformation matrix consider the figure below:

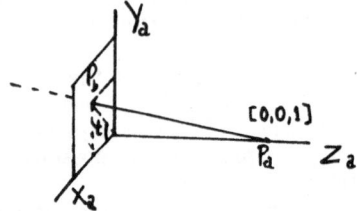

$P_b = [l\cos(t), l\sin(t), 0]$ and $[x,y,z]_b = [x+zl\cos(t), y+zl\sin(t), 0]_a$

So that the transformation matrix takes the form

$$\begin{bmatrix} 1 & 0 & 0 & 0 \\ 0 & 1 & 0 & 0 \\ l\cos t & l\sin t & 0 & 0 \\ 0 & 0 & 0 & 1 \end{bmatrix}$$

For cavalier projection we want $l = 1$ so that $t = 45°$ and for cabinet projection we want $l = 1/2$ so that $t = \text{arccot}(1/2)$ or nearly 63.4°.

1.7 ANALYTICAL AND COMPUTATIONAL TECHNIQUES FOR LINES

[Faux/Pratt,Bowyer/Woodwark]
Implicit Form
A line in two dimensional space may be represented by the equation below:

ax+by+c = 0 or in homogeneous coordinates notation $[wx,wy,w].|A,B,C]^t = 0$

Thus the column vector $[A,B,C]^t$ may be used to denote a line in 2-dimensional space. It can be shown that all the transformations of this vector represent the same line. For fixed A,B and C all number triplets that satisfy $[wx,wy,w]\,[A,B,C]^t = 0$ are coordinates of points on a fixed line. Conversely if $[wx,wy,w]$ are fixed then all numbers triples $[A,B,C]^t$ that satisfy the equation represent lines through the fixed point. For this reason we refer to $[A,B,C]^t$ as a line vector. When C = 0 the line passes through the origin and we have Ax + By = 0.

Now let us see how to transform lines in the plane. The equation of the line before the transformation is $[wx,wy,w].[A,B,C]^t = 0$

After the transformation T is applied the following holds: $[wx,wy,w]_b = [wx,wy,w]_a.T$

The linear equality can be preserved by writing $[wx,wy,w].T.T^1.[A,B,C]^t = 0$

Because $T.T^1$ = identity matrix, if we now write $[A,B,C]^t_b = T^1.[A,B,C]^t_a$

as the transformed line vector, then after the transformation we have a new valid linear equation $[wx,wy,w]_b.[A,B,C]^t_b = 0$

Instead of T^1 it is better to use T^* the adjoint of T, as it differs from T by only a scalar factor det(T) and is not only easier to compute but exists even when T is singular. The column vector $[a,b,c]^t$ representation of a line is made more useful, and potential numerical problems are avoided, by putting it in the canonical or normalised form by imposing the constraint $a^2+b^2 = 1$. This is most simply achieved by multiplying the vector by $1/sqrt(a^2+b^2)$. In the normalised form a and b are direction cosines of the normal, $a = cos(t_x)$, $b = cos(t_y)$, c = -r.

The sign of c may be used to impose a direction on the line. Where the line is to be treated as a boundary it may be called a linear- half plane or half space, because it bisects the plane into two semi-infinite areas.

The Parametric Form
This form of equation consists of two equations which give x and y in terms of a third parameter u: $x = x_0 +a_x.u$; $y = y_0+a_y.u$ (x_0,y_0) is the point on the line corresponding to a zero value of the parameter u. These equations have four constant terms (x_0,y_0,a_x,a_y) as against three in the implicit form. The extra freedom allows us to specify just how the parameter u varies along the line.

If we want u to correspond to real euclidean distance along the line,say, from a point (x_0,y_0) on the line then $x = x_0 + (cos(t_x)).u$, $y = y_0 + (cos(t_y)).u$

Where t_x,t_y are the angles made by the line with the x and y axes respectively. This is the normalised form for this parametric representation of a line. The general parametric form can be normalised by substituting a_x and a_y by $a_x/sqrt(a_x^2+a_y^2)$ and $a_y/sqrt(a_x^2+a_y^2)$ respectively.

In homogeneous vector notation the parametric form can be written as $P = P_0+A.u$ where

$\mathbf{P} = [x,y,1]$, $\mathbf{A} = [a_x, a_y, 0]$ and $\mathbf{P_0} = [x_0, y_0, 1]$. Transforming the parametric form of line is done by transforming $\mathbf{A}$ and $\mathbf{P_0}$ and reforming the parametric equation.

Conversion

The equation $ax+by+c = 0$ is conveniently parameterised as

$$x = -ac/(a^2+b^2) + b.u, \quad y = -bc/(a^2+b^2) - a.u$$

This is also in the normalised form. If the original implicit form was normalised then the division by $sqrt(a^2+b^2)$ can be omitted.

The implicit from of the standard parametric equation is given by:

$$-a_y.x + a_x.y + (x_0.a_y - y_0.a_x) = 0$$

This is normalised only if the parametric form was also normalised.

Distance from a point to a line

If the line is in implicit form (not necessarily normalised):

$$d = (ax+by+c)/sqrt(a^2+b^2)$$

The sign of d indicates on which side of the line the point lies. A 0 value implies the point is on the line, a +ve value implies it is on the half plane side and a -ve value implies it is in the other side of the half plane. This is normally termed as point classification.

If the line is in parameterised form then the distance computation gets slightly complex:

Let $dx = a_y^2(x-x_0) - a_x a_y(y-y_0)$
$dy = a_x^2(y-y_0) - a_x a_y(x-x_0)$

Then $d = sqrt(dx^2+dy^2)/(a_x^2+a_y^2)$

The value of the parameter u, at the foot of the perpendicular from (x,y) is given by

$$u = (a_x(x-x_0) + a_y(y-y_0)) / (a_x^2+a_y^2)$$

Unlike the implicit form there is no direct method of classifying the point with respect to the line represented in the parametric form.

Angle between two lines

Using subscripts 1 and 2 to denote the two lines and t as the angle by which line 1 has to be rotated to align with line 2, for the implicit form we have:

$$t = cos^{-1}((a_1 a_2 + b_1 b_2) / sqrt((a_1^2+b_1^2).(a_2^2+b_2^2)))$$ And for the parametric form we have:

$$t = cos^{-1}(a_{1x}.a_{2x}+a_{1y}.a_{2y})/sqrt((a_{1x}^2+a_{1y}^2).(a_{2x}^2+a_{2y}^2))$$

Equation of a line through two points

Let the points $\mathbf{P_0}$ and $\mathbf{P_1}$ be represented in homogeneous coordinates by $(x_0, y_0, w0)$ and

(x_1, y_1, w_1) respectively. A point with coordinates (x, y, w) will be collinear with them if its coordinates will be linearly dependent on those of P_0, P_1. That is

$$\det \begin{bmatrix} x & x_0 & x_1 \\ y & y_0 & y_1 \\ w & w_0 & w_1 \end{bmatrix} = 0 \text{ or } x(y_0 w_1 - w_0 y_1) + y(w_0 x_1 - x_0 w_1) + w(x_0 y_1 - y_0 x_1) = 0$$

In general this is not in the normalised form. The parametric form is given simply by

$$x = x_0 + (x_1 - x_0).u, \quad y = y_0 + (y_1 - y_0).u$$

Intersection of two lines

The point of intersection between two lines defined by $[a_1, b_1, c_1]$ and $[a_2, b_2, c_2]$ is determined similarly. A third line given by $[a, b, c]$ passing through that point must be linearly dependent on the other two. That is

$$\det \begin{bmatrix} a & a_1 & a_2 \\ b & b_1 & b_2 \\ c & c_1 & c_2 \end{bmatrix} = 0 \qquad \text{or } a(b_1 c_2 - c_1 b_2) + b(c_1 a_2 - a_1 c_2) + c(a_1 b_2 - b_1 a_2) = 0$$

So that the point of intersection is given by

$$x = (b_1 c_2 - c_1 b_2) / (a_1 b_2 - b_1 a_2), \quad y = (c_1 a_2 - c_1 b_2) / (a_1 b_2 - b_1 a_2)$$

If $a_1 b_2 - b_1 c_2 = 0$ then the lines are parallel. (The line between two points and the intersection of two lines demonstrates the duality between points and lines in a plane when homogeneous coordinates are used).

If one line is in implicit form and the other in parametric form then the point of intersection is given by

$$x = (b(x_0 a_y - y_0 a_x) - c.a_x) / (a_x a + a_y b), \quad y = -(a(x_0 a_y - y_0 a_x) - c.a_y) / (a_x.a + a_y.b)$$

At the point of intersection $u = -(c + a.x_0 + b.y_0) / (a_x.a + a_y.b)$

If $a_x.a + a_y.b = 0$ then the lines are parallel. If both lines are in parametric form then the following pseudo code may be used to compute the intersection point and its parametric values:

```
det := a_{2x}.a_{1y} - a_{1x}.a_{2y}
if abs(det) < epsilon then
...the lines are parallel
else
begin
u:= (a_{2x}.(y_{20} - y_{10}) - a_{2y}.(x_{20} - x_{10}))/det;
v:= (a_{1x}.(y_{20} - y_{10}) - a_{1y}.(x_{20} - x_{10})/det;
x:= x_{10} + a_{1x}.u;
y:= y_{10} + a_{1y}.u
end;
```

Where u and v are the parameter values at the point of intersection on the two lines.

Line Equidistant from two points
Implicit form : $x(x_2-x_1) + y(y_2-y_1) - 1/2\ (x_2^2+y_2^2)-(x_1^2+y_1^2)) = 0$

Parametric Form : $x = (x_1+x_2)/2 - (y_2-y_1).u, \quad y = (y_1+y_2)/2 + (x_2-x_1).u$

Normal to a line through a point
Let x_p,y_p be the point and $ax+by+c=0$ the line equation. Then the normal is given by the line equation: $bx-ay+(ay_p-bx_p)=0$. If the line is in parametric then the normal is given by the line equation $x = x_p - a_y.v, y = y_p + a_x.v$

1.8 INTERSECTION OF LINE SEGMENTS

[Guibas/Stolfi,Mairson,Shamos]
In most computer graphics applications one encounters line segments rather than infinite lines. Line segments are most simply represented by their end points. An alternative is to store the parametric equation and the parameter bounds. To determine if two line segments intersect one must check that the parametric values of the intersection point lie within the parametric bounds of the respective line segments.

In a number of applications one needs to determine the intersection amongst not just two line segments but many, say n. This is commonly known as the "pairwise intersection problem". There are three major variants. We may want to know:
(1) whether any two of them intersect
(2) how many pairs of line segments intersect
(3) which pairs intersect

A trivial algorithm (check all possible pairs) can solve all three variants in $O(n^2)$ time. Can we do better than this? It has been shown that the lower bounds for the three variants are as follows: (1) and (2) require $\Omega(nlogn)$ time and (3) requires $\Omega(nlogn+I)$, where I is the number of intersecting pairs.

An algorithm that solves the variant (1) in time $O(nlogn)$ has been known. For variants (2) and (3) no reasonably general algorithm is known that realises $O(nlogn+I)$. The ones that do are restricted to special classes of line segments.

The Plane Sweep or Scan line Method
We shall now introduce a technique that is very common in the processing of geometrical problems, particularly those involving points and straight lines segments. The technique consists of sorting the points that define the problem according to their projections onto a particular axis d and then processing them in that order. We can visualise this process by imagining that the plane is swept (or scanned) by a line perpendicular to d. Whenever this line encounters one of the given points, some "event" occurs and changes the state of the computation. Basically this technique maps a two-dimensional static problem into a one-dimensional dynamic process.

As an example consider the problem of reporting all intersecting pairs among a set of horizontal (H) and vertical line segments. For simplicity no two line segments are collinear. Assume that we shall sweep the plane by a vertical line so that segments and points are sorted according to their X values. As this line is swept we keep a list of horizontal segments, say H-list, that this line currently intercepts. Whenever we encounter the left end point of a horizontal segment we add it to H-list and when we encounter the right end point we delete it. When a vertical segment is encountered. We report one intersection between it and each segment in H-list whose y-value falls between the endpoints of the vertical segment. For maximum speed H-list is maintained as a balanced search tree. When a vertical segment is encountered we locate its ends in this tree and report all in between nodes as intersections. The total time can be easily shown to be O(nlogn+I).

Let us now consider the more complex problem of intersecting a set C of n general line segments. The following observations are important:

(i) The intersections of the line segments with the sweeping line S move continuously up or down this line as S is swept from the left end point to the right. However as long as we encounter no more intersections the vertical ordering of the line segments is maintained (i.e., between successive point encounters the ordering remains). As before we maintain the line segments intercepting S in a search free. Whenever a new left end point is encountered by S, the segment is inserted in sorted order in the search tree, and when its right end point is encountered it is deleted from the tree.

(ii) Two segments can intersect only if they are neighbours in the sorted search tree at some time before the intersection is encountered. Two segments can become neighbours when one of them is inserted or when a segment between them was deleted.

(iii) The sorted search tree must have all its segments sorted according to their intersections on S at all time. Thus when an intersection is encountered the two line segments must be interchanged in S. This is another occasion when two segments may become neighbours. Therefore we must check the two interchanged segments for intersections against their new immediate neighbours.

The total time for this algorithm is O((n+I)logn). There is a special case of the pairwise intersection problem in which the theoretical lower bound Ω(nlogn+I) can actually be attained. This is the case when two sets P and Q of line segments are to be intersected and there are no P-P or Q-Q intersecting segments. It is not within the scope of these notes to discuss that algorithm. Interested readers are referred to [Mairson].

1.9 DISPLAYING STRAIGHT LINE SEGMENTS

[Newman/Sproull,Foley/van Dam,Rogers] Most graphics devices of today incorporate microprocessors which accept end point information and trace out a line between these points. We shall briefly examine this processing of drawing/displaying lines. A raster display can be considered as a matrix of discrete picture calls (pixels) each of which can be illuminated. The process of determining which pixels will provide the best approximation to the desired line segment is known as rasterization. Combined with the process of rendering the picture in scan line order this is known as scan conversion.

Desirable properties for rasterized lines:
(i) lines should start and end properly and appear straight
(ii) lines should have constant brightness along their length independent of their size and orientation.
(iii) lines should be traced out rapidly.

Not all properties are satisfied by the algorithms only. Horizontal, vertical and 45° lines will have uniform brightness. Also the 45° line will appear less brighter than the other two. For reasons of speed integer arithmetic is often used and so end points and line length are only approximated.

Digital Differential Analyser (DDA)

One technique is to solve the governing differential equation:

$Dy/Dx = (y2-y1) / (x2-x1) = $ constant,say, m

so that $y_{i+1} = y_i+Dy = y_i+m.Dx$ or $x_{i+1} = x_i + Dy/m$

For a simple DDA either Dx or Dy, whichever is larger, is chosen as one raster unit. The pseudo code given below may be used:

```
length:= max(x2-x1,y2-y1);
Dx:= (x2-x1)/length;  Dy:= (y2-y1)/length
x:= x1+0.5*Sign(Dx); y:= y1+0.5*Sign(Dy)
i:=1;
while i<length do
  begin
    set-pixel (floor(x), floor(y));
    x:= x+Dx; y:=y+Dy; i:=i+1
  end;
```

The one disadvantage of this algorithm is that it uses floating point arithmetic. The algorithm can be modified to use integer arithmetic only. But it still suffers from end point accuracy and orientation dependence.

Bresenham's Algorithm

Originally developed for plotters with one of the eight possible pen steps, this algorithm is equally suited for use with raster devices. The algorithm tries to select the optimal raster locations to represent a line segment. Depending on the scope of the line it increments by one unit either n or y. The other variable is incremented based on the distance(called error) between the actual line location and the nearest grid locations. Only the sign of this error term need be examined. Consider a line in the first octant.

. If $e_1<1/2$ then (1,0) is a better choice else (1,1).
. $e_2 = e_1+ m$, $e_3 = e_2+m$.
. We only want to look at the sign of e. Hence initialise $e= -1/2$
so that f $e_1<0$ then choose (1,0) else choose (1,1).

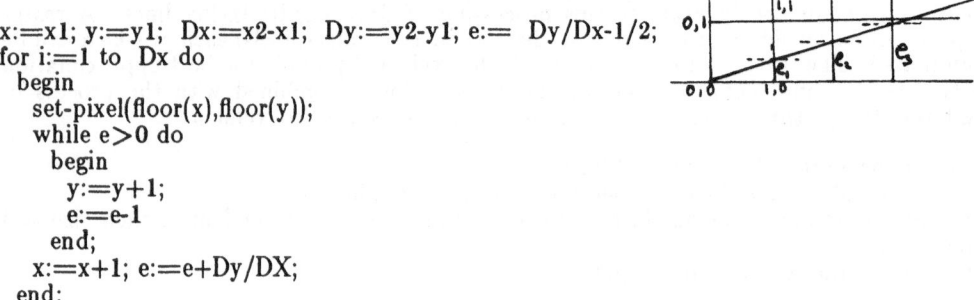

```
x:=x1; y:=y1; Dx:=x2-x1; Dy:=y2-y1; e:= Dy/Dx-1/2;
for i:=1 to  Dx do
  begin
    set-pixel(floor(x),floor(y));
    while e>0 do
      begin
        y:=y+1;
        e:=e-1
      end;
    x:=x+1; e:=e+Dy/DX;
  end;
```

Since only the sign of e is important the above algorithm can be transformed to use only integer arithmetic by the simple substitution of e by 2e.Dx so that we have:

```
x:=x1; y:=y1;  x:=x2-x1;  y:=y2-y1; e:=2*Dy-Dx;
for i:=1 to  Dx do
  begin
    set-pixel(x,y)
    while e>0 do
      begin
        y:=y+1; e:=e-2*Dx
      end;
    x:=x+1; e:=e+2*Dx
  end;
```

The algorithm can be easily extended to display lines in other octants.

1.10 ANTIALIASING

[Rogers,Crow] A basic problem of rasterization is the appearance of the effects of aliasing. Lines and edges appear jagged. In graphics jargon these are known as "jaggies".

There are essentially due to the fact that lines, polygon edges, colour boundaries etc. are continuous whereas a raster device is discrete. For displaying a line it is sampled at discrete locations. (For the line in the first O octant, Bresenham's algorithm samples at points along the axis spaced one raster unit apart). Under sampling can have surprising results.

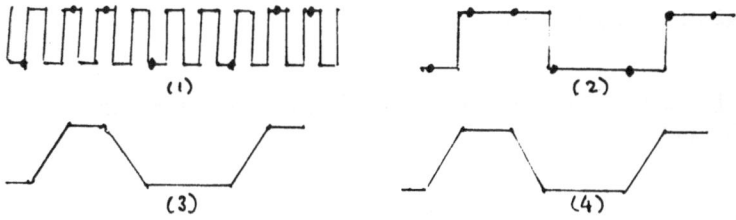

(3) and (4) are aliases. Since (3) is a sample of (1), (4) is also an alias of (1).

Shannon's Sampling Theorem: In order to be able to reconstruct the signal exactly the sampling frequency must be at least twice the highest frequency in the input signal. Note that this theorem does not suggest a method for reconstructing the signal from its discrete signals. It only says that it is possible.

Fundamentally there are two methods for antialiasing. The first is to increase the sampling frequency. This amounts to increasing raster resolution. High resolution CRT's are very expensive. One solution is to sample (compute) at higher resolution and display at lower resolution using some type of averaging. Two types of averaging are uniform averaging and weighted averaging. In uniform averaging, each displayed pixel is divided into subpixels at higher resolution. Display attributes are determined at the centre of each subpixel. The display attributes at the display pixel are obtained as the average of three subpixels.

Somewhat better results can be obtained by considering more subpixels and weighting their influence [Crow].

The second method of antialiasing is to treat a pixel as a square area rather than as an infinitesimal point. A simple modification of Bresenham's algorithm yields an approximation to the pixel area inside the region bounded by the line. This approximation can be used to modulate the brightness of the pixel. Once again consider a line in the first octant.

However if you recall the error term in Bresenham's algorithm you will find that it is e_1+m. Since m is a constant it means that the error term differs from the area by the constant m/2.

In order to modify Bresenham's algorithm let us denote w=1-m. Then note that as long as e<w the situation shown below will note occur. Hence m can be added to e. However if e>w then e has to be reset to "DE" shown in the figure.

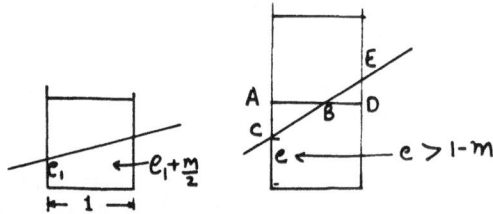

Since DE/BD = m = AC/AB, and BD = 1-AB = 1-AC/m = 1-(1-e)/m.
Hence DE = m.BD = m.$\left(1-(1-e)/m\right)$ = m-1+e = e-(1-m) = e-w.

Breesnham's algorithm for grey scale

```
x:=x1; y:=y1; Dx:=x2-x1; Dy:=y2-y1; m:=Dy/Dx; w:=1-m; e:=1/2;
set-pixel-intensity (x,y,m/2);
while  x<Dx do
  begin
    if e<w then
      begin
        x:=x+1; e:=e+m
      end
    else
      begin
        x:=x+1; y:=y+1; e:=e-w
      end;
    set-pixel-intensity (x,y,e)
  end;
```

1.11 LINES IN THREE DIMENSIONS

[Bowyer/Woodwark,Faux/Pratt]
Parametric Equation :
In three dimensions, the implicit equation of a line is the intersection of two planes. Since more than one pair of planes can describe a given line, the parametric form is to be preferred. It has the form: $x = x_0+a_x.u$, $y = y_0+a_y.u$, $z = z_0+a_z.u$

In the normalised form u would correspond to actual distance along the line from the point $[x_0, y_0, z_0]$. In the normalised form: $a_x^2 + a_y^2 + a_z^2 = 1$

The parametric form can be normalised by dividing the coefficients of u by this quantity. In the normalised form a_x, a_y, a_z are the direction cosines of the line. For a canonical representation the point $[x_0, y_0, z_0]$ can be chosen to be the point on the line closet to the origin of the 3D space. This will facilitate comparison of lines (for identity) and may also avoid some numerical problems.

The normal from a point $[x,y,z]$ in space to the parametric line meets the line at the point U_n given by:

$$U_n = (a_x(x-x_0) + a_y(y-y_0) + a_z(z-z_0)) / (a_x^2 + a_y^2 + a_z^2)$$

If U_0 is the parametric value at which the normal from the origin meets the line the following substitutions will result in the canonical form:

$$x_0 = x_0 + a_x.U_0, \; y_0 = y_0 + a_y.U_0, \; z_0 = z_0 + a_z.U_0$$

Distance between two lines
The minimum distance is given by:

$$d = \frac{\begin{bmatrix} x_{20}-x_{10} & y_{20}-y_{10} & z_{20}-z_{10} \\ a_{1x} & a_{1y} & a_{1z} \\ a_{2x} & a_{2y} & a_{2y} \end{bmatrix}}{\sqrt{\begin{vmatrix} a_{1x} & a_{1y} \\ a_{2x} & a_{2y} \end{vmatrix}^2 + \begin{vmatrix} a_{1y} & a_{1z} \\ a_{2y} & a_{2z} \end{vmatrix}^2 + \begin{vmatrix} a_{1z} & a_{1x} \\ a_{2z} & a_{2x} \end{vmatrix}^2}}$$

The code for this is much simpler:

```
x_21 := x_20-x_10; y_21:=y_20-y_10; z_21:=z_20-z_10;
a_xy:= a_1x*a_2y-a_2x*a_1y;
a_yz:= a_1y*a_2z-a_2y*a_1z;
a_zx:= a_1z*a_2x-a_2z*a_1x;
denom:= (a_xy)² + (a_yz)² + (a_zx)²;
if denom = 0 then
... the lines are parallel ...
else d:= abs(x_21*a_yz+y_21*a_zx+z_21*a_xy)/sqrt(denom);
```

Note: This code does not work for parallel or near-parallel lines. The geometric formulation in this case is inherently unstable and it is best to reformulate the requirement as finding the distance of a point on one line from the other.

Angle between two lines
This is found from the scalar product of their direction vectors. It is not necessary for the lines to intersect.

$$t = \cos^{-1}(a_{1x}a_{2x} + a_{1y}a_{2y} + a_{1z}a_{2z}) / \sqrt{((a_{1x}^2 + a_{1y}^2 + a_{1z}^2)(a_{2x}^2 + a_{2y}^2 + a_{2z}^2))}$$

$t = 0$ implies the lines are parallel and $t = 180°$ implies the lines are antiparallel (i.e., the parameters increase in opposite directions).

Line through two points

If $[x1, y1, z1]$ and $[x2, y2, z2]$ are the two points then the parametric equation takes the form:

$x = x1 + (x2-x1).u$, $y = y1 + (y2-y1).u$, $z = z1 + (z2-z1).u$

This is not in the normalised form.

1.12 ANALYTICAL AND COMPUTATIONAL TECHNIQUES FOR PLANES

[Bowyer/Woodwark,Faux/Pratt,Rogers,Foley/van Dam]
The Implicit form : This is the direct equivalent of the implicit form of the line equation in 2D and is given by: $ax + by + cz + d = 0$

In the normalised form $a^2 + b^2 + c^2 = 1$. Normalization is achieved by dividing the equation by $\sqrt{(a^2 + b^2 + c^2)}$. In the normalised form a,b and c are the direction cosines of the normal to the plane and the absolute value of d is the perpendicular distance of the origin from the plane. The plane may be considered to represent the boundary of a semi-infinite region of space by applying the convention that the normal points array from the region.

The parametric form : Two parameters are required to specify a position in a plane. Given a point (x_0, y_0, z_0) and two different vectors both parallel to the plane say (a_x, a_y, a_z) and (b_x, b_y, b_z), a point in the plane is found by adding a portion of one vector and different proportion of the second vector to (x_0, y_0, z_0):

$$x = z_0 + a_x u + b_x v, \quad y = y_0 + a_y u + b_y v, \quad z = z_0 + a_z u + b_z v$$

If the two vectors are of unit length and are perpendicular, that is

$$a_x^2 + a_y^2 + a_z^2 = 1, \quad b_x^2 + b_y^2 + b_z^2 = 1 \text{ and } a_x.b_x + a_y.b_y + a_z.b_z = 0$$

Then the parameters u and v constitute measurements along orthogonal axes in the plane from an origin at $[x_0, y_0, z_0]$.

Conversion between Implicit and Parametric forms

The parametric values of the foot of the perpendicular from the origin are given by

$$u = \frac{(b_x x_0 + b_y y_0 + b_z z_0).(a_x b_x + a_y b_y + a_z b_z) - (a_x x_0 + a_y y_0 + a_z z_0).(b_x^2 + b_y^2 + b_z^2)}{(a_x^2 + a_y^2 + a_z^2)(b_x^2 + b_y^2 + b_z^2) - (a_x b_x + a_y b_y + a_z b_z)^2}$$

$$v = \frac{(a_x x_0 + a_y y_0 + a_z z_0)(a_x b_x + a_y b_y + a_z b_z) - (b_x x_0 + b_y y_0 + b_z z_0)(a_x^2 + a_y^2 + a_z^2)}{(a_x^2 + a_y^2 + a_z^2)(b_x^2 + b_y^2 + b_z^2) - (a_x b_x + a_y b_y + a_z b_z)^2}$$

If this point on the plane is say $[x_0', y_0', z_0']$ then for the implicit form

$d = \sqrt{(x_0'^2 + y_0'^2 + z_0'^2)}, \quad a = x_0'/d, b = y_0'/d, c = z_0'/d$

Transforming a Plane

The implicit form may be written in matrix notation as $[x\ y\ z\ 1].[a,b,c,d]^t = 0$

If T is the transformation for points in the space then as in the case of lines,

$$[a,b,c,d]^t_b = T^*.[a,b,c,d]^t_a$$

The parametric form can be written in vector notation as $\mathbf{P} = \mathbf{P_0} + \mathbf{A}.u + \mathbf{B}.v$

where $\mathbf{P} = [x,y,z,1]$, $\mathbf{P_0} = [x_0,y_0,z_0,1]$, $\mathbf{A} = [a_x,a_y,a_z,0]$, $\mathbf{B} = [b_x,b_y,b_z,0]$

Transforming this representation is achieved by transforming the vectors $\mathbf{P_0}$, $\mathbf{A}$ and $\mathbf{B}$.

Conversely to convert from the implicit form to the parametric form we define:

$$x_0 = da \ / \ sqrt(a^2+b^2+c^2), \quad y_0 = db \ / \ sqrt(a^2+b^2+c^2), \quad z_0 = dc \ / \ sqrt(a^2+b^2+c^2)$$

Selecting the two vectors $[a_x,a_y,a_z]$ and $[b_x,b_y,b_z]$ is somewhat arbitrary. We choose the first vector in the plane based on external constraints, if any. The second is obtained as the vector product of this and the plane normal $[a,b,c]$. If there are no external constraints for the choice of the first vector then it can be chosen as the vector product of the normal and the coordinate axis corresponding to the smallest of a,b and c.

Distance of a point from the plane

$$r^2 = (a.x+b.y+c.z+d)^2 \ / \ (a^2+b^2+c^2)$$

For the normalised equation the distance is given by $r = a.x+b.y+c.z+d$. The sign of r also indicates the side on which the point lies. A positive value means the point is in the side pointed to by the normal.

Intersection of a line and a plane

If the plane is $ax+by+cz+d=0$ and the line is $x=x_0+a_x.u$, $y=y_0+a_y.u$, $z=z_0+a_z.u$ then the following code may be used:

```
denom:= a*a_x + b*a_y + c*a_z;
if (denom = 0) then
...line and plane are parallel ...
else begin
u0:= -(a*x_0 + b*y_0 + c*z_0 + d)/denom;
x:= x_0 + a_x*u0;    y:= y_0 + a_y*u0;   z:= z_0 + a_z*u0;
end;
```

Other cases may be solved quite simply by using the various conversions discussed earlier.

Intersection of two planes

Assuming that the planes are in implicit form and the line of intersection is determined in the parametric form the following may be used to obtain the coefficients of the parameter t in the line equation:

$$a_x = \begin{vmatrix} b_1 & c_1 \\ b_2 & c_2 \end{vmatrix} \qquad a_y = \begin{vmatrix} c_1 & a_1 \\ c_2 & a_2 \end{vmatrix} \qquad a_z = \begin{vmatrix} a_1 & b_1 \\ a_2 & b_2 \end{vmatrix}$$

Plane through three points

Just as lines and points were duals in 2D, planes and points are duals in 3D homogeneous coordinate space.

The implicit equation is given by:

$$\det \begin{vmatrix} x & x1 & x2 & x3 \\ y & y1 & y2 & y3 \\ z & z1 & z2 & z3 \\ w & w1 & w2 & w3 \end{vmatrix} = 0$$

If we set $w = w1 = w2 = w3 = 1$ then the following code may be used:

```
x21:= x2-x1; y21:=y2-y1; z21:=z2-z1; x31:= x3-x1; y31:=y2-y1; z31:=z3-z1;
a:= y21*z31-z21*y31; b:= z21*x31-z21*z31; c:= x21*y31-y21*x31; d:= -(x2*a+y2*b+z2*c);
```

Using the principle of duality the point of intersection of 3 planes is given by substituting direction cosines variables for coordinate variables and vice versa.

The following code may be used:

```
bc:= b2*c3-b3*c2; ac:= a2*c3-a3*c2; ab:= a2*b3-a3*b2;
det:= a1*bc-b*ac+c*ab;
if (det = 0) then
  ... at least two planes are parallel ...
else
  begin
    dc:= d2*c3-d3*c2; db:= d2*b3-d3*b2;  ad:= a2*d3-a3*d2;
    x:= (b1*dc-d1*bc-a*db)/det;
    y:= (d1*ac-a1*dc-c1*ad)/det;
    z:= (b1*ad+a1*db-d1*ab)/det;
  end;
```

Plane through a point given a normal line equation

Let the point be (xp yp zp) and the line be in the parametric form then the plane equation implicit form is given by:

$$a:= a_x; \quad b:=a_y; \quad c:= a_z; \quad d:= -(a_x*xp + a_y*yp + a_z*zp)$$

1.13 DISPLAYING A PLANE BOUNDED REGION

[Rogers,Foley/van Dam,Newman/Sproull]

The straight line is bounded quite simply by two points on the line. The plane region boundary is however far more complex. It could be a sequence of straight lines or curves or a combination of both or in the highly irregular case be a set of connected pixels in the discrete plane. In any case displaying the plane region as a line drawing would only require the display of the projection of the boundary. The projection would of course depend on the viewing transformation currently applicable. On a raster device displaying a plane region would require intensifying every pixel of the display screen that would be within the projected region of this planar region in 3D. Deciding which pixel is inside the region and which is not is a fairly complex process and we shall take it up in the next lecture. Here we are concerned with the intensity value of the pixels in that planar region. This intensity value depends on a number of parametrics including the plane equation (actually its normal) and the entire process is referred to as shading. Shading presumes the existence of at least one light source as well as knowledge of the optical properties of the surface.

When light energy falls on a surface, it can be absorbed, reflected or transmitted. If all the incident light is absorbed the object is invisible. Reflected or transmitted light makes an object visible. Colour is essentially due to the fact that the surface selectively absorbs some wavelengths in the light energy and not the others.

The light reflected from the surface is also characterised by being either diffusely or specularly reflected. Diffusely reflected light is scattered in all directions. So the observer's position is unimportant.

Lambert's cosine law governs the reflection of light from a point source (assumed to be far away) by a perfect diffuser. It is:

$$I_d = I_p.R_d.\cos(t)$$

where I_p is the incident intensity from the point light source R_d is the diffuse reflection coefficient t is the angle between the surface normal and the light direction.

R_d varies from material to material. It also is a function of the wavelength of the light. For simple illumination models it is assumed constant.

Objects rendered with this simple equation appear to have a dull matte surface. Also because of the point source assumption, objects that receive no light directly from the source appear black. Ambient light in a room represents a distributed light source. The optical formulae for this are very complicated and so a constant term is added to the diffuse equation above:

$$I_d = I_a.R_a + I_d.R_d.\cos(t)$$

where I_a is the ambient light intensity and R_a the ambient diffuse coefficient.

The above model does not distinguish two planes parallel but separated by large distance. Farther the surface lesser the incident intensity i.e., inversely proportional to the square of the distance. Experience has however shown that more realistic results can be obtained by using the linear attenuation law. The illumination model is then:

$$I_d = (I_a.R_a + I_p.R_d.\cos(t)) / (dist+k)$$

where k is an arbitrary constant and dist the distance of the surface from the view point. For view point at infinity dist is zero for the nearest object. For obtaining coloured images the illumination model is applied individually to each of the three primary colours.

Specular reflection of light is directional. The governing equation is the Fresnel equation For a perfect reflecting surface angle of reflection is equal to angle of incidence. So, only an observer located at exactly that angle sees any specularly reflected light. For imperfect reflecting surfaces the amount of light reaching the observer depends on the spatial distribution of the specularly reflected light. For smooth surfaces this distribution is narrow, while for rough surfaces it is more spread out. The highlights on a shiny object are due to specular reflection. Because of the complex physical characteristics of specularly reflected light, an empirical model due to Bui-Tuong Phong [Newman/Sproull] is usually used in simple computer graphics applications. Specifically :

$$I_s = I_p.w(t,l).\cos^n(a)$$

where $w(t,l)$, the reflectance curve, gives the ratio of the specularly reflected light to the incident light as a function of the incidence angle t and the wavelenth l. Here n approximates the spatial distribution (large n for shiny surfaces and small n for rough surfaces). $w(t,l)$ is a rather complex function and so it is usually replaced by an aesthetically or experimentally determined constant R_s. The illumination model or shading function developed so far may thus be written as:

$$I_{ds} = I_a.R_a + I_p/(\text{dist}+k).(R_d.\cos(t) + R_s.\cos^n(a))$$

Recall that individual shading functions are used for each of the primary colours for obtaining coloured images. For multiple point light sources the shading function is obtained by summation as:

$$I_{ds} = I_a.R_a + \sum_j I_{pj}/(\text{dist}+k).(R_d.\cos(t_j) + R_s.\cos^n(a_j))$$

2. POLYGONAL REGIONS

2.1 REPRESENTATION ISSUES

Definition: An open ball with radius $r>0$ around a point x R^2 is defined as the set
$B(x,r) = [y : (y \in R^2) \wedge (\text{dist}(x,y) < r)]$

Definition : A subset X of R^2 is said to be open if it contains an open ball around each of its points. X is open iff $[\forall x : x \in X : \exists r>0 : B(x,r) \subset X)]$

Definition : A subset X of R^2 is said to be closed if (R^2-X) is open.

Definition : A subset X of R^2 is said to be a neighborhood of a point $x \in R^2$ if there exists an open set Y such that $x \in Y \wedge Y \subset X$.

Definition : A point x is said to be
(i) a boundary point of X if $\forall r>0 : B(x,r) \cap X \neq [] \wedge B(x,r) \cap (R^2-X) \neq []$

(ii) an inside or interior point of X if $\exists r>0 : B(x,r) \cap X = B(x,r)$

(iii) an outside or exterior point of X if $\exists r>0 : B(x,r) \cap X=[]$

Definition : The boundary set of X is the set of all boundary points of X.

Definition : The closure of a subset X of R^2 is the union of X with its boundary set.

Definition : A subset X of R^2 is said to be bounded if there exists $r>0$ such that $X \subset B(O,r)$, where $O = (0,0)$ R^2.

Definition : The regularization of a subset X of R^2 is defined as the closure of its interior set. A subset X is said to be regular if it does not change after regularization. Regular sets therefore have non-empty interiors.

Definition : For a given subset X of R^2, the subsets A and B of R^2 form a separation of X, if the following conditions are satisfied:
(i) $(A \neq []) \wedge (B \neq []) \wedge (A \cap B=[])$
(ii) $X = A \cup B$
(iii) No interior or boundary point of A is in B and vice versa.

Definition : A subset X of R^2 is said to be connected if there does not exist subsets A and B of R^2 such that they form a separation of X.

Theorem : A non-empty open set in the plane is connected iff any two of its points can be joined by a polygon (Path) which lies in the set.

Definition : A non-empty connected open set is called a region. The closure of this region is called a closed region. In all our further discussions we shall be concerned with closed bounded regions and hence the prefix "closed" may be omitted.

Definition : A connected subset X of R^2 is said to be multiply connected if the boundary set of X is disconnected.

Definition : A subset X of R² is said to be convex if for any two of its points a,b ∈ X, the straight line segment ab joining them is completely contained in X. Obviously a convex subset cannot be multiply connected and has a single connected boundary.

Definition : A singly connected region is one which can be shrunk to a point. That is it is homeomorphic to an open disk in R². The boundary of an open disk is a circle, which can be analytically represented as a closed curve. The boundary set of a singly connected region can be in the limiting case be represented analytically as a closed curve.

Definition : The boundary of a connected region is oriented in such a fashion that the normal to the curve at any point on the boundary points inwards. The normal is the normal to the tangent line at that point. That is for a simple region the boundary is oriented anticlockwise.

Definition : The winding number of any point p with respect to a region X, w(p,X) is defined as follows: Let r be a ray originating from p in any direction. For any point of intersection x between r and the oriented boundary of X the crossing number is defined as shown below:

(i) If x is not on the boundary of X then count as +1 or -1 depending or whether the boundary crosses the ray from bottom to top or top to bottom.

(ii) If the point x lies on the boundary then the crossing number is counted as shown below:

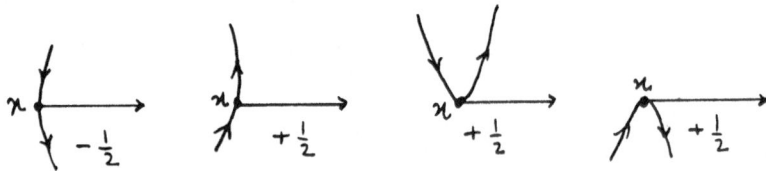

Theorem (Jordan) : The winding number of a point p with respect to a region X is independent of the direction of the ray. Also if X is a singly connected or multiply connected region with non-intersecting boundary curve(s) then the point p lies inside X iff w(p,X)=1, lies outside X iff w(p,X)=0 and on the boundary otherwise.

Simply stated this theorem states that given a closed curve C in R² it is possible to classify any point p ∈ R² with respect to C and say whether p is inside or outside the region whose boundary is C or whether p is on the curve C. Thus the oriented boundary of a region completely characterises the region and its complement in R². In representing homogeneous regions in a computer it is enough if one stores the boundary of the region. There are applications in which the interior is also stored. Typically these are regions in discrete space and are either stored as bit maps or quad-trees or other spatial enumeration structures.

In the rest of this lecture we shall only be concerned with regions represented by their boundary and in particular polygonal regions.

A "simply connected polygonal region" is a closed region whose boundary is a simple polygon. A "multiply connected polygonal region" is a finite connected union of simply connected polygonal regions. It may contain polygonal holes, but no "point holes".

A polygonal region may be specified by a set of circular lists of its vertices (or edges), one for each boundary chain of edges, with the orientation convention: during anticlockwise traversal of an outer boundary chain or clockwise traversal of an inner boundary chain (bounding a hole), the region is towards the left.

A convex polygonal region is convex in the usual sense.

A star-shaped polygonal region is one whose kernel is non-empty. The kernel of a region is the set of points within the region from which the entire boundary is visible; thus a region is star-shaped if there is at least one point that can "see" every point on the boundary. That is the line joining this kernel point and any boundary point is entirely inside the region. Note that convex polygons are star-shaped and the kernel is the entire convex polygonal region.

A polygonal region is said to be monotone along direction d iff intersection with any line perpendicular to d results in atmost one segment. A convex polygonal region is monotone along all directions in the plane.

2.2 AREA OF A POLYGONAL REGION

The triangle is the polygonal region with the smallest number of vertices, namely three, say, P1,P2,P3. The area of a triangle is given by the simple formula below:

$$A = ((x2-x1)(y3-y1) - (x3-x1)(y2-y1))/2$$

The sign of A also indicates the relationship between point P1 and the line P2P3. If A is positive then P1,P2,P3 are in anti-clockwise order and if A is negative then in clockwise order. This test is thus very useful in determining whether a polygonal vertex say Pk makes an acute or obtuse internal angle by checking the triple Pk-1, Pk, and Pk+1.

The area of any polygon represented as a vertex list may be calculated by summing the areas of the trapezia under each side down to the axis. The direction of the sides must be taken into account so that sides on the bottom of the polygon are subtracted from the total. Also if the polygon is a long way from the x-axis then the area of the trapezia will be much larger than the area of the polygon and the accuracy is lost. Temporarily making one vertex the y origin will avoid this problem. The following code may be used:

```
area:= 0.0;
xold:= xn;yold:= 0.0; y0:= yn;
for i:= 1 to n do
  begin
    area:= area + (xold-xi) * (yold + yi-y0);
    xold:= xi; yold:= yi-y0
  end;
area:= area/2.0;
```

The sign is positive for anticlockwise and negative for clockwise traversal.

2.3 CONTOUR FILLING

[Rogers]
One of the unique characteristics of a raster scan device is the ability to display solid areas. The generation of solid areas from simple edge or vertex descriptions is called solid area scan conversion, polygon filling or contour filling. Several techniques can be used to fill a contour. They generally divide into two broad categories: scan conversion and seed fill. Seed fill algorithms are applicable only to raster devices, while the scan line algorithms can be used for line drawing devices as well.

Many closed contours are simple polygons. GKS permits self intersecting polygons while GKS 3D permits multiply connected polygonal regions. The scan line algorithm can be used for filling in self-intersecting contours as well. For the seed fill algorithms to work multiple seeds may have to be provided.

A naive algorithm for filling in a region may be as given below:
for each pixel in the raster window do
    if pixel inside region
        then set pixel to region colour
    else set pixel to background colour;

This technique is rather wasteful as it has to look at all the pixels within the window and can be improved slightly by "boxing" the contour and looking at pixels only within the box. However, the inside test for each pixel is rather expensive. A more efficient technique can be developed by taking advantage of the fact that, except at boundary edges, adjacent pixels are likely to have the same characteristics. This property is known as spatial coherence or scan line coherence in particular. Basically any scan line (y=constant) when intersected with the contour will result in a set of disjoint intervals which are inside the region bounded by the contour.

A Simple ordered Edge List Algorithm
Using this principle a number of algorithms called the ordered edge list algorithms have been developed. Let e1,e2,...,en be the list of edges defining the contour. In case the contour is defined as a circular list of vertices then two successive vertices constitute an edge. A particularly simple algorithm is:

(*prepare the data*)
    1. Determine for each edge the intersection with all the scan
    lines storing each intersection (x,y) in a list.
    2. Sort the list by scan line and increasing X on the scan lines
    i.e., (x1,y1) $<$ (x2,y2) if y1$>$y2 or (y1=y2) (x1$<$x2)
(*scan convert the data*)
    3. Extract pairs of elements from the sorted list, say (x1,y) and (x2,y) of scan line y.
    Set all pixels (x,y) such that x1 $<$ x + 1/2 $<$ x2 to the region colour.

In the above algorithm care has to be taken when the scan line intersects an edge vertex.

Efficiency of the above algorithm can be improved by the following:
(i) Choose scan lines for intersection in order
(ii) maintain for each edge the highest and lowest scan line that intersect the edge, the initial x intersection and x the increment (= Y slope) to be added to x for successive scan lines
(iii) Maintain a sorted list of active edges for the current scan line. This is the same strategy used earlier in the plane sweep technique for intersecting a set of line segments.

Plane Sweep Algorithms

In [Nivergelt/Preparata] an efficient plane sweep algorithm for filling and other operations on polygonal region is described. An important preprocessing step introduced during the sorting phase is the classification of edges/vertices as shown in the figure below:

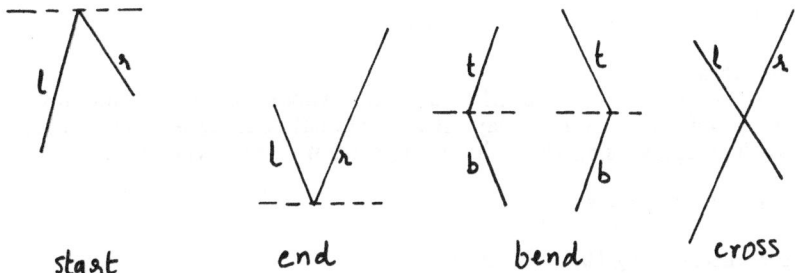

With this classification for every event the processing step is well defined:
(i) start vertex encountered by scan line - start a new active interval or split an existing active interval into two disjoint but asdjacent active intervals.
(ii) end vertex encountered - end of an active interval or merge two adjacent active intervals.
(iii) bend vertex encountered - in active list replace top edge by bottom edge.
(iv) cross vertex encountered - in active list interchange left and right.

Cross vertices are detected as in the earlier algorithm for intersecting a set of line segments by checking newly formed neighbouring edges in the active list.

The Edge Fill Algorithm

The scan line or plane sweep algorithm is powerful and independent of input/ouput details. Each pixel in the display is visited only once. The algorithm's main disadvantage is the expense associated with maintaining and sorting the various lists. The alternate edge fill technique eliminates most of these lists and is described below:

    for each scan line intersecting a polygon edge at (x1,y)
        complement all pixels whose mid points lie to the right of (x1,y),
            i.e., (x,y) such x+1/2 > x1

The algorithm is most conveniently used with a frame buffer. This permits edges to be considered in a completely arbitrary order. As each edge is considered a number of pixels in the frame buffer are complemented when all edges have been considered the frame buffer is ready for display. For complex regions each individual pixel may be addressed many times. By introducing a "fence" this can be reduced. The fence is a vertical line, chosen for convenience to pass through one of the vertices preferably in the central region of the polygon.

The Fence Fill algorithm

```
for each scan line intersecting a polygon edge do
    if the intersection is to the left of the fence,
        then complement all pixels whose mid point lies to the right of the intersection
            and to the left of the fence
        else complement every pixel whose midpoint lies to the left of the intersection
            and to the right of the fence
```

The Edge Flag Algorithm

The edge flag algorithm can be used to fill in a region whose contour has already been painted in the frame buffer or raster display. If a polygonal contour is given it could be easily painted into the display using Bresenham's algorithm. This is the first stage.

The second stage is to fill as below:

```
for each scan line yi intersecting the polygon do
    begin
        inside:= false;
        for x:= 0 to xmax do
            begin
                if pixel-colour(x,yi) = boundary-colour
                    then inside:= not inside;
                if inside then pixel-colour(x,yi) := region-colour
                    else pixel colour (x,yi):= background-colour
            end;
    end;
```

3	2	1
4	P	0
5	6	7

Seed Fill Algorithms

The seed fill algorithms assume that at least one pixel interior to a polygonal region is known. This is frequently the case in interactive graphics wherein the user picks a point within a region for identifying it. Before we describe the algorithm a few definitions are necessary.

Definition: Two pixels are said to be side neighbours (s-neighbour) if the respective cells share a side and corner-neighbours (c-neighbours) if the cells share only a corner vertex. The term N-neighbour, where $0 < N < 7$ is used to denote that pixel whose position is marked with N in the adjoining figure.

Definition : A c-path (or simply path) is a sequence of pixels P1,P2, ..., Pn such that for $k > 1$, Pk-1 is a neighbour (c- or s-) of Pk and for $k < n$, Pk+1 is a neighbour of Pk. The term s-path refers to a similar sequence but instead of being simply neighbours the pixels must be s-neighbours. A simple path is one where all pixels are distinct and no pixel has more than two neighbours in the path. A closed path is one where the first and last pixel coincide.

Definition : A set of pixels S is 4-connected (8 connected) if for every pair of pixels c and d in S there is an s-path (c-path) whose first and last elements are c and d and all its other pixels are in S.

Definition: A region may be either interior- or boundary-defined. If a region is interior-defined then all pixels in the interior of the region have a distinct colour. Similarly a boundary-defined region has all pixels on the boundary set to a unique colour. Interior- or boundary-defined regions may be either 4-connected or 8-connected.

Algorithms that fill interior-defined regions are known as flood fill algorithms and those that fill boundary-defined regions as boundary fill algorithms. We shall discuss only boundary fill algorithms. Flood fill algorithms can be analogously developed. We shall also describe only 4—connected boundary filling. A point to note is that an 8—connected region filling algorithm will fill a 4—connected region but not vice versa.

A simple seed fill algorithm for 4—connected boundary—defined regions
Let b—colour and c—colour be the colour of boundary and interior pixels respectively.

```
procedure seed—fill(seed);
    begin
      if pixel—colour(seed) <> i—colour
        then pixel—colour(seed):= i—colour;
      for s:= 0 to 6 step 2 do
        begin
          if pixel—colour(s—neighbour(seed)) <>i—colour
          and pixel—colour(s—neighbour(seed)) <> b—colour
            then seed—fill(s—neighbour(seed))
        end;
    end;
```

This recursive procedure even if it looks simple can take considerable amount of stack space and procedure calling overhead. The scan line seed fill algorithm attempts to seed only one pixel in any uninterrupted scan line span. The complete algorithm is given below:

```
Procedure scan—line—seed—fill(seed);
  begin (*fill span to right*)
    Repeat
      pright:= 0—neighbour(pright);
      pixel—colour(pright):= i—colour
    until pixel—colour(0—neighbour(pright)) = b—colour;
    (* fill span to left *)
    pleft:= 0—neighbour(seed);
    Repeat
      pleft:= 4—neighbour(pleft);
      pixel—colour(pleft):=i—colour
    until pixel—colour(4—neighbour(pleft)) = b—colour;
    (* check above scan line filled or boundary *)
    p:= 2—neighbour(pleft);
```

```
 while p <> 2—neighbour(pright) do
   begin
     pflag:= false;
       while pixel—colour(p) <> b—colour and
               pixel—colour(p) <> i—colourand p <> 2—neighbour(pright) do
         begin
           pflag:= true; p:= 0—neighbour(p)
         end;
     (* seed extreme right pixel *)
       if pflag then
         begin
           if p = 2—neighbour(pright)
                 and pixel—colour(p) <> b—colour
                 and pixel—colour(p) <> i—colour
             then scan—line—seed—fill(p)
             else scan—line—seed—fill(4—neighbour(p));
                 pflag:= false
         end;
  (* continue checking in case span is interrupted *)
       penter:= p;
       while(pixel—colour(p) = b—colour
         or(pixel—colour(p) = i—colour)
         and p <> 2—neighbour(pright) do p:= 0—neighbour(p);
       if p = penter then p:= 0—neighbour(p);
     end;
(* check scan line below for boundary or c—colour *)
(* this code is similar to the code above *)
   end;
```

2.4 POINT LOCATION PROBLEMS

[Guibas/Stolfi,Lee/Preparata]
We shall now briefly examine the so-called "point location" problem : given a partition
of the plane into two or more regions F1, F2,...,Fm and one or more points P1, P2, ...
Pk determine which points are in which region. A special case is when we have a single
point and just 2 regions a closed region F and its complement; we then have the "point
inclusion" problem.

The point inclusion problem has lots of applications. In interactive graphics it is often
necessary to determine which of the region on the screen the user is pointing using a
locator device like the mouse, the tablet etc.

Convex and star-shaped polygons

One of the simplest instances of this problem is the location of a point with respect to a
convex polygon H. If we take any interior point O of H and list the vertices of H sorted
in order of increasing polar angle as seen from O, then by a binary search we can locate
the angle V_i O V_{i+1} that contains P. It is then a trivial matter to see of the line V_i V_{i+1}
separates P and O. H need not be convex. This method will work for star shaped polygons
as well provided the kernel point is chosen as O. This is an O(logn) test.

Monotone polygons

Instead of ordering the vertices cyclically by their polar angles, as suggested above, we can represent the convex polygon H as two polygon chains, the upper half H_u and the lower half H_l, whose vertices are sorted in x. By binary search we can locate two consecutive vertices $V_i\,V_{i+1}$ on H_l such that $V_i.X < P.X < V_{i+1}.X$; then P will be above H_l iff it is above the line $V_i\,V_{i+1}$. A similar test will tell us if P lies below H_u. It is obvious that this method can be applied to monotone polygons as well. This too is an O(logn) test.

Simple Polygons

For a simple polygon $H = (v_1, v_2, ..., v_n)$, the winding number is given by the expression

$$1/2 \text{*pi} \sum_{1 \leq i \leq n} \text{angle}(V_i, p, V_{i+1})).$$

where the angle is measured in the range (-pi,+pi). The winding number is 0 if p is outside, +1 if P is inside and H is traversed anticlockwise and -1 if p is inside and H is traversed clockwise.

The winding number can also be calculated by chosing an infinite ray originating at p and counting the intersections of this ray with the edges in the polygon. Degeneracies take special handling and the order of both is O(n). If we are prepared to pay for extra storage and preprocessing time we can significantly reduce the query time. One way is to decompose the plane into vertical strips by passing upto n vertices lines $l_1, l_2, ..., l_p$ through the vertices of H and sorted in order of increasing x. The strip between successive lines l_i and l_{i+1} contains no vertices of H, and therefore its intersection with H is a set of trapezia (some degenerating into triangles) whose edges can be linearly ordered along y, say $(e_1, e_2, ..., e_m)$.

Algorithm :

1. If P is left of l_1 or right of l_n, p is outside else locate p (using binary search) between say l_i and l_{i+1}.
2. Using another binary search find e_j and e_{j+1} so that p lies between these edges.
3. If j is odd then p is inside else outside

This algorithm has query time O(logn), storage is (n^2) and preprocessing (n^2).

This algorithm is based on an important principle. Decomposing or subdividing the region(s) into smaller simpler pieces and then determining the piece(s) that includes the given point.

Definition : A planar subdivision is a partition of the plane into f region (faces) with disjoint interiors defined by v vertices and a total of e non-intersecting edges with each edge incident to two vertices, each face bounded by one or more edges and each vertex incident to two or more edges.

We shall be concerned only with straight-line subdivisions, i.e. all edges are straight lines. A straight line subdivision is convex if all faces are convex, and is monotone if all subdivisions are monotone along a common direction d. In a straight line subdivision every face has atleast three edges. If all faces have exactly three edges, i.e. they are triangles then we have a triangulation of the plane.

Euler's Theorem : In any planar subdivision $f - e + v = 2$

Corollary 1 : In plane triangulation $f = 3/2 \; f = 3v\text{-}6$

Corollary 2 : In any straight line subdivision $e < 3v\text{-}6$

Thus the number of edges is a good measure of the complexity of the subdivision.

Any simple polygon can be decomposed into a triangulation of the plane in $O(n\log n)$ time. To locate a point p in this triangulation we can use the algorithm below [Lee/Preparata]:

Let F1, F2 ..., Fm be the faces of the given triangulation and let n be the number of edges in it. It can be shown that there is a family of polyline chains C1, C2, ..., Cm-1 such that
(i) each Ci uses only edges of the triangulation, is monotone with respect to the y axis and is infinite in both directions.
(ii) the chains are consistently ordered by increasing x, i.e. every edge of Ci is on or to the left of Ci+1
(iii) the region between two consecutive chains is a single face of the triangulation.

For example for the figure two chains Ci, Ci+1 could be as follows :

Ci = (16, 11, 8, 13) and Ci+1 = (16, 11, 1, 2, 13)

Because of property (iii) above to locate a point in the face shown shaded we only need to locate it as lying between Ci and Ci+1; this can be done with a binary search on i, at each step checking whether p is to the right or left of the chain. This step requires another binary search along edges of the chain to locate an edge whose y range includes the y of p. The algorithm requires in the worst case $O(\log n)^2$ query time.

It should be clear that the algorithm can be used for any monotone subdivision of the plane.

The data structures and preprocessing are quite complex but the authors show that they are not as expensive as they seem. Preprocessing time is $O(n\log n)$ and storage $O(n)$.

A more recent algorithm [Kirkpatrick] actually reduces the query time to $O(\log n)$. This is based on the observation that by removing an interior vertex and all its incident edges we get a star- shaped polygon with a known kernel point. Once we know that a point is within this star shaped region then in $O(d)$ time we can locate the triangle, where d is the degree of the kernel point in the original triangulation. The degree of a vertex is the number of edges incident at that vertex.

We can consider removing several interior vertices at the same time. As long as these vertices are not adjacent we get a set of disjoint star shaped polygons. These new straight line subdivision can be retriangulated with a lesser number of edges and reformed as star shaped until the entire triangulation ends up as a single triangle. The details of this algorithm are not within the source of this lecture.

2.5 INTERSECTION PROBLEMS

[Newman/Sproull,Foley/vanDam,Rogers]
An important and frequently occuring operation is that of detecting and possibly computing the intersection of one or more geometric objects with one or more regions. The basic intersection problem has many variants.
(i) clipping, the process of extracting a portion of a data base is fundamental to several aspects of computer graphics. In addition to its more typical use in selectively displaying a particular scene or view from a larger environment, it is useful for antialiasing, hidden

line, hidden surface, shadow and texture algorithms as well.
(ii) Boolean operations on regions (intersection, union, difference) have applications in CADD and NC programming. Also the underlying principles are applicable to boolean operations in 3 dimensions, where such operations are fundamental to solid modelling.
(iii) Interference checking is important in VLSI design rule checking, in robot motion planning, pipe layout and a variety of other engineering design situations.

Clipping to a rectangular window
This is a classical problem in computer graphics and has received considerable attention. Basically the problem is : given a set of points and lines, and a rectangular region aligned with the axis determine all the points and portions of line segments lying within the window. Since a large number of points and lines must be clipped for a typical scene, the efficiency of clipping algorithms is of great interest. Hardware or firmware implementation is always preferred.

Let XL,XR be the left and right boundaries, and YT,YB the top and bottom boundaries of the window. Further let $[x_a, y_a]$, $[x_b, y_b]$ be the end points of the line segment to be clipped. Cohen and Sutherland's algorithm may be used to detect completely visible or completely invisible line segments. This is done by assigning to each end point (x,y) a 4-bit code as shown below:

1001	1000	1010
0001	W 0000	0010
0101	0100	0110

first bit (rightmost) set - if $x < xL$
second bit set - if $x < xR$
third bit set - if $y < yB$
fourth bit set - if $y > yT$

If end-code(a), end-code(b) are the four bit codes for the line segment end points a and b then observe the following:
(i) end-code(a) end-code(b) = 0 ('anded' bitwise) implies that the line is completely outside the window region.
(ii) if end-code(a) = end-code(b) = 0 then the line is completely inside the region.

Otherwise the line segment is partially inside or completely outside. Such line segments are intersected with each boundary of the window and those two intersection points which are within the closed window region are selected as the end points of the clipped line segment.

The Sutherland-Cohen Subdivision line-clipping algorithm
This algorithm uses the end-point code to clip away a part of the line segment with respect to a window. The basic algorithm schema is:

```
for each window edge (left,bottom,right,top) do
  begin
    compute end-codes for P1 and P2;
    if P1 P2 is not (totally visible or totally invisible) then
      begin
        if P1 is inside the window then swap (P1,P2);
        replace P1 with the intersection of P1P2 and the window edge
      end;
  end;
```

The Sproull Sutherland Midpoint Subdivision line-clipping Algorithm

The previous algorithm must compute the intersection of the line segment with the window edge. This direct calculation can be avoided by performing a binary search for the intersection by always dividing the line at its midpoint. Implemented in hardware this only requires division by 2 and addition. The basic schema is as follows:

```
procedure visible (P1,P2);
  begin
    if P1,P2 is not completely visible or completely invisible then
    begin
      Pm = (P1+P2)/2;
      visible (P1,Pm); visible (Pm,P2)
    end;
  end;
```

Clipping to a Convex Region

The Cyrus-Beck [Rogers] algorithm for clipping a line to a convex polygon is based on the following observations:

(i) The directed line segment P1,P2 may be represented parametrically as $P(u) = P1 + (P2-P1)u$, $(0 < u < 1)$ and either intersects the polygon at two points say u_l and u_h, with $u_l < u_h$ or does not intersect the polygon at all.

(ii) If n_l is the inward normal at u_l and n_h at u_h of the polygonal region then $(P2-P1).n_l > 0$ while $(P2-P1).n_h < 0$.

(iii) If V_i is a vertex and n_i the inward normal of the same edge e_i, of the polygon then

if $(P1-V_i).n_i$ < 0 then P1 is outside

            $= 0$ then P1 is on the boundary

            > 0 then P1 is inside

the convex polygonal region.

(iv) $u = -(P1-V_i).n_i/(P2-P1).n_i$ is the point of intersection between P1 P2 and e_i.

The Cyrus-Beck algorithm is restricted to convex regions and is order $O(n)$ time complexity. For clipping to non-convex regions one may have to decompose into convex hull regions and then use the algorithm for each sub-region separately.

The emphasis so far has been to clip lines to the interior. The algorithm can be modified easily for clipping to the exterior, i.e. outside the region, visible. Exterior clipping is important in multi-window environments and in hidden line elimination.

In three dimensions the line segments have to be clipped to a view volume, typically a rectangular parallel piped or a frustrum of a pyramid. The Cyrus-Beck algorithm can be extended to handle this case too. We however shall not discuss this extension. The interested reader may refer to [Rogers].

If clipping is to be performed in homogeneous coordinates considerable care must be taken if a perspective transformation is used. The principal reason is that a single plane does not necessarily divide a line segment into two parts - one inside and one outside. The line segment may "wrap around" through infinity such that two disjoint portions are visible inside the region. Blinn [Blinn-2] shows that clipping all line segments before performing the perspective transformation of dividing by the homogeneous coordinate eliminates the segments that return from infinity.

For clipping a line segment to a non-convex polygon no simple algorithm is known. Basically one determines the intersections between the line segment and the polygon boundary edges and orders them in increasing order of u including P1, P2. The visible intervals on this line are then easily determined.

The Intersection of Regions

The fundamental ideas behind all algorithms that intersect regions represented by their boundaries are given below :

(i) If A and B are two polygons to be intersected then divide each edge of A into consecutive intervals such that the interior of one of these intervals can be classified unambiguously as either inside B or outside B. Similarly divide and classify edges of B with respect to A.

(ii) The set of all part edges of A and B marked as inside the other constitutes the boundary of A∩B.

In fact this classification can be used to compute A U B and A - B as well. A U B is the set of all part edges marked as outside the other region. A - B is the set all part edges of A marked as outside B with same orientation and part-edges of B marked as inside A with reverse orientation. These are known as boolean operations. It should be noted that the result of a boolean operation on two regions, not necessarily convex, may result in zero or more disjoint regions. An important requirement of practical algorithms is that the vertices of the resulting regions be output in cyclic order. To be able to do that,in general,rather elaborate data structures and traversal orders have to be incorporated into the algorithms.

The Sutherland and Hodgman Reentrant polygon clipping algorithm clips a polygon to a rectangular window. The basic idea in this algorithm is to clip the polygon against an edge by treating it as a half plane and then to use the resulting polygon as input to clip against the next edge and so on until all the edges of the window are exhausted. The window need not be rectangular but can be any convex polygon.

The Weiler-Atherton [Weiler/Atherton] algorithm is used to clip a polygonal region to another polygonal region, both possibly non-convex and multiply connected, i.e. with holes. The basic idea here is that classification of a part edge changes only at intersection points. So by treating the two polygonal boundaries as directed graphs and introducing intersection points as nodes that link part edges of one polygon with part edge of the other one can define simple graph traversal algorithms that will generate the desired resulting region(s).

The above algorithms are order $O(n^2)$. This is mainly because every edge is intersected with every other. By using the plane-sweep method this can be reduced to $O(n+I)logn)$, where I is the total number of intersecting pairs of edges. In fact using Mairson's technique this can be reduced to $O(nlogn+I)$. Of course the intersection of two convex polygons can be detected very efficiently in $O(n)$ time.

2.6 DECOMPOSITION PROBLEMS

[Guibas/Stolfi,Lee/Preparata]

As we have seen so far it is frequently the case that a geometrical problem involving arbitrarily shaped polygonal regions is much harder to answer than its equivalent for a convex or monotone polygon. Therefore in many cases a convenient solution is to split the given polygon into simpler pieces and, solve the problem separately for each piece and then merge the solutions.

Basically, there are two types of decompositions : partition, in which the interiors of the component parts are disjoint and covering, in which the interiors of component parts may overlap. Sometimes additional vertices, called Steiner points, may be introduced to obtain decompositions with the minimum number of components. We shall only be concerned with the partition type of decomposition.

Theorem : Any simple polygon P of n vertices can be decomposed into n-2 disjoint triangles by adding n-3 new edges.

Theorem : Any simple polygon P of n vertices can be transformed into a triangular subdivision of the plane with 2n-2 regions by adding a vertex at infinity and 2n-3 new edges.

Triangulating a Simple Polygon
A pioneering algorithm [Garey et al] runs in O(nlogn) time. It consists of 2 phases. In the first phase the polygon P is partitioned into a number of monotone polygons in O(nlogn) time, while in the second phase the monotone polygons are triangulated in O(n) time.

Let P be a polygon monotone along the y axis with vertices (P1 P2 ... Pn) sorted in the Y direction. For a monotone polygon this list can be produced in O(n) time. Basically the triangulation algorithm examines the vertices from top to bottom, and outputs a new component as soon as it finds three vertices that define a triangle interior to the polygon. The triangle output is removed. It can be shown that
(i) the remaining polygon continues to be monotone along Y and that if z-1 points have been considered so far then they can be arranged from top to bottom as (s1,s2,...,sk,Pi,...,Pn) with k > 2.
(ii) the points s1,s2,...,sk are all on one side of the boundary of P (i.e. belong to one of the two chains defining P)
(iii) The angles at s2,s3,...,sk-1 are all concave (i.e. result in a clockwise turn)

As a consequence of these properties, we have that the next point Pi is adjacent to s1, or sk or both if it is the last point to be considered.

Algorithm :

```
begin
   s1:=P1; s2:=P2; k:=2;
   for i:=2 to n-1 do
      begin
         if s2 and Pi are on the same side of P then
            begin
               for j:=2 to k do output triangle(sj-1,sj,pi);
               s1:=sk; k:=1
            end
         else
         while k<>1 and angle(sk-1,sk,Pi) is convex do
            begin
               output triangle(sk-1,sk,Pi);
               k:=k-1
            end;
         k:=k+1; sk:=pi
      end;
end;
```

The algorithm for decomposing a simple polygon into monotone pieces is based on the following characterization of monotone polygons:

A simple polygon P is monotone along Y axis iff every concave vertex has one neighbour strictly above it and one neighbour strictly below it.

What this characterization says is that a polygon is monotone iff it has no "interior cusps" pointing up or down of the kind shown below:

downward   upward   Steiner point

The algorithm in [Lee/Preparata] detects such cusps using a plane sweep method and then eliminates them by introducing a "cut" connecting each upward cusp to a visible vertex immediately below it and each downward cusp to a visible vertex immediately above it. For more details of this algorithm the reader is referred to the original paper.

Decomposition into convex components

Optimal decomposition of a simple polygon into convex components is a much harder problem and has been tackled by a number of people. If steiner points are allowed then an $O(n+N^2\log(n/N))$ time algorithm has been reported [Chazelle]. Here N is the number of concave vertices in the polygon.

If an optimal partition is not sought then better running times can be obtained. In [Greene] a monotone polygon is decomposed into convex components in $O(n\log n)$ time. The method is very similar to the triangulation method; removing the convex pieces from the top in such a fashion that the remaining part of the polygon remains monotone. However the fact that the removed pieces are convex polygons instead of triangles forces one to use more complex data structures and to consider many special cases. It has been shown that this algorithm decomposes a simple polygon with atmost four times as many cuts as the absolute minimum needed for convex partitioning of the simple polygon.

2.7 CONVEX HULLS PROBLEMS

[Shamos,Guibas/Stolfi,Lee/Preparata]
The problem is determining the convex hull of a set of n points. The convex hull of a set is the smallest convex region that contains the set. If the points are discrete or form the boundary of a polygonal region then the convex hull is a convex polygonal region. The convex hull problem has been studied extensively and has been the vehicle for the solution of a number of other significant questions in computational geometry. Its application has however been more in pattern recognition, image processing and stock cutting and

allocation problems than in computer graphics.

In one of the first solutions to the convex hull problem [Graham], an O(nlogn) solution is presented. First an internal point I is chosen, say the centroid of 3 non-collinear points. Second the given points are sorted in angular order about I. Next a point with minimum y is chosen. This is guaranteed to be on the convex hull. If this point is V0 and V1,V2,...,Vn are the angular sorted points in a circular list then the following algorithm is used :

```
begin
  V:=V0;
  while next(V) <> V0 do
    if V,next(V),next(next(V)) are anticlockwise
      then V:= next(V)
    else
      begin
        delete next(V);
        if V = V0 then V:= prev(V)
      end
  end;
```

The scan is completed in linear time and so the entire algorithm runs in O(nlogn) time.

Independent of the number of points in the convex hull, the above algorithm takes O(nlogn) time. Jarvis presented an algorithm [Jarvis] that runs in O(nN) time where N is the number of vertices in the convex hull. If N is atmost logn then this algorithm performs better. The approach in this algorithm is the idea of "gift wrapping". Starting with a point V0 on the convex hull, in linear time we can find the next point V1 such that all the points in the set lie to the left of the line V0V1. Th same technique is used successively to obtain V2 V3 ... until VN V0 is formed.

Other interesting algorithms [Shamos,Kirkpatrick/Siedel] use the divide and conquer paradigm and are based on the following principle :
Hull(X U Y) $\subseteq$ Hull(Hull(X) U Hull(Y))
The best amongst these runs in O(nlog N) time. It has been shown that the lower bound for the general convex hull using quadratic tests is O(nlogn). Further that the convex hull problem cannot be solved using a linear test [Yao].

For the special case of finding the convex hull of a simple polygon linear time algorithms exist [Bhattacharya/Gindy,Toussaint/Avis].

3. CURVES AND SURFACES

3.1 REPRESENTATION ISSUES

[Faux/Pratt,Forrest-1]
The representation of a curve by an equation $y=f(x)$ imposes a serious geometrical restriction: A curve so represented must not be intersected at more than one point by any line parallel to the y-axis. Usually, this restriction can be overcome by decomposing the curve into portions each representable in the form $y=f(x)$. Thus a a circle of radius r about the origin is given by the two functions $y=sqrt(r^2-x^2)$ and $y=-sqrt(r^2-x^2)$ defined for $-r<x<r$ However, even for a simple line parallel to the y-axis this device does not work.

More flexibility is obtained by an implicit representation through an equation :
$$f(x,y)=x^2+y^2-r^2=0.$$
As seen earlier any straight line in the plane has an implicit equation of the form $ax+by+c=0$, where a,b,c are constants and a and b do not both vanish; for $b=0$ we obtain a line parallel to the y axis.

The implicit description of a curve has the disadvantage that to find points (x,y) of the curve at all, say for a given x, we must solve the equation $f(x,y)=0$. Except for the straight line this involves solution of non linear equations.

The most direct and most flexible description of a curve is a parametric representation. Instead of considering one of the rectangular coordinates y or x as a function of the other we think of both coordinates x and y as functions of a third independent variable u, a so-called parameter, the point with coordinates x and y then describes the curve as u traverses a corresponding interval. Such parametric representations we have already encountered for the straight line. The circle $x^2+y^2=r^2$ has the parametric representation $x=rcos(u)$, $y=rsin(u)$. Here u denotes the angle at the centre of the circle.

For the ellipse $x^2/a^2+y^2/b^2=1$ we have the similar parametric representation $x=acos(u)$, $y=bsin(u)$, where u is the so-called eccentric angle, that is, the angle at the center corresponding to the point of the circumscribed circle lying vertically above or below the point $P=[acos(u),bsin(u)]$ of the ellipse. We assume here that $b<a$. In both cases the point with the coordinates x, y describes the complete circle or ellipse as the parameter u traverses the interval $0 < u < 2*pi$.

In general, curves C are parametrically represented by two functions of a parameter u,
$$x = f(u) = x(u), y = g(u) = y(u);$$

the shorter notation x(u) and y(u) will be used when there is no danger of confusion.

We assume throughout that f and g possess continuous derivatives unless the contrary is said.

Mapping of Parameter Interval on Curve (Sense of Direction)
For a given curve these two functions f(u) and g(u) must be determined in such a way that the set of pairs of functional values x(u) and y(u) corresponding to a certain interval of values u defines all the points on the curve and no other points. We have then a correspondence between the points of the curve and the values of u in an interval of the u-axis. The parameter representation defines a mapping of the u-axis onto the curve, the original point u on the u-axis being mapped onto the point $x = f(u)$, $y = g(u)$ of C. Since x(u) and y(u) are assumed continuous, neighboring points on to u-axis correspond

to neighboring points on the curve. Since the points of the u-axis are ordered, we may in an obvious manner assign an order or "sense" to the points of C by saying that the point onto which the number u_1 is mapped precedes the point onto which u_2 is mapped if $u_1 < u_2$. The parametric representation thus gives precise meaning to the vague intuitive notion of a curve as a set of points in which the points are arranged in the same order as on a straight line.

Change of Parameters

The values of the parameter u serve to distinguish the different points on the curve C; they play the role of "names" for the individual points of the curve.

The same curve C admits of many different parameter representations. Any quantity that varies continuously along the curve and has different values in different points of the curve can serve as parameter.

If, say, the curve originally is given by an equation $y = f(x)$, we can choose for the parameter u the variable x and describe the curve by the functions $x = u$, $y = f(u)$. Similarly, for a curve described by giving x as a function of y, say $x = g(y)$, we can use y as parameter u and write $x = g(u)$, $y = u$.

For a curve given by an equation $r = h(t)$ in polar coordinates r,t we can choose t as parameter u and obtain the parametric representation
$$x = r\cos(t) = h(u)\cos(u), \quad y = r\sin(t) = h(u)\sin(u)$$

3.2 TANGENTS AND NORMALS TO CURVES

The tangent line to the curve $y = f(x)$ at the point $P(x_1, y_1)$ can be expressed by the equation
$$y = y_1 + D_x f(x_1)(x - x_1)$$
where $D_x f(x_1)$ is the value of derivative of f at $x = x_1$.

It is apparent from the formula that there will be difficulties when the curve has a vertical or near-vertical tangent at P. The difficulty can be avoided by using an implicit equation $g(x,y) = 0$ to describe the curve. The implicit equation of the tangent is then given by
$$D_x f(x_1, y_1)(x - x_1) + D_y f(x_1, y_1)(y - y_1) = 0,$$

where $D_x f(x_1, y_1)$ and $D_y f(x_1, y_1)$ are the values of the partial derivatives of f with respect x and y respectively at the point $P(x_1, y_1)$., The tangent to the curve $x = x(u)$, $y = y(u)$ at the point P with parameter $u = u_1$, is given by the equations
$$x = x(t) = x(u_1) + t D_u x(u_1), \qquad y = y(u) = y(u_1) + t D_u y(u_1)$$

where t is the parameter on the tangent line, and $D_u x(u_1), D_u y(u_1)$ are the values of derivatives at $u = u_1$.

The normal to the curve at P is given by the equations

$$x = x(u_1) + t D_u y(u_1), \quad y = y(u_1) - t D_u x(u_1)$$

3.3 CURVATURE

The radius of curvature p of the curve $y = f(x)$ is given by the well known formula

$$p = (1 + (D_x f)^2)^{3/2}/D_{xx} f$$

Because the radius of curvature becomes infinite at points of inflexion, it is usually better to use the curvature $k = 1/p$, which is finite unless there are cusps in the curve.

The corresponding formula for an implicitly defined curve $f(x,y) = 0$ is given by

$$k = (D_{xx}f(D_y f)^2 - 2D_{xy}f D_x f D_y f + D_{yy}f(D_x f)^2)/((D_x f)^2 + (D_y f)^2)^{3/2}$$

For the parametric curve $x = x(u)$, $y = y(u)$, the expression is

$$k = (D_u x D_{uu} y - D_u y D_{uu} x)/((D_u x)^2 + (D_u y)^2)^{3/2}$$

3.4 CONICS

[Blinn-3,Faux/Pratt]
Implicit Form : A second order curve is defined by an equation having only second powers of the coordinates. The general such equation is:

$$Ax^2 + 2Bxy + 2Cxw + Dy^2 + 2Eyw + Fyw + Fw^2 = 0$$

This can be rewritten in matrix form as

$$[x,y,w] \begin{bmatrix} A & B & C \\ B & D & E \\ C & E & F \end{bmatrix} [x,y,w]^t = 0$$

We will call the 3x3 symmetric matrix Q. All points which satisfy this equation will lie on some two dimensional curve. It satisfies the homogeneous condition that any non-zero scalar multiple of Q represents the same curve.

For the most part, these curves will be conic sections. Examples of some curves and their defining matrices are:

Unit circle: $X^2 + Y^2 = 1$ (or) $x^2 + y^2 - w^2 = 0$ $\quad Q = \begin{bmatrix} 1 & 0 & 0 \\ 0 & 1 & 0 \\ 0 & 0 & -1 \end{bmatrix}$

Parabola: $X^2 - Y = 0$ (or) $x^2 - yw = 0$ $\quad Q = \begin{bmatrix} 1 & 0 & 0 \\ 0 & 0 & -1/2 \\ 0 & -1/2 & 0 \\ 0 & 0 & -1 \end{bmatrix}$

Hyperbola: $1/X - Y = 0$ (or) $xy - w^2 = 0$ $\quad Q = \begin{bmatrix} 0 & 1/2 & 0 \\ 1/2 & 0 & 0 \\ 0 & 0 & -1 \end{bmatrix}$

Some matrices will give degenerate conic sections, that is, the curves are really two intersecting first order curves (lines). This will occur if the original second order equation can be factored into two first order equations with real coefficients. Note that the matrix Q is singular in these cases.

X and Y axes : $X = 0, Y = 0$ (or) $xy=0$ $Q = \begin{bmatrix} 0 & 1/2 & 0 \\ 1/2 & 0 & 0 \\ 0 & 0 & 0 \end{bmatrix}$

Diagonal Lines: $Y = X$, or $Y = -X$ (or) $x^2-y^2=0$ $Q = \begin{bmatrix} 1 & 0 & 0 \\ 0 & -1 & 0 \\ 0 & 0 & 0 \end{bmatrix}$

Another form of degeneracy consists of matrices which are satisfied for one point only. These can also be considered as circles with a radius of zero. This will occur if the equation can be factored but the coefficients are complex. The matrix will be singular in this case also.

Origin : $X = 0, Y = 0$ (or) $x^2+y^2=0$ $Q = \begin{bmatrix} 1 & 0 & 0 \\ 0 & 1 & 0 \\ 0 & 0 & 0 \end{bmatrix}$

The above two cases of degeneracy occur when the rank of the matrix is 2. A further degeneracy occurs when the rank is reduced to 1. In this case, the equation can be factored into two equal terms. The resulting curve is two coincident lines.

X axis twice : $X = 0, X = 0$ (or) $x^2=0$ $Q = \begin{bmatrix} 1 & 0 & 0 \\ 0 & 0 & 0 \\ 0 & 0 & 0 \end{bmatrix}$

A final case can occur in which no points satisfy the equation.

Null Curve : $X^2+Y^2=-1$ (or) $x^2+y^2+w^2=0$ $Q = \begin{bmatrix} 1 & 0 & 0 \\ 0 & 1 & 0 \\ 0 & 0 & 1 \end{bmatrix}$

The above categorizations of quadric curves can be summarized by examining signs of the eigenvalues of the matrix Q. Since multiplying Q by -1 will produce the same curve, flipping the signs of all eigenvalues will yield the same curve type.

$\begin{array}{ll}
(+ + +) \quad \text{or} \quad (- - -) & \text{Null curve} \\
(+ + -) \quad \text{or} \quad (- - +) & \text{Conic section} \\
(+ + 0) \quad \text{or} \quad (- - 0) & \text{Single point (Sphere with radius} =0) \\
(+ - 0) \quad \text{or} \quad (- + 0) & \text{Intersecting lines} \\
(+ 0\ 0) \quad \text{or} \quad (- 0\ 0) & \text{Coincident lines}
\end{array}$

Note that this categorization does not distinguish between shapes which are different only due to homogeneous transformations (perhaps including perspective). Thus an ellipse, parabola and hyperbola are all in the same category.

Modelling
A desired second order curve can be generated from the location of five points by re-writing the original quadric equation in vector form

$$(x^2,2xy,2xw,y^2,2yw,w^2)(A,B,C,D,E,F)^t=0$$

Each of the points yields one row vector as a function of its coordinates. All five points yield a 5x6 matrix which can be used to solve the resulting homogeneous equation for the unknown column vector (A,B,C,D,E,F). This form of definition will not work if the 5 points yield a 5x6 matrix of rank 4 or less. This is analogous to the problem of finding the intersection of two coincident lines, where the algebraic result is the cross product of two parallel vectors. The result, (0,0,0), indicates that there is no geometric solution.

To remove the necessity of solving these equations, Liming uses the following well established classical techniques which illustrate some of the advantages of the implicit form. The first point to note is that if two conics have the equations C1(x,y)=0 and C2(x,y)=0 (or for brevity C1=0 and C2=0), then the equation : (1-a)C1 + aC2 = 0 is satisfied for all points lying on both C1=0 and C2=0. This equation then represents another conic (since it is quadratic) which passes through the intersection points of C1=0 and C2=0, whatever the value of a. As a is varied, a family (or pencil) of conics is formed, two of which are C1=0 (when a=0) and C2=0 (when a=1) The value of the parameter a can in the general case be determined by specifying another point (not an intersection point) which lies on the curve (1-a)C1 + C2 = 0. If the point is $P_1(x_1,y_1)$, then

$$a = C1(x_1,y_1)/(C1(x_1,y_1)-C2(x_1,y_1))$$

We next observe that the equation (a1x+b1y+c1)(a2x+b2y+c2)=0, or (L1)(L2)=0, is a quadratic equation satisfied by all points on the line pair L1=0 and L2=0. It is, in fact, a degenerate conic section obtained by sectioning a cone by a plane through its vertex and parallel to the axis. We may use such line pairs to define non-degenerate conic sections by using the pencil conic equation. Thus we see that the equation (1-a)L1L2 + aL3L4 = 0 represents a family or 'pencil' of conics which pass through the four intersections of the line pairs (L1,L2) and (L3,L4). By specifying a a fifth point we can fix the value of a.

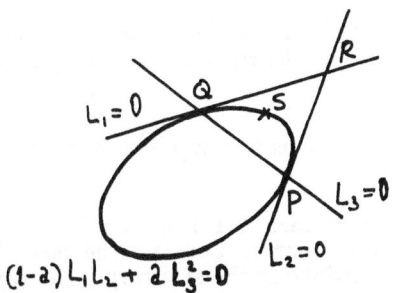

The method can be adapted to find the conic which passes through two points with given tangents and passing through a given third point. If the lines L3 = 0 and L4 = 0 are identical, the equation $(1-a)L1L2 + aL3^2 = 0$ represents a pencil of conics through P and Q with L1 as the tangent at P and L2 as the tangent at Q (see Figure above). The choice of a third point S determines the parameter a.

The conic section can, in this case, be determined by four points: the two points of tangency P and Q the intersection R of the tangents, and some fourth point S known as the shoulder point.

Provided that S is chosen inside the triangle PRQ the conic will always provide a continuous curve between P and Q which lies inside the triangle. If S is the midpoint of the line joining the midpoints of QR and PR, then the conic is a parabola commonly known as the proportional·curve. If S lies between the parabola and the line PQ, the resulting curve will be an ellipse. If it is outside the parabola, the curve will be hyperbolic.

A more natural method of modelling is to define certain standard curves as primitives, e.g. the unit circle centered at the origin. Then other desired circles, ellipses, etc. may be generated by transformations of this primitive in the manner described below. In a sense, once the primitive is specified, the transformation matrix becomes the model.

Transformation

Given a quadric curve matrix, Q_a and a homogeneous transformation matrix, T, it must be possible to derive a new matrix Q_b which represents the transformed curve. That is given

$$(P.Q.P^t)_a = 0 \text{ and } P_b = P_a.T$$

we wish to find Q_b such that

$$(P.Q.P^t)_b = 0$$

for points on the curve. This result is derived in much the same way as was done for deriving the transformation of lines. We first rewrite the equation for transforming points

$$P_a = P_b.T^*$$

Then substitute this expression for P_a into the original quadric curve definition:

$$P_b.T^*.Q_a.(P_b.T^*)^t = 0$$

then expand the parenthesized expression and re-group

$$P_b.[T^*.Q_a.T^{*t}].P_b^t = 0$$

By comparing the expression in brackets with our desired expression for Q_b we arrive at the answer

$$Q_b = T^*.Q_a.T^{*t}$$

That is, to transform a quadric curve, multiply on the left by the adjoint (i.e. generalized inverse) of the point transformation and on the right by the transpose of the adjoint.

Inside Vs Outside

The quadric form we have been using allows us to compute a number for all points on the plane

$$f = P.Q.P^t.$$

If P lies on the curve, the value of f will be zero. If P is not on the curve, the sign of f can tell us if the point is inside or outside the curve. Consider the case of the unit circle at the origin and the value obtained by multiplying the arbitrary point (x,y,w) by its quadric matrix, so that

$$f = x^2 + y^2 - w^2.$$

If f is positive the point is outside the circle, if negative it is inside. Since any nonzero scalar multiple of Q represents the same curve, then, in particular, $-Q$ also represents a circle. For this form, f positive means inside and f negative means outside. The means to distinguish between these cases is the sign of the determinant of Q. Since the inside/outside test must be kept unambiguous we shall make the convention that the determinant of Q should always be negative. Note that any geometric transformation of Q will not change the sign of its determinant.

Another property of the homogeneous representation is the duality principle. Given that all points lying on the curve satisfy

$$P.Q.P^t = 0,$$

the dual form of this statement is that all lines which are tangent to the curve satisfy

$$L^t.Q^*.L = 0,$$

where Q^* is the adjoint of the matrix Q. Consider again the case of the unit circle at the

origin and the vertical line $x=x_0$:
$$L^t.Q^*.L = 1 - x_0^2.$$
The line is tangent to the circle if $x_0=+1$ or $x_0=-1$. If $|x_0| < 1$ the line intersects the circle at two points and the expression x_0^2-1 is positive, if $|x_0| > 1$ then the line does not intersect the circle anywhere.

The above discussion about inside/outside for points can, then, be generalized to lines as; if the product $L^t.Q^*.L$ is positive the line intersects the curve, if zero it is tangent, and if negative it is disjoint.

The line tangency equation allows us to categorize conic sections into the familiar categories of ellipse, parabola and hyperbola. The interpretation is that an ellipse is disjoint from the line at infinity, a parabola is tangent to the line at infinity and a hyperbola intersects it in two locations. The line at infinity has the equation $[0,0,1]^t$ so this product will simply be equal to Q_{33}^*.

The Rational Quadratic [Forrest-3,Faux/Pratt]
The conic can be parametrised in the rational quadratic form and is represented in the homogeneous coordiante space by the following quadratic functions:

$$x=(a1u^2+b1u+c1), \quad y=(a2u^2+b2u+c2), \quad w=(au^2+bu+c)$$

This form has been studied extensively and Forrest has defined the conic segment in terms of its end tangents and its intersection with a typical line segment [Forrest-1, Forrest-3]. This gives control over the shape through three points and a scaling factor that determines the type of conic (ellipse, parabola, hyperbola etc.). Experience with such geometric handles enables the user to develop a good 'feel' for the shape without having to know the exact mathematical forms used to represent the curves.

Super-Conics
Higher order curves in a plane are not widely used in industry and have not been studied extensively. Generalizations of conics, especially of ellipse and hyperbola are known under the name of super-conics [Faux/Pratt, Barr].

In their canonical implicit form these are described by
$$x^{2/n}+y^{2/n}=1 \text{ and } x^{2/n}-y^{2/n}=1,$$

where n is a positive real number.

In the parametric form we express them as
Super-ellipse : $x=[(1-u^2)]^p$, $y=[(2u)]^p$, $w=[(1+u^2)]^p$.
Super-hyperbola : $x=[(4+u^2)]^p$, $y=[(4u)]^p$, $w=[(4-u^2)]^p$.
Super-parabola : $x=u^n$, $y=u^2$, $w=1$.

The super-ellipse has been in use in industry for a number of years [Faux/Pratt]. Other super conics have been introduced recently and may require further experimentation and study in order to be accepted as tools for shape design.

3.5 SPACE CURVES OR TWISTED CURVES

[Foley/van Dam,Smith]

Twisted or non-planar curves extend into 3-D space. The functions x(u),y(u),z(u) should be as simple as possible in order to make the computer applications of these curves easy, economic and efficient. Polynomial functions are very good candidates for defining parametric curves. They are evaluated using a few arithmetic operations. Trigonometric, exponential or logarithmic functions on the other hand require either table look up methods or iterative procedures for their evaluation.

The simplest polynomials that give twisted curves when used as coordinate functions are the cubic polynomials. Quadratic or second degree polynomials can give only plane curves [Peters]. The coordinate functions of a parametric cubic curve are of the form (given below as a vector valued function)

$$r(u) = Au^3 + Bu^2 + Cu + D = [u^3, u^2, u, 1] \cdot [A, B, C, D]^t$$

A,B,C,D are four unknown vectors which, when specified, completely characterize the curve. Two limits u_0 and u_1 may be specified so as to give a segment instead of an entire curve. A common convention is to assume $u_0 = 0$ and $u_1 = 1$, since an appropriate linear transformation of A,B,C,D with $u_0 \neq 0$ and/or $u_1 \neq 1$ gives rise to another set A',B',C',D' with $u_0 = 0$ and $u_1 = 1$, without altering the shape of the segment.

These parametric cubic curves have been in use in computer graphics as well as in a variety of applications for quite some time. The method of specifying the four constants A,B,C,D with $u_0 = 0$ and $u_1 = 1$ relates the curve equations to the geometric shape or configuration that it describes. The relation may be an approximation or an interpolation. This enables the user to convert the shape in mind into the mathematical curve form.

A spline is a piecewise polynomial satisfying continuity conditions between the pieces. We will study piecewise cubic polynomials which are continuous in the first derivative between pieces or in both the first and second derivative. These are called cubic splines, and we will henceforth assume cubic splines in these lectures. One of the two classes of splines presented will be continuous in the first derivative only; the other will be continuous in both the first and second derivative. Since polynomials are continuous in all derivatives, it must be the junctions between the pieces in a spline where continuity is a question. These points are called knots.

The original spline was not mathematical but a real draftsman's tool consisting of a flexible strip of metal or wood and several heavy metal pieces which anchored the flexible strip to the drafting table. The strip curved depending on where these heavy "ducks" (knots) were placed, providing the draftsman with a guide for drawing a general class of curves, more general than provided by a set of French curves. The first mathematical splines were models of this real spline, but the mathematics has now evolved beyond the constraints of reality to the point where modern splines bear little resemblance to their mechanical predecessors. They share with it the notion of graceful curves generated from a small set of discrete points.

Points usually have more than one coordinate, of course. So to spline points together means to spline their x coordinates together, their y coordinates together, and their z coordinates together. Thus it is customary to represent splining of points by presenting a solution for one coordinate, say x, and assuming the same solution for y and z.

The Two Classes of Splines

Interpolating splines are those which pass through their knots. The earliest splines were all interpolating since the mechanical spline from which they were derived (arguably) "interpolated" its knots. The splines of a newer class, the approximating splines, approach but do not intersect their knots, which are often called control points. By analogy, the knots for interpolating splines are also sometimes referred to as control points. So the two classes of splines of interest here are local interpolating splines and local approximating splines.

The interpolating splines have first-order continuity (continuity of the first derivative at knots) and approximating splines have second-order continuity (continuity of the first and second derivative at knots). They are both, of course, infinitely differentiable at points which are not knots. The approximating splines, in a sense, trade off the desirable feature of having the knots on the curve for another desirable feature, increased grace from second-order continuity.

Hermite Form

Let us see how the Hermite form of a cubic is determined from endpoints and endpoint tangents. We are given the points P_0 and P_1 and the tangent vectors S_0 and S_1 at these. We want to find A, B, C and D subject to the conditions listed below: (Note we shall only consider the x coordinate)

$$x(0) = x_0, \ x(1) = x_1, \ D_u x(0) = s_0, \ D_u x(1) = s_1.$$

Let $U=[u^3,u^2,u,1]$ and $C=[A,B,C,D]^t$, so that the parametric cubic is defined by the equation $x(u) = U.C$

Also
$$x(0)=x_0=[0,0,0,1].C \text{ and } x(1)=x_1=[1,1,1,1].C$$

To continue with the tangent vector conditions, we first differentiate with respect to u, obtaining

$$D_u x(u) = [3u^2,2u,1,0].C$$

Then $D_u x(0)=s_0=[0,0,1,0].C$ and $D_u x(1)=s_1=[3,2,1,0].C$
The four conditions for x_0,x_1,s_0 and s_1 can be gathered together into a single matrix equation:

$$\begin{matrix} x_0 \\ x_1 \\ s_0 \\ s_1 \end{matrix} = \begin{bmatrix} 0 & 0 & 0 & 1 \\ 1 & 1 & 1 & 1 \\ 0 & 0 & 1 & 0 \\ 3 & 2 & 1 & 0 \end{bmatrix} [C]$$

Inverting the 4 x 4 matrix achieves our objective of solving for C giving

$$C = \begin{bmatrix} 2 & -2 & 1 & 1 \\ -3 & 3 & -2 & -1 \\ 0 & 0 & 1 & 0 \\ 1 & 0 & 0 & 0 \end{bmatrix} \begin{bmatrix} x_0 \\ x_1 \\ s_0 \\ s_1 \end{bmatrix} = M_h.G_h$$

Here M_h is the Hermite matrix and G_h is the Hermite geometry vector. Applying this result, we obtain $x(u) = U.M_h.G_h$, and similar equations for y(u) and z(u).

Given x_0, x_1, s_0 and s_1, we can evaluate $x(u), y(u)$ and $z(u)$ for $0 < u < 1$ and find all points on the cubic curve from x_0 to x_1 with starting tangent vector s_0 and ending tangent vector s_1.

If we take the product $U.M_h$, we have : $UM_h = [(2u^3-3u^2+1),(-2u^3+3u^2),(u^3-2u^2+u),(u^3-u^2)]$
Postmultiplying this by G_h yields:

$$x(u)=U.M_h.G_h=x_0(2u^3-3u^2+1)+x_1(-2u^3+3u^2)+s_0(u^3-2u^2+u)+s_1(u^3-u^2).$$

The four functions of u in the product $U.M_h$ are often called blending functions, since the first two functions blend x_0 and x_1, while the other two blend s_0 and s_1, producing the "blended" sum $x(u)$.

Cardinal Spline
A local interpolating spline used for many years in computer graphics has gone under several names: the cardinal spline, the Catmull-Rom spline [Catmull/Rom], or the Overhauser spline [Brewer/Anderson]. It has obviously been reinvented several times.

The cubic Catmull-Rom spline may be specified with the following 4x4 matrix:

$$M_{cr} = 1/2 \begin{bmatrix} -1 & 3 & -3 & 1 \\ 2 & -5 & 4 & -1 \\ -1 & 0 & 1 & 0 \\ 0 & 1 & 0 & 0 \end{bmatrix}$$

This matrix is used to generate a spline curve as follows: Given a list of x-coordinates, and a parameter u which will take us along the spline connecting (or approximately connecting) one coordinate x_0 to the next x_1 as the parameter is varied from 0 to 1, a new x-coordinate is obtained from each value of u from the four nearest given x coordinates (two behind, two ahead, along the curve) by $U.M_{cr}.G_c$, where $G_c=[x_{-1},x_0,x_1,x_2]$. Recall that the y-coordinates and z-coordinates of a given set of points to be interpolated would be treated similarly.

The Cardinal Spline A shape parameter called tension causes a spline to bend more sharply; it increases the magnitude of the tangent vector at the knots. The cubic cardinal spline generalization of the Catmull-Rom spline adds tension with the parameter labelled a in the following defining matrix:

$$M_{ca} = \begin{bmatrix} -a & 2-a & a-2 & a \\ 2a & a-3 & 3-2a & -a \\ -a & 0 & a & 0 \\ 0 & 1 & 0 & 0 \end{bmatrix}$$

Clearly for M_{cr}, a = 0.5; Another popular value of a is 1 which, of course, has sharper bends than the Catmull-Rom but a simple integer matrix.

The four curves defined by

$$c0(u) = [u^3,u^2,u,1].M_{ca0}$$

$$c1(u) = [u^3,u^2,u,1].M_{ca1}$$

$$c2(u) = [u^3,u^2,u,1].M_{ca2}$$

$$c3(u) = [u^3,u^2,u,1].M_{ca3}$$

where M_{cai} is the i-th column vector of matrix M_{ca}, called the basis segments for the cubic cardinal spline, and the four curves drawn as one are called the basis function for the cubic cardinal spline. A spline can be thought of as the curve $X(u)$ resulting of the sum of copies of the basis function positioned at each knot and weighted by its magnitude. All splines discussed here have associated basis functions which may be derived similarly.

The parameter a has a simple interpretation which explains the use of the word "tension". The matrix above is used to generate, for each four consecutive points, the part of the spline curve between the middle two points. Suppose these four points are called x_{-1}, x_0, x_1, and x_2. Consider the tangent at point x_0; for cardinal splines it is parallel to the vector $x_{-1}x_1$. Similarly the tangent at point x_1 is parallel to the vector x_0x_2. The magnitudes of these two tangents is proportional to the lengths of the two vectors, respectively, and the constant of proportionality is a.

The cubic cardinal matrix may be easily derived from the two tangent constraints above and the fact that the curve must pass through x_0 and x_1.

Our four constraints may be expressed by the following equations:
$x(0)=x_0$, $x(1)=x_1$, $D_ux(0)=a(x_1-x_{-1})=s_0$, $D_ux(1)=a(x_2-x_0)=s_1$
Thus if s_0 and s_1 represent the slopes, or tangents, at points x_0 and x_1, respectively, then this can be written as

$$G_h = \begin{bmatrix} x_0 \\ x_1 \\ s_0 \\ s_1 \end{bmatrix} = \begin{bmatrix} 0 & 1 & 0 & 0 \\ 0 & 0 & 1 & 0 \\ -a & 0 & a & 0 \\ 0 & -a & 0 & a \end{bmatrix} \begin{bmatrix} x_{-1} \\ x_0 \\ x_1 \\ x_2 \end{bmatrix} = M_{hc}.G_c$$

Substituting in the Hermite form we have : $x(u) = U.M_h.G_h = U.M_h.M_{hc}.G_c$
Defining the product $M_h.M_{hc}$ as M_a we have: $x(u) = U.M_a.G_c$, the cardinal spline.

Bezier Spline
The form for defining a cubic developed by Bezier is also very similar to the Hermite form and differs in the definition of the endpoint tangent vectors [Bezier]. For the Bezier form also four points are used. The tangent vectors of the endpoints are determined from the line segments $P_{-1}P_0$ and P_1P_2. Specifically, the tangent vectors S_0 and S_1 of the Hermite form are defined to have the relation to the four Bezier point P_{-1}, P_0, P_1 and P_2:

$$S_0 = 3(P_0-P_{-1})r \text{ and } S_1 = 3(P_2-P_1).$$

Therefore the relation between the Hermite geometry matrix G_h and the Bezier geometry matrix G_b is

$$G_h = \begin{bmatrix} x_0 \\ x_1 \\ s_0 \\ s_1 \end{bmatrix} = \begin{bmatrix} 1 & 0 & 0 & 0 \\ 0 & 0 & 0 & 1 \\ -3 & 3 & 0 & 0 \\ 0 & 0 & -3 & 3 \end{bmatrix} \begin{bmatrix} x_{-1} \\ x_0 \\ x_1 \\ x_2 \end{bmatrix} = M_{hb}.G_b$$

As before defining the product $M_h.M_{hb}$ as M_b, we have $x(u) = U.M_b.G_b$, which is now the

Bezier form. The matrix M_b obtained from the product $M_h.M_{hb}$ is

$$M_b = \begin{bmatrix} -1 & 3 & -3 & 1 \\ 3 & -6 & 3 & 0 \\ -3 & 3 & 0 & 0 \\ 1 & 0 & 0 & 0 \end{bmatrix}$$

The Bezier curve passes only through x_{-1} and x_2. Hence it is an approximating curve. Two characteristics of the Bezier from tend to make it more widely used in graphics than the Hermite form. First, the geometry matrix (of four points) has intuitive appeal for an interactive user since, by moving the points with a locator device, one can easily mould the curve to a desired shape. With the Hermite form, tangent vectors must be directly specified; this is a more difficult job to do interactively, and the concept is unfamiliar to some users. On the other hand, forcing a curve to match a known tangent vector is easier with the Hermite form. Second, the convex hull of the four control points bounds the Bezier curve. The convex hull is useful in clipping a curve against a window or view volume. Rather than clip the curve immediately, we first test the convex hull, and only if it intersects the window or view volume need we then examine the curve itself.

We can better understand the convex hull property of the Bezier form by taking the product $U.M_b.G_b$: $(1-u)^3 x_{-1} + 3u(u-1)^2 x_0 + 3u^2(1-u)x_1 + u_3 x_2$.
Examining the polynomial coefficients of the four points, we see that each ranges in value between 0 and 1 and that their sum is 1 for $0 < u < 1$. Thus, this expression is just a weighted average of the four control points. It can be shown that the weighted average of n points fall within the convex hull of the n points: this can be seen intuitively by considering n = 2 and n = 3, and then generalizing.

B-Splines

The B-spline cubic representation does not in general pass through any control points, but is continuous and also has continuity of tangent vector and of curvature (that is, its first and second derivatives are continuous at the endpoints) while the Hermite and Bezier forms have only first-derivative continuity at endpoints (but do pass through control points). Thus, we can say that the B-spline form is "smoother" than the other forms. The B-spline formulation is $x(u) = U.M_s.G_s$, where

$$M_s = 1/6 \begin{bmatrix} -1 & 3 & -3 & 1 \\ 3 & -6 & 3 & 0 \\ -3 & 0 & 3 & 0 \\ 1 & 4 & 1 & 0 \end{bmatrix}$$

It is used just as are the other spline matrices above. Its basis segments are generated just as for the cardinal spline. In brief, they are given by $b_i = U.M_{si}$ $0 <= i < 4$. The M_{si} are the column vectors of M_s.

To approximate the control points x_1, x_2 ..., x_n by a series of B-splines, we use a different geometry matrix between each pair of adjacent points. The approximation from near x_i to near x_{i+1} uses

$$G_s^i = [x_{i-1}, x_i, x_{i+1}, x_{i+2}]^t, 1 < i <= n.$$

The first and second derivative continuity at a junction point can be easily shown by evaluating the position, first and second derivatives at u=1 for the ith segment and at u=0 for the $(i+1)^{th}$ segment. It can also be shown that the join points and their derivatives are weighted sums of the three immediately adjacent points.

The convex hull property of Bezier curves holds for B-spline curves as well; the convex hull for the curve from near x_i to x_{i+1} is that of the four control points used to generate the curve : $x_{i-1}, x_i, x_{i+1}, x_{i+2}$. This means that the curve cannot get any "wilder" than its control points, or the polygon defined by its control points. Interpolating splines are not so nice. They can have kinks and wild fluctuations. All generalizations below of the B-spline share this convex-hull property.

Tensioned B-Splines

The B-splines have been generalized to tensioned B-splines by analogy with the generalization of Catmull-Rom splines to cardinal splines. The tensioned cubic B-spline may be specified with the following matrix:

$$
M_{s2} = 1/6 \begin{bmatrix} -a & 12-9a & 9a-12 & a \\ 3a & 12a-18 & 18-15a & 0 \\ -3a & 0 & 3a & 0 \\ a & 6-2a & a & 0 \end{bmatrix}
$$

Clearly for M_s, $a = 1$.

The Beta Splines

Barsky [Barsky] has generalized the B-spline even further by adding not only tension but also what he calls bias. Bias may be described as the tendency for a spline to bunch more to the left than to the right, or vice versa. More precisely, it is the ratio of the velocity right of a knot to the velocity left of the knot The biased and tensioned B-spline is called the Beta-spline. The cubic Beta-spline may be specified with the following matrix:

$$
M_{s,b_1,b_2} = 1/d \begin{bmatrix} -2b_1^3 & 2(b_2+b_1^3+b_1^2+b_1) & -2(b_2+b_1^2+b_1+1) & 2 \\ 6b_1^3 & -3(b_2+2b_1^3+2b_1^2) & 3(b_2+2b_1^2) & 0 \\ -6b_1^3 & 6(b_1^3-b_1)) & 2 & 0 \\ 2b_1^3 & b_2+4(b_1^2+b_1) & 2 & 0 \end{bmatrix}
$$

where $d = b_2+2b_1^3+4b_1^2+4b_1+2$

Clearly $M_s = M_{s,1,0}$. Not so clearly, M_{s2} can be shown to be a special case of M_{s,b_1,b_2}, where $b_1 = 1$ and $b_2 = 12(1-a)/a$.

Knot Spacing

We have assumed throughout this discussion that the knots are uniformly spaced; in fact, they are assumed to be the integers. Parameter u varying, from 0 to 1 takes the spline from one integer knot to the next.

For cubic splines, the first and last knots in a list are used only for starting and stopping conditions (since only the middle two knots of each consecutive four are connected by application of the spline matrix to the four knots). If the spline is not to be a closed curve

- it is not to be a cyclic spline - then it is frequently adequate to double the first and last knots, to give them multiplicity 2. That is, the first and second knot are made identical, and the last and the next-to-last knot are made identical. To make a cyclic spline, simply append the last knot to the first of the list and append the (original) first two knots to the end.

The effect of a knot with multiplicity greater than 1 is to cause an approximating spline to approach the knot more closely. Thus it is like a local tension control but unfortunately not subtle. For interpolating splines, which already pass through the knots, increased multiplicity causes loops, or kinks, at the knots.

To use nonuniform spacing of knots would imply that the basis function changes shape as it is translated along the parameter u axis - i.e., that a nonuniform basis is being used. Since the shape of the spline would certainly change with a different knot spacing, knot spacing might be considered as providing shape control. One method for assigning nonuniformly spaced knots separates them by distances proportional to the distances separating the values at the knots. So tightly bunched data is assigned to closely spaced knots. This technique [Forrest-4] does not make dramatic changes in spline shape, relative that obtained with a uniform spacing, unless the data is tightly bunched. That this is true can be seen considering what happens if the data is so close it actually coalesces into one point. Then the proportional spacing method of nonuniform basis places the corresponding knots atop one another to get, equivalently, a single knot of multiplicity greater than 1. We have already seen that this causes the spline to approach its knot or to kink.

3.6 QUADRIC SURFACES

[Blinn-3]
Second order surfaces are also called quadric surfaces. They are defined by an expression with each term having coordinates to the second power.

$$Ax^2+2Bxy+2Cxz+2Dxw+ \ Ey^2+2Fyz+2Gyw+Hz^2+2Izw+Jw^2 = 0$$

This can be rewritten in matrix notation as:

$$[x,y,z,w] \begin{bmatrix} A & B & C & D \\ B & E & F & G \\ C & F & H & I \\ D & G & I & J \end{bmatrix} \begin{bmatrix} x \\ y \\ z \\ w \end{bmatrix} = 0$$

We will call the 4x4 symmetric matrix Q. The shape of the surface so defined depends upon the algebraic properties of the matrix Q. The various shapes are first distinguished by examining the signs of the four eigenvalues of Q. (Since the matrix is symmetric, the eigenvalues are guaranteed to be real.)

non-degenerate
(+ + + +) or (− − − −) No points satisfy the equation
(+ + + −) or (− − − +) Ellipsoid, hyperboloid of 2 sheets, paraboloid
(+ + − −) Hyperboloid of 1 sheet, hyperbolic paraboloid

degenerate
(+ + + 0) or (− − − 0) A single point (i.e. a sphere with radius=0)
(+ + − 0) or (− − + 0) Cylinder, cone

doubly degenerate
$(+ + 0\ 0\ )$or$(- - 0\ 0\ )$ A single line (i.e. a cylinder with radius$=0$)
$(+ - 0\ 0\ )$ Two intersecting planes

triply degenerate
$(+ 0\ 0\ 0\ )$or$(- 0\ 0\ 0\ )$ Two coincident planes

Note that the classifications do not distinguish between shapes which are different only due to perspective transformations. Thus an ellipsoid, paraboloid and hyperboloid of 2 sheets are in the same category.

Examples of some surfaces and their defining matrices are:

Unit Sphere : $X^2 + Y^2 + Z^2 = 1$ or $x^2 + y^2 + z^2 - w^2 = 0$
$$\begin{bmatrix} 1 & 0 & 0 & 0 \\ 0 & 1 & 0 & 0 \\ 0 & 0 & 1 & 0 \\ 0 & 0 & 0 & -1 \end{bmatrix}$$

Unit Cone : $X^2+Y^2-Z^2=0$ or $x^2+y^2-z^2+w^2=0$
$$\begin{bmatrix} 1 & 0 & 0 & 0 \\ 0 & 1 & 0 & 0 \\ 0 & 0 & -1 & 0 \\ 0 & 0 & 0 & 0 \end{bmatrix}$$

Unit Hyperboloid of one sheet : $X^2+Y^2-Z^2=1$ or $x^2+y^2-z^2-w^2=0$
$$\begin{bmatrix} 1 & 0 & 0 & 0 \\ 0 & 1 & 0 & 0 \\ 0 & 0 & -1 & 0 \\ 0 & 0 & 0 & -1 \end{bmatrix}$$

Surface Normals
A vector normal to a general algebraic surface $F(x,y,z,w)=0$ is formed by taking partial derivatives of the function:
$$N = (D_x F, D_y F, D_z F)$$
This function is defined over all space, but it makes sense as a normal vector only when the derivatives are evaluated at points on the surface. This vector is not necessarily of unit length and must be appropriately scaled if this is a requirement.

For second order surfaces the x component of the normal vector is
$$D_x F = (1,0,0,0)Q(x,y,z,w)^t + (x,y,z,w)Q\,(1,0,0,0)^t = 2(x,y,z,w)Q\,(1,0,0,0)^t$$

and in general
$$N = 2[x,y,z,w]\,Q\begin{bmatrix} 1 & 0 & 0 & 0 \\ 0 & 1 & 0 & 0 \\ 0 & 0 & 1 & 0 \\ 0 & 0 & 0 & 1 \end{bmatrix}$$

Transformations
For second order surfaces the transformation takes the form $Q_b = T^s.Q_a.T^{st}$

Rational Parametric Form
As in the case of conics the quadric can be parametrized so that it can be considered as a

parametric patch: trigonometric and rational quadraticwhich are inter-convertible through simple substitutions.

Below we show the rational parametric parametrizations for some quadric patches. For the standard parametrization, the values of u and v range between 0 and 1 so that the patch does not extend infinitely. These parametric functions, when substituted for the coordinates, indeed satisfy the implicit equation for the surface in the canonical form (with $A=E=H\neq0$). Non canonical forms are obtained through rotation, translation and scaling. The surfaces are described using homogeneous coordinates. Euclidean coordinate functions can be obtained using division by w. For example X(euclidean) = x/w etc.

Parabolic cylinder : $x=u$, $y=u^2$, $z=v$, $w=1$

Elliptic cylinder : $x=1-u^2$, $y=2u$, $z=v(1+u^2)$, $w=(1+u^2)$

Hyperbolic Cylinder : $x=4+u^2$, $y=4u$, $z=v(4-u^2)$, $w=4-u^2$

Cone : $x=(1-u^2)v$, $y=(2u)v$, $z=(1+u^2)v$, $w=1+u^2$

Elliptic Paraboloid : $x=u$, $y=v$, $z=u^2+v^2$, $w=1$

Hyperbolic Paraboloid : $x=u$, $y=v$, $z=u^2-v^2$, $w=1$

Ellipsoid : $x=(1-v^2)(1-u^2)$, $y=(1-v^2)(2u)$, $z=(2v)(1+u^2)$, $w=(1+v^2)(1+u^2)$

Hyperboloid of one sheet : $x=(4+v^2)(1-u^2)$, $y=(4+v^2)(2u)$, $z=(4v)(1+u^2)$, $w=(4-v^2)(1+u^2)$

Hyperboloid of two sheets :
$x=(4+u^2)(4+v^2)$, $y=(4u)(4+v^2)$, $z=(4-u^2)(4v)$, $w=(4-u^2)(4-v^2)$

Super-quadrics
Barr[Barr] has introduced super-quadrics in parametric as well as implicit form. These differ from the corresponding quadrics in the exponents of their terms. Three quadrics are defined in their super form using trigonometric parametrization: **Super-ellipsoid :**
$x=\cos^m(u)\cos^n(v)$, $y=\sin^m(u)\cos^n(v)$, $z=\sin^n(v)$
so that $(x^{2/m}+y^{2/m})^{m/n}+z^{2/n}=1$

Super-hyperboloid of one sheet : $x=\cos^m(u)\sec^n(v)$, $y=\sin^m(u)\sec^n(v)$, $z=\tan^n(v)$
so that $(x^{2/m}+y^{2/m})^{m/n}-z^{2/n}=1$.

Super-hyperboloid of two sheets : $x=\sec^m(u)\sec^n(v)$, $y=\tan^m(u)\sec^n(v)$, $z=\tan^n(v)$
so that $(x^{2/m}-y^{2/m})^{m/n}-z^{2/n}=1$

In addition to these, torus and super-torus are discussed in [Barr]. **Super-torus :** $x=\cos^m(u)(k+\cos^n($
$y=\sin^m(u)(k+\cos^n(v))$, $z=\sin^n(v)$
so that $[(x^{2/m}+y^{2/m})^{m/2}-k]^{2/n}+z^{2/n}=1$.
The special case with $m=n=1$ is known as torus.

3.7 PARAMETRIC BICUBIC SURFACES

[Forrest-2,Foley/van Dam]
We now generalise from cubic curves to bicubic surfaces defined by cubic equations of two parameters, u and v. Varying both parameters from 0 to 1 defines all points on a surface patch. If one parameter is assigned a constant value and the other parameter is varied from 0 to 1, the result is a cubic curve. As with curves, we will work only with the parametric equation for x, denoted by x(u,v).
The form of x(u,v) is:

$$x(u,v) = \begin{array}{llll} a_{11}u^3v^3 + & a_{12}u^3v^2 + & a_{13}u^3v + & a_{14}u^3 \\ a_{21}u^2v^3 + & a_{22}u^2v^2 + & a_{23}u^2v + & a_{24}u^2 \\ a_{31}uv^3 + & a_{32}uv^2 + & a_{33}uv + & a_{34}u \\ a_{41}v^3 + & a_{42}v^2 + & a_{43}v + & a_{44} \end{array}$$

This is more conveniently written as : $x(u,v) = UC_xV^t$
where $U=[u^3,u^2,u,1]$, $V=[v^3,v^2,v,1]$, and V^t is the transpose of V. This is called the algebraic form of representation, because C_x gives the coefficients of the bicubic polynomial. There is also a C_y and C_z which give the coefficients of y(u,v) and z(u,v). Throughout the discussion we shall consider only x(u,v) as the same arguments apply always to the other coordinates.

Hermite Form
We want some approach analogous to that used for curves which allows the use of control points and tangent vectors to define the bicubic coefficients. Consider the hermite cubic curve, with u as the parameter.

$$x(u)=UM_hG_{hx}$$

This we rewrite so that the Hermite geometry matrix is not a constant but rather a function of v:

$$x(u,v)=UM_hG_{hx}(v)=UM_h[x_0(v),x_1(v),s_0(v),s_1(v)]^t$$

The functions $x_0(v)$ and $x_1(v)$ define the x-components of the starting and ending points for the curve in the parameter u. For any specific value of v, two specific endpoints are defined. Similarly, $s_0(v)$ and $s_1(v)$ define the tangent vectors at the endpoints of the cubic in u. We can think of the surface patch as an interpolation between $x_0(v)$ and $x_1(v)$: the initial tangent vector for the interpolation is $s_0(v)$ and the final tangent vector is $s_1(v)$. In the special case that the interpolants are straight lines, a ruled surface is produced. If the curves $x_0(v)$ and $x_1(v)$ are also coplanar, the ruled surface is planar and the surface patches a four-sided polygon.

Now let $x_0(v)$, $x_1(v)$, $s_0(v)$ and $s_1(v)$ each be cubics represented in Hermite form, so that:

$$x_0(v)=VM_h[q11,q12,q13,q14]^t$$

$$x_1(v)=VM_h[q21,q22,q23,q24]^t$$

$$s_0(v)=VM_h[q31,q32,q33,q34]^t$$

$$s_1(v)=VM_h[q41,q42,q43,q44]^t$$

The four cubics can be expressed in a row vector as
$$[x_0(v), x_1(v), s_0(v), s_1(v)] = VM_hQ$$
where Q is the 4x4 matrix of the 16 elements q11,q12,...,q44. Transposing both sides of the equation by using the identity $(ABC)^t = C^tB^tA^t$ gives:

$$\begin{matrix} x_0(v) \\ x_1(v) \\ s_0(v) \\ s_1(v) \end{matrix} = \begin{bmatrix} q11 & q12 & q13 & q14 \\ q21 & q22 & q23 & q24 \\ q31 & q32 & q33 & q34 \\ q41 & q42 & q43 & q44 \end{bmatrix} M_h^tV^t = QM_h^tV^t$$

Therefore

$$x(u,v) = UM_hQM_h^tV^t$$

How is Q defined in terms of points and slopes? Examination shows that q11 is x(0,0) because it is the starting point for $x_0(v)$, which is in turn the starting point for x(u,0). Similarly, q12 is x(0,1) because it is the ending point of $x_0(v)$, which is in turn the starting point for x(u,1). We also see that q13 is $D_vx(0,0)$ because it is the starting tangent vector for $s_0(v)$, and q33 is $D_{uv}x(0,0)$ as it is the starting tangent vector of $s_0(v)$, which is in turn the starting slope of x(u,0).

Using these interpretations, we can write

$$Q = \begin{bmatrix} x(0,0) & x(0,1) & D_vx(0,0) & D_vx(0,1) \\ x(1,0) & x(1,1) & D_vx(1,0) & D_vx(1,1) \\ D_ux(0,0) & D_ux(0,1) & D_{uv}x(0,0) & D_{uv}x(0,1) \\ D_ux(1,0) & D_ux(1,1) & D_{uv}x(1,0) & D_{uv}x(1,1) \end{bmatrix}$$

The upper left 2x2 partition contains the four corners of the surface patch, the upper right and lower left partitions specify the slopes along each parametric direction at the corners, while the lower right partition gives the partial derivatives at the corners with respect to both parameters. These partials are often called the twists, because the greater they are, the greater the twist (like a corkscrew) at the corner of the surface patch. The Hermite form of bicubic surface patches is one form of the Coons' patch [Coon-2]. They are also called Ferguson surfaces. In the coon's form very general blending functions, not just polynomials are permitted.

All other forms of the cubic splines discussed earlier can also be generalised to bicubic surfaces. For example the cardinal spline would have the form:

$$x(u,v) = UM_{ca}G_cM_{cb}^tV^t$$

where a and b are tension parameters which may or may not be equal. Similarly the **Bezier** bicubic surface takes the form:

$$x(u,v) = UM_bG_bM_b^tV^t$$

The geometry matrix G_b consists of 16 control points. Bezier surfaces are attractive in interactive design for the same reasons that Bezier curves are attractive: the control points can be easily manipulated to change the shape of the surface patch. The convex hull property of Bezier curves also holds for Bezier surfaces.

Continuity across patch edges is obtained by making the four control points on the edges equal. Continuity of tangent vector, and hence C(1) continuity, is obtained by additionally making the two sets of four control points on either side of the edge collinear with the points on the edge. In addition, the ratios of the lengths of the collinear line segments must be constant.

B-spline patches are analogous to the preceding cases:

$$x(u,v) = UM_s G_s M_s^t V^t$$

As with B-spline curves, C(2) continuity is obtained. The matrix of 16 control points defines the patch, and in general the points are not on the patch. Also the convex null property is satisfied by this and its derived surfaces.

The **Beta-spline** bicubic surface takes the form:

$$x(u,v) = UM_{sb1b2} G_s M_{sb1b2}^t V^t$$

b1 and b2 may be different for u and v.

Transforming Curves and Patches

To transform a 3D curve or patch, we could calculate points on the curve or patch and then transform the points, one by one. Fortunately, there is a better way: we can instead transform the geometry matrix of points (or of points and tangent vectors) defining the curve or surface and then use this transformed matrix to generate points on the transformed curve or surface. To transform a geometry matrix points are written by adding a 1 as the homogeneous coordinate while for tangent vectors the homogeneous coordinate is set 0.

3.8 PRODUCT SURFACES

[Mudur/Koparkar-1] Basically in the definitions of these surfaces two curves are involved- the cross section or the pattern curve and the spine curve. Let us denote the pattern curve as A(u) and the spine curve as B(v), with u varying from u0 to u1 and v from v0 to v1. The pattern curve is swept along the spine and its various instances are referred to by the parameter v.

The spine as well as the pattern curve are assumed to be well-formed curves. By this we mean that they are continuously differentiable throughout the domain of their parameters so that the tangent, the normal and the binormal are well defined vectors. The curve forms used for computer aided design do generally satisfy these requirements.

Translational Invariant Form

Let us consider the generic point on the spine given by v. The surface is then given by the simple rule "Add the two curves in a coordinatewise fashion". Thus any point (x,y,z) on the resulting surface is given by

$$x=A1(u)+B1(v), \quad y=A2(u)+B2(v), \quad z=A3(u)+B3(v)$$

Note that different 'swept' instances of the pattern curve are all obtained from it by mere translation. No rotation or scaling takes place. In particular, if the pattern curve is planar then all its instances are placed in various parallel planes. Neither do these planes rotate as v changes, nor does the curve rotate within the plane containing it.

When each instance of the pattern curve may be either contracted or expanded (in equal

proportions in all the three directions) without effecting any rotation on it, the resulting surface is termed as a product surface. Yet another function, which we denote B0(v) determines the current scaling factor at each instance that corresponds to the current parameter value v.
The product surface is then given by

$$x = B0(v)A1(u) + B1(v), \quad y = B0(v)A2(u) + B2(v), \quad z = B0(v)A3(u) + B3(v)$$

We may put it in the following matrix form, which represents the resulting surface as the one obtained by applying various transformations to the pattern curve.

$$[x(u,v), y(u,v), z(u,v), 1] = [A1(u), A2(u), A3(u), 1] \begin{bmatrix} B0(v) & 0 & 0 & 0 \\ 0 & B0(v) & 0 & 0 \\ 0 & 0 & B0(v) & 0 \\ B1(v) & B2(v) & B3(v) & 1 \end{bmatrix}$$

The reader may compare it with the standard matrix used for coordinate transformation using homogeneous coordinates for points.

Below we discuss various special cases of the product surfaces.
1) Linear Sweep
This is produced when Bi(v)s are linear while B0(v) is constant. These surfaces are useful in describing 21/2 D objects such as turned and milled parts.
2) Conical Linear Sweep
In this, all Bis including B0(v) are linear. Linear sweep is its special (degenerate) case. The first one may be called the cylindrical sweep in view of the second one being called conical sweep. These are useful in describing tapered parts.
3) Circular Linear
Bi(v)'s are once more linear. B0(v) is arbitrary but A(u) is not any arbitrary curve. A(u) defines a circle or a circular arc in the plane that is orthogonal to the line defined by [B1(v), B2(v), B3(v)] and has its centre as the point of intersection of its plane and the line of the spine B(v). The simplest way to describe it is that A(u) is the circle in z=0 plane while B(v) is the z axis. B0(v) is arbitrary. This is very useful in describing lathe machined parts.
4) Spherical Product
The name spherical product comes from a particular parametrization of the sphere using latitudes and longitudes as parametric lines. For a sphere A(u) and B(v) should be circles. All quadric surfaces can be parametrized as the spherical product of two conics, A(u) and B(v). (This is evident from the parametrizations discussed earlier). Similar statement is true for super-quadrics. The spherical product surface necessarily consists of two plane curves, A(u) and B(v), in x-y and x-z planes respectively, with

$$A(u) = [A1(u), A2(u)], \quad B(v) = [B0(v), B3(v)]$$

We have the surface defined by the equations:

$$x = A1(u)B0(v), \quad y = A2(u)B0(v), \quad z = B3(v)$$

i.e. we set B1(v)=B2(v)=A3(u)=0 to obtain this special case from the general definition of product surfaces.
3-D Sweep or Generalized Sweep
This is the product surface in which no scaling is done. i.e. B0(v) is identically 1. The

resulting form is symmetric in A(u) and B(v) so that any curve can be thought of as being swept along the other

Other suitable forms of product surfaces can also be defined depending upon the requirements of the application. The name product surfaces is chosen in view of the fact that it represents the class of surfaces that are generalized forms of spherical product surfaces.

There are however some disadvantages with the product surface as defined. A locally non-realizable surface results in the degenerate case when the spine is tangential to the pattern curve. Self intersecting surfaces can also arise depending on the relative shapes of the pattern and the spine curves. A solution to this problem is to force the tangent of the pattern curve to maintain a constant non-zero angle with the tangent of the spine curve at every point of the spine curve. This also in many ways complies with the intuitive idea of 'sweeping the pattern along the spine'.

4. THE PROCESSING OF CURVES AND SURFACES

4.1 AN OVERVIEW OF PROCESSING TASKS

Once a shape is represented within the computer there are a variety of processing tasks which need to be performed on these shapes. Typical processing tasks are listed below:

Rendering

    (1) Drawing Curves
    (2) Depicting Surfaces
    . Net of curves (isoparametric or level contours)
    . Planar tessellation (triangulation or polygonal mesh)
    . Hidden line drawings (silhouette and intersection edges)
    . Visible surface shaded images

Spatial Interference

    (1) Interference detection
    (2) Intersection (amongst points,lines,planes,curves and surfaces) It is important to be able to handle degenerate cases (tangencies,singularities) as well

Analysis

    (1) Mass property computations
    . Arc length,surface area,volume,centre of gravity,moment of inertia etc.
    (2) Discretisation (FE Mesh generation)

Manufacture

    (1) Die/Mould Making
    (2) Process Planning
    (3) NC Machine tool programming
    (4) Associated information handling (schedules,inventory and bill of materials,etc.)

The above is not an exhaustive list of tasks. Tasks depend very much on the environment and the application. Some of the above are very difficult to formulate and are very relevant current research topics. Until recently maximum attention has been given to rendering and to intersection curve drawing. We discuss the intricacies of some of these tasks below.

Rendering curves and surfaces
A curve is drawn as a polygon with a large number of sides that approximate it. For implicit form of curves, one coordinate is incremented uniformly while the other is treated as its function and the equations are solved to get the vertices of the polygon. For parametric curves, the increments are uniform in the parameter, while x, y values are calculated. Computation may be reduced using forward difference methods. However, equal increments do not produce equal segments nor do they necessarily produce the number of segments in proportion to the curvature. Bresenham's algorithm for straight lines has been extended to conics [Pitteway]. The basic principle is the same : define a simple error function based on which one can decide whether to illuminate the horizontally or the diagonally adjacent pixel.

Stepping repeatedly along the arc of a curve at a fixed distance requires approximation of the given curve by a polygon having equal sides. Using this any pattern or figure can be repeated along the curve without interference of the consecutive instances .

Different output devices are used for displaying images and these influence some of the algorithms. The objects need not be described in the space of the output device. A projection that maps from the object space to the image space is required. Accordingly, the algorithms used to generate images may be either object space algorithms or image space algorithms. Object space algorithms first process the representations of the curves and surfaces and then project the results into the image space to form an image. Object space algorithms are independent of the output medium or output device used. They depend on the curve and surface types that are used to represent objects. On the other hand, image space algorithms first transform the representations to image space, and then operate on the transformed representations. They are therefore dependent both on the types of curves and surfaces used as well as on the display device.

Thus the main task in rendering is to form a correspondence/mapping between the objects and the intensity values on the screen. For simple surfaces the mappings are simple enough so that one can start painting without resorting to any further division of the object or the screen.

4.2 COHERENCE

For complex surfaces (both combinatorial or component wise) this correspondence is much more difficult to establish. In such cases either the object is subdivided or is looked at within a smaller region of the screen. The discretised nature of the screen is taken into account and the correspondence is defined in a discrete fashion. Three broad ways in which this correspondence is established are discussed below:

Pixel covering (Ray Tracing) method
The screen is assumed to be consisting of discrete pixels and the mapping is defined for those parts of the surface that exactly map on these pixels. To search for such parts a ray is used. The ray emerges from the eye of the viewer and passes through the pixel. The points of intersection of this ray with the surfaces are computed and the attributes for the pixel determined. Alternatively one can subdivide the surface until it covers only a single pixel and thus compute the attributes of that pixel.

The general algorithm for displaying a surface using this technique is quite simple[Blinn]. For example displaying a quadric surface defined by the 4x4 matrix Q consists of a scan across the screen of all the pixels. For each pixel the x and y coordinates are substituted into the quadric equation:
$$(x,y,z,1) \ Q \ (x,y,z,1)^t = 0$$
The result is a quadratic equation in z. If there are no solutions to this equation then the object does not appear in the pixel. If there are solutions the one with the smallest z is chosen. The process though simple is a bit lengthy. Many optimizations may be performed.

For bicubic surfaces this is not as simple. It becomes necessary to intersect a line with the surface.

Intersection between Line and Bicubic

[Faux/Pratt]

Assuming the line is in parametric form as $P(t) = P_0 + At$ its intersection with the surface in implicit form is obtained by substituting for $x(t)$, $y(t)$, $z(t)$ in $S(x,y,z) = 0$. This is a polynomial equation in a single variable t and can be solved analytically for lower order surfaces. Its intersection with a surface of the form $S(u,v)$ is obtained as the simultaneous solution of the three non-linear equations (actually vector equation) given below:

$$S(u,v) - At - P_0 = 0$$

This vector equation can be solved using the Newton-Rhapson or other numerical analysis technique. Alternatively we can solve this by minimising the function $S(u,v)-At-P_0^2$ with respect to t,u and v. This method has the advantage of overcoming the problem which occurs when the line either touches the surface or has no intersection with it. Yet another approach is to represent the line as the intersection of two planes in implicit form, say $a_1 x + b_1 y + c_1 z + d_1 = 0$ and $a_2 x + b_2 y + c_2 z + d_2 = 0$. If the surface is in implicit form then with these two equations and the surface equation one can obtain a polynomial equation in one of the coordiantes. Once the solution for one of the coordinates is obtained the other two can be derived using the two linear plane equations.

For the bicubic one substitutes $x(u,v)$, $y(u,v)$ and $z(u,v)$ in the two equations to obtain a pair of equations in two variables u and v which can be solved using Newton-Rhapson or other numerical techniques.

Scan line covering (Plane sweep) method

This method capitalises on the fact that the raster image is generated in a vertically scanned fashion. Each scan line together with the eye position defines a plane called the scan plane. An intersection of this plane with the surface exactly maps onto the scan line under consideration.

Intersection between a Plane and a Surface

The intersection between a plane and a quadric surface may be null, a single point or a conic section in space [Blinn]. This can be determined by evaluating the following expression:

$$(a,b,c,d)Q^*(a,b,c,d)^t$$

This is analogous to the determination of whether a point lies on the quadric surface. If the expression is 0 the plane is tangent to the quadric, if it is positive the plane intersects the quadric and if it is negative the plane is disjoint. The fact that the plane is tangent to the quadric can be used to solve other useful geometric problems. For example the maximum and minimum Y limits of the surface may be found by intersecting the quadric with the $y=y_0$ plane defined by the vector $(0,-1,0,y_0)$. Multiplying this and its transpose with Q^* will yield a quadratic equation in y_0 which will give the maximum and minimum y values of the quadric.

The intersection of a plane and a bicubic is obtained by substituting the surface defining functions into the plane equation. This would result in an equation in two variables u and v of the form:

$$a.x(u,v)+b.y(u,v)+c.z(u,v)+d=0$$

This equation has an additional degree of freedom and hence represents a curve. For any particular value of u or v the equation reduces to a polynomial in the other variable solving which points on the curve are obtained.

Area covering method

This method considers the screen area covered by the entire surface or part of the surface under consideration. Unlike the earlier cases the area is not resticted to be a pixel or a single scan line.

4.3 REALISTIC IMAGES

In displaying 3-D objects, we add certain edges which separate backfacing parts of a surface from its front facing parts. To depict a sphere, which has no edge, we draw a circle, which separates the back and front facing portions of the sphere. Such an edge is called a silhouette. Detecting silhouettes is an important operation in image synthesis. It is an image space task since the silhouette depends on the point from which the surface is being seen. At any point on the silhouette, the surface normal N is orthogonal to the line of sight E - i.e. the line from the eye position to that point. Thus silhouettes can be calculated by solving the equation N.E=0.

In generating images by computers, more realism is achieved by removing those parts, which are hidden by the opaque surfaces lying between them and the eye. Objects consist of a number of surfaces. Some of these surfaces hide others, depending on the viewing direction. A number of algorithms have been published for removing such hidden parts, each one capitalizing on different features of the surfaces, the display device, the data structures used, and so on. The solution essentially consists of sorting and dividing the surfaces so that rendering in that order will eventually result in an image of the scene as would normally be seen by a viewer in the real world with opaque objects. Sutherland et al [Sutherland et al] present an excellent survey of methods for producing hidden line drawings of plane faced polyhedral objects. Later developments are well documented by Foley and Van Dam [Foley/Van Dam] and Rogers [Rogers].

4.4 SIMPLIFICATIONS

Piecewise linear approximation of a curve segment helps in reducing computational complexity linear segments can be processed in a straightforward way. For all computational purposes, some tolerance is prescribed within which the linearity is checked. Linearity in this sense is a measure of the maximum deviation of the curve segment from a straight line. The reference line for the measurement of linearity is usually chosen to be the chord or one of the end tangents.

Linearity Estimation
[Faux/Pratt]
Let $d(u)$ denote the deviation vector, i.e. the vector perpendicular from the point $P(u)$ of the curve to the line with respect to which the linearity is measured (usually the chord of the segment). $d(u)$ can be expressed using vector analysis in terms of $P(u)$:

Let M be a point where the perpendicular from P meets the chord.

$$M - P_0 = k(P_1 - P_0) \text{ for some scalar k.}$$

$$d(u) = P - M = P - P_0 - (M - P_0) = P - P_0 - k(P_1 - P_0)$$

Taking scalar product with $P_1 - P_0$ and noting that $d(u)$ is perpendicular to it, we have

$$0 = (P-P_0).(P_1-P_0)-k[(P_1-P_0)]^2$$

So that

$$k = (P-P_0).(P_1-P_0) \ / \ [P_1-P_0]^2$$

And hence

$$d(u) = P-P_0 - (P_1-P_0) \ \{(P_1-P_0).(P-P_0)\}/[P_1-P_0]^2$$

At the point of maximum deviation, the curve tangent is perpendicular to $d(u)$ so that $D_u P = 0$ where $D_u P$ denotes the derivative of P w.r.t. u. For a polynomial curve of nth degree this equation reduces to the equation of degree $2n-1$. Since $u-u_0$ and $u-u_1$ are two factors, it reduces further to an equation of degree $2n-3$. For cubics, it gives a cubic equation. In case of rational quadratics the degree is four while for rational cubics, the degree is seven.

For parametric curves, which are modelled using Bezier or B-spline form, the segment lies within the convex hull of its control vertices. It therefore suffices to have a linear convex hull in order to get a linear curve segment. The test checks the control vertices, which are finite in number, for linearity.

Planarity Estimation

Planarity of surfaces is defined analogous to the linearity of curves, using deviation function $d(u,v)$. $d(u,v)$ is derived as below:

Let us consider the plane through P_{00}, P_{01}, P_{10} for reference. Let M be the foot of the perpendicular from P onto this plane.

$$M-P_{00} = h(P_{10}-P_{00}) +k(P_{01}-P_{00}), \text{ for some } h \text{ and } k.$$

$$d(u,v) = P-M = (P-P_{00})-(M-P_{00}) = (P-P_{00})-h(P_{10}-P_{00})-k(P_{01}-P_{00}) = Q-ha-kb$$

with $Q = P-P_{00}, \ a = P_{10}-P_{00}, \ b = P_{01}-P_{00}.$

Taking dot product with a and b and noting that $P-M$ is perpendicular to both of them we have

$$0 = -Q.b + ha.b + k[b]^2$$

$$0 = -Q.a + h[a]^2 + ka.b$$

These may be solved to get values of h and k provided the two vectors a and b are not along the same line and the plane is well-defined. (If not, another plane should be sought).

These values, when inserted, result into an expression for $d(u,v)$ which has the same form as $P(u,v)$.

The points, where maximum value may be sought are given by the simultaneous solutions of the equations

$$D_u\,[d(u,v)] = 0,\ D_v\,[d(u,v)] = 0$$

These non linear equations may be solved using iterative methods from numerical analysis. However, it should be noted that it may not be worthwhile to repeat such a computationally expensive method for each of the subpatches that result out of subdivisions.

A simpler method would be to estimate some upper bound to the deviation instead of measuring its maximum. For parametric surfaces expressed in Bezier or B-spline form, the test of planarity of the surface reduces to the planarity of the convex hull of the control vertices [Lane/Riesenfeld,Cohen/Lychie/Riesenfeld].

Euclidean Bounds and Overlap Tests
Euclidean bounds estimate in some way the extent of the curve or a surface in Euclidean space. The bounds of any curve/surface are defined by the six values

$$<\text{Xmin},\text{Xmax},\text{Ymin},\text{Ymax},\text{Zmin},\text{Zmax}>$$

where any point (x,y,z) on that curve/surface satisfies
$$\text{Xmin} <= x <= \text{Xmax}\ \textbf{and}\ \text{Ymin} <= y <= \text{Ymax}\ \textbf{and}\text{Zmin} <= z <= \text{Zmax}$$

If the object extends over a very small region,say, a single point for all practical purposes, then it can be processed in a straightforward way. A surface patch that covers only one pixel of the final display device is an example. The Euclidean bounds define a region, of some typical shape, around the curve segment/patch, which completely contains the curve segment/patch. The boundary of such a shape is relatively easy and compact to store and evaluate. Circles (bubbles or balls) and rectangular boxes with or without their sides parallel to coordinate axes are two examples that have been used frequently. For a parametric curve in Bezier or B-spline form, the convex hull of their control vertices determine their Euclidean bounds. Determining Euclidean box bounds for curves and surfaces is essentially the problem of determining the extreme values in each of the coordinates. Except for special cases this will generally involve the use of numerical techniques. Euclidean bounds are used in iterference checks. If the boxes do not overlap then obviously the segments/patches contained within cannot intersect.

Mass Properties
In processing geometric objects different properties describing various attributes are required to be estimated. These are collectively called as mass properties. The number of algorithms developed so far for estimating various mass properties is considerably low. The algorithms are generally based on statistical methods such as Monte-Carlo methods. Centre of gravity(mass distribution), area calculation, density, are some examples of mass properties. Ray tracing techniques can also be extended to perform mass property computations.

Exact arc length is given by integrating the differential of the arc segment ds between the two end points. Approximate arc length can be calculated by adding the lengths of sides of the approximating polygon that is used to draw the curve. The accuracy of the estimation depends upon the closeness of the polygon to the actual curve. It may be inaccurate for the portions for which the deviation of the curve from the approximating line segment is substantial. However, by choosing polygon sides sufficiently close to the curve, the reliability of the estimation can be increased.

Area of an arbitrary bounded surface is calculated using the integral of the differential of the area element over the entire surface. Using certain conversion theorems, the integral can be reduced to a line integral, over the boundary of the area However, it may be difficult to evaluate the integral analytically, and numerical methods have to be adopted. An approximate area may be estimated in a simple manner if the surface is approximated by some polyhedron consisting of plane surfaces. The accuracy of this estimate once again depends on the closeness of the polyhedral approximation.

Intersections

Two polynomial or rational curves can intersect in a finite number of distinct points. In their implicit form, their points of intersection are the simultaneous solutions to the equations representing the two curves. Eliminating one or more variables leads to a higher degree algebraic equation. Solving this equation is another problem; it may not be solvable by analytic methods. For parametric curves, the equations for intersections are obtained by equating expressions for x, y etc. These are then solved simultaneously for the parameters. Usually numerical methods are required [Faux/Pratt].

If one of the curves is a straight line, then its intersection with the other curve is detected in a relatively easy manner. On substituting the values from the linear equation into the other equations, one variable is eliminated without increasing the degree of the other. Generally curves used for computer processing have lower degrees, usually 2 or 3, and the resulting equation for the points of intersection can therefore be solved analytically. This feature has been used to great advantage in some algorithms, particularly scanline methods.

Sometimes it happens that the two curves intersect in a common segment instead of an isolated point. For implicit form of curves, this corresponds to the fact that the two functions describing them have one or more common factors.
As an example, consider

$$x^3 + xy^2 = x \text{ and } x^2 + y^2 = 1.$$

These two have a circle, $x^2 + y^2 = 1$ in common. Such a case may be detected using algebraic methods [Bernard/Child].

Since computers work with a finite precision, equality of two curves is always determined within some tolerance. In this case, two curves may be declared to have a portion in common without having any algebraic relationship -such as a common factor-between them. This case needs to be handled appropriately and common segments should be detected within the given tolerance. An intersection between two surfaces is determined only within some prescribed tolerance. In some applications, intersection of a surface with a curve may also have to be determined. Such an intersection may consist of one or more isolated points, or even a curve segment whenever some portion of the curve lies completely on the surface. Generally two surfaces intersect in a curve. Sometimes they may intersect in an isolated point, and sometimes in an area. These cases require special attention in detecting the intersection of two surfaces. The curve of intersection may be calculated analytically, typically in the case of implicit surfaces described by equations of sufficiently low degree. For parametric surfaces, analytic methods are rarely applicable.

4.5 TAXONOMY OF PROCESSING ALGORITHMS

A number of algorithms and methods have been suggested for processing curves and surfaces. Some of them are specific to the applications for which they have been developed; others are more general purpose methods, or can be modified suitably to perform other tasks. A broad classification distinguishes analytic methods from numerical methods, but a finer distinction is necessary to describe the types accurately. Such a classification is based on the strategy or the principle used to devise the method. We now briefly describe the strategies and review the existing methods.

We categorise the basic mathematical/algorithmic strategies in use as below:
  1. Incremental
  2. Convergence
  3. Analytic
  4. Subdivision

In the incremental strategy, coordinates or parameters are fixed and a point (or the value of a property at a point) is obtained from these values in order to process the curve or surface. Whenever a new point (or its property) is to be calculated, one or more of its parameters or coordinates is incremented with some prefixed value and the calculation repeated.

In the convergence strategy, a new point (or property value) is estimated according to some prefixed criteria and then an iterative method is used to converge to the resulting point (property value).

Analytic methods result in relatively simple algebraic equations that may be solved or evaluated in order to determine the point (or property value). Since the required result is mathematically derived, full information about the points (or properties) is available and may be extracted from the equations whenever required.

All the three strategies discussed above are more or less similar and have been at times combined with each other in a particular method or algorithm for processing curves and surfaces. The distinction between them is mathematical rather than algorithmic, and therefore operationally the methods look more or less similar to each other.

Subdivision, is an algorithmically different strategy. It evaluates one or more curve or surface properties for the entire curve or surface under consideration. If it is simple enough for processing, then it is passed to the appropriate process. Otherwise it is subdivided and the same calculation is recursively repeated for each part that results. The terms "properties" and "simple enough" are dependent on the particular task under consideration and on the environment.

The major difference between the incremental/convergence methods and the subdivision methods is that the former seek the solution in a local way by calculating the next point/property value within some neighborhood on the surface; the subdivision methods try to estimate some property for the entire curve/surface and subdivide only if the property indicates that the sub-object is not simple for immediate processing. Thus the subdivision methods are dependent on the nature of the curves or surfaces under consideration, and local properties like curvature etc. are automatically made use of. Analytic methods formulate the solution for the entire curve or surface in one shot.

Analytically deriving the intersection curve for quadric surfaces in implicit form is possible essentially because of the low degree of equations that need to be solved. For parametric bicubics it is not possible because of the very high degree of the equations that result. Use of the incremental strategy relies on the implicit form. Therefore this method too cannot be used for the parametric form. The convergence strategy has been used very convincingly for the implicit form of the quadric surfaces in a number of working systems. A few systems can handle toroidal surfaces as well. For some specific tasks it has been used for parametric bicubics as well. However it works on the assumption that a good initial approximation to the desired result can be made. This implies that the nature of the desired result is known a priori. In general, for higher order implicit forms and for parametric bicubics and higher order bipolynomials, this initial guess is very difficult and very often not possible.

Subdivision methods on the other hand are highly suited to the parametric form. Theoretically x,y,z are unbounded in the implicit form. Bounds, if any, are to be derived from the equations. This may not always be simple. But parameters as well as the coordinate functions are always bounded. Using rational polynomial forms for the quadrics most of the commonly used surfaces in geometric modelling can therefore be handled using subdivision techniques.

4.6 A REVIEW OF EXISTING METHODS

With the various characteristics discussed so far, we now briefly review the existing methods for rendering curved surfaces. The discussion is very brief and only the important points are mentioned. For details, the reader may consult the original papers referenced in this review.

We first discuss the implicit form and then the parametric form. Among each of these, we proceed from the pixel covering, scan line covering to area covering methods.

Ref : [Weiss]
Surfaces : Quadrics (implicit)
Rendering Forms : Hidden line drawings
Strategy : Incremental/Analytic
Weiss' algorithm is a line drawing algorithm for quadric surfaces, and removes hidden lines. The lines that appear in the drawing are:
1) Intersection of two surfaces
2) Silhouette lines

A rough estimate (or rather a loose estimate) of the minimum and maximum values of the coordinates on each surface is made (i.e. Euclidean bounds). This is done analytically, considering different special cases of the surface form. The equation of a quadric surface intersection curve (QSIC) is obtained by eliminating one of the coordinates using Sylvester's method. The points on the QSIC are obtained by incrementing one of the coordinate variables within its bounds and solving for the other. Visibility is tested by examining each calculated point against every other surface. The bounds and intersections of two patches are the same for any particular composition of surfaces (scene), while silhouette is required to be calculated for each viewing position. Points on the silhouette are determined by the coincidence of the two intersection points of a line from the eye point.

Ref : [Woon/Freeman]
Surfaces : Quadrics (implicit)
Rendering Forms : Hidden Line Drawing
Strategy : Analytic/Convergence
Simple curves of intersection are solved for analytically and drawn. For more complicated curves, such as non planar curves, the new point is sought using the Newton Raphson method. The initial guess is provided by the corner point of a solid

where 3 surfaces meet. A corner point may however be difficult to calculate without using some a priori knowledge about the scene. Hidden lines are removed in a manner similar to that used by Weiss. The silhouette is defined as the intersection of a surface and the polar plane of the eye point with respect to the surface.

Remarks: Guessing initial point for a QSIC may require a well defined scene and some a priori knowledge of the QSIC.

> **Ref : [Levin]**
> Surfaces : Quadrics (implicit)
> Rendering Forms : Hidden Line Drawings
> Strategy : Analytic
> Covering : Area

The basic approach is to take a linear combination of the two quadrics to be intersected forming a pencil of quadrics say, $aQ_1 + bQ_2$. If Q_1 and Q_2 intersect, then their intersection curve is the basis curve of the pencil and lies in every surface on the pencil. The basis curve is also the intersection curve for any other two surfaces of the pencil, say $R = Q_2 - AQ_1$ and $S = Q_2 - BQ_1$. Suitable values of A and B can be determined so that simple R and S will result such that their intersection curve is the same as that of Q_1 and Q_2.

The choice of A and B is through a cubic equation, obtained after some manipulation on Q_1 and Q_2. Levin has proved that the pencil essentially contains one or more of the following surfaces and hence the intersection curve can be thought of as an intersection of this surface with some other surface in the pencil (usually Q_1 or Q_2 itself).

These surfaces are
    1) Line
    2) Single plane
    3) Coincident planes
    4) Parallel planes
    5) Intersecting planes
    6) Parabolic cylinder
    7) Elliptic cylinder
    8) Hyperbolic cylinder
    9) Cone
    10) Hyperbolic paraboloid

1 through 5 are planar and yield conics as the intersection curves. With cylinders and cones, their base curve is considered (which is one of the conic sections). Through each point of this base curve passes a generator of the surface which meets the QSIC in some point. Thus a correspondence between the base curve and the QSIC is established. A parameter is selected on the base curve and is given some fixed increment to get points on the base curve. Correspondingly the intersection of the line through this point in the direction of the axis of the surface is calculated by direct substitution of relations between x,y,and z along this direction (given by direction cosines) with the other surface. This gives a second degree equation which when solved, gives the corresponding point on the QSIC. Thus the QSIC is traced.

If the intersection curve lies on the hyperbolic paraboloid then the appropriate transformations are performed to get its equation as uv=w in the new coordinate system (also called the canonical form). The same transformation is applied to the other surface as well. Then u acts as a parameter for the base curve (v=constant) and v acts as the secondary parameter that corresponds to a point on the QSIC. Inverse transformation traces out the QSIC in the non-canonical form.

Remarks: This is a line drawing system. Multiple intersection curves are difficult to handle automatically (the user has to specify the number of lobes for the curve of intersection). Along with the other QSICs, it displays silhouettes (limbs) also. A silhouette can be thought of as an intersection curve of the surface and the polar plane of the view point. Obviously the silhouette is also a conic. The surface normal is calculated as the divergence of the quadratic function at the required point.

The ease with which these two calculations can be made are the advantages of the implicit form.

Ref : [Shapedata]
  Surfaces : Some Quadrics + Torus (implicit)
  Rendering forms : Hidden line drawings and shaded pictures
  Strategy : Convergence
  Covering : Pixel

Romulus uses a marching algorithm for detecting intersection of surfaces (which are called tracks). A precalculated starting point is stored along with the definition of each track. Each new point on the track is first predicted and then refined until it is close to the track, within some prescribed tolerance. The refinement is done through iterations which are referred to as relaxations. The track is created by joining successive points.

Given the starting point the cross product of the two surface normals at it gives the tangent vector. Along this tangent, the new point is predicted with appropriate step length. This point is relaxed repeatedly until a point on the track is obtained. This completes the first step and generates the first point on the track other than the predefined point. For other steps, a new point is predicted along the direction vector that is obtained by joining last two consecutive points. As before it is relaxed until the resultant point lies sufficiently close to the track.

Refinement or relaxation of the predicted point is done by means of a second order convergent process, based on the surface geometry. This method differs substantially from intersection tracks to silhouette tracks.

For intersection tracks, perpendicular to the two surfaces are dropped from the predicted point. The next approximation is the point where the two tangent planes at the feet of the perpendiculars intersect with the plane defined by the two perpendiculars. The process is repeated until a point is obtained with sufficient accuracy (within a prescribed tolerance).

In case of silhouette tracks, a different procedure is used since it is defined by a single surface together with an eye position by the equation N.E=0 . A new point on the track is predicted along that surface tangent which is perpendicular to the vector joining the eye position to the previous point. A perpendicular is dropped from the approximation and the value of N.E is calculated. If it is zero, then we have obtained the point on the silhouette. If it is non-zero then the point is displaced slightly and the steps are repeated to get another value of N.E. This displacement is made in a direction perpendicular to the approximating tangent. Along such a direction, N.E varies approximately linearly so that the two points for which N.E is calculated are considered and a third point is obtained along the line joining them for which the (interpolated) value of N.E is zero. This is usually sufficient to give us the foot of the perpendicular on the silhouette. Otherwise the calculations are repeated.

Generally a stopping point is supplied with the track definition. However, it may not coincide with any of the points obtained on the track in marching. So it is necessary first to ensure that such a point is within the prescribed chordal tolerance of the line of a step, and secondly, its projection on the step line lies within the bounds of the steps.

Remarks: For detection of intersection/silhouette curves the convergence procedure used is not Newton/Raphson. Geometric properties such as tangent plane etc. are considered in seeking successive points on the curves. The method is very fast. The starting point of each curve has to be stored with its definition, and this requires some apriori knowledge about the curve to be handled. Hidden parts are removed using a variation of the Z buffer algorithm for shaded pictures. Shaded pictures are generated using a ray tracing method with any user specified raster size.

Ref : [Mahl]
Surfaces : Quadrics (implicit)
Rendering Forms : Shaded pictures
Strategy : Analytic/Convergence
Covering : Scan line

Intersection of a quadric with a scan plane is essentially a conic. Thus the span occupied by a surface on the current scanline is the projection of some conic. The conic is checked for extreme values of x, which correspond to the passing of a silhouette or a patch edge through it. The conic is subdivided at such points, and back facing portions are culled; the front facing portion determines the span on the scan line. All calculations are performed using numerical techniques. The extent on a scan line is determined from the conic resulting out of intersection of the quadric with the scan plane. On a scan line intensity value is interpolated between two intensity values at the end points. Hidden parts are detected by x-then-z sort in a scan line.

Ref : [Kajiya]
Surfaces : Parametric bicubics
Rendering forms : Shaded pictures
Strategy : Convergence
Covering : Pixel

The method presented is a ray tracing algorithm for rendering bicubic patches. A ray is defined by a pair of intersecting planes, so that as discussed earlier two bicubic equations are to be solved in order to obtain the point of intersection.

Algebraic solution involves the following steps:
   1) The two bicubics are considered to be cubics in a single variable v (with functions of u as their coefficients).
   2) The resultant of the two polynomials is calculated using Bezoults Determinantal form [The resultant of a polynomial is a particular determinant constructed through another determinant of some special kind known as Bezoults determinantal form]. The resultant is a function of u.

3) All zero's of this resultant are calculated Using numerical methods. "The resultant is zero if and only if the two polynomials have a common root". Thus all zeros (in u) give the common roots of the polynomial equations in u.

4) Putting the values of u that are the solutions of "Resultant = 0", into the original equations, equations in v result. After solving them for v we get the (u,v) values of the common solutions to the two equations.

Remarks: The numerical procedure used is due to Laguerre and not Newton/Raphson. This method is cubicaly convergent and therefore takes only one iteration for linear and quadratic functions. It converges to the nearest solution (may be complex). The method is "slow but definite".

Ref : [Catmull-1,2]
   Surfaces : Parametric Bicubics
   Rendering Forms : Shaded pictures
   Strategy : Parametric Subdivision
   Covering : Pixel

The algorithm subdivides each patch until either it covers only one pixel or it lies completely outside the limits of the frame buffer (i.e. until it covers a single or no pixel). At this stage, the intensity value as well as the depth of this small patch is calculated at a prechosen sample point inside the pixel and is stored into the frame buffer. For each of the subpatches generated from other surfaces, in consequent subdivisions, the depth values are compared with those that have already been stored, in the frame buffer. The old values of intensity and depth are rewritten by the new values in case the old patch lies behind the new one. This simple procedure generates pictures with hidden parts removed, in a natural way.

The procedure of testing the size of the patch with respect to the pixel is speeded up by using a polygon that has coincident vertices with the patch. At the same time, it is worth noticing that if a patch lies entirely inside the screen, then all subpatches resulting from it also lie inside the screen, and this test is not applied repeatedly.

The subdivision process is speeded up by the method suggested in [Catmull-1]. It applies to any polynomial. The main feature of the process is that all the operations can be described using additions and shift of bits. A brief description of the method follows:

We illustrate it for cubics. The parametric mid point of a cubic is the average of the two end points minus a correction term.

The cubics can be subdivided with 3 additions.
$$f(t) = at3+bt2+ct+d$$

$$f(t+h) = a(t+h)^3+b(t+h)^2+c(t+h)+d$$

$$f(t-h) = a(t-h)^3+b(t-h)^2+c(t-h)+d$$
So that
$$f(t+h)+f(t-h) = 2f(t)+2h^2(3at+b)$$
i.e., $f(t) = [f(t+h)-f(t-h)]/2 - h^2(3at+b)$.

Now the correction term $h^2(3at+b)$ itself is a polynomial $g(t)$ of t. Thus the value of $g(t)$ can be calculated in the same manner from $g(t+h)$ and $g(t-h)$.

It turns out to be
$$g(t) = [g(t+h)+g(t-h)]/2$$

Thus maintaining f(t+h) and g(t+h), we can determine the values of f(t) and g(t) just using additions and binary shifts. Thus the function evaluation at the midpoint is performed using end values. The method generalizes for two dimensions i.e. for the functions of two variables, in a natural way.

Remarks: This work pioneered the activity on subdivision methods for handling of parametric surfaces. The subdivision terminates when the patch can be said to cover a single pixel. A very fast technique of subdivision using forward differences has been evolved. In spite of this, the method is slow just because of the total number of pixels to be covered. It also fails for some pathological cases, where all the four corners of a patch map onto the same pixel, but the patch itself is much larger.

> **Ref :** [Blinn]
> Surfaces : Parametric Bicubics
> Rendering Forms : Shaded pictures
> Strategy : Incremental/Convergence
> Covering : Scan line

Blinn's algorithm proceeds in two phases:
> 1) Ymax values are determined and patches are sorted.
> 2) As the scanline is processed, the new patches with Ymax = Yscan are added to
the list of patches under processing.

At the same time every edge in the image (may be a patch edge or a silhouette edge) is updated to reflect its intersection with the current scanline. These intersections determine the span covered by the patch on the current scanline. All the silhouette edges are considered to be edges for rendering purpose. Within a scanline, the x values are scanned to generate depth and normal information. All equations are solved using numerical techniques. (Newton-Raphson). The initial guess for this is provided by the corresponding value on the previous scanline. This is referred to as an 'Edge tracker'. Whenever the patch is introduced for the first time, the starting points for the iteration are guessed using heuristic methods. The average number of iterations has been estimated to be 2.5. Use of extrapolation over two previous values reduces this number to less than one, since some initial guesses already satisfy the termination criteria.

Remarks: The method is entirely based on the use of numerical methods for solution of non-linear simultaneous equations. It has difficulties whenever the patch has a singularity, a cusp, a saddle point, or when a silhouette and a patch edge start simultaneously. The start of a silhouette edge is determined by the numerical solution of a set of non-linear equations at every scan step. Hence the algorithm is rather slow.

> **Ref :** [Whitted]
> Surfaces : Parametric bicubics
> Rendering Forms : Shaded pictures
> Strategy : Convergence
> Covering : Scan line

Whitted's algorithm is similar to that of Blinn. It differs only in the processing of silhouette edges. In the initial preprocessing phase, each edge of a patch is checked to see whether it intersects a silhouette or not. If a patch contains a silhouette, it meets the patch boundary in precisely two points. The silhouette equation is interpolated by Hermitian interpolation using the data available at these two extreme points. The patch is then subdivided along this silhouette so that the resulting patches regenerated from their boundaries do not contain silhouette edges in their interior portions. This step simplifies the x scanning along the scanline in the second phase of the algorithm; only two x values appear as intersections of edges with the scanline.

Remarks: The method has difficulties if the patch is excessively curved and the silhouette does not intersect the patch boundary in exactly two points (i.e., when the silhouette intersects the patch boundary in more than two points or just one point or does not intersect the boundary at all).

> Ref : [Lane/Carpenter,Lane et.al.]
> Surfaces : Parametric (C^2 Class)
> Rendering Forms : Plane tessellation drawings, Shaded pictures
> Strategy : Parametric subdivision/analytic
> Covering : Area/Scan line

The algorithm for scanline display of bicubic patches has the following steps:
  1) Patches are sorted by maximum possible y values over them.
  2) As a scanline is processed, the patches with Ymax=Yscanline are subdivided until:
    a) The subpatch has Ymax $<$ Yscanline so that it does not contribute to the current scanline.
    b) The patch is planar with all its sides linear within a prescribed tolerance.
  3) All patches with ymax $>$ yscanline $>$ ymin which are planar (as described in step 2) are compared using standard techniques for scan conversion and the appropriate segment is displayed along the current scanline.

Step 3 can be revised so that the original patch description can be used to achieve more accurate rendering using intensity values calculated from the patch definition instead of the planar approximation. Step 1 can be performed using radix sort which is linear in time. The planarity and linearity tests are performed by measuring deviations of the convex hulls from planes or lines through them. The main advantage of this algorithm over the other methods of scan conversion is that the approximation to the surface by plane faces is not made a priori, but is based on the position of the patch with respect to the current scanline. The method is not restricted to bicubic patches provided that tests for linearity and planarity are available. One such method is presented in [Lane/Carpenter]. This method is based on the Taylor's expansion of functions and therefore assumes the patches to be at least of the class c2(possessing continuous second derivatives). The estimation of the deviation is done through the magnitudes of the residues after second term in the Taylor's expansion, whereby the linear part from which the deviation is measured is provided by the first linear terms of the expansion. The method uses a straightforward manipulation of the terms of the Taylor's expansions. The method provides an upper bound to the deviation as well as the maximum y value which may not be tight bounds.

Using this an initial estimate of the maximum deviation is made for the surface and then this deviation is appropriately reduced for each subdivision. No attempt is made to determine the actual flatness of each of the resulting subpatches. This can lead to too many or too few subdivisions.

Remarks: A method for detecting intersection can be devised from this method, each surface is subdivided until it is planar, and plane-plane intersection methods are applied to all pairs of planes that result. Of course, such a method has the disadvantage that it keeps those portions which may not possibly intersect, throughout the processing, without rejecting them in the initial stages. Cracks may appear in the picture if the tolerance is not sufficiently high. The method applies to all C^2 surfaces.

Ref : [Lane/Riesenfeld,Cohen/Lyche/Riesenfeld]
    Surfaces : Bezier and B-splines and other surfaces satisfying Convex hull and variation diminishing properties.
    Rendering Forms : Plane tessellation drawings, Shaded pictures
    Strategy : Control vertex polygon subdivision
    Covering : Area

Lane and Riesenfeld present methods applicable to Bernstein and B-Spline curves and surfaces [Lane/Riesenfeld]. A brief account follows:

The curve or surface is subdivided at the parametric midpoints by logically subdividing the Bernstein or B-spline polynomials. The polynomial over the parametric range [0,1], is replaced by a combination of two polynomials, one over [0,1/2], the other over [1/2,1], and then each is reparametrized so that it gets defined over [0,1]. The first theorem establishes the necessary formulae.

As the process of logical subdivision continues, the polygon or the polyhedron formed by control vertices comes closer and closer to the curve or the surface. In the limit, where the number of subdivisions approaches infinity, the curve or surface results. Second theorem proves this.

This theorem makes it possible to estimate the shape (length, curvature, area, Euclidean bound or any other property of the shape) using the convex hull of the control vertices.

In rendering, the subdivision process is carried out until the convex hull of the control vertices is linear (for a curve) or planar with linear edges (for a surface), of course within some prescribed tolerance, and then is processed using techniques for line segments or quadrilaterals. In detecting the intersection between two surfaces, non- intersecting convex hulls result in rejection of the corresponding surfaces, otherwise subdivision continues until the surface is planar with linear edges.

These methods have been extended to non-uniform (discrete) B-Splines [Cohen/Lyche/Riesenfeld]. An algorithm (known as OSLO algorithm) provides a method of inserting a new knot at any position with any multiplicity, in such a way that the new vertices can be calculated, which, with the new set of knots give rise to the same shape as before. This technique then easily extends to form two subcurves resulting after a logical subdivision at any point. This is achieved by inserting a knot at such a point where the subdivision is to take place. This non-uniform subdivision makes it possible to choose the subdivision points in a manner that is most appropriate to a given particular task. Thus all the subdivision algorithms that are developed to handle curves and surfaces defined using uniform splines can now be applied to discrete-spline representations.

Ref : [Koparkar/Mudur,Koparkar]
Surfaces : Rational quadratic and bicubic
Rendering forms : plane tesselation, intersection and silhouette detection and drawing
Strategy : Function splitting and subdivision
Covering : Area

The functions defining the curves and surfaces are logically split into parametric intervals at their extremum and inflexion points. The curves and surfaces are now guaranteed to be monotonic within the interval and hence are contained within the bounding boxes defined by their end points in Euclidean space. A simple direct method of estimating linearity of a function within the sub-interval is then provided, using which linearity of a curve is easily determined. The planarity of a surface patch is defined in terms of the linearity of the constituent functions. Using these subdivision techniques for a variety of tasks have been devised. An important point to note is that using this method patches are subdivided only in the direction in which they are curved. Thus if the v function is already linear for a subpatch then it will be subdivided only in u. **Remarks** : The techniques are applicable to all C2 class of curves and surfaces. The convex hull property is not essential. For bicubics and rational quadratics simple functions and procedures have been defined so that most of the tasks can be carried effeciently.

Ref : [Mudur,Mudur/Koparkar-2,Koparkar]
Surfaces : All C1 class parametrically defined curves and surfaces
Rendering Forms : plane tesselation, intersection and silhouette detection and drawing, shading and hidden surface removal
Strategy : Parametric subdivision and Use of Interval arithmetic
Covering : Area

This is a very powerful extension to the previous method. Here the basic observation is that for all subdivision schemes to work it is sufficient to know the range of functions defining properties of the curve or surface. For example, linear deviation of a curve, planar deviation of patch, local visibility function N.E etc. INterval arithmetic with some extensions is used as a method for directly evaluating the bounds of functions, albeit loose bounds.

Remarks : Interval arithmetic provides a powerful methodology for devising subdivision algorithms in a uniform amnner for any processing task on curves and surfaces. The methodology is simple enough to be incorporated into a VLSI implementation for a "geometry engine" for handling parametric curves and surfaces.

REFERENCES

[Ahlberg/Nielson/Walsh] Ahlberg J.H. Nilson E.N. and Walsh J.L. "The Theory of Splines and Their Applications", Academic Press, 1967.

[Askwith] Askwith E.H.: "The Analytic Geometry of the Conic Sections", Adam and Charles Black, 1967.

[Barsky] Barsky B.:"A Description and Evaluation of various 3D models", IEEE Computer Graphics and Applications, Jan 1984.

[Barnard/Child] Barnard S. and Child J.M.: "Higher Algebra", Macmillan and Co., 1952.

[Barr] Barr A.H.: "Superquadrics and Angle Preserving Transformations", IEEE Computer Graphics and Applications, V1, p11, 1981.

[Bezier] Bezier P.: "Mathematical and Practical Possibilities of Unisurf", Computer Aided Geometric Design, Proceedings, Academic Press, 1974.

[Bhattacharya/Gindy] Bhattacharya B.K. and Gindy H.El.:"A new linear convex hull algorithm for simple polygons",J. Alogrithms,V4,p85,1984.

[Blinn-1] Blinn J.F.: "Computer Display of Curved Surfaces", in Supplement to SIGGRAPH 78, Computer Graphis, V12, 1978.

[Blinn-2] Blinn J.F.: "Clipping using Homogeneous Coordinates",Computer Graphics, V12,No2,1978.

[Blinn-3] Blinn J.F.:"The algebraic properties of homogeneous second order surfaces", SIGGRAPH 84 Tutorial Notes on Mathematical Elements for Computer Graphics, 1984.

[Bowyer/Woodwark] Bowyer A. and Woodwark J.:"A Programmer's Geometry", Butterworths, 1983.

[Brewer J.A. and Anderson D.C.,:"Visual interaction wwith Overhauser curves and surfaces", Computer Graphics, Vol 11, p 214, 1977. (Proc SIGGRAPH 1977).

[Catmull-1] Catmull A.A.: "A Subdivision Algorithm for Computer Display of Curved Surfaces", Ph.D. Thesis, University of Utah, 1974.

[Catmull-2] Catmull A.A.: "Computer Display of Curved Surfaces", Proceedings IEEE Conf. on Computer Graphics, Pattern Recognition and Data Structures, p 11, 1975.

[Catmull/Rom] Catmull E. and Rom R.:"A class of local interpolating splines", Computer Aided Geometric Design, Ed:R.E.Barnhill and R.F.Riesenfld, p 317, Academic Press, 1974.

[Cohen/Lyche/Riesenteld] Cohen E., Lyche T. and Riesenfeld R.: "Discrete B-Splines and Subdivision Techniques in Computer Aided Geometric Design and Computer Graphics", Computer Graphics and Image Processing V14, p87, 1980.

[Carlbom/Paciorek] Carlbom I and Paciorek J.:"Planar Geometric Projections and Viewing Transformations",Computing Surveys,V10,No4,p465,1978.

[Chazelle] Chazelle B.:"Computational Geometry and Complexity",PhD thesis,Carnegie Mellon Univ., 1980.

[Coons-1] Coons S.A.: "Transformations and Matrices", Notes, University of Michigan, A Short Course on Computer Grphics, 1975.

[Coons-2] Coons S.A.: "Surface Patches and B-Spline Curves", Computer Aided Geometric Design, Academic Press, 1974.

[Crow] Crow F.C.:" A comparison of antialiasing techniques ",IEEE Computer Graphics and Applications, Vol 1, p 40, 1981.

[Duff] Duff T.: "Families of local matrix Splines", Technical Memo 104, Computer Graphics Project, Lucas Films Ltd., Course Notes of Mathematical Elements in Computer Graphics held during SIGGRAPH 84.

[Faux/Pratt] Faux I.D. and Pratt M.J.: "Computational Geometry for Design and Manufacture" Ellis-Horwood, 1979.

[Foley/Van Dam] Foley J.D. and Van Dam A.:"Fundamentals of Interactive Computer Graphics",Addison Wesley,1982.

[Forrest-1] Forrest A.R.: "Curves and Surfaces for Computer Aided Design", Ph.D. Thesis, University of Cambridge, 1968.

[Forrest-2] Forrest A.R.: "On Coons' and Other Methods for the Representation of Curved Surfaces", Computer Graphics and Image Processing, V1, p341, 1972.

[Forrest-3] Forrest A.R.: "The Twisted Cubic Curve: A Computer Aided Geometric Design Approach", Computer Aided Design, V12, p165, 1980.

[Forrest-4] Forrest A.R.: "User aspects for free-form surface design", Course Notes of SIGGRAPH 82 Tutorial on Freeform Surfaces.

[Garey et al] Garey M,Johnson D.S.,Preparata F.P. and Tarjan R.E.: "Triangulating a simple polygon",Informatio Processing Letters,V7,p175,1980.

[Graham] Graham R.L.:"An efficient algorithm for determining the convex hull of a finite planar set",Information Processing Letters,V1,p132,1972.

[Greene] Greene D.H.:"The decomposition of polygons into convex parts", Advances in Computing Research, Vol 1, (Ed:Preparata F.P.),JAI press,p235,1983.

[Guibas/Stolfi] Guibas L. and Stolfi J. : " Course Notes on Computational Geometry", CS445, Stanford Univ. 1982-83.

[Jarvis] Jarvis R.A.:"On the identification of the convex hull of a finite set of of points in a plane",Information Processing Letters,Vol 2, p 18,1973.

[Kajiya] Kajiya J.T.: "Ray Tracing Parametric Patches", SIGGRAPH V 16, p245, 1982.

[Kirkpatrick/Siedel] Kirkpatrick D.G. and Siedel R.:"The ultimate planar convex hull", Tech Rep 83-577, Dept. of Comp. Sc., Cornell Univ., 1983.

[Koparkar] Koparkar P.A.: "Computational Techniques for Processing Parametric Curves and Surfaces", Phd Thesis, Bombay Univ., 1985.

[Koparkar/Mudur] Koparkar P.A. and Mudur S.P. : "Computational Techniques for processing Parametric Surfaces", CVGIP, Vol 28, p303, 1984.

[Lane/Carpenter] Lane J.F. and Carpenter L.C.: "A Generalized Scan Line Algorithm for the Computer Display of Curved Surfaces", Computer Graphics and Image Processing, V11, p290, 1979.

[Lane et. al.] Lane J., Carpenter L., Whitted T. and Blinn J.: "Scanline Methods for Displaying parametrically Defined Surfaces", Communications of A.C.M. V23, p23, 1980.

[Lane/Riesenfeld] Lane J.M., Riesenfeld R.F.: "A Theoretical Development for the Computer Generation and Display of Piecewise Polynomial Surfaces", IEEE Transactions on Pattern Analysis and Machine Intelligence, V2, p36, 1980.

[Lee/Preparata] Lee D.T. and Preparata F.P.: "Location of a point in a planar subdivision and its applications ", Siam Journal of Computing, Vol 6, No 3, p 594, 1977.

[Lee/Preparata] Lee D.T. and Peparata F.P. : "Computational Geometry: ASurvey", IEEE Trans on Computers, Vol 33, No 12, p 1072, 1984.

[Levin] Levin J.Z.: "A Parametric Algorithm for Drawing Pictures of Solid Objects Composed of Quadric Surfaces", Communications of A.C.M., V19, p555, 1976.

[Mahl] Mahl R.: "Visible Surface Algorithm for Quadric Patches" IEEE Transaction on Computers, V21, p1, 1972.

[Mairson/Stolfi] Mairson H.G. and Stolfi J.:"Reporting and counting linesegment intersections" Tech Report, Dept. of Comp. Sc., Stanford Univ., 1984.

[Maxwell] Maxwell E.A.: "Methods of Plane Projective Geometry Based on the Use of General Homogeneous Coordinates", University Press, Cambridge, 1946.

[Mudur] Mudur S.P.: " A General Schema for handling curves and surfaces in geometric modelling", Proc. Nicograph 83, p 213, 1983.

[Mudur/Koparkar-1] Mudur S.P. and Koparkar P.A. : "Product surfaces and Modulated Surfaces for 3-D shape representation in Computer Vision Systems ",Proc IEEE SMC Conf 1983, p207, 1983.

[Mudur/Koparkar-2] Mudur S.P. and Koparkar P.A. : "Interval Methods for processing geometric objects", IEEE Computer Graphics and Applications, Vol 4, No 2, p 7, 1984.

[Newman/Sproull] Newman W.M., Sproull R.F.: "Principles of Interactive Computer Graphics", Second Edition, McGraw Hill, 1979.

[Peters] Peters G.J.: "Interactive Computer Graphics Applications of the Parametric Bicubic Surface to Engineering Design Problems", Computer Aided Geometric Design, Academic Press, 1974.

[Requicha] Requicha Aristides A.G.: "Representations of Rigid Solids: Theory, Methods and Systems", Computing Surveys, V12, 1980.

[Riesenfeld] Riesenfeld R.: "Applications of B-Spline Approximation to Geometric Problems of Computer Aided Design", Ph.D. Thesis, University of Utah, UTEC-CSc-73-126, 1973.

[Rogers] Rogers D.F. : "Procedural Elements for Computer Graphics", McGraw Hill, 1985.

[Shamos] Shamos M.I.: "Computational Geometry", PhD Thesis, Yale Univ., 1978.

[Shapedata] "New Surface and Track Geometries -Second Draft", Shape Data Ltd., Cambridge, 1980.

[Sommerville] Sommerville D.M.Y.: "Analytic Geometry of Three Dimensions", Cambridge University Press, 1934.

[Smith] Smith A. R. :"Spline Tutorial Notes", Technical Memo 77,Computer Graphics Project, Lucas Film Ltd., Course notes on Introduction to Computer Animation Tutorial held during SIGGRAPH 83.

[Toussaint/Avis] Toussaint G.T. and Avis D. : "On a convex hull algorithm for polygons and its application to triangulation problems", Pattern Recognition, Vol 15, p23, 1982.

[Weiler/Atherton] Weiler K. and Atherton P.:"Hidden Surface Removal using polygon area sorting", Computer Graphics, Vol 11, p 214, 1977 (Proc SIGGRAPH 1977).

[Weiss] Weiss R.A.: "Be Vision, A Package of IBM 7090 Fortran Programs to Draw Orthographic Views of Planes and Quadric Surfaces", Journal of A.C.M. V13, p194, 1966,.

[Whitted] Whitted T.: "A Scan Line Algorithm for Computer Display of Curved Surfaces", in Supplement to SIGGRAPH 78, Computer Graphics, V12, 1978.

[Woon/Freeman] Woon P. and Freeman H.: "A Procedure for Generating Visible-line Projections of Solids Bounded by Quadric Surfaces", IFIP TA6, p81, 1971.

[Yao] Yao A.C. : "A lower bound to finding convex hulls", J. ACM,Vol 28, p780, 1981.

Part II

Hardware for Computer Graphics and Basic Algorithms

A New Generation of Hardware

C. Machover

Introduction

Computer Graphics continues to exhibit exciting growth and future potential. In 1985, more than $6.2 billion worth of commercial hardware, software, systems, and serivces are forecasted to be sold worldwide. Expectations are that will grow to $15,000,000,000 by the end of the decade. The CAD/CAM portion of the market is forecasted to grow from about $3.7 billion in 1985 to about $13.8 billion by 1990. Overall growth rates average more than 30% per year with parts of the industry, like workstations, growing even faster.

The dominance of color raster display systems continues ... some forecasters suggest that except for office automation displays, almost 80% of all raster displays shipped are in color. Much higher performance workstations are becoming available to the point where the picture quality and dynamic performance advantages long attributed to stroke refresh displays are being seriously challenged by some of the new color raster workstations. While touch input and the mouse continue to be widely used as operator input devices, new developments in voice input offer the promise of a resurgence of interest in that technology. While we may be moving closer to a "paperless society", interest continues to be high in various kinds of color hard copy devices. Personal computer based systems are becoming ubiquitous. By 1988, we expect that more than 500,000 personal computers will be used in scientific and engineering applications. Software companies are being required to support an increasing number of display and hard copy devices, and provide tools for the non-programmer, non-computer specialist, to benefit from the graphics revolution.

Displays

The price/performance characteristics of display products have continued to improve ... full color, full graphic raster graphic systems are now available at prices comparable to the lowest cost storage tube of just a few years ago. Tektronix, for example, introduced the 4105 unit which has a 480 x 360 pixel displayable matrix, 60 frame per second non-interlaced image, and the price is slightly under $4,000.

At the other extreme, terminals of increasing performance and functionality have been introduced at surprisingly nominal prices. Pressure from a new performance plateau with regard to flicker free displays was reached in 1983 with the introduction by Tektronix of the 4115 ... a 1,024 x 1,280, full color raster display, operating 60 frames per second non-interlaced. Shortly after the 4115 introduction, several other companies manufacturing both display controllers (such as Lexidata and Raster Technology) and monitors (such as Kratos, SRL and Sabre) began to introduce their products with similar performance. These 64 Hz scan frequency, 100 megahertz video bandwidth products represent the present state-of-the-art of color raster performance. The Tektronix unit sells in the $20–30,000 range depending on configuration, the monitors sell in the $4–5,000 range, and the display controllers sell in the $10–15,000 range.

Because of the pressures of the CAD/CAM users, one can expect that more and more products will begin to appear offering the high resolution coupled with non-interlaced, 60 frame per second displays. Because the scan frequency requirements for 1,000 line, 60 Hz non-interlaced system are essentially the same as for a 2,000 lines, 30 Hz interlaced (although twice the video bandwidth is needed), there will probably be some interlaced 2,000 line products introduced shortly. These products, however, will probably push the limits of the shadow mask CRTs and may, in the short term, not represent a significant picture quality improvement over the present 1,000 line, non-interlaced systems. Several companies, including Sabre and Chromatics, are now offering about 1,200 x 1,600, 60 Hz non-interlaced displays as part of their workstations.

The high performance end is also under pressure to increase the dynamic capability. Products are beginning to appear which permit near real time manipulation of solid-shaded images. One of the first efforts in this direction was the introduction by Lexidata of SOLID-VIEW, a Z-buffer polygon approach which allows a fairly complex solid image to be developed on a CRT within about ten to twenty seconds after the software has defined the image in polygon form. More recently, several other companies like Silicon Graphics, GTI, Witeck, Phoenix Data Systems, Adage, Raster Technologies, and Megatek have shown products which can rotate a solid image in near real time (about one new image in a tenth of a second) once the software has defined the image. Soon one can expect to see these hardware products being added as much lower cost VLSI processors in graphics workstations.

Following the introduction by NEC of a display controller chip (7220) a number of manufactures are beginning to develop their own VLSI chips to enhance the functionality of their workstations. In fact, within the next 2–3 years, various standard CAD software functions (like 2D drafting) will probably appear on chips.

Manufacturers continue to push the performance on their units by speeding up the time to write a pixel (state-of-the-art is in the order of ten nanoseconds per pixel), and adding various kinds of hardware anti-aliasing techniques. AED, Jupiter, Megatek and Seiko, all offer products with some form of hardware anti-aliasing.

Another trend as the terminals grow more intelligent, is an increasing number of microprocessors in the same workstation. Historically, a single microprocessor was used both as a display controller, I/O controller, and programmable unit. Present trends are to use a variety of microprocessors assigned to a number of different tasks.

There is also an increasing interest in a large number of simultaneous colors. Art, animation and imaging areas, forced the increased number of simultaneous colors. The CAD/CAM applications generally started out with eight to twelve colors on the assumption that most of the schematic or line drawings could not make use of more colors than that. However, as the interest in solid modelling for mechanical CAD grows, the need for realistic modelling of solid images grows. This implies that these display terminals need to have somewhere on the order of 256 to 512 simultaneous color capability.

Another factor that became more apparent during the past year was the growing number of Japanese companies entering the display terminal market. The Japanese have certainly dominated the monitor market over the last few years … companies like Matishita, Mitsubishi, Ikegami, and Hitachi have become the major suppliers of computer graphic quality monitors in the United States. Recently, companies like Seiko, Japan Radio Company, Graphics, and Comtec have started to market their products in the U.S. With the IBM PC setting a defacto standard in the PC area, a number of Japanese companies are also beginning to introduce graphics oriented personal computers that can use IBM PC developed software. NEC, Canon, and Sony have been particularly active in that area. To date, however, the Japanese have not made major inroads into the U.S. PC market.

It is estimated that more than $1.2 billion worth of graphic raster displays will be sold in 1985 ... probably 70% of those (if not more) will be color.

While about $80 million worth of storage tube displays will be sold in 1985 and about $160 million worth of stroke refresh displays will be sold, neither represent the mainstream of display interest any longer. The storage tube is essentially a dormant technology, still finding application in very specialized areas where extremely high data density coupled with excellent resolution and picture quality are necessary. The stroke refresh systems still finding application in high performance dynamic areas. However, with the cost, dynamic capability, and picture quality of the raster systems continuingly increasing, the application advantages of the storage tube and refresh displays are rapidly dissipating. Almost every traditional stroke writer display company, such as Adage, Vector General, Evans & Sutherland, Lundy, Megatek, and Sanders have now introduced raster systems. In some cases, the raster systems that were introduced are directly plug compatible with existing stroke writers. For example, using the IBM 3250 as a target, CGX, Spectragraphics, Adage and Vector General have all announced color raster plug compatible products. At the end of 1983, IBM introduced a color raster compatible version of the 3250, the 5080, an extremely aggressive, price/performance product offering. One can expect that other traditional manufacturers of stroke writers, such as Imlac and Vector Automation, will come to market with color raster systems as well.

Sales of the color raster displays are probably growing at rates two to three times faster than the rate of growth of either stroke refresh or storage tube displays.

The cathode ray tube continues to be challenged by other display techniques. Flat panel displays based on liquid crystal and electroluminescent techniques continue to attract interest. U.S. companies like Panelvision and Japanese companies like Sharp are beginning to move aggressively into this area. Color flat panel displays have also been delivered. Flat panel displays will be a major factor in the *portable* workstation market, but will probably not present a significant short-term challenge to the CRT in conventional workstation environments.

Interest continues in the plasma display area. In 1983, IBM announced its 20″ diagonal 1,000 line plasma display available on an OEM basis. IBM has also introduced plasma workstations as alphanumeric terminals for business applications.

Large screen projection displays will become more common. We may begin to see a growing interest in true 3-D displays, especially if the demands of the entertainment industry (commercial broadcasting or video games) can be harnessed to develop a viable true 3-D technique.

Input Devices

On the operator input side, a great deal of attention is being given to the merging use of the Mouse ... which is a trackball turned up-side-down. There are about a dozen companies who manufacture "mice", and units are now available for less than $100.

As the effort to capture the non-computer, non-graphics user continues, touch input devices can be expected to gain dominance. The new HP 150 personal computer features touch input, for example.

Voice input is also a potentially strong input device especially when relatively low-cost connected (or continuous) spreech units become available. Such units have come on the market in about the $2,000 range.

Scanners and automatic digitizers are expected to become more common over the next few years.

Hard Copy

Hard copy, especially color, will continue to be a major part of computer graphics over the next decade. We expect that about $1 billion worth of hard copy equipment will be sold in 1985. Electrostatic continues to be a viable technique, and Versatec introduced an electrostatic color unit in 1983. Announcements of several new competing color electrostatic units are expected shortly. Last year, we thought by 1984, more dollars would be spent on electrostatic hard copy than on conventional pen plotters. However, the literal explosion of low-cost pen plotters due to the personal computer influence, probably will shift the electrostatic take over to the end of the decade. However, electrostatic plotters probably will shortly take over pen plotters in CAD/CAM applications requiring D-size and larger plots. Other companies are trying to refine the jet plotter techniques and today it is possible to buy a full-color jet printer for under $2,000. Thermal ink transfer represents another promising technology. The jet and thermal ink transfer products represent the fastest growing segment of the hard copy market. Both techniques can now be used to make overhead transparencies. In 1984, a series of low cost ($4,000–$7,000) laser printers became available. Although still limited to black and white, the price/performance is impressive. Color should become available before the end of the decade. Mead has demonstrated a "carbonless paper" like color technique that could become commercially viable by the end of the decade.

The film recorders are coming down in price or increasing in performance. Units using 35 mm cameras or Polaroid instant film are on the market now in the $3–5,000 range. Polaroid brought out their own $1,500 film recorder for use with personal computers. At the other end of the spectrum the traditional 2,000 line film recorders which sold for $200–300,000 are being challenged by new low-cost units coming in from companies like Matrix. Matrix is delivering a 2,000/4,000 line film recorder in the $30,000 price range. GE and Dicomed have also announced lower priced, high resolution film recorders. Further, in 1984, both Matrix and Image Resources (now part of CALCOMP) announced 2,000 line film recorder systems selling for about $10,000.

Intelligent Workstations

Over the past two years, major interest has been in the area of lower cost intelligent work-stations. Tektronix desktop computers like the 4051, 4052, and the 4054, are typical of "first generation" systems that had sufficient capacity to allow a user to make use of graphic technology without tying up a host computer ... in effect, just using the host computer as a massive data base or a place for massive number crunching. For the CAD/CAM user, intelligent workstations can improve system response.

Many intelligent workstations have become available in the past few years, most based on 16 and 32 bit CPUs (Intel, Motorola, and National).

Apollo and Sun Microsystems have become almost defacto standards, but Tektronix has made several major workstation announcements in the past year. Hewlett Packard offers the HP 9000 which uses a custom 32 bit microprocessor.

Forecasted World Computer Graphics Market for USA Manufacturers 1985/1990

	1985 Shipments (Millions of $)		1990 Shipments (Millions of $)		Compounded Annual Growth (%)
1. Consumer (includes video games and CRT peripherals for personal computers)	2,600		9,650		30
2. International (shipments by USA mfg. to non-USA customers)	2,300		7,590		27
a) Commercial		1,900		6,270	
b) MIL SPEC		400		1,320	
3. Commericial/ Industrial*	3,200		15,410		37
a) Hard copy		540		1,880	
b) Displays		770		4,190	
c) Software/System		1,620		8,390	
d) Other		270		950	
4. U.S. Government	2,460		9,120		30
a) Commercial		1,110		4,120	
b) MIL SPEC		1,350		5,000	
Totals					
Worldwide, All	10,560		41,770		32
Worldwide, Commercial	6,210		25,800		33

Prepared by Machover Associates Corp., 199 Main Street, NY 10601, USA

Personal Computers

One final systems issue ... the personal computer is becoming an increasingly important factor. Up to the last few years, whenever I talked about the personal computer market, I emphasized that it was the peripherals that offered an advantage. But, that has changed dramatically. The personal computer, itself, is used as a workstation. These systems are used either in a standalone mode, with the graphic quality determined by the PC characteristics, or as a "front-end" to a system capable of producing extremely high quality graphics.

Today, for example, there are several companies, including T&W Systems, Cascade Computer, Personal CAD and Autodesk, that offer CAD/CAM software packages that run on the Apple and IBM personal computers. By the end of 1985, there are expected to be more personal computer CAD systems (not workstations) installed than more conventional maxi-, midi- and mini-based CAD systems.

Market Data

Machover Associates Corporation complete forecasts on the entire worldwide computer graphics market are given in the following table. The numbers represent our estimates of U.S. shipments worldwide. The numbers do not include shipments made by non-U.S.

Forecasted World Computer Graphics Market for USA Manufacturers

Product (All commericial, industrial)	1985 (Millions of $ estimated)		1990 (Millions of $ forecasted)		Compounded Annual Growth (%)
1. Hard Copy	1,050		3,150		25
a) pen		400		1,000	20
b) electrostatic		380		1,160	25
c) film (COM, dry silver, etc.)		200		610	25
d) others		70		380	40
2. Displays/Workstations	1,500		7,010		36
a) storage		80		60	−10
b) refresh		160		130	−10
c) raster		1,200		6,500	40
d) other		60		320	40
3. Software/System/Services	3,140		14,050		35
a) software/services		570		2,550	35
b) systems		2,570		11,500	35
4. Other	520		1,590		25
Total	6,210		25,800		33

Prepared by Machover Associates Corp., 199 Main Street, White Plains, NY 10601, USA

Graphic Displays Forecasted Installations 1983–1988

Application	1 Desk top	2 Graphics Workstation	3 Graphics Terminals	Total
A. Business/prof.	*15,420,000*	*468,500*	*312,700*	
1. Secretary/clerk	1,817,900	–	–	
2. Executive "What if ..." etc.	11,254,000	263,000	156,200	
3. Business Graphics (charts)	2,326,600	195,500	156,500	
4. "Digital" Paint	21,500	10,000	–	
B. Scientific/Engr.	*522,600*	*790,400*	*794,100*	
1. CAD/CAM	23,300	87,200	39,300	
2. Engr/Scientific	499,300	634,200	408,800	
3. Process Control	–	69,000	346,000	
C. Educational	1,224,400	6,900	13,800	
D. Graphic Arts	134,000	101,200	73,900	
Total				

Typical Desk Top Units: PC's such as IBM, Apple, etc., HP 9000, TEK 4051
Typical Graphics Workstations: Florida Computer Graphics, Beacon, Apollo, Orcatech, CADMUS
Typical Graphics Terminals: TEK 4105, 4107, 4109, 4115, IBM 3250, 5080, 3279

Market Definitions:
A.   *Business/Proof* ... Basic business graphics for data representation, "whatif" and graphic solutions to business problems, digital paint/animation
B1.   *CAD/CAM* ... Computer aided design, drafting and manufacturing
B2.   *Engr/Scientific* ... CAE, general engineering scientific data analysis, instrumentation
B3.   *Process Control* ... SCADA, and other mimic board type environments
C.   *Education* ... systems used in schools of all kinds
D.   *Graphic Arts* ... systems used in printing and publishing

suppliers. We estimate that if shipments by non-U.S. suppliers were included, that total values would increase by 10%.

We are also including the table, "Installed Units 1983–1988", which gives Machover Associates Corporation forecasts of installed graphics displays delivered between 1983 and 1988 by application. Note that the display units are dominantly desktop personal computers.

Intelligent Computer Graphics Workstations – An Overview

C. Machover

Abstract

One of the most exciting current developments in the area of computer graphics is the emergence of the microcomputer-based intelligent workstation. A recent market study suggests that over the next decade, sales will grow at about 1.5 times the rate of growth for the rest of the computer graphics industry ... reaching sales of over $1,000,000,000 by the end of the decade. This paper will describe these workstations, discuss present capability and future trends.

Introduction

One of the most exciting current developments in the area of computer graphics is the emergence of the microcomputer-based intelligent workstation. The sales of these stations ... which include graphics capability, processing capability to handle other than simply display generation, communications capability, mass memory, input and output devices ... are growing at a faster rate than almost any other segment of the computer graphics industry. A recent Frost & Sullivan market study[1] in which I participated, estimated that over $35 million of intelligent workstations were sold in 1981, and that volume will grow to well over $1 billion by the end of the decade. This 46% growth rate is 50% faster than the overall industry growth and higher than any other segment of the market. If the workstation concept is expanded to include dumb and smart workstations, as well as turnkey systems, total sales of more that $8.5 billion are forecasted by the end of the decade.

Like most devices which suddenly capture everyone's attention, origins often lie in technology and product which was available years before. If one generalizes the definition of such a workstation to include a "self-contained" unit which not only handles graphics functions, but a number of application functions as well, then surely such early minicomputer-based products such as the DEC 338, 339, and 340, based on the old DEC 8 bit machines and the early IDI IDIIOM based on the Varian 620 series of computers (both introduced in the mid-1960's) qualify as workstations. While, the units had generally limited capability ... from the standpoint of display content, computer capability (typical 12 and 16 bit words), main memory (usually limited to 16,000 words), and mass memory (in the one to two million byte range) they were able to handle a range of standalone applications. These units were relatively expensive ... typically in the $50–100,000 range.

Throughout the late 60's and early 70's, the number of large scale mini-computer based systems continued to grow and other display manufacturers such as, Vector General, Adage,

---

[1]   "The Computer Graphics Workstations Market in the U.S." (A1029), November 1982

Megatek, Imlac, and Evans & Sutherland, added new mini-computer based graphics products to their line. These systems generally employed stroke-refresh graphics and were in the $50,000 to $100,000 range. Megatek and Imlac products were available at about one-half that price, but mass memory and hard copy peripherals could significantly increase the total system cost.

By the mid to late 70's, workstations began to appear whose intelligence was based on custom designed processors rather than commercial mini-computers. Perhaps the first version of this kind of system was the storage tube based Tektronix 4051 which might be termed the first generation of desktop computers. The systems were equipped with up to 32K bytes of memory, various mass memory devices, ability to drive output hard copy and support a variety of input devices. A flurry of new products began to appear in this category ... which have become known now as desktop computers. These included the Hewlett Packard series 45 as a typical example, and the Three Rivers PERQ system.

The Tektronix 4051 represented a major breakthrough from a price standpoint. The early versions of the unit came in under $10,000 ... current versions sell for about $7,000 (although when fully equipped with peripheral devices are anywhere on the order of $15,000). Most recently (late 1970's to the present), newer intelligent workstations are based on a wide range of commercial and custom microprocessors. Some units built around the 8 bit Z80 type processors. Current systems are beginning to migrate to 16 and 32 bit units using micro-processors like the Motorola MC68000 and the Intel 8080 series. Other configurations make use of bit sliced microprocessor configurations. Frequently, several microprocessors are combined in the same units, some to handle graphics functions, some to handle applications functions, and some to hand I/0 (including communication and peripherals control) functions.

Today, there is a huge range of these intelligent workstations available ... from essentially personal computer type systems such as the Apple II and III, the TRS 80, the IBM and DEC personal computers, to extremely sophisticated, high performance, high memory capacity units such as the Apollo Domain series that was brough to market with a fully developed local area networking capability. Today, these intelligent workstations can be obtained in the $5,000 to $80,000 range. The memory is in the range of 4 million bytes and mass memories include the ability to support large capacity (in the order of 50 million bytes) hard disk. Figure 1 is a block diagram and description of a typical contemporary workstation. The product is sold in the USA in the $9,000 to $20,000 range.

Display Characteristics

As noted before, the earliest units were generally stroke refresh display technology. The first desktop ... the Tektronix 4051 ... was based on the storage tube. However, today, essentially all intelligent workstations being offered commercially are raster. Both the stroke-refresh, and storage tube systems were monochromatic, as were the early raster systems. However, now there is a major move toward color raster systems.

From a display standpoint, the earlier raster units had either personal computer type picture quality of about 125 x 125 picture (pixels) elements, or commercial TV picture quality range of about 500 x 500 pixels. Most recently, several products are becoming available in the 1,000 x 1,000 pixel range.

147

SUN Workstation^{TM}

Product Overview

SUN Microsystems Inc
2310 Walsh Av, Santa Clara, CA 95051
408-748-9900

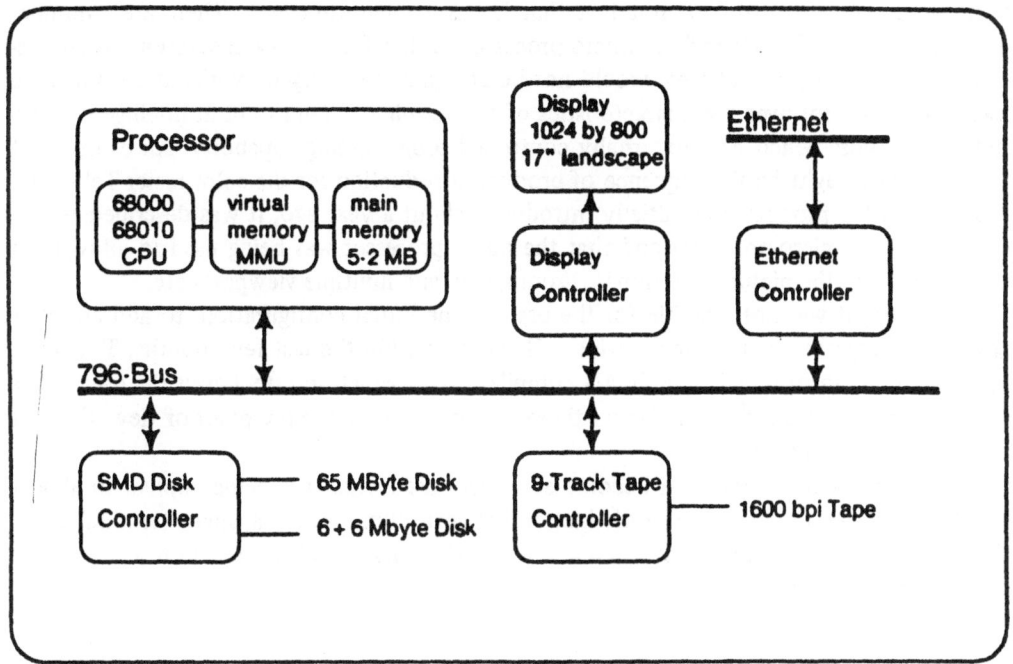

Description

The SUN Workstation is a high-performance graphics workstation suited for scientific, engineering, CAD/CAM, document preparation and other applications.

SUN Workstations are interconnected via the Ethernet into clusters forming a distributed computing environment.

Each SUN Workstation has its own 32-bit CPU, main memory, display, and network interface. Other pheripherals such as disks, printers, etc., can be shared via the network.

In addition, each SUN Workstation can support pheripheral controllers connected to the internal I/0 Bus, the Intel Multibus or 796-Bus. Pheripheral options include a color display, SMD disk interface, 1600 bpi tape interface, and a "mouse" pointing device.

UNIX is a trademark of Bell Laboratories
Multibus is a trademark of Intel Corporation
SUN Workstation is a trademark of
SUN Microsystems Inc.
Note: Specifications subject to change
(c) 1982 SUN Microsystems Inc.

Features

Processor	68000/68010, 10 MHz
Main Memory	256k to 2 MByte with parity
Virtual Memory	2 MByte per process 16 simultaneous processes
Display	1024 by 800 pixel, black & white 17″ landscape display
Network	10 MBit/sec Ethernet (4Q82) 3 MBit/sec Ethernet
Software	Berkeley UNIX 4.2 bsd (1Q83) Unisoft V7 UNIX Core Standard Graphics VT100/4014 Emulators (PROM)
Peripherals	640 by 480 by 8 color display SMD Disk Controller 65 MByte Disk, 20 msec 6 + 6 MByte Disk, 50 msec 1600 bpi 9-track tape Mouse pointing device (4Q82)
Packaging	Desk-Top, H x W x D 19 x 17 x 17″ Power: 110 V, 3.5 A (220 V, 2 A)

Intelligent Workstation

The implication of the earlier definition of intelligent workstations is that the product has some programming capability, not just that it has a micro-processor. There are a number of products available that include micro-processors either for display generation or I/0 control that from my point of view would not be considered intelligent workstations since the user has no control over the characteristics of the terminal. I tend to limit intelligent workstations to those which have externally controlled programming capability. An example of the difference might be the sequence of product introduction for the color raster Tektronix 4113. When the product was initially introduced about a year ago, it was described as having an internal micro-processor and that the micro-processor was being used to allow local manipulation of the picture functions ... zoom, pan, and multiple viewports etc.

However, it was not possible for the user, in the initial configuration, to add any user developed programs to the workstations. However, within the last few months, Tektronix has introduced an optional FORTRAN compiler board which in effect gives the user access to the internal micro-processor. Under those circumstances, from my point of view, the unit is an intelligent workstation.

The term, workstation, has become so widely used, that it is being applied to almost every kind of graphic device. The distinction between dumb terminal, smart terminal, intelligent terminal and workstation is being blurred. However, I will use the term in the sense of a programmable station.

Applications

The applications for these intelligent workstations have been growing enormously and include engineering, business, scientific, educational, artistic and others. The original Tektronix 4051 was very often used in standalone applications to solve relatively simple analysis problems and to operate as a terminal for computer aided education purposes. It was then occasionally linked to a central or host computer and data was transferred between the workstation and the host. Frequently, large data bases were in the host or large analysis programs were in the host, and the device essentially acted as a graphic database entry device.

From a business graphics standpoint, the earliest uses for intelligent workstations were in applications similar to that of Computer Pictures. Their first unit, based on a Chromatics terminal, allowed a user to enter business data and manipulate it for modest analysis purposes and see graphic output of various kinds. That product was also later interfaced to existing databases and host computers such as the Cullinane system so that the user could simply inquire from a given database. Data from the raw database would come across the communication lines and would be formatted to the user's requirement on the face of the CRT, then local manipulation and analysis would be possible.

From a computer aided design and drafting standpoint, the initial interest in intelligent workstations was to relieve the load on the host computer so that the response to an individual's actions would be much more satisfactory. By moving some of the functions to the workstation, it was felt that true time sharing operation (over low grade communication lines) would be possible. And, this would permit a large number of workstations to operate from the same host. Initially, the feeling was that major analysis portions of the CAD function would still be resident on the host. However, in the latest implementations of this kind of environment such as the Auto-Trol Advanced Graphic Workstations built around the Apollo Domain series, essentially the entire CAD package has been migrated to the workstation and each user has a complete software package at his disposal. A mainframe computer may still be part of the local area network, but would handle very large scale analysis programs (such as finite element) rather than all analysis such as volumetric calculations for example.

Future Trends

There is little question that the growth of intelligent workstations will continue. Industry rumors are that "the VAX on a chip" is going to be announced momentarily which would further increase the power available to the individual user. While the cathode ray tube will probably continue to be the dominant display device, flat panel displays based on plasma, LCD, and other technologies, are beginning to appear. As terminal portability (physically) becomes an issue, flat panel displays can be expected to become more common. Workstations which include multiple display heads are also becoming available.

As time goes by, the engineering and business users will need to make a decision about footprint issues. That is, now most of the engineering and office systems are viewed as isolated elements ... word processing is one function satisfied by one terminal ... CAD is satisfied by another terminal ... and business graphics satisfied by a third terminal. It is very possible that as the power of the workstation increases, all of these functions will be funneled into a single physical workstation ... it will become the user's window onto that user's professional world. This is becoming increasingly feasible, certainly from a hardware standpoint in terms of the power capability, responsiveness, display clarity, multiple window capability and so forth, that is currently available. Much work still needs to be done in the software area. The final issue is how the user communicates with these systems and how the user responds to the workstation environment. Keyboards are still widely used. However, as we bring these workstations to a wider population much more attention needs to made in the operator interfaces. One can expect to see growing uses of voice input and various kinds of touch sensitive devices. Ergonomic considerations will continue to grow in importance. The European users community has been much more aggressive in imposing ergonomic constraints on workstation suppliers than have been USA users. However, USA suppliers are becoming increasingly sensitive to this issue, and a number of USA manufacturers, such as Control Data and Florida Computer Graphics, have built product lines which successfully address the ergonomics issues.

And, of course, pushing the traditional workstations suppliers are the myriad personal computers whose power is increasing and whose cost is decreasing. Where a conventional workstation vendor ... such as Tektronix or Hewlett Packard ... might measure its sales in thousands or tens of thousands of units, the PC vendors are viewing their sales in hundreds of thousands and millions of units. When we consider that today we carry on our wrists computers that have the power equivalent to a room full of computers several decades ago, the potential for this technology is staggering.

Representative Suppliers of Workstations

ADVANCED ELECTRONICS DESIGN, INC.
440 Potrero Avenue
Sunnyvale, CA 94086
(408) 733-3555

APPLE COMPUTER
20525 Mariani
Cupertino, CA 95014
(408) 996-1010

APOLLO COMPUTER, INC.
15 Elizabeth Drive
Chelmsford, MA 01824
(617) 256-6600

BOEING COMPUTER SERVICES CO.
2810 160th Avenue S. E.
Bellevue, WA 98008
(206) 763-5250

CADLINC, INC.
1872 Brummel Avenue
Elk Grove Village, IL 60007
(312) 228-7300

CADMUS COMPUTER SYSTEMS
600 Suffolk Street
Lowell, MA 01852
(617) 453-2899

CADNETIX CORP.
5797 Central Avenue
Boulder, CO 80301
(303) 444-8075

CADTEC CORPORATION
2355 Old Oakland Road
San Jose, CA 95131
(408) 942-1535

CADTRAK
823 Kifer Road
Sunnyvale, CA 94086
(408) 730-2591

CELEBRITY COMPUTING
9692 Via Excelencia
San Diego, CA 92126
(619) 271-9940

CHROMATICS, INC.
2558 Mountain Industrial Blvd.
Tucker, GA 30084
(404) 493-7000

COMPANION COMPUTER CORPORATION
7404 Washington Avenue South
Eden Prairie, Minnesota 55344
(612) 944-5022

CONVERGENT TECHNOLOGIES
2500 Augustine Drive
Santa Clara, CA 95051
(408) 727-8830

DATA GENERAL CORP.
4400 Computer Drive
Westboro, MA 01580
(617) 366-8911

DECISION GRAPHICS, INC.
11 Main St.
PO Box 306
Southbrorough, MA 01772
(617) 481-4119

DIGITAL EQUIPMENT CORP.
146 Main Street
Maynard, MA 01754
(617) 897-5111

DIPIX, INC.
Rivers Center
10220 Old Columbia Road
Columbia, MD 21046
(301) 992-3900

FLORIDA COMPUTER GRAPHICS
1000 Sand Pond Road
Lake Mary, FL 32746
(305) 321-3000

FUTURENET CORP.
21018 Osborne Street
Canoga Park, CA 91304
(213) 700-0691

GEOBASED SYSTEMS
725 West Morgan Street
Raleigh, NC 27603
(919) 834-9313

GOULD ELECTRONICS
10 Gould Center
Rolling Meadow, IL 60008
(312) 640-4000

HEWLETT PACKARD
19320 Pruneridge Avenue
Cupertino, CA 95014
(408) 996-9800

IBM INSTRUMENTS, INC.
Orchard Park
PO Box 332
Danbury, CT 06810

INFORMATION DISPLAYS, INC.
28 Kaysal Court
Armonk, NY 10504
(914) 273-5755

LEXIDATA
755 Middlesex Tpke.
Billerica, MA 01865
(617) 663-8550

MASSCOMP CORPORATION
One Technology Park
Westford, MA 01886
(617) 692-6200

MICRO CONTROL SYSTEMS, INC.
143 Tunnel Road
Vernon, CT 06066
(203) 872-0602

MOSAIC TECHNOLOGIES, INC.
47 Manning Road
Billerica, MA 01821
(617) 667-2383

MULTIPLE TECHNOLOGIES CORP.
24681 Northwestern Highway
Southfield, Michigen 48075
(313) 353-3300

NBI, INC.
Technical Products Division
3450 Mitchell Lane
Boulder, CO 80301

OMNI CAD CORPORATION
Burleigh Park
Fishers, NY I 4453
(716) 924-4170

ORCATECH, INC.
2680 Queensview Drive
Ottawa, Ontario
CANADA K2B 8H6
(613) 820-9602

PERKIN ELMER CORP.
2 Crescent Place
Oceanport, NJ 07757
(201) 870-4500

PRIME COMPUTER, INC.
Prime Park
Natick, MA 01760
(617) 655-8000

QUBIX GRAPHIC SYSTEMS, INC.
18835 Cox Avenue
Saratoga, CA 95070
(408) 370-9229

RASTER TECHNOLOGIES
9 Executive Park Drive
N. Billerica, MA 01862
(617) 667-8900

RIDGE COMPUTERS
586 Weddell Drive
Sunnyvale, CA 94086
(408) 745-0400

SABER TECHNOLOGY CORP.
2381 Bering Drive
San Jose, CA 95131
(408) 945-9600

SIGMA ELECTRONIC SYSTEMS LTD
Sigma House, North Heath Lane
Horsham, West Sussex RH124UZ
ENGLAND
(0403) 50445

SILICON GRAPHICS
630 Clyde Court
Mountain View, CA 94043
(415) 960-1980

SUN MICROSYSTEMS
2550 Garcia Avenue
Mountain View, CA 94043
(415) 960-1300

SYMBOLICS, INC.
9600 DeSoto Avenue
Chatsworth, CA 91311
(213) 998-3600

TEKTRONIX, INC.
PO Box 500
Beaverton, OR 97077
(503) 644-0161

TELESIS CORP.
21 Alpha Road
Chelmsford, MA 01824
(617) 256-2300

TERAK CORPORATION
14151 N. 76th Street
Scottsdale, Arizona 85260
(602) 998-4800

TEXAS INSTRUMENTS
12501 Research Blvd.
Austin, TX 78769
(512) 250-4356

THREE RIVERS COMPUTER CORP.
720 Gross Street
Pittsburgh, PA 15224
(412) 621-6250

VERSATEC, INC.
2710 Walsh Avenue
Santa Clara, CA 95051
(408) 988-2800

WESTWARD TECHNOLOGY, INC.
5 Cambridge Center
Cambridge, MA 02142
(617) 492-1890

XEROX
PO Box 1600
Stamford, CT
(203) 329-8700

ZYMOS
477 N. Mathilda Avenue
Sunnyvale, CA 94088
(408) 730-8800

Overview of Raster Graphics Hardware

N. I. Badler and I. Carlbom

Raster graphics display systems offer a wide variety of capabilities, features, speeds, and interfaces. Raster architectures and display processers are rapidly maturing to enable faster generation of more complex objects, higher-resolution displays, and more bit-planes for better color. This development is possible largely by more powerful micro-processors and cheaper memory. Hardware is available for fast generation of solid objects. One of the most dominant trends is the development of workstations, which provide integrated software environment with high-bandwidth graphical I/O as the standard user interface.

It is impossible to do justice to all graphics systems developments. We only highlight three important areas. One area is the "basic" raster graphics frame buffer; another is high performance systems which use custom VLSI chips to expand graphics function performance to near real-time solid object rendering; and the third is the incorporation of graphics display systems (usually relying on bit-mapped graphics) into complete workstations.

Raster Graphics Frame Buffers

A considerable number of vendors manufacture raster graphics frame buffers. These range from single board "add-on" graphics for micros to sophisticated microprogrammable graphics engines. Cost is related in obvious ways to spatial resolution, color resolution, speed, and additional graphics features.

The presentation will show several examples of such displays, but we will not discuss them here for two reasons: (1) they generally have straightforward architectures (as noted in the previous lecture), and (2) there are literally dozens of vendors making such equipment. Highlights from the SIGGRAPH '84 exhibition will be shown.

Two points are worth noting, however: raster graphics is ubiquitous in the personal computer arena, and low cost terminals are increasingly offered with graphics options. It is probably safe to claim that graphics, and especially color graphics, has significantly catalyzed the personal, as well as the small(-ish) business computer marketplace. It is not a great step from a personal computer to a workstation (see below). A short, but handy discussion of personal computers may be found in [1].

Relatively low cost terminals may now be found with, for example, VT100 protocols for direct terminal (character manipulation) use, Tektronix 401x compatibility, and an innate graphics mode. Retrofit boards to add graphics capabilities (usually as a Tektronix 401x emulator) to a VT100-type terminal are quite popular.

High Performance Raster Graphics Systems

There are a number of high performance raster graphics systems available. In general, high performance means faster line or polygon throughput for more "real-time" display update, and shaded or visible polygon renderings for more realism. We briefly examine the IRIS Graphics System, Seillac 7, Lexidata Solidview, Raster Technologies Model 1 series, and the Weitek Tiling Engine.

The IRIS Graphics System [2,3] is a peripheral frame-buffer system which has a processing pipeline similar to that of high-performance vector systems, where several graphics operations occur simultaneously in a sequential set of processors. The central part of the graphics processing pipeline, the geometry subsystem, consists of 12 identical VLSI chips [2]. The chips can be programmed to do dot products, clipping, and scaling. Typically, the pipeline is configured such that the first four chips perform matrix multiplication, the next six clipping, and last two scaling to screen coordinates. One significant difference between this processing pipeline and those of high-performance vector systems (other than it generates solids) is that the geometry engines operate on floating point data.

The IRIS system can be configured as a terminal or as a workstation. The terminal consists of a Motorola 68000 and a geometry-chip pipeline. In the terminal version, the graphics application runs on a host and generates display list commands which are interpreted by the MC68000 and the geometry pipeline. The workstation may have a second processor, a Motorola 68010 which functions as the host. The MC68010 runs Bell Laboratories' UNIX, and can run as a node in an Ethernet environment. The IRIS software includes a window manager which supports mixed text and 3D graphics. Thus, this graphics workstation has a complete environment of operating system, programming languages, tools for program developments, as well as facilities for high-performance three-dimensional graphics.

The performance specifications indicate that 65,000 3D coordinate transformations can be performed per second. If polygons are being displayed, each with an average of four coordinates, then line drawing throughput would be around 16,000 polygons per second. At a 30Hz update rate, about 500 polygons can be manipulated in "real-time."

At the present, IRIS is a 1024x1024 system with a maximum of 12 bit planes for color and shading. The visible surface display algorithm "built-into" the IRIS system is a two-pass priority sort microcoded in the MC68000. The number of polygons that can be processed is therefore limited by the available memory and the time cost of the sort.

Another high performance system is Seillac 7[4]. This is a recent device from Japan, introduced in the United States at SIGGRAPH '83. It has an architecture based on pipelined independent processors and custom VLSI circuits. The channel processor, I/O device controller, display processor, and coordinate transformation processor are separately structured. One option is a 32 bit floating point processor for coordinate transformations. The device interprets a hierarchic display file stored locally. Color shading, polygon filling, and line anti-aliasing are also performed locally into a specially designed frame buffer.

The architecture has been designed support Core-like display techniques (temporary and retained segments) as well as faster modes for direct display and bit-map operations.

The basic system offers 1400x1024 resolution with 12 bit planes, expandable to 24. Since the planes are double-buffered for faster updates, a 12 bit system actually contains 24 planes.

The current specifications include 3D transformation hardware, polygon clipping, 0.5 Mbyte user display list memory (expandable to 8 Mbytes), anti-aliased lines, 400,000 short vectors/second, 20,000 filled polygons/second, and 18 deep segment transformation nesting. Since a line requires 16 bytes of display memory, the standard system (0.5 Mbyte) will hold about 32,000 vectors. At 200,000 vectors/second (in the temporary or retained mode), a full 0.5 Mbyte display list can be refreshed at about 6Hz, or about 6,000 vectors at 30Hz. Assuming about four vectors per polygon, the Seillac 7 should be able to display about 1,500 polygons at 30Hz (about three times more than the IRIS, based on the published specifications).

The display has automatic z-cueing of lines and the ability to smoothly change the intensity or color of a line along its length. Polygon filling and normal vector shading is done in hardware. Visible surface processing, if required, is done in host resident CITRUS software.

Other frame buffers with visible surface processing based on z-buffer bit planes are the Lexidata Solidview and the Raster Technologies 1/25S and 1/80 systems. Solidview offers 12 bits of color and 10 bits of depth per pixel; the Raster Technologies systems offer 24 bits of color and 12 bits of depth. The 1/80 system offers 1000 lines, while the others are medium resolution (around 640x525).

If an installation has an existing high resolution frame buffer, but wants to take advantage of emerging micro technology to improve polygon processing time, the Weitek Tiling Engine may be suitable. The Tiling Engine is an attached processor with 24 bit planes that can be employed to extend an existing 1280x1024 graphics system. The Tiling Engine accepts solid objects represented as polygons, and renders these polygons through a z-buffer algorithm. Of the 24 bit planes, 12 are dedicated to the z-buffer. Incoming (unsorted) concave or convex polygons of up to 256 sides are each decomposed into triangles before tiling, shaded using Gouraud or Phong methods, and then rendered into the z-buffer. Tiling throughput is quoted at approximately 1 msec per triangle; or about 1000 triangles per second.

A transformation processor has been added to form the Weitek Solids Modeling Engine which interprets and displays curved surface (B-spline, Bezier, and Coons) patches. It can tesselate, transform (including perspective divide), clip, scale, light model (with multiple light sources), and shade 120 patches (tesselated into 6000 triangles) in about 3 seconds.

Other features include cutting planes, cross sections, contouring, patterning, and edge highlighting. A transparency effect is available using patterned tiles. Direct polygon picking from the screen is also supported. One option is a polygon (or patch) buffer for local (fast) polygon (patch) editing.

The Solids Modeling Engine can be integrated with a variety of host and graphics terminals, as well as with some workstations.

Workstations

Workstations are built around several principles: (1) each user has a single dedicated CPU, (2) the users are connected through a network, and (3) the user interfaces to the CPU through a high-resolution bitmap display.

The primary applications area for the workstations are not necessarily computer graphics, but they all employ some form of graphics for general interaction, and the workstations support at least some primitive graphics functions. We will briefly review three workstations (or families of workstations) which support a varying degree of graphics functions. As we will see in the next section, a high-performance, three-dimensional graphics system is also designed around the workstation paradigm.

The first family of workstations, the Xerox D-machines, consists of the Dorado (Xerox 1132), the Dolphin (the Xerox 1100), and the Dandelion (The Xerox 1108) which represent a set of extremely powerful workstations, designed primarily for Artificial Intelligence applications. The Dorado, the most powerful of the systems, has the processing power of more than five times that of a Vax 11/780 when running Lisp. (For arithmetic it does not compare as favorably.) The Dandelion runs at about one-third the speed of the Dorado, and the Dolphin at one-tenth the speed. The Dorado can be configured with as much as 8Mbytes of memory; the Dolphin and the Dandelion start at 1.15M and 1.5M bytes of main memory, respectively. The D-Machines have facilities for interfacing to a local communications network.

The D-machines include a high-resolution (1024 x 808 pixels) black-and-white display, and the Dorado can also be equipped with a color display (480 x 640 pixels) with up to 256 colors. The interaction is done through a keyboard and a mouse. The D-machines run Interlisp-D, but Smalltalk and Mesa are also available. Interlisp-D provides simple raster graphics functions: a bit-block operation with texturing, text with multiple fonts, lines, and spline curves. Interlisp-D also provides a display management system which supports multiple windows, menus, and a set of graphics utilities. The graphics functions are integrated into Interlisp-D, which makes it easy to experiment with graphical user interfaces.

The Apollo DOMAIN system is a high-performance local area network of dedicated processors (the DN660, the DN460, and DN300). The highest performance processor, the DN660, is designed around a proprietary 32 bit bit-slice CPU and a 16 bit bit-slice display processor. The DN660 can be configured with up to 4 Mbytes of main memory and 2 Mbytes of display memory. The DN660 can be equipped with a high-resolution (1024 x 1024 pixels) display with up to 256 colors or a medium resolution display (512 x 512 pixels) with full color capabilities (24 bit planes).

The Apollo systems run a proprietary UNIX-like operating system, which supports network wide virtual memory management and interprocess communication. FORTRAN-77, PASCAL and C are available. The operating system's display manager provides multiple windows, with independent processes operating in each window. The interactive graphics functions can run either under the display manager or control the entire display screen.

The display processor performs a variety of graphics functions, such as bit-block transfers, raster operations, vector generation, area fills, and tile fills. High-level graphics software is provided by the ACM SIGGRAPH Core package, which is available from all languages. Apollo also provides icon-driven electronic spread sheets, mail, calendar, and document preparation, and a large variety of application software is available from third party vendors in, e.g., finite element analysis, CAD/CAM, and modeling. The Weitek Solids Modelling Engine has been interfaced with an Apollo system to provide real-time raster graphics. Other workstations, such as the Sun workstations, are built around standard microprocessors, operating systems, and network protocols. The Sun workstations are built around a MC68010 with up to 4 Mbytes of main memory, runs full UNIX 4.2, and support the Ethernet local area network. The Sun workstations support 220 standard UNIX utilities, a multi-window display manager, an implementation of the ACM SIGGRAPH Core graphics package, and high-level third party application programs, to provide a powerful computing environment.

The Sun Workstations employ custom VLSI chips to implement raster operations. The Sun Workstations support high-resolution (1152 x 900 pixels) black-and-white displays, and medium resolution (640 x 480 pixels) color display with 8 bit-planes. The color monitor is used as a peripheral to the monochrome workstation, and the system software, such as the window manager, cannot run on the color monitor.

The IRIS Graphics system is also available in a workstation configuration with UNIX as the local operating system.

Acknowledgements

Much of this information has been freely borrowed from [1] jointly written for Eurographics 1984 by the authors.

References

[1] Badler, N. I., and I. Carlbom, The Computer Graphics Scene in the United States, Proc. Eurographics 1984.

[2] Clark, J. H., The geometry engine: A VLSI geometry system for graphics, Computer Graphics 16(3) (July 1982) 127-133.

[3] Clark, J. H., and T. Davis, Work station unites real-time graphics with UNIX, Ethernet, Electronics (Oct. 1983) 113-119.

[4] Ikedo, Tsuneo High speed techniques for a 3D color graphics terminal, IEEE Computer Graphics and Applications 4(5) (May 1984) 46-58.

Scan Conversion

N. I. Badler

1. Scan converting simple primitives

The concept of SCAN CONVERSION is important in raster graphics since any shape which is to be drawn into the frame buffer must first be decomposed into pixels lying in a regular raster grid pattern. Typical shapes which the graphics display generator may scan convert are POINTS, LINES, RECTANGLES, CIRCLES, CONICS, DISKS, CHARACTERS, SPECIAL SYMBOLS, ICONS, BITMAPS, PATTERNS, and POLYGONS, as well as REGIONS defined by or bounded by pixel values in the frame buffer itself. Some of the perceived power of a raster graphics display depends on the primitive vocabulary of scan converted shapes: the more that are handled by the display processor, the better.

For the most part, we will assume that the shape primitives are supplied to the scan converter in integer device coordinates. We will permit the coordinates to fall outside the physical screen limits; various CLIPPING procedures will insure that only the on-screen (or within viewport) portions are actually drawn. Occasionally we shall permit shape coordinates to be specified as real numbers over the same screen grid. In this way we can easily extend the discussion to the scan conversion of anti-aliased versions of the primitive shapes.

Given the brief presentation, we will be able to just touch on the technical issues, and so a significant bibliography is included. Much of this material can be found in very accessible form in books [13][23] and thus no algorithms will be explicitly given here. The purpose of these notes is to present the scope and pertinent issues surrounding the process of scan conversion.

1.1 Points

The point is the simplest graphical primitive. There are interesting problems, however, if a point is allowed to have real coordinates in which case it must be created by anti-aliasing techniques.

1.1.1 Without anti-aliasing

If the point is visible, write the corresponding pixel. The point is not displayed if it lies outside the screen boundary or the current viewport.

1.1.2 With anti-aliasing

Crow's algorithm [7] will display a dot at any real coordinate location on the screen grid. It represents the display spot as a finite (approximate) Gaussian function, and distributes the point's intensity over three or four adjacent pixels.

1.2 Lines - Incremental schemes

Lines have historically been one of the most basic shapes required of a scan converter. A number of methods exist, mostly characterized by INCREMENTAL calculation and an avoidance of floating point arithmetic. Such a method is given by Bresenham [4][13]. A consequence of the raster grid is that scan converted lines are broken up into short horizontal or vertical sub-segments (unless the line is exactly at an integer multiple of 45 degrees). The process of smoothing (anti-aliasing or dejagging) the line to make it appear as a single, continuous (slanted) line can be done in a number of ways; these are sketched below.

Line clipping to the screen or viewport is a necessary and simple, though non-trivial, task. The method of Sutherland and Cohen is the most common [13]. It is more efficient to clip the line before scan conversion than to discard points generated by scan conversion which happen to lie outside the viewport.

1.2.1 Without anti-aliasing

Bresenham's algorithm works by using an easily computed DECISION VARIABLE to decide which of the two possible next points for a line is actually closer to the real line. Rather than compute the initial value of the decision variable based on the line slope (which would require a real division), one end of the line is translated to the origin (0,0) and the value found by simple arithmetic using the x- and y-extents of the line. Once the initial decision variable is obtained, succeeding ones are computed by simple integer addition, subtraction, and binary shifts (multiplication by 2).

1.2.2 With anti-aliasing

Essentially these techniques fall into two classes: those that modify the incremental line scan converter algorithm to utilize the known error (from the decision variable) between the actual line coordinates and the available screen pixel coordinates [7][14], and those that model the line as a finite width polygon [6]. The former are generally simple and fast enough to be implemented in hardware, but the latter are more general in that they permit arbitrary width lines and proper derivation of the background color at line boundaries.

1.3 Circles

There are several poor ways to scan convert circles: computing sines and cosines while incrementing a small angle is perhaps the worst. Incremental methods for high quality raster circles have been devised [24][5][16][9][20]. These take advantage of the eight-fold symmetry of the circle when its center is positioned over an integral grid point.

Circle clipping can be done on a point by point basis.

Recently, Field has shown how to incrementally generate anti-aliased circles whose centers and radii need not be integral [11].

1.4 Characters, symbols, and patterns

There are basically two ways to store characters and related symbols. The first method stores their component shapes simply as lines, often called STROKE TABLES. The character is scan converted by processing each of its lines. The other method stores a matrix or bit-map of the various pixels and their values to be set when the matrix is actually positioned in some like-sized region of the display. Scan conversion here is simply a matter of setting pixels in the correct region.

1.4.1 Stroke tables

A stroke table is a sequence of incremental moving and drawing commands which define a shape. The individual lines are clipped as needed by the usual line clipper. The character or symbol may be scaled larger or smaller as needed without compromising its shape, though very small characters will suffer from aliasing problems unless steps are taken to dejag lines. Stroke characters are easily rotated or skewed to arbitrary angles, and are especially effective when considered as three-dimensional shapes. Proportional spacing of characters is simple to effect, since the end point of each character may be explicitly given in the table by the final move.

1.4.2 Bitmaps

Usually a graphics display processor will have built into its firmware bitmap representations for all the printable ASCII characters, often in more than one size. If different sized bitmaps are allowed, characters may be proportionally spaced by beginning the next character at the edge of the adjacent one.

The character bitmaps can be scaled up by factors of two, often independently in each dimension. Arbitrary scaling and rotation is quite difficult and must utilize sophisticated sampling techniques. Anti-aliasing may be built into the bitmap [7][31]. Pixels in the bitmap which lie outside the character or symbol may be written into the frame buffer (replacing the previous values) or treated as transparent (letting the previous values "show through").

Special graphics characters, or user-definable characters may be offered. Sometimes a vendor will offer a customer a special character set burned into a PROM in the character generator.

A pattern is a bitmap which can be used by the hardware to fill a region (see below), or sometimes determine a line style during line scan conversion.

2. Scan converting regions

One of the primary attractions of a raster display is the ability to shade solid areas. We can distinguish several cases: where the shape is already defined by some collection of pixels in the frame buffer; where the shape is characterized by a few simple parameters, and where the shape is an polygon. We will deal with the first two cases in this section, and the polygon case by itself in the last section.

Besides the discussion of these filling techniques in [13], a very thorough treatment of the many possible unusual cases and details of several algorithms and their relative efficiency may be found in Pavlidis' book [23]. Other references include [29][21].

A common requirement in scan converting regions is the ability to READBACK pixel values from the frame buffer. This is because the algorithms use the implicit shape defined by the pixel values already present to delimit the filled region. (In the case of scan converting polygons, on the other hand, the fill boundary is given explicitly as a list of line segment edges.)

There are two types of ADJACENCY possible in raster grids: 4-CONNECTED and 8-CONNECTED. In 4-connected adjacency, pixels are considered adjacent if they share a common top, bottom, left, or right edge; in 8-connected adjacency, the four corner pixels are also neighbors. In general, 4-connectedness is better for "foreground" objects, while 8-connectedness is better for the "background." In practice, the user is typically given the choice.

The first two of the three classes of algorithms given below also require the presence of a SEED pixel, supplied by the user, which is known to lie inside the desired region. It may be difficult for a program to determine a seed point algorithmically except in rather simple cases (such as when the region is known to be convex). The third type of fill, parity fill, does not require a seed, but introduces a number of unique complications that are, nevertheless, soluble.

2.1 Flood-fill algorithms

A FLOOD-FILL algorithm [13][22][28] operates on a given existing color in the frame buffer. One such point with that color is selected as the seed, and a new pixel value (color) is given. Any pixels adjacent to the seed having its original value are set to the new value. This process continues recursively until the entire connected region defined by the original seed's value are changed to the new value.

2.2 Boundary-fill algorithms

The BOUNDARY-FILL algorithm [13] is slightly different from flood-fill. In boundary fill the shape to be filled is implicitly delimited by pixels of a given boundary value. When any pixel interior to the boundary is specified, and a new value supplied which is NOT presently in the interior of the implied region, that value is propagated recursively to (4- or 8-connected neighbors) from the seed until the interior is colored entirely in the new value.

Although very simple to state and code, the recursive form of boundary-fill makes somewhat inefficient use of the programming language by relying on its system stack. Pavlidis offers an iterative version in [23].

Recent efforts to create boundary fills with boundaries having two or three colors have been reported [12].

2.3 Parity fill algorithms

The parity fill algorithm is very similar in spirit to the polygon filling algorithms to be discussed below: if there is a bounded region of the two-dimensional pixel plane then a scan-line should alternately enter and leave the region as it crosses the boundary. The notion of PARITY arises due to the observation that runs (sequences) of scanline pixels must be in one of these two states, and must alternate between them. These algorithms, as noted above, do not require a seed pixel and work on arbitrary closed regions. Discussions of parity fill algorithms appear in [23][10].

In EDGE-FILL [1][10] all pixels to the left (say) of the boundary are inverted as the boundary is traversed from any particular starting point on the boundary. (It may be argued that distinguishing such a point makes it a seed, but this is not so. The seed in the above algorithms is distinct and interior to the filling boundary (which we presume to know) while the boundary for parity fill is already available or else is easily found by linear search along a scan line until a pixel of the desired value is encountered.) All pixels outside the region will be inverted an even number of times (once as we pass "down" one side of the contour and once as we pass back "up," since the region is closed. Of course, with non-convex regions a pixel may be inverted several (pairs of) times as the boundary wiggles up and down, but closure insures that they will in fact occur in pairs. By this argument, all pixels within the boundary, therefore, will be inverted an odd number of times, that is, filled.

In a minor variation of edge-fill, the scanline pixel inversion may be performed up to some arbitrary vertical line rather than the left edge of the screen. This line resembles a fence, hence the algorithm is called FENCE-FILL [1]. By choosing the fence from some pixel contained in the region boundary, fewer pixels need be inverted.

By using a scanline buffer, another variant called PAIRWISE-FILL can be defined. Although optimal for convex regions, its performance is quite non-optimal for certain cases such as spiral shapes [10].

2.4 Special cases: Rectangles and disks

There are two special cases where region filling may be done in an iterative (non-recursive) fashion: orthogonal rectangles and arbitrary disks.

Rectangles are almost always found as a primitive of the graphics display processor, since filling an entire rectangular region between two opposite corners is a matter of straightforward array addressing. Rectangle clipping is simply accomplished by checking the rectangle corners against the viewport corners and replacing the former by the latter where the rectangle exceeds the viewport.

For integral corners, anti-aliasing is unnecessary. For non-integral corners, it is probably easiest to treat the rectangle like a regular polygon (see below).

Disks are a bit more difficult. Filling algorithms are possible, but slow, and depend on frame buffer read-back and the existing pixel values. The alternative is to create the disk directly by incremental methods. Badler [2] adapted Horn's algorithm [16] to fill disks with real centers and radii: in this most general case the disk is generated in scanline order. Other disk scan conversions are reported [9][20]. Field creates anti-aliased disks incrementally [11]. An area-weighting scheme was also used by Badler in rendering smooth images of spheres [3].

Disk clipping is simple since all methods decompose the disk into easily clipped horizontal lines, vertical lines, or rectangular elements.

3. Scan converting polygons

One of the most useful primitives that a graphics display can "understand" is the polygon. If a general polygon primitive exists, then wide lines and filled (stroke-based) characters are also obtained. Given as an ordered list of vertices, the polygon can be scan converted into the frame buffer as a solid (or patterned) area, possibly with color interpolation between the vertices, or a different edge color.

By a polygon is meant a CLOSED ORDERED sequence of line segments specified by their endpoints. The lines are not allowed to cross one another, either at a real or implicit vertex, nor be superimposed along any subset of their length: the polygon is SIMPLE. By allowing the polygon to have more than one boundary loop, multiple component polygons or polygons with HOLES may be created. If there is one component entirely contained within another, then the interior of the contained one is usually considered outside the polygon. To avoid semantic difficulties, one adopts some convention such as "the inside of the polygon is always to the left of the edge as we traverse its ordered edge list." With this rule we can unambiguously determine whether an enclosed polygon component is a hole or not.

It is worth noting that the topology of the two-dimensional plane permits the splitting of any convex or concave (planar) polygon with holes into one single (concave) polygon without holes. The essential idea is that one starts at an outside boundary vertex and creates two new edges to a nearby hole: one edge continues the exterior boundary to the hole, the other (exactly superimposed) takes the interior hole boundary back to the exterior. For multiple holes the process is iterated as needed. (The superimposed lines may be eliminated by a slight displacement of their coincident vertices.)

In order to avoid faulty scan conversion problems, the polygon must be clipped to the screen (or viewport) space first. If the polygon is two-dimensional, the new method described by Liang and Barsky [17][18] may be used. If the polygon is three-dimensional, the Sutherland-Hodgman algorithm must be used [30][13]. The main point of these algorithms is that the polygon must be maintained as a simple closed curve in order for filling by scan conversion to be effected. It is not possible to simply clip each of the polygon's constituent lines.

3.1 Convex polygon methods

Let us assume for the present that the polygon we wish to scan convert is closed, simple, clipped, and convex. We will also assume that the vertex coordinates are real numbers.

3.1.1 Scanline method

Given such a convex polygon, each scanline of the display will intersect the polygon in either two, one, or zero places. By shifting any polygon coordinates which happen to fall exactly on an integer scanline coordinate a fraction of a unit (e.g. half) up or down, the case of one intersection may be eliminated. Since the polygon is closed, any scanline with two intersections must therefore start outside the polygon, intersect one edge, proceed through the interior to the other intersection, and finally end in the exterior. By filling the portion in the interior over all such scanlines with two intersections, we fill the polygon.

In practice, an efficient data structure is created to hold polygon edges sorted by y (scanline), and maintain the intersections as they march along the edges. At most two polygon edges are active (i.e. have intersection points) on any one scanline. The active edges can change only as the lower y-coordinate of a vertex is passed. This SCANLINE COHERENCE property speeds the scan conversion considerably. Moreover, the linear character of the edges permits the intersection points to be calculated incrementally (EDGE COHERENCE).

If the polygon is defined in 3D, a similar incremental calculation gives the changing depth of the polygon along the scanline. This fact is used to great advantage in z-buffer systems for visible surface renderings.

3.1.2 Trapezoid fill

The special case of a convex polygon whose top and bottom are parallel to scanlines has been investigated [19]. Degenerate top or bottom edges are allowed (creating triangles). For trapezoids the convex polygon edge lists degenerate to one edge for each side and no polygon vertices are encountered.

3.1.3 Triangle fill

This is also a special case of a convex polygon. All configurations may be explicitly enumerated. An attractive feature of triangles is that they are always planar (unless degenerate); thus a 3D polygon shader can easily fill the triangular region without worrying about possible non-linearity while interpolating the coordinates of the corners.

3.2 General polygon methods

A general polygon scan converter must work with either convex or concave polygons, possibly with holes. There are two possible approaches: confront the problem directly as a generalization of the scanline method above, or decompose the polygon into managable convex pieces.

3.2.1 Scanline method

The scanline method for convex polygons can be generalized by noting that a scanline must intersect the polygon in an even number of points (excluding polygons with vertices or edges coincident with scanlines) [23][13]. If this is the case, the scanline will begin outside the polygon and alternately enter and leave it with each edge intersection. (Interior contained polygons are therefore considered to be holes; if a hole in turn contains a polygon, that polygon is then considered to surround polygon interior, and so on.) Filling is simply a matter of writing color or pattern into the alternating scan line segments in the interior.

The polygon edges are still sorted into scanline ordered lists, but now more than two edges may be active at a time. Again, the active edges can change only as the lower y-coordinate of a vertex is passed. Incremental edge intersections are computed for each active edge.

3.2.2 Decomposing into convex polygons

Since we have already considered the convex polygon case, one possibility to to take the concave polygon and decompose it into convex pieces [21]. A number of algorithms have been used, including decomposition into trapezoids [19], triangles [27][33][15], and any convenient convex shapes [26]. These algorithms generally require time on the order of n log n, where n is the number of polygon vertices. Since the direct, scanline method sorts the vertices anyway, it is not clear whether any computation is actually saved by decomposing. (A bit of thought will show, for example, that the decomposition into trapezoids is nearly exactly what the sorted multiple active edge list in scanline processing must do anyway.) It is, however, easier for hardware (firmware) design to leave the burden of decomposition on the user's program and only implement the simplest cases!

3.2.3 Anti-aliasing issues

Since polygons are so useful, we should like to anti-alias them to improve their appearance on the display. Unfortunately we cannot just scan convert the polygon and then go back and anti-alias the edges, since this would leave darker pixels near the boundary (but definitely in the interior) of the shape. One solution [25] is to anti-alias the edges as the polygon is being filled. At each edge the slope is known, and that value can be used to estimate the amount of polygon color edge pixels must receive. The slope is computed once for each edge; simple incremental arithmetic provides the other values along the edge during scan line processing.

Two problems with this method are the possible generation of incorrect colors at vertices, and poor blends with the background [32]. We cannot always assume that polygons (or any other scan converted shape, for that matter) will always lie on a uniform black background. To handle the general case, filtering, supersampling [8], or area–computation techniques [6] must be employed.

References

[1] Ackland, B.D., and N.H. Weste, The edge flag algorithm – A fill method for raster scan displays, IEEE Trans. on Computers C-30(1) (Jan. 1981) 41-47.

[2] Badler, N.I., Disk generators for a raster display device, Computer Graphics and Image Processing 6(6) (Dec. 1977) 589-593.

[3] Badler, N.I., J. O'Rourke, and H. Toltzis, A spherical representation of a human body for visualizing movement, IEEE Proceedings 67(10) (Oct. 1979) 1397-1403.

[4] Bresenham, J.E., Algorithm for computer control of digital plotter, IBM Systems J. 4(1) (1965) 25-30.

[5] Bresenham, J.E., A linear algorithm for incremental digital display of circular arcs, Comm. of the ACM 20(2) (Feb. 1977) 100-106.

[6] Catmull, E., A hidden surface algorithm with anti–aliasing, Computer Graphics 12(3) (Aug. 1978) 6-11.

[7] Crow, F.C., The use of grayscale for improved raster displays of vectors and characters, Computer Graphics 12(3) (Aug. 1978) 1-5.

[8] Crow, F.C., A comparison of antialiasing techniques, IEEE Computer Graphics and Applications 1(1) (Jan. 1981) 40-49.

[9] Doros, M., Algorithms for generation of discrete circles, rings, and disks, Computer Graphics and Image Processing 10(4) (Aug. 1979) 366-371.

[10] Dunlavey, M.R., Efficient polygon–filling algorithms for raster displays, ACM Trans. on Graphics 2(4) (Oct. 1983) 264-273.

[11] Field, D., Algorithms for drawing simple geometric objects on raster displays, PhD Diss., Technical Report 314, Dept. of Electrical Engineering and Computer Science, Princeton Univ., Princeton, NJ (June 1983).

[12] Fishkin, K.P., and B.A. Barsky, A family of new algorithms for soft filling (Extended Abstract), Proc. Graphics Interface '84, Ottawa, Canada (May 1984) 181-185.

[13] Foley, J.D., and A. van Dam, Fundamentals of Interactive Computer Graphics. Addison-Wesley, Reading, MA, 1982.

[14] Fujimoto, A., and K. Iwata, Jag-free images on raster displays, IEEE Computer Graphics and Applications 3(9) (Dec. 1983) 26-34.

[15] Fujimoto, A., C. Perrott, and K. Iwata A 3-D graphics display system with depth buffer and pipeline processor, IEEE Computer Graphics and Applications 4(6) (June 1984) 11-23.

[16] Horn, B.K.P., Circle generator for display devices, Computer Graphics and Image Processing 5 (1976) 280-288.

[17] Liang, Y.-D., and B.A. Barsky, An analysis and algorithm for polygon clipping, Comm. of the ACM 26(11) (Nov. 83) 868-877.

[18] Liang, Y.-D., and B.A. Barsky, Corrigendum: An analysis and algorithm for polygon clipping, Comm. of the ACM 27(2) (Feb. 84) 151.

[19] Little, W.D., and R. Heuft, An area shading graphics display system, IEEE Trans. on Computers C-28(7) (July 1979) 528-531.

[20] McIlroy, M.D., Best approximations to circles on integer grids, ACM Trans. on Graphics 2(4) (Oct. 1983) 237-263.

[21] Pavlidis, T., _Structural Pattern Recognition_. Springer-Verlag, New York, 1977.

[22] Pavlidis, T., Contour filling in raster images, Computer Graphics 15(3) (Aug. 1981) 29-36.

[23] Pavlidis, T., _Algorithms for Graphics and Image Processing_. Computer Science Press, Rockville, MD, 1982.

[24] Pitteway, M., Algorithm for drawing ellipses or hyperbolae with digital plotter, Computer Journal 10(3) (Nov. 1967) 282-289.

[25] Pitteway, M., and D. Watkinson, Bresenham's algorithm with grey scale, Comm. of the ACM 23(11) (Nov. 1980) 625-626.

[26] Schachter, B., Decomposition of polygons into convex sets, IEEE Trans. on Computers C-27(11) (Nov. 1978) 1078-1082.

[27] Shamos, M., Computational geometry, PhD Diss., Yale Univ. (May 1978).

[28] Shani, U., Filling regions in binary raster images: A graph-theoretic approach, Computer Graphics 14(3) (July 1980) 321-327.

[29] Smith, A.R., Tint fill, Computer Graphics 13(2) (Aug. 1979) 276-283.

[30] Sutherland, I.E., and G.W. Hodgman, Reentrant polygon clipping, Comm. of the ACM 17(1) (Jan. 1974) 32-42.

[31] Warnock, J., The display of characters using grey level sample arrays, Computer Graphics 14(3) (July 1980) 302-307.

[32] Whitted, Turner, "Anti-aliased line drawing using brush extrusion," _Computer Graphics_ 17(3), July 1983, pp. 151-156.

[33] Wordenweber, B., Surface triangulation for picture production, IEEE Computer Graphics and Applications 3(8) (Nov. 1983) 45-51.

Fast Spheres, Shadows, Textures, Transparencies, and Image Enhancements in Pixel-Planes[1]

H. Fuchs, J. Goldfeather, J. P. Hultquist, S. Spach, J. D. Austin, F. P. Brooks, Jr., J. G. Eyles, and J. Poulton

Abstract

Pixel-planes is a logic-enhanced memory system for raster graphics and imaging. Although each pixel-memory is enhanced with a one-bit ALU, the system's real power comes from a tree of one-bit adders that can evaluate linear expressions $Ax + By + C$ for every pixel (x, y) simultaneously, as fast as the ALUs and the memory circuits can accept the results. We and others have begun to develop a variety of algorithms that exploit this fast linear expression evaluation capability. In this paper we report some of those results. Illustrated in this paper is a sample image from a small working prototype of the Pixel-planes hardware and a variety of images from simulations of a full-scale system. Timing estimates indicate that 30,000 smooth shaded triangles can be generated per second, or 21,000 smooth-shaded and shadowed triangles can be generated per second, or over 25,000 shaded spheres can be generated per second. Image-enhancement by adaptive histogram equalization can be performed within 4 seconds on a 512 x 512 image.

1. Introduction

The Pixel-planes development grew out of earlier designs for speeding up raster image generation (Fuchs 1977; Johnson 1979). An enhanced design is described in (Clark 1980). In these designs, the task of generating pixels is distributed between several dozen processors. Even when we were designing these systems, we realized that the bottleneck in raster image generation was "pushing pixels," since bottlenecks earlier in the image generation pipeline could be eliminated by fast arithmetic hardware. Two present examples are the Weitek multiplier chips (Weitek) and a custom "geometry engine" chip (Clark 1982). The limitation of these earlier systems that we sought to overcome with Pixel-planes was that once the number of processors increases to one per memory chip, the bottleneck becomes data movement into the chip. Even if the processor were much faster than the memory chip, in any one memory cycle, only one address-data pair can be put into the chip. Pixel-planes attempts to overcome this limitation by putting computation logic right onto the memory chip, with an entire tree of processing circuits generating many pixels's worth of data in each memory cycle.

Central to the design is an array of logic-enhanced memory chips that form the frame buffer. These chips not only store the scanned-out image but also perform the pixel-level

---

[1] This research supported in part by the Defense Advance Research Project Agency, monitored by the U.S. Army Research Office, Research Triangle Park, NC, under contract number DAAG29-83-K-0148 and the National Science Foundation Grant number ECS-8300970

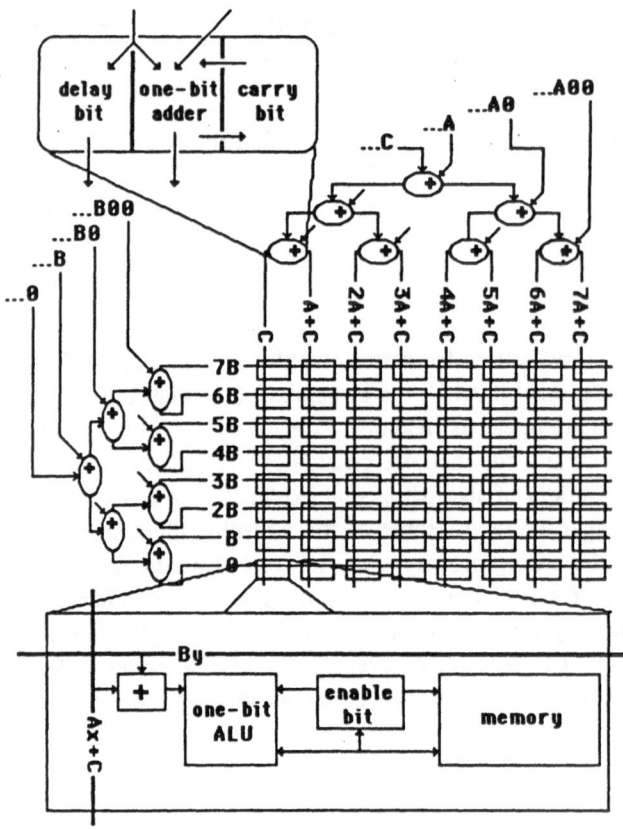

Fig. 1. Conceptual design of an 8 x 8 Pixel-planes chip

calculations of area-definition, visibility calculation and pixel painting. Recently, various individuals have devised other algorithms for the Pixel-planes engine — for computing shadwos, sphere displays, and even image processing tasks. It is increasingly evident that the structure of the machine has greater generality and applicability than first imagined.

Although to many first-time observes Pixel-planes appears to be a variant of the parallel processor with a processor at every pixel, its power and speed come more from the binary tree of one-bit adders that efficiently compute a linear expression in x and y for every pixel in the entire system. Given coefficients A, B, and C, the two multiplier trees and a one-bit adder at each pixel compute $F(x, y) = Ax + By + C$ in bit-sequential order for each (x, y) on the screen (see Fig. 1). If this expression had to be calculated at each pixel with only the one-bit pixel processor alone, the system would take 20 times as long to complete the calculation!

For efficiency in the actual chip layout, the two multiplier trees have been merged into a single-tree and that tree compressed into a single column. Thus, the system contains a unified multiplier tree, a one-bit ALU at each pixel, a one-bit Enable register (controlling write operations of that pixel), and 32 bits of memory (72 bits in the Pxpl4 implementation now being built). Figure 2 illustrates the organization that is used on the actual memory chips.

The system is driven by a transformation engine, which sends vertices of the database to the *translator*. This board converts this data to a series on linear equations which describe

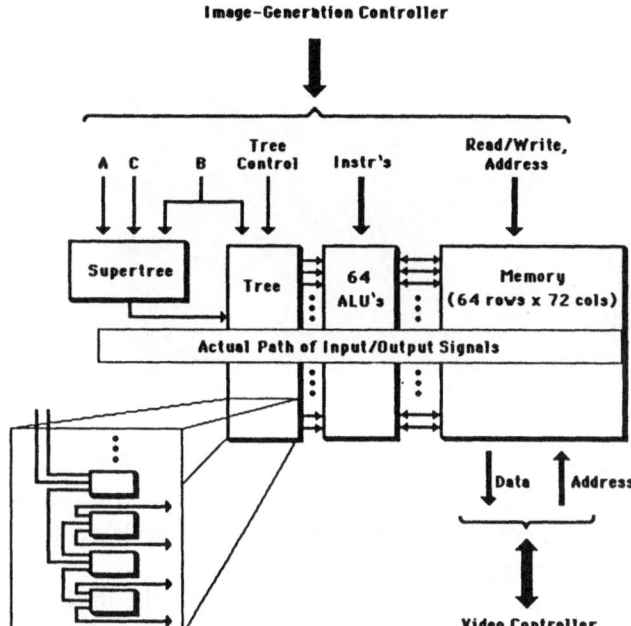

Fig. 2. Floor plan of Pixel-planes 4 chip

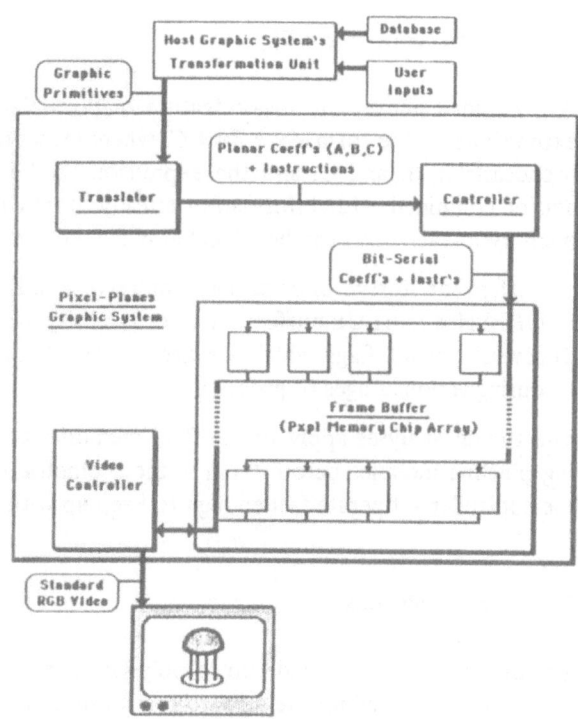

Fig. 3. Logical overview of a 3D graphics system using Pixel-Planes image buffer memory chips

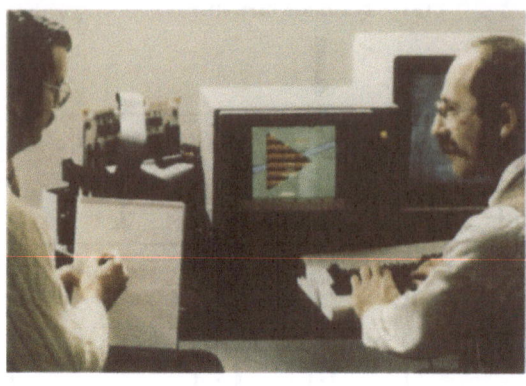

Fig. 4. Pixel-Planes 3 System. John Poulton (left) and Henry Fuchs and the working Pixel-Planes 3 prototype (photo by Jerry Markatos)

the location of each polygon in screen space. Each linear equation, together with an opcode, is passed to the *image generation controller*, which activates the control lines on the frame buffer chips (see Fig. 3). Figure 4 shows our latest small working prototype with the color image being generated by six Pxpl3 chips.

Details of the hardware design and the implementation are in (Paeth 1982) and in (Poulton 1985). The latter of these papers outlines architectural enhancements that may increase the speed of the system by a factor of 5. In the future, we hope to integrate the Pixel-planes architecture with a silicon-based flat-screen display, so that the display itself will handle the display computations (Shiffman 1984; Vuillemier 1984).

2. Algorithms in Pixel-Planes

As explained above, the major feature of Pixel-planes is its ability to evaluate, in parallel, expressions of the form $Ax + By + C$, where (x, y) is the address of a pixel. The controller broadcasts A, B, and C, and the expression $Ax + By + C$ is evaluated and then compared and/or combined with information already stored in the memory in each pixel cell. The memory at each pixel can be allocated in any convenient way. A typical allocation might be:

1) buffers for storage of certain key values (e.g., a ZMIN buffer for depth storage, and RED, GREEN, and BLUE buffers for color intensity values)
2) several one-bit flags which are used to enable or disable pixels (via the Enable register) during various stages of processing.

The timing analyses apply to the Pxpl memories and scanout. They assume image generating pipeline modules before them — the geometric transformation unit, the translator, and the controller — operate fast enough to keep up with the Pxpl memories.

2.1. Convex Polygons

The display of objects made up of polygons is accomplished in three steps: scan conversion of the polygons, visibility relative to previously processed polygons, and shading.

2.1.1. Scan Conversion. The object of this step is to determine those pixels which lie inside a convex polygon. Initially, all Enable registers are set to 1. Each edge of the polygon is defined by two vertices, $v_1 = (x_1, y_1)$ and $v_2 = (x_2, y_2)$, which are ordered so that the polygon lies on the left of the directed edge $v_1 v_2$. Then the equation of the edge is $Ax + By + C = 0$, where $A = y_1 - y_2$, $B = x_2 - x_1$, and $C = x_1 y_2 - x_2 y_1$. Furthermore, $f(x, y) = Ax + By + C$ is positive if and only if (x, y) lies on the same side of the edge as the polygon. The translator computes A, B, and C, and these coefficients are then broadcast to Pixel-planes. A negative $f(x, y)$ causes the Enable register for (x, y) to be set to 0; otherwise the Enable register is unchanged. A pixel is inside the polygon if and only if its Enable register remains 1 after all edges have been proadcast.

2.1.2. Visibility. Once scan conversion has been performed, final visibility of each polygon is determined by a comparison of z values at each pixel. The translator first computes the plane equation, $z = Ax + By + C$, as follows:

Step 1: The plane equation in eye space has the form:

$$A'x_e + B'y_e + C'z_e + D' = 0. \tag{1}$$

The first 3 coefficients, which form the normal to the plane, are found by computing the cross product of the two vectors determined by the first three vertices of the polygon. Alternatively, an object space normal can be part of the polygon data structure and transformed appropriately to produce an eye space normal. Assuming that (x_0, y_0, z_0) is a vertex, the last coefficient is given by:

$$D' = -A'x_0 - B'y_0 - C'z_0 \tag{2}$$

Step 2: Using the transformation equations:

$$
\begin{aligned}
x_e &= (-x - k_1)/(z'r_1), \\
y_e &= (-y - k_2)/(z'r_2), \quad \text{and} \\
z_e &= -1/z'
\end{aligned} \tag{3}
$$

where r_1, r_2, k_1, k_2 are constants related to the screen resolution and the location of the screen origin, we can transform (1) to screen space and still retain the form:

$$z' = A'x + B'y + C' \tag{4}$$

Step 3: Given that n bits are reserved for the ZMIN buffer, and that the minimum and maximum z values z_1, z_2, for the object to be displayed are known, we can rescale the equation so that $0 \leqslant z \leqslant 2^n - 1$ by replacing z' by:

$$z = (2^n - 1)(z' - z_1)/(z_2 - z_1) \tag{5}$$

Combining this with (4) we can write z in the form $z = Ax + By + C$. The visible pixels are then determined by using the standard Z-buffer algorithm (Sutherland 1974) at each pixel simultaneously. The controller broadcasts the plane equation of the current polygon, $z = f(x, y) = Ax + By + C$. Each pixel whose Enable bit is still 1 compares its $f(x, y)$ to the value in its ZMIN buffer. The pixel is visible if and only if $f(x, y) < ZMIN$, so pixels with $f(x, y) \geqslant ZMIN$ set their Enable bits to 0. The controller rebroadcasts A, B, and C so that the still-enabled pixels can store their new ZMIN values.

2.1.3. Shading. To determine the proper color for each pixel, the controller broadcasts 3 sets of coefficients, one for each primary color component. For flat shading, $A = B = 0$ and $C = color$. A smooth shading effect similar to Gouraud shading (Gouraud 1971), created by linearly interpolating the colors at the vertices of the polygon, can also be achieved.

For example, suppose the polygon has 3 vertices (x_1, y_1), (x_2, y_2), and (x_3, y_3) with red components R_1, R_2, R_3. Geometrically, one can visualize linear interpolation of the red component at (x, y) as selecting the third component of the point (x, y, R) that lies on the plane passing through (x_1, y_1, R_1), (x_2, y_2, R_2), and (x_3, y_3, R_3) in xyR-space. The translator computes the equation of this plane as follows:

Step 1: The vector equation

$$(x, y) = s(x_2 - x_1, y_2 - y_1) + t(x_3 - x_1, y_3 - y_1) + (x_1, y_1) \tag{6}$$

is solved for s and t which are written in the form:

$$s = A_1 x + B_1 y + C_1$$
$$t = A_2 x + B_2 y + C_2 \tag{7}$$

Step 2: The plane equation is written in the form $R = Ax + By + C$, where

$$A = A_1(R_2 - R_1) + A_2(R_3 - R_1)$$
$$B = B_1(R_2 - R_1) + B_2(R_3 - R_1)$$
$$C = C_1(R_2 - R_1) + C_2(R_3 - R_1) + R_1 \tag{8}$$

The controller broadcasts A, B, and C, and $Ax + By + C$ is stored in the RED color buffer for pixels that are still enabled after the scan conversion and visibility computations. If there are more than three vertices, the translator checks the colors $R_4, R_5, \dots$ at the remaining vertices $v_4 = (x_4, y_4)$, $v_5 = (x_5, y_5)$, $\dots$. Only in the case that for some i, $R_i \neq Ax_i + By_i + C$ is it necessary to subdivide the polygon by introducing new edges. Note that this subdivision is performed only during the shading stage and is not required during any other phase of processing.

Timing Analysis. The time it takes to process a polygon depends on the number of edges and the number of bits needed for the representation of $Ax + By + C$. Suppose were require an E bit representation for enabling pixels on one side of an edge, a D bit representation for

Fig. 5. The Chapel Hill "Old Well" rendered by a
Pixel-Planes functional simulator with input of
357 polygons. Estimated image generation time
(assuming a 10 Mhz clock) is 9 msec

the depth buffer, a C bit representation for each color component, and N bits for the representation of screen coordinates (usually 2 more than the log of the screen resolution), then scan conversion of an edge requires $E + N + 3$ clock cycles, and the visibility calculation of a polygon requires $2(D + N + 3)$ clock cycles. Once this is determined, shading of the polygon without subdivision requires $3(C + N + 3)$ additional clock cycles, while $3(C + N + 3) + (E + N + 3)$ additional cycles are needed for each subdivision. Hence, the total time to process a "worst case" n-side polygon is:

$$n(E + N + 3) + 2(D + N + 3)$$
$$+ (n - 3)(E + N + 3)$$
$$+ 3(n - 2)(C + N + 3)$$

clock cycles. If we assume that $E = 12$, $D = 20$, $C = 8$, $N = 11$, $n = 4$, and a clock period is 100 nanoseconds, a 4-sided polygon can be processed in 33 microseconds. Hence, about 30,000 such polygons can be processed per second. This permits real-time display of quite complex objects (see Fig. 5).

2.2. Shadows

After the visible image has been constructed, shadows created by various light sources can be determined (see Fig. 6). Our approach determines shadow volumes (Crow 1977) defined as logical intersections of half-spaces. This is most similar to (Brotman 1984) except that explicit calculation of the shadow edge polygons is unnecessary in Pixel-planes. Briefly, the algorithm proceeds as follows:

Step 1: Flag initialisation. For each pixel, a Shadow flag is allocated from pixel memory, and both the Enable register and Shadow flags are set to 0.

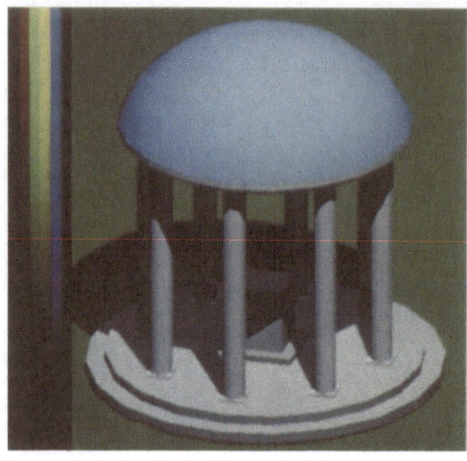

Fig. 6. "Old Well" with shadows (simulation). Estimated time: 13.8 msec

Step 2: Determination of pixels in shadow. For each polygon, the set of visible pixels that lie in the frustum of the polygon's cast shadow are determined and the Enable registers for these pixels is set to 1. The logical OR of Shadow and Enable is then stored in Shadow.

Step 3: Determination of color intensity of shadowed pixels. After all polygons have been processed, those pixels whose Shadow flag is 1 are in the shadow of one or more polygons. The color intensity of these pixels is diminished by an appropriate factor.

The implementation of this algorithm is based on the parallel linear evaluation capability of Pixel-planes, together with *ZMIN* value that is stored for each pixel. The idea is to disable those pixels which are on the "wrong" side of each face of the shadow frustum. We begin by choosing an edge of the current polygon, and finding the plane P determined by this edge and the light source. We want to disable those pixels which are not in the same half-space relative to P as the current polygon (see Fig. 7). The algorithm must handle two cases.

Case 1: P does not pass through the origin in eye space. In this case we observe that if the eye and the current polygon are in the same half-space relative to P, then it suffices to disable pixels that are farther away than P, and if the eye and the current polygon are in different half-spaces relative to P, then it suffices to disable pixels that are closer than P. In order to accomplish this we do the following:

a) The translator determines the equation of the plane P in the form $z = f(x, y) = Ax + By + C$, chooses a vertex (x_i, y_i) of the polygon not on P, and finds the sign of $f(x_i, y_i)$.
b) The coefficients $A, B,$ and C are broadcast so that f can be evaluated simultaneously at all pixels.
c) If $f(x_i, y_i)$ is positive, all pixels whose *ZMIN* is less than $f(x, y)$ are disabled, and if $f(x_i, y_i)$ is negative, all pixels whose *ZMIN* is greater than $f(x, y)$ are disabled.

Case 2: P passes through the origin in eye space. This relatively rare case is easier to process than Case 1. We observe that P projected on the screen is an edge so it suffices to disable

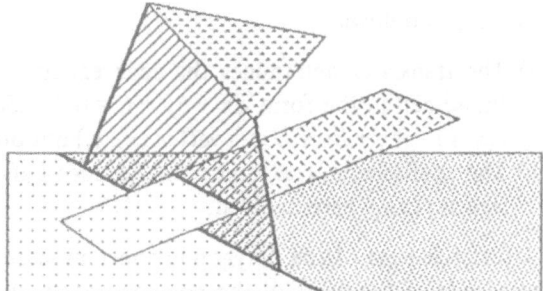

After shadow post-processing of first edge
of triangle

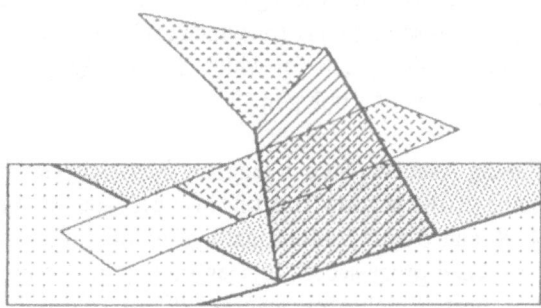

After shadow post-processing of second edge
of triangle

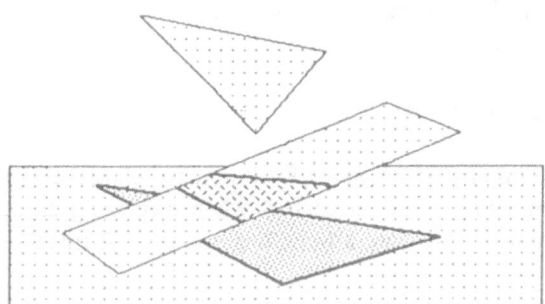

After completing shadow post-processing
of triangle

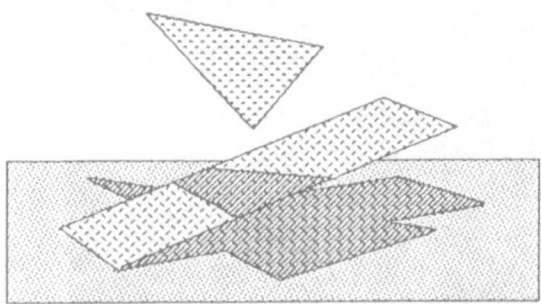

Result of all shadow processing

Fig. 7. Shadowing Algorithm

pixels which are not on the same side of this edge as the projected current polygon. We proceed as follows:

a) The translator determines the edge equation of the intersection of P with the plane of the screen in the form $Ax + By + C = 0$. In addition, the translator determines the sign of $f(x, y) = Ax + By + C$ at a vertex (x_i, y_i) not on P.
b) The coefficients A, B, and C are broadcast and those pixels whose $f(x, y)$ is not the same sign as $f(x_i, y_i)$ are disabled.

After each edge of the polygon has been processed in this manner, the pixels that are on the same side of the plane of the polygon as the light source must still be disabled. We let P be the plane of the polygon itself, and use either Case 1 or Case 2 above, with the one exception that we check the sign of f at the light source. Note that in the same half-space relative to P, we disable pixels for which $ZMIN = f(x, y)$, and if they are in different half-spaces we do not disable pixels for which $ZMIN = f(x, y)$. In this way, we can display either the lit or the unlit side of a polygon.

Timing Analysis. Step 1 requires 2 clock cycles for each polygon. In order to process each plane of the shadow frustum of a polygon, we need $(E + N + 3)$ cycles for the broadcast of A, B, and C and 2 additional cycles for the resetting of the Shadow flag. After all polygons have been processed, $3C$ cycles are required to modify the color component. Hence, in order to process P polygons, we need $P((n + 1)(E + N + 3) + 2) + 3C + 2$ clock cycles. For example, if $E = 12$, $N = 11$, $n = 4$, $C = 8$, and a clock period is 100 nanoseconds, 78,000 polygons can be processed per second.

2.3. Clipping

Clipping of polygons by boundary planes, a procedure usually performed in the geometry pipeline, is not necessary when displaying an image in Pixel-planes. Time can be saved by performing only a bounding box type of trivial rejection/acceptance. Edges which lie wholly

Fig. 8. "Old Well" with shadows cut by hither plane within the Pixel-Planes memories (simulation). 177 polygons after trivial rejection. Estimated time: 8.8 msec

or partially off the screen will still disable the appropriate pixels during scan conversion. Even hither and yon clipping can be achieved by passing (at most) the two edges of the intersection of the polygon plane with the hither and yon planes, and disabling pixels which are on the appropriate side of these edges. The shadow volumes must be similarly clipped, by the addition of the shadow planes determined by the light source and the line of intersection of the plane of the polygon and each of the clipping planes (see Fig. 8).

2.4. Spheres

Fred Brooks suggested to us a method for drawing filled circles in Pixel-planes. We have extended that method to spheres with Z-buffer and an arbitrary light source. Since Pixel-planes is essentially a linear machine, it might seem difficult to display objects rapidly which are defined via quadratic expressions. However, by using an algorithm that, in effect, treats a circle as a polygon with one edge, and by using some appropriate approximations, we can overcome these difficulties (see Fig. 9, 10). Just as in polygon display, we proceed through a scan conversion, a visibility, and a shading phase (Max 1979; Pique 1983).

Step 1: Scan Conversion. Note that the equation of a circle with radius r and center (a, b) can be written in the form:

$$g(x, y) = Ax + By + C - Q = 0 \tag{9}$$

where $A = 2a$, $B = 2b$, $C = r^2 - a^2 - b^2$, and $Q = x^2 + y^2$. A section of the memory at each pixel, called the Q-buffer, is allocated for the storage of $x^2 + y^2$, and is loaded with this value at system initialization time. The translator computes A, B, and C and $f(x, y) = Ax + By + C$ is evaluated at each pixel. The value in the Q-buffer is subtracted from $f(x, y)$ and those pixels for which $f(x, y) - Q$ is negative are disabled.

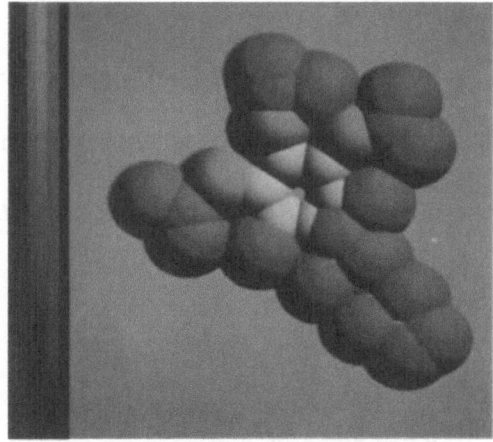

Fig. 9. Trimethoprim (simulation). Presorted data. Estimated time: 1.3 msec

Fig. 10. Trimethoprim with Z-buffer (simulation). Unsorted data. Estimated time: 1.7 msec

Step 2: Visibility. If the eye coordinate system is chosen so that the $z > 0$ half-space contains the sphere, then the visible hemisphere is the set of points (x, y, z) satisfying

$$z = c - \sqrt{r^2 - (x-a)^2 - (y-b)^2} \tag{10}$$

where r is the radius and (a, b, c) is the center of the sphere. We can approximate this by

$$z = c - (r^2 - (x-a)^2 - (y-b)^2)/r \tag{11}$$

which in effect approximates the hemisphere with a paraboloid. Using a method similar to that described in Step 1, the expression in (11) can be evaluated, compared with the existing contents of the ZMIN buffer, and then stored if necessary, in the ZMIN buffer. Visibility is then determined in the same way as it is for polygon display.

Step 3: Shading due to light sources at infinity. The unit outward normal at the visible point (x, y, z) on the sphere with center (a, b, c) and radius r is

$$\bar{N} = (1/r)(x-a, y-b, z-c)$$
$$= (1/r)(x-a, y-b, -\sqrt{r^2 - (x-a)^2 - (y-b)^2}) \tag{12}$$

Let $\bar{L} = (l_1, l_2, l_3)$ be the unit direction of an arbitrary light source. Then the point of maximum highlight on the sphere is $(rl_1 + a, rl_2 + b, rl_3 + c)$. Denote by *CMIN* the ambient color value and by *CMAX* the maximum color value for a given color component. Then for diffuse shading of the sphere, the color value at (x, y) is

$$Color(x, y) = \begin{array}{ll} CMIN + (CMAX - CMIN)(\bar{L} \cdot \bar{N}), & \text{if } \bar{L} \cdot \bar{N} \geqslant 0; \\ CMIN, & \text{if } \bar{L} \cdot \bar{N} < 0. \end{array} \tag{13}$$

Using the parabolic approximation of the hemisphere as we did in Step 2, we can approximate $\bar{L} \cdot \bar{N}$ by:

$$\bar{L} \cdot \bar{N} \approx (l_1(x-a) + l_2(y-b))/r - l_3(r^2 - (x-a)^2 - (y-b)^2)/r^2 \tag{14}$$

Then the color at a given pixel can be written in the form:

$$Color(x, y) = K(Ax + By + C - Q) + CMIN \tag{15}$$

where

$$K = -(CMAX - CMIN)l_3/r^2,$$
$$A = -l_1 r/l_3 + 2a,$$
$$B = -l_2 r/l_3 + 2b,$$
$$C = l_1 ra/l_3 + l_2 rb/l_3 + r^2 - a^2 - b^2 \tag{16}$$

The translator computes A, B, C, and K. Multiplication by K is accomplished by first approximating K by the first n non-zero bits of its binary representation:

$$K \approx \sum_{i=1}^{n} 2^{j_i} \tag{17}$$

Then for each j in the sum, the controller broadcasts $2^j A$, $2^j B$, $2^j C$. Q is shifted by j bits and subtracted from the linear expression determined by the three broadcast coefficients. The resultant value:

$$2^j(Ax + By + C - Q) \tag{18}$$

is added to the contents of the appropriate color buffer, COLBUF. After all the terms in the sum have been processed, we set $COLBUF$ to 0 if $COLBUF < 0$. The constant value $CMIN$ is broadcast and added to $COLBUF$.

Timing Analysis. The initial loading of the Q-buffer requires $37(E + N + 3)$ clock cycles. Scan conversion and visibility are the same as in polygon processing and take $(E + N + 3)$ and $2(D + N + 3)$ cycles, respectively. Shading requires $4(C + N + 3)$ cycles for each term in the sum used to approximate K, and the broadcast of $CMIN$ requires 20 cycles. Hence, if k is the number of terms in the approximation of K, it takes

$$37(E + N + 3) + S((E + N + 3) + 2(D + N + 3) + 4k(C + N + 3) + 20)$$

clock cycles to process S spheres. For example, if $k = 3, E = 20, N = 11, D = 20, C = 8$, then 34,000 shperes can be processed per second.

2.5. Adaptive Histogram Equalization

In computed tomographic (CT) scan displays, CT numbers must be assigned (grey) intensity levels so that the viewer can perceive appropriate degrees of contrast and detail. Because the range of CT numbers is, in general, greater than the range of intensity levels, some compression has to take place. This makes it difficult to control the contrast in both light and dark areas. The standard method, selection of windows in the CT range, results in intensity discontinuities and loss of information. AHE (Pizer 1984) is an assignment scheme that makes use of regional frequency distributions of image intensities. The processed image has high contrast everywhere and the intensities vary smoothly (see Fig. 11, 12). The method proceeds as follows. For each point (x, y) in the image:

Step 1: A "contextual" region centered at (x, y) is chosen, and the frequency histogram of CT numbers in this region is computed. Typically, this region is a circle, or a square with edges parallel to the screen boundaries.

Step 2: In this histogram, the percentile rank, r, of the CT number at (x, y) is determined.

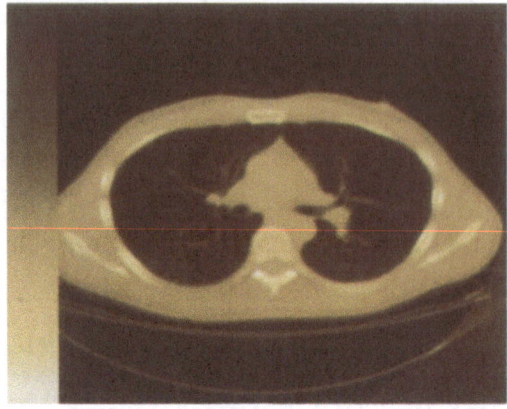

Fig. 11. Original CT scan image

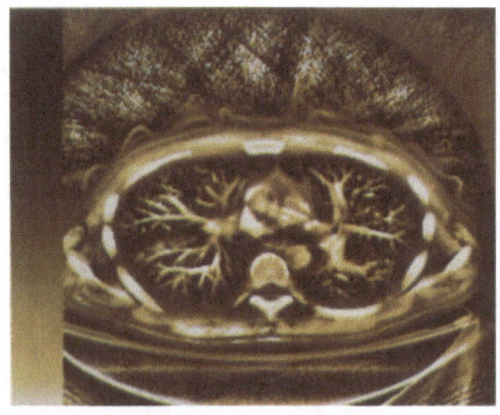

Fig. 12. CT scan image after AHE enhancement (simulation). Estimated time for this 256 x 256 pixel image: 1 second

Step 3: This rank is used to compute an intensity level, i, in some grey scale ranging between, say, i_1 and i_2. Specifically, $i = i_1 + r(i_2 - i_1)$.

This method requires the computation of a CT distribution at every pixel in the image, and so it is far too inefficient for most uses, requiring approximately 5 minutes to compute on a 256 x 256 image on a VAX11/780. A more efficient alternative, requiring about 30 seconds for a 256 x 256 image, is to compute the distribution only at a small set of sample points and use a linear interpolation scheme to approximate the intensity levels at the other points.

An efficient alternative, which finds the exact value at each pixel, can be implemented in Pixel planes. The idea is to make use of the parallel processing capability to construct the rank incrementally at each pixel simultaneously.

Step 1: The CT numbers are loaded into the pixel memories, and a counter at each pixel is initialized.

Step 2: For each pixel (x_0, y_0):

a) The coefficients necessary to disable those pixels that are outside the contextual region centered at (x_0, y_0) are broadcast. For example, if the region is a polygon or a circle, this is equivalent to the scan conversion step discussed earlier.

b) The CT number, $N(x_0, y_0)$, is broadcast and compared, in parallel, to the CT number, $N(x, y)$ which is stored at each enabled pixel (x, y). If $N(x, y) > N(x_0, y_0)$, the counter at (x, y) is incremented.

Step 3: After all pixels have been processed, the counter at each pixel contains the rank of the pixel CT number within its own contextual region. If both the number of pixels in the contextual region and the length of the grey scale are powers of 2, this rank can easily be scaled to an intensity by shifting bits.

Timing Analysis. It requires 25 cycles to load each pixel with its CT value and initialize its counter. It requires $2(E + N + 3)$ cycles to disable pixels outside each contextual region and 40 cycles to broadcast the CT numbers and increment the counters. On a 512×512 display with $N = 11$ and $E = 12$, we have estimated the time required to perform AHE is about 4 seconds.

3. Algorithms Under Development

This section describes algorithms still under development. Only functional simulations (rather than detailed behavioral ones) have been executed and the timing estimates are thus less precise. In particular, we are still exploring speedups for multiplication and division in the pixel processors. The timing estimates given in the figures are conservative (we hope), but still assume a 10 MHz clock.

3.1. Texture Mapping

One way of producing a texture on a polygon is to compute a texture plane address (u, v) associated to each pixel (x, y) and then look up the appropriate color value in a texture table indexed by u and v. The Pixel planes linear evaluator can be used to determine, in parallel, this texture plane address.

To see how this is done, we proceed through some mathematical computations. In order to orient a texture on a polygon in eye space we first choose a point $P0$ on the polygon and 2 orthonormal vectors $\bar{S}$ and $\bar{T}$ in the plane of the polygon. Then to texture address (u, v) associated to the point X on the polygon is given by:

$$u = \bar{S} \cdot (X - P_0),$$
$$v = \bar{T} \cdot (X - P_0). \tag{19}$$

If $\bar{S} = (s_1, s_2, s_3)$, $\bar{T} = (t_1, t_2, t_3)$, $P = (p_1, p_2, p_3)$, and $X = (x_e, y_e, z_e)$, equations (19) can be rewritten in coordinate form as:

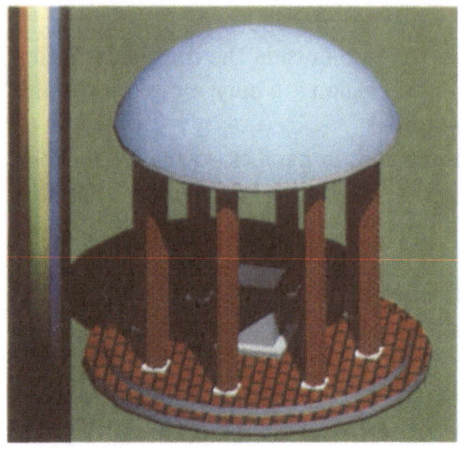

Fig. 13. Bricked "Old Well" (simulation). 66 textured polygons out of a total of 357. Estimated time: 14.3 msec

$$u = s_1(x_e - p_1) + s_2(y_e - p_2) + s_3(z_e - p_3)$$
$$v = t_1(x_e - p_1) + t_2(y_e - p_2) + t_3(z_e - p_3). \tag{20}$$

Substituting the equations (3), which relate screen space to eye space, into (20) and using the plane equation $Ax_e + By_e + Cz_e + D = 0$, we can write u and v in the form:

$$u = (A_1 x + B_1 y + C_1)/z$$
$$v = (A_2 x + B_2 y + C_2)/z \tag{21}$$

The translator computes A_1, B_1, and C_1, and the controller broadcasts them to Pixel-planes. The division of $A_1 x + B_1 y + C_1$ by z (which is already stored in ZMIN) is done in parallel at the pixel level, and the result is stored in a U-buffer. The V-buffer value is found in a similar manner. A texture table is then passed, entry by entry, to Pixel-planes, and each pixel selects a texture value corresponding to its stored (u, v) value. For periodic patterns (checkerboards, bricks, etc.) it is only necessary to transmit a small table defining the unit pattern (see Fig. 13).

3.2. Transparency

Transparency effects can be achieved by disabling patterns of pixels prior to polygon processing. For example, one could broadcast the coefficients $1, 1, 0$ in order to evaluate $x + y$, and disable those pixels for which $x + y$ is even (see Fig. 14).

Transparency effects can also be produced with subpixel mask successive refinement, where transparent polygons are ignored on particular passes over the database. For example, transparent polygons can be ignored every other pass or every third pass, thereby yielding different degrees of transparency.

Fig. 14. "Old Well" with transparent columns (simulation). 64 transparent polygons out of a total of 357. Estimated time: 13.8 msec

3.3. Anti-Aliasing

We have been developing several anti-aliasing techniques for polygons. We have come to believe that the essential difference between various approaches is whether the visibility at the subpixel level is performed before or after the anti-aliasing computations. Our first approach, which aims at producing an image rapidly and "improving" the image with each screen refresh, makes no assumptions about visibility determination before the Pxpl memories. The second approach, which takes more time, but produces a high quality anti-aliased image initially, assumes visibility ordering has already been done.

Method 1: Successive Refinement. Each pixel (x, y), is subdivided into a grid of subpixels so that each subpixel has an address of the form $(x + xoffset, y + yoffset)$. We generate the image several times (16, perhaps), each time offsetting the image slightly by some $(xoffset, yoffset)$ in such a way that the sample points within a pixel's area form a reasonable distribution. (The shift is easily achieved by adding $A \cdot xoffset + B \cdot yoffset$ to the C coefficient of each broadcast triple.) Two sets of color buffers are maintained, one to store the color generated by the latest image generation offset and the other to store a running average as we move around the subpixel grid.

The extra cost of the algorithm over standard subpixel "super-sampling" is the color blending between each pass over the graphic database. This is less than 1,000 clock cycles (100 microseconds) per pass. This particular super-sampling successive refinement technique, however, supports dynamically interactive applications. The initial images appear similar to common anti-aliased images, and significant refinement is produced within a few additional sampling passes.

Method 2: Subpixel Coverage Mask. The polygons are sorted from front to back, perhaps by first transforming the polygon list into a BSP tree (Fuchs 1983). Each pixel is subdivided into a number of subpixels and one bit of the pixel memory is reserved for each such subpixel. During the scan conversion step of polygon processing, the coefficients defining each edge are normalized to yield the distance from the center of the pixel to the edge. The coverage mask and area contribution of an edge can be passed from a precomputed table (Carpenter 1984) in the controller indexed by this distance and A, the coefficient of x. (Note that only one row of the table needs to be passed for any edge.) The number of ones in the mask is used to compute a color contribution which is added to the color buffers. When the number of ones in the coverage mask stored at each pixel reaches the total number of subpixel, the pixel is disabled. Since polygons are processed in front to back order, "leakage" of color from hidden polygons is avoided. This approach is somewhat similar to the one used in the Evans and Sutherland CT-5 real-time image generation system often used for flight training (Schumacker 1980).

4. Conclusions

We have highlighted in this paper the aspects of Pixel-planes that give it computing power and efficiency — the parallel linear expression evaluator embodied in the tree of one-bit adders. We have illustrated this capability by describing a variety of algorithms (shadows, spheres, image enhancement) that appear to run efficiently in this machine. Pictures from the Pixel-planes simulators indicate that high-quality images can be generated rapidly enough for dynamic, often real-time, interaction. The images from the working small prototype (see Fig. 4) are simpler than the images from the simulators due to the small number of custom chips presently available. We expect Pixel-planes 4, with considerably increased speed and resolution, to start working by June 1985. We expect that a full-scale (500–1,000 line) display system can be built with less than 500 Pxpl memory chips in currently available (1.5 micron CMOS) technology. We also hope that the algorithm developments, especially those based on simplifying algorithms into linear form, will be useful for those developing graphics algorithms on other parallel machines.

5. Acknowledgements

We wish to thank Fred Brooks for the basic circle scan-conversion algorithm, Alan Paeth and Alan Bell of Xerox Palo Alto Research Center for years of assistance with the design and early implementations of Pixel-planes, Scott Hennes for assistance with the implementation of the Pxpl3 memory chip, Hsieh Cheng-Hong and Justin Heinecke for discussions about architecture and algorithm interactions, Turner Whitted for discussions about anti-aliasing and transparency algorithms, Eric Grant for 3D data of the Old Well, Steve Pizer, John Zimmerman, and North Carolina Memorial Hospital for CT chest data, Mike Pique, Doug Schiff, Dr. Michael Corey and Lee Kuyper (Corey and Kuyper from Burroughs Wellcome) for Trimethoprim drug molecule data, Trey Greer for T_EX help, and Bobette Eckland for secretarial support. Special thanks go to Andrew Glassner, who supervised the layout and paste-up of this paper.

6. References

Brotman LS, Badler NI (October 1984) Generating soft shadows with a depth buffer algorithm. IEEE Computer Graphics and Applications 5–12

Carpenter L (July 1984) The A-buffer, an antialiased hidden surface method. Computer Graphics 18(3): 103–109 (Proc Siggraph '84)

Clark JH (July 1982) The geometry engine: A VLSI geometry system for graphics. Computer Graphics 16(3):127–133 (Proc Siggraph '82)

Clark JH, Hannah MR (4th Quarter 1980) Distributed processing in a high-performance smart image memory. Lambda 40–45 (Lambda is now VLSI design)

Crow FC (July 1977) Shadow algorithms for computer graphics. Computer Graphics 11(2):242–248 (Proc Siggraph '77)

Fuchs H (1977) Distributing a visible surface algorithm over multiple processors. Proceedings of the ACM Annual Conference, 449–451

Fuchs H, Johnson B (April 1979) An expandable multiprocessor architecture for video graphics. Proceedings of the 6th ACM-IEEE Symposium on Computer Architecture, 58–67

Fuchs H, Poulton J, Paeth A, Bell A (January 1982) Developing pixel-planes, a smart memory-based raster graphics system. Proceedings of the 1982 MIT Conference on Advanced Research in VLSI, 137–146

Fuchs H, Abram GD, Grant ED (July 1983) Near real-time shaded display of rigid objects. Computer Graphics 17(3):65–72 (Proc Siggraph '83)

Gourand H (1971) Computer display of curved-surfaces, IEEE Transcations on Computers 20(6):623–629

Max NL (July 1979) ATOMILL: atoms with shading and highlights. Computer Graphics 13(3):165–173 (Proc Siggraph '79)

Pique ME (1983) Fast 3D display of space-filling molecular models. Technical Report 83-004, Department of Computer Science, UNC Chapel Hill

Pizer SM, Zimmerman JB, Staab EV (April 1984) Adaptive grey level assignment in CT scan display. Journal of Computer Assisted Tomography 8(2):300–305. Raven Press, NY

Poulton J, Austin JD, Eyles JG, Heinecke J, Hsieh CH, Fuchs H (1985) Pixel-planes 4 graphics engine. Technical Report 1985, Department of Computer Science, UNC Chapel Hill (to appear)

Schumacker RA (November 1980) A new visual system architecture. Proceedings of the 2nd Annual IITEC, Salt Lake City

Shiffman RR, Parker RH (1984) An electrophoretic image display with internal NMOS address logic and display drivers. Proceedings of the Society for Information Display 25(2):105–152

Sutherland LE, Sproull RF, Schumacker RA (1974) A characterization of ten hidden-surface algorithms. ACM Conputing Surveys 6(1):1–55

Vuillemier R, Perret A, Porret F, Weiss P (July 1984) Novel electromechanical microshutter display device, Proceedings of the 1984 Eurodisplay Conference

Weitek (1983) Designing with the WTL 1092/1099. Weitek Corporation, Santa Clara, CA (Weitek publication 83AN112.1M)

VLSI-Architectures for Computer Graphics[1]

G. D. Abram and H. Fuchs

Abstract

Both academic researchers and commercial concerns are increasingly interested in applying VLSI technologies to graphics systems:

— For researchers, graphics systems offer an attractive model for study of computer architectures in VLSI: these systems have a small well-defined set of operations and simple data and control structures, making these systems ripe for applying parallelism and modularization techniques; many of these systems, especially the interactive high-resolution color ones, have severe computation demands that are unfulfilled by solutions embodied in current systems.
— For commercial concerns, there is a rapidly increasing market for interactive graphics systems as personal workstations in which graphics displays replace text-only terminals.

In this paper, we cover: a) the conceptual organization of a "generic" graphics system and its realization in several state-of-the-art commercial products; b) the architecture of several recent VLSI chips and systems and their likely effect on the organization of future graphics systems; c) the architecture of several VLSI-based systems that are currently subjects of research. The design strategies used in these systems — the structure of parallelism, intertwining of data and computation, the tradeoff between custom and off-the-shelf parts — may provide insights into other applications as well.

1. Introduction

The design of graphics systems has been a challenging topic of study for several decades; the demands for ever-increasing performance have always pushed the available technology to its limits. The availability of off-the-shelf TTL circuitry in the early 1970's allowed custom designs of minicomputer-level complexity. The advent of large-scale RAMs allowed systems to store complete images and quickly and randomly address any pixel in them; this capability gave rise to the current boom in color raster systems. Inexpensive microprocessors allowed these frame buffer systems to perform many functions independently of the host computer.

The possibility of custom VLSI promises another level of power in affordable graphics systems. The increased plasticity of custom VLSI allows systems designed using this medium

---

[1] Microarchitecture of VLSI Computers, edited by P. Antognetti, F. Anceau and J. Vuillemin, NATO ASI Series E on Applied Sciences, No. 96, published in 1985 by Martinus Nijhoff Publishers, Dordrecht, The Netherlands

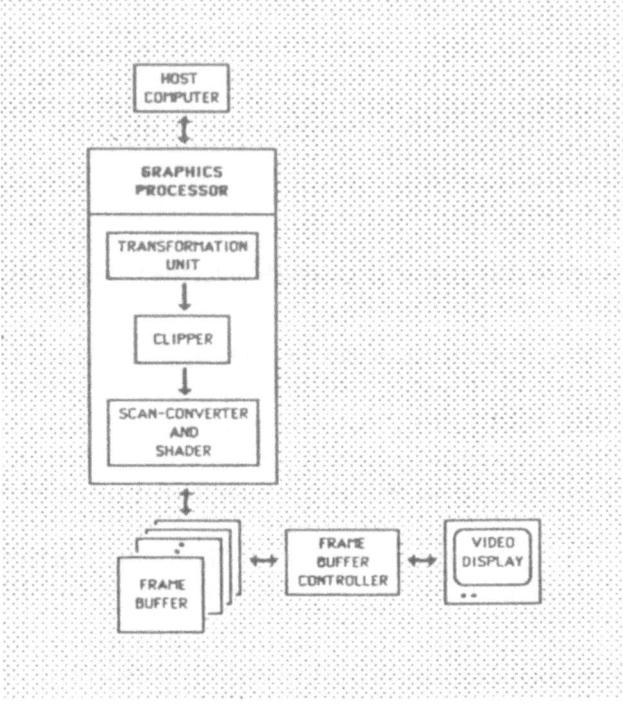

Fig. 1. A typical 3D raster system organization

to take on radically different structures than seen herefore. This paper explores some of these possible structures — a few just recently announced, most yet to come.

We concentrate in this paper on interactive color raster systems aimed at laboratory or office use, mostly for 3D applications; a few related systems that focus on 2D applications are included (Gupta, Sproull et al. 1981). Of course, most of the systems cited can be used for a wide variety of applications, not restricted to 3D. We have intentionally left out systems aimed at the expensive ($1M) flight simulator market, largely due to lack of available information in the public domain (Schachter 1981), although a number of the systems covered in this paper may be used for flight simulator applications.

The overall organization of many raster graphic display systems is quite similar (Fig. 1). The central feature is the frame buffer memory in which is stored the image currently being displayed — and perhaps one or more additional images. To relieve the host computer from low-level tasks, one or more processors are attached to most frame buffers. The nature and organization of these processors is one of the major focuses of this paper. Its major tasks for 3D image generation are illustrated in Fig. 2. An alternate organizations is used for many general purpose workstations, in which the image usually shows one or more pages of mostly textual information (rather than an interactive 3D image). The major tasks involve generation and movement of 2D image data; the typical hardware organization for such systems is shown in Fig. 3.

In studying many graphic system designs currently being developed, several distinct strategies become evident.

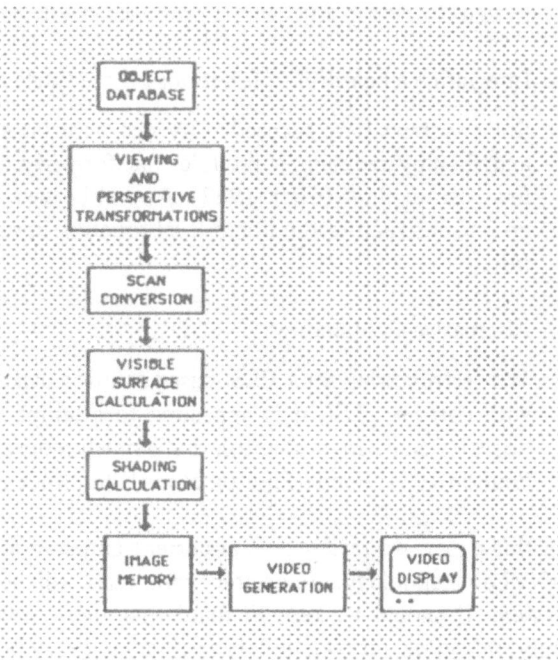

Fig. 2. Functional steps for 3D image synthesis

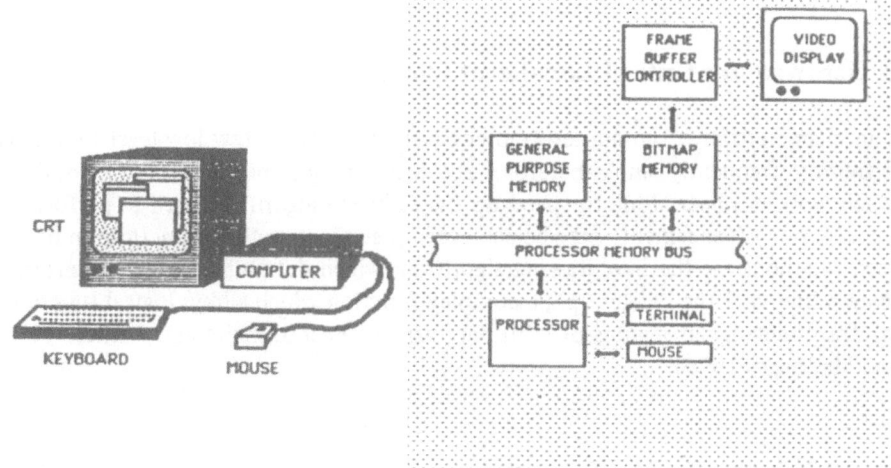

Fig. 3. A bitmap display and typical hardware organization

— Implementing innermost loops in hardware

One obviously reasonable strategy to consider is to transfer an often-executed inner loop from software to hardware (Atwood 1984; T. Ikedo 1984). The details of these designs are discussed in section 2. As some have noted, however, this strategy many not always succeed (Pike 1984). The new hardware inner loop solver may add so much more over-head as to swamp any gains it produces in solving the inner loop faster.

— Integrating a boardful of functions onto a single chip

Some systems have succeeded by restructuring an extant solution into VLSI components and thereby reducing a module that formerly needed one or more boards of parts to a few custom chips (Clark 1982). As will be seen below, however, it is not always obvious how to restructure the board-level function in such a way as to enable a VLSI-based solution.

— Alternative architectures

The restructuring for a VLSI-based solution can extend beyond the board to system level; with custom VLSI, it is appealing to attempt a radical restructuring of the problem in hopes of achieving a solution that's much more attractive in this new medium (Fuchs and Poulton 1981; Fuchs, Poulton et al. 1982; Kedem and Ellis 1984).

In this paper, we review several current and several proposed systems which take advantage of VLSI technology. Associated with each will be a figure noting the structure of such a system. It should be kept in mind that these architectural layouts are conceptual models only, reflecting our own understandings, and may bear only superficial resemblance to actual implementations.

2. Hardware for Critical Low-Level Functions

One characteristic of computer graphics systems is that a few low-level functions are used extremely frequently and, therefore, account for large portions of the total work done. Much work has been done to speed up the software algorithms used to perform these functions. Major advancements may be achieved by supporting these functions in hardware. Two such functions are the line drawing algorithm, which determines which pixels best approximate a line, and the "raster op", a complex function which allows logical functions between arbitrary rectangular regions of a bitmap display (Bechtolsheim and Baskett 1980; Thacker and McCreight 1979).

2.1. VLSI Support for Line Drawing

Although major strides have been made in the design of raster graphics systems, random-scan (also called vector or calligraphic) systems remain the technology of choice for line-drawing applications. This is for two reasons: image generation time and image quality. Raster systems must compute the set of pixels which best approximate lines and set them accordingly; random-scan systems use analog circuitry to drag the electron beam across the CRT screen from endpoint to endpoint. Since raster systems have only a relatively coarse grid of addressable pixels, images show distracting staircasing effects along edges (unless

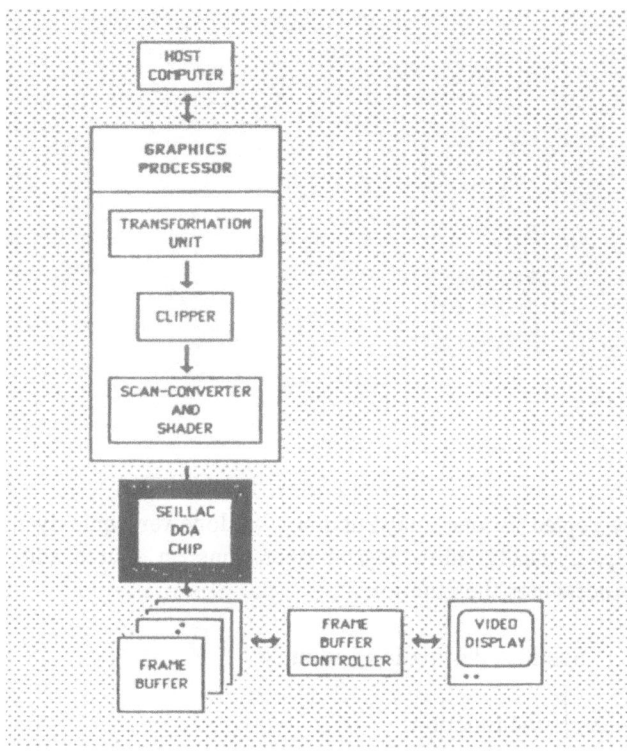

Fig. 4. Organization of system using SEILLAC DDA chip

costly anti-aliasing algorithms are used); in contrast, lines on random-scan systems are smooth.

The SEILLAC-7, a new graphics system built by the Seillac Co., Ltd., utilizes a custom ECL DDA chip to achieve extremely high line drawing rates (Fig. 4). It is claimed to be about five times faster than previous raster systems that lack such special-purpose hardware (though other systems claim similar speeds, such as the Ramtek 2020) (Ikedo 1984). This chip, which achieves a speed of about 40 nanoseconds per pixel in the line, includes a function to modulate the pixel intensity to alleviate the staircasing effects. In doing so, the images generated are claimed to approach stroke-drawn systems both in image quality and in vector drawing speeds.

2.2. Bitmap Manipulations

A recent development in professional workstations has replaced the standard ASCII terminal with a high resolution black-and-white frame buffer system (a "bitmap" display). This approach, pioneered in the Xerox Alto system in the early 1970's (Thacker, McCreight et al. 1971), offers many advantages over standard ASCII terminals; for example, high quality graphics and arbitrary fonts can be used for document preparation.

Bitmap displays require that the graphics system perform operations (Raster Ops) on bitmap memories efficiently (Fig. 5). Scrolling a bitmap window requires that the window

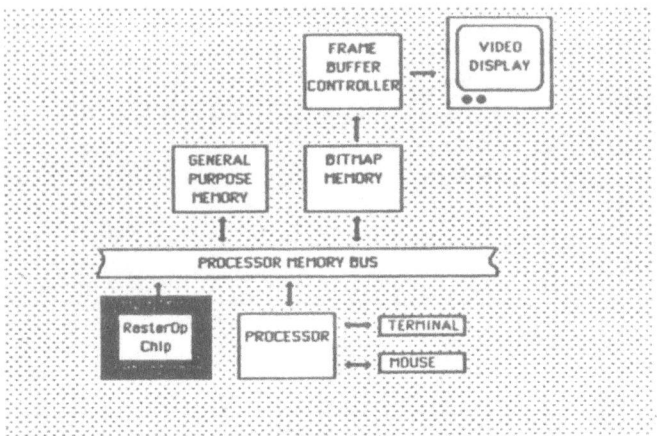

Fig. 5. Bitmap system organization using rasterOp chip

be copied up one line; this must be done very quickly if the display is to be useful. Raster Ops typically allow logical operations on source and destination bitmaps; the copying process uses the function:

f(source, destination) = source

whereas the function:

f(font, destination) = ~ font

may be used to write reverse video characters.

The implementation of the RasterOp function, however, is tricky. First, source and destination areas may overlap; the algorithm must be careful to operate in an order which ensures that data will not be overwritten before it is used. For example, if the destination is to the *left* of the source, the operation must proceed from left to right across the source, whereas if the destination is to the *right* of the source, the pass must be in the opposite direction.

The problem is further complicated by the organization of the bitmap memory. Bitmap displays are often organized with 16 or 32 horizontally adjacent pixels in a single word. Since regions do not necessarily fall on word boundaries, corresponding pixels in source and destination words may fall at different bit positions within the words. In order to operate on the several pixels within each memory word in parallel, *two* source words must be available to be to aligned with the data within the destination data word. The logical operation is then applied to the aligned words, and the result written to the destination locations. This must be repeated for each word which contains a destination pixel.

Silicon Compilers, Inc., in conjunction with Sun Microsystems, Inc., have implemented a chip to support the RasterOp function (Iannamico and Atwood 1984). This chip utilizes a two word FIFO to manage the source data words; the adjacent words are fed to a barrel shifter to align them with the destination data. Alternately, a pattern register is available for repetitive source data (for example, if a background pattern is to be written). The data words are fed to a simple ALU to compute tha logical operation; a function decoder allows the host to choose among 8 possible functions of pattern, source, and destination pixel values. Finally, mask registers can be used to protect bits of the destination data words which lie outside the destination area.

A substantial amount of work remains for an external controller to do (either the host CPU or an external finite state machine). Unlike the Seillac DDA chip outlined above, the looping here must be handled by the controller. The chip has no memory-addressing capability; it must rely on the controller to spoon-feed it input data and to return the results to the destination memory locations. The chip does, however, provide functions which may be costly for conventional microprocessors, including in particular the arbitrary 32-bit shift necessary for data alignment.

3. Integrated System Components

Whereas greater performance can be had by supporting critical functions in hardware, both performance and cost can be addressed by integrating large parts of the conventional graphics system. Some functions typically built out of large numbers of chips can, in fact, be implemented directly on a single (or a very few) VLSI ICs. This substantially decreases the chip count and can greatly improve the performance.

3.1. TI 4161 Memory Chip

Two related problems plague the frame buffer memory designers: 1) contention between image generation and scan-out for memory access, and 2) the high part count (and associated cost) of satisfactory designs (Fig. 6). For a 1024 x 1024 x 1 system refreshed at 60 Hz, a pixel (i.e. one bit of the frame buffer memory) must be available for display every 16 nanoseconds (or less). This rate can be achieved by interleaving the pixel memory among several

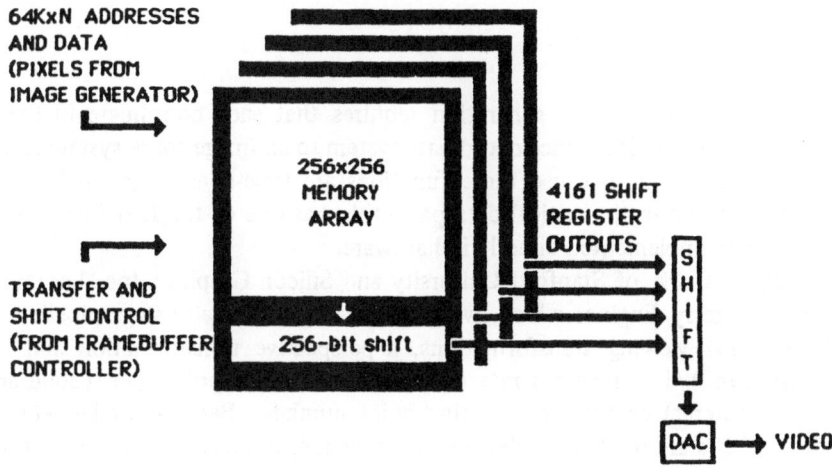

Fig. 6. A possible frame buffer design using TI 4161 RAMs

memory chips, which are read in parallel into a high speed shift register which then shifts pixels out at the desired rate. Assuming that the frame buffer is built using 64Kx1 RAM chips, 16 chips are required for a 1024 x 1024 bitplane, and scanout requires a memory cycle 16 x 16 = 256 nanoseconds, leaving little for image generation (unless very high speed − and therefore expensive − memories are used). Using 16Kx4 RAMs, we use the same number of chips and get 64 pixels in parallel, and we need a memory cycle every 1024 nano-seconds. Unfortunately, we now need four times as many memory chips and the data path is four times as wide. (Also, with these 4-bit wide chips, modifying a single bit is often awkward, necessitating a read-modify-write operation.)

Possible Memory Organizations

memory chip size	desired access rate	data path width
256Kx1	64 nsec.	4
64Kx1	256 nsec.	16
16Kx4	1024 nsec.	64

In other words, achieving the necessary data rates requires using small-capacity RAMs; whereas achieving low parts counts requires using large-capacity RAMs.

Texas Instruments has recently brought to market a special dynamic memory chip to help solve this problem (Pinkham, Novak et al. 1983). Much like conventional 64K RAMs, the TI 4161 memory is organized as 256 rows of 256 columns. The difference is that a 256-bit 40 nanosecond shift register is included. A command causes an *entire row* to be transferred to the shift register; the chip then acts as two completely independent chips; the 256-bit shift register and a normal 64Kx1 DRAM. In this manner, the chip allows a low system parts count while not tying up memory for scan-out (one memory cycle accesses 256 pixels).

3.2. The Geometry Engine

Three-dimensional image generation requires that each coordinate in the scene be transformed from a object space coordinate system to an image space system and then clipped to the visible region. Because these functions are time-consuming (including multiplies and divides) and lie in the critical data path, this was one of the first image generation components to be implemented directly in hardware.

James Clark, of Stanford University and Silicon Graphics, Inc., has implemented a chip (the Geometry Engine) which, when organized in a twelve-stage pipeline, performs three-dimensional viewing transformations, a perspective transformation and clipping (Fig. 7) (Clark 1982). It achieves a rate of 65,000 coordinate points per second and (unlike most earlier systems) operates on floating point numbers. Because a relatively small number of identical ICs are used to implement this pipeline, the cost is low, the cost will be lower still when multiple copies of the present IC will fit onto a single die.

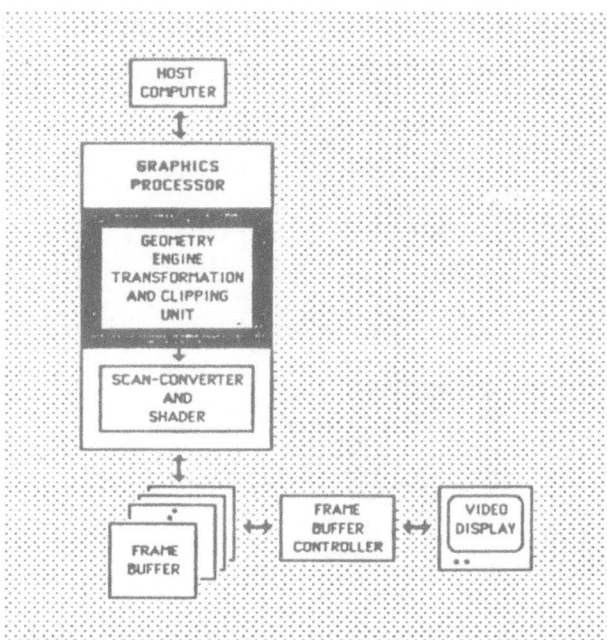

Fig. 7. System with geometry engine
for transformation and clipping

3.3. Graphics Display Controllers

Possibly the first specialized integrated circuits for video generation were single-chip video syne generators. Even with such chips, graphics display controllers typically require large amounts of logic, and hence are quite expensive to build out of off-the-shelf MSI and SSI components. Lately, however, two VLSI graphics display controllers have entered the market, each designed for a specific corner of the graphics market.

The NEC 7220 (second sourced as the Intel 82720) is designed to handle high-resolution (1024 x 1024) color raster graphics systems (such as the Vectrix VX384, a 670 x 480 system with 9 bits per pixel). The 7220 sits between the host processor (often an Intel micro) and the video memory (Fig. 8). Its video generation circuitry provides a great deal of flexibility, including provisions for zooming, panning, and windowing the image, plus the ability to use a light-pen input device. It also supports image generation by on-board line, arc, area fill and other graphic primitive display functions. Using the 7220, a complete high quality graphics system can be added to a microprocessor system at little more than the cost of the memories and the controller itself.

In contrast, the TI TMS9118 family of graphics display controllers are aimed at the low-cost world of video games, requiring only three chips to add graphics capability onto a standard microprocessor (Fig. 9) (Williamson and Rickert 1983). Although they allow only low resolution 256 x 192 images, they contain support for several specialized functions, including 32 so-called "sprites". A sprite is a small object defined by a rectangular grid of pixels whose position on the screen can be set by simply storing the location in a register,

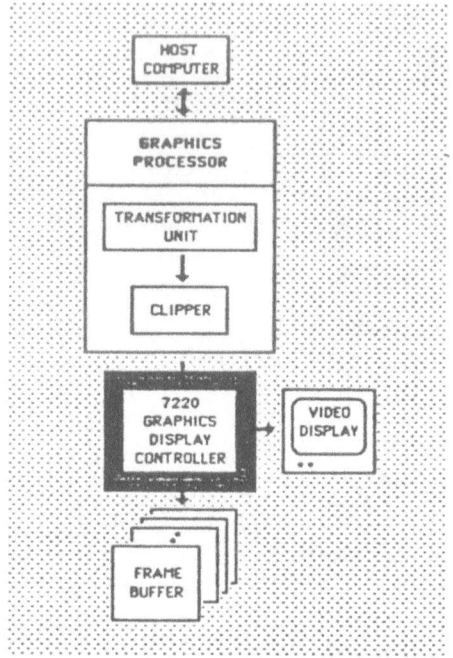

Fig. 8. Graphics system using 7220/82750 graphics display controller

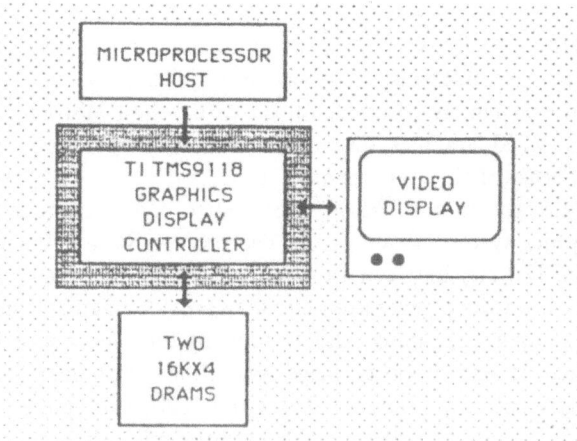

Fig. 9. Low-cost system using TI TMS9118 graphics display controller

rather than actually copying its pixels from place to place in a (full-image) frame buffer. By using sprites for moving objects in the display, even extremely low-cost devices can support certain classes of very high quality interaction.

4. Alternative Architectures for VLSI

Several current research projects are investigating ways to restructure the traditional graphics architecture to take better advantage of VLSI technology; in particular, the capability of applying potentially many specialized processors to the problem of image generation. These alternative architectures divide into two classes: those that divide the problem in image space and those that divide the problem in object space. Image space strategies divide the *image plane* into independent subsets and associate a separate processor to each. Object space strategies instead divide the *object database* and assign a processor to each.

4.1. Image Space Strategies

A hard constraint on the performance of raster systems is the bandwidth into the frame buffer memories. However, we can increase the bandwidth to the memories by splitting the image memory into separate components (on the image generation side; the memory still should look contiguous to the scan-out hardware). By associating pixel generating power with each component, these separate components can be accessed in parallel, effectively multiplying the bandwidth to the memories by the number of separate components. In this section, we look at two such strategies. (For speeding up the restricted case of images composed solely of axis-oriented, filled rectangles, see [Whelan 1982].)

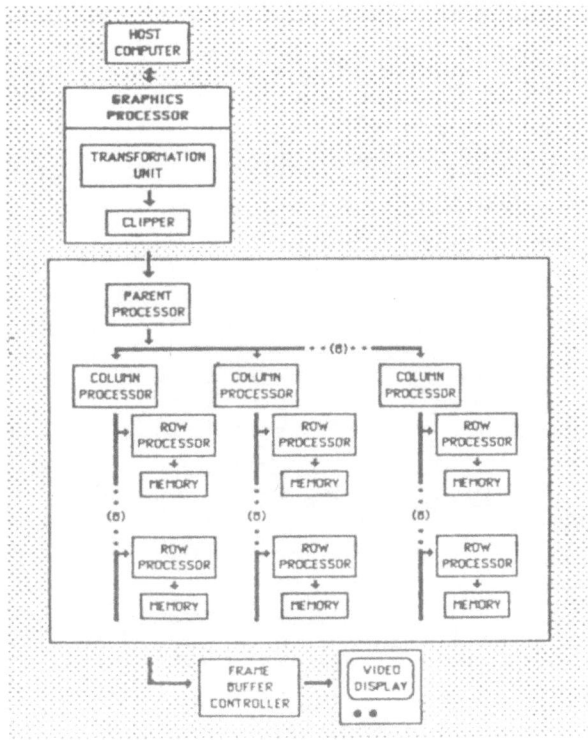

Fig. 10. Clark and Hannah 8 x 8 display architecture

4.1.1. Clark and Hannah. James Clark and Marc Hannah have proposed an image space segmentation approach which splits the image screen into segments the size of the RAM chips used (Fig. 10) (Clark and Hannah 1980). This organization is similar to an earlier system in (Fuchs and Johnson 1979). Both these systems distribute the image buffer in an interlaced fashion in X and Y among many small memories, each controlled by a small processor. For example, a 1024 x 1024 bit plane can be built out of 64 16K RAMs. These RAMs are interlaced so that for any 8 x 8 area of the bit plane, one bit comes from each of the these systems RAM chips. Thus, each memory contains every eight pixel in every eight row.

Clark and Hannah's system contains an intermediate layer of "column" processors between the main "parent" processor and the memory controlling "row" processors. Each of these processors then does a share of the image generation computation. To generate a line, the parent processor first determines the starting column, slope, line width and ending column of the line, and transfers this information to the column processors. The column processors then determine the part of the line intersecting the associated column of the image memory and transfers this to the row processors. Finally, the row processors actually write pixels into the image memory.

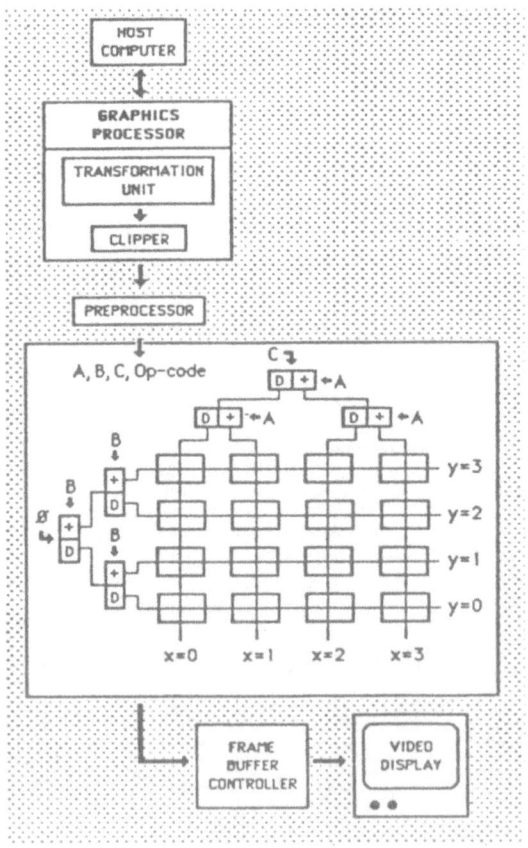

Fig. 11. A pixel-planes system (4 x 4 resolution)

4.1.2. Pixel-Planes. We, together with colleagues A. Paeth and A. Bell at Xerox Palo Alto Research Center, have been working on an image-generating system, "Pixel-planes" that performs low level pixel operations within "smart" custom memory chips that make up the frame buffer (Fig. 11) (Fuchs and Poulton 1981; Poulton et al. 1982). The memory chips autonomously perform, 1) scan conversion (calculating the pixels that fall within a line-segment, convex polygon, or circle), 2) visibility calculations based on the depth ("Z") buffer algorithm, and 3) pixel painting (either "flat" or a limited Gouraud smooth shading).

Efficient implementation is possible because each of the above operations can be performed by variations of the same calculation at every pixel, $F(x, y) = Ax + By + C$ where x, y is the address of the pixel. This function can be efficiently realized on silicon by a complete binary tree with a pixel at each terminal node and a one-bit adder paired with a one-bit delay at each non-terminal node. This circuitry and the other needed processing circuitry (a one-bit ALU at each pixel) is sufficiently compact so that the area of the chips consist of half-standard memory cells and half the processing circuitry described above.

Since both shading and depth can be formulated in similar equations, Pixel-Planes based systems can perform Gouraud-like smooth shading and Z-buffer visible surface computations. Two working prototypes have been built at UNC; the latest prototype's chips each contain 2K bits of memory distributed among 64 pixel processors, each with 32 bits of memory. Based on conservative speed estimates (10 MHz clock), the system is expected to process 25,000 to 30,000 arbitrarily-sized polygons per second.

4.2. Object Space Subdivision Approaches

An alternative opportunity for parallel processing in image generation is to subdivide the *input data*, assigning separate hardware to each subdivision. Some of the earliest real-time flight simulation systems used this approach; unfortunately, at the time hardware had to be built out of a large number of simple parts, and was therefore extremely expensive and limited in scope (Schumacker, Brand et al. 1969). Using VLSI technology, however, small, specialized processors can be built to perform the necessary operations. Several new designs have been proposed along these lines.

4.2.1. Gershon Kedem's CSG Machine. Gershom Kedem has proposed an architecture for the display of objects defined using Constructive Solid Geometry (CSG) (Fig. 12) (Kedem and Ellis 1984). CSG is a strategy for computer-aided design in which designs consist of several primitive shapes (spheres, cones, prisms etc.) which are combined using regularized set operations (UNION, INTERSECTION, ADDITION and SUBTRACTION). CSG structures are very naturally represented as binary trees in which leaf nodes correspond to primitives and internal nodes correspond to the operation which combines the objects described in the two subtrees.

Kedem's approach instantiates the CSG tree directly in hardware. A reconfigurable tree structure is built which consists of two types of nodes: Primitive Classifiers (PCs), for leaf nodes, and Combine Classifiers (CCs), for internal nodes. To compute a pixel value, the PCs compute (in parallel) the intersections of the ray rooted at the eye point and passing through the pixel center with their associated primitive objects. These intersections (actually line segments of the ray) filter up the tree. Each CC takes the line segments of its left and

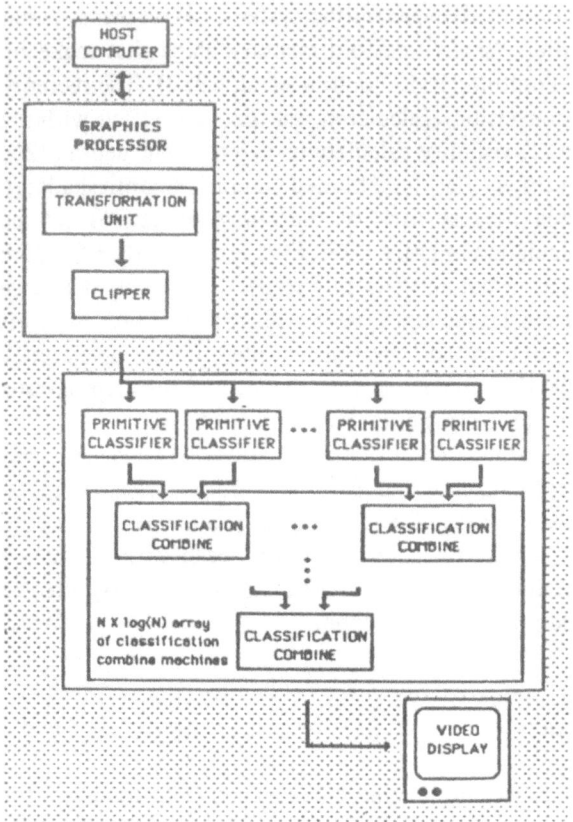

Fig. 12. Kedem's CSG machine architecture

right subchild and applies its operator on them and passes the result up the tree. The final result, produced at the root fo the tree, is then used to compute a pixel shade.

4.2.2. Cohen and Demetrescu. Cohen and Demetrescu, in (Cohen and Demetrescu 1980) have proposed a system that assigns a processor to each potentially visible polygon in the image space (i.e., already transformed world model polygon) (Fig. 13). These processors are connected as a pipeline and are operated in synchrony with the video generation. For each pixel on the screen, a token is passed through the pipeline of polygon processors. This token carries the shade and depth of the closest point found for this pixel. This depth is the distance from the viewing position of the closest polygon encountered at this pixel; thus the shade is the best guess so far of the color seen at this pixel. Each processor in turn tests whether the pixel lies inside its polygon. If the point lies inside, the processor compares this depth with its polygon's depth at this point. If the polygon's depth is closer, its depth and color replace the token's data. For real-time image generation, tokens pass in raster-scan order and travel at video rates; that is, each processor must make each decision in one pixel time.

An elegant feature of this approach is that the pixels stream out of the end of the pipeline in raster-scan order and each value represents the color of the nearest polygon at that pixel; thus the data can be routed directly onto a video display screen.

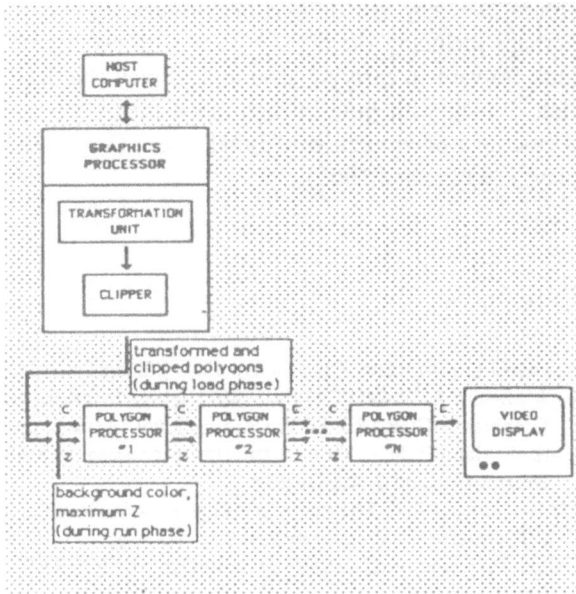

Fig. 13. Cohen and Demetrescu's pipe-lined architecture

Weinberg, in (Weinberg 1981), proposes an elaboration on this design which addresses the problem of anti-aliasing by passing multiple depth-sorted tokens for each pixel along with subpixel masks. Each processor then determines the portion of the pixel covered by its polygon, and compares with the token's mask when the correct position in the depth order is found. If preceding polygons do not completely obscure it, it is added to the token chain. Subsequent tokens are then examined to see if the new polygon completely obscures them, deleting those that are. A filter section at the output uses this data to determine an output shade for each pixel.

This general approach features great modularity; it consists of identical processors hung together in a simple pipeline. It is easily expandable by simply adding more processor chips. The design costs are held down by the fact that only a single IC needs to be developed; manufacturing costs are held down by the simple structure. The only difficulties may be 1) implementing enough processors so that there is one for each and every polygon in the most complex scene in the intended application, and 2) making each processor sufficiently fast to complete all its calculations for a pixel in one pixel time.

5. Summary and Conclusions

As the reader is likely to gather from the above list of designs, we are currently witnessing a blossoming of creative designs for harnessing a new medium to solve an old problem. The good news in all this is that with all this attention, there is likely to be substantial progress; indeed, virtually with each passing month a new system with increased performance is introduced — usually found to contain some custom integrated circuitry. In the next few years, many of the designs described above will, not doubt, be developed, refined, and tested. The effective ones will be adopted, the others will be improved or abandoned. Further in the future, we may see designs that integrate even more of the display system functions — perhaps including the display itself within the processing and image memory. We can then look forward to carrying around a display the size of a book, whose surface is a high-resolution display with built-in high-speed image generating capabilities — thus approaching the predictions of visionaries' "dynabooks" (Kay 1977) and eye-glass mounted "ultimate displays" (Sutherland 1965).

References

Atwood J (1984) Raster-Op chip overview. Silicon Compilers, Inc, Los Gatos, California

Bechtolsheim A, Baskett F (July 1980) High-performance graphics for microcomputer systems. Computer Graphics (SIGGRAPH '80 Proceedings), vol 14, no 3, pp 43–47

Clark J, Hannah M (1980) Distributed processing in a high-performance smart image memory. VLSI Design, vol 1, no 3, 4th Quarter

Clark J (July 1982) The geometry engine: a VLSI geometry system for graphics. Computer Graphics (SIGGRAPH '82 Proceedings), vol 16, no 3, pp 127–133

Cohen D, Demetrescu (1980) Presentation at SIGGRAPH '80 Panel on Trends on High Performance Graphic Systems

Fuchs H, Poulton J (1981) PIXEL-PLANES: A VLSI-oriented design for a raster graphics engine. VLSI Design, vol II, no 3, 3rd Quarter

Fuchs H, Johnson BW (April 1979) An expandable multiprocessor architecture for video graphics. Proceedings of 6th Annual (ACM-IEEE) Symposium on Computer Architecture, pp 58–67

Fuchs H, Poulton J, Paeth A, Bell A (January 1982) Developing pixel-planes, a smart memory-based raster graphics system. Proc. MIT Conference On Advanced Research in VLSI. Artech House, Dedham, MA

Gupta S, Sproull R, Sutherland IE (August 1981) A VLSI architecture for updating raster-scan displays. Computer Graphics (SIGGRAPH '81 Proceedings), vol 15, no 3, pp 71–78

Ikedo T (1984) High-speed techniques for a 3D color graphics terminal. IEEE Computer Graphics and Applications, vol 4, no 5

Kay A (September 1977) Microelectronics and the personal computer. Scientific American, vol 237, no 3

Kedem G, Ellis J (May 1984) Computer structures for curve-solid classification in geometric modelling. Technical Report TR137, Department of Computer Science, University of Rochester

Pike R (1984) Presentation at University of North Carolina at Chapel Hill

Pinkham R, Novak M, Guttag K (July 21, 1983) Video RAM excels at fast graphics. Electronic Design, pp 161–172

Schachter B (1981) Computer image generation for flight simulation. IEEE Computer Graphics and Applications, vol 1, no 4

Schumacker R, Brand B, Gilland M, Sharp W (September 1969) Study for applying computer-generated images to visual simulation. US Air Force Human Resources Lab Tech Rep AFHRL-TR-69-14

Sutherland I (1965) The ultimate display. Proceedings of the IFIP Congress, vol 2

Thacker CP, McCreight M, Lampson BW, Sproull RF, Boggs DR (1979) ALTO: A personal computer. Xerox Corp. In: Siewiorek DP, Bell CG, Newell A (1982) Computer structures: principles and examples. McGraw-Hill, pp 549–572

Weinberg R (August 1981) Parallel processing image synthesis and anti-aliasing. Computer Graphics (SIGGRAPH '81 Proceedings), vol 15, no 3, pp 55–61

Whelan D (July 1982) A rectangular area filling display system architecture. Computer Graphics (SIGGRAPH '82 Proceedings), vol 17, no 3, pp 147–153

Williamson R, Rickert P (August 4) Dedicated processor shrinks graphics systems to three chips. Electronic Design, pp 143–148

Part III

Standards for Computer Graphics

A Reference Model for Computer Graphics Standards

P. R. Bono

Overview of Graphics Standards

Standards codify the exchange of information across an interface between two functional units. Standards specify what is to be exchanged, but not how the functional units carry out their operations. Figure 1 represents an application programmer's model of a graphics system. Two interfaces are central to graphics standardization: the application programmer interface (API) and the virtual device interface (VDI). Standards at both interfaces provide device independence for the user of the standard. That is, the user can deal with one or more abstract ("virtual") graphics devices with a full range of input and output capabilities. The messy details of the particular hardware capabilities of any particular graphics device are hidden from the user. Instead, implementations of the standards must emulate any required facilities not directly supported by the hardware. Furthermore, the implementations

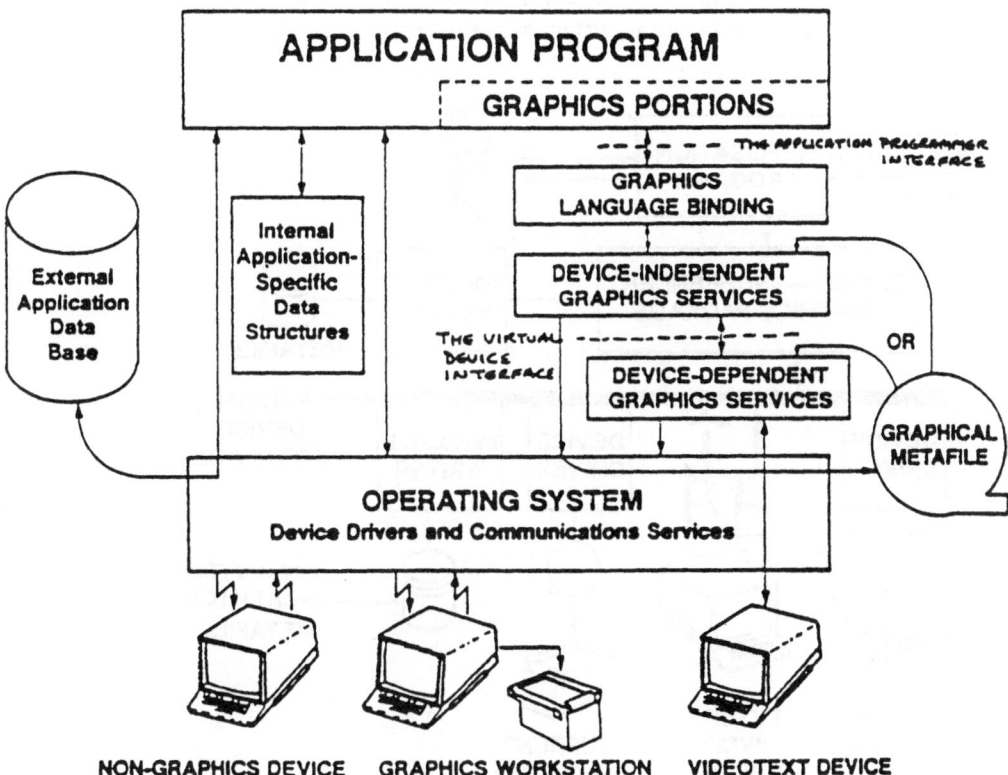

Fig. 1. Programmer's model of a graphics system

mask the peculiarities of the particular command sets used to communicate specific orders to the graphics devices.

The API is represented by three major graphics standards projects: PHIGS, GKS, and GKS-3D, all of which are described briefly in the following. These API standards are typically implemented as a collection of external procedures or subroutines that a programmer can link with his application code to obtain graphical input and cause pictures to be displayed on graphical output devices.

The VDI is internal to the graphics system and concerns system programmers, Independent Software Vendors (IVS's), peripheral device manufacturers, and graphics controller board and graphics chip markers. They require device-independence, without sacrificing performance. The specification of a proper Computer Graphics Virtual Device Interface (CG-VDI) is crucial to the success of distributed graphics systems; the CG-VDI, part of the ISO Computer Graphics Interface (CGI) project, is described in detail in another unit of this tutorial.

To exchange pictures among diverse applications and across separate programming environments, information can be captured at the level of the VDI and placed in a graphical metafile. These files can be sent over telephone lines and computer networks to be stored or processed by the recipient.

There are two phases to the use of metafiles (see Fig. 2). To create the metafile, a metafile "device driver" or metafile writer or generator must be available with a graphics package. To read and redisplay metafiles generated on other computers, a metafile reader or interpreter must be available on the system where the picture is to be used.

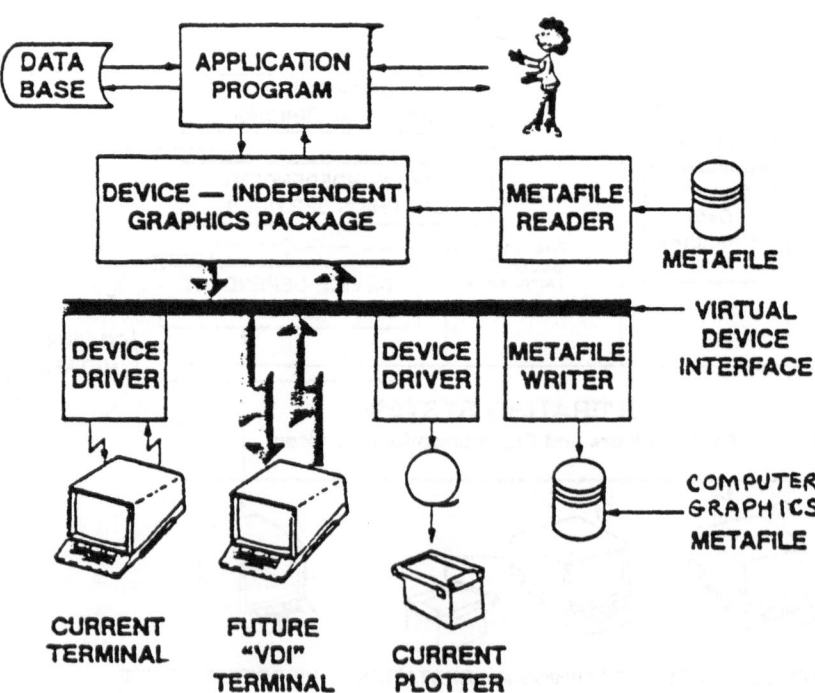

Fig. 2. Generating and interpreting metafiles

PHIGS

The Programmer's Hierarchical Interactive Graphics System is an emerging standard specifying an application programmer's interface to a rich, device-independent graphics environment. PHIGS is designed to support such important applications as CAD/CAE/CAM, command and control, molecular modelling, simulation, and process control. PHIGS emphasizes the support of applications needing a highly dynamic, highly interactive operator interface and expects rapid screen update of complex images to be performed by the display system.

The current state of technology dictates that the initial implementations of PHIGS will be designed to run on nothing smaller than IBM 4300 class and DEC VAX-11/780 class machines using such high-performance displays as the IBM 5080, Tektronix 4115, Megatek Whizzard, and Ramtek 9460. Until fast, floating-point hardware is commonly available, until processor cycle times improve substantially, and until internal word sizes and data path widths increase to 32 bits or more, PHIGS is unlikely to be implemented, *in toto*, on personal computers. However, PC's may play a role in displaying graphics from a PHIGS implementation hosted on larger mainframes and minicomputers, where the PC is just a node in a network of graphics workstations with varying capabilities.

GKS

Like PHIGS, GKS is an API standard. GKS consists of nearly 200 user interface routines that give a programmer the ability to create graphics output and accept graphics input from a wide variety of graphical devices. These include black-and-white and color displays, printers, plotters, and camera systems, as well as mice, data tablets, joysticks, and digitizers. A GKS implementation also typically provides programming access to GKS from several higher-level programming languages such as FORTRAN, Pascal, and C.

As could be readily determined by visiting the Expositions at Computer Graphics '85 in Dallas in April and Siggraph '85 in San Francisco in July, GKS is already being offered by several vendors of personal computer software, including Advanced Technology Center, Cybervision, GIXI, Graphic Software Systems, IBM, Nova Graphics, Prior Data Sciences, and Visual Engineering. The IBM PC/XT/AT line, under both the DOS and UNIX operating systems, is the favorite host environment. A dozen other companies (including DG, DEC, Megatek, Precision Visuals, and Tektronix) are shipping GKS offerings for mainframes and minicomputers. The GGS implementation supports level 2b (full GKS, except for asynchronous input); most other PC implementations support only level Ob (no segments). Several European implementations (including GTS/GRAL, ICL, SIYGRAPH, and UNIRAS) are also commercially available.

Because of GKS's siue and the fact that a program is developed by linking the application to the GKS development library, a hard disk system of 10 MB or more is nearly mandatory for GKS program development. However, once developed, a GKS program can be run on a PC that has only floppy disks. Typical GKS programs written in FORTRAN and linked with the GSS-TOOLKIT Kernel System library average about 110 Kbytes. The same program written in C would be about 15 to 20 Kbytes smaller, due principally to the smaller size of the C run-time library and to the smaller size of the code necessary to provide the Clanguage binding layer.

On the PC, GKS is an extremely attractive software tool that bridges the UNIX and DOS worlds. For application developers, writing graphics in GKS means that, given the proper support environment (described under the topic CG-VDI below), the same program can run in both DOS and UNIX environments. This substantially increase the size of the marketplace, especially for UNIX developers. The door is also opened for running the same programs on the minis and mainframes to which the PC user has access through computer networks.

A single-user PC environment offers opportunities for the GKS developer to offer more flexibility than is usually found in mainframe GKS implementations. For example, the GSS-TOOLKIT Kernel System supports dynamic selection and loading of device drivers at runtime, programmer interfaces from the three most useful higher-level programming languages, a rich selection of over 50 of the most popular graphics input and output devices, and access to multiple, concurrently open input and output workstations. Implemented in C, the GSS-TOOLKIT Kernel System is optimized for size and performance on microcomputers whose memory and speed constraints are difficult to surmount.

GKS-3D

The project to specify extensions to GKS for defining and viewing three-dimensional, wireframe objects is well under way. A draft specification, firm enough for implementors to start product design and implementation, should be available by December, 1985. GKS-3D puts additional demands on the computational and data storage capacity of the host. Perhaps as much as 50% more "horsepower" and 30% more storage will be needed for a GKS-3D implementation when compared with GKS. This stretches the limits of most of today's PC's. However, the newer boxes based on the Intel 80286 and Motorola 68020 processors should have enough power to handle GKS-3D applications, when coupled with new graphics controller boards and chips supplying VDI functional support in firmware and hardware that should start appearing in 1986. Such GKS-3D programming systems should be especially popular on UNIX workstations targeted for the CAD/CAE marketplace.

GKS-3D will provide a software "bridge" for ISV's and "Fortune 2000" companies who desire a single, standard programming environment on their mainframes, minicomputers, and microcomputers. The thickiest part of making a good GKS-3D product involves implementing the viewing pipeline efficiently. Perspective and parallel projections, several clips to viewing volumes, and access to optional hidden line/hidden surface algorithms — all put pressure on the capability of the system to optimize the calculations as points are transformed from world coordinates to device coordinates through three intermediate coordinate systems.

Towards a Graphics Standard for 3D (GKS-3D)

W. T. Hewitt

1 INTRODUCTION

GKS [1] is about to be published as an international standard. For sometime the ISO working group on Computer Graphics (known as ISO TC97 SC21 WG2, formerly SC21 WG5-2 and SC5 WG2) has been investigating, via its 3D sub-group, extensions to GKS. In September 1983 at its meeting in Gananoque, Canada, the group identified two areas appropriate for standardisation [2]. Recognising that for many application programs requiring a computer graphics interface, 2D was not sufficient, the extension to 3D was an obvious choice. For many applications the segment model of GKS is not adequate and the provision of facilities for the hierarchical structuring of (graphical) data is the second area. Of course WG2 has been and is developing other standards associated with GKS, e.g. the CGM and CGI. The aim of working group is to produce, as far as technically feasible, members of a compatible family of graphics standards and NOT competing standards.

The graphics panel of the United States (ANSC X3H31) had been working on structures for sometime and volunteered to submit the project, the Programmers Hierarchical Interactive Graphics System (PHIGS)[3], for review by ISO. The project has recently been approved (February, 1985) by the parent committee (SC21) of the graphics working group, and the 3D group is now starting the technical review.

This paper will review the history and features of GKS-3D. GKS-3D leads PHIGS within the ISO processing of standards. It became a project in September 1983, and was registered as a Draft Proposed International Standard, at the SC21 meeting in February 1985, in Paris. (GKS was registered as a DPIS in 1980, and will become an international standard (IS) in mid 1985.) Further technical review and voting by the member bodies of ISO is required to take GKS-3D from a DPIS to a Draft International Standard (DIS) and also to an IS. As GKS-3D is still a moving target, this paper uses reference [1] as the definition of GKS-3D.

2 GKS-3D HISTORY

In September 1983, at the Gananoque meeting, Paul Ten Hagen and Rens Kessner of the Netherlands volunteered to develop GKS-3D. In December 1983 the first draft was distributed and comments were received from a number of graphics panels. The second version was produced for the next WG2 meeting which was at Benodet, France in June 1984. During that meeting, majority agreement was reached on all the technical issues raised enabling the 3D group to re-draft the document at Benodet[4][5]. Subsequently a new version was issued in September/October 1984. In Mierlo, Netherlands, in December 1984, the 3D group met again and resolved most, although not all of the comments raised [6], [7]. Early 1985 saw the production of the latest version (3.4) [8] which has been registered as a DPIS. The next meeting at Timberline, USA, in July 1985 will review the comments on this version, and decide if it should be submitted for voting and registration as a DIS.

The GKS-3D document (160 pages in length)[8], describes the "changes" to be made to GKS IS 7942 to convert it to GKS-3D. This so called 'delta' document must be read in conjunction with GKS as it describes only the additions and modifications to GKS to convert it to GKS-3D. This approach was taken so that (1) aspects of GKS would NOT be re-opened for discussion. (2) No incompatabilities with GKS would be introduced by repitition of the GKS text in a GKS-3D document, and (3) so that the document was small, and the '3D sections' were easily identified.

3 GKS-3D - SCOPE, GOALS and PURPOSE

The statements in the previous paragraph bring to mind a very simple question: "What is 3D?". At Gananoque WG2 decided, via the development of a Scope, Goals, and Purposes document [2] the answer it would use for this question. GKS-3D encompasses those of GKS:

(a) portability of application programs.

(b) to aid the understanding of graphics.

(c) to serve manufacturers as a guide to the facilities required in graphics devices.

(d) Support of a wide variety of devices.

(e) Support of a wide range of facilities on those devices.

(f) Should be small!

(g) These facilities should be consistent, compatible, complete and orthogonal.

(h) These facilities should be addressed in a device independent manner.

(i) These facilities should be described in a (programming) language independent manner.

For the Extensions to 3D, the following design goals are also important:

(j) The relationship between GKS and GKS-3D should be defined precisely and NOT be implementation dependent.

(k) The format of GKS functions and their parameters should remain unchanged.

(l) Additional capabilities will be added solely to support 3D functionality.

The use of (j) and (k) is obvious, upwards compatibility. A major goal is that GKS programs should run without modification (and produce the same results?) in the GKS-3D environment. (l) recognises that GKS as a standard must be STABLE and prevents rectification of any shortcomings of GKS.

The extension (over GKS) adds the following:

(a) definition and display of 3D graphical primitives.

(b) A mechanism to control the viewing transformation and associated parameters.

(c) A mechanism to control the appearance of primitives, including optional support for Hidden Line / Hidden Surface removal (HLHS), but excluding light sources, shadows etc.

(d) 3D input tools.

(e) Planar primitives, to be specified by lists of 3D coordinates.

4 GKS-3D WORKSTATIONS

As in GKS the workstation is fundamental to GKS-3D. The concept of the GKS workstation have been generalised by assuming the workstation is now able to process with 3D co-ordinate information. The workstation driver software may remove the z co-ordinates when it renders pictures onto the (flat) screen. Similarly the workstation driver must be able to re-create 3D information (possibly by simulation) should GKS-3D request such information. The functions of GKS used to control the workstation have not been altered or added to by GKS-3D.

5 GKS-3D OUTPUT PRIMITIVES

Seven output primitives exist in GKS-3D:

(a) polyline - a set of connected lines defined by a point sequence.

(b) polymarker - a set of symbols centred at the given positions.

(c) text - character string at the given position.

(d) fill area - a polygonal area which may be hollow or filled with a uniform colour, pattern or hatch style.

(e) fill area set - a set of polygonal areas which be hollow or filled with a uniform colour, pattern, or hatch style. This allows for specfying areas with holes or disjoint regiosn (without dummy edges) that mmust be treated as a single entity, particularly for HLHS computation.

(f) cell array - an array of pixels with individual colours (see figure 1).

(g) generalised drawing primitive (GDP) - addresses special geometric output capabilities of a workstation.

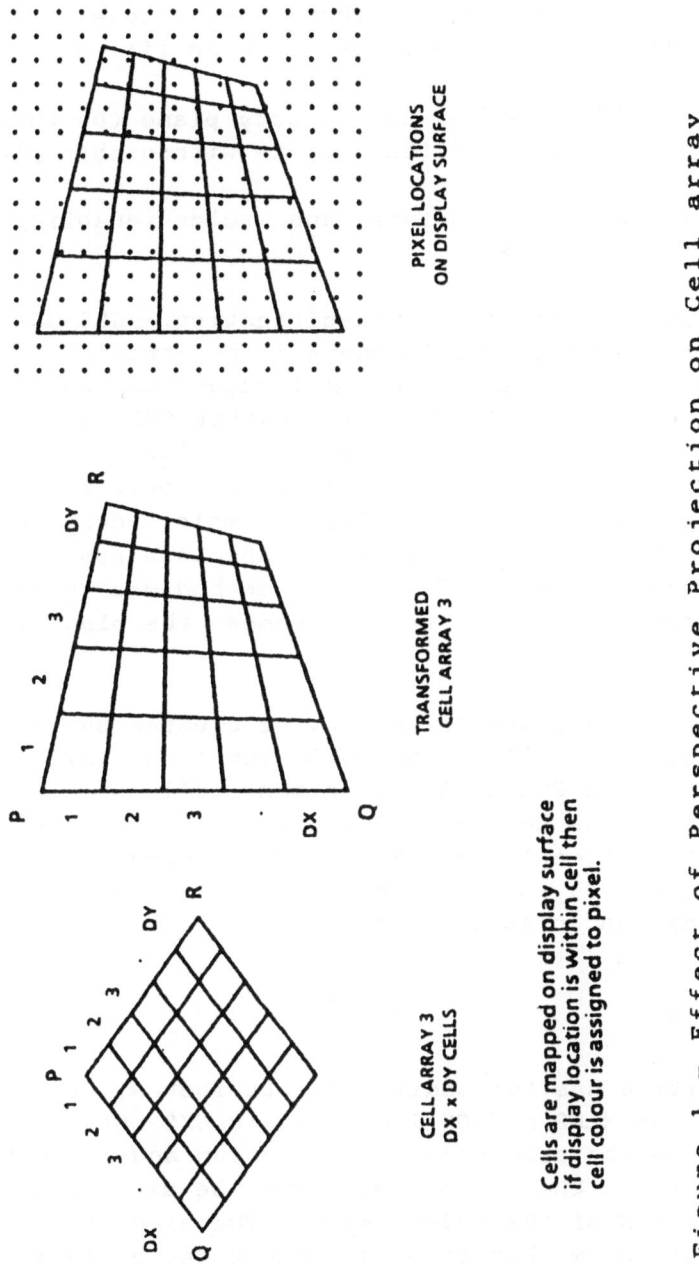

Figure 1 – Effect of Perspective Projection on Cell array

With the exception of polyline and polymarker, all these primitives are planar. All planar primitives have zero thickness and two sides, the obverse and reverse. The text, and/or pattern are 'written' on the obverse, and when the primitive is viewed such that the reverse becomes visible, it will display a 'mirror image' of the text/pattern of the obverse. There are at least two ways of specifying planar primitives, such as fill area:

(a) A specification of an arbitary plane (by three 3D points) and a list of (2D) points within this plane.

(b) A list of (3D) points and rules enabling the plane to be deduced.

With the latter method of specification, GKS-3D must check for planarity. This check is non-trivial as some tolerance must be used, which will depend on the method of representation of the data within GKS-3D (real vs integer), where in the viewing pipeline this is performed, and any number of other factors. The former is not how most of us work. For example, drawing the faces of a cube knowing only its absolute position and size is very difficult. The latter method was chosen and the implementation is free to choose the plane if the points are non-planar.

Each of these (3D) primitives may be created by one of TWO function calls: The GKS function call (e.g. POLYLINE) or the POLYLINE 3 function call of GKS 3D. GKS-3D specifies how the GKS function is converted to a 3D primitive, (see later). Both calls create this 3D primitive, thus the GKS functions for primitives have NEW meanings and create instances of the 3D primitive.

6 ATTRIBUTES

Each primitive has two additional attributes, the VIEW INDEX and the HLHS METHOD INDEX. As in GKS these indices are bound to the primitive upon creation and cannot be altered, i.e. the index may NOT be altered but the REPRESENTATION of the index may be. The view index is an index into a workstation dependent table. This table contains sufficient information to enable the workstation driver to compute a view of the primitives. Thus a primitive can be viewed differently on each active workstation. The view index is intended to behave like the colour look table of raster devices. Each primitve may have a different representation of colour (view) N, and when the colour (view) representation is changed the picture changes (is re-computed if necessary). Devices with transformation hardware should be able to accommodate this feature dynamically; those without such hardware must do an implicit picture regeneration. The default view is an orthographic projection onto the z=0 plane.

HLHS method index, the other new attribute, is used to pass information to any hidden line hidden surface computation. For this index there is no bundle table on a workstation. The meanings of this index (with the exception of zero) are implementation dependent. Zero is to be interpreted, on all workstations as NONE, i.e. this primitive does not take part in any HLHS computation. HLHS computations are optional, and GKS-3D says no more about HLHS, except it identifies the point within the output pipeline where it must take place.

Fill area set has a new bundle table and attribute associated with it, controlling how the edge of the constituent polygons are rendered. It is very similar to the bundle table used for displaying lines. Each bundle table entry has:

EDGE FLAG (on or off).

EDGE TYPE the linestyle used to draw the lines.

EDGE WIDTH SCALE FACTOR how much thicker than a nominal width.

EDGE COLOUR INDEX index to indicate what colour to draw the lines of the edge.

There are also aspect source flags for these aspects. The edge is drawn on top of the interior. Thus, for interior style HOLLOW two lines are drawn. Conceptually the edge is drawn on top of the hollow boundary.

Fill area and fill area set also support mapping of patterns onto the same. For this the pattern reference points have a 3D counterpart the PATTERN REFERENCE POINTS 3. This function has three points as it parameters, which are used to define the plane of the pattern. In general this plane will not be co-planar to the plane of the fill area or fill area set. To map the pattern onto the fill primitives the three pattern reference points are projected along the normal to the fill area (set) plane onto the fill area(set) plane. These 3 projected points define the orientation of the pattern in the fill area plane. If the projected pattern reference points form a degenerate case an implementation dependent technique is used.

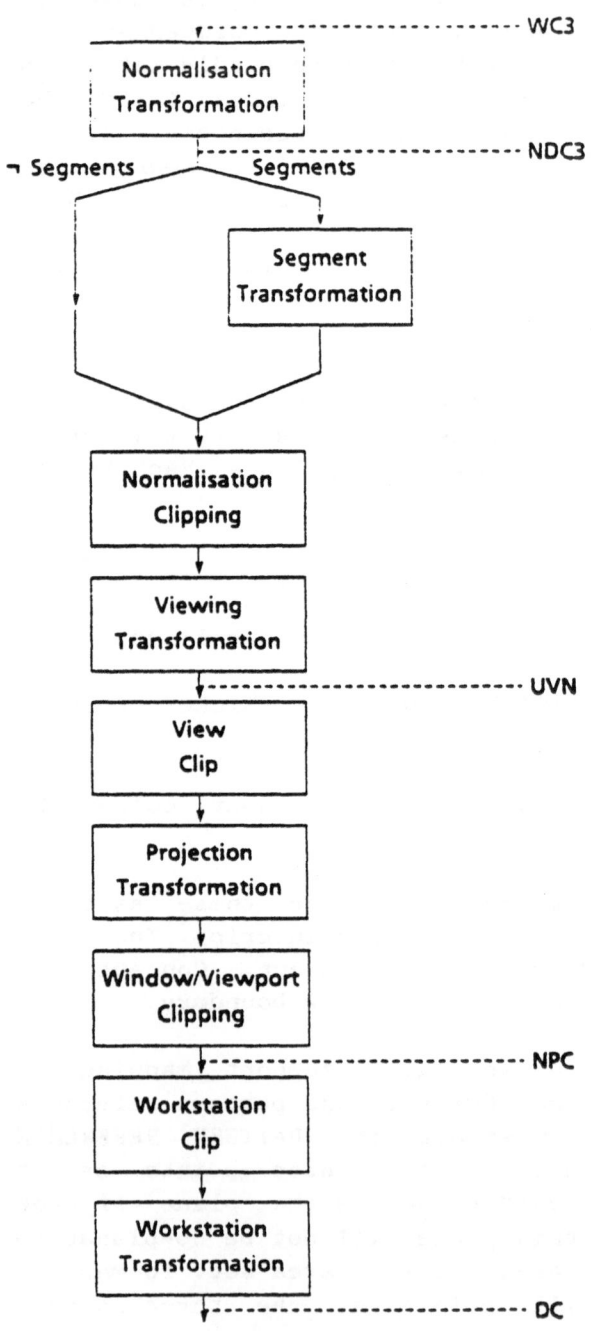

Figure 2
Output Pipleine

7 VIEWING PIPELINE

The viewing pipeline is shown in figure 2. When a primitive is created the current normalisation transformation converts from World co-ordinates (WC3) to Normalised device co-ordinates (NDC3). Any segment transformation is also applied, followed by the normalisation clip. This is exactly as in GKS except mappings are 3D and not 2D. The workstation driver takes over and, continuing to work in 3D, uses the current representation of the view index bound to the primitive to create a view of the primitive. The second part of the view representation controls the projection into Normalised projection co-ordinates (NPC3). Any HLHS computation takes place in this coordinate system. NPC3 is coincident with NDC3 and the workstation transformation is used to map NPC3 to device co-ordinates (DC3). The effect of the view and projection transformation is to re-orientate the primitves within NDC3. Both parallel and perspective transformations are supported. The SET VIEW REPRESENTATION function has a number of parameters which are illustrated in figure 3 for parallel and figure 4 for perspective projection. Also part of this function is a view matrix, which is a 4 X 4 matrix used prior to projection to specify the view of the object. A utility function is provided to enable the matrix to be computed, given a view reference point, a view up vector and the view plane normal.

8 INPUT

Two additional input classes are provided: LOCATOR 3 and STROKE 3. A locator 3 returns a position in world co-ordinates (WC3), a normalisation transformation number, and a view index. Similary STROKE 3 returns a sequence of points in WC3, a normalisation transformation number and a vew index.

For locator 3 (and stroke 3), the workstation driver generates a co-ordinate in DC3. If no 3D digitiser is available, simulation must be used to provide a third co-ordinate, e.g. typing the value on a keyboard. The workstation transformation is used to invert this DC3 value to an NPC3 value. The view index set by INITIALISE

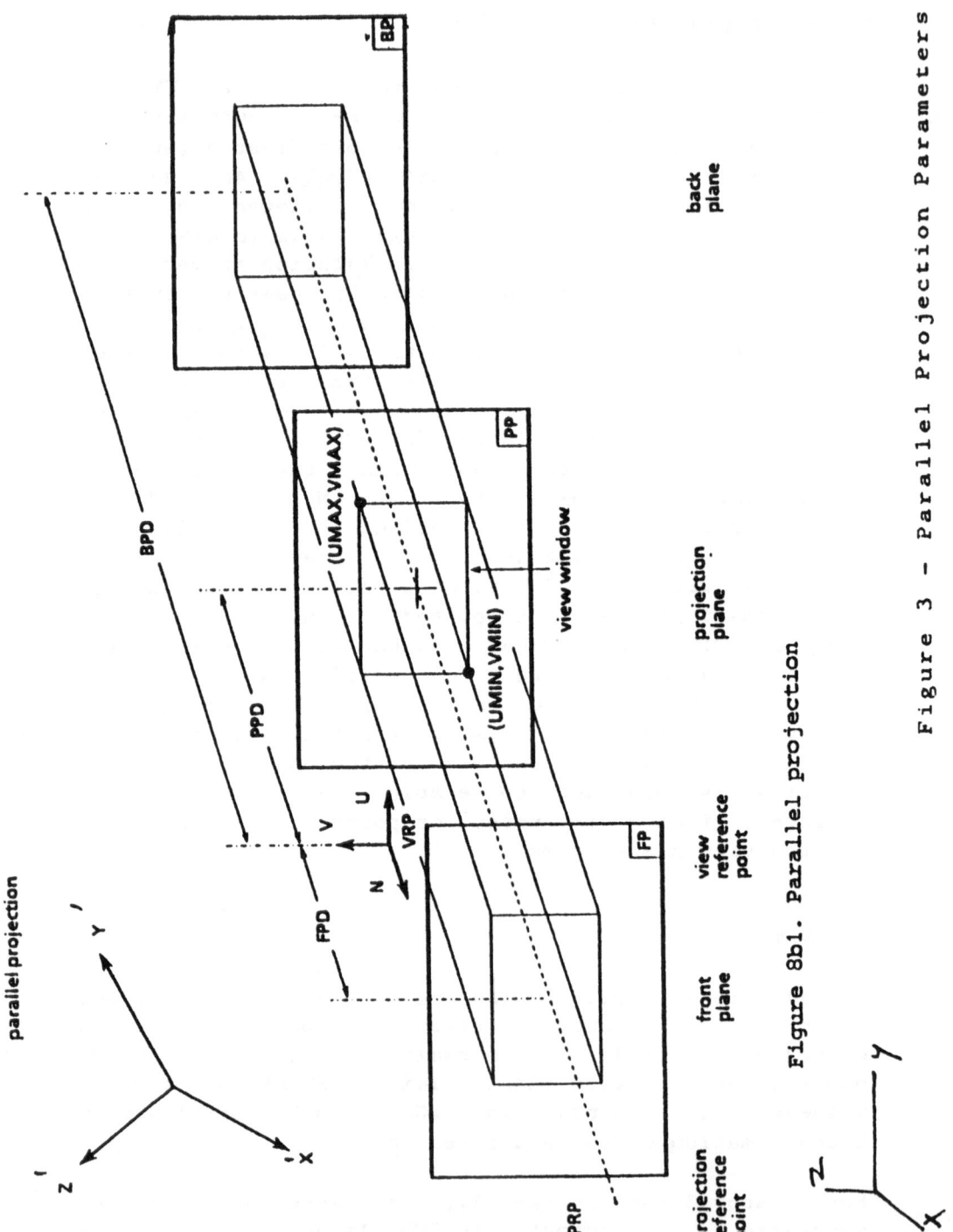

parallel projection

(UMAX,VMAX)

(UMIN,VMIN)

view window

BPD

PPD

FPD

U

V

N

VRP

PP

BP

FP

back plane

projection plane

view reference point

front plane

projection reference point

PRP

Figure 8b1. Parallel projection

Figure 3 - Parallel Projection Parameters

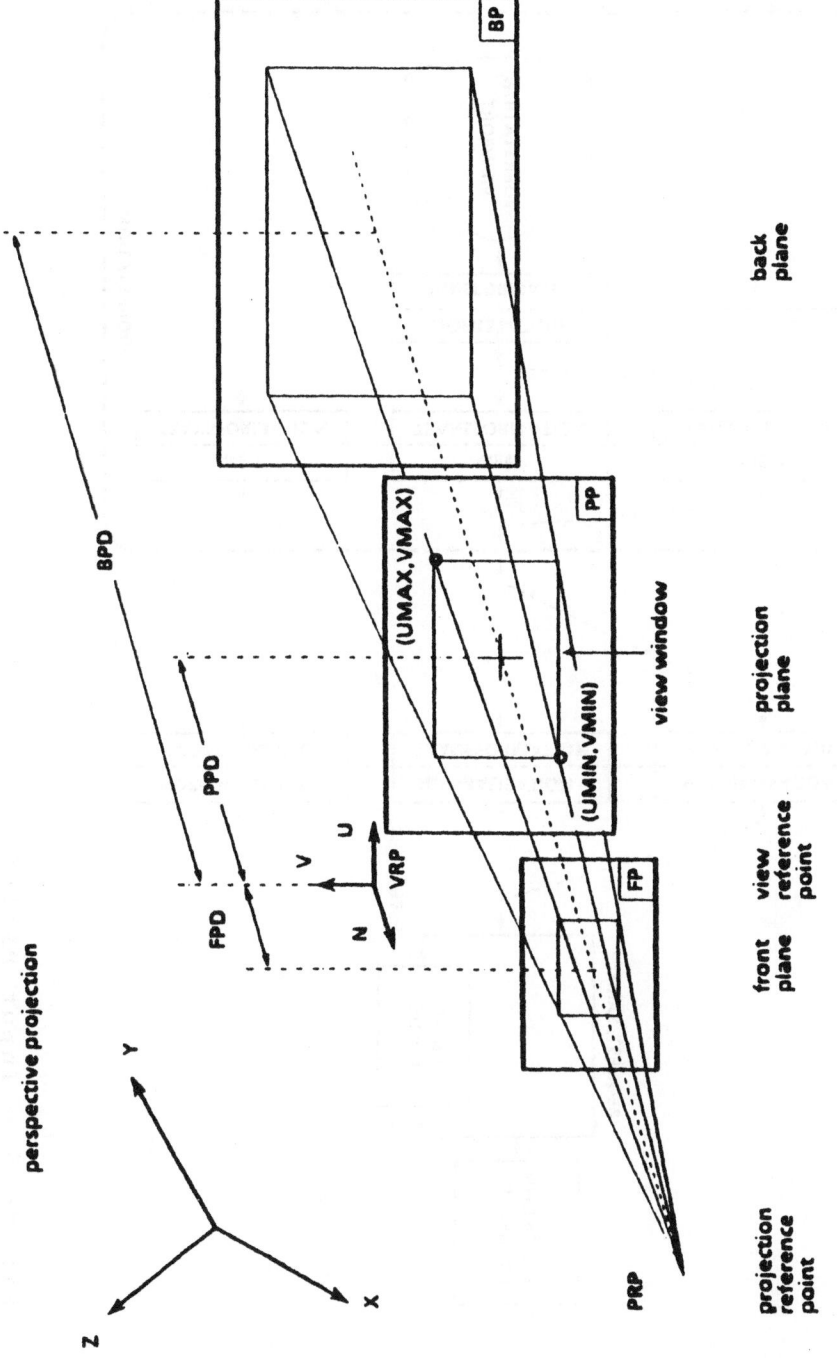

Figure 4 — Perspective Projection Pipeline

222

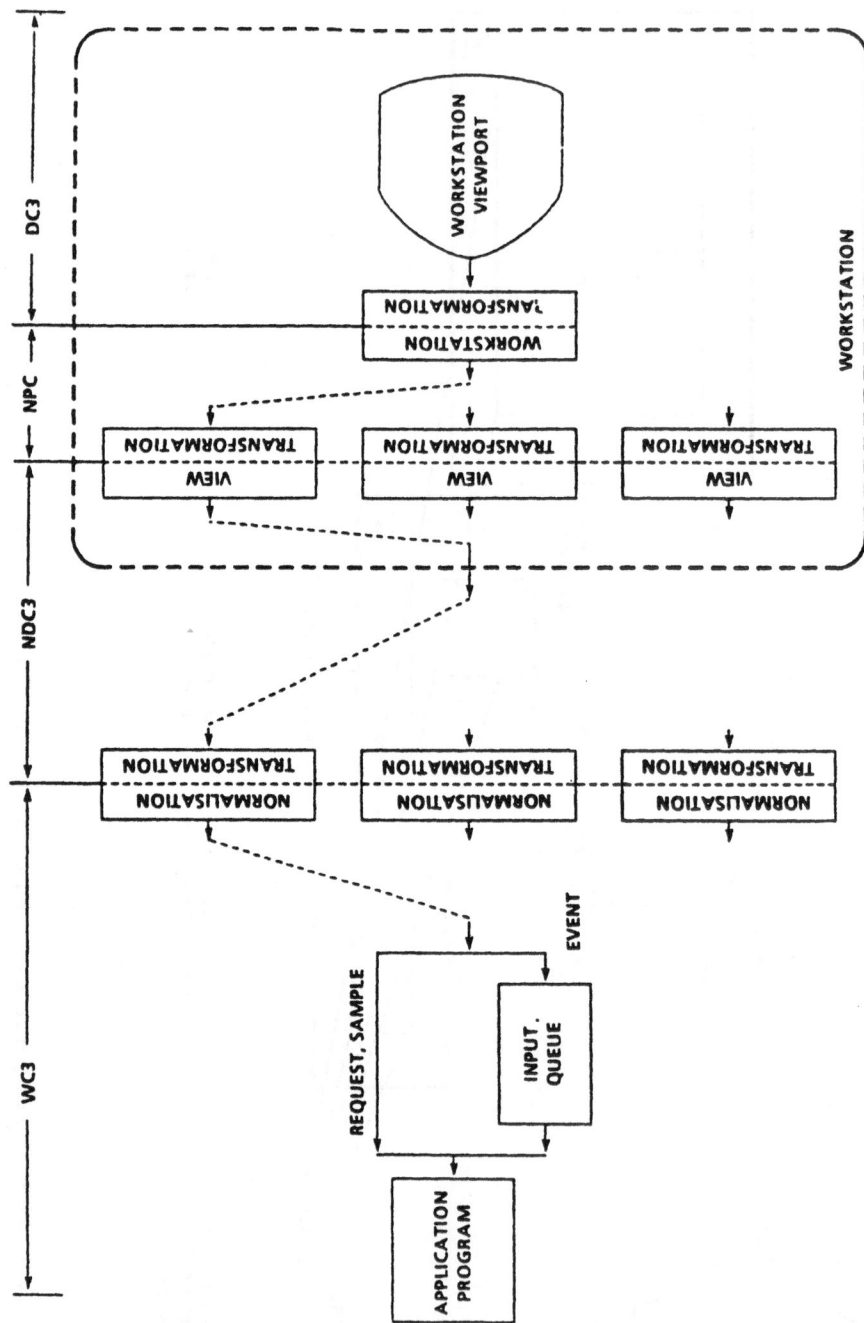

Figure 5 - Input Pipleine

LOCATOR 3 is used to get the view parameters and the inverse of the viewing transformation used to convert from NPC3 to NDC3, see figure 5. As in GKS the normalisation transformations are searched to find the appropriate one to return to the application program. Because the source data is 3D there is always a unqiue inverse.

The GKS functions LOCATOR and STROKE continue to return 2D co-ordinates. These 2D input devices produce data on the z=0 plane. In practice this means for a 2D locator the z co-ordinate can be ignored, as long as the normalisation transformations which do not contain the z=0 plane are excluded. Normalisation transformation number 0 always contains z=0.

9 GKS in GKS-3D

One of the design goals was that GKS programs should work in this 3D system. It was also mentioned that the GKS primitive functions (e.g. POLYLINE) produce a 3D primitive. In 3D the GKS functions define primitives that lie in the z=0 plane. Thus z=0 is added to the parameter lists to make it a 3D primitive instance. Table 1, an extract from the GKS-3D document show the action of the GKS functions whose action must be modified for GKS-3D.

Other possibilities for the placement of the GKS primitives were considered, such as an arbitary settable plane in whcih the 2D functions lie, but wrer rejected because they introduced too many side effects. The default view index its representation, and the workstation transformation are such that GKS programs should run. The major difference is with the metafile. As workstations are 3D devices so is the metafile, and metafile output conatins 3D information. Thus a GKS-3D metafile cannot be read by a GKS program, though a GKS-3D program can read both 2D and 3D metafiles. Upwards compatibility has been achieved, but not downwards compatibility.

Table 1 – Conversion of GKS functions to GKS-3D

4.14 Overview of interpretation of GKS functions in a 3D environment

This table shows how existing GKS functions are interpreted in GKS-3D. Each GKS function call is followed by a GKS-3D function call which has the same effect in GKS-3D. This does not imply that the GKS function calls the GKS-3D function.

- POLYLINE		→	- POLYLINE 3	
n×(x,y)	n×(WC)	→	n×(x,y,0)	n×(WC3)
- POLYMARKER		→	- POLYMARKER 3	
n×(x,y)	n×(WC)	→	n×(x,y,0)	n×(WC3)
- TEXT		→	- TEXT 3	
(x,y)	(WC)	→	(x,y,0),(x+1,y,0),(x,y+1,0)	3×(WC3)
string	(S)	→	string	(S)
- FILL AREA		→	- FILL AREA 3	
n	(I)	→	n	(I)
n×(x,y)	(WC)	→	n×(x,y,0)	n×(WC3)
- CELL ARRAY		→	- CELL ARRAY 3	
(Px,Py)	(WC)	→	(Px,Py,0)	(WC3)
(Qx,Qy)	(WC)	→	(Qx,Py,0)	(WC3)
			(Px,Qy,0)	(WC3)
dimension	2×(I)	→	dimension	2×(I)
colour array	n× n×(I)	→	colour array	n× n×(I)
- GDP		→	- GDP 3	
n×(x,y)	n×(WC)	→	n×(x,y,0)	n×(WC3)
identifier	(N)	→	identifier	(N)
data record	(D)	→	WC content → WC3 content in implementation-dependent way	(D)
- SET PATTERN REFERENCE POINT		→	- SET PATTERN REFERENCE POINTS 3	
(x,y)	(WC)	→	(x,y,0)	(WC3)
			(x+1,y,0)	(WC3)
			(x,y+1,0)	(WC3)
- SET WINDOW		→	- SET WINDOW 3	
transformation number	(I)	→	transformation number	(I)
window limits-			window limits-	
xmin, xmax	(WC)		xmin, xmax	(WC3)
ymin, ymax	(WC)		ymin, ymax	(WC3)
			zmin=0, zmax=1	(WC3)
- SET VIEWPORT		→	- SET VIEWPORT 3	
transform number	(I)	→	transform number	(I)
viewport limits-		→	viewport limits-	
xmin, xmax,	(NDC)		xmin, xmax,	(NDC3)
ymin, ymax,	(NDC)		ymin, ymax	(NDC3)
			zmin=0, zmax=1	(NDC3)

- SET WORKSTATION   →   - SET WORKSTATION

WINDOW			WINDOW 3	
ws ident	(N)	→	ws ident	(N)
window limits		→	window limits	
xmin, xmax	(NDC)		xmin, xmax	(NPC)
ymin, ymax	(NDC)		ymin, ymax	(NPC)
			$zmin = 0$, $zmax = 1$	(NPC)

- SET WORKSTATION   →   - SET WORKSTATION
  VIEWPORT   VIEWPORT 3

ws ident	(N)	→	ws ident	(N)
viewport limits		→	viewport limits	
xmin, xmax	(DC)		xmin, xmax	(DC3)
ymin, ymax	(DC)		ymin, ymax	(DC3)
			$zmin = ws\ zmin$	(DC3)
			$zmax = ws\ zmax$	(DC3)

- INSERT SEGMENT   →   - INSERT SEGMENT 3

segment	(N)	→	segment name	(N)
segment transformation matrix			segment transformation matrix	

$$\begin{bmatrix} M_{11} & M_{12} & M_{13} \\ M_{21} & M_{22} & M_{23} \end{bmatrix} \quad 2\times 3 (R) \quad \rightarrow \quad \begin{bmatrix} M_{11} & M_{12} & 0 & M_{13} \\ M_{21} & M_{22} & 0 & M_{23} \\ 0 & 0 & 1 & 0 \end{bmatrix} \quad 3\times 4 (R)$$

- SET SEGMENT TRANSFORMATION   →   - SET TRANSFORMATION 3

segment name	(N)	→	segment name	(N)
segment transformation matrix		→	segment transformation matrix	

$$\begin{bmatrix} M_{11} & M_{12} & M_{13} \\ M_{21} & M_{22} & M_{23} \end{bmatrix} \quad 2\times 3 \times (R) \quad \begin{bmatrix} M_{11} & M_{12} & 0 & M_{13} \\ M_{21} & M_{22} & 0 & M_{23} \\ 0 & 0 & 1 & 0 \end{bmatrix} \quad 3\times 4 \times (R)$$

10 CONCLUSIONS

Work is also underway on the language bindings, and it is hoped that they will not lag as far behind GKS-3D as they did for GKS. GKS-3D will not compete with GKS, it will supplement it. You must choose the right 'tool for the job'. GKS has one advantage over GKS-3D, it did NOT have to be compatible with anything.

11 REFERENCES

These document are all available through your national standards committee.

[1] ISO DIS 7942 GKS

[2] ISO TC97 SC5 WG2 N193 - 3D Sub-group report of Co-chairs.

[3] PHIGS - ANSC X3H3/84-44

[4] ISO TC97 SC5 WG2 N307 - 3D Sub-groups Chairmans report.

[5] ISO TC97 SC5 WG2 N308 - GKS-3D Resolved Issues List 1.

[6] ISO TC97 SC21 WG5-2 3D/59 - GKS-3D Proposed Resolved Issues List 2.

[7] ISO TC97 SC21 WG5-2 3D/60 - GKS-3D Active Issues List 3.

[8] ISO TC97 SC21 WG5-2 N277 Rev GKS-3D Functional Specification.

Programmers Hierarchical Interactive Graphics System (PHIGS)

W. T. Hewitt

1 INTRODUCTION

GKS and GKS-3D enable graphical data to be grouped into segments and certain operations can be carried out on segments,(thus effecting all primitives within the segment) such as transforming and making it visible or invisible, or deleting. The contents of a segment cannot be edited in anyway. The more expensive (i.e. high performance) refresh display (and now many raster displays) have always been able to support a more sophisticated picture structure than that encompassed by GKS and GKS-3D. Further for many applications the segment model is not sufficient. PHIGS (the Programmers Hierarchical Interactive Graphics System) is aimed at such a market. Its scope:

o definition, display and modification of 2D and 3D graphical data

o definition, display and manipulation of geometrically related objects

o Rapid dynamic articulation of graphical entities

Rapid dynamic articulation can be loosely described as "if I turn a dial (some rotation angle) the appropriate part of the picture is modified in real time". This system has been developed by ANSC X3H31 and in February 1985 was adopted as a work item within ISO.

GKS and GKS-3D are technically very similar, many of the functions in PHIGS being identical to their counterparts in GKS and GKS-3D.

2 CENTRALISED DATABASE

Creation of a picture in PHIGS is a two phase process. First the application invokes (certain) PHIGS functions to define the picture and its structure. The definition of the

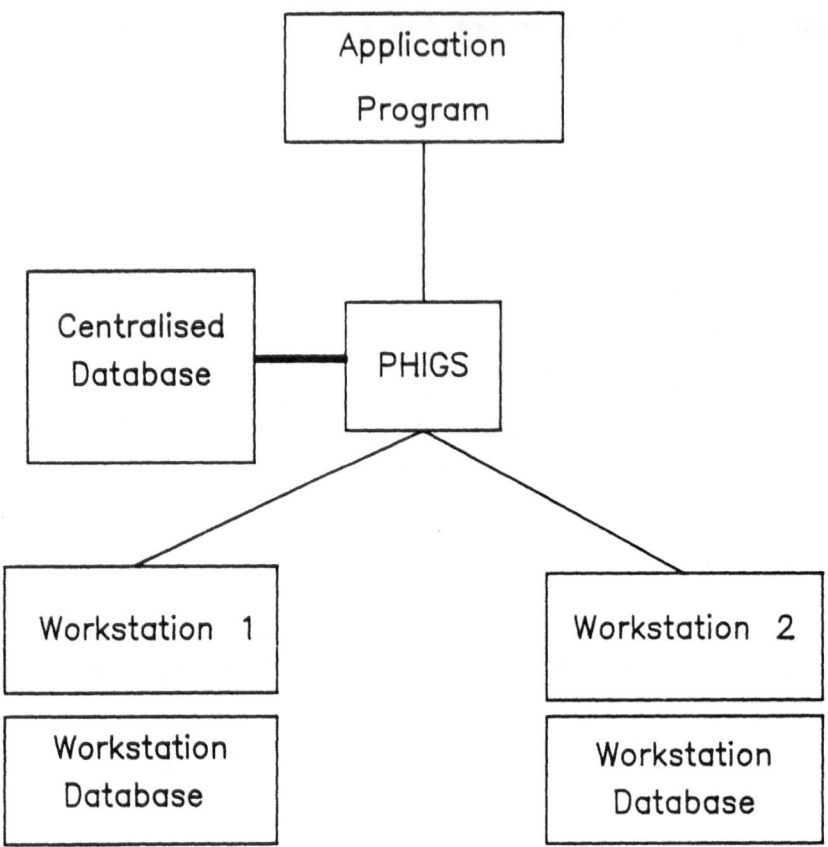

Figure 1 PHIGS Structure

picture is stored in the centralised database. In the
second phase the application program 'POST's part of the
picture to one or more of workstations available. Any
modifications to the (centralised) database are
automatically dispatched to the 'POST'ed workstations; See
figure 1.

3 STRUCTURES

In the centralised database the graphical data (structure
elements) is organised into structures. The structure
elements include all the primitives and aspects that GKS
and GKS-3D allow in segments. Additionally modelling
transformations, labels, application specific data and
calls to other structures (execute structure) are structure

elements.   (The basic unit which is 'POST'ed to a
workstation is a structure, and its instanced structures.)

Because structures contain references to other structures
the   centralised   database   may   represent hierarchical
relationships among the graphics data. A structure may be
executed more than once from another structure, for example
define a structure wheel, which draws a wheel!   The
structure axle would contain structure elements to

o draw the axle

o modelling transform to put wheel on one end

o execute structure wheel

o modelling transform to put wheel on other end of axle

o execute structure wheel

Structure car could then be similar to axle except the
execute structure would execute axle. This is illustrated
in figure 2.

More complex structures are obviously possible, figure 3
shows several examples.

Structure CAR
Modelling transform
Execute AXLE
Modelling Transform
Execute AXLE

Structure AXLE
Modelling Transform
Execute WHEEL
Modelling Transform
Execute WHEEL

Structure WHEEL
polyline

Figure 2 An example Structure

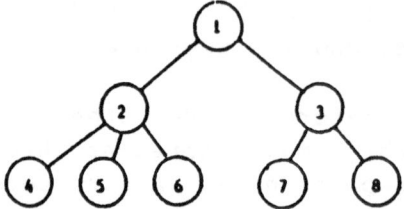

Figure   shows a structure in which 4, 5, and 6 are subordinate to 2, which
is in turn subordinate to 1. Similarly, 7 and 8 are subordinate to 3, which
is in turn subordinate to 1.

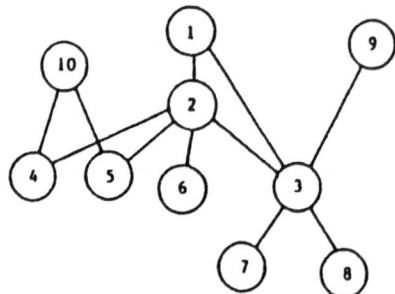

Hierarchical Structures with Three Root Structures

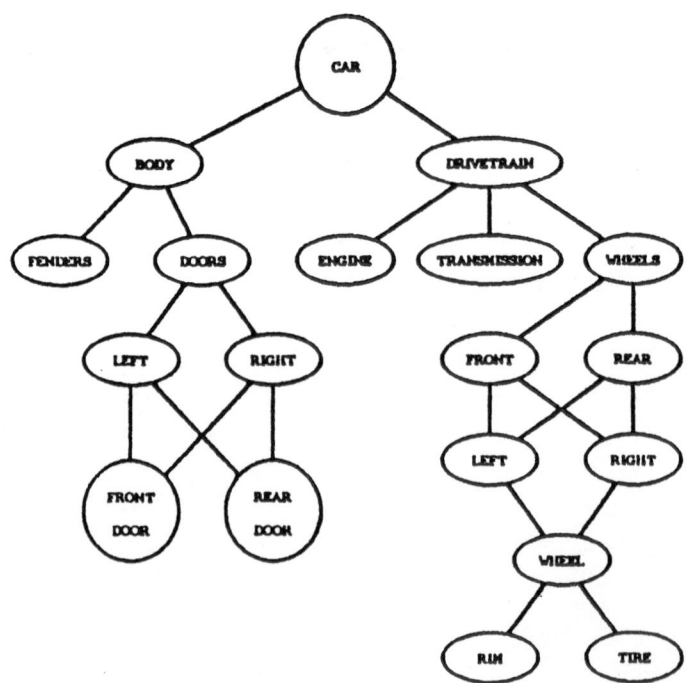

Figure 3 Example Structures

4 ATTRIBUTE BINDING

In GKS and GKS-3D attributes (eg colour index) are bound to the primitive upon creation (in Phase 1). In PHIGS attribute selection functions (such as set polyline colour index) become structure elements. The value of an attribute affects only the structure in which it is defined and subsequent structures below it in the hierarchy. Thus values of attribute used to render primitives are determined in phase 2 (display) i.e. during structure execution or traversal. A primitive may be rendered differently for different instances of the primitive. E.g.

        OPEN STRUCTURE AXLE

        SET POLYLINE COLOUR INDEX 1

        MODELLING TRANSFORM

        EXECTUE WHEEL

        SET POLYLINE COLOUR INDEX 2

        MODELLING TRANSFORM

        EXECUTE WHEEL

        POLYLINE C

        OPEN STRUCTURE WHEEL

        POLYLINE A

        SET POLYLINE COLOUR INDEX 3

        POLYLINE B

In this example polyline A would be rendered with colour 1 for the first instance and colour 2 for the second instance. In both instances polyline B would be drawn in colour 3. Wheel inherits either polyline colour index 1 or 2 whereas (due to the explicit setting within wheel) any structure referenced by wheel would inherit polyline colour

index 3. Polyline C would be drawn with colour 2, the last
set in this or a higher structure, even though wheel reset
the 'current' polyline colour index to 3.

If it was required to have a red/green wheel and a
blue/yellow wheel PHIGS cannot support this directly as
only one (polyline colour index) attribute of each type may
be inherited. It would be necessary for the wheel to be two
structures wheel_A and wheel_B and the parent to invoke
BOTH structures changing the relevant attribute in between
calls.

5 STRUCTURE EDITING

Having defined (and possibly displayed) the structure the
application program can now edit the structure. PHIGS has
the following functions to assist:

o INSERT LABEL   - an application defined label is added as a structure
               element. It is treated as a no operation during
               traversal.

o INSERT APPLICATION DATA - add a data record as a structure element.

o SET ELEMENT POINTER   - make PHIGS 'point' at the structure element
               corresponding to the parameter.

o OFFSET ELEMENT POINTER   - add the offset to the structure element poi

o SET ELEMENT POINTER AT LABEL - make PHIGS 'point' to the structure
               element corresponding to the user defined label

o DELETE ELEMENT   - remove the structure element pointed to by the
               element pointer (current element).

o DELETE ELEMENT RANGE - delete elements in the supplied range.

o DELETE ELEMENTS BETWEEN LABELS - delete elements between the labels,
               leaving the labels in the structure.

o INQUIRE ELEMENT POINTER - return current value of element pointer.

o INQUIRE ELEMENT TYPE & SIZE - what is the current element.

o INQUIRE ELEMENT CONTENT - get the structure element data.

These functions enable data to be inserted into an open structure, deleted or modified. Note it is NOT possible to edit (e.g.) a point of the polyline line, just the whole polyline. To edit a polyline:

```
SET ELEMENT POINTER                    ! point to correct item

GET ELEMENT DATA( ..... PX,PY,PZ.....)    ! get its data

PX(i) = something else                 ! edit the data

SET ELEMENT POINTER                    ! point to correct item

POLYLINE3(N,PX,PY,PZ)                  ! put the data back
```

This editing can be thought of as like a line editor. I.e. it is possible to insert, remove or replace lines of text (structure elements) in a file (structure), but it is NOT possible to edit the CONTENT of a line of text.

6 COORDINATE SYSTEMS AND TRANSFORMATIONS

We have already mentioned that a structure element could be a modelling transform. Primitives are defined in modelling coordinates and during structure traversal one or more modelling transformations may be applied to the coordinate data of the primitives. Modelling transformations are represented by 4 X 4 matricies, and are thus affine transformations. The outcome of the modelling transformation is a primitive defined in World Coordinates (WC3).

[world coordinate] = [Composite transformation] [Modelling Coordinate]

The composite modelling is the product of the current global modelling transformation (a structure element) and the current local modelling transformation (a structure element):

[Composite transformation] = [Global] [Local]

When a structure is invoked the current global and local transformations are saved. Upon return the transformations are returned to this saved state.

The local modelling transformation may be modified in one of three ways by the function SET MODELLING TRANSFORMATION:

o REPLACE

    [Composite transformation] = [Global] [New transform]
    [local] = [new transform]

o PRE-CONCATENATE

    [Composite transformation] = [Global] [Local] [new transform]
    [local] = [local] [new transform]

o POST-CONCATENATE

    [Composite transformation] = [Global] [new transform] [Local]
    [local] = [new transform] [local]

This set of functions is supplemented by a numbr of utility functions to make the creation of the 4 X 4 matricies easier.

World Coordinates (WC3) is a device independent coordinate system used to compose the graphics data in different modelling coordinates for viewing.

The view transform maps WC3 into the View Reference Coordinate system (VRC). This transformation is analagous to pointing the camera at the objects (in WC3) and enables the projection to be specified along the 'Z' axis. VRC and the projection specification are a 3D device independent, workstation dependent coordinate system. The The view mechanism is similar to that of GKS-3D, in that the stucture element is a view index and the view specification is via the workstation view tables. The parameters for the view specification are described in the notes on GKS-3D. The output from the projection transformation are in Normalised Projection Coordinates (NPC3) and the workstation transformation selects all (or part) of the composed views to display, see figure 4.

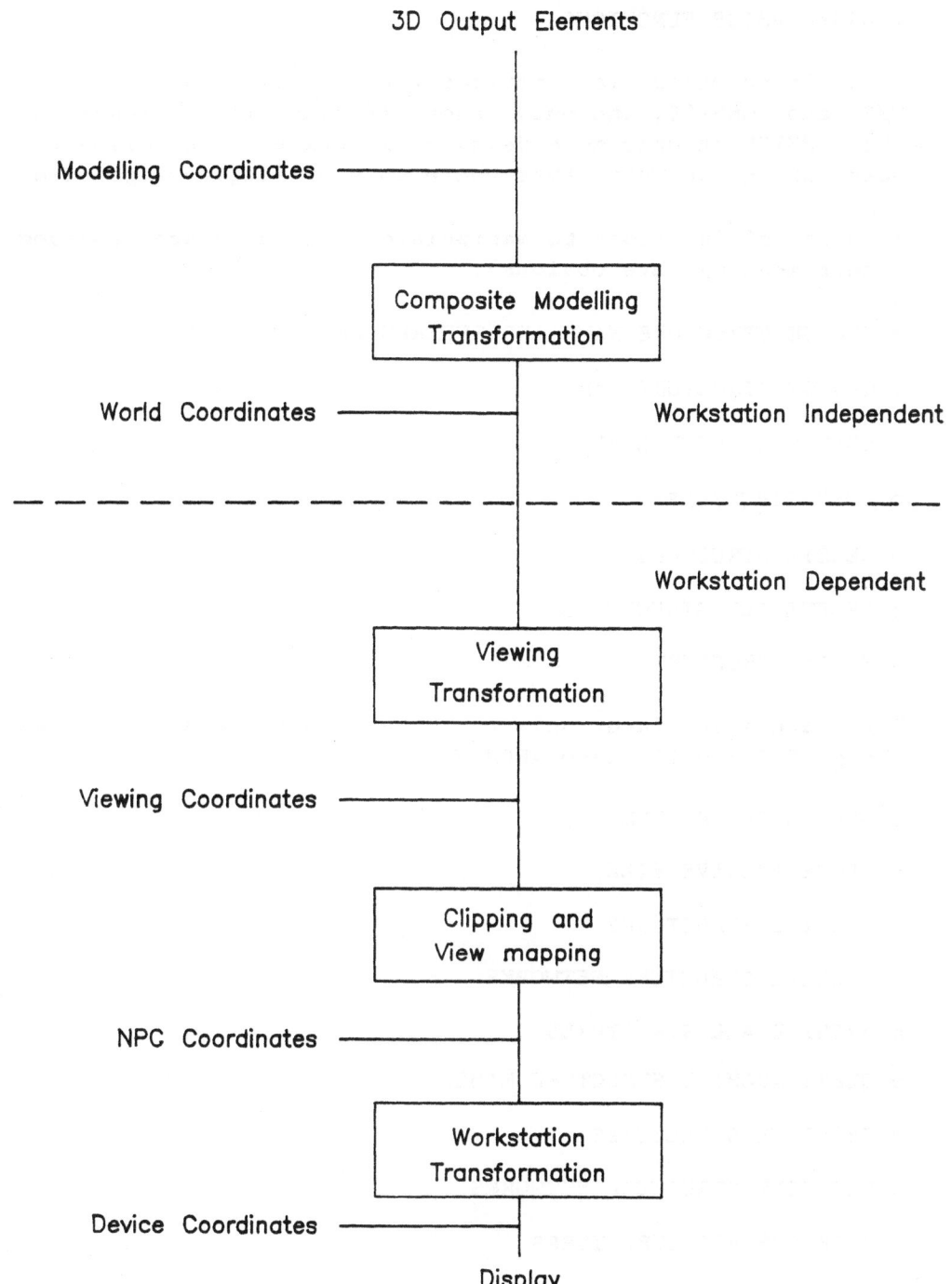

Figure 4 The PHIGS Viewing Pipleine

7 OTHER PHIGS FUNCTIONS

Input is provided via functions very similar to those of GKS and GKS-3D, the only major diference is in PICK input where PHIGS returns more detailed information, enabling the path through the structure where this primitive originated.

A number of functions to manipulate structures are provided (their meanings are obvious):

o CHANGE STRUCTURE NAME AND REFERENCES

o CHANGE STRUCTURE NAME

o CHANGE STRUCTURE REFERENCES

o COPY STRUCTURE

o DELETE STRUCTURE

o DELETE ALL STRUCTURES

o EMPTY STRUCTURE

There are also functions to create and read metafiles though PHIGS calls them ARCHIVEs:

o OPEN ARCHIVE FILE

o CLOSE ARCHIVE FILE

o ARCHIVE STRUCTURES

o ARCHIVE STRUCTURE NETWORKS

o ARCHIVE ALL STRUCTURES

o QUERY ARCHIVE STRUCTURE NAMES

o RETRIEVE STRUCTURES

o RETRIEVE STRUCTURE NETWORKS

o RETRIEVE ALL STRUCTURES

o DELETE STRUCTURES FROM ARCHIVE

o DELETE STRUCTURE NETWORKS FROM ARCHIVE

o DELETE ALL STRUCTURES FROM ARCHIVE

Interfaces and Data Formats for Transfer and Communication in Computer Graphics Systems

J. Encarnação and J. Schönhut

CONTENT

1. Introduction

A Graphics System may be seen as a computer-aided environment supporting the application program. The basic elements associated with it are:

— Operator (User)
— Graphics Support System (Services)
— Other User Interface Support System (Services)
— Application Functions
— Generic Action Routines
— Data Base

The kernel for the communication between the different parts of such a system is composed of the different data items associated with the communication elements.

From the point of view of the user operating such a graphics support system, a simple functional model may be given showing the functional decomposition of the model. The Graphics System is then based on the following basic functional components:

— User (Operator of the Computer-Aided Environment based on a Graphics Support System)

— Graphics
    — Graphics Viewing
    — Request Processing
    — Graphics Metafiles

— Model
    — Model Metafiles (Design Data)
    — Model Data Management

— Application
    — Control
    — Heuristics

This model implies a clean separation between application system, application control, graphics support system and model data management functions. This functionality again is based on the transfer of the associated items stored in the corresponding metafiles (graphics, model).

2. Data Interfaces

The model shown gives the basic functionality of a Graphics System as a computer-aided environment supporting the application program. The model given in Fig. 1 shows the different data interfaces in such a system for which standards have been developed or are in the process of being developed; these are:

— GKS and GKS Language Bindings; this is also the interface required for other graphics functional standards under discussion (e.g. PHIGS)

— the European Videotex Interface CEPT Geometric Encoding (which is a subset of the ECMA Graphics Data Syntax (GDS))

— Computer Graphics Interface (CGI) formerly known as Virtual Device Interface (VDI)

— Computer Graphics Metafile (CGM) formerly known as Virtual Device Metafile (VDM)

— the US Videotext Interface, the North American Presentation Layer Protocol Syntax (NAPLPS)

— Product Definition Data Interfaces like the Initial Graphics Exchange Specification (IGES) for the exchange of product data in connection with the graphic model, the VDAFS Sculptured Surface Interface developed by the German Automobile Manufacturers, SET (Aerospatiale, France) or XBF-2 (CAM-I); other examples are the German work on Transport and Archiving of Product Definiton Data (short TAP) and the related international work on STEP, the planned International Standard for Exchange of Product Definition Data Models.

— Interfaces for the integration of graphics in documents, e.g. the integration of graphics metafiles into documents defined in Standard General Markup Language (SGML) or Office Document Architecture / Office Document Interchange Format (ODA/ODIF).

— Interfaces for Presentation Graphics on the top of graphics standards like GKS.

The coherent and efficient integration of all these standards and developments into a highly functional Graphics Support System is one of the technical goals for the future in the area of Computer Graphics System Design.

Two activities related to GKS will be of specific impact in this development:

— the VLSI support of GKS implementations, and

— the design and implementation of GKS based applications for open communication sytems (e.g. LANs and WANs).

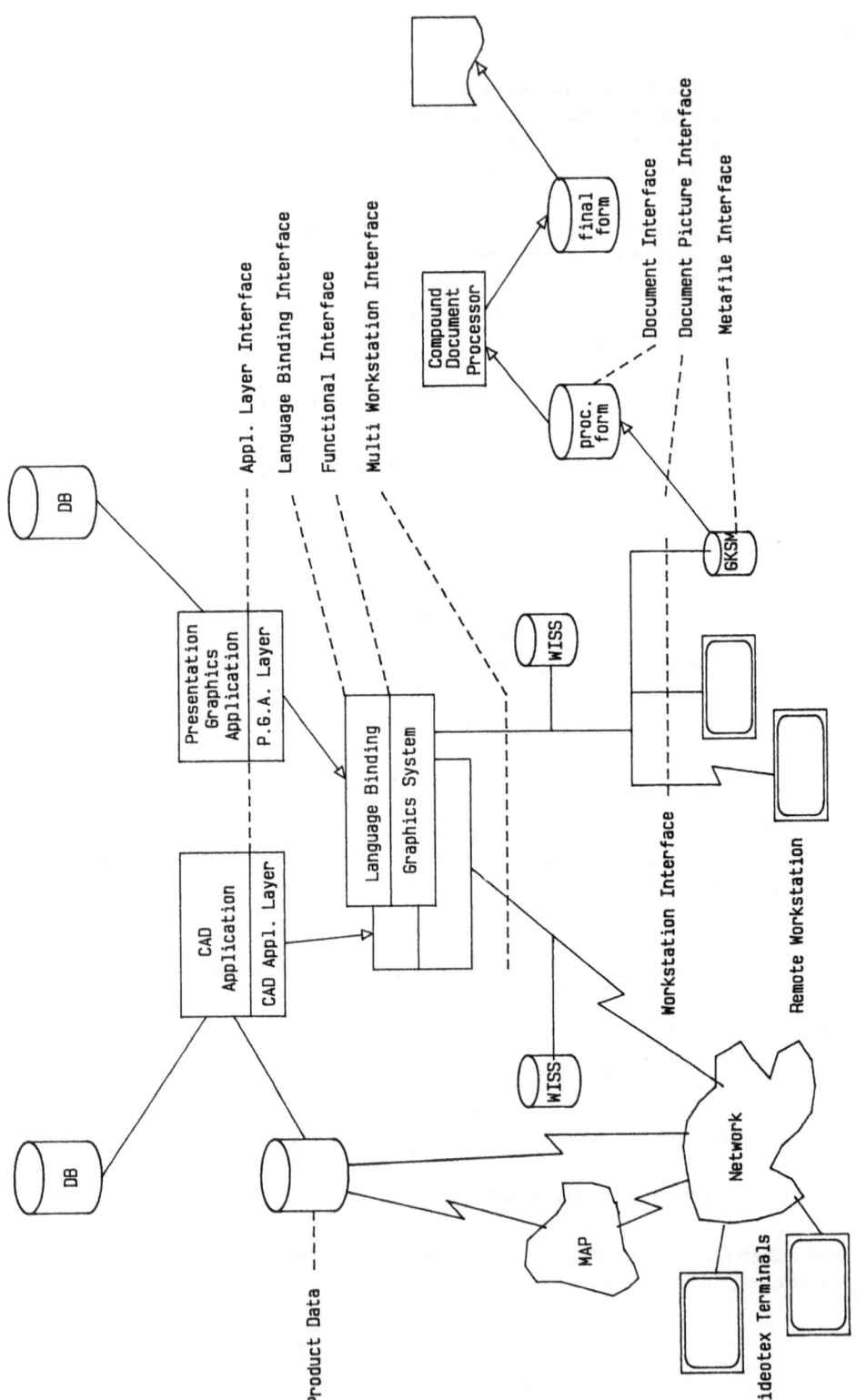

Fig. 1: Functional and Data Interfaces in a Graphics System

3. Standards for Graphics Programming

In the history of Graphics standards development several milestones are to be considered:

— Formation of the Graphics Standards Planning Committee (GSPC) in 1974 by ACM SIGGRAPH /1/;

— Formation of the Committee for the development of Computer Graphics Standards by the German Standardisation Body (DIN - Deutsches Institut für Normung) in 1975 /2,3/;

— The IFIP WG5.2 Workschop SEILLAC I (Methodology in Computer Graphics) organized by R. Guedj in France in 1976 /4/.

Todays scenarium of these standards and projects is shown in Fig. 2. This figure shows the distribution of graphics standards based on their dimensionality (2D and 3D), level of picture structuring (segments and hierarchies), and specification type (Functional Specifications, Language Bindings, Data Encodings):

— The Graphical Kernel System GKS is an already well established and publicised standard (ISO 7942) /2,3,5,6,7/. GKS will not be further discussed here, since it is well documented and discussed elsewhere /2,5/ in substantial detail. GKS is a 2D standard with one level of picture structuring based on segments.

— GKS-3D /8/ provides the application program with the following capabilities:
    — The definition and the display of 3D graphical primitives;
    — Mechanisms to control viewing transformations;
    — Mechanisms to control the appearance of primitives including optional support for hidden line and/or hidden surface elimination, excluding light source shading and shadow computation;
    — Mechanisms to obtain 3D input.

Fig. 3 shows the GKS-3D viewing pipeline. Existing 2D GKS applications should run without modification on systems incorporating GKS-3D, since no changes are made to the existing 2D functions. GKS-3D by now has reached ISO 2nd DP status being registered as ISO DIS 8805 early 1986.

— PHIGS (Programmer's Hierarchical Interactive Graphics Standard) /9/ includes in its functionality three dimensional output primitives and transformations and hierarchical segments, called structures. It has dynamic control over the visual appearance of attributes of primitives within a structure. One goal of PHIGS is to support the most powerful workstations becoming available. The structure of the PHIGS viewing pipeline is shown in Fig. 4.

— GKS Output Level 3 /10/ describes a set of extensions to GKS for segment hierarchy and editing. This GKS level 3 allows a segment to invoke other segments; an existing segment may be reopened for editing; elements may be inserted and deleted. The content of segment elements may be inquired. Segment networks may

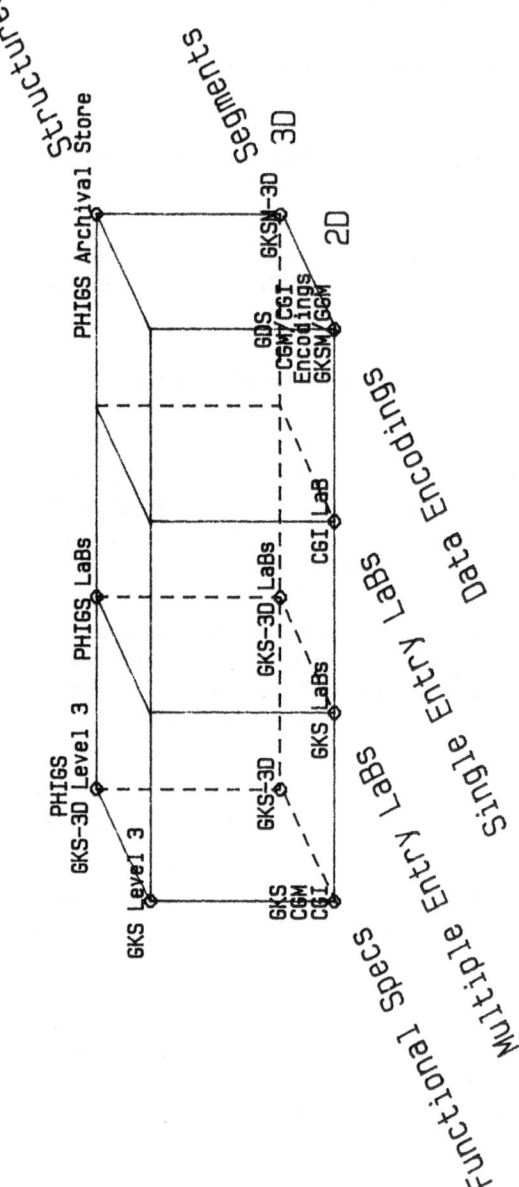

Fig. 2: Classification of Graphics Standards and Projects

243

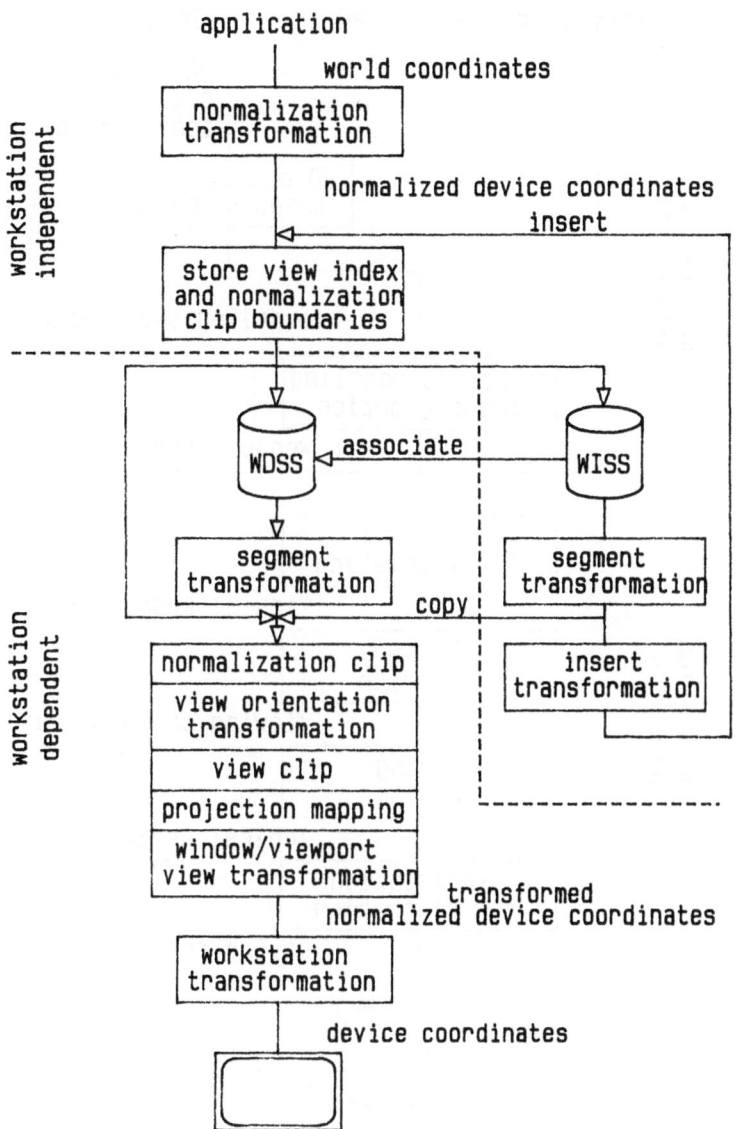

Fig. 3: Viewing Pipeline of GKS-3D

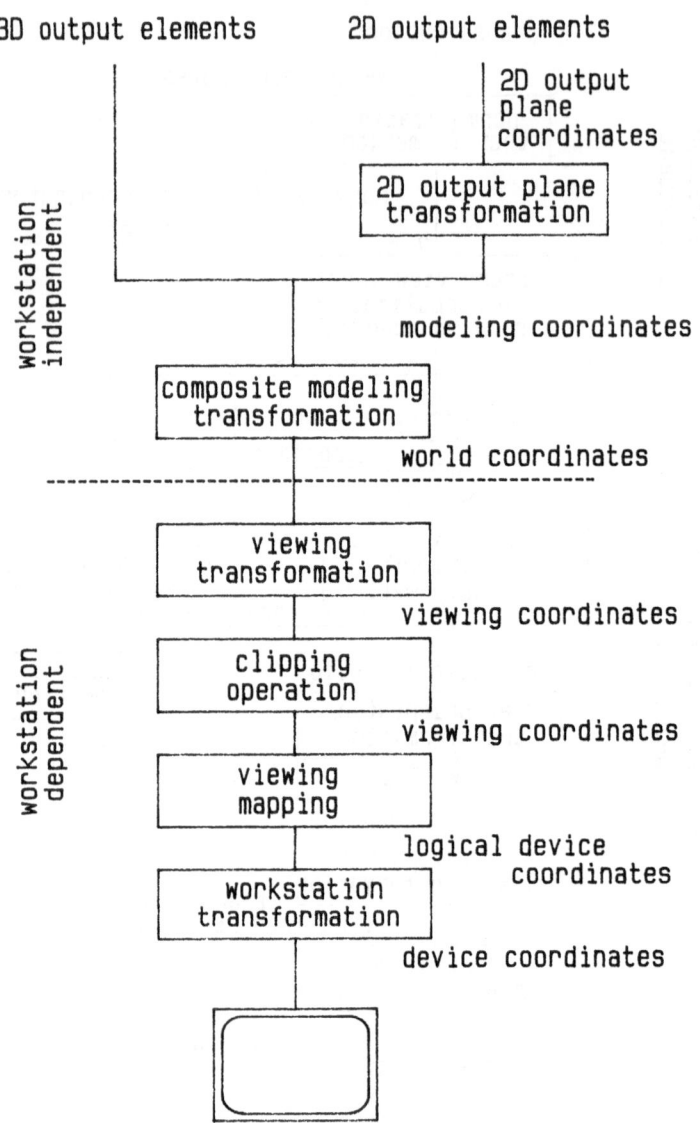

Fig. 4: PHIGS Viewing Pipeline

be stored in metafiles. This GKS level 3 demands only 15 functions in addition to GKS. By now GKS level 3 has no official standing as a standard or standards project but is only a working document; nevertheless it shows an extremely interesting way of extending GKS to handle segment hierarchies with the appeal of needing only very few additional functions. Based on GKS-3D this approach gives (by a minimal extension) a functionality comparable to PHIGS which is at the same time fully compatible to GKS and GKS-3D.

An important issue to be addressed in this context is the migration of applications written for the different standards shown in Fig. 1. The migrations from GKS to GKS-3D or from GKS to GKS level 3 are guaranteed by the fact that the full GKS functionality is a subset of both GKS-3D as well as of GKS level 3. The migration from GKS to PHIGS or from GKS-3D to PHIGS still make some problems because of existing incompatibilities between the functionalities of the GKS Standard and the current document of PHIGS. One of the key technical issues is the attribute binding concept, where GKS binds attribute values at generation time of the primitive, whereas PHIGS does the binding only at traversal time of structures and attribute values may be inherited from the parent structure. It may be that the actual public reviewing of PHIGS will help to solve some of the existing technical problems with the migration of application programs between the GKS Standard and a planned PHIGS Standard.

The "down migration" of applications from GKS-3D (and GKS Output Level 3) to 2D GKS may be solved by using the metafile functionality.

4. Graphics Metafiles

Graphics Metafile Standards ideally define file formats for storing and transmitting pictures in a device and application independent way. In practice they define functionality as well as encodings of formats. They enable the interconnection of various graphical devices and graphics systems in a standardized way. An overview of different encoding methods is given in /11/.

GKSM is the GKS Metafile used by GKS; it is a sequential file that can be written and read by GKS /7/ and is used for long term storage and transmittal of the graphical information produced or to be read by GKS. GKS provides means not only for writing but also for reading of the GKSM. The GKS Metafile contains two dimensional pictures represented by data records (called items) generated as a result of GKS functions involved. The GKSM contains:

—   file/picture header,
—   end item,
—   control items,
—   output primitive items,
—   attribute items,
—   non-graphical, application dependent data (user items).

GKSM is build up of a sequence of logical variable length data records. GKS addresses GKSM like a workstation. Two workstation types are defined for the GKS Metafile:

— the GKSM output workstation and
— the GKSM input workstation.

The functionality of the GKSM is described in the GKS /7/ document. A proposal for a presentation is given in Annex E of this document.

The Computer Graphics Metafile (CGM) /12/ formerly known as VDM (Virtual Device Metafile) defines the functional behaviour (semantics) and form (syntax) or encoding of a set of elements. The following set of elements is specified:

— descriptor elements,
— control elements,
— picture descriptor elements,
— graphical elements,
— attribute elements,
— escape elements,
— external elements.

A CGM is a collection of elements from this set. The descriptor elements give the CGM interpreter sufficient information to interpret metafile elements and to make decisions concerning the resources needed for display /12/.

CGM is expected to be usable as a GKS Metafile at level 0a of GKS if the portability of a CGM for GKS applications has to be ensured.

Since CGM cannot serve as a full GKS Metafile (levels 1 and above) and there is only one format for a GKSM given as example in Annex E to IS 7942, work is now under way to provide a full GKSM which is upward compatible to CGM. This project with the working title Generalized Graphics Metafile (GGM) has been prepared by the DIN working group on computer graphics and is about to be started in the ISO arena.

5. Device and Workstation Interfaces

GKS introduced the concept of workstations. These workstations hide device characteristics from the application programmer and thereby has significantly increased device independence of graphics software. Multiple of these workstations can be concurrently active and can be controlled independently by one application. This multiple workstation concept implies an interface called the multiple workstation interface, i.e. an interface before the data and control stream is splitted up to the different workstations. A second interface is required which adresses the single individual workstation. This interface is called the Workstation Interface (WSI).

The European Computer Manufacturers Association ECMA has defined its ECMA Standard 96 /13/ called Graphical Data Syntax (GDS). ECMA GDS is a character coded binding of almost the complete GKS functionality; the only missing parts are the GKS normalisation transformation and the GKS metafile functions; all other functions including those referring to the Workstation Independent Segment Store (WISS) and the complete input functionality are included. Thus difference to full GKS is minimal.

The development of this standard and the adoption of the output subset by CEPT strongly supports the expectation that in the near future devices with full GKS capabilities will be available at reasonably low cost; another implication of that development is that the appearance of GKS on silicon makes the efficiency complaints about pure software implementations obsolete.

In GDS the functions are coded very efficiently taking into consideration that reduction of the amount of data to be transferred reduces cost significantly.

The WSI specifies the functional separation of the GKS Kernel and the GKS Workstation. It allows the operation of GKS in distributed systems and the exchange of information between kernel and workstation of different implementations. The distribution among different hosts does not put restrictions on the functionality defined by GKS. The WSI is only implicitly defined in the GKS document; a more specific definition is given in /16/. Within ISO a Computer Graphics Interface Standard CGI /17/ is currently under development. It is intended that this standard shall provide at least the full functionality of the Workstation Interface.

For some devices including GKSM and CGM (at level 0) the device interface will coincide with the WSI; for other devices WSI capabilities not available on the device have to be simulated; such devices provide a low level device interface only and need device drivers.

A graphics device driver is that portion of the graphics system software that translates commands and data from the CGI into the form required by the particular input/output mechanism of the device. CGI is an interface which is internally closest to the pysical devices and the last point where device independence can still be achieved.

6. Videotex

Graphics in videotex environment can be represented in three different ways:

— alpha-mosaic character graphics,
— scanned image facsimile mode graphics,
— geometrically encoded graphics.

This last one has been strongly influenced by and come out of the computer graphics standardization at least in Europe.

As already mentioned before CEPT, the European PTTs have adopted as their Videotex Standard Geometric Encoding /16/ the output subset of the ECMA Graphical Data Syntax (GDS) /13/. The influence of this interface cannot be estimated high enough regarding the impact this standard has on the appearance of VLSI based solutions for graphics.

The North American Presentation Layer Protocol Syntax (NAPLPS) /17/ is an older attempt to provide character encoded graphics in a videotex environment. Despite the claim NAPLPS does not encode graphics commands very effieciently, definitely not as efficiently as GDS does; compared to GDS the graphics functionality is poor; the interface is clearly closer to a rather dumb device.

Currently there are strong currents within CCITT to provide a common framework for various videotex standards. One goal of the viedotex development is integration. The functionality of videotex itself currently already integrates text, graphics and facsimile. The availablity of these services in larger integrated networks is another important aspect of integration.

7. Product Data Transfer Formats

The Initial Graphics Exchange Specification (IGES) /18/ is a neutral data format which serves as a communication file to transfer data between CAD/CAM systems. IGES is structured as a five section file, containing the following parts:

— Prolog Section contains user defined text header for the file;

— Global Section contains information about the system, on which the part was developed, including numeric accuracies, scale factors, units of measurement and other environmental parameters; the object data in the file is composed of individual entities;

— Directory Entry Section contains an index to all the entities in the part as well as descriptive attributes for each;

— Parameter Data Section contains the actual data defining each entity;

— Terminator Section acts as a bookkeeping record to check the number of records received and processed.

IGES files are coded in ASCII, with 80 characters per record and appear logically as card deck. The new versions of IGES allow a binary file structure to reduce the data volume. The binary file structure utilises data definitions and relationships identical to the ASCII version, but trades substantial data compression for increased processing complexity. The IGES file concept is strongly directed to the "transfer of drawings" and related information between CAD/CAM systems.

IGES includes three entity types:

— geometry (including point, line, circle, conic, parameter spline, surface of revolution etc.);

— dimensioning/annotation (includes angular dimension, centreline, label, etc.);

— structure (includes standard and user defined associations, drawing relationships, font relationships, view relationships).

IGES is the oldest of Product Data Transfer formats; it became a NBS standard and later on an ANSI standard while still at a rather immature stage. As a result of the problems experienced with IGES ongoing development of follow up standards are going on in various arenas.

The German Standards Organisation DIN e.g. has taken an interest in standards for graphics and CAD systems interfaces for a number of years. In the beginning of 1983, when the demand for standards in product definition data exchange began to be expressed more acutely, a new DIN working group was formed. It was named "Transfer and Archival of Product Definition Data" (briefly TAP). This working group is concerned with issues very similar to those of IGES in the data exchange between CAD systems as well as a medium or long term storage of such data.

In the area of automotive engineering in Germany, the Association of Automobile Manufacturers (VDA) has recently developed a standard format for exchanging curve and surface data, called the VDA Sculptured Surface Interface called VDAFS /19/.

The approach taken here may serve as an example of a low redundancy lean entity set solution. The interface is limited to geometry entities (and comments) and contains only the following set:

— point;
— point set;
— point vector set;
— composite curve (include parametric splines);
— parametric spline surface.

Any geometric representations not contained in this basic set are converted to the standard by the sending system and later reconverted into the local representation of the receiving system. The VDA proposal is currently under review by DIN and will become a German national standard probably in 1986. Pilot implementations exist and have been tested with good success. The VDAFS will also be submitted for international reviewing.

International work in this area is done within ISO TC184/SC4, where an International Standard for the Exchange of Product Model Data (STEP) is being developed. One source comes from the US follow up activities for IGES called Product Data Exchange Specification (PDES). Besides the DIN work another source is from the French SET /20/ (Standard d'Echange et de Transfert) from Aerospatiale.

Process automation is an area of increasing impact in the US as well as worldwide. The keyword there is MAP, the Manufacturing Automation Protocol from General Motors. This is a de facto standard for the integration of Computer Aided Design (CAD), Computer Aided Manufacturing (CAM) and Computer Integrated Manufacturing (CIM). MAP gains more and more industrial acceptance worldwide and it can be expected that this also will influence STEP development too.

By the end of 1983 a new Electronic Design Interchange Format (EDIF), with similar goals to IGES, has been developed by the main semiconductor and computer companies. EDIF enables the communication of various types of electronic data among CAD/CAE tools and systems. The EDIF file consists of four kinds of information blocks:

— Status blocks contain accounting information, such as data, author's name and software level;

— Design blocks provide entry points to the EDIF file contents by indicating which cell in which library contains the top level description of the design conveyed by the file;

— Cell Definition Libraries contain all relevant design information;

— User Data blocks are catch-alls to handle information not otherwise expressible in EDIF.

The EDIF file does not concentrate as much as IGES on the drawings and related data, but more on electronic design information and corresponding data. This file is still in a very early stage of reviewing; the companies involved in this reviewing process are, among others, Daisy Systems, Mentor Graphics, Motorola, Semiconductors, Tektronix, Texas Instruments and University of California at Berkeley. There were also efforts to extent IGES for PCB design.

8. Graphics in Documents

The two major standards developments in the area of documents are the Standard General Markup Language SGML /21/ and Office Document Architecture/Office Document Interchange Format ODA/ODIF /22/. They distinguish between a logical and a layout structure, between a processible and an image form of a document. In SGML as well as in ODA/ODIF proposals are currently under discussion to integrate graphics in form of graphics metafiles. This allows to supply graphics from external sources and integrate them into a document in processible form. The document processing and producing system has to provide capabilities to handle such compond documents. This is a good example of integration of standards of different fields.

9. Presentation Graphics Layer on Top of GKS

For a Presentation Graphics Layer the following three interfaces have to be specified:

(a) Interface "GKS - Presentation Graphics Package"
- primitives
- data structures
- clusters/levels (functionality)

(b) Interface to the Environment
- operating system
- language binding
- interface to the data handling utilities
- interface to the methods handling utilities

(c) Operator Interface
- passive/interactive
- dialog
- interaction techniques

Based on such a specification, special implementations of a presentation graphics package can be realised which at the application layer differ from each other. Their efficiency is then dependent on the methods library and on the data structure handling utilities used. A Working Group of the German GKS Verein (GKS Association) is active in the development of common interfaces (a), (b) and (c) on the top of GKS, to achieve more flexible capabilities for system integration /23,24/.

10. GKS in a Network Environment

The WSI (Workstation Interface; see "Device and Workstation Interfaces") of GKS opens the possiblitiy of using GKS in a network environment. The communication is based on the concept of a Graphic PAD (G PAD), which is an extension of the CCITT standard proposal for alphanumeric communication (PAD). Such a G PAD is a software module, with the functionality of channeling the information received either to an alphanumeric terminal, or to a given process running under the local operating system; this process implements the GKS Workstation. The GKS oriented communication protocol is based on the services supplied by the T.70 transport protocol. In Germany, several institutions are involved in designing and implementing these concepts; these activities are conducted under the sponsorship of the German Research Network DFN (Deutsches Forschungsnetz).

11. Bibliography

/1 / *Encarnacao J, Schlechtendahl EG* (1983) Computer Aided Design: Fundamentals and System Architectures. Springer

/2 / *Enderle G, Kansy K, Pfaff G* (1984) Computer Graphics Programming - GKS - The Graphics Standard. Springer

/3 / *Encarnacao J, Strasser W (eds)* (1981) Geräteunabhängige Graphische Systeme. Oldenbourg

/4 / *Guedj RA, Tucker H (eds)* (1979) Methodology in Computer Graphics, Proc. IFIP WG5.2 Workshop SEILLAC I) May 1976

/5 / *Hopgood FRA, Duce DA, Gallop JR, Sutcliffe DC* (1983) Introduction to the Graphical Kernel System (GKS). Academic Press

/6 / *Duce DA, Hopgood FRA* (1984) Lecture Notes of GKS Tutorial at EUTROGRAPHICS'84, Copenhagen

/7 / *ISO 7942* (1985) - Information Processing - Computer Graphics - Graphical Kernel System (GKS) - Functional Description

/8 / *ISO 2nd DP8805 GKS-3D* - Information Processing - Computer Graphics - Graphical Kernel System for Three Dimensions (GKS-3D) - Functional Description

/9 / *ISO TC97/SC21 N819* (1985) Programmers Hierarchical Interactive Graphics Standard (PHIGS) (working document)

/10/ *Steinhart J* (1984) Proposal for GKS Output Level 3, ISO TC97/SC5/WG2 N309

/11/ *Schönhut J* (1986) Classification of Graphical Metafile Encodings. In: Computers and Graphics Vol.10, No. 2

/12/ *ISO DIS 8632/1-4* (1985) Information Processing - Computer Graphics - Metafile for the Transfer and Storage fo Picture Description Information (Computer Graphics Metafile CGM)

/13/ *Standard ECMA-96* (1985) Syntax of Graphical Data for Multiple Workstation Interface (GDS)

/14/ Structure of a Workstation Interface. Position Paper, DIN NI AK 5.9.4

/15/ *ISO TC97/SC21/WG2 N* (1986) Computer Graphics Interface CGI (2nd Initial Draft)

/16/ *CEPT T/CD6-1 part 2 (revised)* - Videotex Presentation Layer Data Syntax - Geometric Display

/17/ *ANSI X3.110-1983* (Dec. 1983) Vidoetex/Teletext Presentation Level Protocol Syntax (North American PLPS)

/18/ *ANSI Y14.26M* (Sept. 1981) Digital Representation of Product Definition Data

/19/ *DIN 66301 Normentwurf* (1984) - VDAFS Format zum Austausch geometrischer Informationen (Sculptured Surface Interface) German Version

/20/ *SET Specifications Rev. 1.1* (March 1984) (Standard d'Echange et de Transfert). Aerospatiale Direction Technique

/21/ *ISO DP 8879* (1985) Standard General Markup Language SGML

/22/ *ISO DP 8613* (1985) Office Document Architecture/ Office Document Interchange Format ODA/ODIF

/23/ *Paller A, Harendra HB* (March 1983) Management Graphics. CAMP'83 Tutorial, Berlin

/24/ Protokoll der Sitzung der ad-hoc-Gruppe "Präsentationsgraphik" des GKS-Vereins am 10.02.1984in Darmstadt

Videotex and Protocol Systems

C. D. O'Brien and H. G. Bown

INTRODUCTION

Videotex is a name used internationally to represent a class of home
and business information services which disseminate information or
provide for transactional services from public information
suppliers. The system makes use of the home television set as an
essential still-picture display medium where the consumer may select
what is displayed. An eletronic module can be added to the
television set to allow it to assemble and display an image
consisting of characters and pictorial drawings. The information to
be displayed is typically received either from a data connection
over a telephone line or from encoded data in the unused scan lines
of an over-the-air television or cable television signal.

There are a number of such pulbic access information systems under
development in various countries which are designed to operate over
different communication lines and on various types of terminals.
Unfortunately, the major problem with many of these systems is that
the limitations of the particular display hardware, especially with
respect to resolution, are reflected in the communications protocols
they utilize. The protocol presented in this paper is based
primarily on alpha-geometric coding principals and is independent of
the type of display hardware or communications channel.

Rapid advances in the state of the art in electronics in the past
decade have changed the original design constraints for Videotex
systems. The cost of memories has dropped tremendously with the
result that high resolution pictures may now be stored and displayed
on home television sets or other display apparatus at a moderate
cost. In addition, the introduction of inexpensive micro-computers
has allowed sufficient sophistication to be programmed into a
terminal so that a high level, efficient communications code can be
utilized.

The basic design approach for the Canadian Videotex system is based on the premise of independence from particular hardware display apparatus limitations such as the resolution of current display techniques. The concept of forward and backward compatibility is of central importance. Forward compatibility means that the communication codes must be designed in such a way that future terminals will be able to access old data. This allows for growth and means that a future terminal with higher resolution can accept low resolution or otherwise limited data from an established data base. Backward compatibility, which is much more difficult to achieve, means that an installed inventory of terminals can receive and decode all future command formats in an intelligent manner. Again using resolution as an example, a picture which is communicated in high resolution should appear as a low resolution picture on older or less expensive terminals and as a high resolution picture on those termminals equipped to handle high resolution. The broadcast colour television signal format is a good example of a design for both forward and backward compatibility. At one time only monochrome television sets and signals existed, but now the situation is more complex. Colour sets can receive both black and white signals as well as colour signals (forward compatibility). Monochrome television sets can receive black and white singals, and when receiving colour signals, they interpret them as black and white (backward compatibility). Technically, this compatibility was very difficult to achieve with television signals, but it has allowed the introduction of colour television without the need to replace the installed inventory of television sets. The same type of growth potential must be desgined into the Videotex communications protocol from the start.

The content of the information in public data bases is of principal importance. There can only be one format of data otherwise the information marketplace becomes fragmented. In order for videotex services to be commercially viable there must be a "critical mass" of information available. To achieve this the informaton itself must be a commodity. All "authors" may prepare videotex pages in a manner which may be "read" by anyone without any distortion of the information. The standard for encoding the text and graphics presenting the information must be very flexible.

For the above reasons, the North American Presentation Level Protocol Syntax (NAPLPS) includes the Picture Description Instructions which have been defined in terms of the geometric primitives of POINT, LINE, ARC, RECTANGLE, POLYGON and INCREMENT, and which describe the structure of the entity to be drawn. For example, a line is drawn by specifying its endpoints. It is the responsibility of the terminal to decode this high level description and to draw the best line possible between the two endpoints. On a high resolution display, finer increments are used to draw the same line that would be be displayed in a coarse manner on a low resolution display. In this way, both forward and backward compatibility is achieved because drawing commands are described in terms of geometric primitives rather than in terms of some parameter of the display hardware. The accuracy with which coordinate positions are specified to describe these geometric primitives is reflected in the communications code, but this can be dealt with in a compatible manner by allowing the resolution of this description to be varied and by truncating the coordinate description to the accuracy which can be handled by the terminal.

The geometric coding scheme was originally developed at the Communications Research Centre of the Canadian Federal Department of Communications, after many years of research into image communications. This coding scheme was presented to the CCITT (International Telephone and Telegraph Consultive Committee) and resulted in the alpha-geometric model being included in the coding recommendation S.100-1980 and the videotex service recommendation F.300-1980. After some enhancements based on experience gained in field trials in Canada and the USA, consensus developed in North America toward a single common standard for videotex. This resulted in the adaption of the NAPLPS standard jointly by the Canadian Standards Association (CSA) and the American National Standards Institute (ANSI) in October 1983. This standard has since been included as part of the CCITT recommendations in March 1984.

There are many applications of this standardized protocol beyond Videotex public acess information systems. Because of the independence of the coding scheme from display hardware limitations, this common coding approach can be used for describing pictures for all types of computer graphics terminals such as calligraphic vector displays, storage tube displays, raster graphic displays or flat panel matrix displays. The geometric coding scheme can be used as the display-independent coding for computer graphics applications. Similarly, the CCITT has provided for a compatible coding structure for the Teletex business communications service and the Videotex Presentation Level Protocol can provide advanced Presentation level facilities to Teletex.

There are various different service scenarios evolving which utilize many different communications methods. To name a few, there are voice grade telephone lines, cable television lines, optical fibre communication channels, over-the-air broadcast television and digital communications lines such as packet switched channels. These various types of communication channels vary widely with respect to error rate, data rate, bandwidth and the capability to reverse the channel to transmit data back from the terminal to the information source. Standardized terminology has not yet been developed to describe all these services. In fact, some of these services tend to blend together. The general term Videotex is often used to encompass all such text and graphic communications systems even though specific services may have distinct service names.

The term "Teletext" (not yet adopted by the CCIR) is commonly referred to as a broadcast television Videotex service. It is different from "Teletex", a term adopted officially by CCITT to define a specific type of terminal-to-terminal text communications service. This is an area of confusion which has been recognized by both the CCITT and the CCIR and reconciliation of terminology is a matter for further study.

Interactive Videotex is a service based on the use of a two-way communications line between a Videotex terminal and a central data bank. Broadcast Videotex (Teletext) is a service based on the use of one-way communications channels such as over-the-air or cable television signals where the entire repertoire of data pages is continuously transmitted and where the user's terminal waits for and selects the desired page. Except for the nature of the interactive dialogue for information retrieval, the time delay and the amount of information available, both services operate in essentially the same way as far as the user is concerned.

For information retrieval, a subscriber to Videotex would be able to select from a number of pages of material which he or she may wish to display and view. An information supplier would provide a central data bank of information covering a wide range of topics. Typically a subscriber selects which information is to be presented by keying the appropriate selection into a calculator-like keypad or typewriter-like keyboard attached to the television set. As an example, a user who wishes to know the latest sports scores selects the sports page which then presents a menu consisting of a list of sports to choose from. By keying in the menu selection for hockey, the current hockey scores might be presented.

A Videotex system consists of an information source, a communication system to distribute the information data, and a terminal to interpret and display the data requested by a subscriber. Because there will be a large number of terminals in many locations such as homes, offices and schools, the terminal is the most important component of the entire Videotex system with respect to both capabilities and cost. It is envisaged that a number of manufacturers will produce terminals for Videotex of varying levels of cost and sophistication. A high quality terminal capable of very fine resolution may find use in an office situation, while a low cost minimum-feature terminal may be of greatest demand in the cost-sensitive home consumer market. A range of terminals will provide the public with choice. A manufacturer is free to produce any level of sophistication in a terminal he desires as long as the terminal is fully compatible with the Presentation Level Protocol Syntax. Although the Presentation Level Protocol Syntax does not change for different communications media, there could be differences in the manner of receiving data, in error coding, in data flow control and in transmitting interaction commands back to the host data base computer. These differences must be considered in the specifications for the interface of a terminal to a communication line.

For the purpose of this paper, the relative merits of various communications means will not be discussed, although the existence of important systems factors, such as the loading on telephone exchanges and the need for error protection in cable and off-air systems are noted. Rather, the ISO layered system architectural model will be presented which illustrates how the various aspects of a total communications protocol for given services can be made to interwork.

COMMUNICATIONS MEANS

The common aspect to all Videotex-like text and graphic systems is the identical coding format for the information content. The manner in which data is communicated to the home or business terminal has no effect on the presentation coding but does affect the form of the interactive dialogue for the user. Communications over a narrow-bandwidth voice grade telephone line is predicated on the use of one line per terminal so the response to interactions by the user is very good. However, images take time to build up because the data transfer rate is usually 1200 bits per second. Communications over a subchannel of a cable television system offers a higher bandwidth path into the home, but the path is a broadcast channel into all homes with the result that statistical queueing of requests is required. Responses to interactions would be slower but pictures could build up very quickly. Some cable television systems provide a reverse channel for two-way operation, but if this is not available, another channel over a different medium would be required to transmit interaction commands back to the data based host computer. Standards for these various system aspects exist or are under development for different communications systems.

Several unused lines in the flyback (vertical blanking) period of an over-the-air broadcast television signal may be used to transmit images by encoding the information in this unused bandwidth. This technique is commonly called Boradcast Videotex or TELETEXT. Because no reverse channel is possible over the air, a continuous stream of a small number of pages is sent in a cyclic sequence. A terminal waits until the page it has requested is transmitted and then captures the page and displays it. The limitations are that only a small number of information pages may be accessed and long delays may in incurred in waiting for a page to be presented. A detailed specification for the Broadcast Videotex (Teletext) transmission technique is given by the Department of Communications Regulatory Service Broadcast Specification BS-14. This format has been adopted in Canada and the United States of America as the North American Basic Teletext Specification (NABTS).

Other communications means such as digital data services over the telephone local loop and optical fibre data channels are also capable of providing such services to home or business. Of particular interest are combined communications means, for example, the transmission of individual pictures over a circuit-switched medium such as a telephone line; and the transmission of large blocks of data, whole "magazines", over a broadcast facility such as a cablevision subchannel for later off-line use.

RELATED SERVICES

There are a large number of information distribution and computation services using remote terminals existing at present which could be enhanced be the addition of graphics in a hardware independent manner. These services are as diverse as communicating word processor machines, a message oriented Teletex service or the communication of terminals with a central computing facility. For most of these text-oriented services a de facto standard has developed with ASCII as the presentation layer standard. Millions of such "Teletype"[1] - like printing and "Video display units" exist and it is a fundamental requirement that Videotex terminals incorporate the functions of these basic business terminals.

CODING PHILOSOPHY

The North American Presentation Level Protocol Syntax encodes text and graphic information in such a way as to enable it to be easily communicated. Independence of display or communications hardware constraints is achieved by using simple geometric Picture Description Instructions as the basis of the coding scheme.

The standard for encoding text and graphic information is but one of a number of interconnected standards required to provide a Videotex or similar communications service. In terms of the architecture

---

1. Teletype is a registered trademark of Teletype Corporation.

defined in ISO's multilayer reference model of Open Systems Interconnection, the Presentation Level Protocol Syntax forms part of the sixth or Presentation layer.

The ISO layered system architecture is a seven-layered assembly of inter-related protocols required to define an entire communications system. Each layer covers an independent aspect of a communications system in such a way that other protocols may be substituted at various layers in order to operate over different media. For example, the physical layer standard defined for communications over telephone wires is a modem specification, while the physicaly layer standard for transmission over a television broadcast channel is an electrical radio transmission specification. Both the Interactive Videotex and Broadcast Videotex (Teletext) services make use of the same Presentation Level Protocol Syntax, at layer 6, while having wholely different transmission protocols in layers 1 to 5.

The layered system architecture permits communications protocols to be defined in such a manner that many interrelated applications may interwork. Through the work of ISO and CCITT a unified structure is emerging in which compatible protocols can be defined. An example is the packet switched data transmission protocol presented in CCITT Recommendation X.25 which defines a data transmission service totally independent of the coding format or application of the data transmitted over it. Such a protocol is intended to interconnect with different application data presentation coding and service scenarios and is therefore an open system. The layered system architecture allows Open Systems Interconnection (OSI).

In the layered communications architecture, similar functions are grouped together to form distinct layers. Each standardized layer provides a set of services to the layer above it by performing functions internal to the layer and by utilizing services provided by the layer below it. Since all inter-layer interfaces are well defined, each layer can be considered independent of the particular implementations of other layers. The following diagram illustrates the seven functionally separate layers of the OSI model.

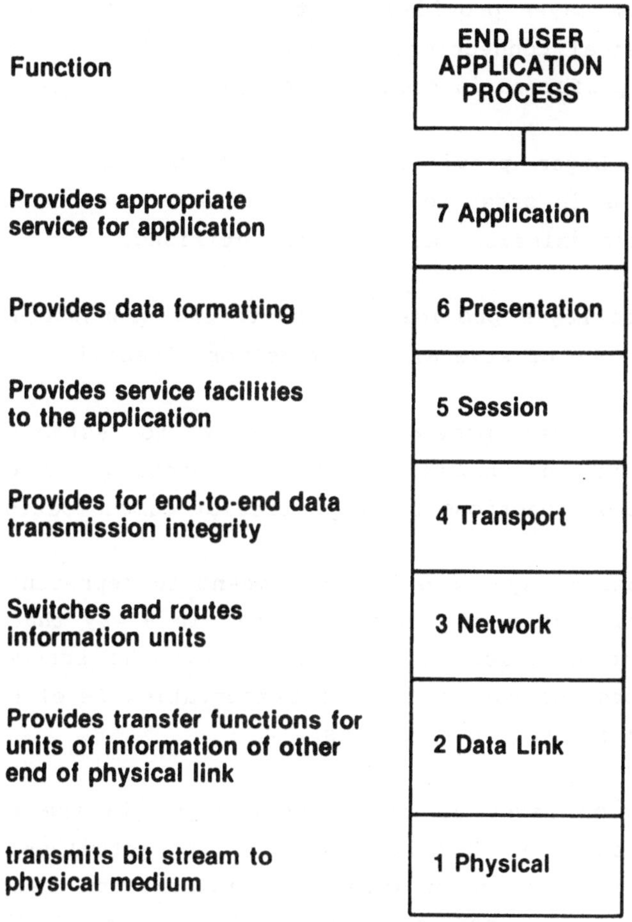

Function	END USER APPLICATION PROCESS
Provides appropriate service for application	7 Application
Provides data formatting	6 Presentation
Provides service facilities to the application	5 Session
Provides for end-to-end data transmission integrity	4 Transport
Switches and routes information units	3 Network
Provides transfer functions for units of information of other end of physical link	2 Data Link
transmits bit stream to physical medium	1 Physical

Figure 1   The seven functionally separate layers of the ISO OSI Model

The seven layers may be viewed in two major groupings. Layers 1 to 4 concern the transference of data while layers 5 to 7 concern how the data is processed and used.

The Physical Layer provides mechanical, electrical and procedural functions in order to establish, maintain and release physical connections.

The Data Link Layer provides a data transmission link across one or several physical connections. Error correction, sequencing and flow control are performed in order to maintain data integrity.

The Network Layer provides routing, switching and network access considerations in order to make invisible to the transport layer how underlying transmission resources are utilized.

The Transport Layer provides an end-to-end transparent virtual data circuit over one or several tandem network transmission facilities.

The Session Layer provides the means to establish a session connection and to support the orderly exchange of data and other related control functions for a particular communication service.

The Presentation Layer provides the means to represent and interpret the information in a data coding format in a way that preserves its meaning. The detailed coding formats for the scheme described in this paper provide the basis of a Presentation Level Data Syntax for Videotex and related applications.

The Application Layer is the highest layer in the reference model and the protocols of this layer provide the actual service sought by the end user. As an example, the information retrieval service commands of a Videotex application form part of the application layer.

Although there is need to define certain standardized application level protocols for information retrieval and other basic applications, the presentation layer and lower layer protocols should be defined in such a way so as to be application independent. There are a large number of services which are also associated with Videotex information retrieval such as "Teleshopping" which have unique application level interaction scenarios. In "Teleshopping" a user answers a number of questions in order to fill out an order form and then transmits the transaction data unit to the host data base computer. This application has much in common with all transaction oriented business data processing services. In fact is is very difficult to define a unique videotex application.

As has been indicated previously, various different transmission media may be used to effect the same service. The coded information retains its meaning regardless of whether it is broadcast or transmitted over a bidirectional data channel. It is the responsibility of the session layer protocol to provide service facilities appropriate to the transmission service, taking into account such factors as the fact that Broadcast Videotex (Teletext) is an inherently one-way transmission medium. A number of different standards are required for the transmission and session layers of these various services.

Since the information coding protocol at the presentation layer preserves the meaning of the information messages in a manner independent of the service or transmission media by which it is delivered, if forms the bridge between many diverse applications.

PRESENTATION CODING STRUCTURE

The most fundamental standard for the information industry is the Presentation Level Protocol Syntax, because it forms a common coding scheme for describing all text and graphic information regardless of the service or application. Data which has been encoded in terms of the Presentation Level (or layer) Protocol Syntax can be used in Broadcast or Interactive Videotex, as well as many related services and in applications as diverse as word processing and computer graphics. The universal, long standing ASCII standard encodes textual information in a manner independent of the terminal device or the application. The North American Presentation Level Protocol Syntax presented here builds upon the existing ASCII standard by including a supplementary character set and a DRCS (Dynamically Redefinable Character Set) capability and includes the Picture Description Instructions and block mosaics to encode pictorial graphics information.

The North American Presentation Layer Protocol Syntax makes use of the existing standards at the presentation layer of the OSI model, such as the well known ASCII standard for text and the techniques for code extension standardized by ISO.

There are a number of existing standards in wide use at the presentation level which encompass the coding of text and graphics information, and which must be taken into account when developing a unified presentation protocol. The most fundamental is the North American standard ASCII code table. ASCII stands for the American Standard Code for Information Interchange (ANSI X3.4 and CSA Z243.4) and has almost universally been adopted by the computer communications industry for the assignment of codes to character coded text. In addition there is an International Reference Version (IRV) code table described in ISO Standard 646 which generalizes the monatary sign. ISO Standard 2022 presents the method of extending the functionality of character coded sequences. The CCITT Recommendations S.100 and F.300 covering Videotex standardize the fundamentals of encoding graphical (pictorial) information, and have been used as the bases of the NAPLPS Data Syntax.

Various existing and enhanced standards have been woven together to form the North American Presentation Layer Protocol Syntax. To understand the NAPLPS completely it is necessary to examine the way in which these codes interweave.

ISO Standard 2022 describes th method of code extention to be used with character coded protocols. It describes the method by which code tables may be "designated " and "invoked". A byte of coded data acts as a pointer into a combined code table consisting of a C control code table and a G set (or text code table). In most applications there are not enough functions (or characters) available in a single G set, so provision has been made in the structure to permit G sets to be swtiched.

The meaning of each of the code tables may be altered by "designating" a set of interpretations to it from the "Repertory". For example, an alternate text alphabet such as the Inuit symbols or the Greek letters could be designated as GO. A particular terminal would be able to accomplish this only if it contained that particular set of code table interpretations in its repertory.

The ISO Standard 2022 for code extension has recently been revised to cover both eight and seven bit coding environments. While the seven bit environment can operate as a direct subset of the eight bit environment, the eight bit environment provides the additional capability of having two G sets as well as both the C0 and C1 sets in use simultaneously with added transmission efficiency. The eight bit b8 is used to address either the right or the left hand side of the expanded code table. Figure 2 illustrates code extension in a 7-bit Environment.

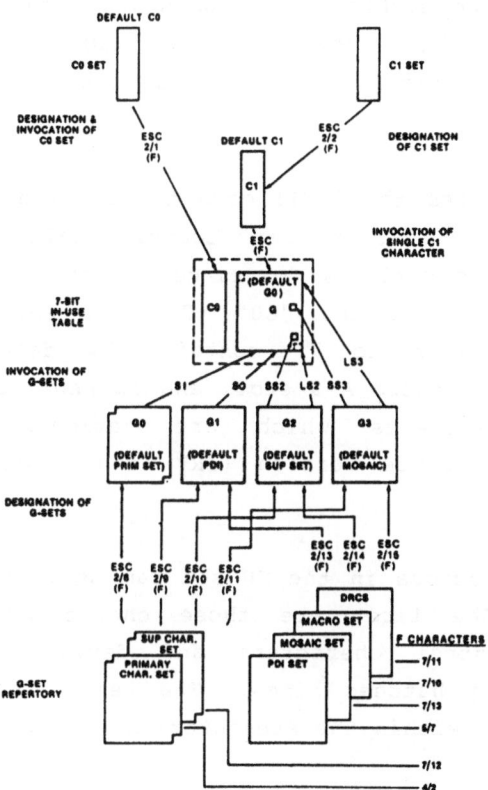

Figure 2   Code Extension in a 7-Bit Environment.

It is necessary to establish within the presentation, session level and transmission protocol whether the eighth bit will be used for parity error checking or for extension to another code table.   In other words, the choice of the eight bit or seven bit code environment at the presentation level is established by the lower layers of protocol for a particular service, or by prior arrangement.

TEXT CODING

In the character coded method of describing text, particular character codes are identified by an eight bit code sequence in which seven of the bits are used as an index into a 128 character code table and the eighth bit is used for parity error checking or extention to another code table of 128 characters. The text standard consists primarily of the code table describing the shapes of characters.

Figure 3 illustrates the ASCII code table. The table is subdivided into two areas. The first area occupying columns 0 and 1 contains control characters such as "carriage return" (CR) and "line feed" (LF) and is known as the "C0" (C zero) set. The second area occupying columns 2 to 7, contains by default the printable alpha-numeric characters A-Z etc., and is know as the "G0" (G zero) set. The characterts which are national variants of the International Reference Version (IRV) code table are indicated by shading.

The control characters in the C0 set can be further subdivided into two classes. The first are those characters which are termed transmission control characters and device control characters, indicated here by hatched lines. The remaining control characters in the C0 set are within the Presentation Layer.

The ASCII code table largely caters to the needs of the English language. For other Latin alphabet based languages where accented letters are an integral part, separate code tables have historically been designed for each linguistic group. In order to alleviate the problems associated with differing code tables, the CCITT in cooperation with ISO has recommended a supplementary character set which contains all the necessary special characters for all Latin based alphabets as well as a method for accenting characters known as the composition method, in which a non-spacing accent character is first transmitted from the supplementary character set and then the character to be accented is transmitted. This method has the great advantage of having total backward compatibility because older, simpler terminals which only implement ASCII (or the IRV) simply ignore the supplementary accent or special character.

In typical usage an accented character would require three bytes to encode. For example, in a seven-bit environment with the primary set designated in its default position as G0 and the secondary set as G2, the coding for an accented character would be thus: an SS2 (position 1/9 in the C0 set) would start the sequence invoking the code table G2 for a single access. The accent would then be specified followed by the primary character. In such a manner the letter é would be coded SS2 ′ e, that is three characters from code table positions 1/9, 4/2, 6/5. The supplementary table of accents, diacritical signs and special characters is illustrated in Figure 4.

b4 b3 b2 b1 \ b8 b7 b6 b5	1 0 0 0	1 0 0 1	1 0 1 0	1 0 1 1	1 1 0 0	1 1 0 1	1 1 1 0	1 1 1 1
	8	9	10	11	12	13	14	15
Row \ Column	0	1	2	3	4	5	6	7
0 0 0 0 — 0	NUL	TC7 (DLE)	SP	0	@	P	`	p
0 0 0 1 — 1	TC1 (SOH)	DC1	!	1	A	Q	a	q
0 0 1 0 — 2	TC2 (STX)	DC2	"	2	B	R	b	r
0 0 1 1 — 3	TC3 (ETX)	DC3	#	3	C	S	c	s
0 1 0 0 — 4	TC4 (EOT)	DC4	$	4	D	T	d	t
0 1 0 1 — 5	TC5 (ENQ)	TC8 (NAK)	%	5	E	U	e	u
0 1 1 0 — 6	TC6 (ACK)	TC9 (SYN)	&	6	F	V	f	v
0 1 1 1 — 7	BEL	TC10 (ETB)	'	7	G	W	g	w
1 0 0 0 — 8	FE0 APB (BS)	CAN	(	8	H	X	h	x
1 0 0 1 — 9	FE1 APF (HT)	SS2 (EM)	)	9	I	Y	i	y
1 0 1 0 — 10	FE2 APD (LF)	SDC (SUB)	*	:	J	Z	j	z
1 0 1 1 — 11	FE3 APU (VT)	ESC	+	;	K	[	k	{
1 1 0 0 — 12	FE4 CS (FF)	APS (FS)	,	<	L	\	l		
1 1 0 1 — 13	FE5 APR (CR)	SS3 (GS)	–	=	M	]	m	}
1 1 1 0 — 14	SO	APH (RS)	.	>	N	^	n	~
1 1 1 1 — 15	SI	NSR (US)	/	?	O	_	o	DEL

Figure 3 . ASCII Code Table

b4 b3 b2 b1 \ b8 b7 b6 b5	1 0 0 0	1 0 0 1	1 0 1 0	1 0 1 1	1 1 0 0	1 1 0 1	1 1 1 0	1 1 1 1
	8	9	10	11	12	13	14	15
Row \ Column	0	1	2	3	4	5	6	7
0 0 0 0 — 0				°	—	–	Ω	ĸ
0 0 0 1 — 1			¡	±	`	¹	Æ	æ
0 0 1 0 — 2			¢	²	´	®	Đ	đ
0 0 1 1 — 3			£	³	ˆ	©	ª	ð
0 1 0 0 — 4			$	×	˜	T.M.	Ħ	ħ
0 1 0 1 — 5			¥	µ	¯	♪	⊞	ı
0 1 1 0 — 6			#	¶	˘	⊟	IJ	ij
0 1 1 1 — 7			§	·	˙	◫	Ŀ	ŀ
1 0 0 0 — 8			¤	÷	¨	⧄	Ł	ł
1 0 0 1 — 9			‘	’	/	⧅	Ø	ø
1 0 1 0 — 10			“	”	˚	◪	Œ	œ
1 0 1 1 — 11			«	»	¸	◩	º	ß
1 1 0 0 — 12			←	¼	▯	⅛	Þ	þ
1 1 0 1 — 13			↑	½	˝	⅜	Ŧ	ŧ
1 1 1 0 — 14			→	¾	˛	⅝	Ŋ	ŋ
1 1 1 1 — 15			↓	¿	ˇ	⅞	ŉ	

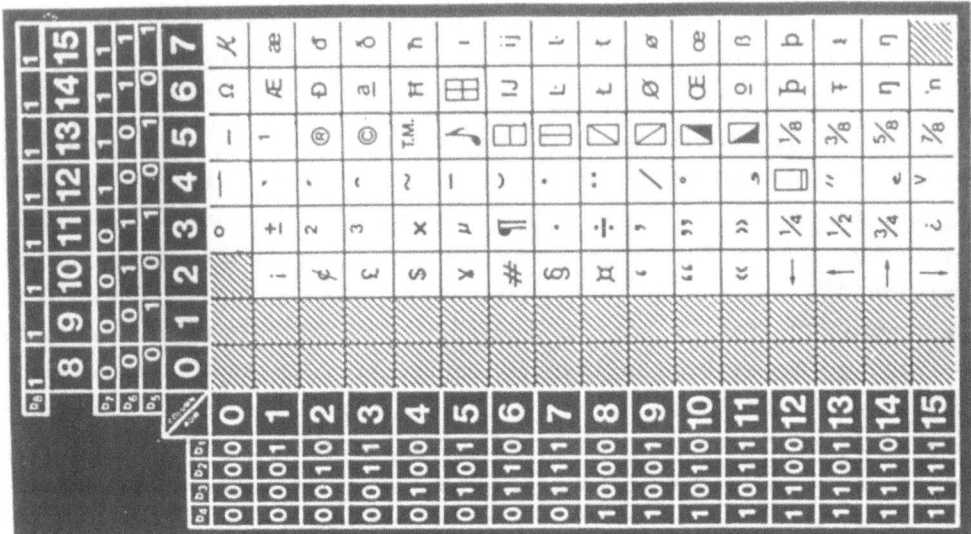

Figure 4 Supplementary Character Table

GEOMETRIC PICTORIAL CODING

The code table technique of defining the functionality of communications codes has been extended to cover pictorial information by the definition of the Picture Description Instructions. These interpretations for the code table consist of sequences of codes to describe graphical operations. The code set is subdivided into two fields, one for operation codes (opcodes) and the other for the numeric data operands associated with an opcode (see Figure 5). A code sequence to perform a drawing operation consists of an opcode to draw a POINT, LINE, ARC, RECTANGLE, or POLYGON, followed by a variable-length sequence of data bytes used to encode numeric parameters for the command. This numeric coding is formed out of codes from table columns 4, 5, 6, or 7, and consists of the least significant six bits of each byte for these code table positions.

Another way of interpreting these code table assignments is to examine the bit patterns of the codes. A PDI code consists of an 8-bit data byte which may include a bit for parity error checking or extension to an additional code table. The format for PDI drawing commands is a 6-bit code field and a 1-bit flag field occupying the 7-bit data field in each byte.

The flag field of the command is used to indicate whether the byte represents a command opcode or data associated with the command. The flag field is 0 for opcodes and 1 for numeric data. The number of bytes in the code sequence associated with a particular drawing command is determined from the flag field. A command's domain begins with its opcode byte and terminates with the start of the next code sequence. A command sequence is terminated by an opcode introducing the next drawing sequence or by any other presentation layer code not from the numeric data section of the PDI code table. Transmission layer control codes should not affect the range of a PDI command sequence as they should be removed from the data stream by lower level processes.

The field of the opcode is further subdivided into a descriptor field and a facilities field (see Figure 6). The descriptor field contains the numeric identifier of each of the eight possible opcodes. The remaining two bits in the facilities field are used

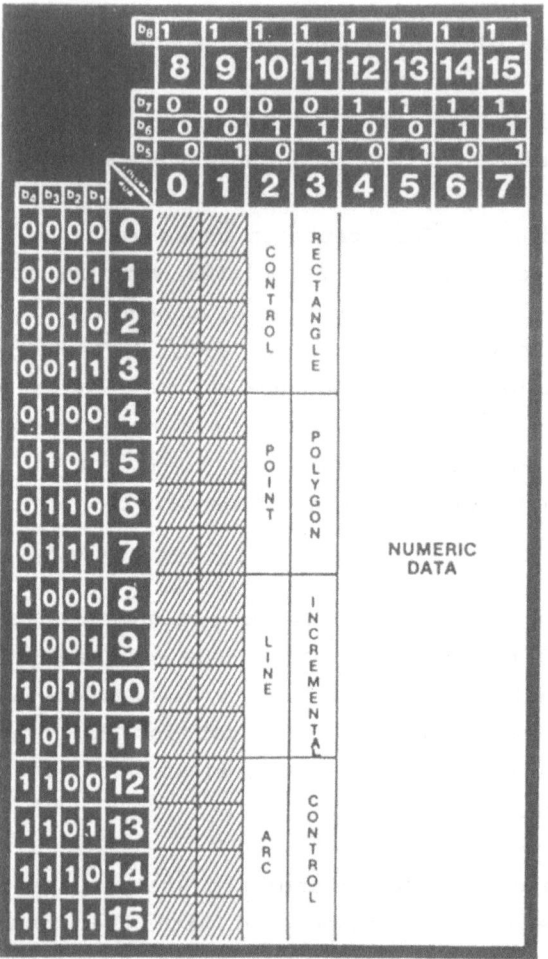

Figure 5 (a) Operation Code and Data Field Assignments

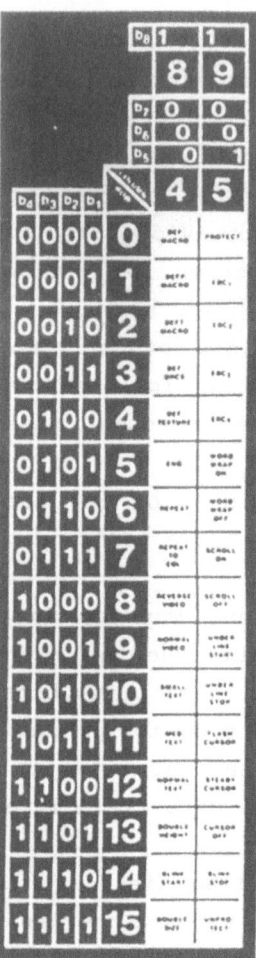

Figure 5 (b) C1 Control Set

for describing optional forms of the instruction. The flag bit (bit 7) equals 0 to indicate an opcode and bit 6 equals 1 to restrict opcodes to columns 2 and 3 from the code table.

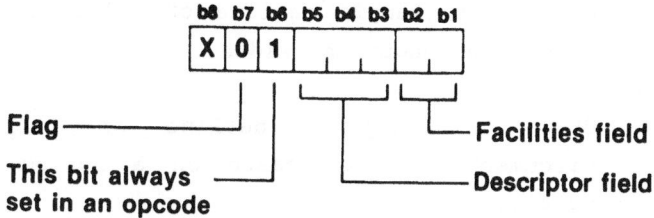

Figure 6   Format of a PDI Opcode Byte

There are a possible total of eight opcodes, each having four
variants defined by the two facilities bits. The eight opcodes
are: POINT, LINE, ARC, RECTANGLE, POLYGON, INCREMENTAL and two of
CONTROL. The first five opcodes in this list are the
alpha-geometric drawing primitives while the remaining opcodes are
used to augment or control these basic drawing commands. A SET
position may be encoded within the basic drawing primitives in order
to increase transmission efficiency. The SET position describes the
start of the drawing operation in Cartesian coordinates (X, Y), on
the screen.

The functions of the opcodes are summarized as follows:

POINT   - sets the drawing point to any position in the
                     display space optionally displays a dot.

LINE   - draws a line based on its end points.

ARC   - draws a circular arc based on the endpoints of the
                     arc and a point on the arc. The endpoints of the
                     arc may be optionally joined by a chord and the
                     area so defined filled in. If more points are
                     given, they define a higher level ARC, a
                     curvilinear line defined by a SPLINE function. A
                     circle is described as an arc whose endpoints
                     coincide and whose intermediate point (with the
                     endpoints) define the diameter.

RECTANGLE — draws a rectangle outline or fills in an area of specified length and width.

POLYGON — draws a polygonal outline or fills in the circumscribed area based on a series of defined vertices.

INCREMENTAL — draws a point, line or polygon in an incremental manner.

CONTROL — provides control over the modes of the drawing commands. One of its major functions is to set up a value or colour of an object.

Figure 7 illustrates the coding of the various forms of the PDI opcodes.

OPCODE	b8	b7 b6	b5 b4 b3	DESCRIPTOR FIELD 0	b2 1	FACILITY FIELD 0	b1 1
CONTROL	X	01	000				
POINT	X	01	001	INVIS	VIS	ABS	REL
LINE	X	01	010	JOIN	SET	ABS	REL
ARC	X	01	011	JOIN	SET	OUTLINE	FILL
RECTANGLE	X	01	100	JOIN	SET	OUTLINE	FILL
POLYGON	X	01	101	JOIN	SET	OUTLINE	FILL
INCREMENTAL	X	01	110				
CONTROL	X	01	111				

INVIS = Invisible
VIS   = visible

ABS = Absolute
REL = Relative

Figure 7   Opcode facilities

Data to be used with a drawing command immediately follows the opcode byte and is distinguished by having the flag bit set to "1". Any number of groups of coordinates or other data may follow a drawing command. The drawing command may be re-executed for each group of data so that, for example, a series of concentrated lines may be specified by one opcode command and followed by the appropriate number of (dx, dy) coordinate pairs. Repeated SET and POINT data can be used to point-plot a graph and repeated RECTANGLE data can be used to draw histograms. Those drawing commands such as POLYGON and ARC (spline), which use a variable amount of data, end their data list upon the next opcode or other presentation level code not from the numeric data section of the PDI code table.

PDI's have been defined to be independent of the physical resolution of the display media. This accommodates future technological advancements in display apparatus without obsoleting current terminals and data banks defined at a lower resolution.

The coordinate specifications are based on a Cartesian 0 to 1 numbering scheme with positions being specified as fractions of this range. This is independent of the physical resolution of the apparatus which may use a television set for display with the order of 256 positions of resolution in the horizontal direction, or a high resolution display apparatus of 1024 positions or any other resolution.

Coordinate specifications may be described to several levels of accuracy because they are represented as fractions of the visible drawing area. Unnecessary least significant bits are eliminated by truncation when the specification is to a greater accuracy than can be handled by the terminal. The numbering scheme 0 to 1 is a single-ended open range, that is, the point 0 is part of the valid drawing area but the 1 is inaccessible.

Display screens with non-square visible areas map into the square drawing area such that (0,0) remains in the lower left hand corner. On a television-like screen with a 4:3 aspect ratio, this corresponds to 0.00 to 0.99... in the x axis and 0.00 to approximately 0.78 in the y axis. Drawing commands into the entire square 0 to 1 grid are permissible but only the circumscribed area is visible.

The default range of the PDI number system is 9 bits occupying 3 bytes of data to describe an x, y coordinate position as illustrated below in Figure 8. It is envisaged that this 3-byte description would be used to communicate the majority of Videotex pictures.

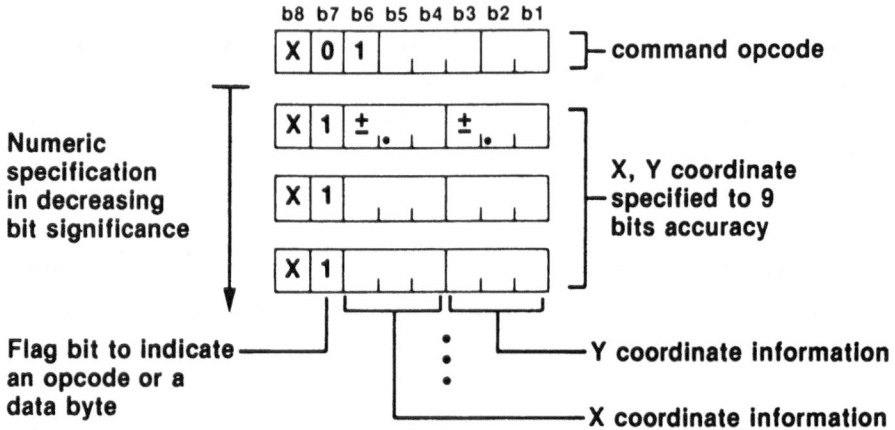

Figure 8   2-D Mode

For images that need to be specified to greater resolution than can be specified in a number range of 9 bits (+256) an additional data byte may be added to the coordinate specifications extending the range to 12 bits. Other higher or lower number ranges may be specified. This number system in no way restricts the terminal manufacturer from implementing any resolution he feels is cost effective at the basic hardware level. The number system merely defines the manner by which pictures are described so that there is display hardware independence in the PDI code. The manufacturer would convert coordinate information from the PDI coordinate system to his working coordinate system. If the hardware number system bears a simple relation to the PDI number system, this would be a trivial conversion. These coding options are made available so that both information suppliers and terminal manufacturers can make these trade-offs in a compatible manner.

OTHER PICTORIAL CODING

The CCITT in its Recommendations S.100 and F.300 present several
mutually exclusive optional methods of coding data for a Videotex
service. In order to provide international compatibility via at
least a gateway function, it is desirable to have a minimum
capability within each terminal to permit data conversion from these
other coding methods. To take the alpha-photographic method of
coding Videotex data is an example, a minimum point-by-point drawing
capability is provided in the INCREMENTAL POINT command. Since the
INCREMENTAL command, like all PDI commands, is defined in a
resolution and hardware independent manner, it is possible to create
an automatic gateway conversion program which will genrate
INCREMENTAL POINT data from alpha-photographic data coded in any
coding scheme.

In the alpha-mosaic approach, the display screen is divided into a
fixed number of character positions, typically 20 rows by 40
character positions per row for a total of 800 characters for a 525
line television system. Each position is fixed, somewhat like the
squares of a chessboard. Coarse graphics is accomplished by
subdividing each character position into six sub areas in order to
define 72 X 80 positions on a European 625 line TV display or 60 X
80 on a North American 525 line TV display. The major problem is
not that the resolution of these display terminals is low, but
rather that it is tied to the hardware resolution limitations of the
particular terminal technology.

There are two alpha-mosaic coding schemes defined in the CCITT
recommendations of Videotex. These two methods, the so-called
serial and parallel attribute schemes make use of entirely different
coding formats to define the attributes (such as drawing colour)
pertaining to the display. Work in CEPT (Conference of European
Postal and Telephone Administrations) has produced rules for
interworking of these two schemes thereby defining what happens when
both schemes are implemented in one terminal or when a gateway is
constructed.

There is a distinct contrast between the approach taken by Canada
and the United States in NAPLPS and by the Postal Administrations in
Europe in the CEPT data syntaxes. NAPLPS is a single data syntax

which is flexible enough to allow forward and backward compatability. The CEPT data syntax is really a collection of up to a dozen different data syntaxes or components of a data syntax which may be optionally selected to form the data syntax for a particular country. Communications between various European countries is limited because translations are required. For example, the format for DRCS selected in France is different and incompatible with that selected in Germany even though both are parts of the CEPT specification, thereby blocking intercommunications.

In addition to the alpha-mosaic schemes defined in CCITT recommendations there are other extremely popular, but incompatible mosaic coding schemes used in the personal and small business computer industry and operating on a different character density, typically 16 rows by 32 characters.

The North American Presentation Level Protocol Syntax contains a basic mosaic shape table of the 2 x 3 sub shapes used within each character cell which may be used in conjunction with the alpha-geometric attribute coding. This permits data conversion from any alpha-mosaic scheme using the 2 x 3 sub shapes by an automatic gateway function. Different character densities may be accommodated by text scaling.

REDEFINABLE PRIMITIVES

NAPLPS defines one other basic method of encoding data. However, this method is very open ended and can be used for a wide variety of purposes. The technique of defining a section of the picture description code to be a "sub-picture" which may be reused several times, is well known in the Computer Graphics field. In the Presentation Layer Data Syntax, this feature may be provided and is called a MACRO drawing primitive.

A MACRO-PDI consists of a sequence of presentation level commands stored under a single character label. When a character from the MACRO code table is transmitted, the sequence is executed. A control sequence is used to delimit the sequence of codes which are buffered to form a MACRO, and an entire G table of 96 character positions is reserved for MACRO names.

A Dynamically Redefinable Character Set (DRCS) capability is provided along with the MACRO capability in order that character sets primarily for non-Latin based alphabets or special alphabets may be defined. DRCS is the TEXT case of the MACRO facility and differs from the macro capability in that the sequences defining DRCS shapes are pre-executed; that is, they are executed at definition time. At execution time, TEXT attributes apply.

For the definition of these redefinable primitives, any presentation level code sequence may be used. It is even permissible for MACRO's to invoke MACROs. When used in conjuction with the WAIT command and the modification of colours using a colour look up table, very sophisticated animations may be produced.

CONCLUDING REMARKS

Electronic Publishing is developing in society as a new and unique information media which will bring with it changes in the amount of information available to the individual. This may be as revolutionary to society as the invention of the printing press or the development of the telephone, radio or television. In effect it brings together the pictorial capabilities of television, the information storage capabilities of the computer and the universal communications access of the telephone.

Videotex is but one part of the emergence of Electronic Publishing. Rapid advances are occuring in parallel in data packet communications, in transactional data services, Teletex, in advanced telephone switching systems, in video storage (video disk and tape), in personal microcomputers, in fibre optics, in direct satellite to home broadcast and in many other areas which will all affect the way one receives information about the world around him.

At the same time as new services such as Videotex are developing the technology upon which they are being constructed is rapidly changing. Dramatic decreases in the cost of electronic memory is rapidly making the bit plane memory technique for construction of terminal apparatus the most cost effective means. The key to handling such extensive change in the developing electrtonic information market place lies in the flexilbiliy of the Presentation

Level Protocol. Since the standard is based on mathematical principals rather than on the hardware capabilities of particular display apparatus various service scenarios on terminal configurations are possible. In this way the coding of information can be done in a common manner for all Electronic Publishing applications. The North American Presentation Level Protocol Syntax will form the base of the information industry.

The major problems which continue to exist in the emergence of Electronic Publishing services are not the problems of how to code data but are the more practical problems of how to generate it, how to store it and how to distribute it. Much more study is necessary on how to organize data banks and integrate electronic means into the existing news and information gathering media.

As new electronic publishing media develop they will effect social changes which are of great importance to society. Government policies need to be developed to maintain privacy for the individual and establish universal availability. The social and policy areas of the Electronic Publishing revolution require urgent study so that these emerging services will develop within an equitable social structure.

BIBLIOGRAPHY

1. ANSI X3.110/CSA T500, "Videotex Teletext Presentation Level Protocol Syntax", October 1983.

2. ANSI X3.4, "American Natinal Standard Code for Information Interchange (ASCII)", 1977.

3. Bell System, "Videotex Standard: Presentation Level Protocol", American Telephone & Telegraph Company AT&T, May 1981 .

4. H.G. Bown, C.D. O'Brien, D.F. Parkhill, W. Sawchuk and J.R. Storey, "Telidon: A Public Access Information System". Journal of Engineering Institute of Canada, April 1979.

5. H.G. Bown, C.D. O'Brien, W. Sawchuk, J.R. Storey and W.C. Treurniet, "Telidon Videotex and User-Related Issues". NATO Converence on Processing of Visable Language 2, Niagara-on the Lake, Canada, Sept. 1979.

6. H.G. Bown, C.D. O'Brien and W. Sawchuk, "Development of the Canadian Videotex System Design". IEEE Transactions on Consumer Electrnics, Vol. CE-25, July 1979.

7. H.G. Bown, C.D. O'Brien and W. Sawchuk, "Development of the Canadian Videotex System: Telidon". Canadian Journal of Information Science, (4) May 1979, pp. 52-59.

8. H.G. Bown, C.D. O'Brien and W. Sawchuk, "Telidon Technology Development in Canada". Presented at Viewedata '80, London, England, 26-28 March, 1980.

9. H.G. Bown, C.D. O'Brien, W. Sawchuk, J.R. Storey and R. Marsh. "Comparitive Terminal Relations with Alpha-Geometric Coding". IEEE Chicago Spring Conference on Consumer Electronics, June 18-19, 1980.

10. Canadian Standards Association, "7-Bit Coded Character Sets for Information Processing Interchange". CSA Standard Z243.4-1973.

11. CBS Television Network; "North American Broadcast Teletext Specificatin.", New York, N.Y. June 1981.

12. CCITT Recommendation S.100, "International Information Exchange for Interactive Videotex", Yellow Book, Volume VII,2 Geneva 1980.

13. CCITT Recommendation F.300, "Videotex Service", ibid., Geneva, 1980.

14. CCITT/Draft Recommendation S.100 "International Information Exchange for interactive Videotex", Draft Red Book, Geneva, 1984.

15. CCITT/Draft Recommendation F.300, "Videotex Service", ibid., Geneva, 1984.

16. CEPT Working Group CD/Se; "European Interactive Videotex Service Display Aspects and Transmission Coding.", Recommendation No. T/CD 6-1. June 1981;

17. Department of Communications, Canada, Telecommunications Regulatory Service, Broadcast Specification BS-14, June 1981.

18. EIA/CVCC (ElectronicIndustries Association/Canadian Videotex Consultative Committee.)", North American Basic Teletext Specification (NABTS)," 1983.

    ISO / 2022.2, "Information Processing - ISO 7-Bit and 8-Bit Coded Character Sets - Code Extension Techniques".., 1983.

19. ISO/DIS 7498, "Data Processing - Open Systems Interconnection - Basic Reference Model", 1983.

20. O'Brien, C.D. Bown, H.G., A Perspective on the Development of Videotex in North America. IEEE Journal on Selected Areas in Communications, Vol. SAC-1,(2): pp 260-266; February 1982.

22. C.D. O'Brien, Bown, W. Sawchuk and J.R. Storey, "The Relationship of Alpha-Geomemtric Videotex Standards to Computer Graphic Standards". Computer Graphics '80, Conference On-line Systems Inc., August 1980.

Part IV

Applications of Computer Graphics

Business Graphics: Graphics Devices and Trends

G. P. Laroff and A. Paller

The next twelve months will be a watershed year for computer graphics in business. The technology is no longer considered frill. Today, nearly every large company recognizes that computer graphics can be a powerful competitive tool in research, marketing, planning, engineering, data processing and financial management. Most companies have targeted this coming year as the time to expand their investment in computer graphics.

Rapid growth and change in the computer graphics field leads some potential users of the technology to delay making decisions. They wait for the day when the choices are fewer and more certain. While they are waiting, however, their competitors are moving forward, using available technology, learning from it, isolating high-pay-off applications and gaining competitive advantages.

A decision continuously facing many users of business and data representation graphics software is the choice of a graphics output device or devices. It is generally recognized that well implemented graphics applications can have very high pay-offs in productivity and profit. Many companies have already learned the secret that the common denominator of high pay-off graphic applications is the production of numerous graphs or, more succinctly, **there are no high pay-off graphics applications that require only a few graphs.** The heart of these systems is found in the new generation of high volume hard copy devices.

In order to address these needs this paper discusses three topics: choosing a graphics output device, high volume production graphics hard copy and the trends shaping the business graphics industry over the next twelve months.

Choosing a Graphics Output Device

We are often requested to list the type of graphics output most applicable to analysis, presentation and publication applications, and then to list technologies and products that best fit the applications requirement. Listing technologies only takes an awareness of the marketplace, but listing brand names, products and pricing can be a dangerous matter, especially if you claim to be as neutral and objective as most of us do. Bowing to continuous pressure from our users, we will name names and list prices. This is a larger task than is initially apparent, and we learned how fast devices are updated, introduced, obsoleted and how often prices are adjusted when we wrote the Hard Copy Devices book (reference 7, below) last year. Nevertheless, with even less homework to confirm this month's product offerings and prices, we will do our best. We apologize in advance for any errors and do suggest most strongly that our readers confirm model numbers, specifications and pricing with the product vendors. This advice is especially valuable when purchasing hardware outside the United States, where prices and model numbers sometimes vary. It should also be assumed that we are making no effort whatsoever to list every device on the market and are only listing devices where we feel an example is required. It is safe to assume that there are at least ten times the vendors and products on the market than we plan on mentioning. Many of today's software users appear to have an almost insatiable appetite for graphics output device information. It is for these people who need updated device information that we have written a number of articles and booklets on choosing graphics devices. For your convenience, some of these references, in chronological order, are listed below:

1. Olps, Darrell M.: "Devices: Introduction and Overview," <u>ISSCO Graphics Week '82</u>, Feb. 1982, pp. 1-16.

2. Laroff, Gary P.: "Choosing the Right Graphics Devices," <u>ISSCO Graphics Week '83</u>, Feb. 1983, pp. 1-13.

3. Laroff, Gary P. and Darrell Olps: "Setting Up a Graphics Workstation," <u>ISSCO Graphics Week '83</u>, Feb. 1983, pp. 1-18.

4. Laroff, Gary P.: Choosing the Right Graphics Devices, ISSCO, San Diego, 1983.

5. Laroff, Gary P.: Wie man die richtige Grafik-Peripherie waehlt, ISSCO Deutschland GmbH Computer-Grafik, Koblenz (West Germany), 1983.

6. Laroff, Gary P.: "Choosing the Right Hard Copy Output Device," ISSCO Graphics Week '84, Feb. 1984, pp. 1-21.

7. Laroff, Gary P.: Choosing Hard Copy Devices for Visual Information Systems, ISSCO, San Diego, 1984.

The importance of **device independence** and **device intelligence** cannot be overstated. **Device independence** lets you, the user, freely choose the devices that best suit your applications. **Device intelligence** takes advantage of the inherent hardware capabilities of your devices. This can reduce computer and communications time and expense. Some of today's major graphics software vendors offer both device independence plus device intelligence so that you can be confident that your hardware investment will be productive.

An optimally effective computer graphics operation will almost certainly be a mixed vendor environment. Film recorder vendors won't have high resolution color devices for previewing; plotter vendors won't have inexpensive black and white devices for previewing; some CRT vendors have no hard copy devices. It is the purpose here to list a number of devices of each type that are supported by the most popular graphics software and that do indeed work with each other.

Computer peripherals vary greatly in cost and performance. We will show you how the application determines what the performance should be and offer a base level of knowledge which will allow informed decisions to be made. Fortunately, the seemingly endless variety of possible applications can be grouped into three broad categories: analysis, presentation and publication. Further, the variety of media which best suits communicating these applications to audiences can also be summarized: soft copy on display screeens, flipcharts, transparencies and slides. With today's technology, you can create charts directly on devices that produce these media.

Table 1. Popular Output Media

Analysis	Soft Copy	Raster Terminals Storage Tube Terminals
	Black-and-white Paper	Demand Hard Copy Pen Plotter Laser Printer COM Recorder
	Color Pages	Pen Plotter Impact Printers Thermal Transfer Ink-jet Color Xerography
Presentations	Flip Charts	Pen Plotter Color Electrostatic
	Transparencies	Pen Plotter Thermal Transfer Ink-jet Laser Printer Film
	Slides	Film Recorder
	Paper Copy	See list under Black-and-white Paper as well as Color Pages, above.
Publications	Black-and-white paper	Pen Plotter Ink-jet Laser Printer Electro-erosion COM Recorder

Today's better software is capable of satisfying the quality demands of the most discerning individuals. The device independence of this software frees the user to choose the output device(s) which best suits his or her application. Although people are often attracted to advertisements for high resolution color displays and 8-pen plotters, these aren't always the optimum devices to fulfill the final objectives. Non-graphics terminals and personal computers are now often used as terminals with software such as ISSCO's DISSPLA or TELL-A-GRAF to provide an effective previewing medium prior to producing medium or higher resolution hard copy. It is easy to be awed by all the devices available today and overlook present and future needs.

Graphics Terminals

Graphics terminals are the most popular devices used to input commands, interact with graphic development and preview output. A terminal used to be the initial item to be considered when choosing graphics devices, but is now often being taken for granted with most of the decision time being used for choices of hard copy devices. The terminal is still a critical element and is unique in its ability to allow input of textual and graphic data; allow interaction with the command set and graphic development and produce both preview and sometimes final graphics displays. Some terminals even support demand screen copy in color or black-and-white for working or final hard copy. Terminals let the user economically design charts and graphs before expending time, effort and expense generating hard copy.

There are essentially four display technologies used in graphics terminals, but one now predominates: raster refresh, also called raster scan. For an overview of the four display technologies: random scan (or directed beam), storage tubes (or DVST), raster refresh and plasma panels, the reader is directed to references 4 and 5, listed at the beginning of this article.

The mainstay of the computer graphics industry for about ten years, the storage tube terminals by Tektronix, have largely been replaced by raster refresh technology. Raster refresh, besides supporting multiple colors versus the storage tube's green on green screen, compensated for the other weaknesses of the storage tube. Raster refresh supported erasability of parts of the display, such as backspacing to erase words, supported panel fill with color or patterns versus the storage tube's stroking in of any shading, made up for the lack of screen brightness, bringing the graphics user out of artificially darkened rooms and supported movable objects on the screen. Of the legendary strengths of the storage tube, only one is really missed: high resolution. The smaller of the storage tubes (11") had a resolution of 1024 x 780 (almost double the resolution of the average raster refresh display in use today) and the more popular larger one had a remarkable resolution of 4096 x 3120. Software users preparing and previewing what will eventually be high resolution black-and-white output, will find the closest representation of what will be their final hard copy graphics on such terminals as the Tektronix 4014, 4015, 4016, 4114 and 4116 and on the IBM 3277-GA.

Most of us though, will be doing our graphics design and preview work on raster refresh displays. The two old mainstays, the Tektronix 4027 in the ASCII world and the IBM 3279 in the BISYNC and SDLC world are largely being replaced by bright new versions with very attractive features.

The 7 features to check out when buying a raster refresh terminal are display refresh rate, resolution, screen size, number of colors, computer overhead, demand hard copy capability and price.

1. Display refresh rate is literally how fast the terminal screen is redrawn. In the United States it seemed previously to be the rule for raster terminals to rewrite (or refresh) half the screen (really every other line) every 1/60 of a second, therefore rewritng the entire screen every 1/30 of a second. This scheme is known as a 30 Hz. interlaced refresh mode. It's the least expensive way to design and build a raster refresh terminal, but the end result is a device which flickers and can cause eye fatigue. In Europe, where the basic electrical frequency is 50 Hz., terminals of this variety are often 25 Hz. interlaced which causes even more eye fatigue as the refresh rate is below the flicker fusion frequency of the human eye. The alternative is for the terminal manufacturer to rewrite the entire display at one time instead of just every other line, a technique know as non-interlaced. When non-interlaced displays are refreshed at a frequency over 50 Hz., most of us view the display as being rock solid, without even a hint of flicker. Some people feel that they can see a difference between 45, 50 and 60 Hz. interlacing, but this author has never been able to tell the difference. When possible, go for an interlaced display. For example, the newer Tektronix 41XX series have interlaced displays, but not the older 402X series. The newer IBM 3270-PC/G series have interlaced displays, but not the older model 3279.

2. Resolution, which has a more formal definition than we shall use, is essentially the number of rows and columns of dots (called pixels for picture elements) on the terminal screen. We used to insist that the horizontal axis needed over 500 elements to be readable or even tolerable, with the aforementioned IBM and Tektronix terminals sporting 640 (horizontal) x 480 (vertical) elements or dots. In reality, for displays that are interlaced, lower resolution is acceptable with the Tektronix 4105 (resolution 480 x 360) being

reasonable for all day viewing.

For most people, though, the minimum resolution that seems comfortable is 640 x 480 on a screen up to about 15" with 19" screens requiring roughly 1024 x 780. Resolution above these values is generally considered to be a very welcome feature. With the passage of time and the improvement in technologies and manufacturing processes, what used to be a major price differential for increased resolution has become only a minor and quite reasonable pricing increment.

3. Screen Size, seems to come in two varieties, those around 15" and those around 19". An inch or two either way doesn't seem to matter to most people. 12" and under is a little small. 25" is a bit difficult to watch at one time. We noted above that people prefer to go to higher resolution when going to a larger (above 17") display. The logic is quite simple: If your televison screen at home is too large, you simply sit back further, but with a terminal if the screen is too large for the resolution, it is inconvenient to sit back further than arm's length.

4. Number of Colors inherently supported by the terminal is critical. Some personal computers support only 3 or 4 colors on the screen at one time, and that is rarely sufficient. If your budget is limited, 8 simultaneously viewable pure colors from a palette of 64 is minimal. The nicer terminals support 16 simultaneously viewable out of a palette of 4096. The Tektronix 4115B and the AED 1024 support 256 simultaneous colors out of a palette of some 16.5 million and the Seiko 2414 supports 1024 out of a palette of 32,768 colors.

5. Computer Overhead required by a terminal should be minimized. These days, local terminal intelligence and memory is smoothing out differences in terminals. The terminal you choose should support the concept of "hardware characters" and polygon fill of any random shape without limit to the number of vectors and cross-over points. The IBM 3270-PC/G and 3270-PC/GX are far more efficient to drive than the older 3279 and the Tektronix 4107 is somewhat more efficient and flexible than the previous model 4027.

A few terminals are summarized here with both their screen size and resolution:

Table 2. Some Representative Color Graphics Terminals

Vendor	Model	Resolution	Screen Size
Hewlett-Packard	2627	512 x 390	10.4"
Tektronix	4105	480 x 360	13"
Envision	220	640 x 480	13"
Envision	230	640 x 480	13"
Ramtek	6211	640 x 480	13"
Ramtek	6221	640 x 480	13"
Tektronix	4107	640 x 480	13"
Tektronix	CX4107	640 x 480	13"
Digital	241	800 x 240	13"
IBM	3270-PC/G	720 x 512	14"
Seiko	1104	1024 x 780	14"
Tektronix	4109	640 x 480	19"
IBM	3270-PC/GX	960 x 1000	19"
AED	1024	1024 x 767	19"
Tektronix	4115B	1280 x 1024	19"
Seiko	2414	1280 x 1024	20"

---

6. Demand Hard Copy Capability is a feature that has a different value placed on it by each user. This author places an extremely high value on being able to press a key on the terminal keyboard and have a nearby hard copy unit generate a full color copy of the screen. A similar capability has long existed in the IBM GDDM environment where a single terminal function key

instructs the mainframe based software to produce a hard copy of the same graphics on a designated device. The capacity to drive a hard copy unit usually has no effect on the price of the terminal, and color copy units are now often available for under $2,000. If this is important to you, don't forget it when choosing a terminal.

7. <u>Price</u> for terminals is based on the features listed above. Contrary to belief, there is much more to the price of a terminal than the resolution and name of the manufacturer. Higher resolution for a given screen size generally raises the price. Passing other thresholds, such as refresh rate and supporting some intelligent features such as zoom, pan, transforms and graphics input sometimes adds the cost of more exotic technologies to the terminal. Terminal price is greatly effected by the amount of memory included in it. Memory is needed in more places than just for storing images and segments. For terminals that support the same number of colors on the screen, doubling the resolution on each axis multiplies the memory requirements by 4. The minimal number of colors is "2" (black and white, on and off, red and green, etc.). For every two-fold increase in the number of viewable colors after that (2, 4, 8, 16, 32, ...) you have to add yet another "memory plane." As an example, let's consider comparing a 640 x 480 resolution terminal with a 1280 x 1024 resolution terminal. With double the resolution on each axis, the second terminal requires 4 times as much memory as the first. If the first terminal can support 4 colors at a time (2^2) and the second one can support 256 colors at a time (2^8), then the color capability of the second terminal is also 4 times as memory intensive. The combination of resolution increase and increase in the number of colors in this example increases the memory requirements of the second terminal 16-fold. Adding more power, segment handling capability and some local intelligence further adds to the price of a terminal with more capability.

High quality color raster refresh terminals will rarely be priced under $4,000. $6,000 to $8,000 buys you somewhat more than $20,000 did a few years ago. $20,000 today will buy a stripped-down version of a very high powered terminal, which you should expect to cost around $35,000 once all the options, bells, whistles and memory planes have been added.

Hard Copy Devices

Most users of business and data representation graphics software require graphics hard copy output. The soft copy of the terminal display is rarely the final copy unless one is only perusing formats or is making decisions based on previously stored graphics, as in the ISSCO IVISS Manager browsing routines. More often than not, the professional now places the choice of a hard copy device over the choice of computer terminal and that copy device now usually provides color output.

To help eliminate the confusion over purchasing a hard copy device, we recently published an entire book on the subject. Titled Choosing Hard Copy Devices for Visual Information Systems, published by ISSCO, the book discusses the trends in hard copy purchases, the major and upcoming technologies, the important performance variables and the trad-offs associaited in choosing one technolgy over the other. For more in-depth discussions than we can possibly include in this article, please refer to the aforementioned book.

The person trying to make a purchase decision on a color or high resolution monochromatic hard copy unit can evaluate major varialbes and trade-offs to eliminated most of the confusion. The five major variables are image quality, resolution, speed, equipment cost and cost per copy. These are discussed at length in our book, reference 7, above. For the 9 major technologies presently employed in making hard copy, Table 3 lists comments on the image quality and specifications commonly encountered on the number of pure colors supported, resolution, speed (time for an "A"-size copy), cost per copy and approximate equipment cost.

Table 3. Hard Copy Specifications Comparison

	Impact		Non-Impact						
	Pen Plotter	Impact Printer	Electro-Photographic	Color Electrostatic	Thermal	Thermal Transfer	Ink-Jet	Laser	Camera Systems
image quality	high	low to medium	medium (B & W)	high	low	medium to high	medium to high	very high (B & W)	very high
pure colors	up to 10	8	1	8: Versatec ECP-42	1	8	8	8: Xerox 6500 only Others: 1 color	"unlimited"
resolution (points or line pairs per inch)	250-1000	100-360	125	100-200	50	100-240	80-150	100: color 240-600: (B & W)	8×10": up to 800 Slides: 3000
speed (8½×11")	3-10 min. or more	3 min. approx.	20 sec.	1 min. (approx.) 8 min. for "E"-size	20 sec.	45-120	1-5 min.	0.2-6 sec. (B & W) 20 sec.: color	1-2 min. (Polaroid) hrs. - days (processing)
cost per copy	$0.01 paper $0.50 acetate	$0.04 - $0.15	$0.05 - $0.15	($0.09) $1.44 for "E"-size		$0.25 paper $0.65 acetate	15 - 20¢ paper $0.85 - $1 acetate	6¢ color 0.4¢ - 2¢ (B & W)	$7 - $10
approximate equipment cost	$700 - $1,660	$4,450 - $11,500	$4,400 - $7,900	$98,000	$1,000 - $5,000	$4,500 - $5,000	$800 - $17,500	color: $39,000 (B & W) $22,000 - $390,000	$6,600 - $200,000

Pen Plotters

Pen plotters are the historical hard copy system in which you get continuous lines and not the dot structure that results from the use of various raster print technologies.

Pen plotters are the workhorses of computer graphics hard copy. They are relatively inexpensive and can be shared by many users. Historically these devices were run off-line using tapes. The only devices which now are being sold as off-line plotters are major systems for high-volume production of graphics. The newer pen plotters are intended for remote on-line use. Pen plotters have multiple pens and a few are capable of continuous output on a number of different media, such as paper and mylar (for use as overhead transparencies).

When choosing between pen plotters, the features that differentiate them are pen speed (usually measured in inches per second), pen accelleration (usually measured in G's), the manner in which the pens are changed in order to change color (which translates into how long it takes to change pens and start plotting again), reproducibility (which is also stated as accuracy), whether continuous roll or sheet feed is available for continuous plotting and, of course, price.

As most data representation graphics is on A-size ($8\frac{1}{2}$" x 11") or B-size (11" x 17") paper, a comparison of plotters in these sizes is usually sufficient. The primary performance difference usually comes down to speed, and there can be a very big difference in how fast your graphics is produced when going from one plotter to another. As a matter of perspective, just a few years ago, the typical business graphics plotter from companies such as Hewlett-Packard and Tektronix were in the $5,000 price range, handled one to four pens and plotted much slower than most of today's plotters.

Today, at the low price end ($395) is the Epson America HI-80 with 4 pens and a pen speed of 9 ips. (The fastest plotter in our discussion is the Hewlett-Packard 7550A at 31.5 ips.) The Epson is clearly not the slowest plotter in its class and is probably positioned at the personal computer marketplace. Other low-end plotters include the Enter Sweet-P with one pen and speed of 6 ips for $695, the 2-pen Houston DMP-40 at 3-4.2 ips at $995, the 1-pen Strobe 100 at $795, the 8-pen Strobe M260 at $995 and what seems to be the undisputed high-volume leader in the personal computer arena and at the low price end, the 2-pen Hewlett-Packard 7470A with a speed of 15 ips, an accelleration of 2G and a list price of $1,095. Most graphics software supports some of the plotters mentioned above.

The mainstream of mainframe business and data presentation graphics is served by plotters with slightly more performance and generally a slightly higher price tag. As with the HP 7470A mentioned just above, accelleration specifications are usually available for these plotters. Accelleration data is vital in making your plotter purchase decisions especially considering the fact that the plotter spends a great percentage of its time accellerating from dead zero either after changing pens, or finishing a vector or finishing printing a character. Plotters that either don't stop between vectors or which accellerate very rapidly, finish the plot much faster than those that don't keep moving. A few plotters are availble in the just under $2,000 price range. The Hewlett-Packard 7475A is a 6-pen, 15 ips plotter with an accelleration of 2G and a reproducibility of 0.001" for $1,895. CalComp's 8-pen, 18 ips, 0.004" resolution M-84 plotter is priced at $1,995. Nicolet's Zeta Sprint is a 6-pen, 14 ips, 0.004" resolution plotter at a price of $1,549. The Enter Sweet-P 600 Six-shooter is a 6-pen, 14 ips, 3G accelleration, 0.004" resolution plotter at the low price end of $1,095. With the exception of the CalComp M-84 (A-size), all of the plotters in this category can handle up to B-size paper. Any of these plotters should do a respectable job with your graphics.

At the slightly higher price end are the production workhorse plotters. Not to be relegated only to production work, these plotters will run all day with better than average speed, clearly outrun the plotters in the previous category and run essentially unattended since they either advance roll paper or feed themselves sheet paper. Nicolet's Zeta 8 has a pen carriage that carries all eight pens simultaneously, an approach which is much faster than most other manufacturers' method of sending the pen carriage over to the side of the plotter to change pens and is also roll fed with either paper in a number of qualities and finishes or mylar for transparencies. It runs at a very respectable 20 ips with a somewhat unbelievable accelleration of 4G producing plots with a resolution of 0.001". The speed, accelleration, 8-pen carriage and internal smarts, such as an internal circle generator, add to the Zeta 8's high-volume continuous roll paper to make it ideally suited to the production graphics environment. Price $5,950. In essentially the same ballpark is the Hewlett-Packard 7550A with 8 pens, 31.5 ips plotting speed, high speed accelleration, 0.001" resolution and a rather nifty paper sheet feeder. Price $3,900.

For the IBM environment, plotters essentially identical to the Hewlett-Packard 7470A and 7475A are available as the IBM models 7371 and 7372 and are supported by IBM software on ASCII ports. The only pen plotter supportable on IBM mainframes in the SNA/SDLC environment is the Nicolet Zeta 887, which is essentially the Zeta 8 with an IBM protocol interface. Price $7,950.

Plotters of larger sizes by such vendors as CalComp, Hewlett-Packard, IBM, Nicolet and Tektronix are, of course, often supported by software that supports the smaller plotters.

Impact Printers

Impact printers are essentially line printers that can address individual dots and permit the printing of graphics and not just lists of alphanumeric characters. They use an arrangement of tiny hammers to strike a ribbon, in a manner similar to that used in a typewriter, to produce a dot matrix image on paper. Various colors are available by changing ribbons. The main advantage of the impact printer is the low cost per copy, especially for black-and-white. The impact printer market is shrinking, if not just holding its own, but although not the most exciting technology, impact printers are reliable and in wide spread production graphics usage. To be fair to both the technology and the products involved, some 90% of the quality problems that people attribute to impact printers would be alleviated if the users would only change the ribbons every now and then. With pen plotters and ink-jet plotters you either add more ink or you get no more graphics. Despite the bargain price of plots from impact printers, we all seem to squeeze another hundred plots or so from long since warn out ribbons and then mumble under our breath about the poor plot quality. Before discounting a particular impact printer, try a new ribbon.

Products, which have been on the market for some time, include the Dataproducts 132, Printronix P300, Texprint Inc.'s DECPLOT, which is a color field upgrade to a standard one-color Digital LA 120 or DECWRITER 3, Texprint Inc.'s TEXPLOT upgrade to Texas Instrument's Silent 700, the Trilog ColorPlot 100 ($11,500), the older Ramtek 4100 and the fairly new (black-and-white) Digital LA-12, LA-50 and LA-100.

Somewhat more popular, and quite prevalent in the IBM environment is the model 3287 and its somewhat faster replacement, the 3268 model 2C. The 3268 model 2C is a 4-color wire matrix ribbon impact printer which can operate at a maximum of 340 characters per second and prints approximately 2.7 times fster than the 3287 at a comparable price of $8,990. Graphics plots are generated in about 2 minutes at a cost of approximately 15¢ each. The unit is driven through IBM's GDDM rasterizing software.

Electrophotographic CRT Copiers

The historical procedure of pushing a button and copying the screen of a storage tube display also works on some refresh raster terminals. Using fairly expensive silver coated paper, black-and-white and grey scale paper copies are produced from devices such as the Tektronix 4631, 4632 and 4634. Prices range from about $6,000 to $8,000.

Electrostatic Printer Plotters

Electrostatic printer plotters have traditionally produced black-and-white copies with images produced electrostatically by electrodes placing charges on dielectric paper, which is then passed through a toner.

Electrostatic printer plotters by such vendors as Benson, CalComp and Versatec, especially those producing large C-, D- and E-size plots are commonplace in engineeringand CAD/CAM environments.   They are far less common in data representation applications.   Common black-and-white A-size terminal screen copiers are the Tektronix 4611 and 4612.

At present there is still only one color electrostatic plotter, the Versatec ColorPlotter model ECP42. Producing full color copy with a high 200 dot per inch resolution over a large 34" x 44" page in only 8 minutes at a low $1.44 cost per copy, the ECP42 is a good performer presently alone in its class. Device price of $98,000 is a bit steep for the average business graphics environment, but engineering organizations with multiple graphics output requirements have found the Versatec ECP42 attractive. The device is driven via Versatec's VersaPlot software.

Thermal Transfer Plotters

One of the two major competing non-impact technologies (ink-jet is the other one), thermal transfer plotters, are getting more reliable and less expensive all the time. Instead of liquid ink, most use a low-melting-point wax transfer ink. On the surface, the products hold the promise of simplicity, reliability, quietness and low cost hardware.

Although announced and priced, most of these devices are manufactured in Japan and not all of them are available in single quantities to end users. The low priced winner is reported to be the Okidata Okimate 20 with a fairly high resolution of 144 dpi at the price of $268. We have yet to see this device and doubt that it can do graphics at this price, if indeed the price is correct.

The thermal transfer plotter used as a basis for most comparisons is the Seiko model

CH-5201B which has been priced at $10,950, has a resolution of 150 dpi, makes copies at the rate of one per minute and is supported as either a demand screen copier of the Seiko D-Scan family of terminals or via the Lasergraphics UI-100S vector to raster converter. The Gulton CP-80C has a resolution of 100 dpi, takes 45 seconds for a copy and is priced around $4,950. Shinko Electric has two families of thermal transfer plotters. The CHC-30 Series of four units are 100 dpi resolution plotters which take about 45 seconds for an A-size plot. The model CHC-35 can be driven digitally and sells for between $5,000 and $6,000. The Shinko CHC-65 produces B-size plots with 200 dpi at 2 minutes per copy. No price is noted for the model CHC-65. Toshiba has the model TN-5400 which produces 200 dpi A-size plots in a minute. The Gulton CP-80C, Shinko CHC-35, Shinko CHC-65 and Toshiba TN-5400 are supported by the Lasergraphics UI-100 Series of vector to raster converters, which are in turn supported by the applications software package.

Ink-jet Plotters

Along with thermal transfer plotters, ink-jet plotters are among the major non-impact printer innovations in the past few years. Ink-jet copiers output high-quality color paper and transparency graphics.

The Advanced Color Technology ACT-II has a resolution of 140 x 85 dpi, a 1.5 minute copy time and a price of $6,150. The fairly similar PrintaColor TC-1040 has a resolution of 120 x 85 dpi, a one minute copy time and a price of $5,495. Both are supported via Lasergraphics UI-100 Series vector to raster converters. With a similar resolution, the Tektronix 4695 has a resolution of 120 dpi, a copy time of about 2-3 minutes, a price of $1,595 and is supported as a demand screen copier of selected Tektronix terminals and via the Vector to Raster Conversion software supplied by software vendors via a Tektronix terminal. Towards the higher resolution end are the Tektronix 4691, Tektronix 4692 and Benson ColorScan 800. The Tektronix 4691 has a resolution of 150 dpi, a copy time of 2 minutes for A-size and 4 minutes for B-size and a price of $12,950. The model 4692 makes A-size copies only with a resolution of 154 dpi at a price of $5,995. The high resolution winner, with 203 dpi, is the Benson ColorScan 800 which makes A-size copies in 3.5 minutes but can also produce B-size plots and is priced around $17,500. ISSCO, for example, supports the Tektronix 4691 via the ISSCO Vector to Raster Conversion software on the DEC VAX computers, through the Lasergraphics UI-100T interface and via the Tektronix 4510 rasterizer. The Tektronix 4692 is supported via the Lasergraphics

UI-100T as well as the Tektronix 4510. The Benson ColorScan 800 is supported via the KMW VP-10 and VP-30 rasterizers.

Laser Printers and Other High Resolution Black-and-White Printers

Fulfilling the need for high resolution black-and-white printers in production graphics as well as publication quality graphics are a large number of devices with varying prices and throughput rates. At the lower price end, are the QMS Lasergrafix models 800, 1200 and 2400. The Symbolics LGP-1 and Imagen Imprint-10 are also often supported. All of these are in the $25,000 and under price category.. In the same general price range are the Xerox 2700, Digital (DEC) LN-01 and Digital LN-03 which are interfaced to via the Plot 27 rasterizing software from Image Research. At the higher price end are found the high volume laser printers such as the Xerox 8700 and 9700 which graphics software vendors interface to via the Xerox EPIC software as well as the Image Research Plot 97 software. In the IBM environment, software vendors support the QMS Lasergrafix family listed above, the IBM 4250 (600 dpi) electro-erosion printer and the IBM 3800 model 3 laser printer. In addition, ISSCO supports the Computer Output Microfilm (COM) recorders from Infomation International Inc. (III) known as the models COMp 80 and COMp 80/3. Not every device in this category is supported on every graphics software company's supported operating systems.

In the color laser printer category, one can support the Xerox 6500 CGP via the Lasergraphics UI-100X universal interface.

Film Recorders

Most people use film recorders to produce slides, but some devices also produce other format films and some produce 8 x 10" Polaroid prints directly. There are three generic types of film recorders:

1.   Terminal driven film recorders
2.   Stand-alone film recorers
3.   Direct drive film recorders

1.   Terminal driven film recorders are independent of the computer and graphics software and only have to match the terminal to which they are connected. Any of the

fine products from companies such as Celtic, Image Resource, Kodak, Lang, LogE/Dunn, Matrix or NISE should fulfill your needs. These camera systems vary widely in their capability and should be investigated carefully relative to your needs.

2.   Stand-alone film recorders are intended for high volume, photo-ready, high accuracy output. Typical devices in this category are the Celco CFR-4000, Dicomed D148CR and D148SR and the Information International Inc. (III) models COMp 80/3 and FR 80/A. Various formats are available, such as 16mm, 35mm, 105mm microfilm or microfiche. Some graphics software vendors support a number of graphics output devices in this category, but you should check with both the software and the hardware vendor to ensure that the configuration that you intend to purchase will work with the application software on your specific operating system.

3.   Direct drive film recorders or slide composition systems are becoming quite popular and available in ever lower price ranges. Typical products include the Dicomed DICOMEDIA family and the Genigraphics 100C, 100D and 100V. Application software vendors' interfaces are available to many of these larger systems. The newer desktop systems which tend to cost from $1,500 to $25,000 without rasterizing equipment are either currently supported or rapidly being added to some vendors' device interface list. The Matrix QCR-D2000 (resolution 2048 x 1366) and QCR D4/2 (resolution 4096 x 2732) are both supported via the Lasergraphics UI-100Q interface as well as the Matric QCC interface. (These Matrix film recorders are manufactured by IMAPRO, of Canada, which distributes them in that country. Honeywell distributes them in numerous European countries.) The Polaroid Palette is supported as the Lasergraphics MPS-2000 which produces slides with a resolution of 2048 x 1366 pixels. The CalComp Samurai, priced at around $10,000 produces anti-aliased slides with a resolution approximately 4096 x 2732 and is driven by a standard host resident software interface through an IBM PC containing necessary Samurai interface components. The most recent announcement is the self contained Bell & Howell Color Digital Imager IV (CDI-IV) film recorder, which at $7,500 is one of the lower cost offerings and has a resolution of 832 x 630. The CDI-IV doesn't require either external interfaces nor a personal computer.

Conclusion on Choosing a Graphics Output Device

With this discussion we hope to have updated you with some of the recent announcements in graphics devices as well as commenting on the degree and manner of driving these devices from graphics software running on your mainframe computer. We certainly hope that the numerous mentions of graphics devices, as requested by users in the past, has been of benefit to you.

High Volume Production Graphic Hard Copy
—The Corporate Productivity Tool of the 1980's

Three days after a Midwest-based franchisor closed the books on its 1984 fiscal year, operators of 1,500 company-owned outlets began receiving a four-page computer-generated graphic report showing each individual store's financial performance.

Producing graphs customized for 1,500 sites required 6,000 original black-and-white charts generated from the corporation's data base using DISSPLA software. Accomplishing the task required the corporation's Versatec model VP-80 electrostatic plotter to produce an average of two plots per minute over a 60-hour period.

It was a prodigious effort, but one that is no longer uncommon. More organizations are successfully leveraging their graphics expertise to take advantage of a relatively new high pay-off application -- high volume production graphics. The Midwest franchisor, for example, is already researching high-speed laser printers in anticipation of producing 24,000 charts in a three-day period to supply all 6,000 outlets with customized four-page financial graphic reports.

Many companies, like the franchisor which asked to remain anonymous, consider production graphics so competitive that they are reluctant to publicly discuss their systems. The heart of these systems, however, is found in the new generation of high volume hard copy devices that have introduced high payoff applications previously unthinkable to anyone who has fed paper and changed pens at a two-pen plotter.

The common device features required by most organizations using high volume production graphics devices include:

1. Speed in excess of one copy per minute of A-size (8½" x 11") black-and-white, about a minute for one A-size full color copy and a bit longer for much larger black-and-white and color plots.

2. Cost per A-size copy less than 2-cents for black-and-white and around 25-cents for color on paper. Larger black-and-white generally costs less than 3-cents per square foot with large color electrostatic plots about 12-cents per square foot.

3. Resolution over 250 dots per inch for black-and-white and over 150 dots per inch for color.

4. Image quality from both the software and hard copy device so charts don't look like they were generated by a computer.

5. Device costs that fit any departmental budget. Moderate speed laser printers (8 to 24 pages per minute) and high volume color page printers range from $5,000 to $30,000. The majority of newer color thermal transfer and ink-jet plotters are priced below $15,000. Very high speed laser printers (70-300 pages per minute) cost between $200,000 and $400,000.

"Throwaway Graphics"

The era of "throwaway" graphics has arrived. It is as easy and practically convenient to provide a manager every Monday with several pages of graphs as a stack of print listings. The merit in replacing listings with volume production of graphs lies in visuals' superior ability to quickly make a point so managers can analyze data faster and more effectively.

The potential of high volume production graphics is reflected in the $15 billion worldwide electronic printer market, which represents just one branch of high volume devices. Dataquest Inc., a San Jose, California based market research firm, estimated that page printers will grow from 13.7 percent of the total market in 1983 to 30.2 percent by 1988. The highest growth rate will take place in the 0-60 page per minute segment, which is predicted to grow at an annual rate of 225% from 1983 to 1988.

A number of organizations have already implemented leading-edge production graphics systems designed to deliver data in visual format to decision-makers.

Bankers Trust New York Corp., the nation's 10th largest commercial bank, prepares dozens of financial graph portfolios monthly to arm its representatives with detailed, specialized presentations when they approach major potential accounts. The charts are generated using TELL-A-GRAF software and produced on a Seiko model CH-5201B color thermal transfer printer plotter.

Amoco Production Company produces more than 100,000 computer-generated maps and cross-sections annually to analyze prospective lease tracts in the intensely competitive off-shore oil business. The company has long used the Applicon IJP ink-jet plotter for color maps and is currently migrating toward the Versatec ECP-42 full color E-size (34" x 44") electrostatic plotter.

More than 1,000 charts plotted daily and requiring over 2 miles of paper each week show the 10-day world weather forecast at the European Centre for Medium Range Weather Forecasts in Reading, England. For reliable unattended operation, the complex multicolor maps and charts produced with custom software and DISSPLA are plotted on Hewlett-Packard model 7586B pen plotters and Benson model Colorscan 800 ink-jet plotters for color work and both Versatec electrostatic plotters and QMS model Lasergrafix 2400 laser printers for black-and-white output.

Boston-based New England Telephone has made a three-page-a-minute color Xerox 6500CGP printer a central component of the utility's visual information system that includes sophisticated sharing of hard copy devices.

The shared devices environment is an important strategy organizations are adopting as they integrate relatively new high-volume devices with their current devices. Mark Borgmann of New England Telephone said the shared environment gives many users access to high quality output equipment.

Borgmann points out six advantages of a shared devices environment:

1. Operation of devices is transparent to users (even when a vector-to-raster conversion may be required).

2. Eliminates users fussing with paper, ink, toner and film.

3. Reduces capital expenditures for devices.

4. Improves device maintenance by delegating the responsibility to a particular group.

5. Makes cost-justification easier by spreading the price of new high quality, increased throughput devices among many users.

6. Frees end-users' terminals for continued use rather than locking them out while waiting for hard copy.

Establishing a successful shared devices environment, Borgmann said, requires device-independent software that "can keep pace with rapid technological advances of the computer graphics market."

Production Graphics Checklist

The advent of production graphics was 1982 when Xerox added graphics capabilities to its model 9700 laser printer capable of producing 120 standard-sized pages of black-and-white graphics every minute with good quality. The price of a typical configuration is $400,000. Since that time, a number of vendors have entered the market offering high quality graphics printers capable of producing eight to 300 pages per minute and priced between $4,000 and $400,000.

Most of the available products have been produced by adding a raster image processing module to print engines from companies such as Canon, IBM, Ricoh and Xerox. In many environments, the method of driving the print engine is the only limitation of throughput rates and often determines the success or failure in implementing high volume production hard copy.

A checklist for evaluating criteria of hard copy devices should include image quality, resolution, speed, equipment cost and cost per copy.

Image quality and resolution govern page appearance. The most common specification for judging resolution is "dots per inch" (dpi), which is a good relative indicator but not a measure of true resolution, or the number of line pairs that can be discerned in one inch. The higher the dpi rating, the better the image quality will be.

In most instances, the quality of a 150 dpi plot is suitable only for personal analysis. An original of a 300-dpi plot is sufficient for distribution within a company or for inclusion in a report. A second generation copy suffers from fuzzy edges and loss of fine details. A 300 dpi chart composed and printed on a $400,000 Xerox 9700 or a $7,000 Apple LaserWriter will usually serve its purpose in a document or report, but the quality required for typesetting is different.

According to Seybold Publications, Inc. of Media, Pennsylvania, 300 dpi laser xerographic printers are regarded as interim proof devices rather than final output devices. For typeset-quality output, either the IBM 4250 with 600 dpi or the Information International (III) COMp 80/3 with about 1,500 dpi is preferred.

Cost per copy usually refers only to consumables and is generally around 5 cents per sheet for a dry toner laser printer, 30 cents per sheet on the IBM 4250 electro-erosion printer and 60 cents to $1 a sheet on a phototypesetter using 11 inch resin coated (RC) paper.

Throughput, or copy speed, is the factor that most differentiates today's A-size black-and-white printers. The low end devices running from about a half minute per page to two minutes per page include screen copiers from Tektronix, higher resolution printers and the IBM 4250 electro-erosion printer. Laser printers run the gamut from eight to 300 pages per minute. See chart.

Device costs are usually a product of resolution, speed and durability. Sustained high speed printing demands a more rugged and expensive printer. Laser printers limited to producing 30 pages per minute rarely exceed $30,000 while printers capable of 70 pages per minute start at $200,000.

Table 4
High Volume A-Size Black-and-white Graphics Output Devices

Manufacturer	Model	Technology	Resolution (dpi)	Copy Speed	Cost per Copy	Approximate Equipment Cost	Remarks
Apple	LaserWriter	dry toner	300	8 ppm		$6,995	PostScript Language
Digital	LN01	dry toner	300	12 ppm	1.2¢	19,995	host rasteriz.
	LN01S	dry toner	300	12 ppm	1.2¢	29,995	vector driven
	LN03	dry toner	300	8 ppm	2.1¢	4,195	host rasteriz.
IBM	3800/3	dry toner	240	215-300 ppm	4¢	330,750	channel attach.
	3820	dry toner	240	20 ppm	4¢	29,900	GDDM driven
	4250	electro-erosion	600	1.5 ppm	30¢	21,000	GDDM driven
III	COMp 80/3	film	1,500	few minutes	60¢	140,000	vector driven
Imagen	8/300	dry toner	300	8 ppm	3.5-4¢	7,995	vector driven
	12/300	dry toner	300	12 ppm	3-3.5¢	17,500	vector driven
	24/300	dry toner	300	24 ppm	3-3.5¢	29,950	vector driven
QMS	Lasergrafix 800	dry toner	300	8 ppm		7,995	vector driven
	Lasergrafix 1200	dry toner	300	12 ppm		19,995	vector driven
	Lasergrafix 2400	dry toner	300	24 ppm		29,995	vector driven
Tektronix	4611	dry toner	--	2 ppm	--	5,050	screen copy
	4612	dry toner	--	2 ppm	--	5,065	screen copy
	4632	photographic	--	3 ppm	--	6,500	screen copy
Versatec	V-80	electrostatic	200	8 ppm	2-4¢	8,900	11 in. wide by long
Xerox	2700-II	dry toner	300	12 ppm		17,995	host rasteriz.
	3700	dry toner	300	12 ppm		29,995	host rasteriz.
	4045 Laser CP	dry toner	150 or 300	10 ppm		4,995	host rasteriz.
	8700	dry toner	300	70 ppm		212,000	host rasteriz.
	9700	dry toner	300	120		390,000	host rasteriz.

Driving Hard Copy Devices from a Computer

Most high volume hard copy units and new generation color output devices are inherently raster oriented. While a pen plotter draws a line (vector) from point A to point B, raster oriented devices produce pictures by assembling a large number of tiny dots layed down in a highly structured fashion. Vector driven devices let the user draw lines in any place and any order. A raster driven device, however, requires that the user figure out where the lines should appear, convert the lines into dots and transmit the dot information to the printer in a predetermined fashion. Although this sounds complicated, raster oriented hard copy devices benefit from better output quality and throughput compared to vector devices.

High volume devices also have been adapted to handle an enormous number of picture elements, or pixels, each of which can have two or more colors (a raster). For example, there are 7.2 million pixels (or dots) on a typical 300 dpi laser printer page, 28.8 million for a page of IBM 4250 output and 239 million dots for an E-size plot off the Versatec ECP-42 color electrostatic plotter.

Raster printers clearly place a heavy computational burden on the driving computer. The computers must store all the pixels, deliver the pixels in the order required by various printers and deliver pixels at a data rate that maintains the high volume capability of the printer. In the case of the IBM 3800 model 3, an incredible data rate of 23 million dots per second must be maintained to achieve a 300 page per minute output of 240 dpi. For this reason, the 3800 model 3 is directly channel-attached to larger IBM mainframes to drive them effectively.

The newer raster oriented hard copy devices are so attractive that many attempts have been made to introduce them to a broad spectrum of users. There are now four ways to drive raster oriented hard copy units: Screen Dump, Host Rasterization, Off-board Vector-to-Raster Converters and On-board Vector-to-Raster Converters. Not all devices are supported by each method, and no single method is best for all users.

Screen Dump transmits graphics in rasterized form from the screen of a graphics terminal to the copy unit without requiring additional rasterization in the computer. Although efficient, the disadvantages of this method include low resolution copies and dedicating printers which keep other users from using the printers. Also, the terminal cannot be used during the copy process because the copier uses the terminal's memory.

Host Rasterization adds special software to the the computer to convert high-level graphics primitives into full-resolution raster in order to take full advantage of the resolution capabilities of raster printers. The rasterized image requires many megabytes, so the image is usually stored on some secondary storage, such as a disk, until rasterization is complete and the copier is ready for transmission. This process provides the advantages of utilizing the printer's full capabilities, allowing the printer to be used as a shared resource and eliminating the cost of a vector-to-raster converter. Disadvantages of host rasterization include the immense amount of compute power sometimes required for rasterization, the large amount of memory or disk space required to store the rasterized image and the heavy I/O burden to transmit that image to the copier at speeds that will keep the copier running at an efficient rate. Examples of host rasterization products are the Image Research Corporation PLOT97 and PLOT27 software for driving the Xerox 9700, 8700 and 2700 and the Versaplot software used to drive the Versatec brand electrostatic printer plotters. IBM's GDDM software includes host rasterization and in the case of IBM brand peripherals, is often the only method of driving these devices.

Vector-to-Raster Converters are hardware devices that look like a sophisticated pen plotter to the computer and application software on their input side and feed rasterized data to the hard copy devices on their output side. In their simplest mode, converters can accept plotter commands, which makes interfacing to them extremely easy. A converter is attached directly to the computer and can act as a shared device so all users have printer access. Some of the units can accept high-level graphics primitives as input, thereby saving the application program from having to generate these functions with vectors. In general, because they do the rasterization and store the resultant raster image, converters save computer power and decrease both memory and disk utilization. On the down side, vector-to-raster conversion hardware, whether as a separate unit or as a built-in module, represents an additional hardware cost and one device is generally needed for each printer to be supported.

Off-board Vector-to-Raster Converters, often referred to as universal rasterizers or universal interfaces, tend to be more flexible than the built-in variety since they were designed to support numerous printers with varying feature sets. The Lasergraphics Universal Interfaces support over 20 different devices covering the widest range of printing technologies, including color xerographic, color ink-jet, color thermal transfer and color photographic film recorders. Other vector-to-raster converters for use with color printers described below are available from Benson, KMW and Tektronix.

On-board Vector-to-Raster Converters are often referred to as raster image processors and are added to a raster print engine and sold as a single product. The conversion is essentially done in the device which means that the user drives the device as if it were vector driven. The converter is part of the product supported by the vendor and the user doesn't have to worry about rasterization. Examples of products including both print engines and on-board vector-to-raster converters are the Digital LN01S and the laser printers from Imagen and QMS.

The best way to drive a hard copy device depends on the site and the application. Whatever the hard copy need, there are now sufficient products on the market to provide the flexibility for almost any environment. The hardware devices are supported by such mainframe graphics packages as SAS/GRAPH, TELL-A-GRAF, DISSPLA, TELLAPLAN and GDDM.

All graphics is not 8½ x 11 inch black-and-white pages, so we conclude our discussion of high volume production hard copy with an overview of appropriate A-size color and large size black-and-white and color graphics output devices.

A-size Color Hard Copy Devices

Color hard copy in a report or for limited distribution used to be an expensive luxury. Working color hard copy was unheard of. In the last few years, A-size color printers have proliferated and now produce reasonable resolution plots in high volume at production rates for a reasonable cost.

The best known device is the Xerox 6500CGP dry toner laser printer based on a color office copier which has been around 10 years. With a resolution of 100 dpi, it makes Xerox originals at the rate of three per minute at a copy cost of 5-6 cents each. Device cost is $39,000 plus a Lasergraphics UI-100X rasterizer priced at $11,995. Color thermal transfer printers are available from a number of vendors and produce color plots in less than a minute at a cost of under 25 cents per copy.

Table 5
High Volume A-Size Color Graphics Output Devices

Manufacturer	Model	Technology	Resolution (dpi)	Copy Speed	Cost per Copy	Approximate Equipment Cost	Remarks
Benson	B-90	thermal transfer	240	17 sec	5¢	$6,995	host rasteriz.
	Colorscan 800	ink-jet	203	3.5 min	<25¢	14,850	A- & B-size
Digital	LCP01	ink-jet	154	2 min	<25¢	14,595	includes rasterizer
Panasonic	EMP T-801	thermal transfer	200	1 min	<25¢	2,300	OEM only
Seiko	CH-5201B	thermal transfer	150	1 min	<25¢	12,650	requires rasterizer
Tektronix	4691	ink-jet	150	2-3 min	<25¢	12,950	A- & B-size
	4692	ink-jet	128-154	1-2 min	<25¢	5,995	fast plot preview
Toshiba	TN-5400	thermal transfer	200	1 min		5,000	not widely available
Xerox	6500CGP	dry toner	100	20 sec	6¢	39,000	Lasergraphics rasteriz.

At the high priced end, the Seiko CH-5201B ($12,650 plus $4,495 for a Lasergraphics UI-100S rasterizer) produces 150 dpi plots at 1 per minute on paper or transparency material. The device cost includes considerable memory resident in the printer itself. This allows the printer to run unattended making as many "originals" of a single plot as required without holding up the rasterizer or mainframe.

Downloading a plot to the Seiko CH-5201B takes only one-half second. At $5,000 plus $7,950 for a Lasergraphics UI-100TN rasterizer, the Toshiba TN-5400 produces 200 dpi full color copies in under a minute.

Of the color thermal transfer printers, the Benson B-90 is the highest resolution at 240 dpi with a reported 17 second copy time. Priced at $6,995, the B-90 requires host rasterization or can run through a Versatec emulator. High volume hard copy often includes those devices that are slower than a-copy-per-minute but run unattended in a spooled environment. The ink-jet plotters from Benson, Digital and Tektronix fit this description. The Tektronix 4692 ink-jet plotter, nominally a 154 dpi 2-3 minute per copy device, has a lower resolution (128 dpi) high speed (1-2 min. per copy) mode for plot preview or time critical applications.

Large size Black-and-white Hard Copy Devices

Electrostatic plotters came on the market mainly as pen plotter replacements. Current models rival many pen plotters for image quality and run considerably faster than pen plotters. For example, the CalComp 5744 electrostatic plotter is 7 times faster than CalComp's high speed 1077 pen plotter, while the model 5742 electrostatic is 10 times faster than the same pen plotter.

Electrostatic plotters provide high (200 dpi) to very high (508 dpi) resolution with a cost per copy in the 2-3 cents per square foot range. Copy speed in the accompanying table is for an 11 inch long plot. Since electrostatic plotters are from 24 to 44 inches wide, 3 to 5 A-size pages can be cut from each of these to increase the overall throughput. Nevertheless, copy time for an 11 inch strip is less than 15 seconds for all 200 dpi and 400 dpi models. The 508 dpi Benson models produce an 11 inch strip at about the same speed as the IBM model 4250 600 dpi electro-erosion plotter discussed above. Each strip can be cut in to 3 to 5 A-size plots thereby more than tripling the 4250 rate. Device costs are between $26,000 and $80,000, with the price based on both resolution and plot width. Electrostatic plotters require host rasterization with software provided by the hardware vendor.

Large size Color Hard Copy Devices

None of the devices listed in the accompanying table produce a large E-size color plot in under one minute. E-size plots (34 in. by 44 in.) are easily cut into 16 A-size plots. Companies such as Grumman Aircraft use this technique to produce high volume color hard copy output. Production, self paper-feeding, multi-pen plotters are available from CalComp, Hewlett-Packard and Nicolet. For any but the simplest of plots, they generally require more than one minute per page. The high resolution, 400 dpi Hitachi model HJP-1610 ink-jet plotter is included due its intended production applications in engineering graphics.

For high speed, though, a color electrostatic plotter should be considered. Until recently, only the Versatec ECP-42 was available and it sold well at $98,000 per printer. It produces large full-color 200 dpi E-size plots for $1.50 each in 8 minutes. This averages to 19 cents each for A-size plots at the rate of 2 per minute, which is somewhat faster and less expensive per copy than the thermal transfer plotters. In July 1985, Versatec is planning to announce two more members of this product family which will produce smaller plots faster at a lower cost per copy.

At the May, 1985 NCGA show in Dallas, Benson demonstrated an engineering prototype of a one-pass high resolution color electrostatic plotter which is due to be available soon in widths of 24, 36 and 44 inches. The Benson one-pass approach (in contrast to the Versatec 5 pass approach) promises to generate plots faster than the Versatec model ECP-42. Progress has been rapid in the large size color graphics output device market with many new and exciting products expected in the years to come.

Table 6
High Volume Large Size Black-and-white Graphics Output Devices

Manufacturer	Model	Technology	Resolution (dpi)	Copy Speed	Cost per Copy	Approximate Equipment Cost	Remarks
Benson	9624S	electrostatic	400	7.33 sec	2-3¢/sq. ft.	$35,490	24 in. wide
	9436	electrostatic	400	—	"	48,985	36 in. wide
	9436S	electrostatic	400	11 sec	"	56,010	36 in. wide
	9644	electrostatic	400	—	"	61,225	44 in. wide
	9644S	electrostatic	400	13.75 sec	"	72,030	44 in. wide
	9824	electrostatic	508	44 sec	"	44,485	24 in. wide
	9836	electrostatic	508	1.22 min	"	61,875	36 in. wide
	9844	electrostatic	508	1.83 min	"	79,875	44 in. wide
CalComp	5732	electrostatic	200	10 sec		26,215	24 in. wide
	5734	electrostatic	400	10 sec		31,460	24 in. wide
	5742	electrostatic	200	10 sec		36,710	36 in. wide
	5744	electrostatic	400	10 sec		41,995	36 in. wide
	5754	electrostatic	400	10 sec		57,995	44 in. wide

Table 7

High Volume Large Size Color Graphics Output Devices

Manufacturer	Model	Technology Speed	Resolution Copy	Approximate Copy Cost	Cost per Copy	Equipment	Remarks
Benson	new 24 in.	electrostatic	"high"	--	--	--	single-pass
new 36 in.	electrostatic	"high"	--	--	--	color	
new 44 in.	electrostatic	"high"	--	--	--	--	
CalComp 1077	1075 pen plotter	pen plotter 0.0005 in	0.0010 in	--	-- 24,800	$20,500 and cut-sheet	dual mode, roll-fed
Hewlett-Packard 7586B	7550A pen plotter	pen plotter 0.0001 in	0.001 in	--	-- 21,900	3,900 E-size	B-size E-size
Hitachi	HJP-1610	ink-jet	400 dpi	16.5 min	--	148,000	24 x 36 in.
Nicolet	ZETA 8	pen plotter	0.001 in	--	--	5,950	11 in. wide
ZETA 887	pen plotter	0.001 in	--	--	17,950	IBM SNA/SDLC	
ZETA 824	pen plotter	0.001 in	--	--	9,900	24 in. wide	
ZETA 824CS	pen plotter	0.001 in	--	--	11,900	24 in., cut sheet	
ZETA 836	pen plotter	0.001 in	--	--	12,900	36 in. wide	
ZETA 836CS	pen plotter	0.001 in	--	--	14,900	36 in., cut sheet	
Versatec	ECP-24	electrostatic	200 dpi	5.5 min	87¢	--	24 in. wide
ECP-36	electrostatic	200 dpi	6.5 min	$1.45	--	36 in. wide	
ECP-42	electrostatic	200 dpi	8 min	$1.50	98,000	42 in. wide	

Conclusion on High Volume Production Graphic Hard Copy

High volume, high quality production graphics hard copy has already been implemented in high payoff applications by organizations that have leveraged standardization on device independent software. The variety of devices is sufficient to fulfill most of today's needs, both in black-and-white and in color. When choosing a plotter, do more than look at the initial cost and cost per copy. Ask yourself "Is the output quality good enough for you and your customer and better than your competition?" If the quality is good enough, then ask "Does the plot now have to go through a printing process?" Image quality is lost in reproduction. If the original is good enough, will it copy good enough? If the original quality was marginal, you will either have to give everyone originals or go to another device to produce originals with double the resolution for suitable reproductions. If you plan to distribute originals, make sure the machine is fast enough to make all the copies that you need. In general, high volume production graphics means sufficient image quality, resolution and speed to please the end recipient of the copies. Hard copy is the visible result of your labors that everyone sees. Look at the product offerings; there is one out there just right for you.

The Next Twelve Months:

The Trends Shaping the Business Graphics Industry

Because it is difficult to act confidently when new announcements seem to obsolete equipment that was new only months earlier, this updated version of "The Next Twelve Months," includes "action items" telling when large organizations can take advantage of each trend.

How These Trends Are Identified

To find these trends, we looked inside the offices of the leading-edge users. These pioneers have already begun using equipment and applications that will be important to four to five million new users of computer graphics over the next three years. Some trends are not yet in common use. To find these, we looked to the leading vendors: IBM, ISSCO and the Japanese, to identify the new products that will alter the technology that we use for computer graphics. By combining the experiences and desires of the leading users with the announced and soon to be announced products of the leading vendors, we are able to paint a clear picture of the major trends. Here, in a nut shell, are those trends.

1. Low Cost Laser Printers

The new laser printers are fast, reliable, and inexpensive. A single printer, costing less than $15,000, can serve the high- quality, black-and-white graphics needs of dozens of users. While the printer is not making charts, it does excellent text printing. It can even integrate text and graphics. The key to its effective use is to install it as a peripheral on a shared computer where it may be accessed from terminals, form communicating PCs, and from batch jobs. (Acquiring one or more graphics laser printers is a 1985 action item.)

2. Ink Jet Printers and Color Thermal Printers

Ink jets have had little success in the business graphics market. Their fortunes should begin to improve, however, in 1985 because of three developments.

1. More speed: up to one page per minute.

2. More resolution: up to 180 dots per inch.

3. Hardware rasterizers: which off load picture processing.

A high speed ink jet printer with a hardware rasterizer provides reasonable quality color charts and can be used as a shared graphics printers. It will be found alongside laser printers in many organizations. The laser will provide high volume black and white graphics. The ink jet will meet requirements for color.

Color thermal printers are an emerging threat to ink jet printers. These Japanese creations provide similar speed, resolution and price to inkjets. Several new varieties will be announced during 1985. As you look for color hard copy, look both at ink jets and color thermal.

(This is a possible 1985 action item for organizations which are not now providing shared color graphics hardcopy.)

3. Micro-Mainframe Graphics Linkages

The vast majority of today's PC users have no access to high quality graphics hardcopy equipment. Only about ten per cent of them purchased digital plotters, and most of those users found they were forced to stand by the plotter feeding it paper any time they needed charts. Their time was too valuable to become plotter operators.

To solve the problem of access to high quality hard copy equipment, a major trend has developed that links micros to mainframes for graphics. In 1984, users created the link by making the PC into a graphics terminal using software or hardware extensions to into a graphics terminal using software or hardware extensions to their PCs. They requested charts from the PC, previewed them there, and routed them to high-quality shared graphics equipment like film recorders, laser printers, and continuous plotters.

In 1985, the PC-as-graphics-terminal trend will continue, but it will be complemented by a new trend linking programs like LOTUS 1-2-3 directly to main frame graphics programs like TELL-A-GRAF. Under the new links, LOTUS 1-2-3 and SYMPHONY will be used in their standard fashion. Users will look at data and view instant charts in stand-alone mode on the PC. When a LOTUS user makes a chart that s/he wants to show to others, however, s/he will use a new "button" inside those packages which will automatically instruct the PC to send the LOTUS Worksheet to TELL-A-GRAF on the mainframe. There it will be converted into a high-quality slide or chart.

(The action items for 1985 are (1) be sure that the PC's you buy have communications capabilities, (2) be sure that the high quality graphics hardware you buy for your mainframes is installed as shared devices, and (3) acquire the linkage software when you need it.)

4. Interactivity

Interactive capabilities will begin to emerge in business graphics software, offering users the ability to point to the location where labels and messages are required. Interactivity is the strength of paint programs such as Dr. HALO and MacPaint. Now the bar chart/line chart/ pie chart programs will begin to have it as well.

This trend was apparent in PC packages in 1984. It will be seen in 1985 especially in mainframe graphics software.

(No action is needed. Software vendors will offer interactivity as an update to existing software.)

5. Graphics Standards' Surprise

GKS (Graphics Kernal System) has now officially eclipsed CORE, the old SIGGRAPH proposal. The leading graphics software vendors have embraced GKS, offering options to their graphics software packages that comply with the GKS standard.

Because GKS is perceived as a device independent standard, most buyers think GKS will make their software support all graphics equipment. However, users are in for a surprise when they learn that GKS software in no way guarantees that any particular graphics device will be supported. Unless the software vendor supplies a "device driver," each graphics device will be incompatible with GKS software. ISSCO's large library of device drivers, covering 270 different devices, protects it users. Other vendors will have to develop device drivers one at a time for several years.

(When buying new hardware users should ask their software vendor, not their hardware vendor, whether a graphics device is "supported" by the software.)

6. IBM PC's With More Power and New Operating Systems (The Mainframe on the Desk)

Today's IBM PC's will soon be eclipsed by two new waves of IBM equipment and software. First, the IBM PC/AT will soon be joined by a series of new IBM PC's which will run the VM operating systems. With the new operating systems, these PC's will be a target machine for mainframe graphics software, especially TELL-A-GRAF and DISSPLA. User organizations will then be able to offer a uniform family of graphics software tools on all machines from the mainframe to the desktop.

(This trend will not lead to an action item until late in 1985. However, knowledge of it has caused most large organizations to delay acquistion of PC graphics packages, other than Lotus and paint programs, until they learn which desktop computers will run the mainframe graphics software they already have.)

7. In-House Publishing

Billions of dollars are spent each year in typesetting, line art, plate making, and printing, so that documents may be published. Until 1985, automation has played a small role, but new hardware and software will allow the computer to do more of the job. When it comes, automation will lower costs and increase responsiveness of the publishing process.

Commercial publishers, such as TIME magazine, have already automated the color control and page layout process. In-house publishers, particularly in the automotive and aerospace industries, are next. Commercial publishers bought systems which were oriented toward color and cost millions of dollars. Newer systems for in-house publishers on the other hand, are oriented toward black and white publishing. They solve the publishing problems of technical documentation and their prices are plummeting as low as $100,000 or less. To organizations whose publishing bills run into the millions of dollars, these lower cost systems are cost effective.

Design workstations and mainframe based publishing systems will both gain from this trend. Stand alone design workstations will be purchased for smaller jobs. Mainframe-based publishing systems will be acquired where large numbers of pages must be created. Mainframes will also be used where text and graphs are created on word processors and graphics software and need to be brought together for final publication.

8. Graphic Project Management Systems Forge Ahead

Project management systems are among the oldest management application of computers. These packages calculate schedules and budgets. They report on tasks that need to be complete by any particular date, and they determine the critical path. Most large companies have project management systems, but they are not as effective as they should be.

A new class of **graphic** project management software is being recognized as an important improvement over the older systems. Organizations have found that graphic project management systems, in particular, TELLAPLAN, which is the first of the new type, is being used 10 to 100 times as much as the older project management systems. Where older systems were used only for the largest projects, the new tools are popular for every project on which schedules are important: auditing, computer systems development, research, marketing, and dozens of others. Part of the difference is ease-of-use, because the new system can be learned and used almost instantly by secretaries and managers. A produce presentation quality charts that show management the schedule and cost status of projects.

(Adding graphic project management to your computer is an action item for 1985 if you have a VAX, PRIME, or IBM mainframe. If you have only a PC, you many want to wait for the next generation PC's. The PC software does not have the needed flexibility and quality.)

9. Graphic Expert Systems

Few of the millions of users of graphics are experts on design, so new software tools have been created to assist those users make charts that look right. The new tools offer three knowledge- based functions: chartbooks, layout intelligence, and color pallette selection. Chartbooks are predesigned graphics. Users tell the computer to "Make Chart 25." The computer looks up the data or asks for it; then it makes the chart. The charts are designed by professionals, so they look good.

Layout intelligence is the second function. It relies on a data base of facts about how to format charts. Examples are (1) how big to make charts so they will fit inside overhead transparency frames, (2) what the length-to-width ratio should be for 35mm slides, and (3) how large to make the chart and the lettering for quarter page or half page publication charts.

Color pallette selection is the third function. It solves the problems created by new graphics systems that offer thousands of colors. "Smart" graphics software chooses combinations of colors that look good together. The user asks for a "look" such as "spring" or "winter." The software selects a pleasing set of colors.

(No action is necessary on this trend. The leading graphic software vendors are adding these capabilities to their products. You will get the new capabilities with updates of those products.)

10.   **Visual Early Warning Systems (Graphic Decision Support System.)**

Software tools are coming to offer push button graphic management for executives. The new tools meet the needs of executives. All traditional computer graphics software packages served the people who created charts. None served the needs of managers who just wanted information, and wanted it graphically. Today, organizations from London to Los Angeles are building or buying new systems that instantly deliver information, in graphic formats at the touch of a button. Of the 100 largest organizations in the United States, 20 have already built or ordered such systems and half of the rest plan to put them in during 1985.

The systems are variously called visual early warning system or graphic decision support systems (DSS). They consist of libraries of charts and tables, automatically updated whenever the underlying data change. Every chart is available at the touch of a button. Another button starts automatic creation of 35mm slides, overhead transparencies, and paper charts.

Visual early warning systems have been created on computers ranging from Altos micros to IBM mainframes, but the trend is toward the mainframes for this application. The mainframe is needed because the data are on the mainframe and because many people need to share the information in those charts. Only the mainframe offers the combination of data, graphics software, storage capacity and network, essential for success of these systems.

(Pent up demand for these systems is enormous. Implementation of a visual early warning system should be the first priority for computer graphics in 1985.)

Geometric Modelling

I. C. Braid

1 Introduction

The application of computers to drafting and design dates back to
Sketchpad, a remarkable program devised by Ivan Sutherland at MIT in the
early 60s [Sutherland]. Sketchpad illustrated the power of combining
interaction in real time between user and computer, with
computer-generated pictures on a cathode ray screen. Here was an ideal
tool by means of which electrical and mechanical engineers could record
their designs. It was the perfect piece of paper: the "drawing" could
be changed any number of times, was accurate, and best of all, could be
"read" by the computer. Thus the recorded information could be used
again when analysing or manufacturing a design. Clearly these
techniques would revolutionise engineering by offering a new medium for
recording and transmitting design data.

The hopes excited by Sketchpad have not been fulfilled as rapidly as one
might have expected, especially in the case of mechanical engineering,
an ancient craft resistant to computer methods. But the steady progress
of geometric modelling, the subject of these talks, suggests that the
early promises may yet be realised.

1.1 Drafting systems

Sutherland had shown how the techniques of Sketchpad could be applied to
circuit design and this quickly led to commercial products. In this
case, the data to be recorded was a graph of nodes and links in which
connectivity or "topology" was important. Applied to engineering
drawings, the same technique required not just a network of nodes and
links, but further geometric data to record the position of each node
and the shape of the curve of each link. The distinction between
geometric and topological information holds good today in drafting
systems and solid modellers.

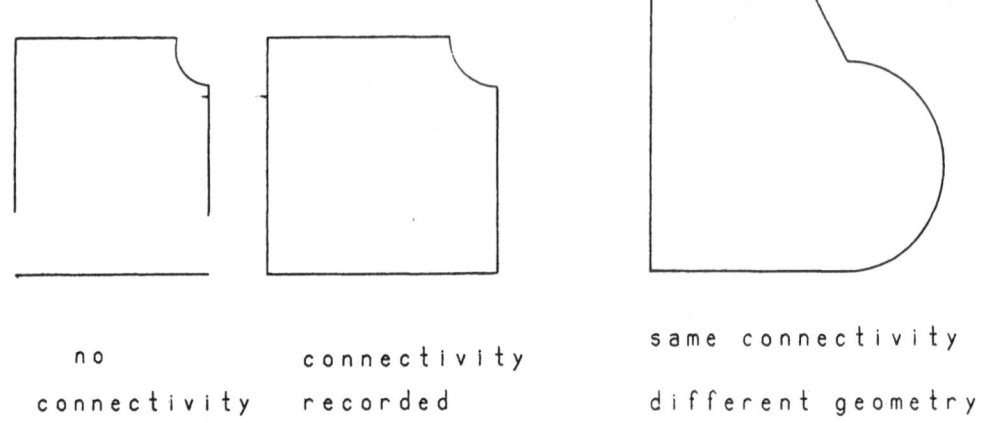

no
connectivity

connectivity
recorded

same connectivity

different geometry

Fig. 1.1 Topology and geometry

Sketchpad led not only to systems for circuit design; it was also the progenitor of drafting systems. These gave a means of capturing drawings as lines and text in 2D, in other words, as marks on paper. The meaning of drawings represented in this way was still left to human interpretation. Nevertheless such systems were able to raise the productivity of drawing offices. Although initial input of a drawing might not be greatly speeded up, the editing of a drawing would be much faster. Introduction of such systems was not too difficult since they affected only a single part of an organisation — the drawing office which continued to produce drawings as before but better and cheaper.

Drafting systems progressed, firstly in the amount of structure captured and in the variety of graphic entities represented, and secondly by moving from two to three dimensions. Lines in 2D became lines in 3D — the so-called wire-frame models. Perspective views could be generated but removal of hidden lines had still to be done interactively by the user splitting lines where they crossed and deleting the correct pieces of lines.

A further step in the progress of drafting systems was to allow 3D wire-frame models to be "surfaced". The user indicated which wire edges were to bound a face end either gave the surface of the face explicitly, or left it to the system to deduce the surface. For simple parts with only planar and cylindrical surfaces, the surfacing process could often be performed automatically.

DRAFTING SYSTEMS

2D only

2D plus depths

3D wire frame

3D wire frame
plus surfaces

Fig. 1.2 The evolution of drafting systems

The surfacing of a wire-frame model is equivalent to the embedding of the graph formed by its edges and vertices. It creates what we shall term a boundary model of a solid. Hidden-line pictures can now be calculated automatically, as can volumes and other geometric properties.

1.2 Surface systems

At the same time that drafting systems were making their appearance, the aircraft and motor industries were developing systems for designing complex 3D surfaces. To begin with these tended to be direct computer implementations of the traditional lofting process whereby cross-section curves were set up in a sequence of parallel planes, and then surfaces were passed through them. The impetus to apply computers in these areas was the inadequacy of the 2D drawing technique to capture 3D surfaces accurately. Unlike the drafting systems which ran on mini computers, the surface systems generally used shared main-frame machines. The mathematical basis of the surface systems was gradually improved and now most are based on parametric curves and surfaces. Much ingenuity went into making the complex mathematical forms amenable to use by non-mathematicians. Even so, the intrinsically four-sided nature of

parametric surfaces meant that the user had to arrange four-sided
patches to suit practical problems where regions with other than four
sides would occur. These systems also called upon the user to assist in
finding intersections between patches, by providing starting points from
which intersection curves were calculated. [Forrest, Faux]

1.3 Systems for classes of parts

A third type of system addressed the problem of designing classes of
parts. Typically these systems covered not only design, but analysis
and manufacture. Programs for a family of pumps, for example, might
present the designer with a small number of parameters to be set. The
program would then generate pictures of the pump, calculate design
properties such as cross-sectional areas, and finally output nc tapes
for cutting prototype volutes or impellers. Wing design is another area
where there exist specialised programs that allow the designer to
specify the properties required of a new wing and which can then create
a wing design and generate hundreds of working drawings in a few days.

These specialised systems are very useful in practice. Being tailored
to a particular problem and embodying knowledge of the terminology and
practice in that area, they are easier and safer to use. They span
design, analysis and manufacture, and so give a much greater pay-off by
reducing the chance of error in transmitting data from stage to stage.
Their drawback is that they are expensive to write and develop, and they
can act as a barrier to progress since they embody certain design rules
which new knowledge may make obsolete.

1.4 Stages in engineering

As well as systems for drafting, there have of course been others for
analysis and manufacture. For analysis, there are systems for analysing
stresses using the finite element technique, and others for kinematic
and dynamic analysis. They require input of a description of the shape
of a part, often in a carefully idealised and simplified form. Other
data will also be supplied to specify loads and material properties, for
example. The analysis model may have to be described by giving yet more
data such as the size of a finite element mesh. These systems are
designed to be used by the analyst whose skill and judgement is still
very much required. Much effort goes into deducing the data from
drawings and checking that the data entered is correct.

After analysis comes manufacture and here again we find specialised
systems for process planning and generation of numerical control data.
Once again data is prepared manually from drawings, some of it being
shape information such as the surfaces supplied in an APT part program,
and other data like motion statements, feeds and speeds, being required
for the manufacturing process.

1.5 Why modelling?

It easy to see why a single complete model of a part should be desired.
The same data is being repeatedly entered - at design, analysis and
manufacture. If the information were captured in a suitable general
form at design time, it could be used again for analysis and for
manufacture. Mistakes would be avoided, and time and money saved.

The question then is to decide on a product representation that will be
suitable for all further computations. It must be accurate, must
contain enough information for all subsequent enquiries to be made
rapidly, and should be concise.

Whether a single representation can meet all these requirements is
debatable. Multiple representations are acceptable provided we can
transform between them when necessary. Certainly we shall also have
additional models for analysis and manufacture - such as finite element
meshes and tool paths.

1.6 Types of modellers

In practice two main types of product model have emerged. One, an
implicit model, is known as the constructive solid geometry (csg) model
[Requicha]. It records a shape as a collection of simpler primitive
shapes such as cubes and cylinders, and their positions in space. The
primitives are represented as the terminal nodes of a tree structure,
and the non-terminal nodes record how the primitives are combined, that
is, added or subtracted or intersected by means of boolean operations.
The model is equivalent to the instructions given to a modeller such as
"Get a cube", "Position it at (4,5,6)", "Get a cylinder", "Position it
at (2,3,4)", "Subtract the cylinder from the cube", and so on.

The csg description, whilst compact and easily deduced from the user's
input, is not convenient for producing pictures. It must first be
transformed into a boundary model, a model that is logically equivalent
to the surfaced, 3D wire-frame model we have already met. This model
records the boundary of a solid in a piecewise manner, dividing it up

into faces such that each face lies on a single surface (planar, cylindrical, toroidal and so on).

The connections between faces are modelled by recording the edges and vertices in which the faces meet. Edges and vertices lie on curves and points respectively. Curves and points may be deduced as intersections of two or more surfaces, or they may be stored explicitly. The latter arrangement, though it introduces redundancy, speeds up the generation of pictures which is important for giving rapid feedback to the user.

The second type of modeller, known as a boundary modeller, emphasises the explicit boundary model rather than the implicit instructions given by the user. The main difference in the internal algorithms is that in a pure csg modeller, boundary models are always deduced from the csg model, whereas in a boundary modeller the primitive volumes are also held or generated as boundary models, and thus the boolean operations accept boundary models as input, and produce boundary models as output. This suits the incremental process of building a design by making successive changes to a single model.

In practice, the distinction between the two types of modeller has gradually lessened. Csg modellers frequently record boundary models of partial results so that boolean operations can be speeded up on subsequent re-evaluation.

The boundary modellers have an advantage in allowing other ways of changing models - for example by blending an edge, tilting a face, moving, scaling or deleting a hole. These local operations recall the local changes permitted by surface systems where portions of a b-spline patch can be altered whilst leaving the remainder of the patch unchanged. It is simple to attach other information such as dimensions, surface finishes or threads to the faces or edges of a boundary model.

A recent development is the introduction of features to boundary modellers. Collections of faces or edges can be named and modified as a group by being moved, rotated, copied, deleted or "pulled off" from the body to which they belong. Features can also carry attributes. From the designer's point of view, features correspond closely to the way he sees a part in terms of its functional items such as slots, holes and grooves.

One variant of the boundary modeller approximates all surfaces by polyhedral facets. The chief advantage of faceted modellers is the speed with which they can be developed and made reliable. Another is their ability to make use of special hardware to create hidden line and hidden surface images very quickly. Boolean operations are carried out on the faceted model. If the facets also carry links to the accurate surfaces to which they approximate, the resulting models can be improved: polygonal approximations to intersection curves can be moved back on to the accurate intersection curves, and facets that are adjacent and refer to the same original surface, can be grouped into faces. However these faces may not be exactly the same as those that would have been obtained by performing the boolean operations on the accurate model. Another disadvantage is that local operations, many of which depend on the topology not changing, are difficult to provide. For these reasons, faceted modellers have tended to be applied to preliminary rather than detail design.

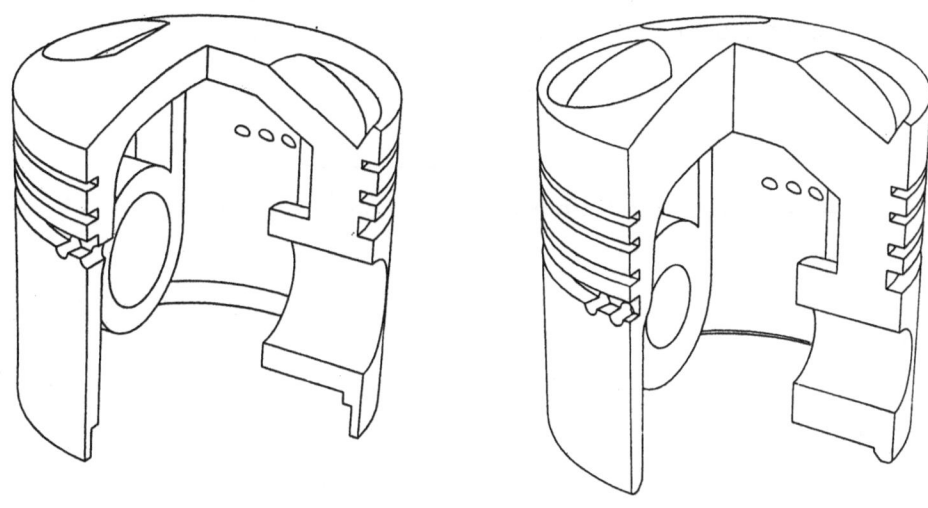

Fig. 1.3   Local operations

1.7 Other types of modeller

Two other types of modeller should be mentioned. One is a variant of the csg modeller where pictures are produced by ray-firing rather than by building a boundary model [Goldstein]. These modellers have been very successful at the task for which they were designed - making pictures, but are not so easily adapted to other applications such as producing nc output.

A second type of modeller is based on the octree method [Meagher] where a shape is approximated by a collection of juxtaposed cuboids obtained by successive binary division of 3D space. Boolean operations and picture production are very rapid on such a model. However, rotations of one object relative to another are expensive (since they require regeneration of the octree model), and storage requirements become large when high accuracy is demanded. It seems likely that these modellers will be confined to picture production and preliminary design studies.

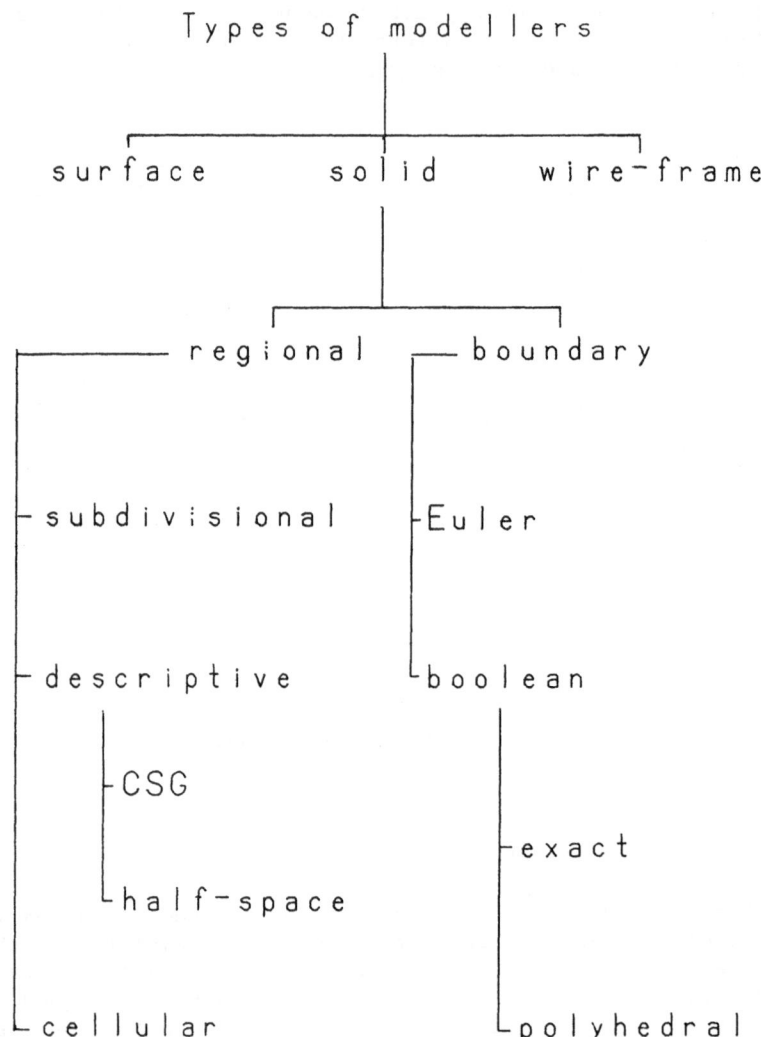

Fig. 1.4 A taxonomy of modellers ([after Hillyard, 1982])

2 Models

We first consider what it is that we wish to model, and then describe ways of doing it.

2.1 Assemblies

Engineers design products which are generally assemblies rather than single components. Thus our model must cater firstly for assemblies. The model must also acknowledge that assemblies frequently have multiple occurrences of identical components or sub-assemblies (they will need to be added up and shown on parts lists). In fact by adding the notion of instances to assemblies, we can also economise on storage space needed by the model, since the instanced item need now be recorded only once. In computer terminology, the assembly-instance structure forms a directed acyclic graph with assemblies at the non-terminal nodes, components at the terminal nodes and instances in the links between the nodes (see fig 2.1).

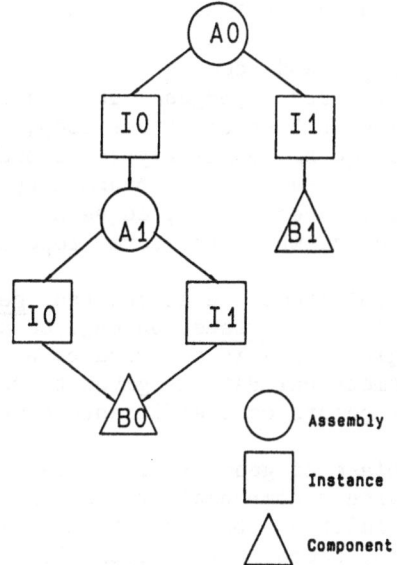

Fig. 2.1 A simple assembly

In order that multiple instances of a component or sub-assembly can be positioned in different places, there must be further information contained in an instance, to specify position and orientation of the instanced sub-assembly or component. Usually position and orientation will be given relative to that of the assembly owning the instance. We thus define an hierarchy of co-ordinate reference frames, one for each assembly or component.

Assemblies will contain a list of instances; other items to be associated with assemblies will be mentioned later.

2.2 Components

Components, the terminal items in the directed graph, will need to stand for solid objects. However, for practical purposes it is useful in addition to provide different models for two special kinds of solid exemplified by sheet metal and pipes, which can be idealised respectively as surfaces plus thickness, and as curves plus cross-section shape. Not only are these idealisations useful for designers, they frequently form the basis of analysis and can be put to advantage in deriving simple views. The 2D idealisation we shall call a sheet and the 3D idealisation a wire.

We shall model the bounding surface of a solid body in a piecewise manner, by representing it as a collection of connected faces. Faces meet one another in edges and edges meet at their ends in vertices. Thus a face will be bounded by edges. The edges are formed into loops. A singly-connected face is bounded by one loop, and a multiple-connected face by two or more loops. Similarly faces are connected into shells. A body with no interior voids will be bounded by one shell only. These items - bodies, shells, faces, loops, edges and vertices - together form the ´topology´ of a solid, where the term ´topology´ is used loosely.

With certain topological items are associated geometrical items, that is, a face is matched to a surface, an edge to a curve, and a vertex to a point. The topological data is recorded by a network of nodes and links whereas the geometrical data is given by real numbers representing co-ordinate values of points or coefficients of equations.

A further important class of geometry is termed construction geometry. This is associated with a component or assembly in order to fix it in a co-ordinate frame of reference but is not associated with topological items such as faces, edges or vertices. It is needed since designers frequently set out construction surfaces, curves and points before and during a design. Often a team of designers will need to work to agreed construction geometry before detailed solid objects are specified. It may also happen that some aspects of a design such as an aerofoil are specified as pure geometry for some time before they are finally translated into solid form.

Yet another kind of data will be needed to cover information like material specification, surface finish, small blends and chamfers. We shall model these items by a general purpose attribute which can be attached to an assembly, instance, body, shell, face, loop, edge or vertex, or to a geometric item i.e. a surface, curve or point. We shall allow attributes to stand for data associated with a single topological or geometrical item. The need for attributes referencing more than one item seems to be limited to a few well-defined cases which will be treated specially. Attributes contain data in the form of one or more numbers or items of text, possibly a unit, and an update class which governs the way the attribute will change as the model alters (see below).

The attributes referring to more than one item, are dimensions and features. A dimension will usually refer to two items, most often two faces, but it may refer to one alone. It may also refer to datum items, which can be modelled as special kinds of body that contain a point.

A feature is a set of faces or edges. So far there has been no need of other types of feature though these could be accommodated if desired. We shall also permit features to carry attributes. Thus a feature will typically stand for a part of a body significant for function or in manufacture: a boss, pocket, or hole, for instance.

Fig 2.2 shows the node types and some of their connecting relations.

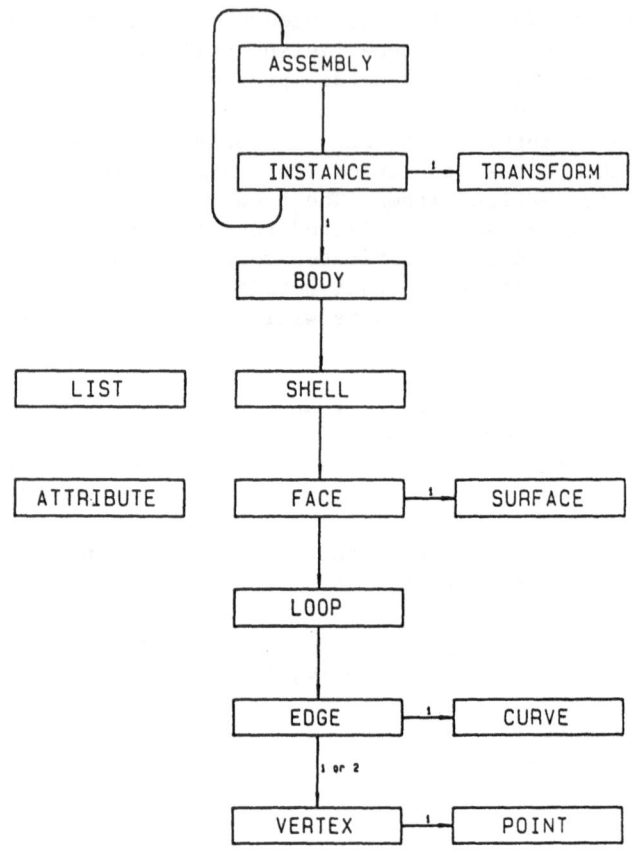

Fig. 2.2   A boundary model

If we consider just the edges and vertices among the topological items, we see they form a general graph. The adding of faces effects an embedding of the graph, a process that occurs in 3D wireframe systems when the model is surfaced, automatically or with use assistance. This is one strategy that can be followed to build up a topological data structure. Another is to build faces separately, each with their edges and vertices, to position them correctly in space and then to sew them up along common edges. A third strategy is to arrange that the edge-vertex graph is always embedded. The Euler operators, to be described below, together with a suitable data structure, ensure this. One possible data structure [Baumgart] is shown in fig 2.3.

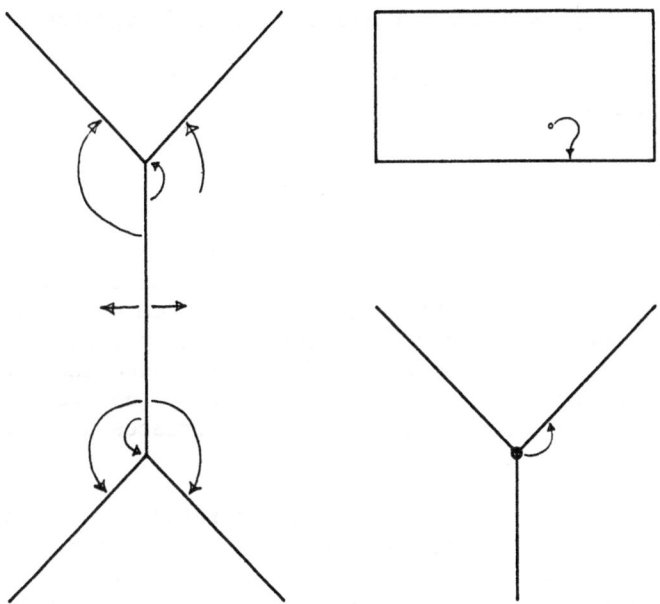

Fig. 2.3 Baumgart's winged-edge data structure

This data structure carries most information attached to edges. An edge node refers to the start and end vertex of the edge, to the faces (or loops) to the left and right of the edge, and to the four winged edges (being the neighbouring edges of the left and right faces, connected to the edge). A face (or loop) need only carry a pointer to one edge of the face, and similarly a vertex need carry only one pointer to an edge having the vertex as an end point. The structure makes searching rapid since the winged-edge pointers provide a two-way chain linking the edges round a face or round a vertex. Storage allocation is simple since face, edge and vertex nodes all carry fixed numbers of pointers.

Other schemes are possible. Ensaldi et al [Ensaldi] propose a data structure where the faces carry most of the information and Woo [Woo] analyses a number of different schemes. One should remember that since engineering components will usually have trivalent vertices (vertices with more than three edges are difficult to produce by machining), the average number of edges round a face will be a small constant. For a simple solid like a cube or a prism, we have:

$$f + v = e + 2 \quad \text{(Euler's rule) and}$$

$$3v = 2e \quad \text{(trivalent vertices)}$$

and hence

$$e/f = 2 + 6/f \text{ which for large f approaches 2.}$$

Since every edge meets two faces, the number of edges round a single face on average will be 4.

2.3 Geometry

Having discussed how to model topological information, we now consider geometry. Surfaces are the most important item of geometry. They are what we machine and measure. Curves and points arise as the intersection of surfaces though for convenience and speed we usually store them too. Only in construction geometry do we sometimes find curves defined in terms of points, and surfaces defined by curves or points.

There are three main choices open to us in recording a surface. We may represent it by an implicit function $f(x,y,z)=0$, or by a bi-parametric, vector-valued function $\underline{P}(u,v)$, or we can approximate the surface by a polyhedral ´surface´. In the first two cases, we then have the choice of adopting a uniform representation or not. For example, some modellers like Build [Braid] or Design [Hillyard], have employed quadric surfaces throughout and have recorded them by storing the coefficients of a symmetric 4x4 matrix e.g. M in

$$[x \; y \; z \; 1] \; M \; [x \; y \; z \; 1]^t = 0.$$

Other systems such as Romulus prefer to record common surface types separately. Thus a plane is given by a point $\underline{Q}$ and unit normal $\underline{n}$ in $(\underline{P}-\underline{Q}).\underline{n}=0$. A cylindrical surface is represented by a point and direction for its axis and a radius. Similar data are stored for conical, spherical and toroidal surfaces. Multiple representations like these lead to more complex code but they also preserve useful information about the particular surface types, which can be put to good effect in speeding up tests and in improving reliability. One source of numerical problems is the calculation of surface intersections when surfaces meet tangentially. Although statistically one might suppose these cases to be rare, in fact they are common since designers often want to join two surfaces without change of slope in order to achieve a desired appearance, to avoid higher stresses or to facilitate withdrawing a part from a mould. Keeping surfaces in individual representations helps in detecting tangent cases in advance and in taking action to ensure that intersection calculations to do not come to grief.

As to whether implicit or parametric surfaces should be employed, the main arguments in favour of parametric surfaces rest on their local properties that permit parts of a surface to be altered without change to other parts. The b-spline surfaces enjoy this property and are popular for design of car bodies and other sculptured surfaces, and there is no doubt that a general modelling system must provide them or some equivalent form of parametric surface.

As the rational polynomical bi-parametric surfaces can also represent quadric and toroidal surfaces exactly, it has been suggested that these might form a universal geometric representation. There are drawbacks to this scheme. Firstly, as with universal implicit surfaces, useful information about particular surface types like cylinders and cones is lost. Secondly, the parametrisation gets in the way. For example, it requires a cylindrical surface extending through 360 degres to be represented by at least two (in practice usually four) separately parametrised patches. Further, extra information must be supplied to fix a parametrisation of no intrinsic interest to the user: in effect we are recording an artifact of the model - the parametrisation - which is not wanted by the user.

A last point to be borne in mind is that algorithms for intersecting parametric surfaces with the accuracy and reliability expected by geometric modellers, tend to be quite slow. One only has to consider the speed with which one can determine that a cylinder intersects a normal plane in a circle to see how much slower it will be to discover the same fact by first intersecting two general sets of rational parametric patches, and then testing the result to see if it is a circle to within a given tolerance. It seems unlikely that even the advantage of special-purpose hardware will overcome such a drawback in this simple case.

The foregoing amounts to a plea for geometrical simplicity in the model. It can be matched by a similar demand for topological simplicity. Some modellers have done without loops by the expedient of using extra edges to link the multiple loops that would otherwise occur round a multiply-connected face. Other modellers, including at one time Build and Romulus, have added "props" down the side of cylinders (see fig 2. 4).

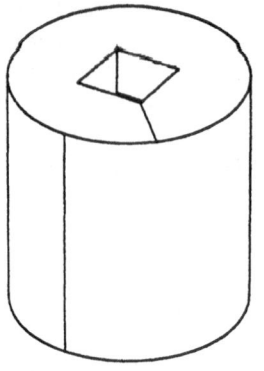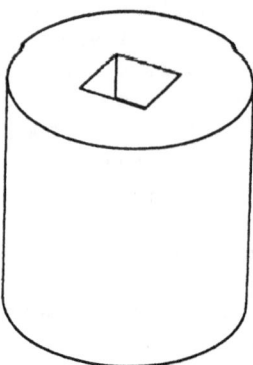

Fig 2.4 Props and links

These too are artifacts of the model or modelling process (as indeed are facets) and should be avoided. Without them, the model provides obvious, easily understood attachment points for attributes and dimensions. There are no hidden edges or faces to immobilise local operations such as tweaking a boss around a cylinder (see fig 2.4) and the model is both simpler and smaller.

Mention should be made of incomplete models. An engineering design in progress is certain to be incomplete and may quite possibly be inexact. Computers always find inexactness difficult to treat, but we can accommodate incompleteness to an extent by allowing the geometry of a face to be suspended or absent (Romulus rubber face). It is possible to let boolean and other operations work on the non-rubber faces so that progress in one region of a complex body is not held up by delays in specifying another region.

Blending surfaces have been an unsatisfactory area of modelling for a long time. At a blend the designer requires slope continuity, but is less fussy about position or curvature; he also expects blends that overlap to do so smoothly. Romulus has recently incorporated a new implicit surface designed expressly for blending between faces meeting at an edge. Control is given by setting range and thumbweight. The range controls the points at which the blend leaves one face and arrives at the other; different ranges may be set for either side if desired.

The thumbweight governs how closely the blend surface follows the underlying faces: a thumbweight of zero gives a chamfer, a thumbweight of one produces an approximately circular blend (exactly so if the cross-section of the faces in a plane normal to a point on their intersections, are straight lines); as the thumbweight becomes large, the blend surface approaches the faces. Fig 2.5 shows examples of blending. The blend characteristics can vary along an edge.

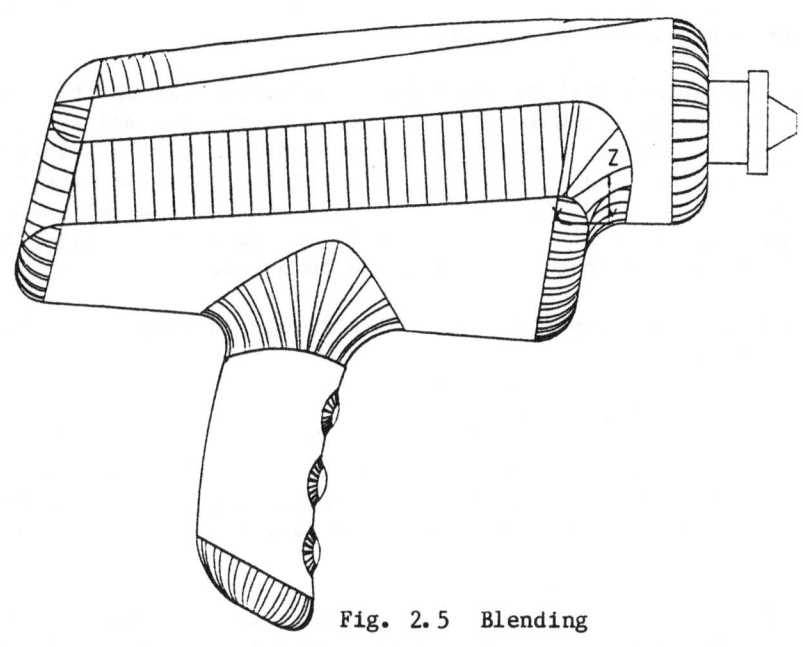

Fig. 2.5 Blending

2.4 Standard models

Several standard models have been proposed. The solid IGES model (PDES), presently being evaluated, covers csg and boundary models, and follows a similar scheme for topology to that described above. There is a practical problem in transmitting boundary models from one modeller to another. Models are made to a certain accuracy governed by the length tolerance in force at the time the model is made. It determines the fineness of detail that will be modelled as well as placing a limit on the distance by which a model containing redundant information, may depart from the ideal of a perfectly self-consistent model.

The safest course is to ensure that any modeller always works to the same tolerance so it can read its old models.

3 Operations

Having described the form of the model in the previous chapter, we now consider ways of building and changing models, beginning with low-level operations which we need for initial creation of simple objects such as cubes and cylinders.

3.1 Euler and other low-level operators

The low-level operations will be the Euler operators [Baumgart] which give a convenient and consistent way of creating and modifying the topological data of a solid model. They also provide a useful internal interface to routines that change the data structure by creating nodes and setting pointers. Once those routines have been tested, we can be sure that the topological structure of the data is always in a consistent state when control is outside the Euler routines.

We have already met the simple form of Euler's rule in chapter 2 above. The general form is

$$2f - 1 + v - e = 2(s - g) \qquad\qquad (3.1)$$

where 1 is the number of loops, s is the number of shells, and g is the (total) genus of the body or bodies. A sphere has a genus of 0, a torus has a genus of 1, and a cube with n non-intersecting through holes a genus of n.

Equation 3.1 describes a discrete surface in 6D. The surface includes the origin, and the numbers of topological entities in every solid must be a point (f,1,v,e,s,g) on the surface. We can arrive at such a point by beginning at the origin and applying a sequence of Euler operators that carries us from point to point along the 6D surface. There are many possible sets of Euler operators [Braid]; here is one:

    1)   create shell, face, loop and vertex
    2)   add edge and vertex
    3)   add edge, face and loop
    4)   add genus and loop, remove face and loop
    5)   add loop, remove shell, face and loop

Although they will not be listed, we shall also need the reverse operators such as "remove edge and vertex" in order to delete bodies using the Euler operators. In practice the low-level operators will also set geometry as well as topology so that we always obtain Euler objects that can be drawn.

The first operation makes what is sometimes termed an "acorn", the simplest non-null Euler object that consists of one shell, face, loop and vertex. The vertex will be given a coordinate point but the surface of the face is left unset (Romulus refers to this as a "rubber" face).

The second operation adds an edge and vertex at a given vertex of a particular face. Thus having made an acorn, we can add edges to it to make a wire object lying in the rubber face of the acorn. This is the basis of the edge-based construction method that Romulus combines with its construction geometry to offer a low-level but powerful means of making any solid (fig. 3.1). Wire objects are useful in their own right, for example, as a visible model for the centre lines of pipework.

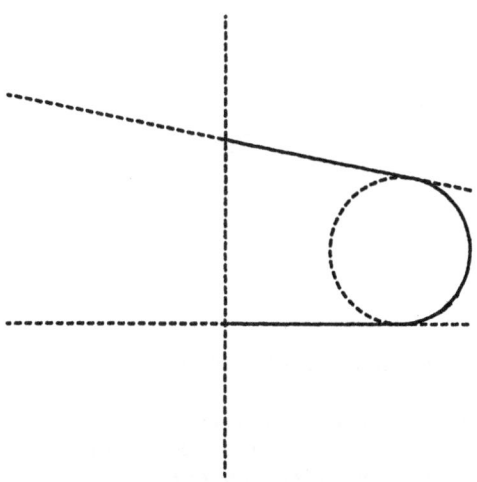

Fig. 3.1 Making a wire object

An open wire object may be closed by means of operation (3) which adds an edge and a face to make a sheet object bounded by a loop of edges and having a face to either side. The surfaces of the faces are determined from the geometry of their bounding edges, a process termed "fixing" the geometry of the face. It is up to the user to ensure the wire edge geometries are consistent.

Romulus uses sheet objects to form an idealised model of sheet metal bodies. In this case the two faces have the same surface geometry but with opposite sense.

3.2 Scribing and piercing

Having selected a face of a sheet (or solid) object, we may draw edges on it using a higher-level operation termed "scribing" (fig. 3.2). If the edges fall within the face, they will form a new loop; if they lie across the face, they will divide it into two faces.

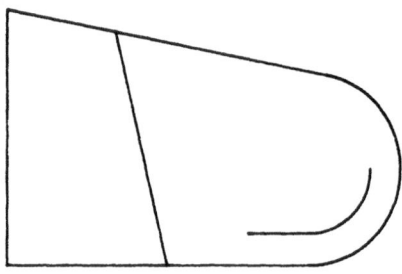

Fig. 3.2 Scribing edges on a face

If a closed loop is formed within a face of a sheet body, it can be "pierced" through to the back face by means of Euler operation (4), thus creating a hole through the sheet object.

3.3 Sweeping

In order to create solid objects from sheet objects, we introduce another higher-level operation termed "sweeping" which is implemented in terms of Euler operators. A face may be swept linearly to make a prismatic shape, or around an axis to make an object of revolution. Some systems provide more general sweeps that allow a face or an open wire to move along another wire so as to sweep out more complex objects. Sweeping raises the dimensionality of the body by one: sweeping a wire makes a sheet; sweeping a sheet makes a solid. A face of a solid may also be swept to make a boss or blind hole. If the base of a blind hole coincides with and lies within another face of opposite sense, it too

may be pierced to make a through hole using Euler operation (4).
Similarly, if a boss is swept up to another face, it may be joined to it
using Euler operation (4) or (5) depending on whether the other face
belongs to the same body or to a different one.

Fig. 3.3 Sweeping

With the operations described so far we are in a position to make
primitive volumes such as a cuboid, cylinder, cone or torus.

3.4 Move, rotate and scale a body

The solid body transformations for moving or rotating a body are
implemented by changing the geometry of a body directly. Thus if a
straight line held as a point and a direction is to be moved, we merely
move the point and leave the direction unchanged. Rotating a straight
line will require changes to the point and direction. It is usual to
provide routines that apply a solid body transformation to each
geometric type (point, curve or surface).

Movement or rotation of an assembly is performed by making changes to
the transformations in the instances belonging to the assembly (and to
any contruction geometry it may own).

Most modellers allow equal scaling of bodies though strictly a scaled body may require changes to the topology. Scaling down may cause two distinct points that were more than a minimum distance apart to be less than the minimum dictance in which case they should be merged into one point. Similarly, scaling up may make inconsistencies that were previously of no importance (being less than the discriminant) significant. The purist solution is to insist that bodies are never scaled but are always made again at a larger size.

Unequal scaling brings further problems. In modellers that represent circles and ellipses in different ways, for example, clearly unequal scaling will cause changes in the representation. Equally, spherical and toroidal surfaces will become elliptical and for unequal scaling to be possible, the modeller must also handle these more general surface types.

3.5 Local operations

An advantage of a boundary model is that changes can be made to parts of it, that is to certain faces, without affecting most of the remaining faces. Changes of this kind we call local operations. They have many advantages. They are well suited to the design process which often consists of making small adjustments to a design until a satisfactory shape has been achieved. Computationally they are fast and need only access a small portion of the model. They are much more convenient than boolean operations for making changes such as blends and chamfers, since to fashion and position a correctly shaped body to perform the blend or chamfer is extremely difficult for the user. Their only drawback is that self-intersecting boundaries can result. It is possible to make the operations check for self-intersections on request, but usually the user will prefer to make the checks visually and so gain speed.

3.6 Features

To specify a local operation requires that part of the boundary (one or more faces or edges) be identified. We term this a feature. The modeller should provide for features to be named, and should give a variety of means for selecting a feature - for example, by pointing or by geometric characteristic such as "all planar faces", "all circular edges with axis parallel to Z and radius 5", "all faces adjacent to this face", or "all faces cut by this ray". It must also be possible to compose features from other features ("all faces common to two features", "all edges in one feature but not in another").

Having defined a face feature, it can be moved or rotated relative to the rest of the body provided the arrangement of faces that results (the topology) is unchanged. The curves of the edges in which the feature meets the rest of the body will be recomputed as will the points of the vertices at their ends.

A feature can also be tapered in order to give a draft to a part so that it can be removed from a die or mould. The taper is specified by the taper angle (usually just a few degrees) and a plane. The taper is calculated so that to one side of the plane the cross section of the feature increases while to the other side it diminishes.

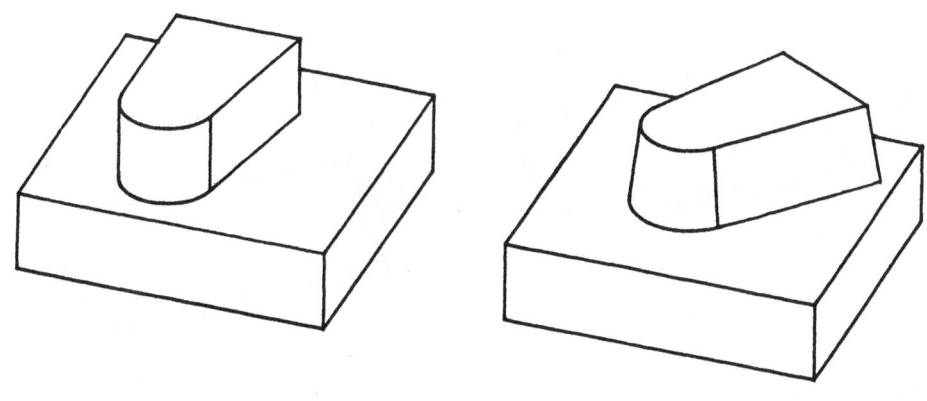

Fig. 3.4 Moving, rotating and tapering a feature

3.7 Tweaking

Tweaking, of which taper is a special case, consists of making changes to geometry while leaving the topology unaltered. Thus a planar face can be replaced by a slightly spherical face; this may be done for aesthetic reasons. Or the diameter or a hole may be altered. A face may sometimes have to be moved on to a surface offset from the original surface, or an implicit surface may be replaced by a parametric surface (one way of introducing parametric surfaces into a model).

3.8 Stretching, bending and twisting

In principle these operations which introduce strain, shear and torsion into models, could be provided. Bending is certainly useful from a practical point of view. It changes the topology but in a well-defined way. For design of sheet metal, it is essential that bend (and unbend) operate on thick slabs and on sheet objects. Bend should also make allowance for the stretching that occurs in physical bending, if the user so requests.

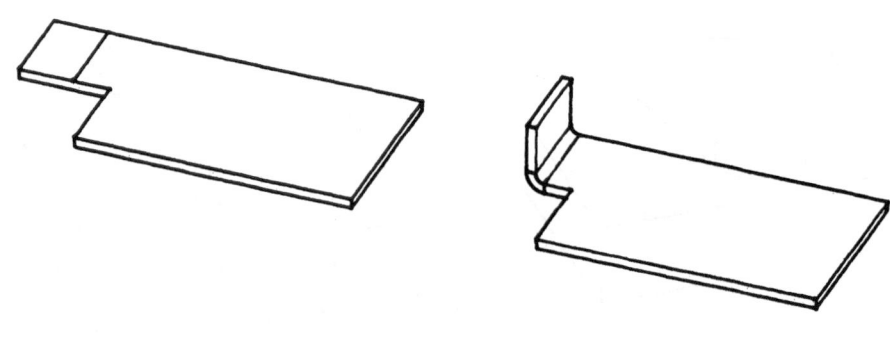

Fig. 3.5 Bending

3.9 Blending

The final stage in the design of many engineering components is to round off or chamfer sharp edges – to avoid high stresses, to allow for extraction from moulds and dies, or to improve safety or appearance. On drawings blends may be expressed implicitly ("round all edges to .1") or be drawn out in full. In a modeller it is valuable to have implicit and explicit blends and chamfers too. Thus a blend or chamfer can be recorded as an attribute of an edge, or it can be modelled explicitly by inserting a new face.

As already described above, Romulus uses a blending technique where a blend is specified by giving the range to either side of the edge being blended (roughly how far the blend surface extends into the face on either side), and the "thumbweight" which determines how closely the blend hugs the surfaces being blended. Overlapping blends are handled by creating new blend surfaces as an amalgam of the overlapping surfaces.

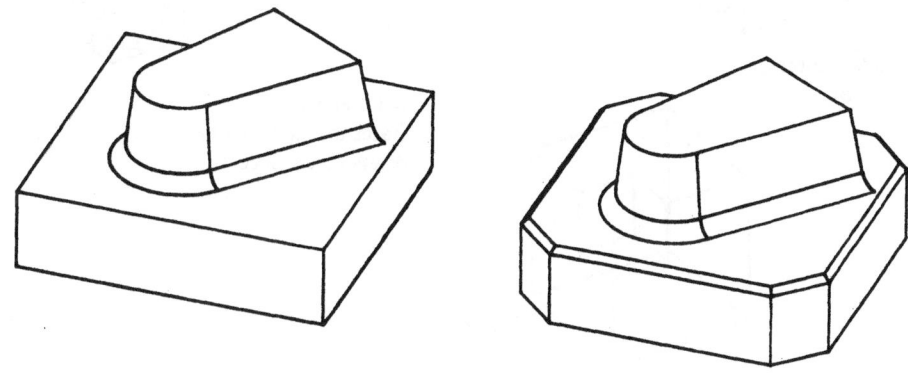

Fig. 3.6 Blend and chamfer

3.10 Boolean operations

These are the most powerful operations without which no system can call itself a solid modeller. In the case of a boundary modeller, they require each face of one body to be compared with each face of another. If the faces intersect, new edges will be inserted along their curves of intersection. When all faces have been thus compared and edges inserted, then depending on the kind of boolean operation (union, intersection or difference), portions of the boundary of each body will be discarded and the remaining pieces linked up again to form boundaries of new bodies. Romulus uses the Euler operations to perform the edge insertions (similarly to scribing discussed above).

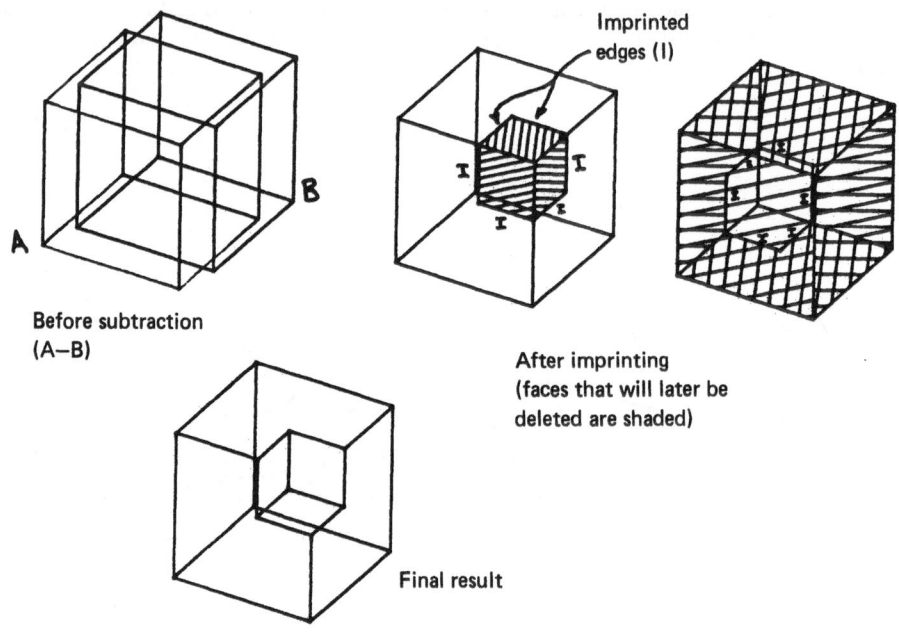

Before subtraction
(A–B)

After imprinting
(faces that will later be
deleted are shaded)

Final result

Fig. 3.7   Imprinting and relinking

The greatest difficulty in building a modeller is to make the boolean operations reliable. Firstly, the geometric intersections of surface with surface or curve must be utterly robust since there can be no user intervention deep inside a boolean operation if anything goes wrong. Secondly the topological changes must be made with care. Difficulties tend to arise with coincidences, or worse, near coincidences, either of position or slope or in higher drivatives. (A good exercise for any modeller is to try subtracting a body from a copy moved or rotated by a small amount.) As tests must be done with respect to a small discriminant, we have to contend with the fact that a ≐ b and b ≐ c does not imply a ≐ c, and algorithms must not make this assumption. One might suppose that coincidences would be rare statistically. Quite the reverse is true since designers want faces to line up and frequently create planar faces with tangent cylindrical neighbours.

4   The user view

Having described the operations that a modeller can perform, we now consider how a user can conveniently direct those operations and follow the progress of a modelling session.

4.1   User interfaces

User interfaces are a hotly debated topic and advocates of particular styles of interaction hold to their views with great fervour. None the less one can discern certain general properties of all interfaces. The interface must convey to the user the current status of the modeller and model. The state of the model is best given by one or more pictures. The state of the modeller, in particular, the state of the input system or what has been entered already, must be conveyed textually or in some other way. The interface must also make clear what options for further input are open to the user, and should minimise the chance of his entering incorrect data, by restricting what may be given. The restrictions should cover both syntax and semantics of the user interaction. Sometimes syntax may depend upon semantics. For example when giving an arc by end points, angle and radius, in the one case where the angle is 180 degrees, a further point must be given in order to avoid ambiguity (two arcs are possible).

Just as text editors have advanced from being driven purely by command interfaces, to the point where most editing can be done simply by pointing and pressing one or two of a small number of keys, so we find a similar trend in interfaces to modellers. Early systems were command-driven with model entities such as bodies and faces being referred to by name. The user had to remember the syntax of each command. This might include a sequence of numeric values each standing for some quantity such as radius, angle or height (e.g. "CYLINDER 5 12"). If the user made an error, the whole line had to be entered again. Many computer operating systems are still at this stage of development since their designers, being computer literate, have grown accustomed to that style of input.

4.1.1   Keyword-value pairs

To save the user having to remember the correct order and meaning of the values, we can include keywords (e.g. "CYLINDER RADIUS 5 HEIGHT 12"); we can also allow alternatives (e.g. "CYLINDER HEIGHT 12 DIAMETER 10"). Although these commands take longer to type, they are easier to read and understand. The effort in typing them is unimportant if the commands are actually entered by menu actions.

4.1.2 Prompting and menus

The system can help the forgetful user still more by prompting him when asked. Thus in Romulus if the user gives "CYLINDER @P", the system might respond with "HEIGHT, RADIUS?". We can arrange that the "prompts" are given in a row or column, in other words, as a menu, an item of which can be selected by pointing or by giving a number n for the nth item in the list. Selection of a menu item by number is economical in user actions and well-suited to the experienced user. Picking is slower since it requires hand-eye coordination but is likely to be preferred by the new user or one unused to typing. It is also helpful to provide the option of more extensive prompts that explain what an entry stands for.

4.1.3 Form-filling

Yet another method of organising input is form-filling. Here the computer will display e.g. "CYLINDER HEIGHT ... RADIUS ..." The form entries can show default values or perhaps the value entered last time, and can automatically advance from one entry point to the next. The form immediately shows what has already been given, and makes it easy to change a value already entered. Still more sophistication is possible. We can arrange that the computer checks values already given to ensure that they lie in predefined ranges for example, or replaces values by variables or expressions as in a typical spreadsheet program. The user should also be able indicate units for values, or at least to give them if units are different from a preset default unit.

Some systems distinguish between beginners and expert. Thus Romulus´ command input can be switched to prompting by the user; it does so automatically if the user makes an error.

4.1.4 A macro language

Every modeller has an implicit model in that the inputs given to it can be expressed as a sequence of textual commands, and in many modellers the command language has been upgraded into a programming language thereby greatly enriching the class of available implicit models. In Romulus, the macro language MCL provides for declaration of variables of type number, vector, logical, string or list. There are operators on the variable types from which expressions can be constructed. The results of the expressions can be assigned to variables or inserted into Romulus commands. Other statements invoke pre-defined macros, which may have arguments, and yet others control looping and branching.

As the macro language incorporates read and write statements, it can be used to encode simple translators to access the model and output data in some standard form suitable to be read by another system, or to read in data and then build or change the model.

The macro language must be supplemented by a set of enquiry functions that return values from the model. The enquiry functions in Romulus mostly take as argument the name of a model item such as a body, face or edge, and deliver one or more values as result. For example, RADIUS returns the radius of a circular edge or cylindrical or spherical surface (or face), POSITION finds a point on a face and DIRECTION gives the vector along a straight edge or the direction of the axis of a cylindrical, conical or toroidal surface (or face). In Romulus, a generalised naming scheme allows connected entities to be found. Thus the function ROMLIST("b0-edges") will return all the edges of body b0, in a list of strings.

The following MCL fragment "unmachines" grooves in a turned part. First the modeller command "RECEIVE" is given to read a model from disc. Then another macro UNDERCUT (not shown) is called to recognise simple grooves, each of rectangular cross-section, and returns them as a set of faces "ucut", each face in the set being the face at the base of the groove. Having found the faces adjacent to each base face, the routine determines the dimensions of the groove. An annular ring is made with these dimensions and united with the body in order to fill the groove. Note the use of a feature defined as those faces "AGAINST" another face, that is, those faces bordering on the given face.

```
        RECEIVE tmod
        DO 'undercut'
        LET k=0
        FOR i IN ROMLIST('ucut-faces')
           LET edg_list=ROMLIST('<i>-edges')
           LET r=RADIUS(edg_list(1))
           DEFINE FEATURE:end AS AGAINST <i>
           LET n=0
           FOR j IN ROMLIST('end-faces')
              LET n=n+1
              LET length_list=POSITION('<j>')
              LET l<n>=length_list(1)
              DEFINE FEATURE:dia AS AGAINST <j> LESS <i>
              LET edg_list=ROMLIST('dia-edges')
              LET r<n>=RADIUS(edg_list(1))
           NEXT j
           LET k=k+1
           IF l1 LT l2 THEN GOTO make
           LET temp=l1
           LET l1=l2
           LET l2=temp
   make:CREATE ucut<k> CYLINDER R 90 FROM <l1>,0,0 TO <l2>,0,0
           CREATE hole CYLINDER R <r> FROM 0,0,0 TO 180,0,0
           SUBTRACT hole ucut<k>
           IF r1 GT r2 THEN LET r1=r2
           CREATE filler<k> CYLINDER R <r1> FROM <l1>,0,0 TO <l2>,0,0
        NEXT i
        FOR i FROM 1 TO k
           UNITE filler<i> tmod
        NEXT i
```

More elaborate applications may require the writing of code to be
compiled and linked with the modeller. This will be necessary when the
task demands the efficiency of compiled code as with translators that
must handle large amounts of data, or when new enquiry routines are
needed for the macro language and cannot be expressed in terms of the
enquiries already provided.

4.1.5 The user's mental model

When designing a user interface, one has to consider not only what
happens within the modeller, but what the user thinks is happening.
This is termed the user's mental model. An infrequent user cannot be
expected to retain a complex mental model of the workings of a geometric
modeller. It is often wise to eschew powerful but complicated

operations in favour of sequences of simple ones. Similarly, operations
with special cases that that the user must avoid or with unexpected side
effects, all complicate the user´s mental model and should not be
admitted if possible. Implicit models are also more difficult for a
user to comprehend, especially when the form of the model is not evident
graphically. Is a blend face actually recorded as a face or as a tagged
edge? The user cannot tell from a picture unless the picture is
specifically annotated. Assembly-instance structures introduce similar
complexities. The four bolts a user sees on the screen may be separate
copies of one bolt, four instances of one bolt, or two instances of two
sub-assemblies, each consisting of two instances of one bolt.

4.2 Graphics

A significant part of a user´s time (and perhaps half the cpu time) goes
in verifying the results of modelling actions, or in examining from
different points of view models already created whilst deciding what to
do next. For speed of response, feedback will often be in the form of
wire frame pictures. Their well-known drawbacks can be mitigated in
various ways. Adding perspective helps, as does modulation of intensity
to indicate depth perpendicular to the screen. Dynamic rotation,
movement and scaling is also extremely effective in giving the user an
understanding of a complex assembly. This is especially true for a
designer who is likely to "know" the part or assembly well. For others
such as subcontractors who have to understand a drawing of a part, a
coloured shaded picture can be of great help, so much so that it may be
economic to model a part simply to make a picture. Hardware is
available now to generate shaded pictures rapidly from polyhedral
models, and is clearly well-suited to polyhedral modellers. Accurate
boundary modellers must first tesselate their models, a process that is
practicable if it can be carried out face by face so that the costs are
spread over multiple modelling operations (each operation is likely to
change only a few faces).

4.3 Incremental update

There is a general problem of keeping derived data such as graphic data
structures up to date as the model changes. We would like to avoid
having to regenerate the derived data each time. If the derived data
can be related back to the model, and we arrange that the modeller
reports model changes as they occur, we can equally arrange that the
derived data is updated automatically. Romulus announces changes in a
"bulletin board" that records births, deaths and changes to topological
items such as faces and edges. The board can be read after each

command, or after a sequence of commands. The bulletin board also makes
it possible to create drawings that emphasise the changes that have
occurred to a part (e.g. by using different line styles or colours for
new, changed or deleted edges), and so help reduce a common problem for
readers of engineering drawings - to discover what has changed.

4.4 Realism or not?

Often it seems that the aim of computer graphics is to achieve greater
and greater realism in the generated images. However for views of
engineering components we should be prepared to enlist the aid of tricks
familiar to artists. They deliberately depart from reality in order to
make a picture easier to understand. Superimposing edges on a shaded
picture (outlining) is often helpful. Another trick is to thicken the
lines that divide a part from the background. Suppression of fine
detail may also be necessary to aid comprehension. Much remains to be
done to make modellers handle realistic complexity effectively, both in
their models and in pictures of models.

5 Applications

We have seen how a macro language extends the usefulness of a modeller.
Not only can programs in the language encode families of parts, they can
also embody design rules, feature recognisers, translators for sending
data to or from external systems, and a host of other applications.
There is the further advantage that since the language is interpreted,
programs can be created at run-time without the need for time-consuming
compilation and linking.

Considering applications in general, we find there are three ways to
connect a modeller and an application (fig. 5.1).

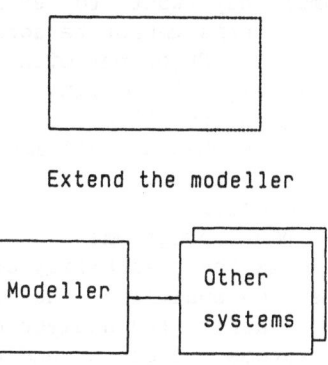

Extend the modeller

Modeller Other systems

Link to other systems

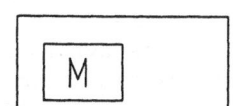

Make the modeller a sub-system

Fig. 5.1 Linking to applications

The first possibility is to extend the modeller by adding further code
(compiled or as macro langauage statements). Extra commands could be
added or further enquiry routines provided in the macro language.

A second method is to send data to or from the application. For
example, geometric data in the model might be output in APT format to a
system for part programming, or in another form for an fe mesh
generator. These processes require first a selection from the model
(putting geometric or tological items into a "bucket"), and second a
transformation (pouring the contents of the bucket down a "funnel"
marked e.g. APT or Patran). The funnel may re-order the data, expand
or change it (e.g. implicit to parametric form, or in the case of

curves, to polygonal form), it may invent and insert names (e.g. names of points), and may precede the data by a header giving title, date and so on.

The application is started and reads the file. The user, such as a part programmer or stress analyst, may edit the data received from the model, and will certainly add further data to specify motion statements and feeds and speeds in the nc case, or, for fe, mesh size details and a description of load forces.

While this process is a considerable advance on creating data manually from a drawing, and does much to reduce errors, there are difficulties. The application programmer may want to examine the extracted data together with the part, but this cannot be done since only an extract of the part model has been made. Or he may wish to change the part, for instance to remove detail that will be ignored in a stress analysis. He may also wish to derive geometry based on the part model but not directly contained in it as when a shell model is derived from a solid model. In the nc case, the generation of APT data leaves out much useful information in the model (effectively the topology) which has to be re-created by the part programmer when he gives the motion statements. Then there is the possibility of the part model changing, perhaps as a result of stress analysis: the whole extraction process must be repeated again. Lastly, the analyst or part programmer has the burden of learning two systems - modeller and application.

The third method in fig. 5.1 has the modeller built in as a subsystem of the application. Now the user need learn only the application system. Since it contains a modeller, it can read in the complete product model and all model data is available to it. Extraction of data from the model can be done at any time from within the application and may indeed be controlled by it (as in the case of adaptive mesh generation [Wordenweber]). All the facilities of the modeller are there for the application to use if need be. Hence the model can be changed, extra construction geometry can be created, and the modeller may be used to model other aspects of the application world such as tooling or partly-machined shapes in the case of process planning.

Provided that a suitable matching of model details and application data can be made, there is the possibility of updating the application data structure as the model changes - another case where the modeller's bulletin board can be put to good use.

So far there is no accepted standard for interfaces to modellers. The creation of such a standard depends on agreement on a "virtual modeller" and on its set of operations. With such a standard, writers of application code would have the possibility of changing modellers should better ones appear. CAM I have sponsored the design of one such interface [CAMI] arranged as a library of routines to be called by Fortran programs. It is to be hoped that an equivalent standard organised as a data interface will be developed; it would be more flexible in that programs in any language could call it, and would be better suited to multi-processor architectures.

From this discussion, the building in of the modeller into an application seems to have most to offer. The first method, of extending the modeller to cover applications, will lead to an ever larger system as further applications are added, and is surely impracticable. The second method has the virtues and drawbacks of modularity. The third method appears to offer the best match to the world of engineering, providing different systems for different specialists. In effect, it depends on the product model capturing all the information needed for subsequent analysis and manufacture, which seems possible since drawings fulfill that role now.

The same approach is possible when the modeller is the recipient rather than the sender of information. Applications of this kind are less common at present, but are growing in importance. We already have the example of the wing design program as well as others for designing turbine blades and other high technology components. As design problems are better understood, and the knowledge needed to perform design is encoded, for example, by means of an expert system, we shall see modellers forming subsystems in more and more design applications. The macro language described above, gives another way for designers or specially-trained assistants to encode design practices.

5.1 Data bases

So far we have envisaged a collection of systems for design, analysis and manufacture, each sharing a common modelling capability. There are other systems too of course in which the modeller plays no part, such as those for purchasing and scheduling. Yet another system, more central even than the modeller, is the data base. Linked to it is the system for configuration control. The data base is the receptacle for data of all kinds including models. Configuration control oversees the product description as it changes and keeps track of the interdependencies amongst the various kinds of data. Essentially it works in the same way as existing manual systems, requiring individuals to examine dependent data following say a design change, to ascertain whether that data must be altered in consequence. There are many practical difficulties - for example, to do with assemblies, and the relationships between implicit and explicit models - but few principles stand out.

5.2 Future possibilities and problems

5.2.1 Hardware

Probably the most important future development is the arrival of new computers, powerful enough to run geometric modellers and cheap enough to give one to each designer or application engineer. The arrival of the workstation is a recognition that people are prepared to pay to remove uncertainty - in this case, uncertainty of response time. More powerful computers also mean that we need no longer trim our modelling techniques to suit computer power (or lack of it); instead we can use the techniques most convenient for the user. These are based on models that have the great merit of being simple, and free from artifacts.

Although we shall no doubt see new hardware for visualising models more rapidly, the development of special hardware for modelling itself is more uncertain. Modelling has so many characteristics of general-purpose computing that modelling-specific machines will be hard-pressed to compete with the price advantage enjoyed by mass-produced general-purpose computers.

5.2.2 Modelling problems

In geometric modelling itself, there are several areas where more research is needed. One concerns patterns and levels of detail: no modellers handle these issue satisfactorily at present. Another source of difficulty is that of modeller reliability. Even though modellers are approaching the point where they are sufficiently reliable to do useful work, it would be a great advance if the problem was better understood. The third area that stands out is that of dimensions and tolerances. Although some years have passed since initial results were published [Hillyard,Light], there is still much to do before useful methods are available for treating dimensioning and tolerancing fully. A fourth problem has been mentioned already - that of converting between boundary models made to different tolerances (a model laundry).

5.2.3 Better design and manufacture

Much work is already in progress on new methods for design and manufacture. Often it relies on artificial intelligence techniques but it has tended to be studied in isolation. There is a gap to be bridged between modelling and AI applied to design for assembly, for manufacture and so on. This occurs at the level of features which must be recognised automatically and in the context of the problem being addressed, rather than being given already defined in the input data. Of course the recognition of features is itself an AI problem, but one whose solution is better attempted with the help of a modeller. At a purely practical level, there is the difficulty of combining modellers written in archaic languages with AI systems expressed in AI languages, something that would be solved by the standard data interface mentioned above.

References:

Baer, A., Eastman, C., Henrion, M. (1979):"Geometric modelling: a survey", Computer Aided Design vol. 11, no. 5, pp 253 - 272.

Baumgart, B. G. (1974): "Geometric modelling for computer vision", Stanford Artificial Intelligence Lab. report STAN-CS-74-463.

Braid, I. C., Hillyard, R. C. and Stroud, I. A. (1978): "Stepwise construction of polyhedra in geometric modelling", proc. IMA conf. on Mathematical Methods in Computer Graphics and Design, Academic Press.

CAMI (1980): "An interface between geometric modellers and application programs", Computer-Aided Manufacturing International Inc., report no. R-80-GM-04.

Ensaldi, S, Floriani, L de, Falcidieno, (1985): "Geometric modelling of solid objects by using a face adjacency graph representation" (to appear).

Faux, I. D. and Pratt, M. J. (1979): Computational geometry for design and manufacture, Ellis Horwood.

Forrest, R. A. (1968): "Curves and surfaces for computer-aided design", Ph D diss., University of Cambridge.

Goldstein, R. A. and Nagel, R. (1971):"3D visual simulation", SCI Simulation Vol. 16, no. 1.

Hillyard, R. C. (1978): "Dimensions and tolerances in shape design", Ph D diss., University of Cambridge.

Hillyard, R. C. (1982): "The Build group of geometric modelers", IEEE Computer Graphics and its Applications, vol. 2, no. 3, pp 43-52.

IGES (1983): "Initial Graphics Exchange Specification (IGES), version 2.0", US Dept. of Commerce, NBS, report no. NBSIR 82-2631 (AF).

Light, R. A. (1980): "Symbolic dimensioning in computer-aided design", MSc diss., MIT.

Meagher, D. (1982): "Geometric modeling using octree encoding", IEEE Computer Graphics and Image Processing, vol. 19, no. 2, pp 129-147.

Requicha, A. A. G. (1979): "Mathematical models of solid objects", University of Rochester, College of Engineering and Applied Science, Tech. memo. 28.

Sutherland, L. E. (1963): "Sketchpad - a man-machine communication system", MIT Lincoln Laboratory Technical Report No. 296.

Woo, T. C. (1985): "A combinatorial analysis of boundary data schemata", IEEE Computer Graphics and Image Processing, March, 1985, pp 19-27.

Wordenweber, B. (1981): "Automatic mesh generation of 2 and 3 dimensional manifolds", Ph D diss., University of Cambridge.

Interactive Geometric Modelling for Integrated CAD/CAM

M. J. Pratt

INTRODUCTION

Although many other interesting applications are now emerging for
solid modelling systems, the goal of their original developers was
to use them to provide unified descriptions of parts and assemblies
in an integrated design and manufacturing context. This goal has
still not been achieved, despite fifteen years of intensive effort
for reasons which are now becoming clear. In what follows the
motivation for the development of solid modellers is first examined;
various approaches to the computer representation of solid objects
are then described and illustrated by reference to specific
modelling systems. There follows a section on applications,
mostly in the field of mechanical engineering which is where many
major problems remain to be solved. Finally, some aspects of the
user interface to solid modelling systems are discussed and an
account is given of moves towards standards for communication
between different modellers and between modellers and applications
programs.

MOTIVATION FOR SOLID MODELLING

Computer-aided manufacturing requires a detailed description, in
machine-understandable form, of the shape of whatever is to be made.
Certain other information is also important; for example, details
of the manufacturing process will depend upon the type of material
required, the surface finish desired and various other factors.
However, geometry is clearly of paramount importance in determining
the method of manufacture. The sum total of geometrical and
nongeometrical information which is required for this process may
be termed the 'product definition' or 'product model'.

The traditional means of product definition is the drawing, with
associated textual information. Drawings may be manually produced
on a drawing board, though nowadays they are increasingly generated
by the use of CAD systems. In either case three orthogonal views
of the object are typically given, supplemented by cross-sectional
or other information where necessary. From the point of view of
the integration of computer aided design and manufacture the drawing,
which is the output of the design process, has a major drawback; it
is not intelligible to a computer, even in its internal storage
format in a CAD system. If computer aided manufacture is to be
used, this means that the geometry shown on the drawing must be
reinterpreted in some way, with a human operative as an
intermediary, so that the computer can make use of it. For
example, a part programmer may write a computer program in a
specialised language such as APT. The first part of such a
program contains formalised details of the surface geometry of the
object in three dimensions. This is followed by specifications
of motions, with respect to those surfaces, of a computer-controlled
cutting tool. If the tool motions are correctly programmed the
shape of the desired object will be cut automatically from an
initial stock volume of material.

The important thing to notice about this last example is that the
part program contains a geometric description of the object, which

must in some sense be equivalent to the geometric information on the drawing. However, the transformation of this information from one form to the other is achieved by a human operative. What is needed for true integration of CAD and CAM is for the product model created during the design process to be already in a form which can be used directly by the manufacturing process. The most promising type of product representation for CAD/CAM appears at present to be that generated by a geometric modeller (sometimes called a solid modeller).

It is important to realise that many of the sophisticated CAD/CAM systems currently in use today are not solid modellers. These are mostly 'wireframe' systems, which allow a part to be modelled as a set of lines or edges in space. In the simplest cases this is achieved by adding depth information to lines in a 2D drawing to generate a wireframe representation of what is called a $2\frac{1}{2}$D object. For automated applications, however, edge information is not enough. There are many applications for which information is needed concerning the surfaces of the object; these include automatic computation of volume and mass, automatic generation of instructions for computer-controlled machining, and automatic hidden line or hidden surface removal in the generation of graphics.

The $2\frac{1}{2}$D wireframe representation of an object results from a fairly obvious extension of the 2D draughting process. In such objects all edges will be either horizontal or vertical, and the nature of the surfaces is obvious; they will either be horizontal planes or cylindrical surfaces (in a general sense) with vertical generators. Many existing wireframe CAD/CAM systems now permit the generation of fully 3D wireframe objects, however. For such objects it is in general no longer possible to infer the nature of the surfaces from the nature of the edge data stored. For example, if an object face has five coplanar edges the system may reasonably 'guess' that the face lies in a plane. On the other hand, if the five edges are not coplanar, the system cannot make an automatic choice of geometry for the face they enclose.

In some wireframe systems the user is allowed to attach faces to his model. This is usually rather a tedious process; first each of the edges bounding the proposed face must be selected, and then the geometric nature of the desired surface indicated. Furthermore, it is the responsibility of the user to ensure that he has attached all the faces necessary to give his object a complete boundary dividing its interior from its exterior. By contrast, the true solid modeller is designed to ensure the integrity of the product model automatically, relieving the user of this responsibility. It also provides much more efficient means for the construction of the product model. Additionally it stores not only geometry but also topology, i.e. information about how all the various faces, edges and vertices of the model are linked to each other. This data is of great importance for automated manufacturing applications. The type of data structure used by most solid modellers is such that additional technological data needed for such applications can readily be linked in if desired.

In summary, solid or geometric modelling systems generate product representations which in principle enable the answer to any desired interrogation to be provided by the computer. Although this should enable many different applications programs to be integrated with a solid modeller, integration has only been achieved for a limited range of engineering applications at present. These will be discussed later, as will the improvements which are needed in solid modelling systems before the range of applications can be widened to provide true integrated CAM.

TYPES OF MODELLER

Existing solid modelling systems may be divided into three classes. Firstly there are systems which are based on a spatial decomposition of a volume containing the modelled object into an array of cells which may be occupied or unoccupied. These are referred to as cellular or spatial occupancy systems. Secondly, there are systems in which the modelling process consists of building up complex objects from relatively simple volumetric building blocks or primitive volumes. If these primitive volumes retain their explicit representation in the data structure which describes the final model, such a system is often referred to as a constructive solid geometry (CSG) modeller. Finally, there are the boundary representation systems, which, as their name implies, model only the boundary of the object. The boundary changes during the creation of a particular model, and details of the method of its construction are lost. In the next three sections these approaches to the modelling of solids are examined in more detail.

Cellular Methods

The basis of the cellular method is conceptually very simple. A finite volume of space entirely containing the object to be modelled is assumed to be divided into a large number of discrete cuboidal cells. In the simplest case these are all of the same size so that a regular 3D mesh arises. The modelling system then simply records whether each particular cell is (a) occupied by material, or (b) unoccupied. The necessary data structure is a 3D matrix in which each element corresponds to one space cell.

The cellular method has the advantage of simplicity. However, in order to obtain good resolution on the boundary of the object it is necessary to use a large number of cells, which leads to problems of computer storage.

The existing solid modellers using the cellular approach overcome the resolution problem by using a relatively coarse mesh which is refined in the region of the object's boundary, its most important feature for practical purposes. The TIPS-1 system, developed at Hokkaido University in Japan (TIPS Working Group 1978), functions largely in terms of a relatively coarse mesh and divides cells into three types rather than two. Those which are completely full or completely empty are comparatively uninteresting and easily dealt with computationally. It is those cells which partly contain material which have to be treated in more detail to provide an accurate representation of the object boundary. The refinement is obtained in this system by making reference to the exact boundary surfaces which are expressed by implicit equations of the form $f(x,y,z) = 0$. For the computation of the volume, mass and moments of inertia of the object represented the boundary cells are further subdivided into a regular array of 125 subcells.

More recently, what is known as the octree method has risen to prominence (Yamaguchi, Kunii and Fujimura 1984). Here only two types of cell are distinguished, full and empty. If a boundary cell is detected which falls into neither class then it is subdivided into a regular 2 x 2 x 2 mesh of 8 subcells. These

are again tested, and boundary subcells further subdivided in the
same manner. This method allows the achievement of any desired
order of resolution on the object boundary. The result of the
subdivision maybe represented as a tree structure, with the single
original cuboidal volume containing the object as root. Each
boundary node of the tree gives rise to eight branches each leading
to a further node which corresponds to a full, empty or boundary cell.
Full or empty cells do not give rise to further branches. Storage
requirements are still large if good boundary resolution is desired;
the use of specialised hardware offers great potential for the future
of this method.

Spatial subdivision methods lend themselves to certain types of
engineering applications, and some solid modellers which are not
basically of this type nevertheless employ subdivision for specific
purposes. The BOXER system, developed at Leeds University, is an
example. It employs a cellular method to determine a machining
strategy for manufacturing the modelled object (Carey and de
Pennington 1983).

Constructive Solid Geometry Methods

Constructive solid geometry (CSG) modellers are those which build up
representations of complex objects in terms of representations of
simple volumetric primitives. These primitives typically include
cuboids, circular cylinders, cones, spheres and sometimes toruses.
Boolean or set operations are provided which allow the set union,
set difference or set intersection of volumes to be represented.
The data structure for a modeller of this kind is based on a binary
tree. For example, if A and B are cuboidal blocks and C is a
cylinder then $(A \cup B) - C$ could be an L-shaped bracket (the union of
A with B) with a cylindrical hole (formed by subtracting C). The
CSG tree for this object is as follows:

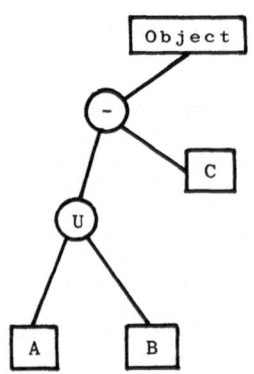

Note that the tree is evaluated from the bottom upwards. The nodes
are set operators, and the leaves primitives. In practice the data
structure is rather more complex than this, since the same primitive
or combination of primitives may be referenced more than once, with
translational, rotational or scaling transformations applied.
Nonetheless the diagram illustrates the essential nature of the CSG
data structure. It should be noted that the geometry of the object
modelled is defined entirely in terms of the geometry of the original

primitives, and that the data structure incorporates a 'history' of the object's mode of creation.

In most CSG systems the actual primitives are represented in terms of half-spaces. Any surface which apportions 3D space into two disjoint regions defines two half-spaces. Thus the plane $x = 0$ divides space into the half-spaces $x < 0$ and $x > 0$; similarly, the cylinder $x^2 + y^2 = 1$ defines half-spaces $x^2 + y^2 < 1$ and $x^2 + y^2 > 1$. Note that a half-space need not be infinite in extent, since the interior of the sphere $x^2 + y^2 + z^2 = 1$ is a half-space.

A cuboidal primitive has six bounding planes, and may be represented as the intersection of six planar half-spaces. If each half-space is of the form

$$ax + by + cz > 1$$

then it requires three numbers a,b,c for its specification. Hence the cuboid may be completely determined by 18 numbers, three for each half-space. In fact we can do better than this by using the fact that opposite boundary planes are parallel and that the planes are otherwise mutually orthogonal. This reduces the requirement to 9 numbers for the cuboid. Other types of primitives can be represented in terms of a similarly small amount of data. The tree structure for a CSG model therefore has only modest requirements for data storage.

It has been shown (Requicha 1980) that provided the original primitive volumes are defined in a valid manner then any object built up from them is also a valid one, provided that the set operations used are interpreted as being regularised. A full understanding of regularised set theory is not necessary for present purposes, but an example will serve to illustrate why its use is necessary. Suppose that two identical cubes are brought into contact so that two of their faces are coincident. The set intersection of these cubes (i.e. the volume common to both) will then consist of the set of points forming the coincident faces, a surface of zero thickness. This is not a well-defined solid object; neither is it an entity of much use in a practical context. The regularised set operations whose use prevents such occurrences are based, roughly speaking, on the idea that an object may be defined in terms of three types of points: interior, exterior and boundary. In order to perform a regularised set operation we proceed as follows:

    (i)   remove all boundary points from each object;

    (ii)   perform the desired set operation on the resulting sets of interior points;

   (iii) put a boundary back on the resulting 'open' set of points.

All this is only conceptual, of course, since the actual computations are not carried out in the manner described, but it does mean that the CSG method is incapable of defining physically unrealisable objects providing the operations it uses are considered to be of the type described.

We now briefly discuss the advantages and disadvantages of the CSG approach before going on to mention some examples of its use. The

characteristics of the method stem mainly from its use of the CSG
tree as the primary data structure.   For most applications, even
such a basic application as graphical visualisation, details are
required of the edges of the model.   However, these are not explicitly available in the data structure, which it will be recalled
contains geometry only in the form of boundary surfaces of
primitive volumes.   Edge information must therefore be determined
whenever required, by computing surface/surface intersections.
Further, the vertices which bound the edges must be computed by
intersecting the computed curves with further surfaces.   Face
information, when needed, must be obtained by computing all the
edges bounding the face, although the equation of the underlying
surface will be available explicitly in the data structure.

The original CSG data structure is said to be unevaluated.   The
process of calculating explicit geometric information concerning the
object boundary from the CSG tree is called evaluation, and it is
a very significant computational task for all but the simplest
objects.   It is usual to store the results of this computation in
a secondary data structure so that it is available for any
subsequent purpose.   The secondary or evaluated data structure is
of the graph-based type used by the boundary representation
modellers described in the next section.   However, it is less
complex since it is essentially a static structure and does not
have to be optimised for the various types of dynamic modification
used in the boundary representation systems.   In early examples
of CSG modellers the evaluated data structure is recomputed from
scratch each time it is required.   However, there is now an
increasing tendency to provide incremental modification of the
secondary data structure as the CSG tree is built.   This can lead
to problems of maintaining consistency between the two representations.

With these ideas in mind we may now list the pros and cons of the
CSG approach:

Advantages:

    (i)   conceptual simplicity,
    (ii) robustness, in the sense that there is little which
        can go wrong,
   (iii) small primary storage requirements,
    (iv) guaranteed integrity of model,
    (v)   ease of representation of 'parametrised' part
        families.

This last point needs some explanation.   Due to the small primary
storage format it is possible to define the dimensions of some
primitives or combinations of primitives as variables.   The result
is a kind of macro, which can be run whenever required with
different values specified for the variables to specify different
members of a family of objects.   This facility has many uses in an
engineering context.

Disadvantages:

    (i)   the method of object construction is largely
        limited to the use of Boolean or set operations
        with primitives;
    (ii) computationally cheap 'local operations' are not
        possible (these are explained in the section on
        Boundary Representation methods);

(iii)   it is difficult to associate auxiliary information
        such as colour, surface finish etc., with individual
        faces of the object, since these are not explicitly
        represented in the primary data structure;

(iv)   it appears to be difficult to incorporate free-
        form parametric surface geometry in CSG modellers -
        such surfaces do not define half-spaces;

(v)   it is comparatively expensive to obtain explicit
        geometry from the model for applications purposes.
        It is true that fast and efficient algorithms have
        been found for computing intersections of the
        common quadric surfaces (Sarraga 1983), but the
        torus still presents problems and matters will
        become worse as other more complex surface types
        are introduced into CSG systems.

Finally, some examples of CSG modellers will be given.   First
there is a family of modellers based on work originally carried out
at Rochester University in the U.S.A.   PADL-1 was the first of
these systems.   The only two primitives provided were the cuboid
and the circular cylinder, and the cuboid edges and cylinder axes
were restricted to being parallel with the coordinate axes of the
modelling space.   Nevertheless, PADL-1 could model more than 40%
of parts manufactured by some typical engineering companies.   Its
development, PADL-2, (Brown 1982) no longer has the restriction on
primitive orientation;   it also provides cones, spheres, and a
limited implementation of toruses in which intersection curves are
restricted to being circles (a case of frequent occurrence).   This
system can model more than 90% of parts from the same companies as
previously surveyed.   Other members of this family of modellers
are UNISOLIDS (a commercial implementation of PADL-2 by McDonnell
Douglas Automation), BOXER (Wickens 1983) a commercial version of a
modeller developed at Leeds University, where there are close ties
with the Rochester team, and GMSOLID (Boyse and Gilchrist 1982),
developed by General Motors but based on PADL philosophy.   Another
interesting system of CSG type is the Finnish UNIBLOCK (Nykanen,
Nystrom and Katainen 1983).   In this modeller each type of
primitive volume is defined in terms of its own natural coordinate
system.   Thus a cuboid is defined in terms of cartesian coordinates,
a cylinder in terms of cylindrical coordinates and so on.   This
enables each primitive to be specified by simple bounds on
coordinate values rather than by nonlinear surface equations.
UNIBLOCK also has other novel features worthy of study.

Boundary Representation Methods

The Boundary Representation approach is to use an evaluated data
structure as the primary and only description of the object.
Details are stored of all the elements which make up the object's
boundary (most notably faces, edges and vertices), together with
what is called topological information which describes how these
elements are linked together.   Typically, the data structure used
is of the graph type, and organised hierarchically in the manner
shown below:

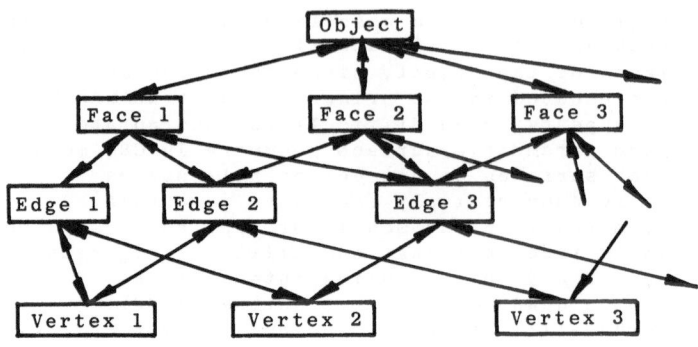

Here the boxes may be considered to contain geometrical information
concerning the entity they represent, though it is possible that
they may contain other associated information in addition.   The
arrows are pointers, and enable answers to be obtained to questions
such as 'Which edges bound Face 1?', or 'Which edges meet at
Vertex 1?'.   The faces, edges and vertices are said to be
topological entities, and the way in which they are linked together
is indicated by the pointers.   The underlying geometric entities
are respectively surfaces, curves and points.   The separation of
geometry and topology is typical of boundary representation modellers.
The topology alone may be considered to define a deformable or
'rubber' object, whose precise form is determined only when the
geometry is specified.   In practice, systems of this type often
have other levels of hierarchy in the data structure;   in particular
it is found very useful to have explicit details of the loops of
edges bounding the faces of an object, and a level of loops may be
found between the edge and face levels.   It should be noted in this
context that faces may contain holes, and that a face boundary may
therefore comprise two or more disjoint loops of edges.

In a boundary representation modeller the data structure is built up
incrementally as model creation proceeds.   This means that a wireframe picture may be drawn quite quickly at any stage;   explicit
edge details are present in the data structure, and it is only
necessary to use an edge-following algorithm with the appropriate
viewing transformation.   Most such systems provide Boolean or set
operations, but these are computationally expensive since surface/
surface intersections must be computed, new edges and vertices inserted
into the data structure and so on.   Consequently, to avoid frequent
long waits by the user for these operations to be performed, a
range of other methods of object construction is usually provided.

One of the basic constructional methods is called sweeping.   A plane
closed 2D profile may be defined and subjected to a linear sweep to
generate a volume.   Alternatively, the profile may be swept
rotationally about an axis in the same plane which does not intersect
the profile.   An open profile may also be used to generate a
rotational solid by rotation about an axis through its end points.
Although sweeping is very useful for the initial stage in the creation
of a complex object, it may also be used at later stages.   For
example, a profile may be defined on a plane face of an object and
subjected to a perpendicular linear sweep inwards (to generate a
depression) or outwards (to generate a protrusion).   These

operations may be used to avoid the use of an expensive Boolean
subtraction or union respectively to obtain the same results.

Other available means for the manipulation of boundary models
come under the heading of local operations. These are operations
which modify the topological aspect of the data structure only
slightly, if at all, and again they are much more efficient than
the Boolean operations which would be needed to achieve the same
results. One type of local operation simply changes the geometry
of a face of the object without changing its topology at all.
For example, a horizontal plane face may be redefined to have a
slight slope on it. This may not affect the number or relative
disposition of the object's faces, edges and vertices, though it
will necessitate a few local changes in the geometry of edges and
vertices in addition to the change in face geometry. The amount
of computation required is modest, however. Local modifications
may also be made implicitly. An edge may simply have a label
attached to it which indicates that it is rounded or bevelled.
The change may be evaluated if required (which will usually involve
the interposition of a new face along the edge in question), but the
implicit change alone would be sufficient for many practical purposes.

We saw earlier that in the case of CSG modellers the theory of
regularised sets provides a guarantee that valid models are always
generated. It has recently been shown (Mantyla 1984) that the
same type of guarantee can be provided for boundary representation
modellers if the underlying modelling process is based on the use
of Euler operators. These are derived from Euler's Law, which in
its simplest form $F - E + V = 2$ asserts a relationship between the
number of faces, edges and vertices of a polyhedral object. For
solid modelling purposes we need a generalisation of this equation
known as the Euler-Poincare formula:

$$F - E + V - H = 2(M - G).$$

In this equation the variables have the following significance:

F = No. of faces of the object(s)
E = No. of edges of the object(s)
V = No. of vertices of the object(s)
H = No. of hole loops (disjoint interior
        edge loops of faces) of the object(s)
M = No. of objects
G = Total genus (the sum of all the through
        holes in all the objects).

Note that the equation is valid for an assembly of objects as well
as a single object; it is also valid for objects with non-planar
faces.

An Euler operation is any operation which changes the values of two
or more of the six variables in the Euler-Poincare formula whilst
retaining its validity. For example, we may add 1 to the values
of E and V. This simply corresponds to the creation of a new
vertex on an existing edge, which then becomes two edges. If we
perform this operation on two opposite edges of a cube, we may
then create a new edge joining the two new vertices. In doing so
we split the original face into two faces, which provides another
example of an Euler operation in which 1 is added to F and E.
Infinitely many Euler operations may be defined, but it is usual,
in modellers which implement them, to work in terms of a convenient
set of about ten. In such systems all modelling operations which

involve topological changes are broken down into sequences of Euler
operations; the topological integrity of the model is thereby
always assured (Braid 1979, Mantyla and Sulonen 1982).

The advantages and disadvantages of the boundary representation
approach are as follows:

Advantages:

(i)   A wider range of model creation techniques is
available than is the case for CSG modellers.
Some of these, including sweeping and local
operations, are cheap and efficient computationally;

(ii)   The data structure provides convenient 'handles'
for the attachment of associated non-geometric
data (e.g. tolerance data, surface finish or
heat treatment requirements for a face);

(iii)   It is easy in principle to implement free-form
or 'sculptured' surface geometry;

(iv)   There is quick and efficient access to the
geometric information which is required for
drawing or for any other modeller application.

Disadvantages:

(i)   Boundary representation models require much more
storage than CSG models, even when the latters'
evaluated secondary data structure is taken into
account. This is because the boundary representation
data structure is highly redundant, containing many
more pointers than are necessary to provide a minimal
representation of the modelled object. The purpose
of this is to optimise the structure for various
types of dynamic modification and to enable a wide
variety of interrogations to be performed quickly;

(ii)   The integrity of the model cannot be guaranteed
unless Euler operations are used;

(iii)   Boundary representation modellers are inherently
less robust than CSG systems. This is because
the successful creation of a complex evaluated
data structure is crucial to the modelling process,
and it may fail due to the computer's inability
to answer certain delicate geometric questions
such as 'Is Plane 1 tangent to Cylinder 2?' or
'Does Face 5 of Object 1 lie in the same surface
as Face 8 of Object 2?' The problems here are
those of computational ill-conditioning and numerical
rounding errors, and very careful attention to
numerical tolerancing on geometrical calculations is
required if a reliable system is to result;

(iv)   It is not easy to provide a facility for modelling
families of parts. The problems of using variable
parameters in a complex data structure, of maintaining
consistency between them in their multiple occurrences
and providing constraints on them so that topology
violations cannot result due to their variation are
probably insuperable. Families of parts must be
defined using a high-level macro approach (rather akin to
CSG language input) and a macro processor which builds up
the corresponding evaluated data structure.

Before leaving the subject of boundary representation modellers it
should be mentioned that some of these systems employ techniques in
which curved surfaces are represented approximately as polyhedral

assemblies of plane facets.   This leads to the following advantages:

  (i)   All surface/surface intersections are plane/plane
        intersections and easy to compute (though a fine
        surface subdivision will require a great many such
        computations);
  (ii) Hidden-line and hidden-surface computations are
        simpler.

However, realism may be lost in drawings of the modelled objects.
Most systems employing faceting techniques also provide some form of
exact representation of the modelled surfaces, though it is not
usually clear what is the precise relationship between the faceted
and exact representations of the object in the internal data
structure.   Systems of this type include the commercially available
modellers EUCLID (Matra-Datavision), GEOMOD (Structural Dynamics
Research Corporation) and Medusa (Cambridge Interactive Systems).

Geometric Coverage

On the whole it is the boundary representation modellers which
provide the greatest range of geometric coverage.   As already
stated, most of the CSG systems provide a range of simple geometric
primitives restricted to the cuboid, cylinder, cone, sphere and
torus.   Exceptions include TIPS-1 (Tips Working Group 1978), which
partakes of a dual CSG/cellular nature, and Synthavision (Goldstein
and Malin 1979).   In both cases, however, the definition of free-
form primitives is a rather cumbersome process for the user, and it
is not easy to define the kinds of surfaces needed to provide the
blends and fillets which feature on many engineering parts.   Fillet
surfaces of the type generated by a rolling ball in contact with
two surfaces are currently under development in PADL-2.

Examples of boundary representation modellers providing free-form
surface facilities include BUILD (Jared and Varady 1984), EUCLID
(Theron 1984) and GEOMOD (Klosterman, Ard and Klahs 1982).   The
first is a research modeller developed at Cambridge University, in
which a novel type of double-quadratic surface has been implemented.
EUCLID is a faceting system allowing the use of Bezier surfaces,
while GEOMOD is another faceting system employing rational B-spline
curves and surfaces.   A version of ROMULUS (Shape Data Ltd 1983)
will shortly be released which allows the exact representation of
blends and fillets in terms of implicitly defined surfaces.

A good idea of the geometric coverage available in a range of
systems may be gained from the proceedings of the CAM-I Geometric
Modelling Seminar held in Cambridge in December 1983.   Here eleven
different systems attempted to model three standard test parts, one
of which included a complex blend between a conical and a toroidal
surface (Faux 1983).

ENGINEERING APPLICATIONS

We turn now to applications of solid modellers.   It should be
pointed out that these systems have a history of fifteen years or so,
and that they have only recently entered industrial use.   At present
their only completely automatic applications, once a product definition has been created, are for the calculation of mass properties
and for purposes of visualisation pure and simple.   However, the
former can save a great deal of laborious hand calculation, and the
virtues of flexible 3D visualisation are manifold.   Most solid
modellers can generate line drawings of the modelled object from any

desired viewpoint, either in wireframe form or with hidden lines removed (which gives better visualisation but requires significant extra computation). Conventional 3-view drawings can be produced if desired, and cross-sectional views can be calculated automatically. Colour shaded graphics are now increasingly commonly provided; these can generate pictures of startling realism, which not only greatly aid the designer in visualising the product but are also ideal for use in advertising material, in technical documentation and so on.

Other applications are also available with solid modellers, but these are usually interfaced rather than integrated, so that a good deal of user interaction is necessary in reformatting geometric information into a form acceptable to the application program. Most modellers, for example, provide interfaces to finite element mesh generation programs which were originally written independently. Many modellers also now have interfaces to numerical control software particularly to 2D systems such as GNC, which will generate instructions for contour milling. More advanced is the 3D ROMAPT interface between ROMULUS and APT, developed by Chan (1982).

Modeller development teams, having devoted most of their early effort to problems of geometric definition, are now increasingly turning their attention to the actual integration of applications programs. Some noteworthy work in this direction includes that of Wordenweber (1982) in automatic finite element mesh generation, Grayer (1977) in automatic generation of data for numerical machining of $2\frac{1}{2}$D parts and Kyprianou (Parkinson 1983) in automatic recognition of features (machining elements) of 3D models. The Structural Dynamics Research Corporation IDEAS package (Klosterman Ard and Klahs 1982) integrates a program for static and dynamic analysis of assemblies and mechanisms with the solid modeller GEOMOD, which is used to model the individual components. These are just a few examples of achievements in the applications area.

Despite these advances we are still some years away from true integration of CAD and CAM. The procedure for determining how a part is to be manufactured is known as process planning; ideally, it takes into account not only the geometry of the part but also associated information concerning part material, surface finish, tolerances and so on. Furthermore, the way in which a part will be made is company-dependent, since different companies will have different types of manufacturing facilities. Process planning must therefore take into account the availability of a variety of machine tools, each of which will have different capabilities and running costs. Suitable feeds and speeds (linear and rotational cutting tool velocities) must be chosen, and consideration given to the number of times the part being made must be repositioned and clamped during the manufacturing process. A variety of other factors is also involved, but these will serve to show the complex nature of the problem. The objective is to find the cheapest feasible means of making the part subject to the engineering constraints imposed upon it.

Numerous computer-aided process planning systems exist, but these are mostly stand-alone programs requiring a high degree of user interaction. In particular, the user is required to input details of the geometry of the part to be manufactured. In an integrated CAD/CAM system this will not be necessary; the part geometry and other necessary information will be supplied from a geometric model of the part.

Most attempts at automated process planning have so far been
based on boundary representation modellers, because of the
problems of associating non-geometrical technological data in a
convenient way with elements of CSG models.   Progress has been
slow, and it is now becoming clear that the main problem is the
low-level nature of the information in a boundary representation
data structure.   Process planners work in terms of 'part
features' or 'form features' such as holes, slots and grooves in
a part.   There is a close correspondence between such features
and the manufacturing operations needed to produce them.
However, in boundary representation terms a feature is (in most
cases) a collection of faces.   Methods for the automatic
recognition of features are known (Parkinson 1983), but it will
not be until geometric modellers are enhanced to allow the
representation and manipulation of features as entities in their
own right that significant process will be made towards automated
process planning.   These matters are further discussed in
Pratt (1984).   A related problem is that of dimensions and
tolerances, which are also required for process planning.   The
dimensions to which manufacturing tolerances are applied are often
not explicitly present in the solid modeller data structure, and
some means must be found of providing them as required.   However,
tolerances on an individual part are usually specified on elements
which are related to features of the part, which provides a further
powerful motivation for the explicit representation of features by
modellers.   The ROMULUS system (Shape Data Ltd 1983) already
provides a feature representation capability;   it is the first
commercially available modeller to do so.

USER INTERFACE

Interactive geometric modelling involves a two-way exchange of
information between the user and the system.   We deal first with
the way in which the system communicates with the user, which is
primarily by means of the display on a graphics screen.   The main
purpose is to help the designer visualise the object he is
designing, and to this end various means are available for enhancing
the realism of the 3D object depicted on a 2D screen.

On a line-drawing display, the most convenient type of picture to
generate from a solid model is a wire-frame drawing.   This simply
involves drawing all the edges from whatever is the chosen viewpoint.
Some geometric modellers allow the user to generate multiple wireframe views simultaneously, typically three orthogonal views plus an
isometric projection.   The addition of profile or silhouette lines
to a wireframe drawing greatly aids visualisation and is relatively
cheap computationally.   Depth cueing (the modulation of line
intensity according to distance from the viewer) is also useful on
displays affording this possibility.   The generation of pictures
with hidden lines removed is obviously highly desirable, but
this is computationally expensive and can cause very long response
times for complex objects.   'Local' hidden line removal is a
cheaper alternative which is sometimes provided.   In this method an
edge is judged to be hidden if the two faces on either side have
normal vectors with components pointing away from the viewer.   The
technique often gives the correct answer but fails, for example,
when an edge is only partly hidden.   The resulting pictures look
less anomalous if 'hidden' lines are drawn with dashes rather than

altogether omitted.   Probably the best aid to 3D visualisation of
a wireframe model is real-time rotation, made possible on some of
the more expensive graphics devices by the use of programmable
analogue controls.   Real-time rotation of hidden-line views is
not currently possible due to the time-consuming nature of the
hidden-line elimination process.

The use of raster graphics makes it possible to produce hidden
surface drawings.   The technique used is generally of the ray-
firing type, and the image produced may be generated either with
respect to the exact object or to some faceted approximation of it.
The use of colour and shading greatly enhances the results.   One
virtue of the shaded surface drawing is that it sometimes shows up
flaws in the definition of free-form surfaces which cannot be
detected from examination of the corresponding wireframe
representation.   The use of specialised hardware for real-time
rotation of hidden-surface objects has already been demonstrated,
and this facility may eventually be widely available.   The
ultimate representation of a solid model, of course, would be a
genuine 3D one.   The use of holograms for this purpose appears
to be some way off, but Genisco have announced and demonstrated a
device, based on a vibrating mirror, which does generate a 3D
image.

Turning now to the means by which the user communicates with
the system, we have a range of input devices available with
different systems.   Some are entirely keyboard-oriented, while
others use cursor-based techniques with visual feedback.   Control
of the cursor may be by joystick, light pen, tablet and stylus
etc., as for other interactive graphical systems.   Some systems are
menu-based while others use command languages.

We shall not dwell on these purely mechanical details of the user
interface, however, but concentrate rather on the procedural aspects
of model creation.   It was noted earlier that CSG modellers
usually require the user to work in terms of primitive volumetric
elements which are used to build up complex objects by means of set
operations.   This is an inherently 3D process; the components,
having been created, must be translated, rotated and scaled
until they are the required size and have the required position
and orientation for the set operations to be applied.   Many
present-day designers, accustomed to working in two dimensions
on a draughting board, do not find it easy to work in this manner.
They much prefer the approach adopted in certain boundary
representation systems, in which the designer can work largely in
2D.   MEDUSA (Geisow 1983) is a prime example; the system may
be used as a 2D draughting system in the initial stages of
design.   After three orthogonal views of a part have been
constructed in the traditional manner, the addition of some
further information in the form of 'link lines' between the views
enables the system to generate a solid model of the part.   It
should be noted that the orthogonal views alone do not generally
define an unambiguous model.   MEDUSA is a popular system, possibly
by virtue of its resemblance to something with which designers feel
familiar.   It is an open question whether we should or should not
encourage future generations of designers and draughtsmen to become
more proficient at working in three dimensions.

When working with a CSG system there are some simple shapes which
can only be created in a rather roundabout way.   If it is wished to

round off one edge of a cube, for example, a square prism must
first be subtracted to leave a step in place of the edge.   The
height and width of the step must be equal to the desired radius.
Then a cylinder of the desired radius and with length equal to
one side of the cube must be created.   If this is now correctly
positioned with respect to the stepped cube a union operation
will give the desired result.   Most boundary representation
modellers allow this object to be created much more simply.   It
is only necessary to define a square 2D profile with one rounded
corner and to perform a translational sweep to generate the
desired solid.   It must be pointed out however that this
strategy is not sufficient if it is wished to round off all the
edges of the cube.   Some modellers, for example BUILD (Hillyard
1982), allow edge-rounding to be performed as a local operation as
described earlier.

One respect in which many modellers are deficient is in the
provision of means for positioning objects relative to each other.
For example, if it is desired to 'glue' two cubes together then
the second must be transformed so that one of its faces is in
contact with a face of the first.   This requires the user to
work in terms of the dimensions, positions and orientations of
both cubes if he is to specify the correct translations and
rotations.   The computer arithmetic will of course be subject
to rounding errors, and a subsequent union operation may fail to
generate a unified object because the two cubes do not in fact
quite touch.   It would be much more convenient to be able to
position the second cube with respect to the first, which would be
made easier if the standard primitive volumes were provided with
local datums.   Such entities would be useful not only for design
purposes but also for manufacturing.   Consider, for example, the
creation of a cylindrical hole by Boolean subtraction of a cylinder.
If the axis of the cylinder is retained as 'auxiliary geometry'
associated with the model this can later be used to specify the path
of the centreline of a drill in the manufacture of the hole.

Expanding on this last suggestion, there is much to be said for
providing the designer with a user interface allowing him to
design in terms of features such as holes, pockets and slots.
Each feature could then automatically be created with its own set
of datums.   This would allow easy positioning of a feature on an
object, and also provide some of the necessary 'handles' for the
attachment of dimensioning and tolerancing information.   The nearest
approach to this situation is found in the MARS system developed
at the University of California, Los Angeles (Arbab et al. 1982).
In this system an object is actually designed in terms of the
manufacturing operations needed to make it.   As pointed out
earlier, there is a close relationship between features and
manufacturing operations, and so MARS may be thought of as a
feature-oriented modeller.   However, design by features is not
without its problems.   The features created by the designer are
not always the same as the features seen by the process planner, and
the development of a user interface based on the suggested
approach will require considerable effort if the result is to be
acceptable to all concerned.   The rewards will be significant if
this can be achieved.

STANDARDS FOR COMMUNICATION

There is currently a great deal of interest in the development of

standards for transmission of data between different CAD/CAM
systems. The most advanced transmission format is at present
IGES (Initial Graphics Exchange Specification). Version 1.0 of
IGES is part of an American national standard (ANSI 1982) and
Version 2.0 is an improved version already in widespread use.
IGES is designed in the first instance for the communication of
CAD/CAM data between systems of wireframe type, although it is
also possible to transmit specifications of conventional types
of free form parametric surfaces. Textual information and
conventional draughting symbols may be communicated together with
the geometric data. IGES may be used in transmitting information
between different systems within a single company or in different
companies with a primary/subcontractor relationship. The principle
underlying the use of a 'neutral' data transmission format such as
IGES is that each CAD/CAM system needs two translators, one to
translate an IGES file into the system's native format, and one to
translate in the reverse direction. Then only 2N translators are
needed for communication between N different systems, rather than
N(N - 1) if separate translators are written for all possible
pairs of systems.

The problem of transmission of solid modelling information in a
similar manner is complicated by the fact that topological as well
as geometrical data must be transmitted. An Experimental Boundary
File (XBF) for this purpose has been developed and tested by CAM-I
(Computer Aided Manufacturing International, Inc.). This is based
on the IGES format but contains the necessary extensions for solid
modelling (CAM-I 1981, Pratt and Wilson 1984). The committee
concerned with developments to IGES has considered the CAM-I
Experimental Boundary File in drawing up its provisional
specification for IGES 3.0, which is intended to handle solid
modelling data. This specification is currently frozen for a period
of evaluation and testing, and many of the features from the XBF have
been incorporated in it.

Another recent development by CAM-I is a specification for a standard
Applications Interface (CAM-I 1980). This is intended to provide a
standard means of communication between user-written applications
programs and geometric modelling systems. Ideally, each modeller
will be provided with an implementation of the Applications
Interface so that the user can extract the information he needs for
his application or can input information into the modeller by
calling a standard set of FORTRAN subroutines. The Applications
Interface documents give specifications of all these subroutines as
regards their subroutine headings, their arguments and their proposed
function. One great advantage of the idea is that the same
applications program could be run with any one of several
modelling systems provided they each had an implementation of the
Applications Interface. The concept has so far only been
partially tested in practice, but an implementation for ROMULUS
is nearing completion and it is hoped that other implementations
will be available in the near future.

REFERENCES

ANSI (1982) Digital Representation for Communication of Product
Definition Data.   ANSI Y14.26M - 1981, American National Standard,
American Society of Mechanical Engineers, New York.

Arbab F, Cantor DG, Lichten L, Melkanoff MA (1982) The MARS CAM-
oriented Modelling System.   Proc. Conf. on CAD/CAM Technology in
Mechanical Engineering, Massachusetts Institute of Technology,
March 1982, MIT Press.

Boyse JW, Gilchrist JE (1982) GMSolid: Interactive Modelling for
Design and Analysis of Solids.   IEEE Computer Graphics and
Applications, March 1982, 27 - 40.

Braid IC (1979) Notes on a Geometric Modeller.   CAD Group
Document No. 101, Geometric Modelling Group, Cambridge University
Engineering Dept.

Brown CM (1982) PADL-2: A Technical Summary.   IEEE Computer
Graphics and Applications, March 1982, 69 - 84.

CAM-I (1980) An Interface between Geometric Modellers and
Applications Programs (3 vols.).   Report No. R-80-GM-04, CAM-I
Inc., Arlington, Texas.

CAM-I (1981) CAM-I Geometric Modelling Project Boundary File
Design (XBF-2).   Report No. R-81-GM-02.1, CAM-I Inc., Arlington,
Texas.

Carey CG, de Pennington A (1983) A study of the Interface between
CAD and CAM using Geometric Modelling Techniques.   Proc. 3rd
Anglo-Hungarian Seminar on Computer Aided Geometric Design,
Cambridge, September 1983, published by Cambridge University
Engineering Department.

Chan BTF (1982) ROMAPT: A New Link between CAD and CAM.
Computer Aided Design 14:261-266.

Faux ID (ed.)(1983) Proc. 2nd CAM-I Geometric Modelling Seminar,
Cambridge, December 1983; Report No. P-83-GM-01, CAM-I Inc.,
Arlington, Texas.

Geisow AD (1983) Results of Benchmarks using MEDUSA.   Proc. 2nd
CAM-I Geometric Modelling Seminar, Cambridge, December 1983;
Report No. P-83-GM-01, CAM-I Inc., Arlington, Texas.

Goldstein R, Malin L (1979) 3D Modelling with the Synthavision
System.   Proc. 1st Ann. Conf. on Computer Graphics in CAD/CAM
Systems, Cambridge, Mass., U.S.A., April 1979, 244-247.

Grayer AR (1977) The Automatic Production of Machined Components
from a Stored Geometric Description.   Advances in Computer Aided
Manufacture (D. McPherson, ed.), North-Holland Publ. Co.

Hillyard R (1982) The BUILD Group of Solid Modellers.
IEEE Computer Graphics and Applications, March 1982, 43-52.

Jared GEM, Varady T (1984) Synthesis of Volume Modelling and
Sculptured Surfaces in BUILD.   Proc. CAD 84, April 1984, Brighton,
England, IPC Science and Technology Press.

Klosterman AL, Ard RH, Klahs JW (1982) A Geometric Modelling Program
for the System Designer.   Proc. Conf. on CAD/CAM Technology in
Mechanical Engineering, Massachusetts Institute of Technology,
March 1982, MIT Press.

Mantyla M (1984) A Note on the Modelling Space of Euler Operators. Computer Vision Graphics and Image Processing 26: 45-60.

Mantyla M, Sulonen R (1982) GWB: A Solid Modeller with Euler Operators.   IEEE Computer Graphics and Applications, September 1982, 17-31.

Nykanen M, Nystrom M, Katainen A (1983) UNIBLOCK Modelling System.   Proc. 2nd CAM-I Geometric Modelling Seminar, Cambridge, December 1983;   Report No. P-83-GM-01, CAM-I Inc., Arlington, Texas.

Parkinson A (1983) Feature Recognition and Parts Classification in BUILD.   CAD Group Document No. 112, Engineering Department, Cambridge University.

Pratt MJ (1984) Solid Modelling and the Interface between Design and Manufacture.   IEEE Computer Graphics and Applications, July 1984.

Pratt MJ, Wilson PR (1984) IGES-based Transmission of Solid Modelling Data.   Proc. MICAD 84, Feb/March 1984, Paris, Hermes Publishing.

Requicha AAG (1980) Representations of Rigid Solids - Theory, Methods and Systems.   ACM Computing Surveys 12: 437-464.

Sarraga RF (1983) Algebraic Methods for Intersections of Quadric Surfaces in GMSolid.   Computer Vision Graphics and Image Processing 22: 222-238.

Shape Data Ltd. (1983) Modeller Test: ROMULUS.   Proc. 2nd CAM-I Geometric Modelling Seminar.   Cambridge, December 1983; Report No. P-83-GM-01, CAM-I Inc., Arlington, Texas.

Theron M (1984) L'Algebre des Solides et la CAO en Mechanique; un example: le Systeme EUCLID.   Proc. MICAD 84, Feb/March 1984, Paris, Hermes Publishing.

TIPS Working Group (1978) TIPS-1 Technical Information Processing System.   Institute of Precision Engineering, Hokkaido University, Sapporo, 060 Japan.

Wickens LP (1983) Presentation of University of Leeds Modelling System (BOXER).   Proc. 2nd CAM-I Geometric Modelling Seminar, Cambridge, December 1983;   Report No. P-83-GM-01,CAM-I Inc., Arlington, Texas.

Wordenweber B (1982) Automatic Mesh Generation on Two or Three Dimensional Curvilinear Manifolds.   Technical Report No. 18, Camputer Laboratory, Cambridge University.

Yamaguchi K, Kunii TL, Fujimura K (1984) Octree-Related Data Structures and Algorithms.   IEEE Computer Graphics and Applications, January 1984, 53-59.

Interactive Production Planning CAM

B. Moseng and J. Hygen

TABLE OF CONTENT

1   WHAT IS CAD/CAM?

1.1   Introduction

<u>Industrial needs</u>: Working conditions for the mechanical industry,
has changed during the last years. The demands seems to be harder
and harder due to

- shorter lifetime of new products
- increased requirements on new products
- smaller lotsizes
- higher productivity
- increased needs for flexibility

All these factors will influence and put strong demands on strategies,
tools and systems to be used in the future. Figure 1.1 indicates the
situation in manufacturing. High efficiency in production will often
result in poor flexibility (line production). Ordinary workshops have
normally high flexibility but poor efficiency. The desired goal
(fig. 1.1) seems like a fata morgana so far.

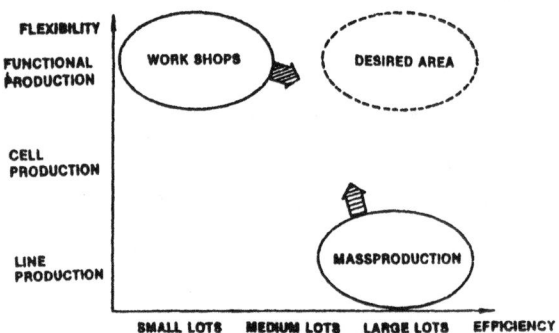

Figure 1.1 Flexibility versus efficiency in manufacturing

<u>CAD/CAM</u>: One important set of tools to meet the mentioned problems
will be extensive use of computer aided systems. New techniques and
reduced computercost will enlarge the use of such systems. By using
CAD (Computer Aided Design) and CAM (Computer Aided Manufacturing)
systems a lot of tasks in the design phase (design, calculations,
variant design, drawing generations etc.) and the production phase
(process/operation planning, NC programming, material planning etc.)
could be done faster, more precise and at a higher quality.

A lot of definitions has been given to CAD-CAM during time. In this context we will use the terms as an abbreviation for all computer aided tools in the area of design and production planning.

Information handling: All CAD and CAM functions deals with handling of information. Figure 1.2 shows very roughly the information flow from design to production. The amount of information which is generated to describe the product is very big. CAE (Computer Aided Engineering) is another very much used term which includes CAD-CAM).

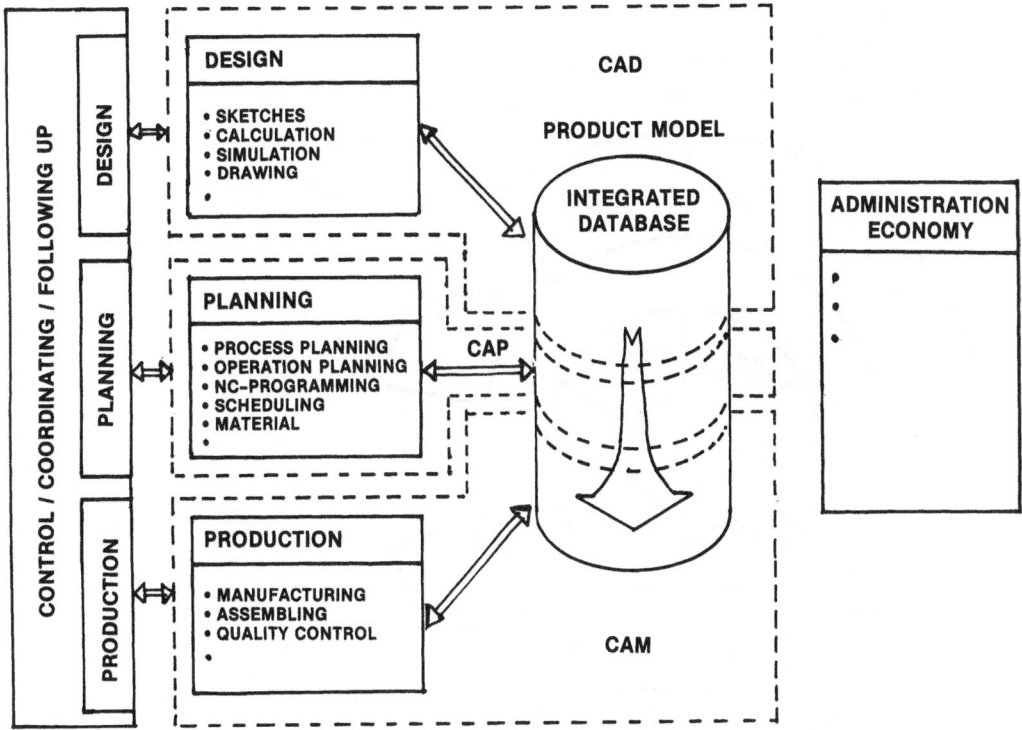

Figure 1.2   CAE as an information flow

History: Design and Production have traditionally been separated professions in most companies. The design department has the responsibility to perform the design and produce drawings. The production department is responsible for planning and performing the production. This division between professions has influenced the system development. Most of the systems developed the last 20 years are directed either towards design (CAD) or manufacturing (CAM).

However, in the last 5-10 years some integrated CAD/CAM systems has been introduced on the market.

1.2   CAD-CAM modules

In the following we will limit our talks to CAD/CAM in mechanical industry. As mentioned earlier different functions could be put into the terms of CAD and CAM. A very rough description will be given on the following pages.

<u>What is CAD?</u> A lot of different CAD systems are available to solve different tasks in the design phase. It covers a wide spectrum of problems from previous design via advanced geometric modelling and calculations to generation of drawings (fig. 1.3). Some keywords are:

- preliminar design
- parametrization
- geometric modelling (3D)
- dimensioning
- calculations
- bill of materials
- drawing generation

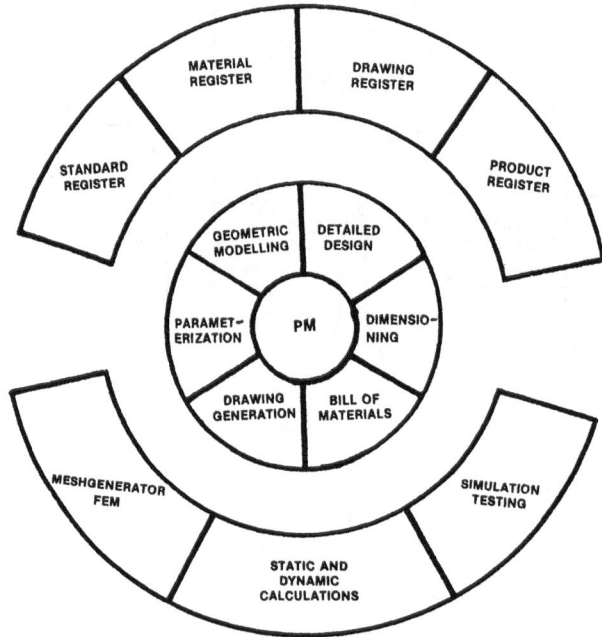

Figure 1.3 Modules in CAD

Most of this activities includes interactive man-machine communication and extensive use of graphic tools. The systems covers a broad spectrum of problems - from very advanced systems to handle 3D volums (ex. hidden line removal) to simpler systems for 2D drawings. The next figures give some examples.

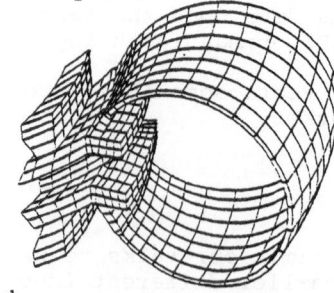

Figure 1.4 a   FEM mesh

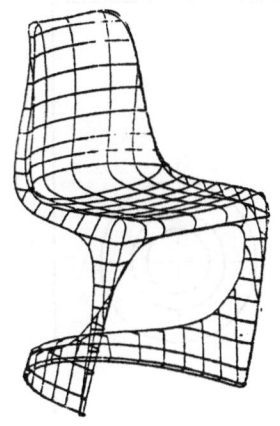

Figure 1.4 b Sculpture surface

Figure 1.4 c Volume modelling

Figure 1.4 Types of geometric modelling

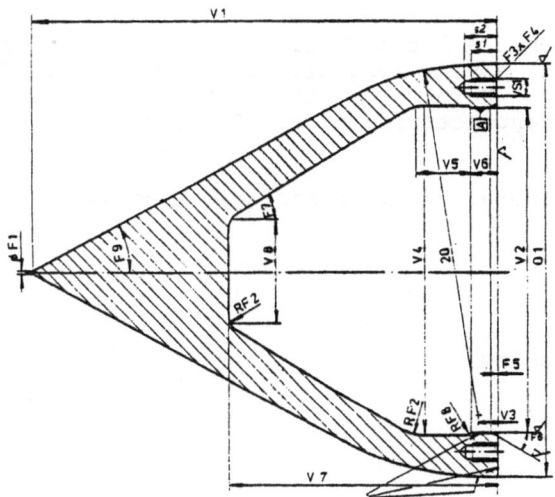

Figure 1.5 Parameterization in design of Pelton turbine
(Kværner Brug)

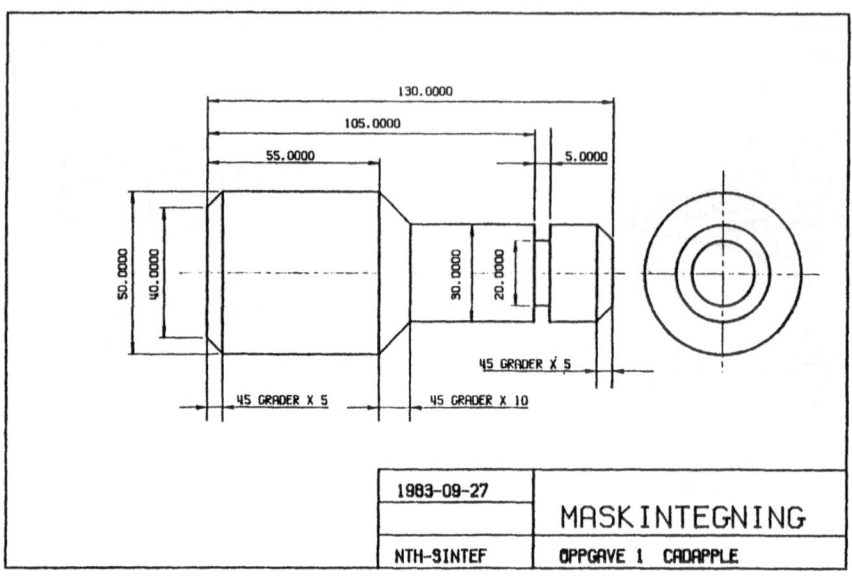

Figure 1.6   Generation of drawings

<u>What is CAM?</u> As already mentioned a lot of definitions and meanings
of CAM has been introduced. For a very long time CAM was identified
with generation of NC-programs. Here we use it as a term for all
computer aided systems on the manufacturing side. 3 major areas
could be mentioned (fig. 1.7)

        Technological planning (generation of technological documents)

        - process planning
        - operation planning
        - NC programming
        -

        Material and Resource planning

        - master planning
        - material planning
        - scheduling
        - assembly planning
        -

        The Manufacturing Process

        - CNC controllers
        - cell systems
        - FMS systems
        -

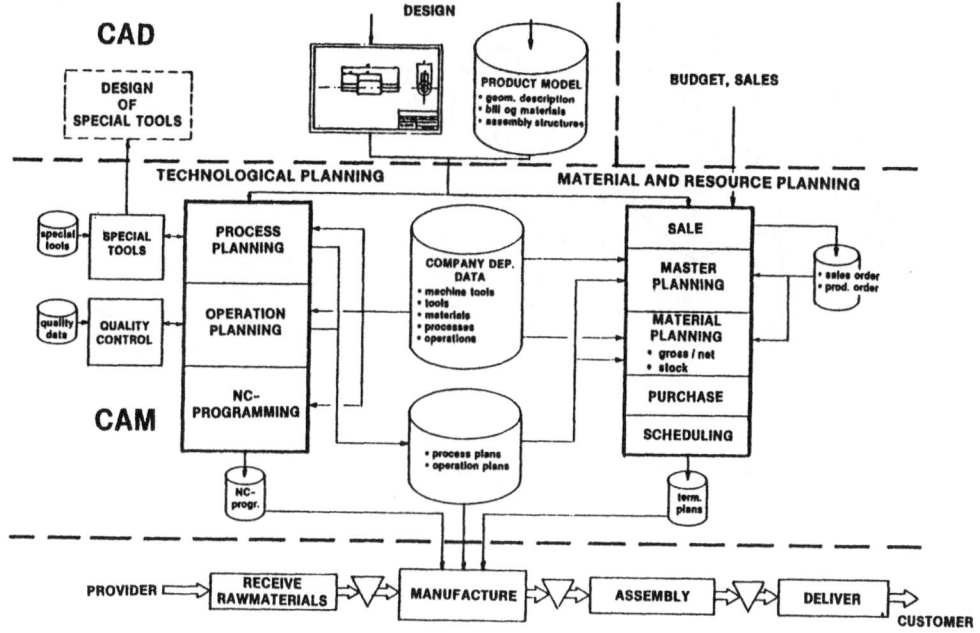

Figure 1.7   Modules in CAM

Many of this activities includes use of graphics in different ways -
from simulation of NC-paths (fig. 1.8) and robotics (fig. 1.9) to
graphic visualization of production plans (fig. 1.10)

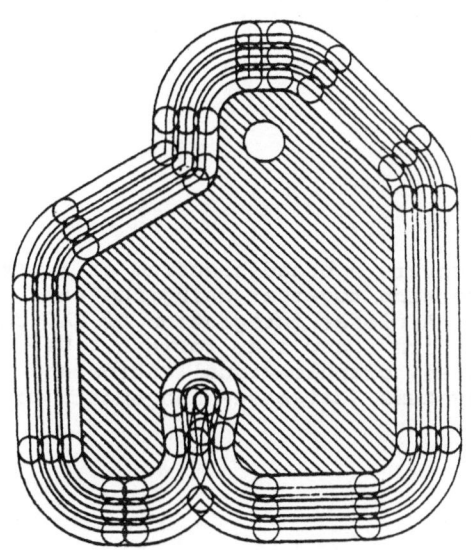

Figure 1.8   Simulation of NC paths

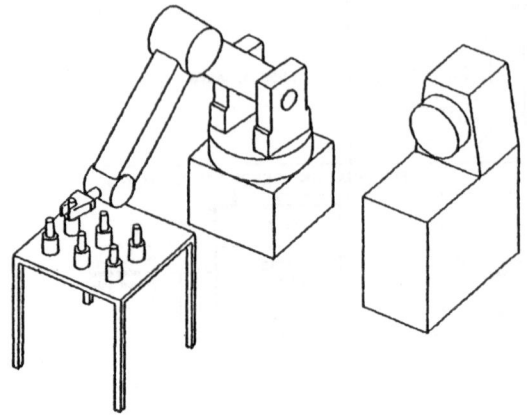

Figure 1.9   Simulation of robot movements

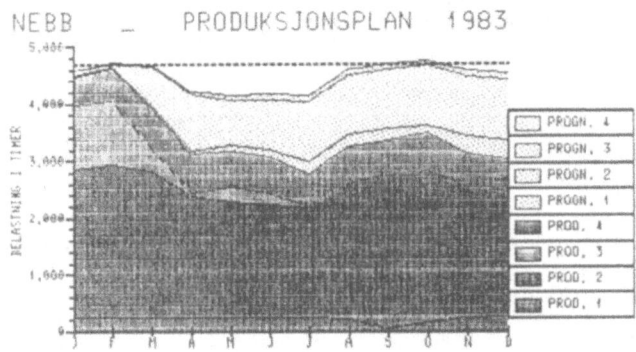

Figure 1.10   Production plan (NEBB)

1.3   Integration

As already mentioned CAD and CAM covers a broad spectrum of functions.
However, most of the systems is working together using the same
registers and by exchanging data. A closer integration of CAD-CAM
will therefore be necessary to perform a new step forward. Use of
interactive communication techniques, graphic visualization and product models implemented on DBMS systems (database-management) will
lead to this progress.

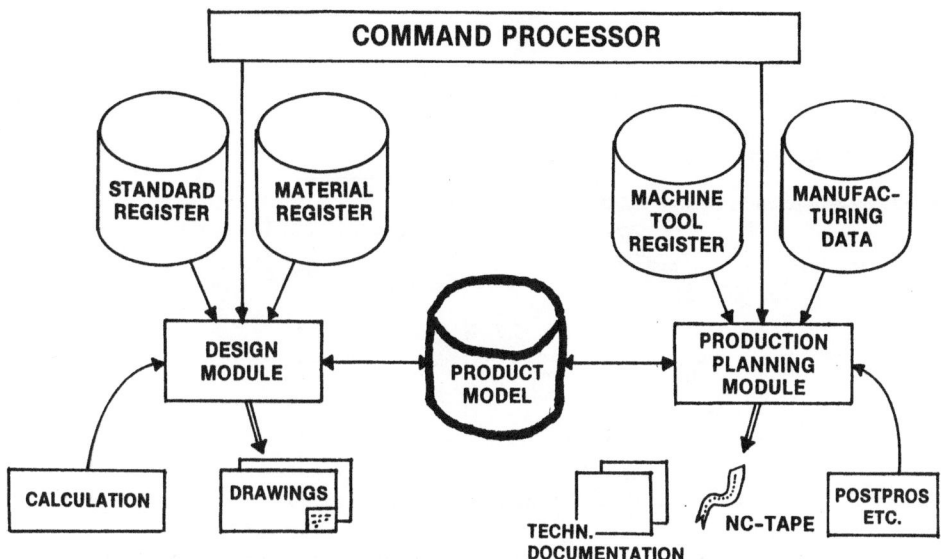

Figure 1.11   Integration CAD/CAM (ex. WZL Aachen)

1.4   CAD/CAM workstation

In the last years modern CAD/CAM workstations has been introduced.
Those workstations have very strong facilities to support the
designer or production planner with interactive system tools. Using
tablet, mouse, multiprocessing, multiwindowing, graphic techniques
etc., a much more human-like way of working is obtained. By coupling
such workstations together using datanets different users can communicate and share common resources.

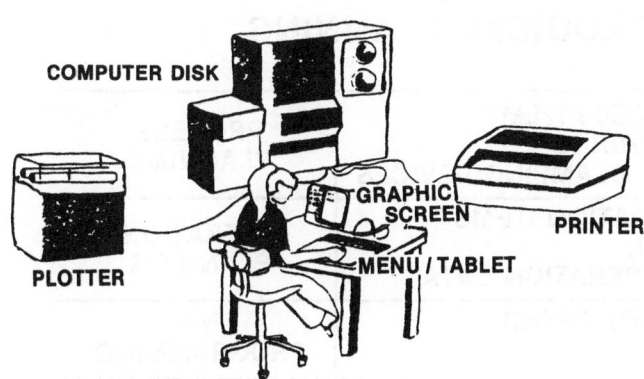

Figure 1.12   CAD/CAM work station

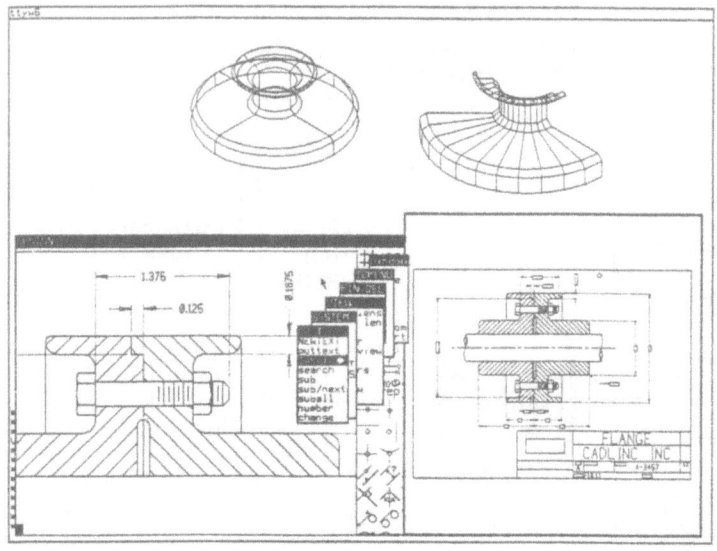

Figure 1.13 Man-machine communication (pop-up menues CADLINC)

2   TECHNOLOGICAL PLANNING

2.1 Overview

The goal of technological planning (TP) is to generate all the technical documents needed for an optimal manufacturing of the product. The
start point is the result from the design process which is found on
the drawing or in the computer. This includes all geometric descriptions, technical information (tolerances etc.), bill of materials,
raw material requirements etc. determined by the designer. Modifying
factors are available machine tools and resources in the company.
Technological planning could be divided in 3 areas (fig. 2.1)

TECHNOLOGICAL PLANNING

1. SEQUENCE OF PROCESS ITEM 2. SELECTION OF MACHINES 3. DETERMINATION OF CLAMPING DEVICES	PROCESS PLANNING
4. SEQUENCE OF OPERATION ITEMS 5. SELECTION OF TOOL 6. CALCULATION OF OPERATION DATA	OPERATION PLANNING
7. GENERATION OF TOOL PATHS 8. POSTPROCESSING	NC PROGRAMMING

Figure 2.1 Technological planning

In the following chapters those 3 areas will be described further. Use of interactive graphics will be specially focused.

2.2 Process planning (PP)

<u>General</u>: Process planning (PP) is perhaps the most difficult task in the area of production planning. It is the first task to be performed after the design phase and it establish the necessary link between CAD and the manufacturing. The main purpose of PP is to select manufacturing processes and operations, machine tools and clamping devices for an optimal production. Needs for quality planning and design of special tools are also often initiated from the PP phase. The PP has to be done in respect of available resources and techn. know how in the company, and is therefore dependent on very skilled planners. Very few good sw-systems exist.

<u>Strategies for PP</u>: Traditionally two different strategies for PP is mentioned (fig. 2.2)

- variant planning (retrieval and editing of old plans)
- generativ planning (generation of new plans using decision
                    tables and rules)

Both strategies has advantages and disadvantages. A fully automated generative PP-system for a broad spectrum of processes and workpieces are not available and will be impossible to implement in practise. A mixture of the two strategies including graphic features will probably be the best user friendly system in the future.

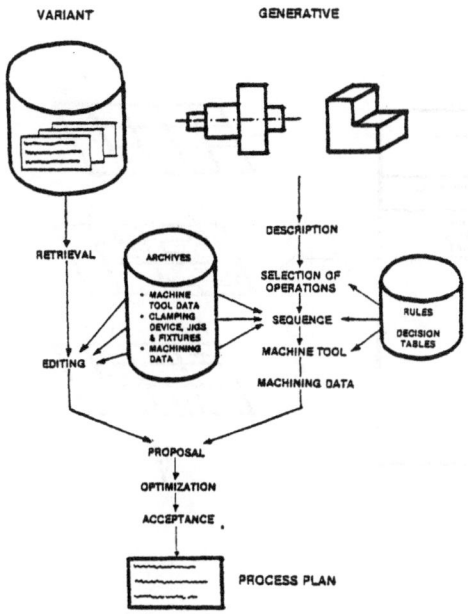

Figure 2.2 Methods of Process Planning

392

Classification - part families: In both methods of PP classification and grouping of products in families are important. From the geometry and techn. description of the workpiece a unique classification number could be defined. This number is later used for archive and retrieval. Today most of this systems are based on alphanumeric information. In the future much more graphics will be used for retrieval functions. An example is given in fig. 2.4 (APS' project)[1].

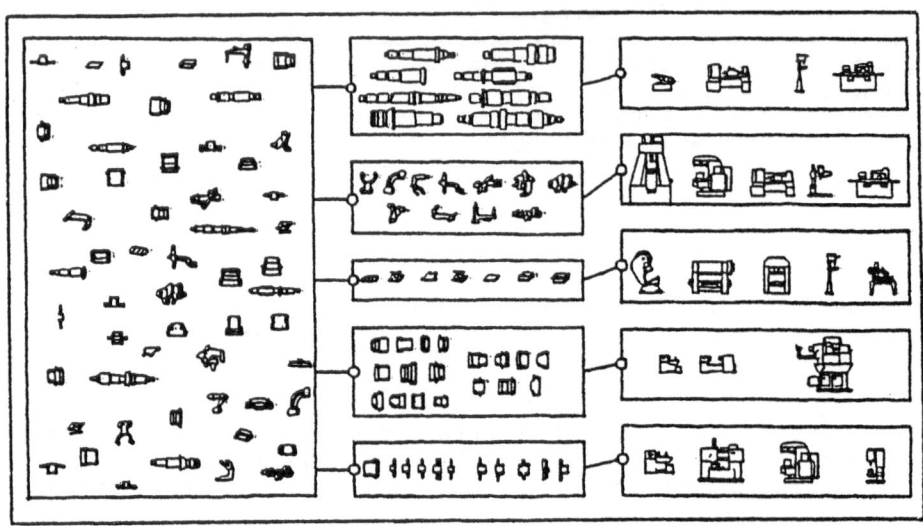

Figure 2.3 Classification in part families

Figure 2.4 Retrieval of process plans using graphic symbols

1 APS - Advanced Production System, German-Norwegian CAD/CAM project

2.3 Operation planning (OP)

The goal of operation planning is a further detailing of the results from process planning. While the PP is the most creative part, OP is more based on selection of existing data from tables and simple calculations. Different phases in a typical operation planning sequence for rotational parts is shown in fig. 2.5

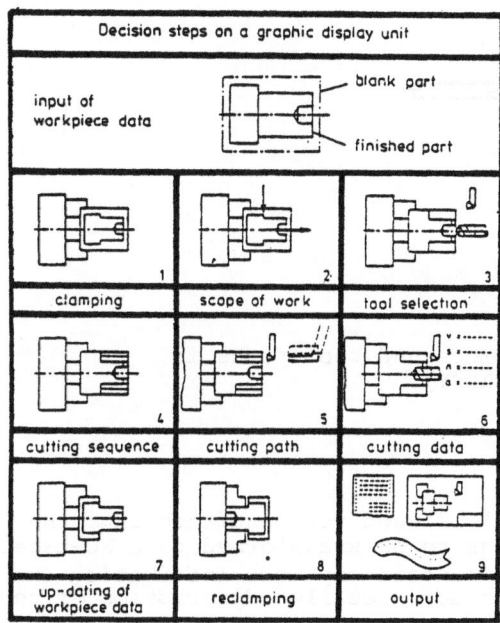

Figure 2.5 Different stages in operation planning (CAPSY)

Interactive graphics are extensively used in operation planning. During the different stages a lot of graphic interaction takes place. Figure 2.6 shows an example of clamping, tools, workpiece and tool paths for a rotational part.

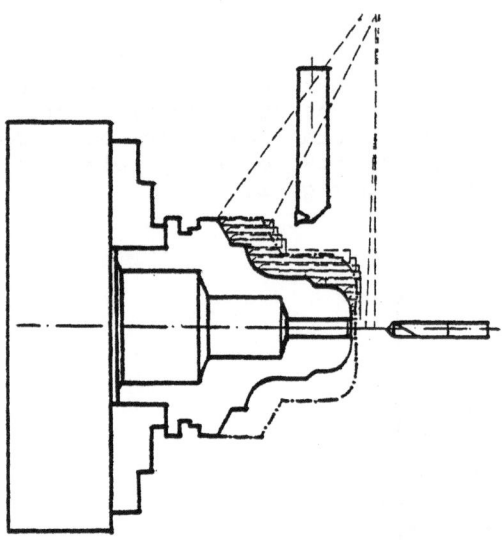

Figure 2.6   Clamping, tool, workpiece and tool paths in
             operation planning (CAPSY)

2.4   NC-programming

If numerical control machines (NC) is used for manufacturing, the
results from operation planning has to be transformed to a NC-tape.
In principle the NC-tape does not contain any more information than
the operation plan - except a much more detailed description of the
tool paths.

Verification of tool paths: A lot of different NC-programming systems
exists.   The most advanced systems offer interactive graphic tools
for complex machining (5-axis).   Figure 2.7 gives some examples of
existing systems.

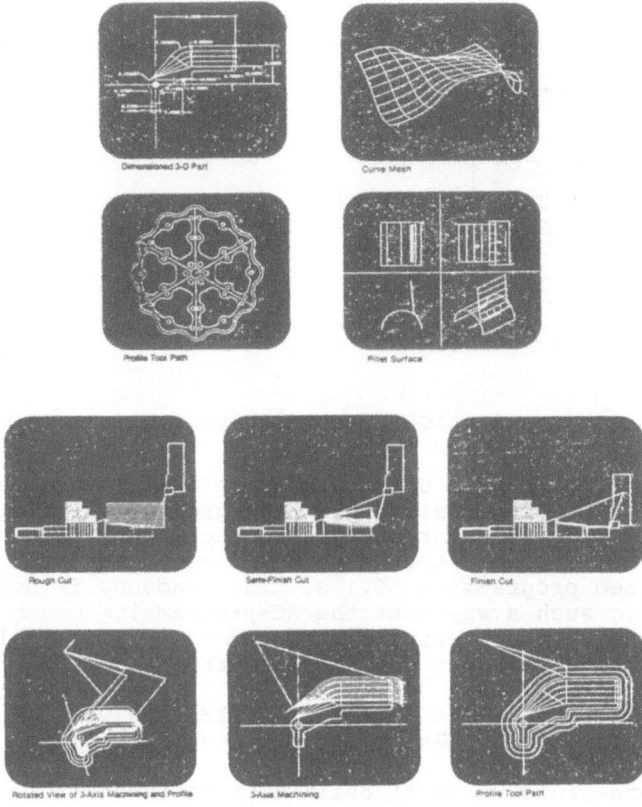

Figure 2.7 NC-programming systems (GRAFTEK)

<u>Nesting of parts:</u> A very important feature in NC-programming is
nesting of parts for flamecutting. Using interactive graphics techniques the different parts is positioned on the plate to have an
optimal cutting and minimum loss of material. Figure 2.8 shows an
example.

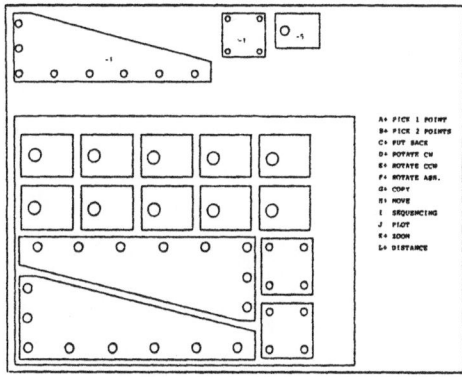

Figure 2.8 a Nesting of parts (VTLNEST)

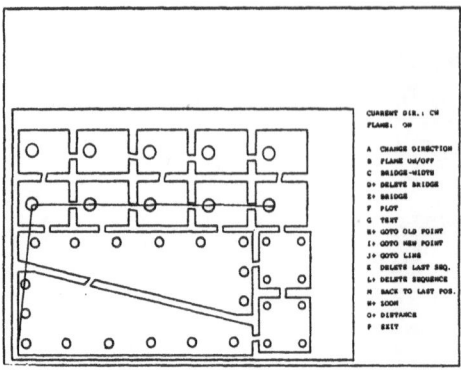

Figure 2.8   Nesting of parts, generation of burning sequence (VTLNEST)

New generation NC-programming tools: Using a conventional machine
tool the operator takes a lot of decisions and have great flexibility
to control and change the process.   Introducing NC-techniques very
much of this possibilities is eliminated.   The NC-programming is
often done in a centralized programming office.   The tendency is now
to develope new systems in such a way that the NC-programming can be
moved back to the operator.   Some NC-controllers offers very flexible
and "easy to use" programming features on the NC control panel.

Another project in this direction is going on at SINTEF and will be
shortly mentioned in the following.   Basis for the development are

- geometry (blank and finished part) definition is taken from
  actual CAD system

- all decisions are taken by the operator using graphic menues

- selection from menues and geometry (coordinates) input is
  done by pointing on the screen (plasma)

- tool and cutting database are avaiable

The operator is always working towards graphic menues on the screen.
He can ask for geometry fig. 2.8, choose cycles (fig. 2.10), define
new cycles, specify tool paths etc. by touching the plasma screen.

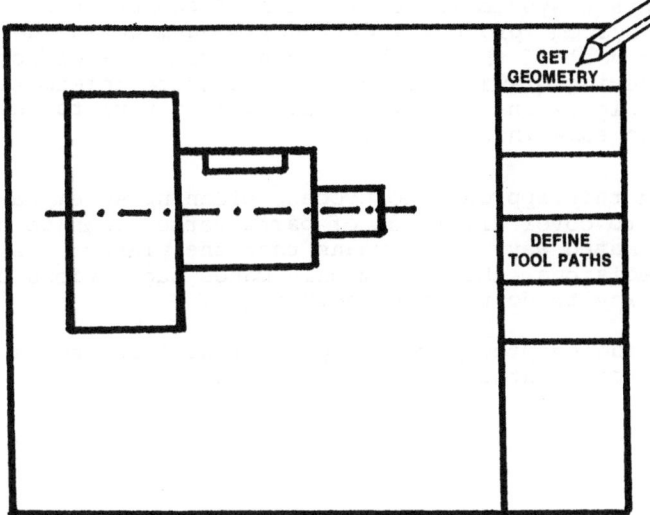

Figure 2.9 Picking up workpiece geometry

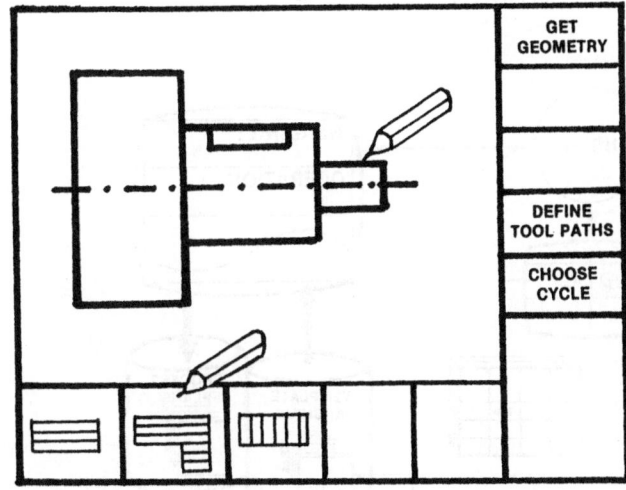

Figure 2.10 Choose cycles (turning)

2.5 Interactive use of product model - coupling to CAD

<u>Coupling to CAD</u>: Today most PP-systems are running as stand alone
systems. In the future a much closer coupling to CAD is natural and
necessary. Integration of CAD and CAM by using Product Models (containing all information about the product) gives new possibilites to
perform a lot of tasks. The designer could ask for and check technological restrictions early in the design phase, and the process planner
could use the geometry descriptions (and geometric modelling tools)
for PP purposes. A lot of information (geometric and technological)
could easily be extracted from the product model.

To meet such requirements a system for extraction of geometric and techn. inf. from a CAD system (product model) has been made in the APS[1] project. The main goal of this work is to evaluate the effect of replacing the engineering drawings used to communicate information from CAD to CAM with a highly interactive module which supports the process planner with the same information.

The PP environment: In this approach to process planning we emphasize the possibilities to cover all kinds of parts rather than to do the planning in an automated way. This means that the planner has to do all the important decisions, the system only makes suggestions of what might be the best way to do the manufacturing.

To assist him in the planning procedure the planner utilizes tools like archives and registers containing information of

- machine tools
- jigs and fixtures
- special tools
- setup times
- raw materials
- etc.

Standardized process plans and recommended operations are found in a template archive by use of a hierarchical matrix system.

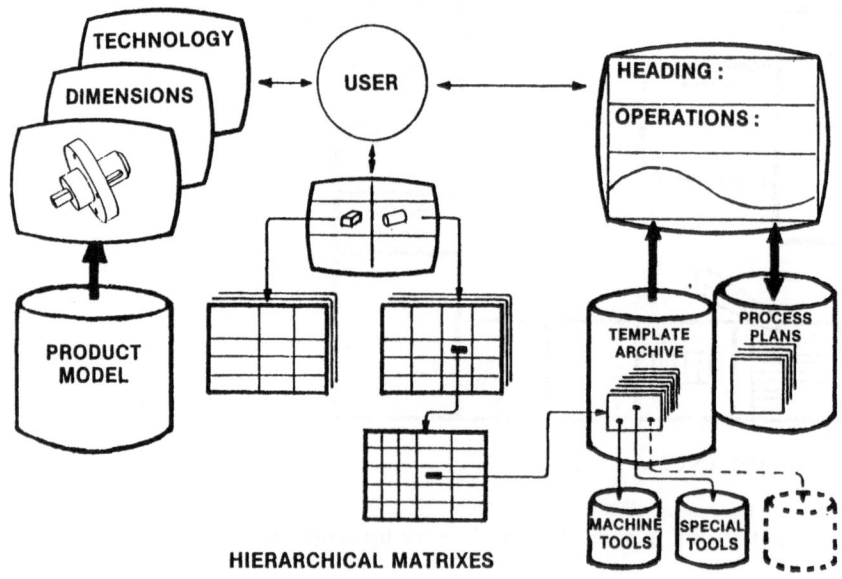

Figure 2.11   Interactive use of Product Model in Process
              Planning environment

Communication with PM: All necessary information about the part is stored in the product model. One important part of the product model

1   German-norwegian CAD/CAM project

is the geometric model and along with this there are also geometric
modelling tools available. In the future (see chapter 2.6) such
tools will be used for geometric manipulations and simulation of
manufacturing processes, delta volume compositions etc.

The commands are collected in 3 groups (fig. 2.12). The process
planner can ask for

- visualization of geometry
- dimensions
- technological data

VISUALIZATION MODULE	DIMENSIONS MODULE	TECHNOLOGICAL MODULE
GEOMETRIC MODEL WIREFRAME MODEL HIDDEN LINE MODEL ROTATE NUMERICAL ROTATE GRAPHIC ZOOM OPTIMIZE WINDOW	DIAMETER LENGTH BETWEEN FACES LENGTH OF EDGE POSITION	TOLERANCES SURFACE INFORMATION SPECIAL ELEMENTS TECHNOLOGY INFORMATION DELETE SYMBOLS

Figure 2.12   Commands for interactive use of Product Model
              (implemented on COMPAC data structure)

Visualization of geometry: The geometry of the part resides in a
datamodel provided by a geometric modelling system. Through call to
this system the geometry of the part can be displayed on the grahpical
screen of the workstation. The routines of the geometric modeller
offers three ways of displaying the geometry.

1. As a wireframe model but without virtual lines

2. As a wireframe model

3. With hidden lines removed

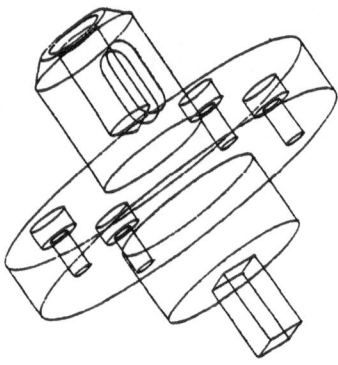 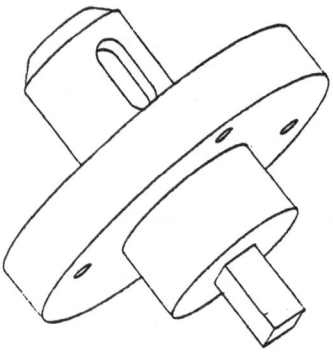

a) Wireframe model   b)   Hidden line removed

Figure 2.13   Visualization of geometry

<u>Dimension module</u>: Through this module the planner can get information
of the geometric dimensions. All dimensions of the part are found
in the geometric model or can be calculated.

<u>Technological data</u>: Through the modul for fetching technological
data the user can obtain such information usually found on engineering
drawings. The information is divided in 3 groups

   - surface information (roughness etc.)
   - tolerances (dimensions, shape, position)
   - special elements like threads, bevels, keyways etc.

The way of interacting in this module is to ask the system to indicate
which geometric elements that contains technological information. If
the process planner is asking for holes with threads in the product
fig. 2.14 shows the result on screen. The thick lines will blink and
indicate the threaded holes.

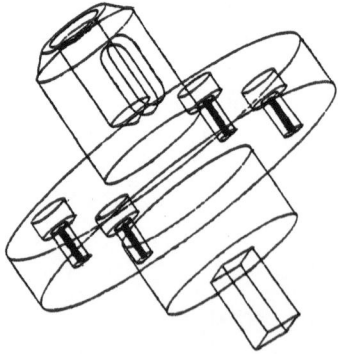

Figure 2.14   Indication of holes with threads (APS)

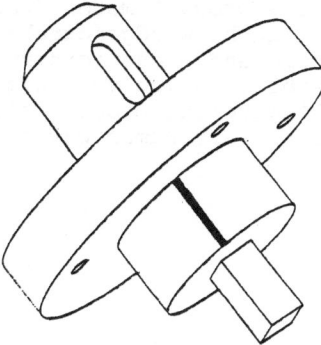

Figure 2.15 Indication of surface information

System architecture: The system is implemented on a VAX 11/780 and an ICAN CAD/CAM workstation is used for interaction. This workstation has one graphic refresh display, one alpha numeric screen and local graphic processor. From a software point of view the features of this workstation is very beneficial for making userfriendly interaction

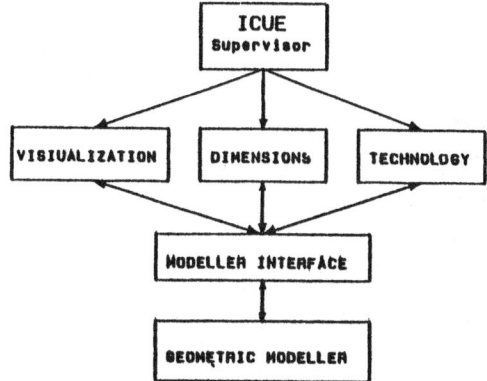

Figure 2.16 The main architecture of the system

The modeller interface: The three modules make calls to a geometric modeller interface. The purpose of this interface is to allow exchange of the modeller. In this particular implementation the geometric modeller COMPAC from IPK in Berlin is used. This modeller has the capability to handle connected information, and also systems for loading technological information is available. In this respect this modeller is suitable for this purpose.

2.6 Graphic simulation in Process Planning

As already mentioned the PP systems of tomorrow will offer a lot of features for graphic simulations. Figure 2.17 shows some possibilities

402

which should be possible. Starting with the product model (geometric description), the rawmaterial description and knowledge databases (experience cost, time data etc.), geometric and economic simulation of the different processes should be possible. Using very high level and user friendly communication tools will give the process planner new possibilities to check alternatives in a very human way of working.

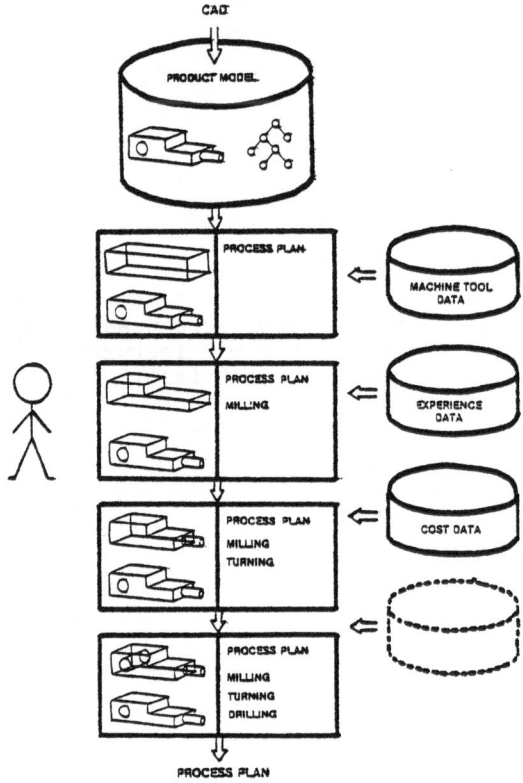

Figure 2.17 Graphic simulation in PP

3   MATERIALS AND RESOURCE PLANNING

3.1 The use of computer graphics

The essential information in the production cycle (as opposed to the product cycle) is not related to the geometry of the part, but to the progress in production. Cost, time and quality are the main objects to be controlled.

The reason for using computer graphics for these systems are to ease the user dialogue and understanding by presenting information in a condensed and comprehensive way. The formats of presentation are well known from the discipline of business graphics; bar charts, histograms, pie charts, staple charts, etc.

Administrative planning systems can use computer graphics in several ways

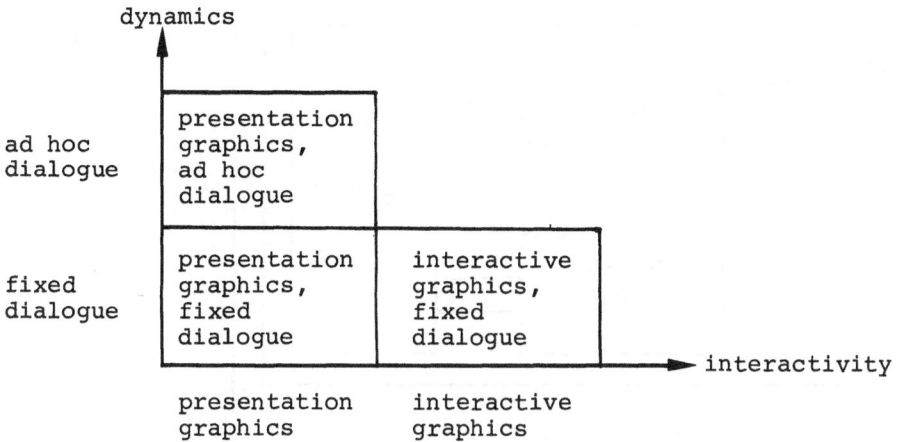

Figure 3.1 Classes of graphic systems

Fixed dialogue means that the user has access to information through a set of preprogrammed transaction for storing, updating and retrival. This is the normal situation in production management applications (stock control, scheduling,...). Ad hoc dialogue means that the user spontanously defines his information needs in non-procedural way, hence getting access to selections/combinations of information not foreseen by the preprogrammed transactions. Ad hoc dialogue should be possible only for information retrieval, as the information contained in the system else could be changed in an uncontrolled way.

Presentation graphics means that information is retrieved from the database and presented to the user as diagrams.

Interactive graphics means that the user can change a picture presented to him and update stored information through such changes.

3.2 Master planning

The master plan is an agreed budget in terms of production volume, between sales management, production management and general management. The master plan is expressed in end products, typically for a period of 1-3 years.

The master plan is essential for the overall factory control, for various reasons:

- it is an agreed objective which all production units are aiming at

- it gives overall loads in the factory, assuring that capacity and load are in balance

- it determines needs for critical purchased and produced parts in due time, as lead times for components often excess required delivery times for end products.

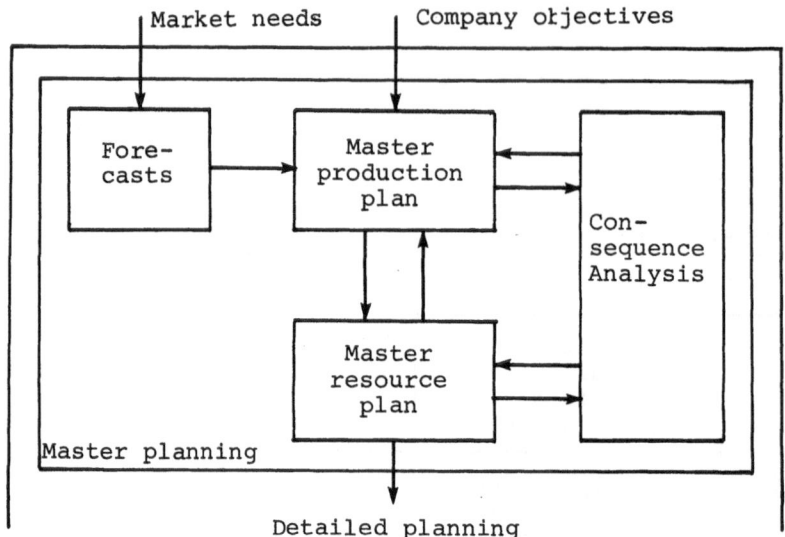

Figure 3.2 Master planning as part of production management

The production volume to be considered in master planning is

- orders already scheduled
- orders not scheduled
- series production
- basic load (repairs, etc.)
- forecasts

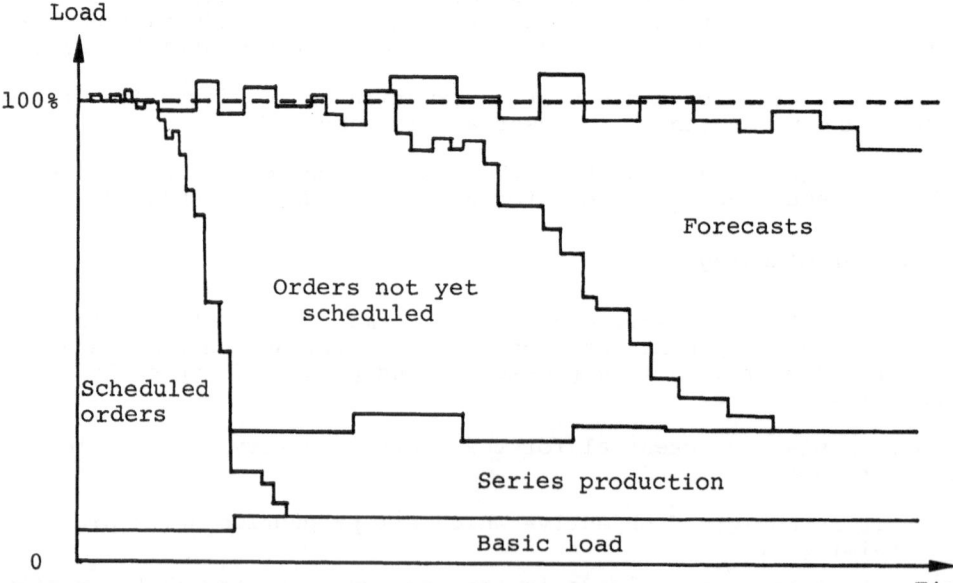

Figure 3.3 Capacity load in master planning

<u>Orders already scheduled</u> have been through operations planning and scheduling, and capacity needs are calculated quite accurately.

For <u>orders not scheduled</u> capacity needs are calculated from experience, often by the use of load patterns for the various types of products.

<u>Series production</u> is related to standard products delivered from stock.

<u>Basic load</u> is experienced load in workshops, not related to delivered products.

<u>Forecasts</u> are related to market expectations, factory load is calculated as for orders not scheduled.

The use of computer graphics in master planning is illustrated by describing FAGROS, a master planning system developed for A/S NEBB by A/S NEBB and Production Engineering Laboratory NTH-SINTEF. The system development was sponsored by Royal Norwegian Council for Technical and Industrial Research.

FAGROS is an interactive master planning system, with a combination of graphic and alphanumeric transactions.

The system is implemented in a customer-order controlled production environment, with three major groups of products

- Generators for hydroelectrical power (customized single products long lead time)

- Electrical machinery (frequent batches, short lead times)

- Railway equipment (few batches, long lead times)

When calculating capacity requirements, the product groups are further divided into product types.

<u>Load calculations</u>

Loads are calculated by the use of load patterns. A load pattern determines the load for producing one unit of given type, as function of time. For one resource unit, there is one load pattern for each product type that flows through that unit.

Load patterns are stored as normalized S-curves, based on experienced data. When actually used, they are transformed to actual values for load and throughput time.

For each product type and workshop, expected load and throughput time are also stored, relative to total load and throughput time. This makes a load distribution per workshop and period possible, when total load and throughput time are given.

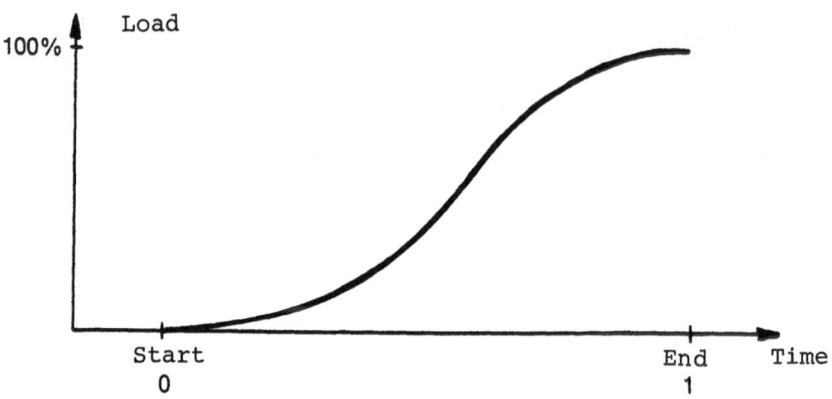

Figure 3.4 Normalized load pattern (cumulative load)

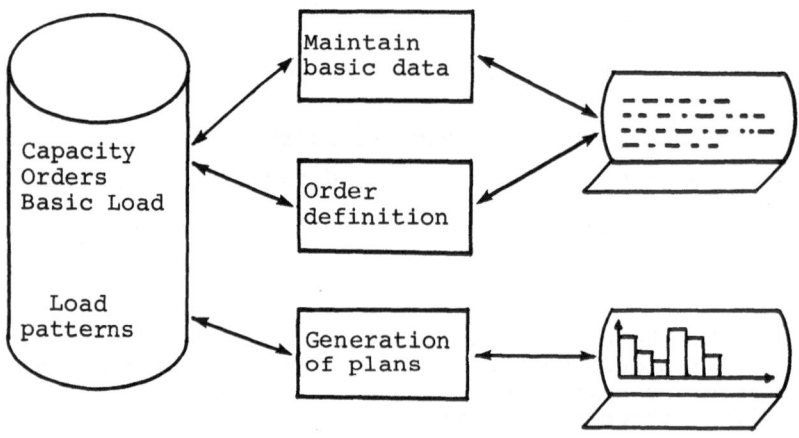

Figure 3.5 System overview

Basic data

The database contains semipermanent information <u>per workshop and product type</u>. This information can be reviewed and changed

- capacity (optimum and maximum)
- basic load per production period
- load patterns (load as function of time)
- load share (fraction of total load)
- throughput time and due date (relative to total throughput time and due date)

Order definition

The database further contains information about all orders (fixed orders and forecasts). The load and throughput time for each work- shop are calculated from total load and throughput time for the order.

The user can override the calculated values. For hydrogenerators
there even is a possibility for calculating total load and throughput
time from physical dimensions of the generator.

Generation of plans

When all orders and prognosed orders are defined, and all loads and
throughput times are calculated, a variety of graphic presentations
can be selected.

Load graphs can be generated for any combinations of

- the whole factory, sums of workshops, one workshop, one
  key machine
- all product groups, combinations of product groups or one
  group, product types within one group
- fixed orders, forecasts, or both

The user can select a surface chart or bar chart representation, with
or without explanatory text.

Bar charts. Two views are possible. The first version is showing
the flow of one production order, through all workshops.

The second version is showing the flow of production orders through a
given workshop. Information content can be selected as for the second
and third criterium described for load graphs.

Load patterns

The time-phased load for a given order, for the whole factory, per
workshop or sum of workshops, or per key machine can be displayed.

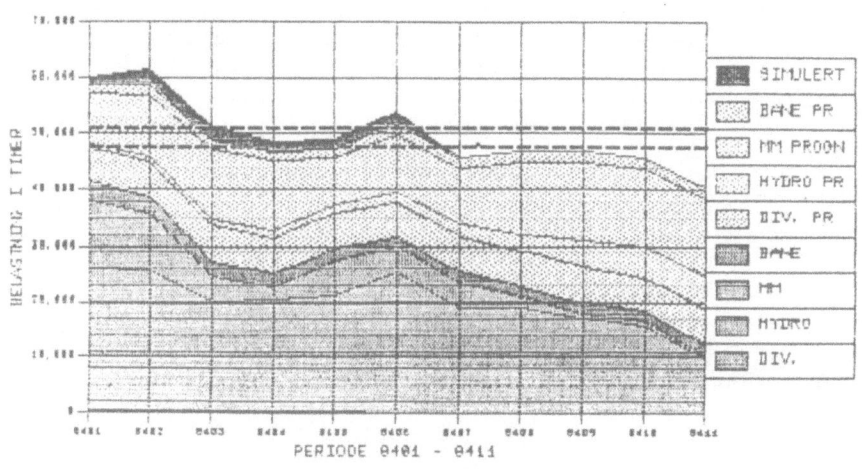

Figure 3.6   Load graph for the whole factory (surface chart with
              explanatory text)

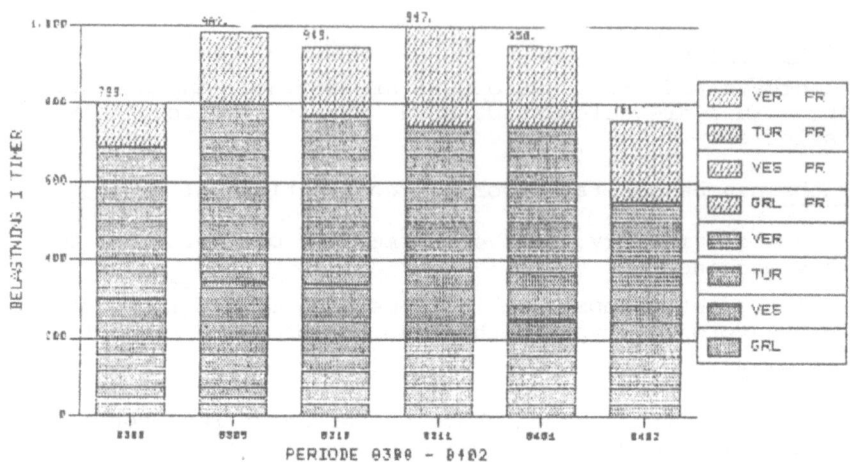

Figure 3.7   Load graph for a key machine (staple chart with explanatory text)

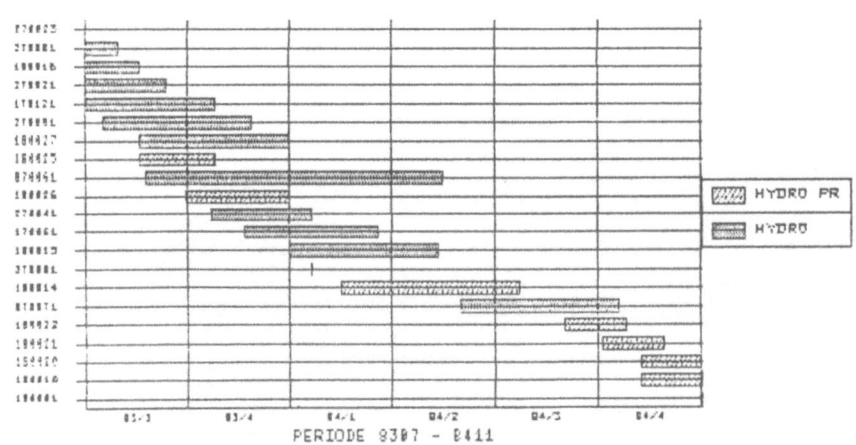

Figure 3.8   Bar chart for a workshop

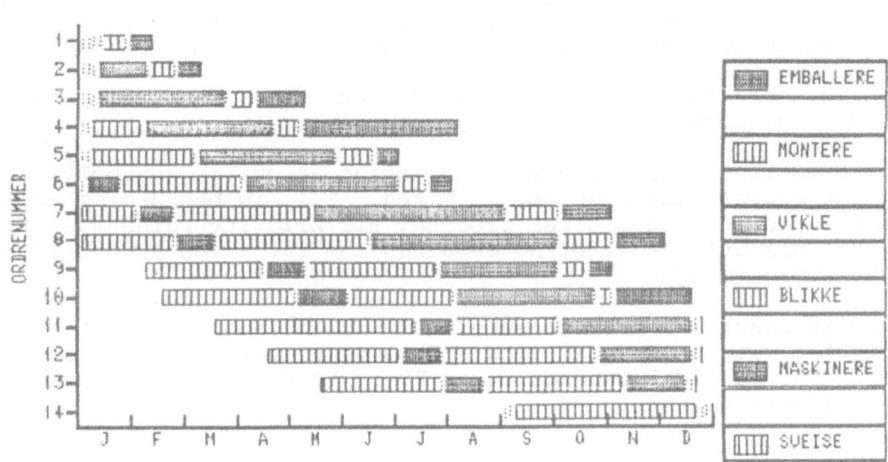

Figure 3.9 Bar chart for production orders

Simulation possibilities

An important part of the master planning process is creating an
optimum plan by trying different alternatives. The system supports
this process, since it is possible in interactive modus to create,
eliminate or move orders, and to change throughput times. The
resulting diagram is immediatedly displayed. Specific orders can be
selected and presented in a special colour in the generated diagrams.

System implementation

A/S NEBB is operating within an IBM mainframe environment. The system
is implemented in this environment. The database system is IMS-DL/1
and programming tools are ADF for alphanumeric transactions and PGF/
GDDM for graphic transactions.

The system is operated from an IBM 3279 semigraphic colour screen
(7 colour) and output can also be directed to a 4-colour hard copy
printer.

3.3 Scheduling

Time-phased needs for individual components are calculated by the
nets requirement calculation process. Rules about batch quantities
and frequencies are applied. The result is a production target per
period for each individual component.

Each component is manufactured through a sequence of operations.
The objectives of the scheduling process is to create a sequence for
each manufacturing unit which allow all batches of components to meet
their target dates. Economics requires this to happen with low level
of work in process and short throughput times.

The scheduling process is often done on a planning board, with calendar time on the horizontal axis, and one line per work station to be planned. Each operation for an order is then represented by a bar with a length corresponding to its duration.

Calculation of duration can be done quite accurately, when the production method is defined (process and operation planning).

There have been tremendous efforts in creating automatic scheduling programs, but success has been very limited. This is because scheduling is not a closed mathematical problem, all priority rules are not formal. Thus effective scheduling requires the intuition and creativeness of the human thought.

The idea of interactive, graphic scheduling is to combine the strengths of the computer with these qualities. This is illustrated by describing a prototype developed for Volvo BM by Production Engineering Laboratory NTH-SINTEF.

Limitation of the problem

The planning period is 1/8 of a year (224 hours). The factory is divided into departments (responsibility of one supervisor), which each is scheduled as a separate unit. The factory is product-oriented to a large extent, the products goes through sequences of operations in the same departement.

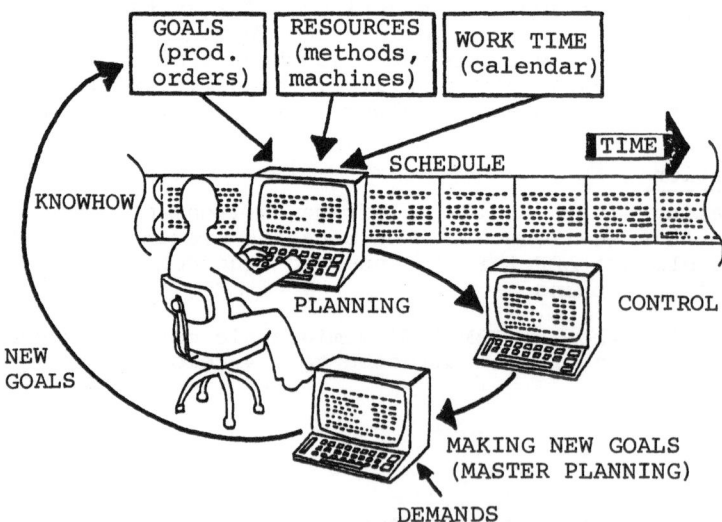

Figure 3.10   Interactive Scheduling by Computer Graphics

Production objectives (volumes and due dates) are set by applying net requirement calculation to the master plan. The scheduling results in a detailed sequence of production for each work station. Conformance in production with schedule has to be checked before a new schedule is made.

The following information is needed for the scheduling

- calendar, defining the time span for each week in the actual period

- <u>station,</u> defining each workstation in the department, the experienced degree of utilization of its capacity, and the time margin to the next workstation. Time margin is used for calculation of transfer time between operations

- <u>production orders,</u> defining the operation sequence for each production order, with calculated times and workstations to be used. For each production order the earliest valid start time and latest valid finish time are defined. It is also stated if overlap between operations is allowed

- <u>shift,</u> defining the shift situation in each station. Shift(s) can be allocated to a workstation during the scheduling process, thus doubling the capacity within certain interval(s).

Graphic Representation

The graphic representation is shown in fig. 3.12 (although not in colours). For each workstation (S 1 --- S 7) the following information is given:

- experienced degree of capacity utilization (UTN.FAKT)
- time margin to next station (TIDMARG)
- number of occupied hours for the workstation (BEL)
- the planned operations as horizontal bars

The planned operations are identified by the colour assigned to the production order, but also names as shown in fig. 3.11.

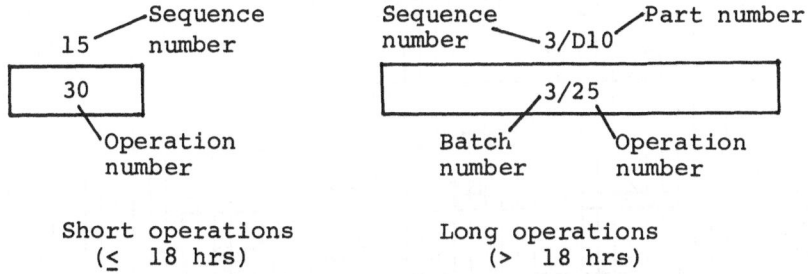

Figure 3.11   Identification of Operations

These numbers have the following meaning:

Sequence number - Each operation entered into the schedule is given a computergenerated sequence number, in order to ease the user dialogue. One operation can be identified either by sequence number or by part number/batch number/operation number.

Part number   - Defining the part to be produced.

Batch number   - Used to discriminate between different production orders for one part within a time period.

Operation number - Identifying the operations necessary to produce the part.

The operation is normally displayed as a bar in the lower position. If it is not room for it, it is shown in upper position. The planner

then has to create sufficient room by moving operations, or by adding
shift or overtime.

Scheduled overtime for an operation is displayed by cutting the operation at the end and displaying the cut-off above the remaining part.

Shift time can be planned for intervals at each station. Operations
in the shift interval are displayed at half the length, but with the
thickness doubled.

The lower, part of the diagram is displaying the manload for the
department (ANTAL OPERATØRER), according to the schedule which is
worked out.

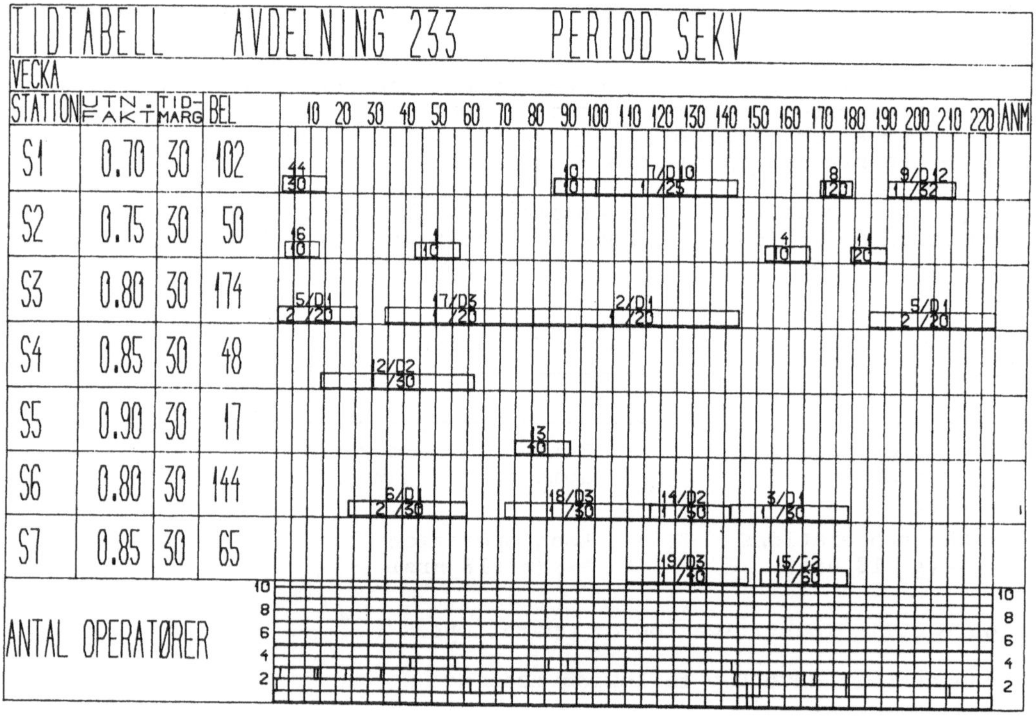

Figure 3.12 Graphic Schedule

The Interactive Graphic Dialogue

By a variety of transactions, the user can enter, move or remove the
operations defined by the production orders. The dialogue is alphanumeric, but the results are immediately represented graphically.
While working the screen is used as a scetch pad, but whenever desired the changes can be made permanent (database update). Whenever
desired a schedule can be stored, and then later on displayed and
revised.

The system allows the planner to make all decisions, but warns him if

- start or finish time is exceeded
- transfer time between operations are to short, or operation sequences are wrong
- two operations in one workstation is overlapping. One of them is then shown in upper position

The following functions are available

- Entering operations

  NO - A single operation
  - given start time
  - in front of an existing operation in the station
  - following an existing operation in the station
  - as close as possible in front of the next operation for the order
  - as close as possible behind the previous operation for the order

  NA - All operations for an order
  - given start time for the order
  - given finish time for the order

- Moving operations

  FO - A single operation
  - to a given position
  - a number of hours (left/right)

  PS - Pack a station
  - packing operations within an interval (left/right)

- Changing capacity

  LS - Shift is allocated to an interval in a workstation

  LO - Overtime is allocated to an operation

- Removing operations

  TO - A single operation

  TA - A production order

  TR - A sequence of specified operations

- Database communication

  OK - Update database

  AU - Return to last update

  SL - Finish (with or without update)

- Service translations

  OP - Calculate manload

  KT - List errors

  VG - Calculate throughput times for product

  LS - List operations not yet scheduled

  PL - Hard copy plot

414

System implementation

The system is running on a VAX 11/780, with a Tektronix 4027 graphic
screen. It is programmed in FORTRAN with use of the GPGS graphic
software.

3.4   Other Applications

In above sections two applications of computer graphics in production
management are covered quite detailed. Other interesting applications
are

Stock control

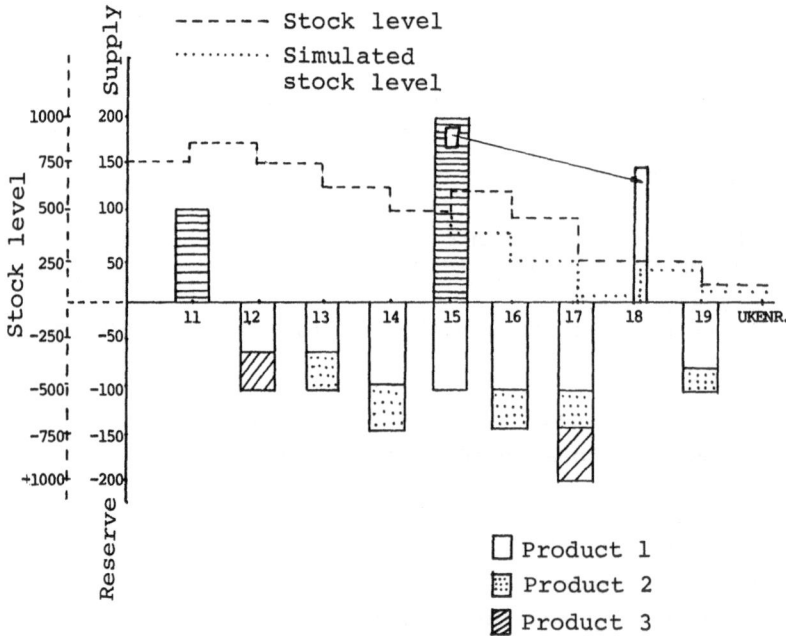

Figure 3.13   Stock movements for an article

Graphical representations of planned supplies and reservations, with
resulting levels gives better insight. By different colours, different
sources of reservations and supplies can be identified.

Consequences of moving supplies/reservations in time, or by changing
volumes are easily shown (narrow staple, dotted line).

Project planning

Delivery of large, complex products (offshore modules, hydroelectrical
power stations) are often planned as projects. Networks analysis has
proven to be an efficient project planning and control method.

Computerized systems for network analysis ease the lots of calculations necessary. However, maintaining the network itself (with hundreds of activities and relations), are as a rule done manually. An efficient graphic interface which allows interactive editing of a computerstored network, would largely increase the power of computerized network analysis systems. See fig. 3.14.

Progress monitoring

The chart in fig. 3.12 could with small changes be used for progress monitoring. By drawing a vertical line showing due date and wiping out operations or parts of operations already performed, the chart would give excellent status information. This require a close feed back from production.

Key figures

Key figures from computerized production management could be extracted and represented graphically, often as functions of time. Examples are

- service level
- planned vs actual load
- capacity load level
- throughput times
- stock levels
- stock turnover (fig. 3.15)
- productivity development (fig. 3.16)

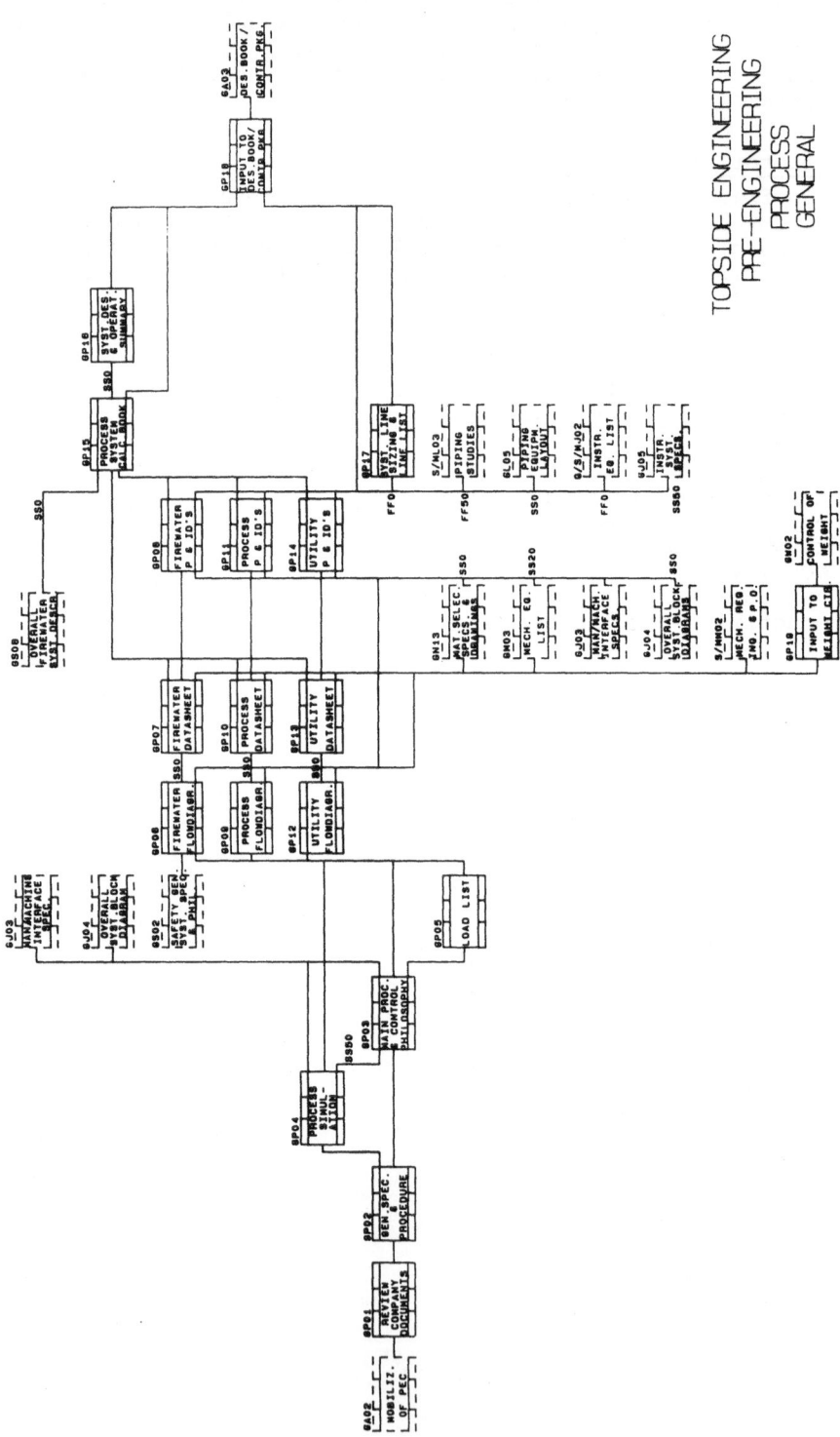

Figure 3.14   Computergenerated network

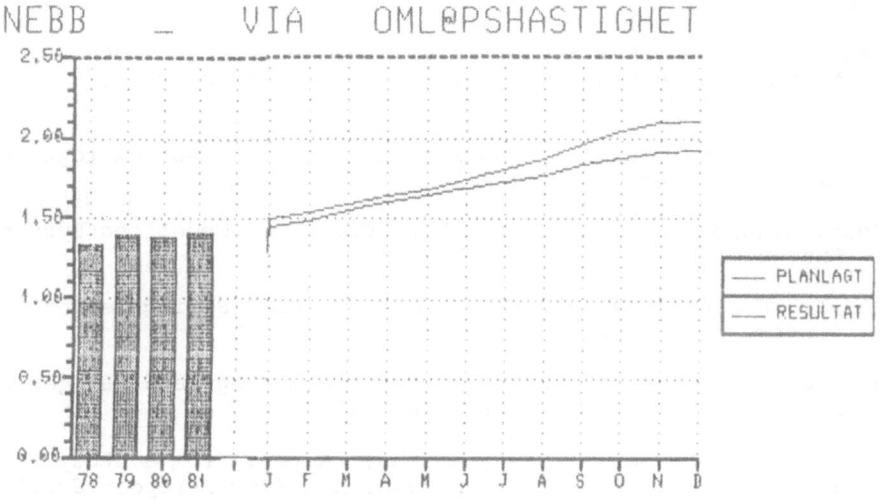

Figure 3.15 Stock turnover

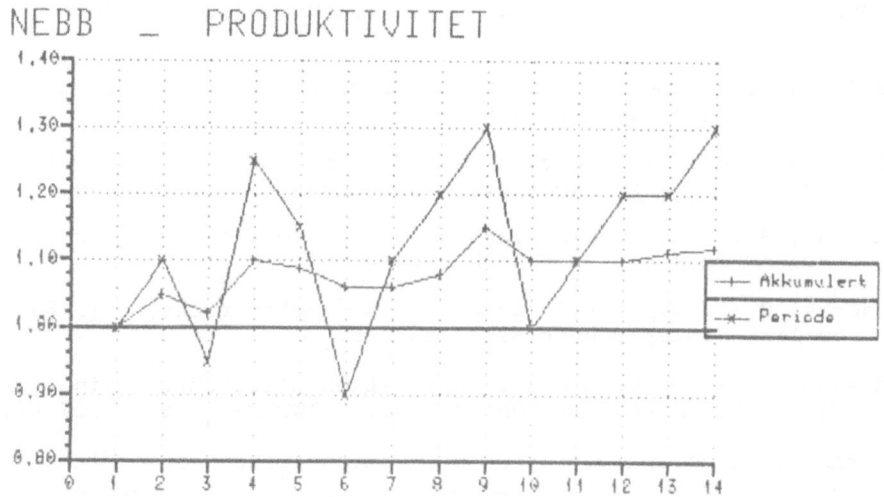

Figure 3.16 Productivity development

REFERENCES

[1]   Wisnosky, D.: ICAM - The Air Force Integrated Computer Aided
       Manufacturing Program. Astronauties & Aeronauties,
       February 1977.

[2]   CAM-I: International spring seminar "Getting CAD/CAM together".
       Arlington, Texas, April 1977.

[3]   Spur, Krause etc.: A Survey about Geometric Modelling Systems,
       Annals of CIRP, Vol. 28/2/1979.

[4]   CAM-I: Proceedings 1980 CAM-I International Spring Seminar,
       Denver, April 1980.

[5]   Bjørke, Ø.: Interconnection between Technology and Management
       Systems, SINTEF-report STF17 A80041.

[6]   Estensen, Gulbrandsen, Lien, Moseng: Report from a study-tour
       in Japan and USA 1982 (in norwegian), SINTEF-report STF17
       A83042.

[7]   Mevåg, H.: CAD/CAM in Design and Production of Waterturbines
       Kværner Brug (in norwegian), NORCAD-83, Oslo February 1983.

[8]   Stokland, Moseng, Bjørke, Gulbrandsen, Estensen: CAM-technique,
       what is status? (in norwegian), SINTEF-report STF17 A82056,
       October 1982.

[9]   Spur, Eversheim, Weill: Survey of Computer Aided Process
       Planning Systems.

[10]   APS Advanced Production System. Progress Report 2, February 1983,
       Kernforschungszentrum Karlsruhe.

[11]   Haaøy Nes, B.: Interactive use of a Product Model. CAM-I
       Product Modelling Seminar, Copenhagen, June 1984.

[12]   Moseng, B.: The Processplanners Workplace (in norwegian), Nordic
       CAD/CAM days 84, Stockholm 1984-02-07.

[13]   Bjørke, Ø.: Computer Graphics in CAM Applications, CAMP'83,
       Berlin, SINTEF-report STF17 A83008.

[14]   Moengen, V.: Do we present information efficiently? (in norwegian)
       NIF-course Materials Control 1981, SINTEF-report STF17 A81094.

[15]   Aaram J., Nodeland O.: FAGROS - Computerized Master Planning
       System using Graphics (in norwegian), SINTEF-report STF17
       A83058.

[16]   Aaram J., Arnøy E.: Presenting Production Management Information
       by Computer Graphics (in norwegian), SINTEF-report STF17
       A83059.

[17]   Birkenes, L.: Interactive Scheduling by Computer Graphics (in
       norwegian), SINTEF-reports STF17 F82035 and STF17 F82076.

Advanced Image Synthesis – Anti-Aliasing

F. C. Crow

Effects and Their Causes

Those who work with digital imagery are familiar with the symptoms of aliasing. In still images, jagged edges caused by the regular structure of dots making up the image are often evident [fig 1a]. In animated sequences the jagged edges come alive, with apparent armies of ants running back and forth along the edges of objects. Small or narrow objects can suffer random changes in shape and even deletion from the image [fig. 1b]. Regular arrays of shapes, such as the windows on the side of a tall building may appear to "swim", or undulate, in an animated sequence.

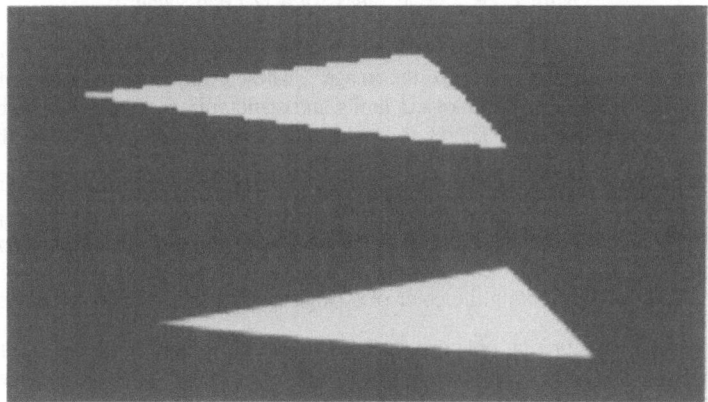

Figure 1a: Jagged edges.

Figure 1b: Disappearing Detail.

The term "aliasing" refers to the effect caused by "sampling" (taking discrete measurements of) a signal at an inadequate number of regular intervals. A 12 cycle signal sampled at 10 regularly spaced positions appears identical to a 2 cycle signal over the same interval and sampled at the same positions. Thus the 2 cycle signal is an "alias" of the 12 cycle signal [figure 2].

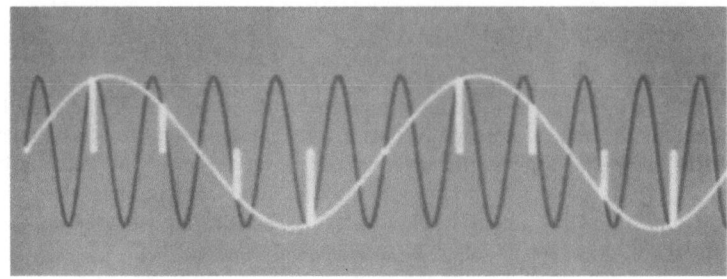

Figure 2: A 2 cycle "alias" of a 12 cycle signal.

An inadequate sampling interval when synthesizing digital images causes small errors in representing the positions of the edges which characterize the image. These errors, in turn, cause all the problems mentioned above. Unfortunately, technological limits and standardized equipment prevent most of us from choosing our sampling interval. Therefore we are left trying to make the best of what we have.

To put it another way, the effects of aliasing are caused by attempts to force the positions of details in an image to coincide exactly with the positions of the individual spots ("pixels") of the physical image structure. In virtually all displays capable of showing shaded images, the physical image structure consists of a regular array of pixels, upon which individually calculated intensities are displayed. An image is most simply calculated by representing the color of a single surface at each of these pixels.

However, if a pixel can represent only one surface then the boundaries between objects in the image must fall between pixel positions. This forces such boundaries to be jagged in shape except where they are perfectly aligned with the pixel array (horizontal or vertical, in most cases). Such boundaries can be made to appear smooth by blending the colors of two or more surfaces at the pixels involved. Methods for calculating that blend and deciding when it is necessary to do so provide the basis for the methods suggested below.

If a display is viewed from an adequate distance, details the size of a pixel cannot be resolved. Therefore, variation in intensity over a few pixels can be used to "suggest" the position of an edge. By such means it is technically feasible to make an image which is indistinguishable from one of much greater resolution. In order to do this we must achieve the same level of intensity at each pixel as would be seen over the equivalent small area in an image of much higher resolution. This can be done by properly considering all the details which contribute to the area represented by each pixel.

In theoretical terms, aliasing cannot be entirely eliminated. In practical terms, however, it can be diminished to the point where it is undetectable. All successful techniques for diminishing aliasing involve increasing the amount of information upon which the image is based. The array of pixels making up an image represent samples from a conceptual scene defined by the input data. The information content of the image can be improved by increasing the number of samples or by taking more information into account when taking each sample.

Treatments of the theoretical underpinnings of the aliasing problem can be found in [CROW77] [KAJIYA81, OPPENHEIM75]. Algorithms for solutions to various aspects of the problem have appeared in [CATMULL78, CATMULL80, CROW77, CROW78, CROW81, FUCHS79, FEIBUSH80, GUPTA81, WARNOCK80].

Easy Solutions

The most straightforward way to reduce the effects of aliasing is to increase the resolution at which the image is calculated. For example, four pixels may be calculated for every pixel on the display. The displayed intensity may then be made the average of the four calculated intensities. Attempts have been made to measure the costs and benefits of this approach [CROW81].

Increasing the resolution, while generally easy to implement, can be very expensive. In general terms, the cost of generating an image varies directly with the number of scanlines for calculations involving the surface definition (vertices, edges, etc.), and with the square of the number of scanlines for calculations involving the shade of an individual pixel [WHITTED82]. Therefore, higher resolution can be very expensive where highlights, texture, or other expensive shade calculation techniques are applied. Furthermore, even for the least expensive shading techniques, the cost of generating the image rises directly with the resolution.

Many of the effects of aliasing may be lessened by processing the image after it has been computed (postprocessing). For example, where the effects are subtle, as along edges across which there is only small contrast, adding noise or blurring the image may be sufficient. For high-contrast edges, a combination of edge detection and smoothing algorithms can have quite satisfactory results [BLOOMENTHAL83]. Standard thresholding techniques may be used to determine where high-contrast details are to be found. Local edge slopes may then be determined by following the edges and pixels may be blended by utilizing the local slope.

The performance of methods which process the completed image is fairly straightforward. Blurring techniques are usually applied globally. Therefore performance is a function of the extent of the blur (how many pixels are involved in the calculation of a single blurred pixel) and the square of the image resolution. Noise addition may in some cases be provided gratis by the equipment (eg. very grainy photographic film) or display algorithms (eg. dithering techniques). In other cases it should cost no more than one or two simple operations per pixel.

Edge-smoothing techniques, on the hand require two stages. First edges must be found. This requires a pass over the entire image, making nearest-neighbor comparisons. Cost is a function of the square of the resolution. Then edges must be processed by blending colors in pixels along edges. The cost of this stage is dependent on the amount of high-contrast detail in the image.

While blurring and edge smoothing techniques may be used to enhance the appearance of images, such methods cannot recover detail which has been lost in the process of making the image. Small or thin objects may still disappear or be distorted. While a still image may be processed to remove clear evidence of aliasing, animated sequences can still reveal problems. Most problems may be avoided by insuring that the data describing the image contains no details below a certain size. However, this will usually require human intervention or much more carefully prepared data than is desirable.

Understanding The Nature Of The Problem

The methods of the previous section have disadvantages because of ineffectiveness in the case of postprocessing techniques or expense in the case of higher-resolution techniques. To do better, it is necessary to have a better understanding of the problem.

The process of making a synthetic image involves taking samples of a 2 dimensional function defined by the surface fragments forming the input data (transformed polygons, patches, etc.). The simplest algorithm for determining the color of a pixel is to evaluate the intersections of all surface fragments with a ray emanating from the eye. The intersecting surface closest to the eye determines the color of the pixel. Areas lying between the rays will be lost. Since such rays are infinitessimally thick, we can argue that virtually everything is lost.

As was stated above, more information must be brought to bear on the problem of computing the shade of a pixel. Instead of using a ray emanating from the eye we should be using a solid angle. The area of each visible surface within the angle must be computed. The color of a pixel is just the average of the colors of all surfaces represented weighted by their respective areas covered within the solid angle.

Calculating such areas is equivalent to a signal processing operation know as "convolution". We "convolve" a "filter" with an image by superposing the filter function over the image function at each pixel position and integrating over the product of the two. The effect of a convolution, for the cases in which we are interested, is to smooth over abrupt changes in color, thus diminishing the strength of higher spatial frequencies in the image.

Fourier theory says that the highest frequency that can be represented in a digital image is one which has a cycle of two pixel widths. Taking a sine wave of that frequency and using the Fourier transform to find the corresponding frequency spectrum we get an impulse function at the highest representable frequency [figure 3a].

Constructing a frequency function which is constant up to the highest representable frequency and then drops to zero, we then take the inverse Fourier transform to find that the corresponding spatial representation is the sinc (sin x / x) function with a central lobe having a width of two times the interpixel distance [figure 3b].

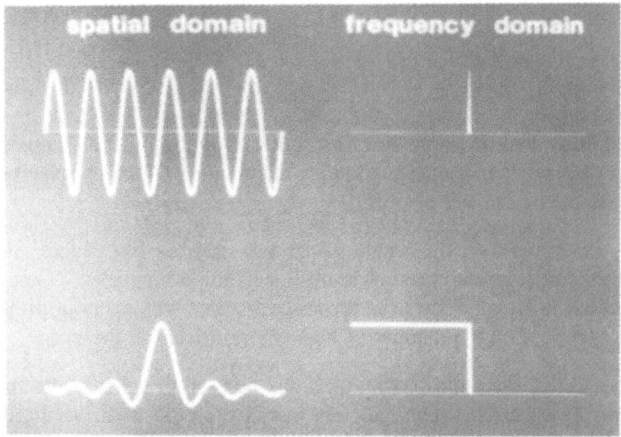

Figure 3: Spatial and frequency domain images of [a] sin x and [b] (sin x) / x.

Now, it turns out that convolving with a filter function has the same effect as multiplying the frequency spectra. Thus convolving with the sinc function is the same as eliminating frequencies above a sharp cutoff, exactly what we want to do.

Unfortunately, the sinc function is infinite in extent and therefore impossible to apply as a filter. However, we can use the general shape of the sinc function to lead us to a practical filter shape. The most important feature to note is that most of the area lying under the sinc function is in the two pixel wide central lobe.

A test pattern was generated to try different filter shapes, with the results seen in fig. 4. Each image shows a synthesized test pattern made using the filter function shown at the bottom. The hatch marks represent pixel spacing. The commonly used filter shapes are (a) an impulse function, or no filter, (b) 16 samples per pixel, (c) 64 samples per pixel with weighting, (d) 64 samples per pixel, (e) 256 samples per pixel with weighting, (f) a box function, or Fourier window, (g) the triangle function, (h) the central lobe of the sinc function, (i) the Gaussian distribution function. Filters wider than 2 pixels such as (j), a weighted version of the 3 inner lobes of the Sinc function, are sometimes used.

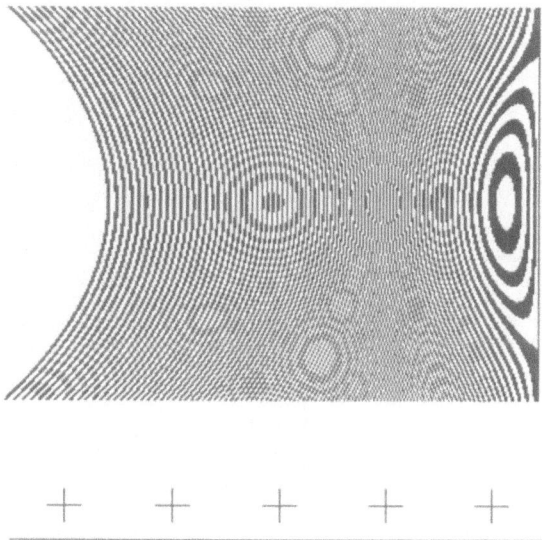

Figure 4a: Impulse (equivalent to a single sample per pixel).

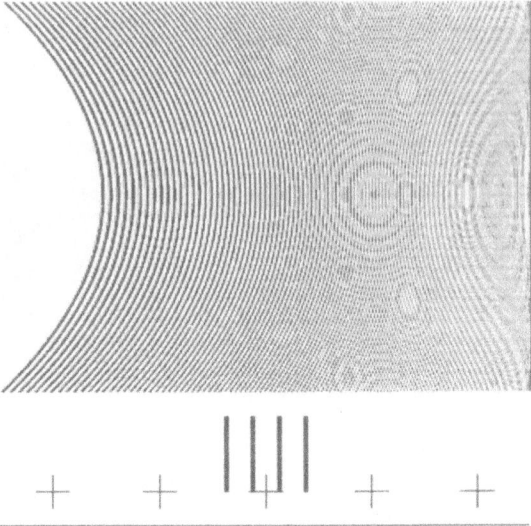

Figure 4b: Four impulses across one interpixel distance (16 samples/pixel).

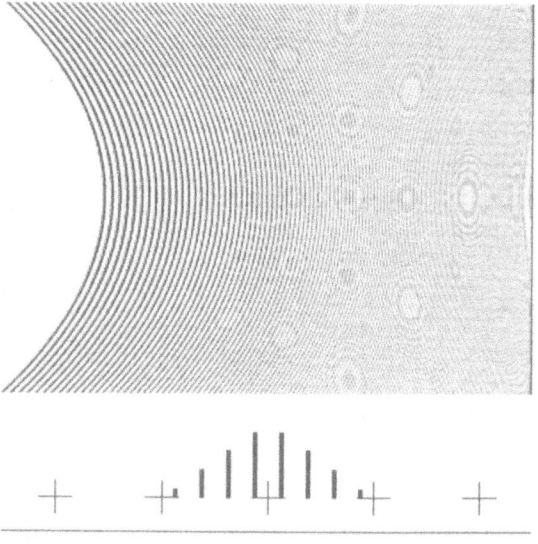

Figure 4c: Eight weighted impulses in 2 interpixel distances (64 samples/pixel).

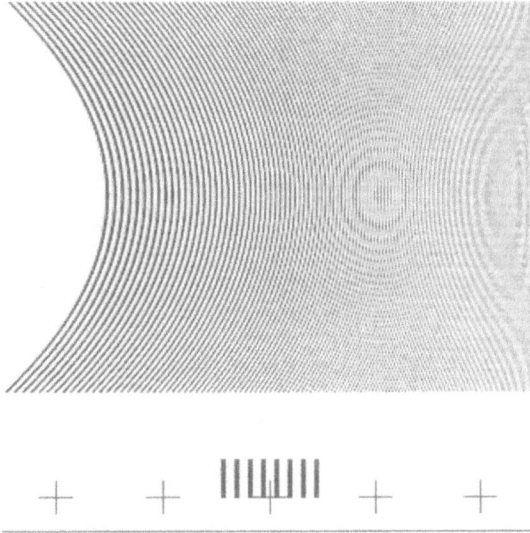

Figure 4d: Eight impulses across one interpixel distance (64 samples/pixel).

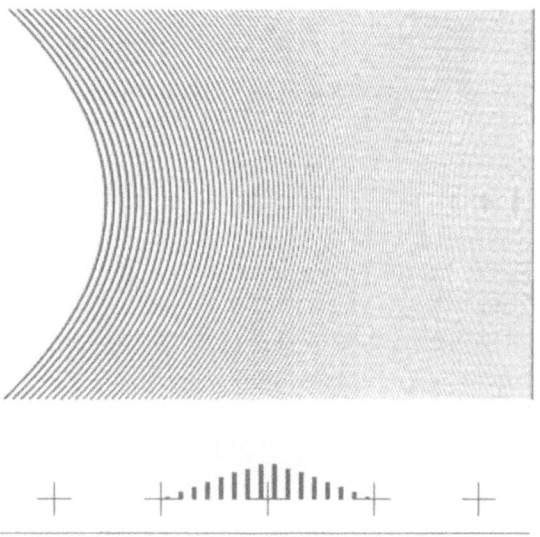

Figure 4e: 16 weighted impulses in 2 interpixel distances (256 samples/pixel).

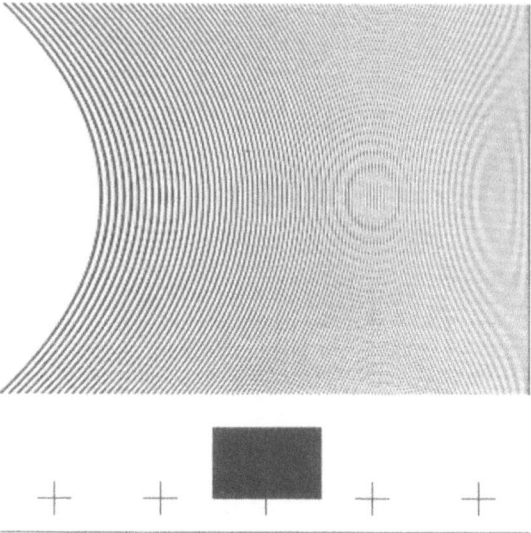

Figure 4f: Box function across one interpixel distance.

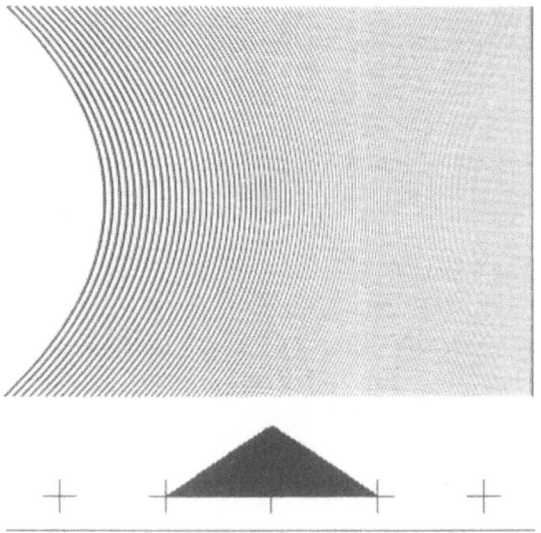

Figure 4g: Triangle across 2 interpixel distances.

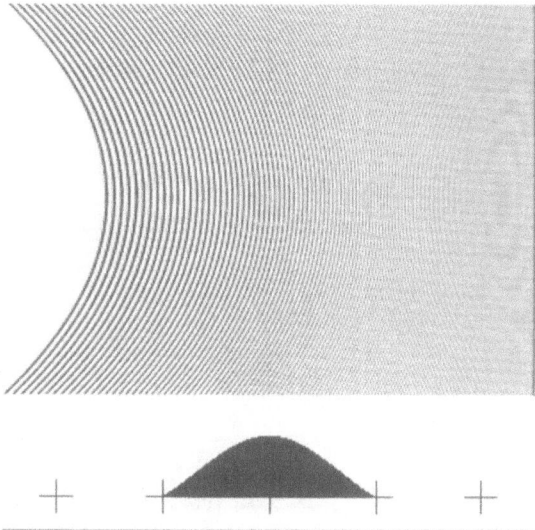

Figure 4h: Central lobe of sinc function across 2 interpixel distances.

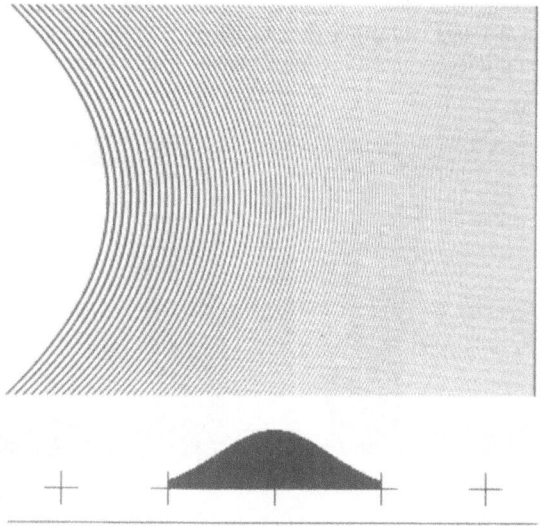

Figure 4i: Gaussian distribution across 2 interpixel distances.

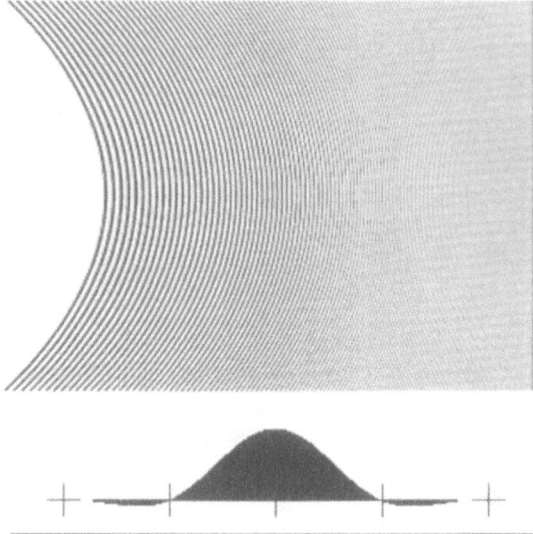

Figure 4j: Weighted sinc function across 4 interpixel distances.

It should be clear from figure 4 which filters work best on an extreme case. However, it is important to test various filters on images typical of those to be used in a given environment (see figures 5 and 6). The more effective filters are also more expensive. In cases where there are no small, highly contrasting details, the less expensive filters will often do adequately. However, line drawings and text are two examples of very common imagery including lots of small, highly contrasting details.

Figure 5: Lines scan-converted using a 1-pixel box filter (left) and a 2-pixel triangular filter (right).

Figure 6: Images calculated at 4096 lines then averaged 8 lines into 1 interpixel distance (equivalent to 64 samples per pixel) to make the top 512-line image and averaged with weighting 16 lines into 2 interpixel distances (256 samples per pixel) to make the bottom 512-line image.

Restricting The Domain Of Application

Different features in an image require differing amounts of care to hide aliasing. Broad areas in which the shade changes slowly obviously can be reproduced with very little information. On the other hand, areas with sharp detail carry a much greater density of information and must be treated more carefully. Areas with extremely fine detail, of course, may not be representable, given the display resolution. In such cases, the proper representation is a smudge of the correct intensity.

Expensive anti-aliasing measures can be practical if it may be determined in advance of their application where they are really necessary. As was seen in the previous section, it is possible to isolate those pixels which contribute to the problem by looking for contrast thresholds. Knowledge of the surface definitions from which the image is to be made allows the display algorithm to know where those high-contrast details are likely to occur. Using such knowledge, the domain of application of anti-aliasing techniques may be restricted to just those areas where they are needed. Furthermore, such information can be used during the generation of the image, avoiding loss of detail which is irrevocable after the image is generated.

Most currently practical images have large regions of sparse detail. It is therefore inefficient to use brute force techniques such as computing the entire image at a much higher resolution then averaging many samples into one displayed pixel. This may not be true for future images of much greater complexity. For the moment, however, algorithms which treat detailed areas with special care remain important enough for study.

Generally, the pixels which need special care are those which contain part of one of the edges defining a surface. If the pixel is considered to represent a very small image from the scene being generated, then the color of each surface visible within that image must contribute to the color of the pixel. The pixel color is determined by summing all the contributing surface colors, each weighted by the area it subtends within the pixel. Thus where an edge passes through a pixel, the surface colors on either side of the edge are blended by a weighted average.

During the generation of an image involving objects with smooth, non-glossy, untextured surfaces, all aliasing problems must occur where the defining edges of surfaces pass through pixels. Therefore the domain of application of anti-aliasing measures may be restricted to those pixels. In an image of a simple environment this greatly reduces the amount of computation required. On the other hand, as image complexity grows, the the number of pixels which must be processed for anti-aliasing becomes more significant. However, it remains computationally impractical to make pictures of a complexity great enough to suggest that global methods such as those of the previous section would be more efficient.

Frequently, curved surfaces are represented by polygonal approximations. This poses a problem in that it is necessary to use a large number of polygons to approximate a curved surface closely enough to avoid a polygonal silhouette [figure 7]. This means that the large majority of edges defining the surface are not evident in the image and therefore require no anti-aliasing measures.
Therefore, one way to cut down the number of pixels subject to additional computation would be to use non-linear surfaces such as piecewise continuous patches. However algorithms for direct rendering of nonlinear surfaces are more difficult to implement, generally less efficient, and sometimes more restrictive than those for polygonal surfaces [BLINN80]. On the other hand, with polygonal approximations to curved surfaces, it is reasonably straightforward to isolate the edges which need extra attention.

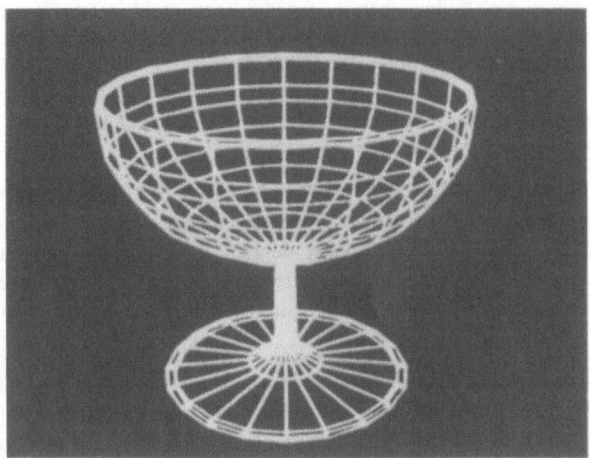

Figure 7: Approximating curved surfaces requires many polygons

The high-contrast edges in an image of a curved surface fall along the silhouette of the surface. If the silhouette can be characterized in the data, then only those pixels involved in the silhouette of the object need be treated for aliasing. There is a relatively easy way to determine silhouette edges. In a polygonally-approximated surface, silhouette edges are those edges shared by a polygon on the visible side of the surface (a "frontfacing" polygon) and one on the far side of the surface (a "backfacing" polygon). Hidden-surface algorithms generally cull the backfacing polygons before rendering a surface [SUTHERLAND77]. If a data structure which provides pointers to the neighbors of a given polygon is used [figure 8], silhouette edges may be determined straightforwardly.

Therefore, for curved surfaces, edges which require special attention are those which are shared by a frontfacing and a backfacing polygon or those which belong to only one polygon. The latter case consists of those polygons which lie along the edge of an open surface (one which does not close on itself).

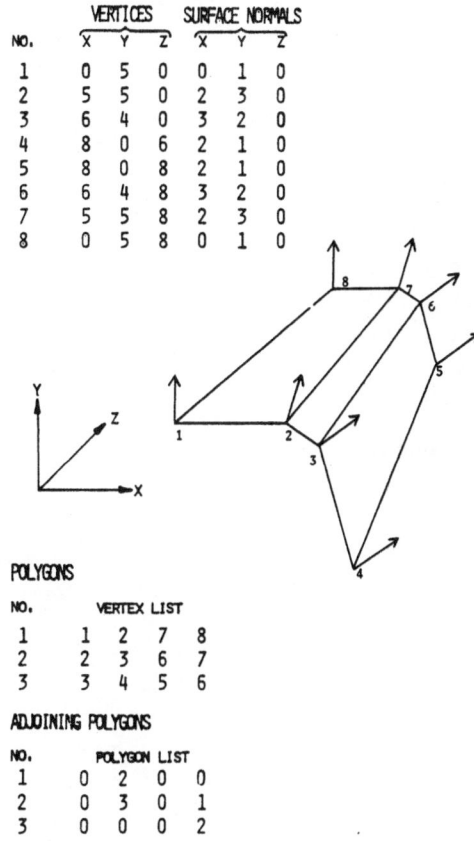

NO.	VERTICES			SURFACE NORMALS		
	X	Y	Z	X	Y	Z
1	0	5	0	0	1	0
2	5	5	0	2	3	0
3	6	4	0	3	2	0
4	8	0	6	2	1	0
5	8	0	8	2	1	0
6	6	4	8	3	2	0
7	5	5	8	2	3	0
8	0	5	8	0	1	0

POLYGONS

NO.	VERTEX LIST			
1	1	2	7	8
2	2	3	6	7
3	3	4	5	6

ADJOINING POLYGONS

NO.	POLYGON LIST			
1	0	2	0	0
2	0	3	0	1
3	0	0	0	2

Figure 8: A data structure with pointers to neighboring polygons

Calculating Subpixel Areas

In order to calculate the intensity of a pixel which represents parts of more than one surface, the area covered by each surface within the pixel must be estimated. Area estimation algorithms can take a number of different forms. However, the algorithm must be relatively quick if it to be used with complicated scenes.

There are two widely used models for the area subtended by a pixel. (1) The image may be considered a grid wherein each square hole represents a pixel area. In this model, pixels abut and completely fill the image area [figure 9]. (2) The image may be modeled more closely to its physical realization on a CRT. Here, the pixels are larger and overlap one another by half [figure 10]. In addition, the importance of a sub-area varies over the pixel; details toward the middle of the pixel area are weighted more heavily in computing the pixel intensity. Various weighting functions have been used [CROW77, KAJIYA81] all of which are similar in general shape to the Gaussian distribution of intensity produced by a focussed electron beam (ie. symmetric with most of the weight in the middle).

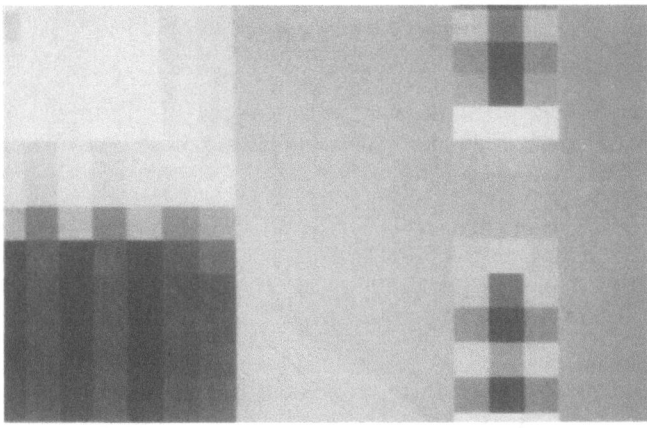

Figure 9: Pixels modeled as abutting squares

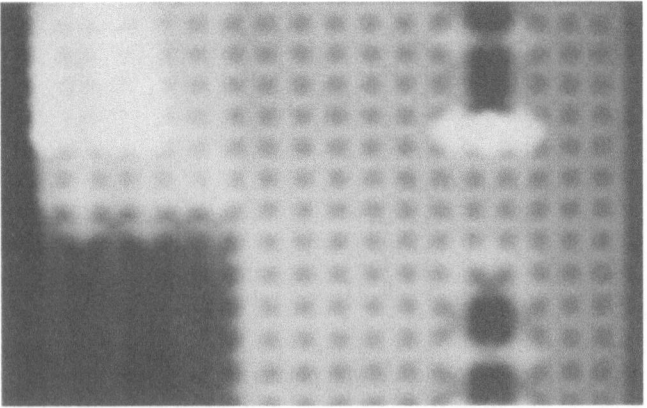

Figure 10: Pixels modeled as overlapping Gaussian bumps

Obviously area estimation algorithms based upon the first model can be somewhat simpler [CATMULL78, CROW78]. The differences in these models, however can be quite important in areas of fine, highly contrasting detail [CROW81] and when rendering lines and characters [CROW78, KAJIYA81]. For the most part, images have been made with the simpler model [CATMULL78, FUCHS79, PITTEWAY81] with varying degrees of success.

Area estimation is most correctly done by calculating a simplified hidden surface algorithm at each affected pixel [CATMULL78, FUCHS79]. However, quite adequate images can be made by simpler approximations.

In order to compute a mini hidden surface algorithm at a pixel, either a "scan-order" algorithm [CATMULL78] or a "cookie-cutter" (polygon subdivision) algorithm [WEILER77] must be used. The scan-order algorithms tend to be complicated and thus hard to implement. The cookie-cutter algorithms have yet to be fully expoited. However, the primary example [WEILER77] is not well suited to complicated images since its computational cost increases with the square of the number of polygons involved.

Many hidden surface algorithms have been inspired by the rapid acceptance of random-access "frame buffers" (bit-map image memories). Relatively simple algorithms can be constructed by sorting the surfaces involved to a "priority" order (closest surfaces have highest priority) and then writing the surfaces to the frame buffer in order. However, when the surfaces are individually scan-converted, there is no way to distinguish whether two surfaces which partially cover the same pixel area both cover the same part of the pixel (overlap), cover different parts of the pixel (abut), or do some of both [figure 11].

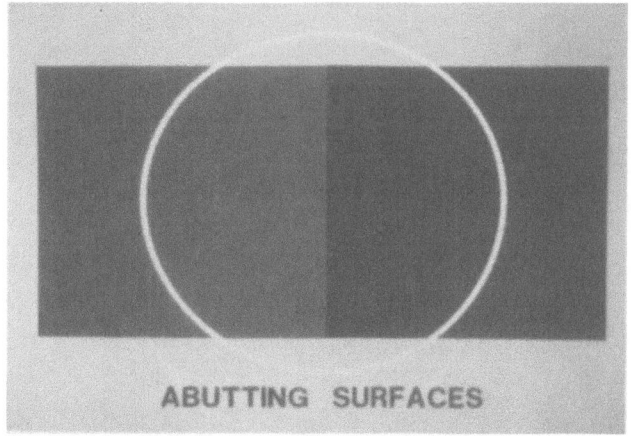

Figure 11a: Abutting surfaces in a pixel

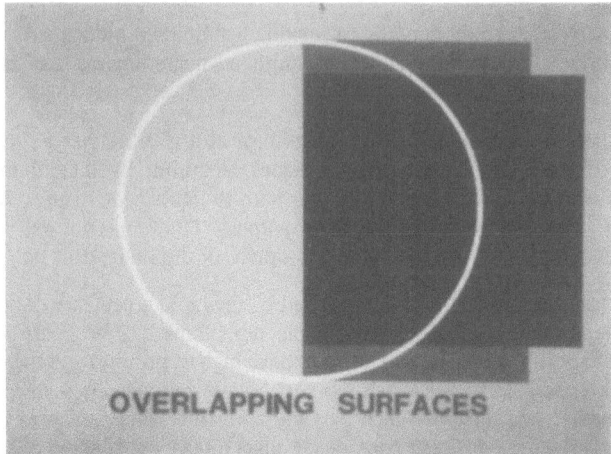

Figure 11b: Overlapping surfaces in a pixel

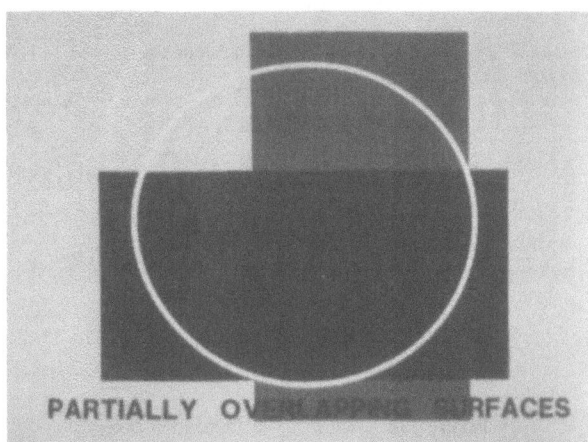

Figure 11c: Partially overlapping surfaces in a pixel

In the simplest case, the "painters algorithm", surfaces are scan converted in reverse priority order. Thus the most distant surface is written to the frame buffer first. Subsequent surfaces are then written over earlier surfaces to hide them. If only part of a pixel is covered by a surface then the proper color for the pixel is a weighted average of the color already stored for the pixel and the color of the surface being scan-converted. The weight for the average must be just the percentage of the pixel area covered by the surface. The painter's algorithm models the situation where all surfaces partially overlap.

Unfortunately a smooth surface modeled by polygons will reveal its seams when rendered with the painter's algorithm [figure 12]. As neighboring polygons are rendered, the first polygon to be rendered will fill pixels along the polygon edge with a color representing a blend of the background color and the polygon color. When the neighboring polygon is rendered, the previously painted pixels along the common edge will be given a color blended from the first blend and the color of the new polygon. Therefore some of the background color will show through along polygon edges.

Figure 12: Seams show through when using the painter's algorithm

A reversed painter's algorithm in which polygons are painted front to back is slightly more successful. Here an additional few bits per pixel can be used to store the "coverage" (the fraction of the pixel's area which is covered by a surface) for each pixel [CARPENTER84]. Now when neighboring polygons are rendered, the first one will give its color to the pixel and store the fraction of the pixel covered. The neighboring polygon now can blend its color for the pixel with the previous color knowing what fraction of the polygon is covered by each. The coverages are then summed. Note that this assumes that surfaces abut. Pixels which are not completely covered are filled in by a background process which blends background color with previously written colors using the coverage information.

This method has problems where backfacing polygons are retained. Since multiple polygons contributing to a pixel are assumed to be abutting, the coverage is overestimated where they overlap instead. This causes edges to be incorrectly represented at contour edges where a backfacing and a frontfacing polygon affect the same pixel [figure 13]. Since backfacing polygons need only be retained where the inside of a surface can be seen, this problem can be avoided much of the time by modeling the inside of an open surface as an additional surface spaced a small distance inside the outer surface. As long as the wall thickness thus defined leaves roughly a pixel width or greater between the inner and outer surfaces, there will be no problems.

Figure 13: Jagged edges due to improper calculation of overlapping surfaces

Happily, many images can be made without worrying much about the distinction between overlapping and abutting surfaces. The defects due to aliasing which draw the eye, are those which produce regular patterns (jagged edges) or those which cause sharp changes from frame to frame (details flashing on and off). If two surfaces which overlap in a pixel are treated as though they abut, the error in shading will be consistent from frame to frame. Therefore, no sharp changes will produced to draw the eye.

In general, it should be somewhat less expensive to use either of the above approaches than to calculate a mini hidden-surface algorithm at every point. The area within the pixel covered by each surface must be calculated no matter what algorithm is used. Additional computation to find what part of which surface covers what other can only add to the cost. However, it should be noted that the cookie-cutter algorithms work in such a way as to allow calculation of only the visible portion of areas partially covering the pixel. So, at least for this purpose, they can be regarded as superior.

Shading and Texture

So far we have concentrated on handling aliasing problems caused along the edges or silhouettes of objects. Modern shading techniques have opened a wealth of new opportunites for aliasing defects by allowing small details to be created independently of surface edges. For example, where highlights are to be calculated on a cylindrical surface, it is possible to produce long, thin, bright features in the image which, if improperly treated, appear jagged [CROW81].

We have made successful images by using higher resolution in highlights, where needed. Since highlights can be calculated independently of the remaining shading components, it is possible to integrate several computations to get a better representation. The problem lies in deciding when such efforts are justified. Without a heuristic for selecting difficult cases, highlights would be very expensive.

We have used a heuristic which estimates local surface curvature based on the surface normal vectors used to calculate the highlights. By using a threshold curvature, highlight resolution can be selectively increased [figure 14]. Unfortunately, we don't have an algorithm for selecting the threshold. The threshold is determined manually, by feedback, a process open to unforseen errors.

Figure 14: Jagged and anti-aliased highlights

The addition of texture to surfaces has allowed some spectacular images to be produced. Very roughly, texture is provided by taking intensities from an image of the texture desired and mapping them onto the surface being scan-converted. Variations on this scheme allow environmental reflections, color patterns, or surface relief to be represented [BLINN76, BLINN78, FEIBUSH80]. However texture can look absolutely horrible if aliasing ruins it [figure 15].

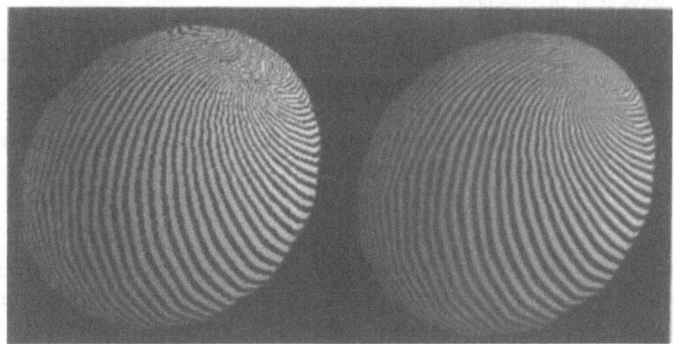

Figure 15: Jagged and anti-aliased texture

Unfortunately, properly calculating the shade of an individual pixel in a textured region involves integrating over a region of the texture image. Since the texture contribution to each pixel representing a textured surface must be calculated, this becomes an expensive proposition. It is especially expensive where there is a significant mismatch in the density of the texture image pixels and the scan-converted pixels. In these cases, large numbers of texture image pixels may have to be integrated when computing the intensity of a scan-converted pixel.

Integrating over large numbers of texture pixels to get a color for display can be avoided by selectively bandlimiting the texture function at such places. Three approaches to this have been published.

(1) A texture function summed from terms with known frequencies can be used [NORTON82]. The texture value can then be looked up using only those terms with frequencies below a computed threshold.

(2) A series of texture images can be precomputed each one with half the resolution of the previous one. The pixels in each image are derived by averaging four pixels from the previous image, yielding at each pixel the average over a rectangular area of a larger image. The texture value is then found by interpolating between values given by 2 adjacent texture images in the series [WILLIAMS83].

(3) A summed representation of the texture can be computed in which each value represents the sum of all texture values below and to the left of the the current one. The summed intensity over a rectangular region of texture can then be recovered quickly. Dividing by the area yields an average value which serves well for the texture value [CROW84].

Catmull and Smith [CATMULL80] have published another approach to texture mapping which decomposes the 2-dimensional mapping process into two passes of a 1-dimensional process. This considerably simplifies the process, so much so that it can be implemented in hardware [AMPEX]. Unfortunately, as of this writing, the 2-pass method has yet to be demonstrated in an all-purpose image generation system. The current use is primarily for manipulatng video images in their entirety.

Temporal Aliasing

In addition to the problems discussed up to this point, there is another form of aliasing which can cause problems in animated imagery. Each frame of an animated sequence is a sample in time of a continuous function. Sampling in time poses the same problems with aliasing as does sampling in space. A frame from a computer-generated sequence has typically represented a single impulse-based sample in time. The effects of the resulting aliasing are perhaps most familiar to us from experiences with conventional motion picture images. The most common effect results in spoked wheels appearing to run backwards (most often seen in "westerns").

In computer-generated animation, the effects of aliasing in time are most noticeable where either some object in the image or else the simulated camera is moving rapidly. In such cases the image appears to hop across the screen in a series of jumps, sometimes creating the illusion of multiple images, rather than moving smoothly. If we apply the lessons learned in spatial anti-aliasing, we can propose to either (1) increase the sample rate, or (2) somehow integrate over time to get a blurred representation of fast-moving objects.

(1) As with spatial anti-aliasing, increasing the sample rate is not the best solution, or even possible, in all cases. The rate at which images are presented cannot be changed under normal circumstances. Standard film presentation provides the viewer with 24 frames per second, each frame flashed twice to limit flicker. Increasing the sampling rate would suggest calculating several frames and averaging them to get each presented frame. Unfortunately, for small numbers of frames, this just leaves the impression of multiple copies of fast-moving objects. Calculating a sufficient number of frames to make this method effective appears to be unnecessarily expensive.

When preparing images for video presentation, the situation is slightly better. All current broadcast standards call for interlaced displays. Generally, one produces a single image for all scan lines at once. However, the sampling rate in time can be effectively doubled by taking advantage of the fact that the odd-numbered lines are presented in between presentations of the even-numbered lines. By calculating half-frames (just the even-numbered or odd-numbered lines) at twice the time rate, temporal aliasing can be greatly diminished.

(2) For several years, researchers in computer animation have been looking for a practical method of presenting objects properly blurred by motion. Early thoughts on the subject were severely hampered by the desire to make images inexpensively enough to be able to afford animation. In recent years, there has been a greater willingness to spend previously incomprehensible amounts of computer time on computer imagery with the result that algorithms for motion blurred imagery are appearing in increasing numbers over the past two years.

Reeves [REEVES83] modeled a class of objects by sets of particles, then blurred fast-moving particles by representing them with a line connecting the extreme positions occupied by the particle during the sample period. Korein and Badler [KOREIN83] implemented a system using blurred discs to represent figures, and proposed a more general algorithm.

Potmesil and Chakravarty [POTMESIL83] used a postprocessing blurring function. Their approach was to take pixels from a rendered portion of an image and blur them after scan conversion. They used a convolution algorithm for doing the blurring which operates by multiplying the frequency-domain versions of the image and the convolution filter. This technique when combined with matting techniques for combining images [CARPENTER84] could be quite effective.

These algorithms for blurring all depend either on modifying the data [REEVES83, KOREIN83] before scan conversion or [POTMESIL83] post-processing the pixels after scan conversion. A more integrated approach was first reported by Cook et al [COOK84]. In this approach, multiple samples are generated at each pixel. Instead of varying just the spatial position of each sample, as is customary for this approach to anti-aliasing, the temporal position of each sample is varied as well. This idea has occurred to others as well who are now publishing their findings [DIPPE85, GRANT85, LEE85, MAX85].

Temporal anti-aliasing is currently a very active area of research. Multiple sample techniques for anti-aliasing can usually be made much more efficient by limiting application of the technique to those places where it is really needed. We will certainly see reports on such techniques explored in upcoming publications.

References

[AMPEX]   --. ADO: Ampex Digital Optics (special effects system for TV studios), Ampex Corporation

[BLINN76]   James F. Blinn, Martin E. Newell. "Texture and Reflection in Computer Generated Images," Communications of the ACM *19* 10. October 1976, pp542-547.

[BLINN78]   James F. Blinn. Computer Display of Curved Surfaces. PhD thesis, University of Utah, December 1978.

[BLINN80]   James F. Blinn, Loren C. Carpenter, Jeffrey M. Lane. "Scan Line Methods for Displaying Parametrically Defined Surfaces." Communications of the ACM *23* 1. January 1980. pp23-34.

[BLOOMENTHAL83]   Jules Bloomenthal. "Edge Inference with Applications to Anti-Aliasing," Computer Graphics (Siggraph '83) *17* 3. July 1983, pp157-162.

[CARPENTER84]   Loren Carpenter. "The A-Buffer, an Anti-Aliased Hidden Surface Method," Computer Graphics (Siggraph '84) *18* 3. July 1984, pp103-108.

[CATMULL78]   Edwin E. Catmull. "A Hidden-Surface Algorithm with Anti-Aliasing," Computer Graphics *12* 3. August 1978.

[CATMULL80]   Edwin E. Catmull, Alvy Ray Smith. "3-D Transformations of Images in Scanline Order," Computer Graphics (Siggraph '80) *14* 3. July 1980, pp270-285.

[COOK84]   Robert L. Cook, Thomas Porter, Loren Carpenter. "Distributed Ray Tracing," Computer Graphics (Siggraph '84) *18* 3. July 1984, 137-145.

[CROW77]   Franklin C. Crow. "The Aliasing Problem in Computer-Generated Shaded Images," Communications of the ACM *20* 11. November 1977, pp799-805.

[CROW78]   Franklin C. Crow. "The Use of Grayscale for Improved Raster Display of Vectors and Characters," Computer Graphics (Siggraph '78) 12 2. July 1978.

[CROW81]   Franklin C. Crow. "A Comparison of Anti-Aliasing Techniques," IEEE Computer Graphics and Applications *1* 1. January 1981.

[CROW84]   Franklin C. Crow. "Summed Area Tables for Texture Mapping," Computer Graphics

(Siggraph '84) *18* 3. July 1984.

[DIPPE85]   Mark A. Z. Dippe, Erling Henry Wold. "Anti-Aliasing Through Stochastic Sampling," Computer Graphics (Siggraph '85) *19* 3. July 1985.

[FEIBUSH80]   Eliot A. Feibush, Robert L. Cook, Marc Levoy. "Synthetic Texturing Using Digital Filters," Computer Graphics (Siggraph '80) *14* 3. July 1980, pp294-301.

[FUCHS79]   Henry Fuchs, Jose Barros. "Efficient Generation of Smooth Line Drawings on Video Displays," Computer Graphics (Siggraph '80) *13* 2. August 1979.

[GRANT85]   Charles W. Grant. "Integrated Analytic Spacial and Temporal Anti-Aliasing for Polyhedra in 4-Space," Computer Graphics (Siggraph '85) *19* 3. July 1985.

[GUPTA81]   Satish Gupta, Robert Sproull. "Filtering Edges for Grey-Scale Displays," Computer Graphics (Siggraph '81) *15* 3. August 1981.

[KAJIYA81]   James T. Kajiya, M. Ullner. "Filtering High Quality Text for Display on Raster Scan Devices," Computer Graphics (Siggraph '81) *15* 3. August 1981.

[KOREIN83]   Jonathan Korein, Norman Badler. "Temporal Anti-Aliasing in Computer Generated Animation," Computer Graphics (Siggraph '83) *17* 3. July 1983, pp377-388.

[LEE85]   Mark E. Lee, Richard E. Redner, Samuel P. Uselton. "Statistically Optimized Sampling for Distributed Ray Tracing," Computer Graphics Computer Graphics (Siggraph '85) *19* 3. July 1985.

[MAX85]   Nelson Max, Douglas M. Lerner. "A Two-and-a-Half-D Motion Blur Algorithm," Computer Graphics (Siggraph '85) *19* 3. July 1985.

[NORTON82]   Alan Norton, Alyn P. Rockwood, Philip T. Skomolski. "Clamping: A Method of Antialiasing Textured Surfaces by Bandwidth Limiting in Object Space," Computer Graphics (Siggraph '82) *16* 3. July 1982..

[OPPENHEIM75]   A. V. Oppenheim, R. W. Schafer. Digital Signal Processing. Prentice-Hall, 1975.

[PITTEWAY80]   M. L. V. Pitteway, D. J. Watkinson. "Bresenham's Algorithm with Grey Scale," Communications of the ACM *23* 11. November 1980, pp625-626.

[POTMESIL83]   Michael Potmesil, Indranil Chakravarty. "Modeling Motion Blur in Computer-Generated Images," Computer Graphics (Siggraph '83) *17* 3. July 1983, 389-399.

[REEVES83]   William T. Reeves. "Particle Systems - A Technique for Modeling a Class of Fuzzy Objects," ACM Transactions on Graphics) *2* 2. April 1983. 91-108.

[TURKOWSKI82]   Kenneth Turkowski. "Anti-Aliasing Through the Use of Coordinate Transformations," Computer Graphics (Siggraph '82) *16* 3. July 1982.

[SUTHERLAND77]   Ivan E. Sutherland, Robert F. Sproull, Robert A. Schumaker. "A Characterization of Ten Hidden-Surface Algorithms," Computing Surveys *6* 1. March 1977, pp1-55.

[WARNOCK80]   John E. Warnock. "The Display of Characters Using Grey-Level Sample Arrays," Computer Graphics (Siggraph '80) 14 3. July 1980, pp302-307.

[WEILER77]   Kevin J. Weiler, Peter A. Atherton. "Hidden-Surface Removal Using Polygon Area Sorting," Computer Graphics (Siggraph '77) *11* 2. July 1977, pp214-222.

[WHITTED82]   J. Turner Whitted. "Processing Requirements for Hidden-Surface Elimination and Realistic Shading," Proceedings, IEEE Spring CompCon February 1982

[WILLIAMS83]   Lance Williams. "Pyramidal Parametrics," Computer Graphics (Siggraph '83) *17* 3. July 1983, pp1-12.

Advanced Image Synthesis – Shading

G. Lorig

INTRODUCTION

Shading is one of those terms which when placed within the
right context can be taken to mean almost anything. For the
purpose of this tutorial, however, I shall use it to denote
the algorithms and processes employed to determine the final
color of a pixel. Covered in this section are such topics as
lighting models, light source models, texture mapping, and
environment mapping. Conspicuously missing, however, is any
discussion of anti-aliasing, since this will be discussed
later in the tutorial.

MATHEMATICAL NOMENCLATURE

M - Matrix

V - Vector (All vectors are assumed to be normalized)

s - Scalar

$A·B$ - Inner product of vectors A and B

Right handed coordinate systems, 350 years of
mathematical tradition couldn't be all wrong!!!!

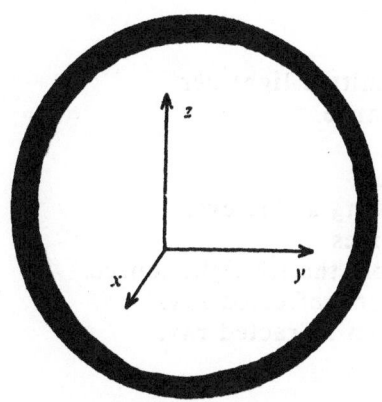
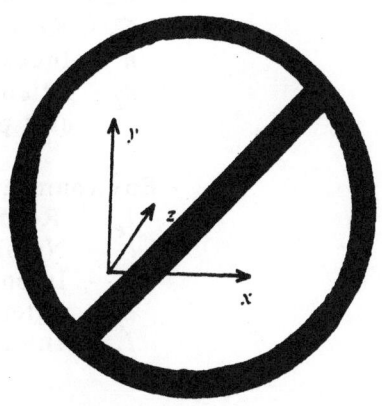

LIGHTING MODELS

The lighting model is the most important yet most often neglected portion of an image synthesis system. It is where the renderer attempts to mimic the interaction of light and surface. The success with which this is accomplished has a profound impact upon the realism of the finished image. Over the past two decades lighting models have undergone a slow evolution becoming increasing complex and realistic. This growth has been due in large part to new rendering techniques, such as ray-tracing which make it possible to more accurately model the phenomena of light and its interaction with objects.

Light models most often consist of some number of pieces, each piece designed to simulate some aspect of light. Below I present one such model, building it up term by term. While many different models exist, this one is fairly representative of those currently in use. The references section of this paper contains a number papers on other lighting models [1][2][3].

Constants and variables used in the lighting model.

- Geometric topology
    - X - Viewing ray from surface to eye.
    - N - Normal to surface at point of interest.
    - L_i - Ray from surface to the ith light source.
    - R - Reflection of viewing ray from surface.
    - T - Refracted viewing ray propagating through solid.
    - d - Length of path through refractive solid.

- Surface characteristics.
    - C_s - Color of surface.
    - k_a - Ambient lighting coefficient.
    - k_d - Diffuse lighting coefficient.
    - k_s - Specular lighting coefficient.
    - e_s - Specular exponent.
    - C_r - Reflective color.
    - C_t - Refractive color.
    - n - Index of refraction.
    - a_t - Attenuation of transmitted light per unit propagation distance.

- Environmental coefficients.
    - I_e - Resultant light arriving at the eye.
    - l - Number of light sources.
    - I_{li} - Intensity of light from the ith light source.
    - I_r - Intensity of light from reflected ray.
    - I_t - Intensity of light from refracted ray.

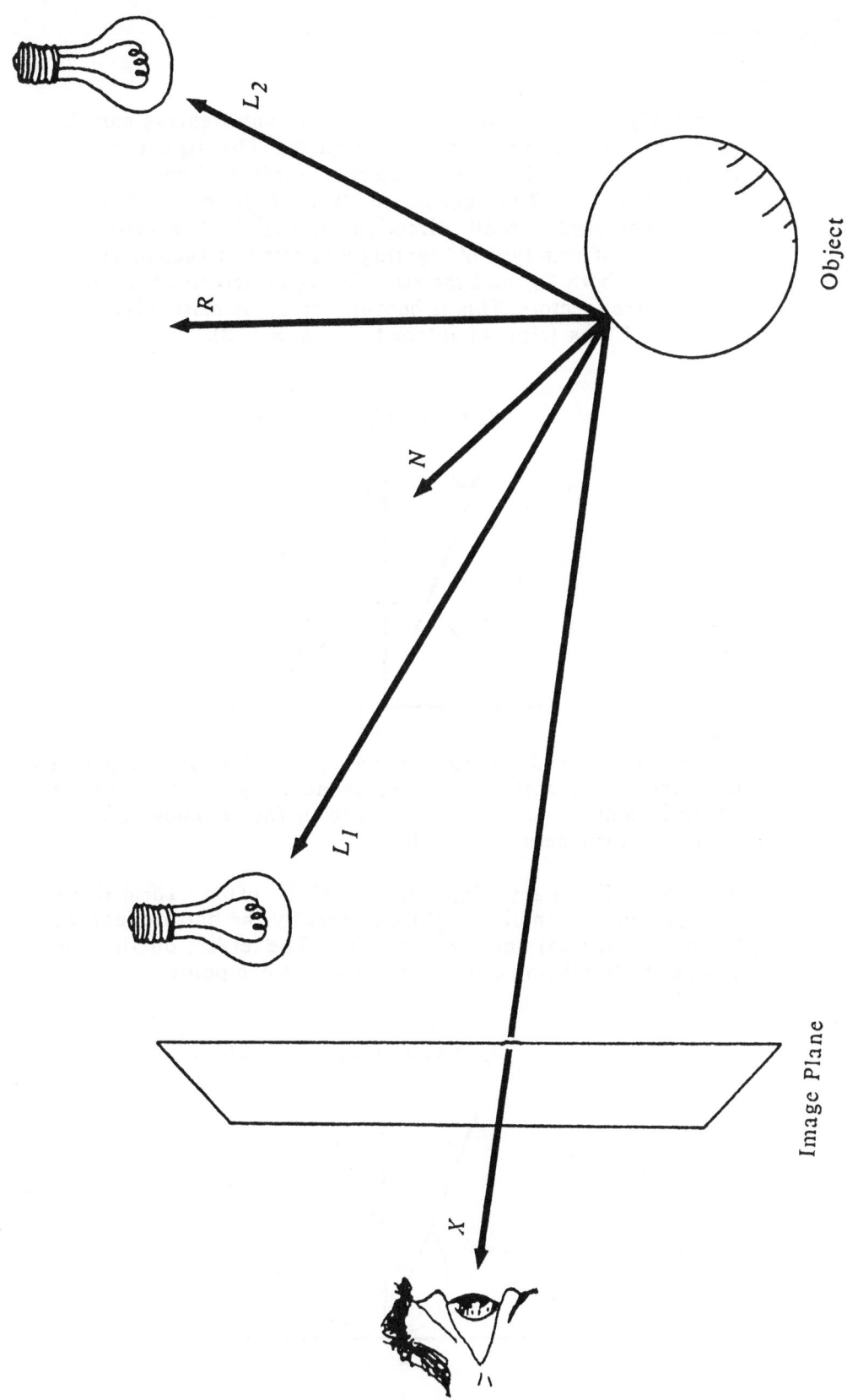

Image Plane

Object

AMBIENT

Invariably the first and simplest term in any lighting models
represents the effects of ambient lighting. This light energy
is sourceless, striking an object's surface from all
directions evenly. The light is, in turn, radiated from the
surface uniformly in all directions. Equation 1 models the
interaction of this type of lighting and some surface of color
C_s. Notice both C_s and the resulting light perceived by the
eye, I_e, are vectors. This is because color is most often
represented as a triple of intensities (e.g. R,G,B).

$$I_e = k_a * C_s \qquad (1)$$

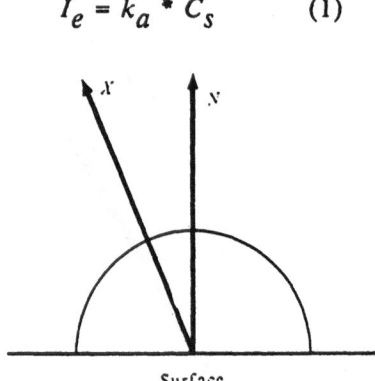

Surface

Notice that the ambient term conveys no information about the
the slope of the surface. Images made using purely ambient
lighting contain no visual cues as to surface topology other
than which surfaces are visible.

A very rudimentary lighting model is often formed by
multiplying the ambient lighting term by the dot-product of
the surface normal and the eye vector. The effect obtained is
equivalent to placing a light source at the eye point.

$$I_e = k_a(N \cdot X)C_s \qquad (2)$$

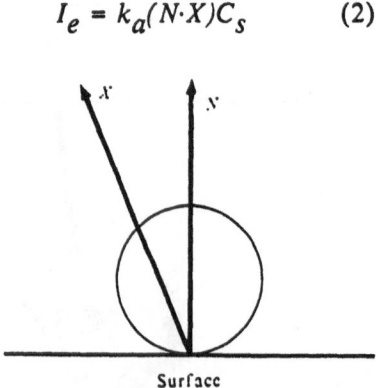

Surface

DIFFUSE

The diffuse lighting term represents light which is emitted from a specific light source, strikes the surface in question, and is then radiated uniformly. As the name implies, diffuse shading is responsible for the more subtle effects of light upon objects. Objects possessing only diffuse lighting attributes appear as if made of a dull smooth plastic. Since multiple light sources may be present within the scene, both this term and the next are summed over the set of all light sources.

$$I_e = k_a C_s + \sum_{i=1}^{l} I_{li}(k_d C_s (N \cdot L_i)) \qquad (3)$$

Ambient   Diffuse

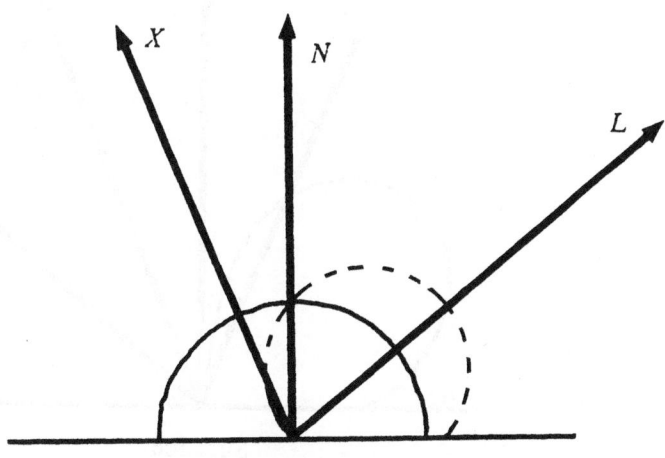

Surface

SPECULAR

The specular lighting component is designed to simulate the reflection of light off of a surface in some distribution about the angle of incidence. This term is responsible for the highlights we associate with glossy surfaces. By increasing the value of the specular exponent, the highlights become smaller and more sharply defined - the surface appears shinier. Notice that the color of this highlight is not controlled by the surface color, but by the reflective color.

$$Ie = k_a C_s + \sum_{i=1}^{l} I_{li}(k_d C_s(N \cdot L_i) + k_s C_r(R \cdot L_i)^{es}) \qquad (4)$$

| Ambient | Diffuse | Specular |

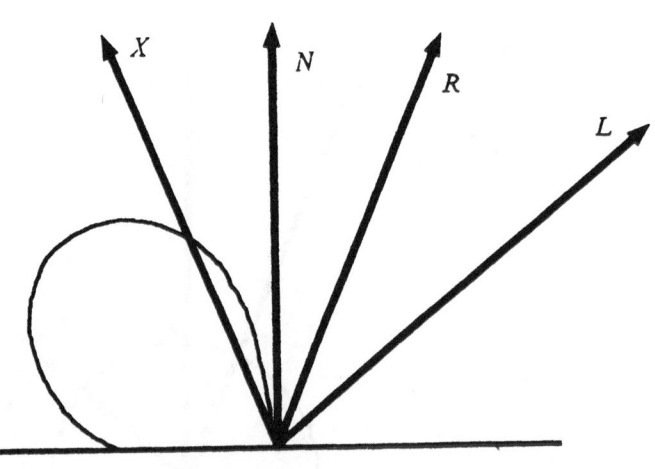

Surface

LIGHT SOURCE CHARACTERISTICS.

Both the specular and diffuse lighting components rely upon two pieces of light source information, the intensity of the emitted light, I_l, and the direction to the light source, L. An easy but half-hearted implementation of light sources involves treating both I_l and L as constant. By holding L fixed throughout object space the resulting effect is of a light source located infinitely far away in the L direction. Since L is invariant large flat objects show no shading changes across their surfaces. A more realistic approach is to represent the light source as a point in object space. This means that each time a point on a surface is to be shaded the vector L must be calculated since it is position dependent. While computationally more expensive the results represent light source placement far more realistically.

By holding I_l constant a light source is modeled as radiating light uniformly in all directions. To simulate flood and wash lights I_l can be made to reflect some directional dependance [4][5]. Equation 5 is a simple example of such a relationship. U is the direction the light source is pointing and k is a constant which controls the distribution of light about that direction. The minus sign in the equation results from L pointing towards the light source instead of away from it.

$$I_l = \frac{(-L \cdot U)^k}{0} \qquad \begin{array}{l} \text{for } L \cdot U \leq 0 \\ \text{else} \end{array} \qquad (5)$$

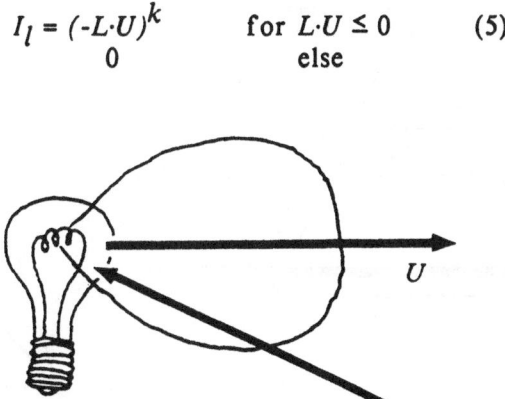

Shadows can be simulated by varying I_l in proportion to the amount of light source visible from the point on the surface being shaded. If the light source were completely obscured, I_l would equal zero and as a result both the specular and diffuse terms would drop out. On the other hand, if no object stood between the surface point and the light source, I_l would equal the unattenuated value of the light source intensity. Because both point and constant direction light sources have no volume and thus occupy no solid angle from the point of view of the point to be shaded, either they will be completely obscured by another object or not at all. This results in sharp distinct shadows composed of only an umbra. Unfortunately, light sources in every day life almost always occupy some finite non-zero volume. As a result the shadows they cast contain both umbra and penumbra regions. The light reaching a point on a surface is equal to the light source intensity integrated over the visible (unobstructed) portion of the light source. Performing this integral is quite messy and very expensive! A common method of avoiding this problem is to model the light source as some number of point light sources [6]. Unfortunately to really do an adequate job of this large numbers of point sources are needed. The extra overhead involved in processing the point sources often makes the use of finite volume light sources rather unappealing. Another approach, well adapted to ray-tracing, involves randomly varying the position of a point light source within the confines of the volume of the finite volume light source [7]. If enough samples of I_l are taken when determining the diffuse and specular lighting components, the average value for I_l will equal that which would have been obtained through integration. This is really nothing more than a Monte Carlo method of determining I_l.

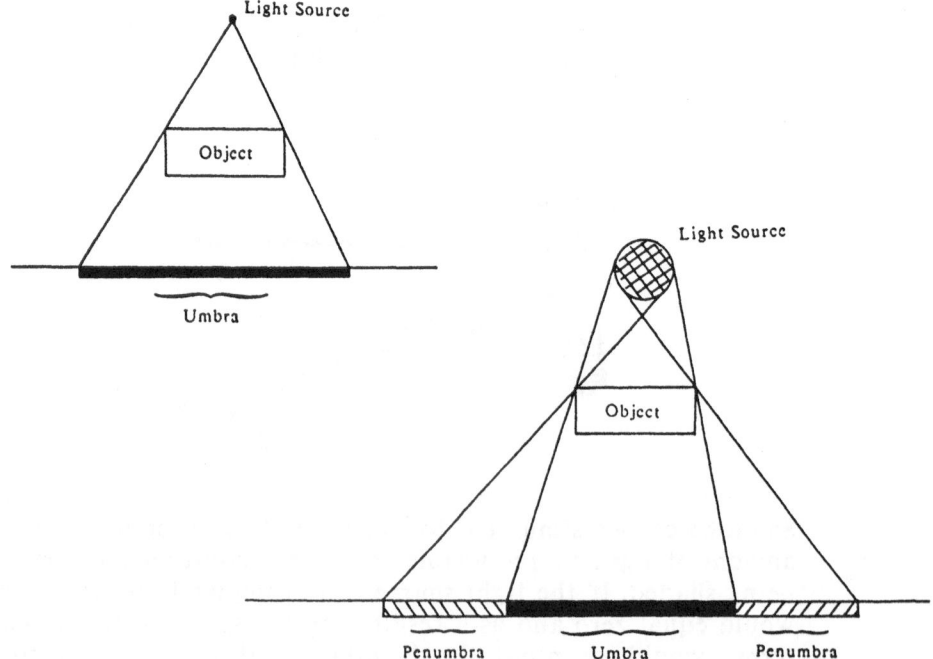

REFLECTED AND REFRACTED LIGHT.

With the advent of ray tracing and other rendering techniques it has become possible to now add to our lighting models a number of secondary lighting effects, most notably reflection and refraction. Given a slowly varying normal vector both, the reflected and refracted images should appear clear and sharp. By inducing small random perturbations in the normal vector such effects as frosted or dull surface can be obtained.

$$Ie = k_a C_s + \sum_{i=1}^{l} I_{li}(k_d C_s (N \cdot L_i) + k_s C_r (R \cdot L_i)^{es})$$

$$+ C_r I_r + C_t I_t (1 - a_t)^d \qquad (6)$$

Reflected   Refracted

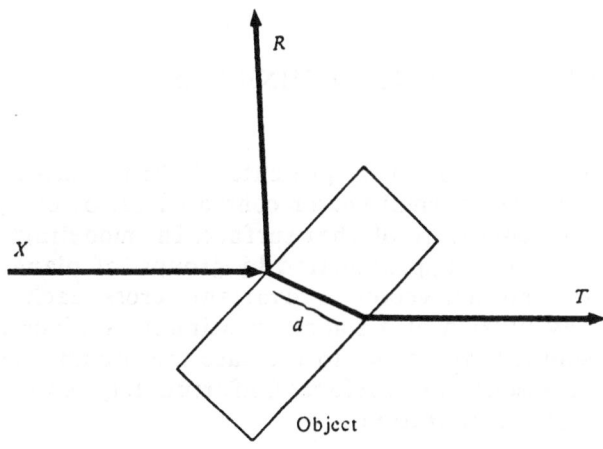

Handy equations for calculating reflected and refracted rays:

$$R = 2(X \cdot N)N - X \qquad (7)$$

$$n = n_1 / n_2 \qquad (8)$$

$$T = -nX - (\sqrt{1. - n^2(1. - (X \cdot N)^2)} - n(X \cdot N))N \qquad (9)$$

CHROMATIC ALIASING.

Most image rendering systems treat color as a three valued vector of intensities, most notably Red, Green, and Blue. This color system has its roots buried in the physiology of color perception. The representation of color in a trichromatic system is basically a form of sampling. While it may be possible to represent any color using this type of system, at least as far as perception is concerned, chromatic aliasing problems arise when manipulation such as those present in lighting models are applied to the color vectors. As with almost any aliasing problem the answer is to take more samples. To minimize chromatic aliasing artifacts the visible spectrum should be divided into more than three regions. Experience indicates that dividing the spectrum into nine regions provides adequate results without increasing the computational time much. The formulas necessary to convert between RGB and the higher resolution color space have proven messy enough to be a deterrent to wide spread use of this system. A discussion of this topic can be found in [2].

SURFACE SMOOTHING TECHNIQUES.

As the previously presented lighting model would suggest, a surface's normal vector controls most of our perception of the true curvature of that surface. In modeling, smooth surfaces are often approximated by groups of planar patches. Because the normal vector is invariant across each of these patches any illusion of a smooth continuous surface is lost. A simple solution would be to increase the number of patches used to represent the surface. Unfortunately more patches means much more computation.

One solution to this problem, known as Gouraud shading [9], involves first calculating the normal vector of each planar facet. Each vertex of each patch is then assigned a normal vector by averaging together the normals of all of the patches sharing that vertex. The color of each vertex is calculated using the averaged normal vectors. The patches are then shaded by interpolating the vertex colors across their surfaces.

Phong shading [10] provides a more realistic yet computationally demanding alternative to Gouraud shading. In this style of shading the normal vector instead of the color is interpolated across the patch. The light model calculation is performed for each pixel using the interpolated normal vector. Because of the nice smooth normal vector field produced by interpolation, far more realistic highlights result. The exponentiation involved in calculating the specular lighting component term tends to be far more sensitive to the behavior of the normal vector.

TEXTURE MAPPING

The phrase "texture mapping" refers to a group of techniques used to systematically alter the characteristics of a surface. By controlling color, reflectivity, and refractivity, complex materials such as wood can be easily and economically simulated. Scene realism can be greatly enhanced without having to increase the complexity of the actual geometry.

Images of either natural or synthetic origin are commonly used as textures. A digitized photograph of a brick wall, for example, can be mapped on to a large box to simulate a bricked area. These mapping images can be thought of as functions in U and V. Given some U and V, a corresponding texture value can be found within the image by treating U and V as the X and Y coordinates of a pixel.

Mathematical functions provide another very useful source of textures. Using Fourier series, a wide range of different effects can be obtained from one simple construct [12]. Stochastic processes in general make wonderfully powerful tools for simulating a wide range of naturally occurring surfaces [13].

The normal vector's control over the perceived slope of a surface makes it an excellent candidate for texture mapping. By perturbing a surface's normal vector in accordance with a map it is possible to create the illusion of surface irregularities or bumps [15]. For this reason this form of mapping is often referred to as "BUMP" mapping. The values used to control the normal perturbations can either be stored as a form of "image", or generated on the fly by some form of mathematical function. Complex structures with very fine surface detail can be modeled using a large crude shape with the finer detail bump mapped on. It should be noted that while this technique provides the appearance of surface detail the actual position of the surface is not altered. For this reason the object's silhouette will always betray it's true shape.

The technique first employed to map a texture onto a surface involved parameterizing the surface in terms of U and V. This U and V was then used either as the input variables into some texture generating function, or as the coordinates of a value within a texture image. The advantage of this method is it's simplicity, most types of surfaces in use are quite easily parameterized making the determination quite fast and painless. Unfortunately, the close relationship between the surface parameterization and the U and V used to determine the texture value makes arbitrary positioning of the texture map upon the surface difficult at best.

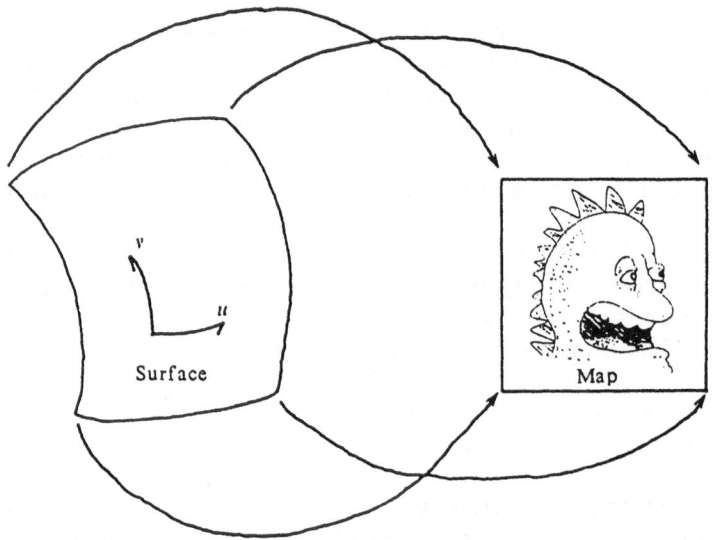

Normal vector intersection mapping places a level of indirection between the surface to be mapped and the map itself. A map template is suspended above the surface to be mapped. The template is a simple, easily parameterized surface such as a rectangle or sphere. The texture value for a particular point on the surface is determined by intersecting the normal vector at that point with the map template. The point of intersection provides a U, V pair to then be used in finding the texture value. Because the map template can be positioned independent of the surface's orientation the map is free of any surface parameterization that may exist and may be positioned arbitrarily. Because of the strong reliance upon the normal vector of the surface, curved surfaces will tend to distort the map in often unpleasant fashions.

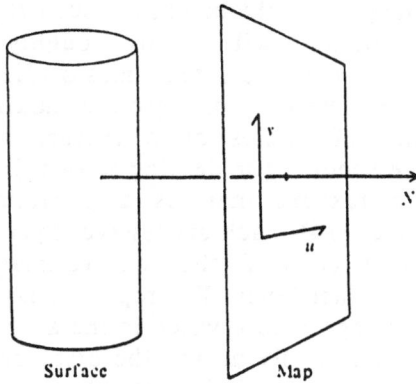

Space- filling texture maps utilize the concept of a mapping template, but in a slightly different manner. The two dimensional mapping template is extruded through space in a direction normal to the map, thus producing a 3-dimensional mapped volume. The texture value at a point on a surface is determined by finding the position of that point within the solid map extrusion. This position can be represented by U,V, and W, where W is the distance along the axis of extrusion. U and V can then be used as the inputs to some mapping function or as the coordinates of a value with in a texture image. Because W provides an added dimension to the map, 3-dimensional textures can also be implemented.

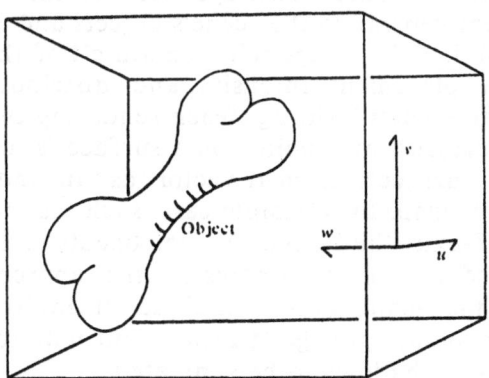

One common problem in texture mapping is that of over and undersampling the mapping image. When a map is of too low a resolution or too close to the eye, the individual pixels in the image become noticeable. If, on the other hand, the mapping image is of too high a resolution or too far away, important details of the map may slip between the samples and disappear. To assure proper sampling results the resolution of the mapping image should be chosen such that in the finished image one pixel of map will occupy roughly one pixel of final image. In animation this is often times difficult. Objects can move from foreground to background making it necessary to store a number of copies of a texture map at varying resolutions. One scheme for dealing with this problem involves representing a texture map as a pyramid of different resolution images [14]. Each successive layer of the pyramid is occupied by a copy of the texture image at half the resolution of the last layer. The top-most layer is occupied by a one pixel image whose value is the average of every pixel in the original image. By noting the distance from the eye to the surface being mapped it is possible to select a level in the pyramid which will yield a texture map at close to the correct resolution. By interpolating between adjacent layers a continuum of texture resolutions can be approximated. This is necessary if animation artifacts caused by jumping between layers are to be avoided.

ENVIRONMENT MAPPING

Simulating the complex lighting environments often found in the real world can be quite difficult and computationally demanding. An interesting alternative to geometrically modeling this environment is to use a texture map to represent the lighting present within a scene. The first step in this process is to construct a fish-eye view of the light sources from a point central to the scene's objects and facing towards the eye point. This image will contain all of the information about light placement, intensity, and distribution needed to describe the scene's lighting. When rendering the final image, the light present at a point on a surface is determined by using the surface's normal vector as an index into the environment map. In a simple case, such as the eye looking down the Z-axis, the X and Y components of the normal vector can be used as the coordinates of the appropriate lighting value in the map. This technique of environment mapping produces astoundingly good results, but will not permit such phenomena as shadows to be simulated.

REFERENCES AND OTHER EXCITING BEDTIME READING.

1. Torrance, K. and Sparrow, E., Theory for Off-Specular Reflection from Roughened Surfaces, J. Opt. Soc. Am., 57(9), pp. 1105-1114, September, 1967.

2. Hall, R. and Greenberg, D., A Testbed for Realistic Image Synthesis. IEEE Computer Graphics and Applications 3, 8 pp. 10-20, November, 1983.

3. Cook, R. and Torrance, K., A Reflectance Model for Computer Graphics, Computer Graphics (SIGGRAPH '81), 15(3), pp. 307-316, August, 1982.

4. Warn, D., Lighting Controls for Synthetic Images, Computer Graphics (SIGGRAPH '83), 17(3), pp. 13-21, July, 1983.

5. Verbeck, C. and Greenberg, D., A Comprehensive Light-Source Description for Computer Graphics, IEEE Computer Graphics and Applications, 4(7), pp. 66-75, July, 1984.

6. Brotman, L. and Badler, N., Generating Soft Shadows with a Depth Buffer Algorithm, IEEE Computer Graphics and Application 4(10), pp. 5-12, October, 1984.

7. Cook, R., Porter, T., and Carpenter, L., Distributed Ray Tracing, Computer Graphics (SIGGRAPH '84), 18(3), pp. 137-145, July, 1984

8. Goral, M., Torrance, K., Greenberg, D., and Battaile, B., Modeling the Interaction of Light Between Diffuse Surfaces, Computer Graphics (SIGGRAPH '84), 18(3), pp.213-222, July, 1984.

9. Gouraud, H., Continuous Shading of Curved Surfaces, IEEE Transactions on Computers, C-20(6), pp. 623-628, June, 1971.

10. Buit-Tuong, Phong, Illumination for Computer-Generated Pictures, Communications of the ACM, 18(6), pp. 311-317, June, 1975.

11. Heckbert, P. and Hanrahan, P., Beam Tracing Polygonal Objects, Computer Graphics (SIGGRAPH '84), 18(3), pp. 119-127, July, 1984.

12. Gardner, G., Simulation of Natural Scenes Using Textured Quadric Surfaces, Computer Graphics (SIGGRAPH '84), 18(3), pp. 11-20, July, 1984.

13. Haruyama, S., and Barsky, B., Using Stochastic Modeling for Texture Generation, IEEE Computer Graphics and Applications 4,3, pp. 7-19, March, 1984.

14. Williams, L., Pyramidal Parametrics, Computer Graphics (SIGGRAPH '83), 17(3), pp. 1-11, July, 1983.

15. Blinn, J., Simulation of Wrinkled Surfaces, Computer Graphics (SIGGRAPH '78), 12(3), pp. 286-292, August, 1978.

Advanced Image Synthesis – Surfaces

F. C. Crow

Introduction

To make realistic, or otherwise interesting, images of objects, it is necessary to find the position and orientation of the surfaces of those objects. To do this, the surfaces must be defined in a way convenient for algorithms which calculate shading from surface orientation, and priority (for determining the visible surfaces) from surface position. We will look first at structures in which to store surface description data, then at geometrical calculations for clipping and intersecting surfaces, then at methods for producing shape descriptions, and finally at algorithms for computing surface priority.

It musty be noted that objects may be described by the surfaces that bound them or by the volume that they occupy. Generally the surface-oriented description has been the more useful for making images while the volume-oriented description has been preferred for many other aspects of computer-aided shape design.

Originally, nearly all synthetic surface imagery was generated from polygonal models. However, more recent images have frequently been made using higher-order surfaces. These surfaces can be classified as either parametric or implicit. A parametric surface is defined by a form such as $F_x(s,t)$, $F_y(s,t)$, $F_z(s,t)$ while an implicit surface takes the form $F(x, y, z)$. Parametric descriptions are used to defined quadratic and cubic "patches" Implicit descriptions have been more frequently used for solids modeling systems and the simplest of the ray-tracing algorithms.

Polygonal surfaces offer the advantage that all elements (in this case the polygons) of the surface are linear. Therefore geometric calculations (e.g. intersection and transformations) are quick and stable. Furthermore, any shape may be approximated arbitrarily closely with an arbitrarily large collection of polygons. However, it does take an enormous number of polygons to approximate a complicated curved surface closely enough that no visible artifacts show when making shaded images. Furthermore, the large number of polygons required for curved surfaces brings all the problems inherent in handling large amounts of data for any purpose.

While the higher-order surface descriptions allow more compact descriptions, they do require more computation. Calculating an intersection between two surfaces can be quite difficult for non-linear surfaces, for example. Furthermore, a solution is not always guaranteed. Iterative techniques for determining the point on a surface through which a ray passes may not converge. Therefore, a bit more sophistication in numerical technique is often required when using higher-order surfaces.

Data Structures

A polygonal surface may be described by just listing, for each polygon in order, the coordinates of the vertices for the polygon. However, since most vertices are shared by more than one polygon, a more compact representation may be had by first listing all the vertices then describing each polygon by listing just the names or numbers (as defined in the vertex list) of the vertices it uses. Enhancements to this general structure which have been used at one time or another include: (1) the surface normal vector for each polygon, (2) the normal vector for each vertex, (3) color, glossiness, or texture at each vertex, (4) pointers to the neighboring polygon across each edge of a polygon, etc.

In a similar vein, non-linear surface patches can be defined by first giving a list of coordinates of control points (the points which determine the surface), then a list of point names which give the control points for each patch in turn. This points-followed-by-polygons structure makes even more sense in the case of nonlinear surfaces since a given point may participate in an even larger number of patches. For example, many bicubic patches require 16 control points in a 4 by 4 mesh. To define a smooth B-spline surface, for example as many as 48 other patches may share at least one control point with a given patch.

Implicit object descriptions are less consistent in form. Generally, a few parameters describe the position and shape of an object. These parameters vary with the nature of the surface type. For example a system in which everything is modeled by ellipsoids [DUFF80] requires only a position, and two vectors giving the size and orientation of the major and minor axes (the orientation of the minor axis could be used to affix texture).

More complex objects, built up from a number of simpler surfaces, require extensions to the above structure. Some objects may be assembled simply as a collection of intersecting surfaces. In these cases, the surface for each subobject may be listed individually. Surface characteristics such as color, glossiness, texture, etc. can be applied to an entire subobject and can, therefore, be entered in a separate structure from that defining the surface shape.

In other cases, smooth joins between subobjects may be desired. In these circumstances, subobjects must share data. A data structure which first lists all vertices or control points, grouped into independently movable parts, and then lists the polygons or patches, works well for such objects. This allows coordinate transformations to be applied to part of the coordinate data (by transforming just one part) causing some surface pieces to change shape while the parts remain smoothly joined together.

The usual reason for assembling a complicated object from many subobjects is to be able to independently move the parts. A transformation, placing each part in its relationship to the whole is generally part of any such structure. In some cases, however, the use of subobjects is a convenience allowing data to be reused in multiple instances. For example, a humanoid figure is usually modeled as symmetric, meaning that the data for one side of the figure can be used (through a mirror transform) to define the whole figure. In such cases the subobject definitions should be separate from the surface definitions. Each subobject should contain data for its surface characteristics (color, etc.), a transformation which positions it relative to the whole object, then a name which identifies the surface data to be used to define the shape.

Geometric Calculations

To render images of surfaces, it is necessary to be able to (1) reposition and reorient them using linear transformations, (2) to clip them to the limits of the field of view, (3) to find their representations in perspective, (4) to calculate intersections between them, and (5) to determine, in some cases, whether parts of the surface are inherently hidden just by their orientation.

For surfaces defined using polygons, all of the above are straightforward. (1) Surfaces may be repositioned and reoriented by applying shape-preserving transformations (rotations, translations, uniform scaling, and mirroring) to the vertex coordinates. (2) Clipping algorithms are also quite straightforward with standard algorithms long available in the literature [NEWMAN73, FOLEY82] although variations continue to pop up [LIANG84, ROGERS84].

Generally, perspective representations for polygons are easily found by first transforming to a space where the eye position lies at the origin and the direction of view lies along the z axis (usually called the eye space) then dividing the x and y coordinates by the z coordinate for each vertex. Of course, a clipping algorithm must be applied to ensure that all such coordinates lie sufficiently far on the positive side of the $z = 0$ plane that no numerical problems will be caused by dividing by extremely small values of z.

Perspective calculations for polygons are slightly less straightforward when depth calculations are to be done in perspective space. In this case, a transform must be supplied for the z-coordinate which preserves planarity in perspective space. For example, if x and y are divided through by z, and z is used intact, planes will be turned into hyperbolas, yielding incorrect intersections. To preserve planarity all coordinates should be divided by the same quantity. A frequently-used technique is to subtract a constant from z before dividing. Usually the constant is the closest allowed depth.

A good way of maintaining planar polygons through perspective and maximizing the depth resolution available in perspective is to use an extra coordinate, w, as follows. Determine the closest and most distant points of interest and clip the data to those confines. Call the closest distance "hither" and the most distant, "yon". Apply the following transformation:

$$x' \leftarrow x;$$
$$y' \leftarrow y;$$
$$z' \leftarrow (z - hither) / (yon\text{-}hither);$$
$$w' \leftarrow z;.$$

Then divide everything through by w':

$$x_p \leftarrow x' / w'; \quad y_p \leftarrow y' / w'; \quad z_p \leftarrow z' / w';.$$

This ensures planarity and limits the values of x_p and y_p to the range $-1.0 - 1.0$ and z_p to the range $0.0 - 1.0$. The depth may then be scaled to fully take advantage of the number of bits available for storage of depth values.

(4) Calculating intersection between polygons is also relatively straightforward. First the plane equation for one of the polygons must be found, then the edges of the other polygon may be clipped against the plane of the first.

The plane equation for a polygon may be found as follows. (1) find a vector normal to the polygon. This can be done by taking the cross product of vectors formed by any three non-colinear vertices of the polygon:

$$[a, b, c] \leftarrow CrossProd[[p_2 - p_1], [p_3 - p_1]];$$

or,

$$a \leftarrow v_1[y]*v_2[z] - v_1[z]*v_2[y];$$
$$b \leftarrow v_1[z]*v_2[x] - v_1[x]*v_2[z];$$
$$c \leftarrow v_1[x]*v_2[y] - v_1[y]*v_2[x];$$

where $v_1 = [p_2 - p_1]$ and $v_2 = [p_3 - p_1]$.

Using the normal vector, the plane equation is given by

$$a*x + b*y + c*z + d = 0.$$

Since a, b, and c are known, d can be found by substituting the coordinates of one of the vertices of the polygon (known to lie in the plane) for x, y, and z in the equation and then solving for d.

Since everything is linear, substituting the coordinates of any vertex not on the plane will yield a value whose magnitude is proportional to the distance of the vertex from the plane. This fact can be used to find the intersection point of an edge which pierces the plane.

Given two points, p_1 and p_2:

$$d_1 \leftarrow a * p_1[x] + b * p_1[y] + c * p_1[z] + d;$$
$$d_2 \leftarrow a * p_2[x] + b * p_2[y] + c * p_2[z] + d;$$

If d1 and d2 have opposite signs then the intersection point, q, is given by:

$$alpha \leftarrow d_1 / (d_1 - d_2)$$
$$q[x] \leftarrow p_1[x] * (1.0 - alpha) + p_2[x] * alpha;$$
$$q[y] \leftarrow p_1[y] * (1.0 - alpha) + p_2[y] * alpha;$$
$$q[z] \leftarrow p_1[z] * (1.0 - alpha) + p_2[z] * alpha;.$$

When these calculations are done using floating point numbers, it cannot always be determined whether or not an edge actually intersects a plane or not. When one or more vertices are very close to the plane, calculations taken in different ways may yield different answers. In many cases, a bias may be added to the calculation to ensure that if an intersection is found, using the bias, then unbiased calculations are guaranteed to find an intersection. However, it is considerably safer to do intersection calculations in the fixed point arithmetic usually used for pixel-based calculations, when possible.

(5) If polygonal data is taken consistently, so that the vertices of a polygon always appear in clockwise order, for example, from the outside of a closed object, then it is possible to determine that some faces are hidden from view just by their orientation. In particular, the z-coordinate of the vector normal to the plane of the polygon in perspective space can be used to make that determination.

If the above formulation for the cross-product is used, the resulting vector should be directed to the outside of the object if a left-handed space, such as the eye space described above and the polygon vertices are taken clockwise as seen from the outside. Therefore, in perspective space, where the z-axis is taken as positive in the direction of depth, a normal vector with a negative z-coordinate implies that a polygon lies on the near side of an object and is therefore potentially visible. On the other hand if the z-coordinate is positive, the polygon is being seen from the inside and must therefore be hidden by a closer portion of the surface.

A similar computation can be done in other spaces such as the eye space or the world coordinate system in which the objects are originally defined. If consistently taken normal vectors point to the outside of an object, then the dot product of the normal vector for a polygon with a vector formed by subtracting the eye position from the position of one of the polygon vertices will be positive if the polygon lies on the far side of the object from the eye position and negative if the polygon lies on the near side.

One problem with determining the plane of a polygon is that the vertices may not always lie in a plane, where there are more than three vertices. This can cause a number of problems. If polygons found to be on the far side of objects are ignored, then visible parts of an object will be missing where

nonplanar polygons are incorrectly determined to be entirely on the far side. A simple solution for this is to always divide larger polygons down into triangles. Another approach is to evaluate the normal at all vertices and only ignore those polygons found to be consistently on the far side. If non-planar polygons are allowed, however, the scan conversion algorithms must be robust enough to handle them properly.

For non-linear surfaces the above calculations are sometimes useful and sometimes inapplicable or impossible. (1) The same transformations which can be used to manipulate polygonal objects can be applied to the position and orientation parameters of non-linear surfaces. (2) Clipping algorithms, on the other hand, pose more of a problem.

Most non-linear surface formulations do not include ways of describing surfaces composed of a nonlinear surface clipped by a plane. Therefore clipping algorithms for such surfaces must operate in two places. First, a bounding volume or convex hull can usually be found for a non-linear surface. The bounding volume is used to determine whether the surface lies totally within or totally outside the field of view. If neither of these conditions holds then the surface must be treated by a later process.

The later process is usually intimately entangled with the rendering, or scan conversion, process. As pixels are computed they may be scissored (ignored if they are found to be outside the limits of the display). On the other hand, many rendering techniques use a subdivision technique for non-linear surfaces. Here, the surface fragments need only be checked after each subdivision to determine whether the smaller bounding volumes lie inside or outside the field of view. If the determination cannot be made then the subdivision process must continue. Subdivision can terminate when the resulting surface covers a pixel or less, or when it can be adequately approximated by a polygon.

(3) Finding the perspective representations of nonlinear surfaces is less straightforward than it is for polygons. While some formulations, such as rational cubics, are valid under perspective transformations, most are not. In the latter cases one can either evaluate the surface at intervals and interpolate between them or use iterative techniques to determine the surface point which transforms to a given pixel [BLINN80].

(4) Finding intersections between nonlinear surfaces poses problems similar to those of clipping and the solutions are similar. When making an image, if the actual edge of intersection is not important but

only its visual representation, the intersection technique often falls out naturally as a byproduct of the scan conversion process. If two surfaces are scan converted together, they can be compared, pixel by pixel, and the frontmost one determined. The apparent edge of intersection, while never calculated, is quite clear in the image.

When the edge of intersection is needed to greater precision or required for other purposes, it can sometimes be calculated directly by solving systems of equations. More often, though, a subdivision process is used to iteratively calculate the edge. Since the subdivision does not proceed nicely along the edge of intersection, the trickiest part of such an algorithm often comes in the process of assembling the line segments resulting from the subdivision process [CARLSON80, THOMAS84].

(5) It is considerably more difficult to determine whether a nonlinear surface is hidden by virtue of its orientation. In many cases, such as in systems where spheres or ellipsoids are the primitive elements [MAX79, KNOWLTON77, PORTER78, DUFF80], the notion is meaningless. In other cases, such as bicubic Bezier or B-spline patches, the convex hull may be found and a determination made based on the polygons thus formed. This subject has been generally ignored in the literature.

Getting the Shape Data

Before one can synthesize three-dimensional imagery, one must synthesize three-dimensional surface models to represent. Much effort has been given to this subject under the rubric of Computer Aided Design. However, surfaces which are produced strictly for the purposes of display can be generated with fewer constraints. The surfaces need not be physically realizable, for instance.

One of the problems of early workers in synthetic imagery was that of coming up with interesting shapes to display. Most early work used shapes either made up by hand or digitized from existing objects. Objects could be digitized using standard machinists tools for measuring heights and displacements from a vertical plane. However, such efforts are tedious enough that many inventive techniques for automating the capture of three-dimensional data were spawned.

A good deal of work went into photogrammetric techniques for recovering three-dimensional data. In the simplest mode, orthographic (front, top, side) views of an object can be photographed and then placed on a digitizing tablet. By being exacting about measuring multiple views of a point on the surface at the same time. Three-dimensional information can be recovered. If the position of certain objects in the photographs is known in advance, the multiple views need not be orthographic [SUTHERLAND74].

Mechanical digitizers have been made which use various angular and linear measuring techniques to determine the position of the tip of a probe. Some of these devices have even been offered commercially. However, it has been difficult to get adequate accuracy by such means, so perhaps greater efforts have gone to electronic measuring techniques.

Devices which measure the time lapse between stimulation of a transducer and the arrival time of the sound generated have been produced commercially. An set of microphones can be carefully arrayed to sense the arrival of a sound with special characteristics. Both ultrasonic and spark generators have been used to produce the sound. A few straightforward geometric calculations to convert the straight line distances from the sound source to three-dimensional coordinates are needed. The main potential difficulty with techniques using sound is interference from ambient noise. Use of unusual sounds has kept this problem to a minimum, however.

Another approach to three-dimensional digitization has been to measure the incoming angle of a light beam. If a collection of pinpoint light sources, LEDs for example, can be made to turn on and off in sequence, then a sequence of measurements of the location of each individual light can be made. If this process can be made to run fast enough, natural motion can be measured by hanging the lights on a moving person or other object of interest. The lights must be considerably brighter than the background for this to work. Either specially-prepared black rooms (which are difficult to see in) or special light frequencies (such as infrared) are generally necessary.

Linear CCD sensor arrays offer a natural way of measuring light angles, a slit can be used to catch the light and direct it onto a limited number of cells or a knifedge can be placed in front of the array putting some portion of the cells in shadow. Each array provides one dimension. If the arrays are arranged orthogonally, all three dimensions can be measured. Extra sensors can be placed strategically to limit the problems caused by lights which become hidden by other parts of the body being measured.

It is also possible, and increasingly practical, to use existing video technology and image processing techniques to do position tracking. Either light sources or very efficient reflectors can be used to produce bright spots in a video image which can then be digitized and measured. Two or more camera-digitizer units can be set up to measure more than two dimensions. As prices for video cameras and digitizers drop and speeds of image processing equipment increase, standard equipment of this sort will probably prove more practical than specialized devices just for three-dimensional position measurement.

Of course much of what is interesting about synthetic imagery is the ability to represent surfaces that don't or can't exist. Three-dimensional digitization is of little interest in these cases. Many surfaces of interest are generated from mathematical models. In these cases the surface definition is implicit. However most shapes are the product of human imagination and don't have a straightforward algebraic expression.

Many shapes have been generated very laboriously by hand, sketching a design out on graph paper and then recording a sufficient collection of points from the paper. However, interactive computer aids for accomplishing the same ends can yield useable data much more quickly, although usually with some limitations.

A number of systems have been built which use a set of primitive shapes (cube, sphere, cylinder, etc.) as building block from which to assemble more complicated objects. The limitations of such a system lie in the limited set of primitive objects. It would be a very time-consuming task to assemble a spherical shape from a lot of little cubes, to make a somewhat far-fetched example. However, such systems usually allow the primitive shapes to be used as negative volumes as well as positive expanding the realm of easily-realized shapes.

Many shapes are very easily generated algorithmically. Surfaces of revolution, for example, require only the input of a profile which can be easily sketched interactively. Prisms can easily be made by duplicating an interactively sketched outline and connecting the original and duplicate by polygonal edges. Tubular shapes can be generated from a space curve fleshed out to a constant or varying diameter. A generalization of the surface of revolution which allows different profiles at different positions around the axis and also allows non circular sections at different positions along the axis can be a powerful tool.

The above shapes all have a limitation in that it is hard to represent protruding portions or holes (eg. a handle). To assemble more complicated objects from the relatively simple set of shapes available, a geometric editor is a good thing to have. A geometric editor allows shapes to be edited by providing a number of ways of combining and modifying objects. For example an object may be clipped against a plane and then closed by constructing a capping polygon over the clipped part.

There are many interesting problems in geometric editors which are still the subject of investigation. For example, combining nonlinear surfaces remains difficult, especially where the join between the surfaces has to meet some criterion of smoothness. Other interesting problems arise out of applying constraints to a situation, requiring an object to be tangent to another or contained within another, for example.

A small collection of algorithmic shape generators combined with a geometric editor allowing shapes to be combined and re-used, generally can produce enough shapes to fit the needs of commercial houses making a business of computer graphics. However, any such system limits the scope of one's imagination by making some things much easier than others. Artistic applications of computer imagery may be excessively hampered by the use of such aids.

So far it has been assumed that the modeler is interested in specifying every last detail of the shape. This isn't always the case. Recent efforts in terrain modeling, for example have endeavored to give just the barest description of the terrain and then let a stochastic process fill in the details [MANDELBROT77, FOURNIER82]. Certainly when creating very complex imagery, it is likely that not every last detail is crucial. In those cases a process may as well fill in the details with something of the right character. There should be a good deal more activity along this line of reasoning in the future.

Computing Surface Priority

A major problem in rendering synthetic imagery lies in determining which surface should be rendered at a given pixel, the heavily-worked "hidden-surface" problem. In fact many think it should be called the "visible surface" problem since the result of interest is the visible surface rather than the potentially many surfaces hidden by the visible one. In any event the problem is to find, for each pixel in an image which surface, if any, is closest to the eye position and thus obscures the others. Of course in the case of transparent surfaces, the problem is to order the surfaces so the proper blend of surface colors may be calculated. We speak of determining surface "priority" to decide which surfaces should obscure which others.

A crude classification of surface priority ordering algorithms can be based on how often the priority is computed. (1) Some algorithms compute the priority at every pixel (or even more often for some anti-aliasing schemes). (2) Other algorithms organize the data so that the priority need only be calculated at those points along a scan line where a surface begins or ends, a "scan segment". (3) Still other algorithms base the ordering on an entire surface element, a polygon or nonlinear patch.

The simplest algorithms are those which determine priority at each pixel. A commonly used technique since memory has become relatively inexpensive is to use the "depth buffer". A large section of memory is set aside for the purpose of storing the depth of the closest surface at each pixel. Between 16 and 32 bits are usually employed for storing a depth. If images are being made using 768 lines of 1024 pixels each then 1.5 to 3 megabytes of storage are needed for the depth information. If devoting that much memory is no problem then the depth buffer is a simple approach.

Each surface is scan converted by whatever means is best suited to produce the color and a consistent depth measure at each affected pixel. This has the advantage that completely different algorithms may be used for scan converting, say, bicubic patches or ellipsoids than are used for scan converting polygons, as long as the depth measures are consistent. As each surface is reduced to pixels, the depth at each pixel is stored in the depth memory ("depth buffer" or "z-buffer"). Then when a later surface is scan converted, the depths thus calculated may be compared with the depths stored earlier to determine which surface is obscured. If the older surface is obscured then the depth and color of the newer surface is stored.

The depth buffer has the advantage of simplicity. However, some restrictions must be accepted. As mentioned above, transparent surfaces must be properly ordered to calculate the resulting shade. Since a depth buffer guarantees only that the topmost surface will be found, it is inadequate for the representation of transparency. Also, since there is normally no information available to compute the effect of partially covered pixels, anti-aliasing is difficult using depth buffers.

Another popular algorithm which computes the priority order at each pixel individually is the ray-tracing algorithm [GOLDSTEIN71, WHITTED80]. Here a ray is traced from the eye position through a virtual pixel position in the world coordinate system and all surfaces intersecting the ray are ordered. Ray tracing allows spectacular shading effects since secondary rays may be traced to calculate reflections, refraction etc. However, doing the ray calculation anew for each pixel is very expensive.

Frequently, the information which determines the shade at a given pixel is nearly identical to that which determines the shade at its neighbors. Algorithms can be made to run more efficiently when they can take advantage of that fact. Many early hidden surface algorithms were designed to produce the image in scan-order [WYLIE67, BOUKNIGHT70, WATKINS70] for just this reason. Once it is determined which surface is closest a some point along a scan line, then the same surface will remain closest for the remainder of its extent along that scan line, if there are no surface intersections. The early algorithms either did not allow intersections or developed clever techniques for quickly finding out when there were not any. Since intersections tend to be rare, except in contrived circumstances, a quick test for intersections gains more performance than a fast way of calculating them.

The algorithms which determine priority on a scan segment basis form the second category. They are generally those known as "scan-order" algorithms. These algorithms work by assembling the information on all surfaces affecting a given pixel and then calculating the shade of the pixel with full knowledge. This has the advantage of providing all the information needed for anti-aliasing and calculating transparency and other shading effects. On the other hand, since all information must be present at each pixel as the image is scanned, rather elaborate (and large) data structures must be maintained throughout the process, causing a large bookkeeping overhead. The necessity to maintain these structures also limits the complexity of the image that can be made to that for which the data structures can be stored at one time.

Generally, scan order algorithms work something like the following. First all surface elements are ordered by their order of appearance from top to bottom on the image. Since, the order can only be determined to the vertical resolution of the image, very quick sorting techniques are available for this step [SUTHERLAND77]. An array of bucket structures can be declared, each of which represents a scan line and holds a pointer to a surface element and a pointer to an overflow area where pointers to additional surface elements first appearing on the same scan line may be stored. One pass through the data fills the bucket structure. A second pass made as the image is being generated. All surface elements which first appear on the scan line currently being computed can be quickly recovered and merged with the surface elements already in use.

Once all surface elements affecting a given scan line are assembled, they can be ordered with respect to their first appearance on the scan line proceeding from left to right. This order can then be traversed as the scan line is generated, keeping a list of surfaces which lie under each scan segment in turn.

The key to efficiency in such an algorithm lies in developing incremental forms for all the surface elements. A polygon edge would be described by its intersection point with the current scan line and the increment which yields its position on the next scan line, for example. As the calculation proceeds down the image all that is necessary to get all the information for the next scan line is a series of additions, plus the calculations for merging new surfaces and discarding spent ones.

There are several advantages to this kind of algorithm. There is no image memory required (this has become less important recently). For images the data structures for which will fit in memory, the growth in computation increases roughly linearly with the growth in the number of surface elements. all information is available at a pixel, making aliasing and transparency fully solvable.

The disadvantages come in the complexity of the algorithm. It is difficult to manage all the incremental forms and keep track of everything. Most algorithms are built so that intersecting surfaces cause significantly greater computational load. Most importantly, the complexity of images is limited by the amount of data that can be effectively utilitized by a single process. Without virtual memory, this is a major problem. With virtual memory, it becomes a problem of the number of memory pages which must be touched in a given amount of time.

Extensions to the scan-order algorithms have achieved greater efficiency by noting that one scan line is often very similar to the next. In particular if no new surface elements enter over a span of scan lines, then scan segments spanned by a single surface element can be expanded to trapezoids over several scan lines [SECHREST81].

Algorithms which determine priority for an entire surface element at once form the third category. These are often called "priority order" algorithms. These algorithms try to order the surface elements and then render them in order, either most distant to least distant or vice versa. There are several advantages to this approach. The surface element order is very easy to determine for a large class of objects. Once the order is determined, each element may be written to the screen independently in a "painter's algorithm" order, each one overwriting whatever lay underneath it. Thus the visible surface is just the last one written at any given pixel.

If surfaces can be characterized as being non intersecting, having roughly uniform sized surface elements, and all being reasonably distant from the eye position, then a very simple ordering algorithm can be used. It turns out that objects made of surfaces obeying these restrictions can be ordered by a bucket sort technique similar to that described for the scan-order algorithms. In this case the buckets are arrayed in depth rather than height.

Given the restrictions just mentioned, any two surface elements which sort to the same bucket are guaranteed to belong to the same surface and to be abutting on that surface or else substantially separated in the image. Therefore, surfaces close in depth will need no further sorting [CROW82]. This is a rather crude way of doing things, but it is very efficient and works well for a very large class of images when it is necessary to produce images economically.

More elaborate sorting techniques come in many forms. One class of priority sort algorithms is best exemplified by the algorithm of Newell, Newell, and Sancha [NEWELL72]. This style of algorithm first sorts all surface elements by depth, then tries to separate elements which overlap in depth by testing for overlap in the image. Elements which overlap both on the image and in depth are subjected to further separation tests. An attempt is made to pass a plane between the elements, for example. Failing that, an intersection between the two is found, and one of them is divided. The end result is an ordered set of surface elements which may then be rendered in order.

Some interesting subtleties pop up in such algorithms. One is the problem of cyclically obscuring surface elements. Element A partially obscures element B which in turn partially obscures element C. However element C partially obscures element A. When there is a large set of elements involved, such as in a model of a turbine, some extra steps must be taken to ensure that the ordering process doesn't continue forever. Newell, Newell and Sancha fixed this problem by tagging elements whose order had been determined after finding them to overlap both on the image and in depth. If a later element violated the order of tagged elements then that element was split to resolve the ambiguity.

Some disadvantages to priority algorithms lie in the necessity of doing comparisons between surface elements in order to do the sort. This introduces a tendency toward computational cost related to the square of the number of surface elements. This can be ameliorated by several techniques. One such technique is to use a hierarchical sort, first sorting clusters of objects, then objects, then surface elements within an object. As long as the number of surface elements which must be compared is small, the computational growth law of the sort algorithm is less important.

Where static environments (strictly nonmoving objects) are being rendered, priority can be determined for use from many different views. Early flight simulator architectures used such an organization [SUTHERLAND77] and recent work [FUCHS80] has revisited the issue.

Static prioritization operates on two levels. At one level, many objects, in particular convex polyhedra, have static priority. In convex polyhedra all faces have equal priority if faces on the far side of the object are discarded. Therefore the priority in independent of position. At another level, the environment can be divided into regions where the priority is constant. A tree structure can be constructed which divides space and imposes a priority on the data. The priority order for any given position is a matter of walking the tree in the proper order. The tree walking order is given by finding the cell into which the observer position falls [FUCHS80].

Priority algorithms lie between the depth buffer algorithm and the scan-order algorithms in the ability to handle anti-aliasing and transparency. Transparency is no problem since the surfaces are ordered. However, anti-aliasing causes some problems. An edge can be properly blended to the background but there is no way to determine how surfaces interact within a pixel.

The various advantages and disadvantages of the different types of algorithm lead one to think about hybrid algorithms which can offer the best of all worlds. A number of people have combined the depth buffer notion with the scan-order algorithm by using a single scan line depth buffer. This retains much of the simplicity of the depth buffer algorithm while not requiring the immense amounts of memory of a full depth buffer.

A number of systems have used matting processes to combine partial images. This allows simpler images to be made representing, say, the foreground, the mid-range, and the background. These partial images can then be combined since they have a known priority. If a static background is used with an animated foreground, then clearly the background need be computed only once. The newly computed foreground image can then be combined with the background anew with each frame.

One notion which has arisen over and over is the idea that if you have specialized data, then the most efficient way to render it is with a specialized algorithm. There have been many algorithms geared the presentation of only spheres [KNOWLTON77, MAX79] or quadric surfaces [GOLDSTEIN71] or other special surfaces [MAX81].

The logical extension of this idea was proposed by Newell [NEWELL75] and partially implemented by Crow [CROW82] and Whitted [WHITTED81]. That idea is to let each object in an image render itself. That is, let the object carry with it the procedure for rendering it (or at least the procedure's name). Then each object can be rendered by a procedure tailored to its characteristics. The practical difficulty with this approach is that it is just too hard to write lots of little specialized rendering algorithms. However the general approach has a lot of utility for environments with a small number of different surface types.

References

[BLINN80]   James F. Blinn, Loren C. Carpenter, Jeffrey M. Lane. "Scan Line Methods for Displaying Parametrically Defined Surfaces," *Communications of the ACM 23* 1. January 1980, pp23-34.

[BOUKNIGHT70]   W. Jack Bouknight. "A Procedure for Generation of Three-D Half-Toned Computer Graphics Representations," *Communications of the ACM 13* 9, September 1970, pp527-536.,

[CARLSON80]   Wayne E. Carlson. "An Algorithm and Data Structure for 3D Object Synthesis Using Surface Patch Intersections," *Computer Graphics 16* 3, July 1982, pp255-263.,

[CROW82]   Franklin C. Crow. "A More Flexible Image Generation Environment," *Computer Graphics 16* 3, July 1982.,

[DUFF80]   Tom Duff. "The Soid and Roid Manual," New York Institue of Technology, Sept. 1980.

[FOLEY82]   J. D. Foley, Andries Van Dam. "Fundamentals of Interactive Computer Graphics," Addison-Wesley, Reading Mass., 1982.

[FOURNIER82]   Alain Fournier, Don Fussell, Loren Carpenter. "Computer Rendering of Stochastic Models," *Communications of the ACM 25* 6, June 1982, pp371-384.

[FUCHS80]   Henry Fuchs, Zvi M. Kedem, Bruce F. Naylor. "On Visible Surface Generation by A Priori Tree Structures," *Computer Graphics 14* 3, July 1980, pp124-133.

[GOLDSTEIN71]   E. Goldstein, R. Nagle. "3D Visual Simulation," *Simulation 16* 1, January 1971, pp25-31.

[KNOWLTON77]   Kenneth C. Knowlton, Lorinda Cherry. "ATOMS-A Three-D Opaque Molecule System for Color Pictures of Space-Filling or Ball-and-Stick Models," *Computers & Chemistry 1* 3, 1977, pp161-166.

[LIANG84]   You-Dong Liang, Brian Barsky.   "An Analysis and Algorithm for Polygon Clipping," *Communications of the ACM 26* 11, Nov. 1983, pp868-877.

[MANDELBROT77]   Benoit B. Mandelbrot. *Fractals - Form, Chance, and Dimension,* W.H. Freeman, San Francisco, 1977.

[MAX79]   Nelson L. Max. "AtomLLL: Atoms with Shading and Highlights," *Computer Graphics 13* 2, August 1979, pp165-173.

[MAX81]   Nelson L. Max. "Vectorized Procedural Models for Natural Terrains: Waves and Islands in the Sunset," *Computer Graphics 15* 2, August 1981, pp317-324.

[NEWELL72]   Martin E. Newell, Richard G. Newell, Tom L. Sancha. "A New Approach to the Shaded Picture Problem," *Proc. ACM National Conference,* August 1972, pp443-450.

[NEWELL75]   Martin E. Newell. "The Utilization of Procedural Models in Digital Image Synthesis," Ph.D. Thesis, University of Utah, Salt Lake City, UTEC SCc-76-218, 1975.

[NEWMAN73]   William M. Newman, Robert F. Sproull. "Principles of Interactive Computer Graphics," McGraw-Hill, New York, 1973.

[PORTER78]   Thomas Porter. "Spherical Shading," *Computer Graphics 12* 3, August 1978, pp282-285.

[ROGERS84]   David F. Rogers, Linda M. Ryback.   "On an Efficient General Line-Clpping Algorithm," *IEEE Computer Graphics and Applications 5* 1, January 1985, pp82-86.

[SECHREST81]   Stuart Sechrest, Donald P. Greenberg.   "A Visible Polygon Reconstruction Algorithm," *Computer Graphics 15* 3, August 1981, pp17-27.

[SUTHERLAND74]   Ivan E. Sutherland. "Three Dimensional Data Input by Tablet," *Proc. IEEE 62* 4, April 1974, pp193-204.

[SUTHERLAND77]   Ivan E. Sutherland, Robert F. Sproull, Robert A. Schumaker. "A Characterization of Ten Hidden-Surface Algorithms," *Computing Surveys 6* 1, March 1977, pp1-55.

[THOMAS84]   Spencer W. Thomas. "Modelling Volumes Bounded by B-Spline Surfaces," PhD Thesis, University of Utah, 1984.

[WATKINS70]   Gary S. Watkins. "A Real-Time Visible Surface Algorithm," Ph.D. thesis, U. of Utah, Salt Lake City, UTEC-CSc-70-101, June 1970.

[WHITTED80]   J. Turner Whitted.   "An Improved Illumination Model for Shaded Display," *Communications of the ACM 23* 6, June 1980, pp343-349.

[WHITTED81]   Turner Whitted, David Weimer. "A Software Test-Bed for the Development of 3-D Raster Graphics Systems," *Computer Graphics 15* 3, August 1981.

Computer-Assisted Animation – An Overview

P. Baudelaire and M. Gangnet

TABLE OF CONTENTS

INTRODUCTION

Above all, animation is the art of movement.
The accomplished animator can bring life to
just about anything - a series of drawings or a
tin can. (from [LAY 79].)

There is an amazing variety of techniques for creating
animation. Among this panoply, computer animation can be
looked upon, both as a totally new technique in its own
right and as a new way for producing conventional
animation such as cartoons. As a *new technique*, it is
explored for its strengths, its specific styles and its
limitations; as a *production tool* it is evaluated for its
efficiency, productivity and aptitude at producing
"usual" animation.

This ambivalence has puzzled and continues to intrigue
practitionners of computer-assisted animation, whether
interested in research or production. This interrogation
is compounded by the duality of the discipline: few
animators are computer scientists and few computer
scientists have been trained as animators. Computer
scientists involved in computer animation may have
sometimes underestimated the subtlety of the animation
craft and the complexity of the animation trade, while
overestimating the power of processors and algorithms.
Similarly, animators may have had difficulties assessing
the strenghts and limits of the computer process in
proper relation with the aesthetic and economic needs of
their industry, as well as sorting out computer
developments applicable to animation production from
purely experimental and research work.

Nonetheless, computer animation has significantly evolved
since the pioneering days of John Whitney, Stan
VanDerBeek, Lillian Schwartz, Ken Knowlton and Peter
Foldes in the late 1960's. A variety of computer tools
and applications have been demonstrated. Reels and reels
of animated films have been produced with computer
assistance. Animation studios have been equipped with
computer production systems. New frontiers are being
explored, such as 3D animation.

This tutorial presents an overview of computer-aided
animation tools, techniques and systems in the mid 80's.
It starts with a quick review of conventional animation -
a prerequisite since computer techniques are in most
cases intertwined with traditional methods.

1. CONVENTIONAL ANIMATION

1.1 ANIMATION TECHNIQUES

Animation techniques are numerous, as the following list suggests:

o Animating objects.
o Time-lapse and pixilation.
o Animating still images: kinestasis and collage.
o Sand and paint-on-glass.
o Cutout and silhouette.
o Clay and puppet animation.
o Pinscreen.
o Optical printing, matte effects.
o Rotoscoping.
o Line and cel animation: this is the traditional cartoon or character animation (covered in more detail in section 1.3).

For more complete coverage of these techniques, see [LAY 79].

1.2 CLASSES OF ANIMATION PRODUCTS

A study of the application of computer technologies to the animation field and industry must encompass *economical* as well as *technical* aspects. The success of the computer as an animation production tool will not simply depend upon its technical merits. In addition to offering the tools necessary to produce the new "high-tech" animation, it must also provide a close match with the aesthetic and budgetary needs of the more traditional animation products that the marketplace expects. The following is a broad classification of major animation products.

1.2.1 Theater animated feature film

This type of animation film, in the classical sense, has three main characteristics:

- It is a *movie* product: traditionally recorded and distributed on 35mm *film*; its visual quality (resolution, colors) must satisfy the requirements of large screen projection.
- It is a *single* show: original story, long script (one hour to one hour and a half), numerous characters, high quality of animation, quality of backgrounds, etc.

- Loose budgetary constraints: quality is a prime objective.

The usual model for of such productions is the Walt Disney movie. These are unfrequently produced today because of their very high cost. Up to now, such feature films have not been a fruitful domain for the application of computerized techniques since their high standards of visual quality have been hard to meet with these methods.

1.2.2 Television animation special

This animation product is also a *single* show, but it is fundamentally different in two respects:

- It is a *video* product: recorded and distributed on video tape.
- Image quality requirements are not as high, budgets are smaller.

This product starts to be, today, within the range of computer-aided animation production.

1.2.3 Television series

This is the quintessential animated *video* product:

- Recorded and distributed on video tape (typically one inch C format).
- Follows *repetitive* and *systematic* production patterns (stereotyped scripts, episode structure, repeated situations) leading to high rates of reutilisation of backgrounds and animation frames.
- Highly competitive marketplace creating a need for cost effective and cheaper production techniques.

This is today one of the prime application areas for computer-aided systems.

1.2.4 Commercial spot

This is typically a unique, short duration product (from a few seconds to several minutes) in which visual quality and quick delivery are essential. Budgets are in proportion to quality requirements and length: the sky is the limit.

Computer animation is used extensively in this type of animated product, with emphasis on special effects and 3D images. The "high-tech" look, rather than increased productivity has probably been the driving factor for introduction of these new techniques.

1.2.5 Miscellaneous animated products

- Computer animation has been applied successfully in a number of short animated *video* products characterised by mechanically or geometrically defined animation:

    . instructional films presenting schematics, diagrams, mechanical parts, numerical data, etc.
    . movie credits, TV station logos, etc.

- Spectacular 3D image synthesis, with simple forms of animation (moving objects as opposed to body animation), has been used recently in science fiction feature films (*Tron, The Last Starfighter*). The future of this type of production is unclear.

1.3 CONVENTIONAL ANIMATION PRODUCTION PROCESS

Conventional animation production is a complex and elaborate process. It follows a rigorous sequence of production steps, each step being handled by specialists. We briefly describe here a typical production process for *line and cel* animation, represented in a diagrammatic fashion in Figure 1. The exact organisation of the process may vary between different animation studios. Figure 2 illustrates the production technique employed at Hanna-Barbera.

o *Storyboarding*

A film usually starts as a *script*. The next description stage has a graphical form: the *storyboard*.

The storyboard is a general conceptual planning aid. It presents the film in outline form, and depicts its key moments; it also specifies its visual style and all aspects of sound, movement, composition and color. *Storyboards* are typically hand-drawn on large sheets of paper, in a variety of styles and presentations (see examples in [LAY 79]).

Other conceptual documents are also used or created during this preparatory phase. *Model* sheets specify drawing styles and colors for each character. In some animation studios, *stock animation notebooks* are used to list prototypical gestures and movements for each major character: these animation sequences may be re-utilized or copied.

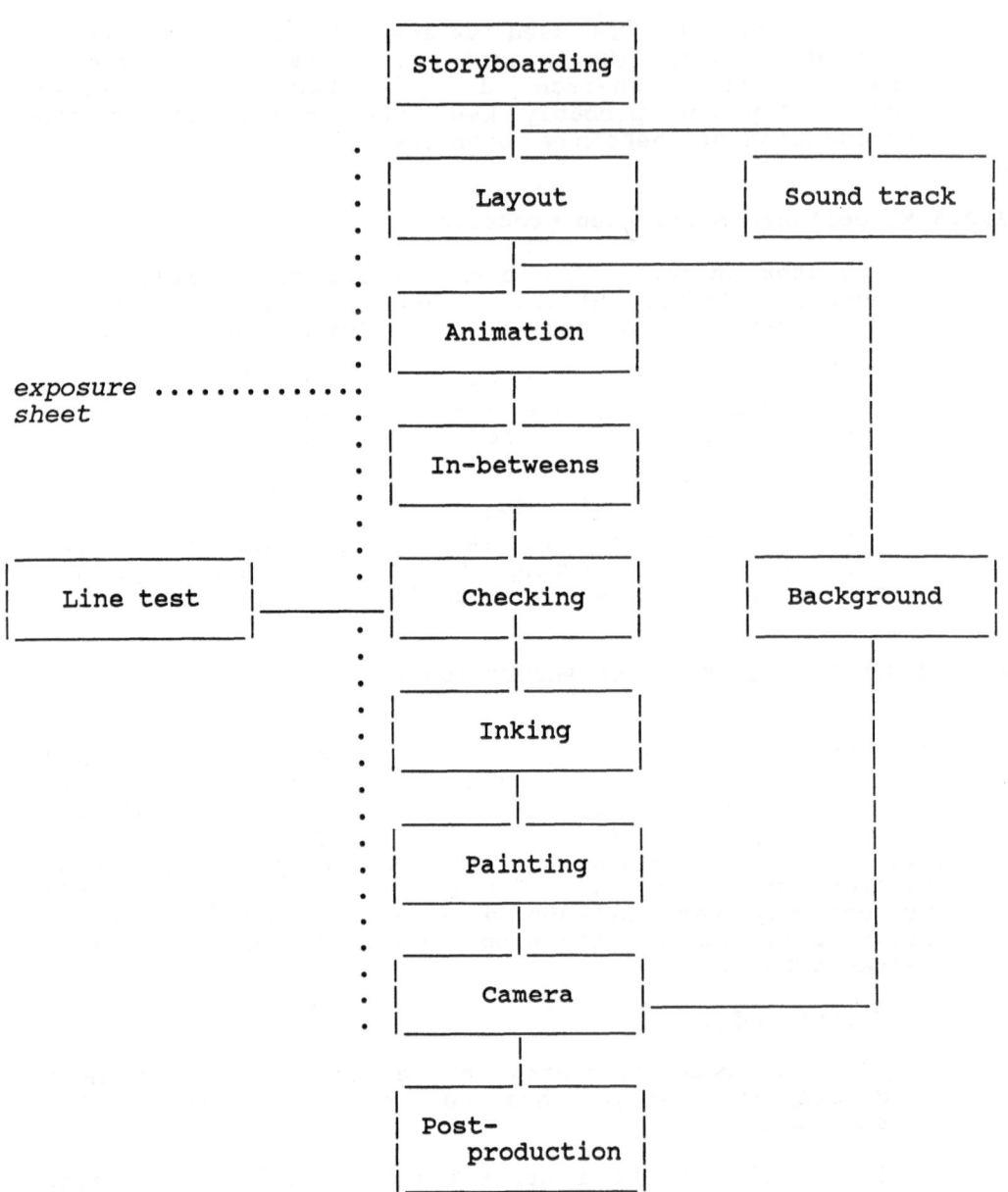

Figure 1 : Typical production process for conventional animation.

475

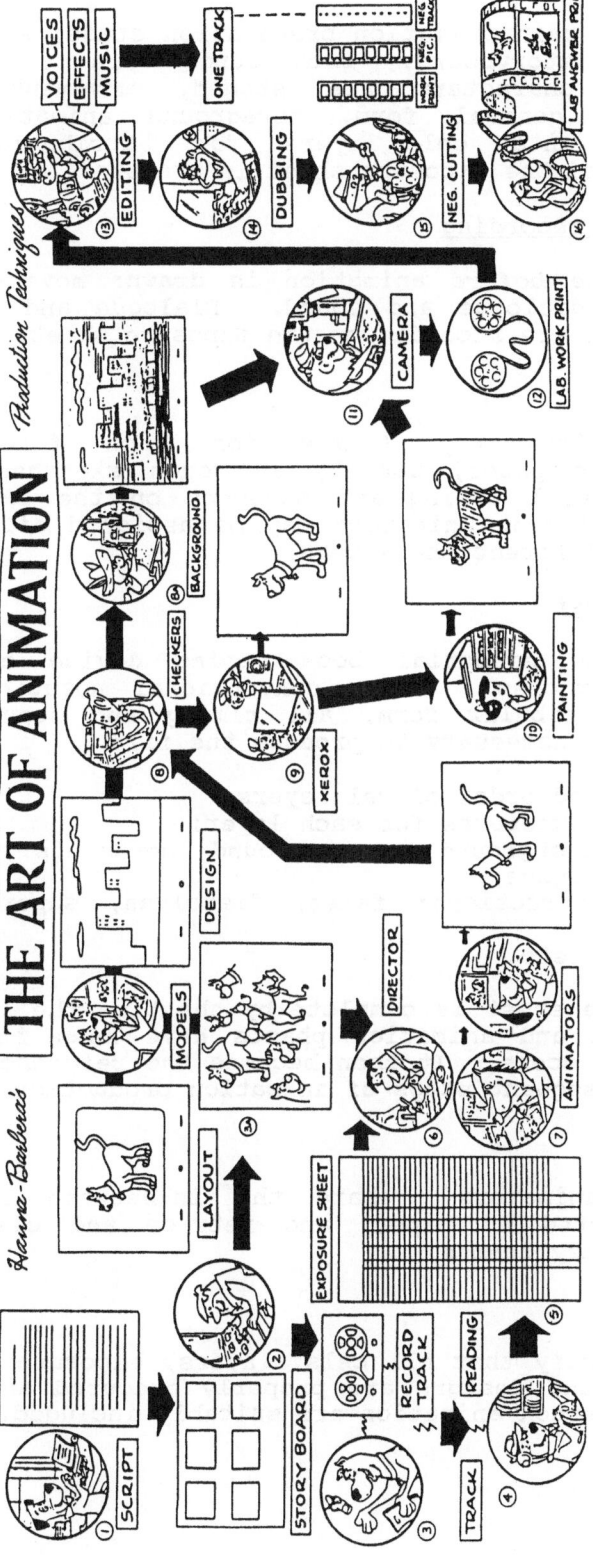

Figure 2: Animation process at Hanna-Barbera Productions.
(Courtesy of Hanna-Barbera Productions).

o *Layout*

This is the main animation preparation stage; starting from the storyboard, backgrounds are sketched, foreground characters are staged, movements are defined in general form, foreground animation is subdivided into cel layers for attribution to animators and the exposure sheet is prepared.

o *Sound track recording*

This is done *before* animation is drawn: movement is matched to dialogue and sound. Dialogue and timing informations are recorded on the exposure sheet.

o *Animation*

Animators draw *key frames* for each foreground character on paper, usually as rough sketches, and specify general timing and movement on the exposure sheet. Different animators may be assigned different scenes or different characters.

o *Exposure sheet*

This is the essential book-keeping device of the animation process. Using conventional notation, it records in tabular form, all timing and sequencing informations necessary to produce the film.

. sequence and order of cel layers;
. number of exposures for each layer;
. camera, background or compound movements: pans, zooms and spins;
. camera instructions: fades, dissolves, superimpositions;
. dialogues, etc.

The exposure sheet is complete by the time the layout, sound track and animation phases have been finished for a given scene. It then becomes the reference data for all subsequent steps of animation production.

o *In-betweens*

Assistant animators prepare the in-between frames, also completed on paper, and retrace and clean up animators' key frames.

o *Checking*

Checkers verify that all cels, layers, exposure sheets and background designs are properly executed and that cycles and stock animation are suitably included.

o *Line test*

Quick shooting of uncolored sketched frames is
sometimes done to verify the quality of animation, as
part of the checking phase.

o *Background*

Working from background designs provided with the
layout, each background is then painted.

o *Inking*

Animators' pencil drawings are transferred to
transparent acetate cels and inked. This is done
today by making photocopies onto acetate, a process
known in the trade as "xeroxing".

o *Painting (or opaquing)*

Each cel is painted on its *backside* to produce opaque
color images.

o *Camera*

Final photography of composite animation (background
and layered cels) on color film, usually 35mm. This
is done either manually or on an automated animation
stand.

o *Post-production*

Editing and sound-dubbing. At this stage, it might be
decided to redraw or re-shoot certain scenes.

Typical breakdown of production costs for these different
phases is as follows:

storyboarding	6%
layout and sound track	17%
animation, in-betweens	27%
backgrounds	6%
inking and painting	24%
camera (animation stand)	10%
post-production	10%

Another significant number is the number of cels per
second of animation: 4 to 10 cels per second being
average figures. They may vary significantly, however,
according to the type of animation product.

2. COMPUTER TOOLS FOR ANIMATION

In this chapter, we outline the various categories of *computer tools* that can be applied in computer assisted animation production, each having its specific hardware and software aspects. These tools often correspond to a process or method within the conventional production scheme described earlier (section 1.3 and Figure 1) suitably transposed to a computer environment, e.g. coloring cels or painting backgrounds.

Other tools are specific to computer-based techniques, for instance key frame in-betweening. As such, they may bring more than simply increased productivity: they may have a strong impact on all the graphical and artistic aspects of the animators' art. This effect may be perceived in opposite ways by animation professionals: on one hand, he or she may see openings toward new animation styles made possible by these techniques; on the other hand, he or she may only see the technical restrictions that prevent the exact replicas of habitual animation forms. Ultimately the animators must be judge. In this overview of the computer animation toolbox, we give attention to the specific and essential technical aspects of each tool.

2.1   IMAGE REPRESENTATION

Of the various *digital representations* of images that are technically possible, two major forms play a key role in computer animation. It is important to summarize their distinct properties. Because of a lack of standard terminology, we shall use the following two neologisms in this document:

a) *Pictogram*

This is an image represented as an *array of pixels* (picture element = the basic element of a *sampled* image).

o Advantages:

- Quality of graphical rendering, subtlety of texture and colored nuances;
- Allows the simulation of traditional graphics tools: free hand stroke, ink and paint, nibs and brushes, airbrush, etc;
- Compatibility with scanned in images.

o Disadvantages:

- Bulky data;

- Scaling, zooming and geometric transforms difficult or costly;
- Imprecise representation and difficult handling of 2D geometrical shapes;
- Interpolation between images difficult to impossible;
- Structuring of images unapplicable.

o Associated properties:

- Spatial resolution: number of scanlines, number of pixels per scanline;
- Representation of colors:
  . Number of primaries per pixel, number of bits per pixel;
  . Color system: Red-Green-Blue, Hue-Saturation-Brightness;
  . Direct color or color-table;
  . Notion of transparency.

o Display and output hardware: *raster* devices only.

b) *Vectogram*

The image is represented as a *structured* collection of basic *geometric shapes* such as: points, lines, polygones and polylines, arcs and curves, splines, patches, etc. Each shape is defined by its characteristic points (end points, vertices, control points, etc) in a simple plane (2D), in multiple planes ($2\frac{1}{2}$D) or in space (3D).

o Advantages:

- Precise representation of shapes;
- Compact data;
- Automatic coloring of shapes defined by their boundaries;
- Easy scaling, zooming and geometric transforms;
- Interpolation between images possible;
- Convenient structuring of images;
- Allows 3D animation (3D models and sets).

o Disadvantages:

- Limited or "mechanical" quality of rendering;
- In 2D, allows only cartoon-like animation: solid colors and line art.
- Needs anti-aliasing treatment to avoid "jaggies" on limited resolution display devices (e.g. broadcast video).

o Associated properties:

- Data precision ("world" coordinate system);
- Graphical properties of lines and curves: color, thickness, texture, etc;
- Color of filled areas and patches;

- Spatial layering (2½D and 3D).

o Display and output hardware:

- Vector drawing devices: line art and wire frame rendering;
- Raster devices: full rendering.

2.2 IMAGE SCANNING

2.2.1 Definition

Capture of an original image or drawing on conventional media (black and white line art or colored image) into digital form: *vectogram* or *pictogram*.

2.2.2 Equipment

- Digitizing video camera or line by line flat-bed scanner.
- Frame buffer.
- Video monitor.

2.2.3 Input control function

- Framing:
  . Optical adjustment (field of view) and mechanical adjustment (camera and image positioning);
  . Manual, mechanical or numerical controls.
- Digitization control: threshold, contrast, gain and dynamic range, intensity and color compensation for device non-linearity.
- Miscellaneous manipulations: filters, paper feeder, etc.

2.2.4 Image representation

o Black and white line art:

- Direct one pass scanning in yields a *pictogram*. Good image quality requires grey levels to avoid line jaggies: 4 bits per pixel appears sufficient. Original line-art usually is at the final recording scale and orientation to avoid scaling and rotating the pictogram. Typical scanning resolution is 512 by 512 pixels. The resulting pictogram may exhibit speckles within blank areas or gaps in lines: these defects are usually corrected manually at the coloring stage (2.5).

- Scanning followed by pattern recognition yields a *vectogram*, i.e. a vector, polyline or curve description of the drawing. The resulting geometric representation may, in principle, quicken the coloring process and allow scaling and rotation of the image, thereby reducing the number of original drawings to be scanned in. However, preserving the texture and line thickness variation of the original is difficult.
- Original line art should be clean and traced (ink or "xeroxed" pencil). Remaining blue pencil marks would require special treatment or filtering.

o Color image:

- Scanning in three passes yiels a RGB *pictogram*. Typical resolution is 512 by 512, 8 bits per primary color , 24 bits per pixel. A color table may be built up on the fly to allow finer color definition (10 to 12 bits per primary color).
- Scanning very large images, such as panoramic backgrounds, as multiple adjacent pictograms requires careful registration and specific pixel processing at the pictogram boundaries to ensure exact joining of the images.

2.3 PAINTING

2.3.1 Definition

Interactive creation or manipulation of a color *pictogram* with an "electronic paintbox". Used to create or retouch backgrounds or certain kinds of animation frames.

2.3.2 Equipment

- Requires a dedicated computer or raster graphics workstation.
- Color video monitor.
- Frame buffer, may contain an image larger than the display area.
- Mouse or digitizing tablet with stylus or puck.
- Keyboard, and optionally, a character terminal.

2.3.3 Painting functions

A typical set of painting functions might include [SMI 78]:

- Choosing or building brushes and nibs: shape, color, texture, etc.

- Painting modes, including special effects (airbrush, transparency, etc).
- Drawing of anti-aliased lines, curves and basic geometric shapes.
- Filling solid areas from a seed point; choice of filling material: solid color, varying color, pattern, texture, another pictogram, etc.
- Manipulation of areas: rectangular, polygonal or arbitrary boundaries; copying or moving; geometric transforms: translation, rotation, scaling, symetry, etc.
- Zooming for working at pixel level.
- Creating and manipulating color tables in RBG or HSB domain.
- Text layout.
- Libraries of brushes, nibs, color tables, stored pictograms, fonts, etc.
- Handling of very large images : panning, reduced views.

2.4 2D SHAPE CONSTRUCTION

2.4.1 Definition

Interactive creation of 2D geometrical shapes in *vectogram* form, possibly in several independent overlays (2½D). Used essentially for key frame creation.

2.4.2 Equipment

- Requires a dedicated computer or graphics workstation (raster or vector drawing).
- Monochrome video monitor or vector drawing display.
- Frame buffer or display list memory.
- Mouse or digitizing tablet with stylus or puck.
- Keyboard, and optionally, a character terminal.

2.4.3 Drawing functions

A typical set of drawing functions includes:

- Creation of basic shapes:
  . Specification of characteristic points: line end points, polyline vertices, spline control points, etc.
  . Fitting of free hand strokes.
  . Predefined shapes with "handles": rectangle, circle, ellipse, etc.
- Grouping and aggregation of shapes.
- Manipulation of shapes: copying or moving; geometric transforms.

- Miscellaneous adjustments: smoothing, cleaning line crossings, vertical or horizontal alignments, etc.
- Zooming for detail work.
- Specifying: line thickness, texture and color, area color, pattern and texture.
- Libraries of shapes.

2.5 COLORING

2.5.1 Definition

Coloring by semi-automatic *filling* of line art drawings usually represented in *pictogram* form. Could also apply to *vectogram* form. This is the direct equivalent to cel coloring, typically applied to scanned in animation frames (2.2).

A painting system usually provides similar color filling functions. However, specialized coloring systems have been developed for filling black and white line art drawing, for efficiency and graphical quality reasons. Specific *tint fill* techniques have also been devised for areas bounded by anti-aliased lines [SMI 79], [STE 79], [LEV 81], [FIS 84].

2.5.2 Equipment

- Requires a dedicated computer or *raster* graphics workstation.
- Color video monitor
- Frame buffer.
- Mouse or digitizing tablet with stylus or puck.
- Keyboard, and optionally, a character terminal.

2.5.3 Coloring functions

A typical set of coloring functions includes:

- Color filling (see 2.5.4), allowing anti-aliased or invisible contours.
- Visualisation of "missed" pixels for color touch up.
- Miscellaneous painting functions for speckle removal and line gap closing.
- Zooming for pixel level touch up.
- Creation and manipulation of color table.
- Specification of colors from animation *character models*.
- Automatic coloring of *successive* animation frames.

2.5.4 Coloring techniques

There are two basic techniques.

a) *Area filling*:

A *semi-automatic technique* applied to a *pictogram* image stored in a frame buffer: a *seed point* is specified interactively by an operator pointing on a display screen; all *contiguous* pixels having some common *attribute* are set to the same filling color. In general the filling attribute is the original color of the pixels (for instance a neutral background color for animation frames) but it could be any other visible or invisible value stored with the pixel.

Special techniques, *soft fill* or *tint fill*, have been devised for treating not only solid areas but also grey pixels on anti-aliased contour lines. On a series of closely related images, such as successive frames of an animation sequence, many of the seed points may be automatically deduced from those provided for the first frame.

The resulting image is a *pictogram*.

b) *Contour scan-conversion*

On images represented as *vectograms*, where contours are coded as polylines or curves, coloring is obtained *automatically* by usual scan-conversion methods. Colors must be specified at the shape construction stage, when frames have been drawn interactively (2.4), or at the image scanning stage, when frames are obtained by vectorization of original drawings (2.2).

A particular topological representation method for line art images, complementary to the vectogram form, *planar maps*, has also been applied to animation frame encoding [MOI 84]. It speeds up the coloring process.

The resulting image is also a *pictogram*.

2.6 IN-BETWEENING

2.6.1 Definition

This is the process by which a complete animation sequence is *automatically* or *semi-automatically* produced from a series of *key frames*, the in-between frames being generated by computer .

2.6.2 Equipment

- Dedicated computer or graphics workstation.
- Mouse or digitizing tablet with stylus or puck.
- Vector drawing or raster graphics monitor.
- Keyboard, and optionally, a character terminal.

2.6.3 In-betweening techniques

We cover here 2D and 2½D animation. Although 3D animation relies on similar ideas, it is discussed separately: see 2.7, 2.8 .

There are two basic techniques for computer generation of intermediate frames from key frames in an animation sequence: *interpolation* and *transformation*. Both methods relying on geometrical algorithms, key frames must therefore be represented as *vectograms*. These are produced either by vectorizing scanned images (2.2) or by interactive shape creation (2.4). Both techniques may be easily combined.

a) *In-betweening by interpolation*:
   [PAL 83], [KOC 84], [COM 84]

   - Decomposition of key frames into individually interpolated geometrical elements: typically open or closed lines and curves.
   - Establishing a one to one correspondence between interpolated elements in two or more consecutive key frames, as well as between matching points in corresponding elements (this controls the deformation of the element). The animation is smoother for higher degree interpolation (more than two key frames).
   - Defining the interpolation trajectory: straight line or curve.
   - Defining the interpolation rhythm or animation timing, i.e. the positions of the in-between frames on the interpolation trajectory.

b) *In-betweening by geometric transforms*:

   - Decomposition of key frames into individually transformed elements: lines, curves, polylines, basic geometric shapes, etc.
   - Defining transforms applied to each element: rotation, scaling, symmetry, stretching and combinations. Transform factors may be constant or may vary between key frames, for instance by interpolation.
   - Defining the transform trajectory or translation factor.

- Defining the interpolation rhythm or animation timing.

In conclusion, it should be pointed out that in-betweening techniques have not been able, up to now, to generate effectively cartoon-like animation. A new style of animation can be achieved using these techniques but a lot of work remains to be done until the smoothness and richness of hand-made animation is reached.

2.7 3D MODELING

The main difference between 2D and 3D animation is the fact that the latter uses 3D models of characters and objects to be animated. Backgrounds can also be described as 3D models.

Once the tedious work of model building has been completed, 3D animation has several advantages over 2D. The main one being that the computer performs all hidden-surface, shading and lighting computations which are in fact rendered manually in 2D animation with numerous hand drawn frames.

3D modeling techniques are common to several fields of computer graphics: computer-aided design, simulation, image synthesis. Many kinds of data structures are used to store the geometrical and topological information needed. See [NEW 79], [FOL 82] and [REQ 80] for a general overview. Among the data structures most often used for 3D animation, we find:

- Polygon meshes and polyhedra,
- Quadric and super-quadric surfaces,
- Surface patches: bi-linear or bi-cubic (Coons, Bézier, B-spline).

Structured models are build from elementary components using tree-like structures. This allows the animator to define the articulations of a model and to animate each component as a single entity, see 2.8.

Two problems are important for 3D modeling:

- User interface: because of the huge amount of data needed to define a model, specific interaction techniques are necessary.

- Level of details: because of the movements of the camera or of the model, *temporal aliasing* occurs in 3D animation. So, one has often to define several models of the same object or character according to the viewer's distance.

2.8 SPATIAL ANIMATION

Spatial animation has been the subject of extensive work in recent years. See [BAD 79], [REY 82], [ZEL 82a], [ZEL 82b], [WIL 82], [GOM 84].

Tree-like structures allow for geometric transformations at each node defining a subset of the scene. But spatial animation is not limited to moving objects in space. It should also permit dynamically changing display and rendering parameters, such as color and lighting models.

Interpolation techniques are of great importance in spatial animation and several methods are used. The user must be provided with tools for the interpolation of key positions and timing (e.g.: pacing, easing-in and out, and holding). Synchronization of movements is also mandatory. Languages like ASAS or MIRA, and interactive techniques like BBOP or TWIXT have been devised to deal with full-control motion.

2.9 LINE TEST

2.9.1 Definition

Quick production of a simplified animated sequence for verification of animation quality. Typically executed with line drawing characters and objects without colors or backgrounds.

2.9.2 Real-time animation

The quickest solution is real-time animation: each frame is either stored (in *vectogram* or *pictogram* form) or computed on the fly (in *vectogram* form, with real time interpolation or transformation). Because of access time requirements (at least 12 to 25 frames per second), storage must be in main memory: as a result, typical real-time line tests last only a few seconds.

Equipment required:

- Dedicated computer or graphics workstation.
- Possibly, specialized real time graphics processor.
- Large amounts of random access main memory.
- Vector drawing or raster graphics display.

2.9.3 Quick turn-around video recording

Line-tests may also be produced with quick turn-around video recording equipment, on the same principle as the final recording process (2.10) but with the appropriate short cuts and simplification.

Equipment required:

- Analog magnetic video disk.
- Single frame video tape recorder.
- In the future: writeable digital video disk.

2.10 RECORDING

2.10.1 Definition

This is the process of combining the various layers of images composing the final image. This process is usually controled by the *exposure sheet*.

2.10.2 Recording techniques

The combining and recording process can take place in the *digital* or the *video* domain.

a) The digital technique relies on the use of a frame buffer in which each layer of the image is written from bottom (background) to intermediary cels to top (foreground), with proper handling of "transparent" pixels. This frame buffer feeds digital-to-analog converters driving either broadcast video recording equipment (videotape recorder or analog video disk) or a higher-resolution image recorder for film production.

All images (background and cels) must be converted to *pictogram* form at this stage of the production process. Two particular issues raise difficult problems in relation to picture quality:

- Camera zooms which require either scaling the background image or storing images of different sizes.
- Anti-aliasing of contour lines.

b) The combining and recording process can also be done with digitally controled video processing equipment, chroma key mixers and other television studio systems. A distinct advantage of this approach is to allow mixing live action, real scenes and objects, within animated sequences. However the produced image quality is inferior to images treated in the digital domain.

The distinction between these two domains may well disappear in the not so distant future as video technology becomes digital.

2.11 PRODUCTION MANAGEMENT

2.11.1 Definition

The production of an animated film is an elaborate multi-stage process: an animation studio is in essence a production plant. There is a need for managing large quantities of data in a large variety of forms, not the least of which being a great number of images, as well as scheduling and monitoring numerous production steps.

2.11.2 Equipment

- Multi-user time sharing mini-computer system.
- Image filing server.
- Character or semi-graphical terminals.

2.11.3 Production management functions

- Animation process control:
  . *Layout*: framing and camera movements,
  . *Exposure sheet*,
  . *Animation sequence re-utilization*.
- Library of character *models*.
- Planning and scheduling.
- Cost control and production accounting.

Of all the above, the interactive entry and editing of exposure sheet information is the only management function that is often encountered on computer-assisted animation system. It is typically the driving information for the recording process (2.10). Computer implementation of this function usually follows the habitual tabular form and notational convention of the traditional exposure sheet.

3. COMPUTER ASSISTED ANIMATION SYSTEMS

3.1 GENERAL SYSTEM ARCHITECTURE

The computer animation tools presented above (chapter 2) may be combined in a variety of ways, often together with conventional techniques, to constitute complete animation production systems. Within such systems one can usually distinguish three main, somewhat independent "modules":

- *animation* per se: the creation of animated characters and objects. In 2D line and cel (or cartoon like) animation, these are treated as *foreground* figures over a static background. In 3D animation, characters and setting are more intimately linked through a common modeling space.

- *background creation* : in 2D animation, backgrounds can be treated in a largely independant fashion from character animation.

- *recording* : the merging process by which final images are composed, on film or video media, by combining background and animation.

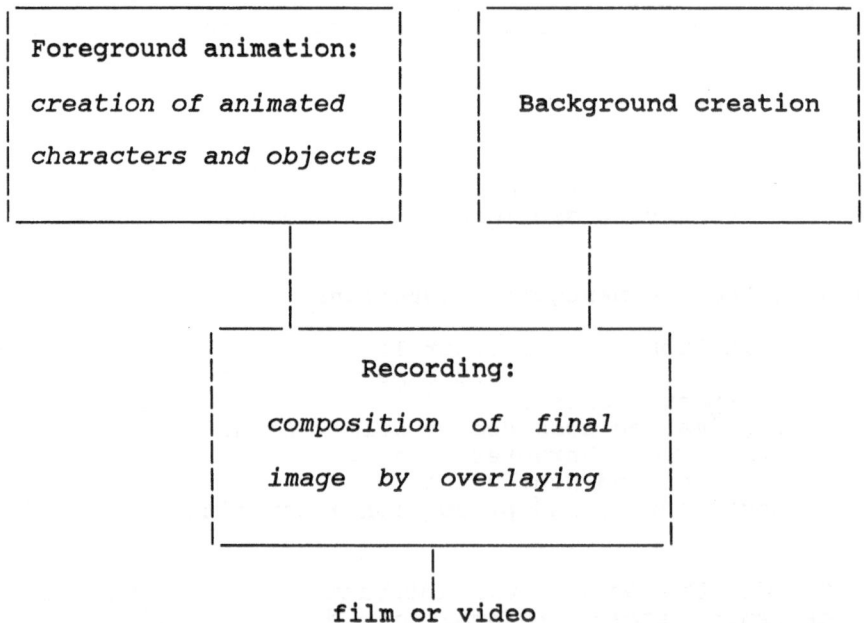

Figure 3: Basic architecture of
computer-assisted animation.

This general architecture of a typical computer-assisted animation system is illustrated on Figure 3. It is a framework for presenting the main categories of systems. The separation between these three principal processes becomes fuzzy in the case of 3D animation (see 2.7 and 2.8). For 2D line and cel production one can distinguish two basic classes of *foreground animation* systems:

- *Frame by frame* animation (3.2),

- *Key frame* animation (3.3).

Background creation is a topic in itself covered in 3.4. The *recording* process is described in 2.10.

3.2 FRAME BY FRAME ANIMATION

This is a general class of systems in which *each* frame requires some form of human intervention.

o *Paintbox systems*

Small scale systems have been developed that rely totally on the computer as a sketching, coloring and painting tool in which all frames are interactively created. These systems are usually build as single-user graphics workstations integrating several of the basic functions discussed above, typically: *painting, 2D shape construction* and *recording*. Limited line test or a quick replay function is sometimes provided.

Such systems are only suitable for commercial spots, instructional animation and other video oriented short length productions.

o *Cel coloring systems*

These are large *production oriented* systems mixing conventional cel production methods with computer based coloring and recording processes.

Production follows the conventional process of Figure 1, up to but not including the inking stage. Computer processing starts here: cleaned hand-drawn animation frames (pencil on paper) are scanned in, as well as painted backgrounds; animation frames are interactively colored on a graphics screen; exposure data is fed in; recording proceeds automatically.

There are two representative systems of this type:

. the Computer-Aided Animation System (CAAS) from Computer Graphics Lab, originating from the New-York Institute of Technology,
. the Hanna-Barbera Productions system.

492

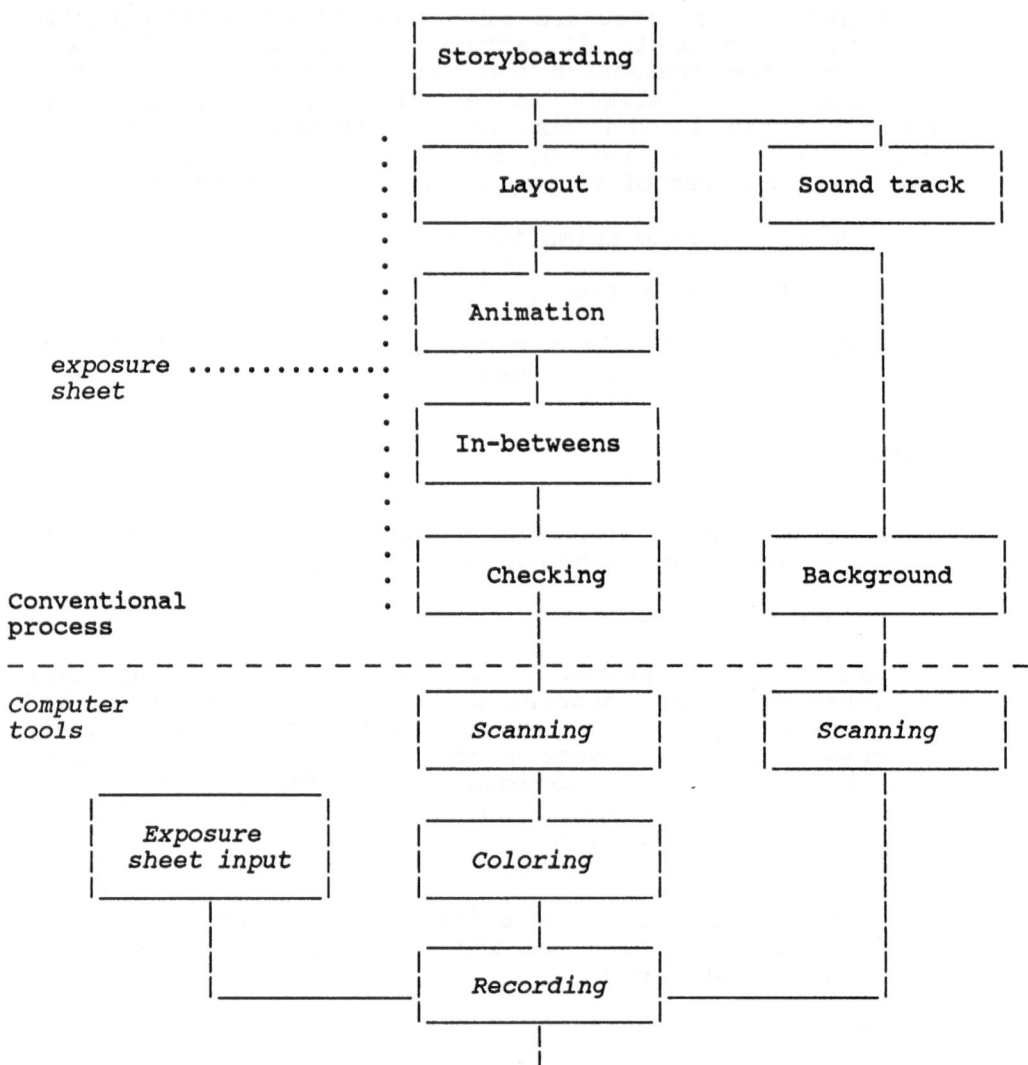

Figure 4 : Computer-assisted cel coloring system.

They are both multi-user systems designed and built along similar principles. They integrate on a multi-machine configuration (VAX) several of the basic functions described in the previous chapter: *image scanning, painting, coloring, recording* and *production management* (exposure sheet). This is summarized in Figure 4.

These systems are oriented towards large scale production of cartoon animation and television series.

3.3 KEY FRAME ANIMATION

This is the general class of systems in which the computer is used to generate intermediate frames. In principle, the animator has only to draw key frames: the in-betweening process is automated. The general process is illustrated in Figure 5.

Key frame techniques have not proven their applicability for cartoon and character animation. Beyond the experimental films of Peter Foldes, in-betweening based on interpolation of lines has produced rather poor results. Other techniques based on shape transformation and interpolation have produced interesting results [COM 84]. However, these techniques introduce a new style of animation akin to flat puppet animation rather than a new way for producing character animation. Their success will depend on how well they are adopted by animators.

Automatic in-betweening is nonetheless convenient for a range of simple animation using simple movements (translation, rotation, scaling) applied to constant shapes or sub-images.

3.4 BACKGROUND PRODUCTION

There is no unique solution for the production of backgrounds. To satisfy the variety of styles and the range of budgets, many methods and tools are applicable. Nonetheless, backgrounds are images of a specific kind:

- A background is often a *panoramic* image, spanning several times the screen area (vertically and horizontally), allowing traveling and camera movements. In addition, it may be desirable to produce an illusion of depth with perspective views.

- It is usually a high quality image requiring more subtle graphical rendering and a wider gamut of color than foreground animation.

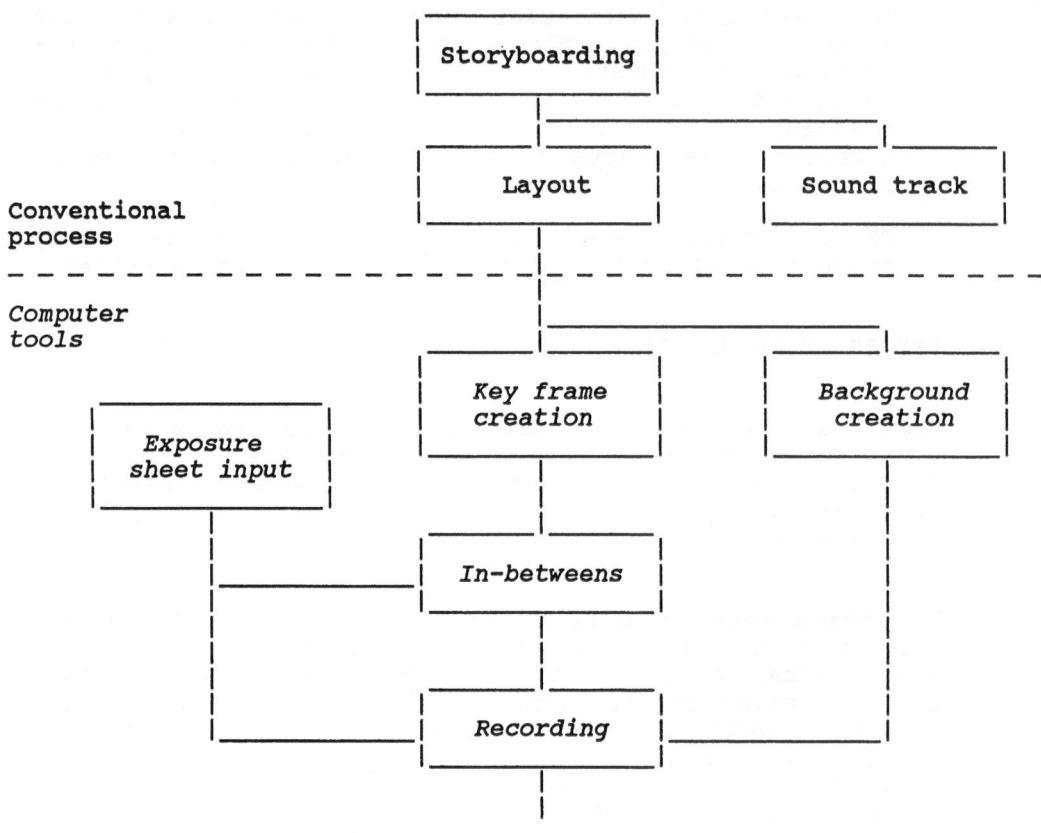

Figure 5 : Key frame animation system.

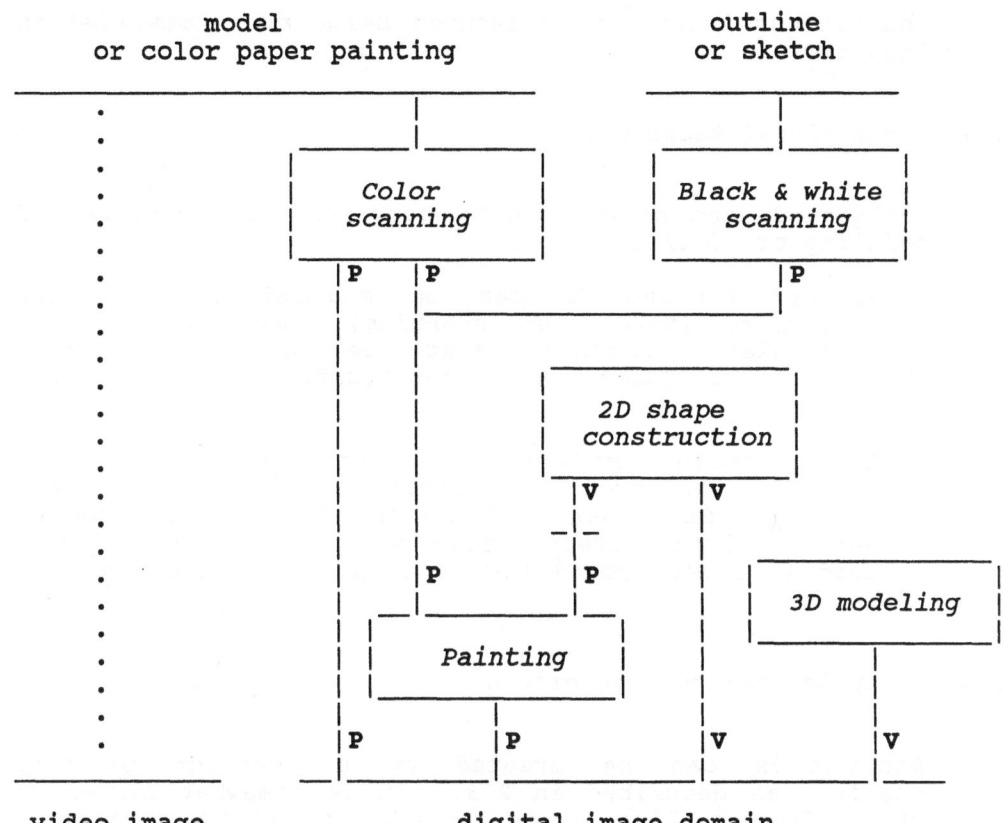

Figure 6 : Background creation.
(**P**= *pictogram*, **V**= *vectogram*)

The various techniques presented below are summarized in Figure 6.

3.4.1 Traditional techniques

Backgrounds can be created by conventional techniques of *painting* or *modeling*.

- Painted backgrounds can be scanned in as color *pictograms* (three-pass scanning): see section 2.2. Particular attention must be given to color correction, color table construction and panoramic images.

- Reduced-scale models are sometimes convenient solutions for producing varying views of a recurrent setting. Still views of the model may be scanned as above. Alternatively, video shots of the model may be used as a background for video mixing, chroma keying, etc.

3.4.2 Computer painted background

Backgrounds can be created on a computer painting station, as described in 2.3. It is somewhat easier to start from a line image (black and white pictogram) obtained by one-pass scanning of a sketch or outline of the background. Again, color control and image size are prime technical issues.

3.4.3 2D synthetic background

Simplified 2D, or $2\frac{1}{2}$D, backgrounds can be rapidly produced with an interactive 2D shape creation tool (2.4) generating images in vectogram form. Advantages such as: quick production, automatic coloring, easy handling of panoramic images and camera movement, have to be weighed against the somewhat simplistic look of such backgrounds. Alternately, these images may serve as sketches for computer painted backgrounds (3.4.2).

3.4.4 3D synthetic background

This is the fully computerized version of a traditional model: it offers realism (sometimes with the "high-tech" look), and total control of view point and movement. Although fully compatible with 2D line and cel animation, it has to be treated in the framework of 3D animation (2.7 and 2.8).

BIBLIOGRAPHY

[BAD 79]   Badler, N.I., and Smoliar, S.W., "Digital Representations of Human Movement", *ACM Computer Surveys*, Vol. 11, No 1, March 1979.

[COM 84]   Comparetti, G., "Outil de production industrielle de dessin animé par ordinateur", *Colloque CESTA*, Biarritz, May 1984.

[FIS 84]   Fishkin, K. P., and Barsky, B. A., "A Family of New Algorithms for Soft Filling", *Computer Graphics*, Vol. 18, No 3, July 1984.

[FOL 82]   Foley, J., and Van Dam, A., *Fundamentals of Interactive Computer Graphics*, Addison-Wesley, Reading, Mass., 1982.

[GOM 84]   Gomez, J. E., "Twixt: A 3D Animation System", Proc. of *EUROGRAPHIC'S 84*, Sept. 1984.

[KOC 84]   Kochanek, D., and Bartels, R., "Interpolating Splines with local Tension, Continuity and Bias Control", *Computer Graphics*, Vol. 18, No 3, July 1984.

[HAL 68]   Halas, J., and Manvell, R., *The Technique of Film Animation*, Hastings House, New York, 1968.

[HAL 76]   Halas, J., ed., *Computer Animation*, Hastings House, New York, 1976.

[LAY 79]   Laybourne, K., *The Animation Book*, Crown Publishers, New York, 1979.

[LEV 78]   Levoy, M., *Computer-Assisted Cartoon Animation*, Masters thesis, Cornell University, 1978.

[LEV 81]   Levoy, M., "Area Flooding Algorithms", *SIGGRAPH'81*, Tutorial on 2D Computer Animation, Aug. 1981.

[MAD 69]   Madsen, R. P., *Animated Film: Concepts, Methods, Uses*, Interland, New York, 1969.

[MOI 84]   Moissinac, J.C., *Aides informatiques à la réalisation de dessins animés*, thèse, Ecole des Mines de Saint-Etienne, 1984.

[NEW 79] Newman, W., and Sproull, R., *Principles of Interactive Computer Graphics*, 2nd Ed., McGraw-Hill, New York, 1979.

[PAL 83] Palyka, D. M., "A brief Description of an In-between System", *SIGGRAPH'83*, Tutorial on 2D Computer Animation, 1983.

[REQ 80] Requicha, A., "Representations of Rigid Solids: Theory, Methods and Systems", *ACM Computing Surveys*, Vol 12, No 4, Dec 1980.

[REY 82] Reynolds, C. W., "Computer Animation with Scripts and Actors", *Computer Graphics*, Vol 16, No 3, 1982.

[SMI 78] Smith, A. R., "Paint", Technical Memo No 7, Computer Graphics Lab, New York, 1978. Also: *SIGGRAPH'81*, Tutorial on 2D Computer Animation, 1981.

[SMI 79] Smith, A. R., "Tint Fill", *Computer Graphics*, Vol. 13, No 2, Aug. 1979.

[STE 79] Stern, G., "SoftCel - an Application of Raster Scan Graphics to Conventional Cel Animation", *Computer Graphics*, Vol. 13, No 2, Aug. 1979.

[WIL 82] Williams, L., "BBOP", *SIGGRAPH'82*, Tutorial on 3D Computer Animation, July 1982.

[ZEL 82a] Zeltzer, D., "Motor Control Techniques for figure Animation", *IEEE Computer Graphics and Applications*, Vol. 2, No 9, Nov. 1982.

[ZEL 82b] Zeltzer, D., "Representative of Complex Animated Figures", Proc. *Graphics Interface 82 Conf.*, 1982.

Design of a Human Movement Representation Incorporating Dynamics

N. I. Badler

ABSTRACT

Characteristics of a human movement representation are discussed, including distinctions between hierarchic levels and interacting features. Representations for dynamic as well as spatial properties are necessary for effective performance (simulation) of movement. Connections are demonstrated between dynamic properties of several sorts and an existing qualitative notation system called "Effort-Shape."

Keywords and phrases: Motion understanding, movement representation, dynamics, robotics, simulation, computer graphics.

1.0 INTRODUCTION

A significant portion of our activities and perceptions are associated with the performance, observation, description, or recording of human movement. It is a challenge to the current state of knowledge in artificial intelligence to similarly represent, simulate, and integrate these differing manifestations of human movement since they touch on such seemingly diverse areas as computer graphics, computer vision, robotics, and computational linguistics [Badl80b]. In this brief exposition we shall discuss the methodology and philosophy behind our research into the computational understanding of human movement, concentrating on the issues of movement representation, movement synthesis, and task specification.

Movements of human or robot agents may be characterized at many different levels. A purely geometric level of description as changing coordinates, though necessary, is insufficient for most practical purposes. A simple gesture such as closing the hand may be described by joint angles, by paths of the fingertips, by flexion of muscles, by the concept "grasp," or by the intention "shake hands." Each type of description is useful in different contexts, and a natural hierarchy of levels seems to appear. To discuss a movement representation therefore is to establish what descriptive levels are important and what attributes or characteristics are adequate to completely "cover" the space of possible movements at each level.

While viewing movement hierarchically helps focus attention on descriptive or conceptual levels, the performance of a particular motion is the interaction or combination of effects from many sources, rather than the refinement (or generalization) of a movement at a different level of detail. Geometric object descriptions, for example, lend themselves to the latter view [Clar76, Badl78a, Marr81]. Movement, on the other hand, is dictated by simultaneous influences --- muscle tension, external forces, joint limits, path constraints, expressive purpose and intention --- as well as by the context of temporally adjacent activities. A better approach to movement understanding therefore would cover the following aspects of a movement:

* The geometry, kinematics, and dynamics of the agent.

* Any goal-directed acts the movement was part of.

* What, if anything, it signified.

For example, sign language research [Klim79] shows that certain seeming variations in a movement are understood as the same sign, while others are not. Often movements along the same spatial path and toward the same spatial goal may signify very different intents, such as "touch, "press" and "punch."

Our current research on human movement has evolved from several areas: computer graphics for motion synthesis [Badl79b, Kore83], computer vision for motion and shape analysis [ORou80], Labanotation for movement notation [Hutc70, Webe78], language analysis for motion verb characterization [Badl75], and robotics for path planning and goal-directed behavior [Kore82]. In this paper we shall discuss the central "core" of the methodology - the movement representation and its interpretation by computer simulation.

2.0 MOVEMENT REPRESENTATION

A movement representation is a system in which any movement may be decomposed into "primitives" with implementable semantics. We require these primitives to have descriptive significance, thus eliminating things like semi-infinite film libraries, artist-drawn animation, or unprocessed natural language. A more appropriate vocabulary appears to consist of goals, paths, positions, dynamics, and relationships.

In constructing a movement representation we have been very concerned with its capabilities to describe sufficient information for a "performance" via computer synthesized graphic images [Badl79b]. This point of view has been very fruitful in deciding what characteristics of a movement description, and hence of an adequate representation, are necessary. The important concept is that movement synthesis considerations demand consistent implementable semantics. If a computer system could produce any movement specified by the appropriate descriptive parameters, then it would also verify that a representation was an adequate knowledge base with which to describe or notate observed movement. Thus, for example, if the representation cannot express the differences between "press" and "punch," it would not have sufficient means to distinguish these actions if actually observed.

Symbolic representations of many movement properties are found in Labanotation [Hutc70], a movement notation system originated over 50 years ago by Rudolf Laban. Our choice of Labanotation over other systems was based on its redundant means of expressing a movement, its capabilities for arbitrary frames of reference, its incorporation of goal-directed actions, and its essentially "digital" symbol system [Badl79b]. We abstracted these Labanotation properties into a set of five "primitive movement concepts" [Webe78]: directions, revolutions, facings, contacts, and shapes. These primitives were not concerned with dynamic effects (force, acceleration, torque, etc.), muscular movements (bulges, contractions, etc.) or facial expressions [Plat81, Park82], only with the location and relations of body joints or surfaces in space. Thus a motion specification in this system actually describes the final goal and some constraints on the path rather than the internal method by which it is achieved [Badl78b].

We have recently come to view movement somewhat differently. That is, it appears more useful to distinguish four different kinds of movement primitives: "changes" such as rotations by a given angle or motion along a given path or direction; "goals," such as achievement of a given location in space for a joint or a given orientation for a body segment [Kore82]; "relationships," such as between body parts or the body and its environment; and "dynamics," such as how much force or effort is expended. A chart summarizing the function of the motion categories of the "old" representation [Badl79b, Webe78] with respect to this new representation appears in Table I.

Table I
Comparison of "old" and "new" movement representations.

"old"	"new"
DIRECTION (movement)	Change on position
DIRECTION (position)	Reach goal
REVOLUTION (rotate)	Change in rotation (halfplane, deviation)
REVOLUTION (twist)	Change in twist
FACING	Orientation goal
SHAPE (movement)	Sequence of reach goals, or "keyframe" locations
SHAPE (position)	Sequence of "keyframe" positions
CONTACT	Sequence of reach and orientation goals

In Table I, the "keyframe" concept refers to a single three-dimensional state (for example, joint angle configuration) for the body. "Relationships" are not discussed further at this time, except to note their connection with higher-level motion and task planning concepts [Badl83, Zelt83].

The evolution of the motion representation is motivated not only by current efforts in three-dimensional computer animation, but also by recent practice in robotics [Paul79, Holl80, Loza79, Derb83] and motion analysis [ORou80]. One application of this research, in fact, would be to build a very high level motion control language on top of robot control systems such as AL [Fink75] or AUTOPASS [Lieb77].

3.0 DYNAMICS

A key feature of human movement which we virtually ignored in our earlier representation efforts is its dynamic quality, that is, the manner in which the body moves in terms of "force," "effort," "exertion," "energy," or the like. This may be more significant, in an expressive or intentional sense, than the actual path. For example, variations in dynamics can alter the message conveyed in American Sign Language [Klim79, Loom83]. Dynamics considerations only appear implicitly in the representations derived from the study of Labanotation (such as our own) because:

1. that notation system itself (nor for that matter, nearly any other) did not convey dynamic information other than timing (duration) and perhaps "accent,"

2. motion semantics have been mostly concerned with "smooth" implementation of each primitive motion, not of the "details" of that motion during its execution nor with its continuity in the context of the temporally adjacent motions, and

3. the computational models must include capabilities for understanding some minimal physics associated with body mass, force, inertia, gravity, balance, and so on [Badl80a].

Computer animation done without concern for motion dynamics looks "flat" or "mechanical" at best; discontinuous or jerky at worst.

Previous efforts at incorporating dynamics into computer generated animation have focused on explicit velocity or acceleration functions [Meze71, Speg75, Catm72, Herb78], artist-drawn keyframes [Burt76, Reev81], smooth spline functions [Will82, Shel82], or actual human dynamics [Calv80, Baec69, Zelt82]. The problem has been investigated more mathematically in robotics [Holl80, Lee82, Brad83]. Our own examination of the dynamics problem has focused on alternative notation systems combined with physical and graphical motion models.

In searching for a representational basis for the dynamic qualities of movement, we examined a notation system complementary to Labanotation called Effort-Shape notation [Dell70]. Unfortunately, the semantics of this system are not defined quantitatively, so we have taken some liberties in interpretation. We believe this to be a reasonable approach since our intent is not to "computerize" Effort-Shape, or another other notational system as we and others have attempted to do. Rather, we use these systems to aid in comprehending the scope of human movement so that our representations are more likely to cover the space of possibilities. In the remainder of this paper we describe a dynamics representation and sketch possible implementations of its semantics.

4.0 EFFORT-SHAPE NOTATION

Effort-Shape Notation is a system for representing the qualities of movement rather than its actual method of achievement by the body. Of the two major components of the notation, "Shape" is less important to the present discussion and appears to be at least partially derivable from the positional and directional information already present in our existing representation. On the other hand, the Effort component provides some interesting insights into new properties not already present in our system.

Figure 1. EFFORT dimensions and rough characterizations of their qualities.

SPACE

INDIRECT		DIRECT
flexible		channeled
deviating		undeviating
spiraling		straight

FORCE

LIGHT		STRONG
weightless		forceful
bouyant		vigorous
delicate		emphatic

TIME

SLOW		QUICK
sustained		sudden
lingering		fleeting
languid		rushed

FLOW

FREE		BOUND
uncontrolled		controlled
swingly freely		constrained
cannot be easily stopped		can be stopped instantly

The Effort dimension (Fig. 1) consists of four "factors": effort flow, weight, time, and space. "Effort flow" describes the changes in the quality of muscle tension in the body as it varies between "free" and "bound"; "weight," changes in body or limb weight between "light" or "heavy"; "time," changes in the quality of a movement between "sustained" and "sudden"; and "space," changes in the spatial focus between "direct" and "indirect".

Our research on incorporating dynamics into computer movement simulation is proceeding along four different dimensions. The first introduces controllable randomness into motion, the second involves representing physical characteristics of a specific joint and its "constellation" of muscles; the third models gross acceleration and velocity parameters, and the fourth phrases sequences of movements.

4.1 Joint Changes, Goals, And Randomness

We first remark on one distinction drawn from the Effort parameters. Executing a movement depends on knowing whether or not a particular goal point is intended. The "space" Effort factor allows the expression of "direct" or "indirect" actions. Only the former can be interpreted as a positional goal in space; for the latter, a positional goal is inappropriate. A reasonable interpretation is that "indirect" movements are described by changes in joint angles rather than by goal positions. A movement described solely by joint rotations (changes) is apt to have a weak sense of focus or directionality at the end of the moving limb. One way, therefore, to obtain less "direct" movements is to express them by joint rotations only.

The point we must make here is that indirectness is a quality which may be desirable in certain human movements, and we should seek to control its presence, not avoid it in the representation. It is perhaps not surprising that people have difficulty reaching specific goals or positioning other mechanisms such as robots when restricted solely to motion changes by specific joint angles. Recent work in robotics, for example, has come to appreciate "Cartesian" or rectilinear control of end effector position (goal) over numerical specification of joint angles [Paul79]. Position control through teleoperators or direct manipulation of the three-dimensional body or linkage can overcome this limitation but this option is not normally available to the graphical animator. Some of the problems with this approach are the lack of suitable sensors to digitize the actual human body positions and the necessity to control and generalize the motions thus input [Calv82, Gins83]. We would expect that the class of motions best input by such direct sensing techniques should be the "indirect" ones; indeed this is supported by the extreme difficulty in using joint angle positions alone to achieve convincing goal directed motions such as walking. One further problem is encountered if joint angle changes to a human figure model are implemented carelessly: the relative changes introduce a small but measurable amount of numerical error into the joint position. The problem and its numerical analysis solution in a human animation environment have been neatly documented by Herbison-Evans and Richardson [Herb81].

Another mechanism for achieving indirectness is by stochastic motion processes: large-scale Brownian or fractal motion [Mand77] applied to the motion of body joints. Similar stochastic motion processes have been used for fire and fireworks special effects [Reev83]. While we have not yet attempted to create such fractal (and hopefully indirect Effort) motions, incorporating a suitable random number generator and its parameters into the existing motion control structure is not difficult. It appears that such randomness is orthogonal to the joint angle or cartesian control issue. Since that issue is already covered by motion expression (changes or position) in the representation, we associate a separate "randomness" quality with the "space" Effort factor. Its initial value would be established from the indirect Effort quality for greater ("indirect") or lesser ("direct") disorder. A random perturbation of goal point could then appear quite different from a similar random fluctuation in joint angles, and increasing randomness would produce unique motions in either case.

We speculate that small amounts of disorder may give rise to many "natural" gestural and postural effects, since the living body cannot remain in abject rigidity very long. Removing the "stiffness" of the computer graphic body should go very far toward enhancing the realism of synthesized human motion. Moreover, there is no reason why such perturbations cannot follow quasi-regular patterns; it is merely a matter of what function is chosen to implement the semantics of randomness. This point of view could integrate natural motion cycles (gait), gestural cycles (eating, breathing), and positioning cycles (nervousness). Repetitious motion under these conditions has yet to be investigated.

4.2 Muscle Tension And The Flow Parameter

For an individual body joint, dynamics are characterized by the "flow" dimension which may be taken as the overall muscle tension at a joint, varying from no tension ("free") to maximum tension ("bound"). Our present simulation [Badl80a] corresponds to maximum tension since no external (gravitational) or internal (inertial) forces can alter the prescribed path. By incorporating the ability to vary tension into our simulation, we will be better able to model target over- or undershoot and more realistic reaction to external forces. One way to accomplish this is to feedback through a "flow valve" the computed position and velocity of the limb end modified by the current set of active forces (Fig. 2). "Bound" movements correspond to a closed valve, hence no adjustment (the usual computer graphics animation approach). A fully open valve ("free") corresponds to the forces acting on the limb end as if it were in free fall, that is, with essentially no muscle tension opposing it. Inbetween values create a mix of the two cases and, hopefully, more natural movements.

At the present time we believe that two independent valves are necessary: one to feedback inertial forces generated by the mass of the limb and another to feedback external loads (gravity or held objects) on the limb. Robot arm motion equations separate these forces explicitly [Holl83]. The valve outputs are combined vectorially to determine the next position of the limb, that is, the result of feedback is a displacement vector times the "gravity" valve opening plus another displacement vector times the "inertial" valve opening. An example of this kind of situation might be holding a brick in the air. Vertical movements against gravity are relatively bound, else the brick would fall. Sideways movements, however, may be more free since the inertia of the hand in a horizontal plane would be more difficult to overcome [Hutc82].

4.3 Motion Variation Along A Spatial Path

The geometric form of the path of a body joint or a limb end effector changes as the rate of movement changes. Since a specific positional goal may be expected, we must select a model which allows both control over the path and constraint to goals. Mathematically, the path of a particle depends on its inital position, its velocity, and its (changing) acceleration. A weakness of

Fig. 2. Where dynamics influence movement.

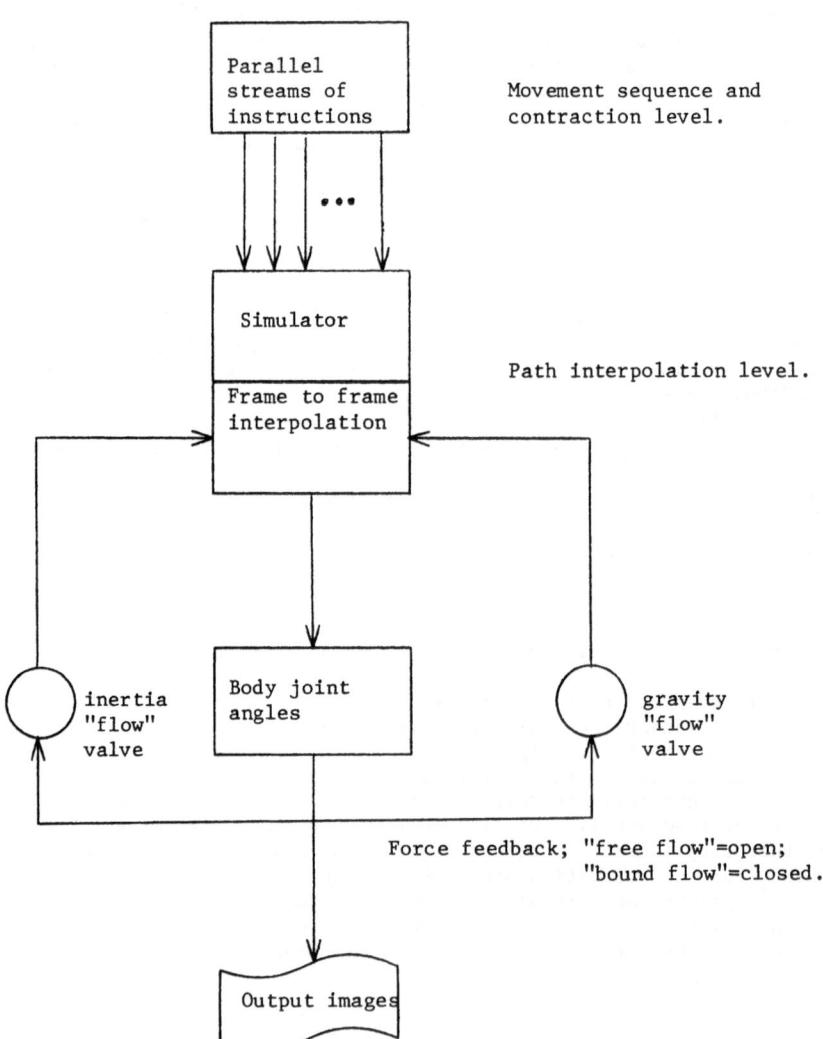

Labanotation and, consequently, of our initial motion representation, is the failure to provide specifics for motion parameters beyond average velocity. To attempt a remedy, we look closely at definitions of the "weight" and "time" Effort qualities.

A qualitative definition of "light" weight is "as if the limb were weightless." This appears to imply an apparent reduced mass of the limb. By simple physics, force equals mass times acceleration. Since naive perception does not measure force directly, and since the mass of the limb is not inherently changable, the only way the apparent mass can be altered is by a real change in the acceleration. Increasing the acceleration induces a perceived reduction in mass. Conversely, the "strong" Effort quality ("as if the limb had significant weight") is conveyed by a decrease in acceleration.

The "time" Effort quality contributes additional information. "Sustained" time implies no change in velocity, that is, an acceleration of zero; "sudden" implies a quick change in velocity, hence a rapid change in acceleration. Unfortunately, the Effort quality gives no specifics on the direction of change, and Dell is rather ambiguous on this point. A possible resolution of this situation may be based on two observations:

1. Arbitrarily assume that every primitive motion by itself starts at rest and ends at rest. (We will return to examine the end conditions in the following section.)

2. The "weight" factor appears to function primarily at the terminus of a motion where "force" to transferred to another object or projected into space.

In the interests of symmetry (and in fact, in most of Dell's examples) "suddenness" would appear to function primarily at the beginning of a motion. This interpretation meshes satisfactorily with our surprise at motion with a sudden onset.

We are therefore drawn to the conclusion that the "time" and "weight" Effort qualiies provide qualitative acceleration information. Clearly the weight (force) information interacts (physically!) with the mass of the moving limbs to determine the joint accelerations [Holl83]. Our challange is to utilize this information in a fashion which avoids the significant calculations necessary for actual robotic control. Our goal, after all, is graphical simulation. We may trade-off physical exactness for convincing motion quality. For instance, we may permit a slight shift in timing or a position correction from feedback near the end of a motion path as long as the "efforts" appear correct or appropriate. It is tantalizing to imagine that this situation is in fact obtained during the execution of unique or novel motion by a real person, and that repetition (practice) is necessary to actually iterate to complete achievement of all motion and timing constraints.

By modeling joint paths as parametric curves [Faux79], such as B-splines, both goals and path geometry may be represented and interpreted by the movement simulator (Fig. 2). The use of polynomial curves to model (robot) end effector trajectories is not new [Paul72, Derb83], nor is their use to model changing velocities and accelerations [Will82, Shel82]. Our studies are directed toward more formal derivations of the form of these curves to generate movements with specific Effort qualities. The role of the animator is therefore moved to a higher level than the mere manipulation of the curves or their control points directly.

For example, the default semantics of a path described by a B-spline curve might be equally-spaced control points or better yet, somewhat closer spacing at the start and end to avoid sharp accelerations. A "light" Effort then spreads the control point spacing more evenly, while a "strong" Effort compresses them more at the destination, causes a quicker deceleration, and results in the appearance of more force per unit mass.

4.4 Movement Phrasing

Another dynamic effect that we are studying is movement phrasing, that is, the smooth blending of a sequence of movements. Again the B-spline interpolated curves are useful here, as individual movements can be smoothly blended. A special case of quadratic velocity functions for smoothing has been used [Herb78] but no phrase structuring has been designed.

A related aspect of phrasing is how a sequence of movements can change over time as the performer becomes either more skilled and experienced, on the one hand, or more tired or rushed on the other. As has been observed in both speech [Frie75] and American Sign Language [Klim79, Fris78], certain types of movements will be lost, and others replaced with a related gesture towards the original target, when a person is involved in everyday discourse. Such changes are not derivable purely from the original movement specification, but require a sense of "fast speech" or "fast action" rules as well.

5.0 CONCLUSIONS

To summarize, we have described how the qualitative factors of Effort-Shape notation might serve to extend existing movement representations. One strong motivation for this quantification is the tantalizing use of English verbs to characterize the Effort "extremes" (Fig. 3). Using these factors as the core concepts of an animation system based on natural language input, we can imagine modeling particular actions by adverbial modifications of the closest motion verb [Tsot80]. These concepts appear to come much closer to the expressiveness or intent of an action than the spatial descriptions of Labanotation, graphical languages, or robot control systems. Work on a high level animation system where actions are sketched out (like a storyboard) and modified through these language concepts is underway. In the next section we present a more global view of the entire TEMPUS system for movement specification and simulation.

Fig. 3. The eight extremes of the Effort qualities.

3 Effort Combinations	Word Equivalent
direct-light-sudden	dabbing
direct-strong-sudden	punching
direct-light-sustained	gliding
direct-strong-sustained	pressing
indirect-light-sudden	flicking
indirect-strong-sudden	slashing
indirect-light-sustained	floating
indirect-strong-sustained	writhing

Acknowledgements

This investigation has been greatly aided by discussions with many colleagues and students, especially Bonnie Webber, Jim Korein, and Steve Platt. Moral support from Ann Hutchinson Guest on issues of dynamics and Effort-Shape Notation is much appreciated.

This research is partially supported by NASA Contract NAS9-16634.

References

[Badl75]   Badler, N.I. "Temporal scene analysis: Conceptual descriptions of object movements," PhD. Dissertation, Dept. of Computer Science, University of Toronto, Toronto, Canada, 1975.

[Badl78a]   Badler, N.I., and R. Bajcsy, "Three-dimensional representations for computer graphics and computer vision," Computer Graphics 12(3), Aug. 1978, pp. 153-160.

[Badl78b]   Badler, N.I, S.W. Smoliar, J. O'Rourke, and L. Webber, The simulation of human movement. Technical Report, Dept. of Computer and Information Science, University of Pennsylvania, Philadelphia, PA, 1978.

[Badl79a]   Badler, N.I., J. O'Rourke, and H. Toltzis, "A spherical representation of a human body for visualizing movement," IEEE Proc. 67(10), Oct. 1979, pp. 1397-1403.

[Badl79b]   Badler, N.I., and S.W. Smoliar, "Digital representations of human movement," Computing Surveys 11(1), March 1979, pp. 19-38.

[Badl80a]   Badler, N.I., J. O'Rourke, and B. Kaufman, "Special problems in human movement simulation," Computer Graphics 14(3), July 1980, pp. 189-197.

[Badl80b]   Badler. N.I., J. O'Rourke, S. Platt, and M. A. Morris, "Human movement understanding: A variety of perspectives," Proc. AAAI Conf., Stanford, CA, 1980, pp. 53-55.

[Badl83]   Badler, N.I., B.L. Webber, J.U. Korein, and J.D. Korein, "TEMPUS, A system for the design and simulation of mobile agents in a workstation and task environment," Proc. IEEE Trends and Applications Conference, 1983, pp. 263-269.

[Baec69]   Baecker, R., "Picture-driven animation," Proc. AFIPS Spring Joint Comp. Conf., Vol. 34, AFIPS Press, Montvale, NJ, 1969, pp. 273-288.

[Bapu81]   Bapu, P., S. Evans, P. Kitka, M. Korna, and J. McDaniel, User's guide for COMBIMAN programs, Univ. of Dayton Research Institute, U.S.A.F. Report No. AFAMRL-TR-80-91, Jan. 1981.

[Brad83] Brady, J.M., J.M. Hollerbach, T.L. Johnson, T. Lozano-Perez, and M.T. Mason. Robot Motion: Planning and Control MIT Press, Cambridge, MA, 1983.

[Burt76] Burtnyk, N., and M. Wein, "Interactive skeleton techniques for enhancing motion dynamics in key frame animation," CACM 19(10), Oct. 1976, pp. 564-569.

[Calv80] Calvert, T., J. Chapman, and A. Patla, "The integration of subjective and objective data in the animation of human movement," Computer Graphics 14(3), July 1980, pp. 198-203.

[Catm72] Catmull, E., "A system for computer generated movies," Proc. ACM Annual Conf. 1972, pp. 422-431.

[Clar76] Clark, J., "Hierarchical geometric models for visible surface algorithms," CACM 19(10), Oct. 1976, pp. 547-554.

[Dell70] Dell, C. A Primer for Movement Description, Dance Notation Bureau, Inc., New York, 1970.

[Derb83] Derby, S., "Simulating motion elements of general-purpose robot arms," International J. of Robotics Res. 2(1), Spring 1983, pp. 3-12.

[Dool82] Dooley, M., "Anthropometric modeling programs -- A survey," IEEE Computer Graphics and Applications 2(9), Nov. 1982, pp. 17-25.

[Faux79] Faux, I., and M. Pratt. Computational Geometry for Design and Manufacture, Ellis Horwood, Chichester, England, 1979.

[Fink75] Finkel, R., R. Taylor, R. Bolles, R. Paul, and J. Feldman, "An overview of AL, a programming system for automation," Proc IJCAI-4, 1975, pp. 758-765.

[Frie75] Friedman, J., "Computer exploration of fast speech rules," IEEE Trans. on Acoustics, Speech, and Signal Processing 23(1), Feb. 1975, pp. 100-103.

[Fris78] Frisberg, N., "The case of the missing length," Communication and Cognition 11(1), 1978, pp. 57-67.

[Gins83] Ginsberg, C.M. and D. Maxwell, "Graphical Marionette," Proc. ACM SIGGRAPH/SIGART Workshop on Motion: Representation and Perception, April 1983, pp. 172-179.

[Hend73] Hendrix, G., "Modeling simultaneous actions and continuous processes," AI Journal 4, 1973, pp. 145-180.

[Herb78] Herbison-Evans, D., "NUDES-2: A numeric utility displaying ellipsoid solids, version 2," Computer Graphics 12(3), Aug. 1978, pp. 354-356.

[Herb81] Herbison-Evans, D. and D. Richardson, "Control of round-off propagation in articulating the human figure," Computer Graphics and Image Processing 17(4), 1981, pp. 386-393.

[Holl80]   Hollerbach, J.M., "A recursive lagrangian formulation of manipulator dynamics and a comparative study of dynamics formulation complexity," IEEE Trans. Systems, Man, and Cybernetics 10(11), Nov. 1980, pp. 730-736.

[Holl83]   Hollerbach, J.M., Dynamic scaling of manipulator trajectories, A.I. Memo No. 700, MIT, January 1983.

[Hutc70]   Hutchinson, A. Labanotation, Theatre Arts Books, New York, 1970.

[Hutc82]   Hutchinson, A. Personal Communication, 1982.

[King81]   Kingsley, E., N. Schofield, and K. Case, "SAMMIE-a computer aid for man-machine modelling," Computer Graphics 15(3), Aug. 1981, pp. 163-169.

[Klim79]   Klima, E., and U. Bellugi. The Signs of Language, Harvard Univ. Press, Cambridge, MA, 1979.

[Kore82]   Korein, J.U., and N.I. Badler, "Techniques for goal directed motion," IEEE Computer Graphics and Applications 2(9), Nov. 1982, pp. 71-81.

[Kore83]   Korein, J.D, and N.I. Badler, "Temporal anti-aliasing in computer generated animation," Computer Graphics 17(3), July 1983, pp. 377-388.

[Lee82]   Lee, C. S. George, "Robot arm kinematics, dynamics and control," IEEE Computer 15(2), Dec. 1982, pp. 62-80.

[Lieb77]   Lieberman, L. and M. Wesley, "AUTOPASS": An automatic programming system for computer controlled mechanical assembly," IBM Journal of Research and Development 21(4), July 1977, pp. 321-333.

[Loom83]   Loomis, J., H. Poizner, U. Bellugi, A. Blakemore, and J.M. Hollerbach, "Computer graphic modeling of American Sign Language," Computer Graphics 17(3), July 1983, pp. 105-114.

[Loza79]   Lozano-Perez, T., and M. Wesley, "An algorithm for planning collision-free paths among polyhedral obstacles," CACM 22, Oct. 1979, pp. 560-570.

[Marr81]   Marr, D., and H. K. Nishihara, "Representation and recognition of the spatial organization of three-dimensional shapes," Proc. Royal Soc. London B200, 1981, pp. 269-294.

[Meze71]   Mezei, L., and A. Zivian, "ARTA, an interactive animation system," Proc. IFIP Congress 1971, North Holland Pub., pp. 429-434.

[ORou80]   O'Rourke, J., and N.I. Badler, "Model-based image analysis of human motion using constraint propagation," IEEE Trans. PAMI 2(6), Nov. 1980, pp. 522-536.

[Park82]   Parke, F. "Parameterized models for facial animation," IEEE Computer Graphics and Applications 2(9), Nov. 1982, pp. 61-68.

[Paul72]   Paul, R.P., Modelling, trajectory calculation and servoing of a computer controlled arm. Stanford AI Project Memo No. 177, Stanford Univ., Nov. 1972.

[Paul79]   Paul, R.P., "Manipulator cartesian path control," IEEE Trans. Systems, Man, and Cybernetics 9(11), Nov. 1979, pp.702-711.

[Plat81]   Platt, S., and N.I. Badler, "Animating facial expressions," Computer Graphics 15(3), Aug. 1981, pp. 245-252.

[Reev81]   Reeves, W., "Inbetweening for computer animation utilizing moving point constraints," Computer Graphics 15(3), Aug. 1981, pp. 263-269.

[Reev83]   Reeves, W., "Particle systems - A technique for modelling a class of fuzzy objects," Computer Graphics 17(3), July 1983, pp. 359-376.

[Rieg80]   Reiger, C., and R. Stanfill, "Real-time causal monitors for complex physical sites," Proc. AAAI Conf., Stanford, CA, 1980, pp. 215-217.

[Shel82]   Shelley, K. and D. Greenberg, "Path specification and path coherence," Computer Graphics 16(3), July 1983, pp. 157-166.

[Speg75]   Spegel, M., Programming of mechanism motion. Tech. Report CRL-43, Div. of Applied Science, New York University, New York, 1975.

[Tsot80]   Tsotsos, J., J. Mylopoulos, H.D. Covvey, and S.W. Zucker, "A framework for visual motion understanding," IEEE Trans. PAMI 2(6), Nov. 1980, pp. 563-573.

[Webe78]   Weber, L., S. Smoliar, and N. Badler, "An architecture for the simulation of human movement," Proc. ACM Annual Conf. 1978, pp. 737-745.

[Will82]   Williams, L., "Bboop," 3D Animation Seminar Notes, SIGGRAPH 1982.

[Zelt82]   Zeltzer, D., "Motor control techniques for figure animation," IEEE Computer Graphics and Applications 2(9), Nov. 1982, pp. 53-59.

[Zelt83]   Zeltzer, D., "Knowledge-based animation," Proc. ACM SIGGRAPH/SIGART Workshop on Motion: Representation and Perception, April 1983, pp. 187-192.